THE

Progressive Historians

D1120892

Richard Hofstadter

THE

PROGRESSIVE

HISTORIANS

Turner, Beard, Parrington

VINTAGE BOOKS
A Division of Random House
New York

First Vintage Books Edition,
February 1970

Copyright © 1968 by Richard Hofstadter

All rights reserved under International and Pan-
American Copyright Conventions. Published in the
United States by Alfred A. Knopf, Inc., New York,
and Random House, Inc., New York, and simultane-
ously in Canada by Random House of Canada Limited,
Toronto. By arrangement with Alfred A. Knopf, Inc.

Library of Congress Catalog Card Number: 68-23944

Manufactured in
the United States of America

To

B.K.H., D.H., S.K.H.

Acknowledgments

For their kind assistance I wish to thank librarians at the College of Emporia, The Henry E. Huntington Library, and at the following universities: Columbia, Cornell, DePauw, Harvard, Yale, the University of Washington, and the University of Wyoming. I have also received cordial aid at the Oral History Collection of Columbia University. Quotations from Charles A. Beard's letters to Oswald Garrison Villard are with the permission of the Harvard College Library; from his letters to Carl Becker with the permission of the Cornell University Library; from his letters to Harry Elmer Barnes with the permission of the library of the University of Wyoming. Quotations from the letters of Frederick Jackson Turner are with the permission of The Henry E. Huntington Library. If I refrain from acknowledging the several scholars who read drafts of chapters, it is only to spare them association with my judgments and to avoid the impression that this work aims to convey something like a professional consensus; but they will know that they have my gratitude. Alfred A. Knopf gave me access to the relevant portion of his own memoir in the Columbia Oral History Collection; Arthur Schlesinger, Jr., permission to consult that of his father; Harry Elmer Barnes to consult his correspondence with Charles and Mary Beard. Others provided me with distinctive information or unpublished materials: Ray Allan Billington, Stuart Bruchey, E. H. Eby, Isabel Grossner, Alfred Kazin, Everett Sims. Vernon Parrington, Jr., generously made available the papers of his father and the use of his study, corrected some errors in my first drafts of Chapters 10 and 11, and tolerantly bore with many criticisms he thought excessive. The completion of this work was hastened by a fellowship in 1966–7 from the John Simon Guggenheim Memorial Foundation, and at other times by the assistance of the Henry P. Kendall Foundation. My research assistants, Edwin G. Burrows and Michael Wallace, brought to this undertaking exceptional diligence and warm concern, as well as independent views. It would be hard to enumerate the many contributions of my secretary, Jane Slater, not least her keen interest in the development of the argument. As always, I have relied more than I can say upon my wife's taste and candid judgment, and her informed feeling for American history. To my daughter, Sarah K. Hofstadter, armed with a copy of Fowler and an exceptional dialectical hardihood, I owe my reluctant decision to depart from a habit of long standing and write "a historian" instead of "an." A version of Chapter 10 was given as the Stephen Allan Kaplan Memorial Lecture at the University of Pennsylvania, November 1967; a version of Chapter 12 as a lecture before the Charles Warren Center for Studies in American History, Harvard University, March 1968. Some sequences from Chapters 6 and 7 appeared in *Dissent*, January–February 1968.

Note to the Vintage edition: A number of small stylistic changes have been made, and for the correction of important biographical errors on pages 168 and 288–89 I am most grateful to Beard's daughter, Mrs. Alfred Vagts.

October, 1969   R.H.

Contents

INTRODUCTION · xi

PART I · THE BACKGROUND

1 · *Historical Writing Before Turner* · 3

PART II · FREDERICK JACKSON TURNER

2 · *Turner and the Western Revolt* · 47
3 · *Frontier and Section and the Usable Past* · 84
4 · *The Frontier as an Explanation* · 118

PART III · CHARLES A. BEARD

5 · *Beard and the Progressive Mind* · 167
6 · *The Constitution as an Economic Document* · 207
7 · *The Constitution and Political Thought* · 246
8 · *Reconsiderations* · 285
9 · *The Devil Theory of Franklin D. Roosevelt* · 318

PART IV · V. L. PARRINGTON

10 · *Economics and Criticism* · 349
11 · *Criticism and Political Thought* · 396

PART V · THE AFTERMATH

12 · *Conflict and Consensus in American History* · 437

Bibliographical Essay · 467
INDEX · *follows page* 498

Introduction

This book began as a study of three central works of twentieth-century American historical writing. I intended at first to write rather full essays on the setting and influence of Frederick Jackson Turner's *The Significance of the Frontier in American History*, Charles A. Beard's *An Economic Interpretation of the Constitution of the United States*, and V. L. Parrington's *Main Currents in American Thought*, and to set in order my own views on the issues raised by the large body of criticism that has grown up around them. As I went on, the historical setting in which these works emerged and their sources in the lives of the authors began to compel my attention. I found myself writing not merely historiographical criticism but a certain measure of intellectual history and even, in a limited way, of biography. It seemed less sensible than I had first imagined to write about Turner's ideas on the frontier without giving some attention to his other notions—on sectionalism, for example—or on Beard's study of the Constitution without saying a good deal about his use of the economic interpretation of history, his approach to the problem of historical knowledge, and finally his ideas on foreign policy. But in some respects the original design of this book is still evident in its present form. The reader who wonders why I have given so much more attention to Beard's book on the Constitution than to all his other writings taken together must remember that it was my first intention to write about that book alone, and that whatever I have done with his other concerns has been in the hope of illuminating the leading ideas and the particular style of thought that are evident in this basic work.

Few readers, I believe, will be puzzled as to why I started with works by these three men. I might easily have written also about Carl Becker, who had a subtler mind and wrote better prose than any of them and who might have qualified too as a "Progressive" historian. But no single book of Becker's compared in its effects with the three I began with; and quite aside from my wish to keep a long book from getting still longer, and my awareness of two admirable books on his historical thought by Cushing Strout and Burleigh Taylor Wilkins, Becker's influence on our thinking about American history was not to be compared with that of my trio. My criterion was, above all, influence; and among writers on American history it was Turner, Beard, and Parrington who gave us the pivotal ideas of the first half of the twentieth century. It was they who seemed to be able to make American history relevant to the political and intellectual issues of the moment. It was their ideas that seemed most worth exploring and testing, and it was they who inspired one young man after another to take up history as a profession.

In grouping these three as Progressive historians I do no more than follow the precedent of other recent writers on American historiography. Not one of them was, to be sure, an easily classifiable partisan in the day-to-day national politics of their time, but all of them took their cues from the intellectual ferment of the period from 1890 to 1915, from the demands for reform raised by the Populists and Progressives, and from the new burst of political and intellectual activity that came with these demands. They were directed to their major concerns by the political debate of their time; they in turn contributed to it by giving reform politics a historical rationale. It was these men above all others who explained the American liberal mind to itself in historical terms. Progressive historical writing did for history what pragmatism did for philosophy, sociological jurisprudence for law, the muckraking spirit for journalism, and what Parrington called "critical realism" for letters. If pragmatism, as someone has said, provided American liberalism with its philosophical nerve, Progressive historiography gave it memory and myth, and naturalized it within the whole framework of American historical experience.

If I call these men Progressive historians, however, it is not because of a desire to group them together as an altogether unitary "school," still less to suggest that they took precisely the same view of the political changes of their age.

Although they came from the same region and belonged roughly to the same class and generation, they had different experiences, they were different in temperament, and their ideas did not always coincide. Beard, for example, was quick to see that the frontier idea, though linked at certain points to American insurgency, was also overlaid with a kind of conservatism and even of nationalist complacency. Both he and Parrington responded more positively to the leftward tendencies in the heterogeneous movement that we loosely describe as Progressivism, while Turner might be said to have belonged to its conservative wing. And in the New Deal era, just when Turner's ideas were beginning to be questioned sharply by a new generation of historians, the ideas of Parrington and Beard probably reached the peak of their influence. Even between these two, who stood closer to each other intellectually than either did to Turner, there were some important intellectual differences. There was in Beard, except for the last years of his life, a pervasive note of hard-boiled iconoclasm about most aspects of the American tradition, which made it impossible for him to celebrate with Parrington's warmth the legacy of Jeffersonian liberalism. To such differences in personal style and thought I hope I have done justice in the text.

I have asked myself why I wrote this book, and why at this time. From a public, impersonal point of view, there is excellent reason for it: the past twenty years have been a period of exceptionally rich productivity and lively argument in American historical writing, in the course of which the Progressive historians have been scrutinized very closely, criticized elaborately, sometimes ferociously, and subjected to a thorough revaluation. Very little of the relevant literature is known to the general intellectual reading public, and though it has been bruited about that, say, Beard's book on the Constitution is no longer so highly thought of as it once was, few laymen have more than the vaguest idea why. Yet I cannot quite say that I began this as an effort at popularization, a worthwhile task in its own right but not one of my pre-eminent interests. I started this book out of a personal engagement with the subject, out of some

sense of the incompleteness of my reckoning with my intellectual forebears, out of the feeling I have about this
and other subjects that I do not quite know what I think
until I have written it, and the conviction that if I did
not write about these men now the clarification that I hoped
for from such a reckoning might never take place. At the
point at which I began to have some identity as a historian, it was the work of these men, particularly Beard and
Parrington, that interested me as supplying the guiding
ideas to the understanding of American history. Along with
many other professional historians of my generation, strange
as it seems to me now, I took up American history under
the inspiration that came from Charles and Mary Beard's
The Rise of American Civilization; and my first professional
essay, published thirty years ago, was an attempt to take issue
with some of their suggestions about the origins of the Civil
War. Later, at a time when my own conceptions of our history were beginning to take form, I found myself impelled
to write again about all three of these men and to take
some note of their critics.[1] A good deal of what has gone
into this book is then a reprise of that perennial battle we
wage with our elders, particularly with our adopted intellectual fathers. If we are to have any new thoughts, if we
are to have an intellectual identity of our own, we must
make the effort to distinguish ourselves from those who preceded us, and perhaps pre-eminently from those to whom
we once had the greatest indebtedness. Even if our quarrels are only marginal and minor (though I do not think
that can be said of the differences discussed here), we must
make the most of them.

It has occurred to me in some of my wrier moments that
as I feel myself all too rapidly becoming an elder in my
turn, there may be some reassurance in recalling or re-
enacting my own parricidal forays. But there is surely some-

[1] See "The Tariff Issue on the Eve of the Civil War," *American
Historical Review,* 44 (1938), 50–5; "Parrington and the Jeffer-
sonian Tradition," *Journal of the History of Ideas,* 2 (1941), 391–
400; "Turner and the Frontier Myth," *American Scholar,* 18
(1949), 433–43; "Beard and the Constitution: The History of An
Idea," *American Quarterly,* 2 (1950), 195–213, reprinted as
"Charles Beard and the Constitution," in Howard K. Beale, ed.,
Charles A. Beard (1954), 75–92.

thing more than the generational gap at stake in all the criticism to which the Progressive historians have been subjected. Turner was born in 1861, Beard and Parrington within ten years of the end of the Civil War, and they all came of age just at the time when the movements of protest against the evils of late nineteenth-century industrialism were coming to a head. Their leading critics have been born in the twentieth century, many of them after the First World War. Progressive history had been written to meet several needs that are no longer felt in the same way, and it began to seem, to members of my generation, somewhat too insular and too nostalgic. Those of us who grew up during the Great Depression and the Second World War could no longer share the simple faith of the Progressive writers in the sufficiency of American liberalism. We found ourselves living in a more complex and terrifying world, and when we set about criticizing the Progressive historians I believe it was with a keener sense of the difficulties of life and of the problem of rendering it in intelligible historical terms. Even those of their guiding ideas that still seemed to be valid now seemed marginal rather than central; and many of their interpretative ideas rested on some kind of identification of the past and present that we could easily see through, not because we were cleverer but because *their* present was no longer ours. Gradually they ceased to be the leading interpreters of our past and became simply a part of it.

So much of the historiographical criticism of the past twenty years has been destructive that my own task has inevitably been destructive also, but I hope some signs of my affection for these writers are still visible. Perhaps at points a tentative note can also be heard. At one time or another I have changed my mind about each of these men, and it is by no means inconceivable to me that on some counts I may change it again. The historical returns are never complete; even now we are beginning to hear from some precincts we had forgotten about, and some of the revisions are being revised, perhaps to good effect. A very large part of what historians differ about boils down to questions of emphasis, to arguments about how much stress we want to put on this factor rather than that, when we all admit that both were at work. And I see no way of arriving at a final consensus on questions of this kind. I take comfort in a remark Carl Becker once made in objecting to the very idea of a definitive history: "Who cares to open a book that is without defect or amiable weakness?"

I have tried to keep criticism within fair bounds at every point, but it has occurred to me at the end that I have committed one injustice to my subjects which can now be remedied only by bringing it to the attention of the reader. What I have done is to test Progressive historical writing against the work that has come *after* it; by comparison, my efforts to set it against the work that preceded it are relatively spare and perfunctory. I might have conveyed a keener sense of the original merits of the Progressive writers had I made a fuller and more elaborate study of the generation that came before them. Though I have indeed begun with a chapter on historical writing before Turner's day, it is not a detailed analysis of the state of historical work just before the Progressives arrived on the scene, but a long impressionistic leap through our historical writing from the early nineteenth century. In sparing myself a close and intense reckoning with the voluminous literature of the period from 1870–1900, I may have spared the reader as well as myself some tedium; but I suppose that the Progressive historians would have emerged somewhat stronger if I had said at length what I have said in brief. The Progressives opened up arguments in areas where there had been too much agreement and too much complacency. They took the writing of American history out of the hands of the Brahmins and the satisfied classes, where it had too exclusively rested, and made it responsive to the intellectual needs of new types of Americans who were beginning to constitute a productive, insurgent intelligentsia. They were in the vanguard of a new generation of Midwestern scholars who were deeply involved in the critical ferment that was felt at the beginning of the century, rebellious about the neglect of their own region, eager to make up for the past failure of historians to deal with the interests of the common man and with the historic merits of movements of reform. They attempted to find a usable past related to the broadest needs of a nation fully launched upon its own industrialization, and to make history an active instrument of self-recognition and self-improvement. Something important we do indeed owe them, and I hope it will not be smothered here in the folds of criticism.

Wellfleet, Mass.
New York, N.Y.   R. H.
June 1966–March 1968

PART

I

The Background

CHAPTER 1

Historical Writing
Before Turner

> *What should be done for the stop, the turn of this Degeneracy? . . . I'll shew them the Graves of their dead Fathers.*
> —Cotton Mather, *1702*

> *I regard any concession as to popular illusions as a blemish.*
> —Henry Adams, *1890*

I

MEMORY is the thread of personal identity, history of public identity. Men who have achieved any civic existence at all must, to sustain it, have some kind of history, though it may be history that is partly mythological or simply untrue. That the business of history always involves a subtle transaction with civic identity has long been understood, even in America where the sense of time is shallow. One of our early nineteenth-century promoters of canals and public works was also a promoter of historical collections because he understood with perfect clarity that there was some relation between the two. "To visit a people who have no history," he wrote, "is like going into a wilderness where there are no roads to direct a traveller. The people have nothing to which they can look back; the wisdom and acts of their forefathers are forgotten; the experience of one generation is lost to the succeeding one; and the consequence is, that people have little attachment to their state, their policy has no system, and their legislature no decided character."[1]

The historians of the nineteenth century worked under the pressure of two internal tensions: on one side there was the constant demand of society—whether through the nation-

---

[1] Archibald D. Murphey, quoted in David D. Van Tassel, *Recording America's Past* (1960), 104.

state, the church, or some special group or class interest—
for memory mixed with myth, for the historical tale that
would strengthen group loyalties or confirm national pride;
and against this there were the demands of critical method,
and even, after a time, the goal of writing "scientific" history.
Again, history had a double vocational inheritance of its
own. It had originated as a branch of literature, or of literature modified by certain philosophical objectives. It was now
increasingly put to the task of modeling itself after nineteenth-century science, of responding to imperatives of craft
that had nothing to do with literature and whose advocates
sometimes even scorned the idea that history is a literary
art. All this the historians of the United States shared with
their fellows elsewhere, but they had peculiar problems arising
out of distinctive aspects of American experience. "It's a complex fate, being an American," Henry James once said, and
American historical writing bears witness to him. The problem of American identity, especially poignant because the
business of becoming American involved at some point in
every family tree the shock of deracination and the trial of
starting anew, was also multifarious because regional and
national loyalties pulled against each other, as did the imperatives of different classes, ethnic groups, races. Americans
seem, too, to make remarkably intense demands upon their
history, perhaps because they have so little of it, because
so much of the heritage of the human past had no remainders
or monuments on these shores, and that therefore some kind
of mythological substitutes had to be *devised*. And, while it
is no doubt true to some degree everywhere that history
doubles for political theory and has even in secular ages
taken on some of the work of theology, it is perhaps more
keenly true in the United States. An intensely political people
with some remarkable political achievements to take pride in,
the Americans nonetheless produced, despite the unquestionable brilliance of John Adams and James Madison, not a
single political theorist of the first rank, and the best of their
political thinking was done before the eighteenth century
was over. A religious people, as modern peoples go, they
steered away from doctrine, and produced, at least after
Edwards, no great theologians. But the writing of history,

in which they showed remarkable distinction, producing an impressive number of capable writers and a few great ones, seems to have taken on a considerably enlarged burden, both in expressing their politics and embodying their values in one or another variety of historical theodicy. When the New Englanders ceased to believe, they wrote history; when the Southerners went down to defeat, they did the same.

Time is the basic dimension of history, but the basic dimension of the American imagination is space. The lessons and the inspiration Americans crave from their history they have had to find in the face of their grossly foreshortened sense of time and their recurrent disposition to look rather disdainfully upon the remoter past. We have, it is commonly said, no monuments, no ruins, no palpable reminders of the ancient history of the race. On our own shores, for all practical purposes, American history begins with the seventeenth century, cut off from feudal and prefeudal memories. West of the Appalachians it begins (except for a few areas) only with the eighteenth century, and is largely a thing of the nineteenth. Most important, what could still be called not so long ago the entire first half of American history—that is, the colonial period down to about the 1760's—has largely been lost to the American imagination. For that epoch we have no sense of history, only an episodic mythology. Even to the instructed popular mind there is no sense of an American past running continuously back into those times, no meaningful sequence of events covering this long period in which the separate pattern of American life emerged and our institutions took on much of their distinctive character. What we do have as a substitute for a historical conception of this span of time is a series of tableaux, of timeless, frozen vignettes, each one of which seems to establish a moral or convey a message: the Pilgrim fathers and pioneer courage; John Smith and early hardships; Cotton Mather and Puritan intolerance; Roger Williams and heroic dissent; John Peter Zenger and freedom of the press; Colonial Williamsburg and the charm of the olden times. Americans seem to conceive of their history within a very shallow time span, in which one age is very much like another, in which the Founding Fathers become timeless oracles, to be consulted for wisdom on perplex-

ing current problems. There is something comfortable about
this, but it is grossly deceptive; it encourages anachronism,
the blurring of historical lines, the failure to develop a sense
for what is distinctive about each epoch and how one gives
way to another. Both the conservative nationalist historians
of the Gilded Age and the Progressive historians of Charles A.
Beard's generation sometimes fell into this trap, converting
the episodes of the past into mere counters to be deployed on
the checkerboard of contemporary controversies.

What Americans have lacked in a sense of time they
have tried to make up by an enlarged sense of space. Their
thoughts tend not to run backward into an antiquity they do not
know but rather outward into a larger geographical theater
of action, the theater not of the past but of the future. Even
in the earliest days, John Cotton, arguing that the exile of
Roger Williams for his heresies was really punishment of a
very benign sort, remarked that the jurisdiction from which
he had been banned was small and "the Countrey round about
it large and fruitful: where a man may make his choice of
variety of more pleasant and profitable seats, than he leaveth
behinde him. In which respect, Banishment in this countrey
is not counted so much a confinement, as an enlargement."
For Americans, uprooted from many soils and stemming
from many ancestries and thrust into the open natural environment of the new continent, the very possibility of freedom
quickly became associated with the presence of empty space,
and also with the freedom to move, to get away from the
physical proximity of others, to escape from society itself
into the innocence of nature. It was Frederick Jackson Turner's essential merit, as well as the source of some of his defects, to be the first historian to try fully to incorporate this
awareness of space, this delight in movement, this yearning
for rebirth under natural conditions, into our historical
thought. But of course this passion for space and movement,
which had its delusive aspects for the pioneer, has also made
its difficulties for the historian. The distinctive business of
history is with society, with the development of social institutions, and in itself space is no more than marginal as a
social category. The American mind, as our imaginative writers have given witness over and over again, has craved what

the fresh continent promised, the natural and the innocent; but the progress of society across the continent steadily brought the perplexities of institutional life and the despoiling hand of man—neither Natty Bumppo nor Daniel Boone could ever get far enough from the sound of the axes tearing away at the forests.

And here lay the nub of the intimate American quarrel with history: the difficulty of combining the pastoral, or still worse the primitivist, sense of the ideal human condition with another equally deep intellectual craving, the belief in progress. The heritage of the Revolution, combined with the American penchant for "natural" and innocent conditions, provided a difficult starting point. In the common American opinion, the heroic conduct that made the Revolution and the wise statecraft that made the Constitution showed that the country was launched under the leadership of men who were virtual demigods and under institutions that were close to perfection. The country was believed also to have a social condition about as close as man can get to pastoral innocence. As one looked back, one looked back always to wiser men and better times. Yet how could one reconcile this belief—hardly less strong for being latent and imperfectly articulated—with the general American commitment to what Herbert Butterfield has called the Whig interpretation of history, in which the idea of progress is a central tenet? How can a people progress if they have started near to perfection?

American historians in the nineteenth century were in the main a conservative class of men writing for a conservative public. But they were obliged to account for the life of a nation that had originated in a revolution, had gone on from this to develop a particularly vigorous and egalitarian democracy, and then in time to experience a disastrous Civil War and after that an orgy of material development marked by the emergence of a vulgar plutocracy and crass machine politics. Somehow national pride and confidence had to be reconciled with all this. Somehow the Revolution had to be tamed and naturalized, distinguished from other, more mischievous revolutions. The ghastly political failure of the Civil War had to be accommodated to the notion that American institutions are superior. The whole tumultuous and seamy

history of the nineteenth century had to be squared with
the idea of progress.

The Civil War was a particularly troublesome challenge.
All that had gone into it, the oppressive evil of slavery, the
sectional quarrel, the bloodletting itself, accorded neither with
the American's boasts about the perfection of his political
system nor with his faith in progress. The fascination of the
war as a historical subject could not quite distract attention
from the shock of failure: the political order that was supposed to be the best in the world had broken down completely,
and after four years of fraternal strife had been so badly
patched up that the wounds never really healed. It seemed
necessary to deny or dismiss or manipulate or simply quarrel
with a good deal of American history: How could the war
have been avoided? Whose fault was it? Was it really an irrepressible conflict? In the schools the young would be taught
to pledge allegiance to "one nation, indivisible, with liberty
and justice for all"—a phrase awkwardly designed to minimize
the fact that the whole early history of this nation rumbled
with threats of its divisibility, and that it had in fact been
divided in the most costly way; or that liberty and justice
for all were so far from having been achieved that the nation was periodically shaken with the consequences of their
denial. The approved histories of the country have struggled
constantly against the profound disparity between national
ideals—unity, democracy, equality, freedom, tolerance—and
the disturbing realities: state and regional particularism, the
issues of slavery and race, ethnic mixture and a system of
exclusion and discrimination, extraordinary outbursts of intolerance and violence, the constant erosion of the original
American Eden.

II

The first writers of American history after national independence were mainly localists. Their animating subject,
of course, was the Revolution—its origins, its vindication, its
heroes. But for the most part they wrote about South Carolina
or New York or Massachusetts, not about the Revolution as a
national phenomenon. Some of the best work of the age,

notably David Ramsay's *History of the Revolution of South Carolina* (1785) and Jeremy Belknap's three-volume *History of New Hampshire* (1784–92), which Tocqueville praised for its thoughtfulness, was done in this vein. It is hard to decide how far this localism was the result of the prevailing loyalties—after all, most of the states had had a century and more to form a pattern of allegiance whereas the nation was still to prove itself—and how far it was merely a response to technical difficulties like the unavailability of good libraries, archival collections, and printed records, and the hardships of travel. Even as late as 1826, when the indefatigable Jared Sparks went on a 3,500-mile trip in search of original records, it took him all of six hours by stage to get from New Haven to Hartford. In the period just after the Peace of Paris, so little documentary material was available that an astonishingly high proportion of the historical writers of the era, including no less a man than John Marshall, yielded to the temptation to plagiarize a large part of their work from the contributions of Edmund Burke and others to the *British Annual Register*. Much, indeed, of the most vital material for the study of the American past was in distant English archives.

Under such conditions practicality confirmed what long habit and old loyalties had established. It was hard to find the materials to tell in much depth of detail or with much accuracy the whole story of the American people; it was relatively easy to collect state records and to form, on the strength of local pride, historical societies that would be concerned with state or local lore. To have come to America in the first instance was a radical step that had to be vindicated. The first colonial histories had been colored by this motive; they had been promotional, celebratory, and then perhaps (as in the case of the Puritans) nostalgic or defensive; and after 1776 the state historians built upon this legacy a literature touting the revolutionary merits of their own states, commemorating local heroes, and dwelling poignantly on the particular grievances each one had against British policies. At the beginning of the nineteenth century there were as yet no general histories of the United States, no established patterns for national historians. Abiel Holmes, the father of Oliver Wendell Holmes, compiled a respectable two-volume chronicle in 1805. Benjamin Trumbull, who published a general history in 1810, got no further than the events of 1761. Even in 1839, when Sparks lectured at Harvard on the American Revolution from 1763 to 1783, he had to use as his textbook the work of an Italian writer, Carlo Botta, because he could get no other, "all the other historians of the same period being out of print."[2]

Much of the work of forging national loyalty was done in biographies. The outstanding leaders of the Revolution were, after all, more than simply local heroes, and through the portrayal of their days and deeds, one of the most popular forms of writing, the pull of national sentiment made itself felt. Washington, the ideal subject, benefited not only from the efforts of Parson Weems, who told historical lies in order to impress upon the young the importance of telling the truth, but also from a biography by John Marshall (1804–07) and from the basically useful, if somewhat bowdlerized, twelve-volume *The Writings of George Washington* (1834–7) by Jared Sparks. William Wirt's *Patrick Henry* (1818), Sparks's Library of American Biography series, and the nine volumes of John Sanderson's *Biography of the Signers of the Declaration of Independence* (1820–7) also gave testimony to the demand for such literature and the possible profits of writing it, and served the double function of strengthening national feeling and defining character models for the young.

In time the prospects for serious historical work improved. By the 1820's and 1830's, the first great compilers had begun to work. Hezekiah Niles brought out his *Principles and Acts of the Revolution in America* in 1822, Jonathan Elliot his invaluable edition of the debates over the ratification of the Constitution during 1827–30, Jared Sparks his *Diplomatic Correspondence of the American Revolution* during 1829–30, and Peter Force began his *American Archives* in 1837. By 1830 some two dozen historical societies had been formed; personal papers and collections, most of which Sparks had found still in private hands, were beginning to pass into more accessible public repositories. The states were starting their own collections of documents. It was beginning to be possible

---

2 H. B. Adams, *Life and Writings of Jared Sparks* (1893), II, 375.

to write general American history out of authentic sources, though a great mass of the basic colonial material could be found only in England.

Still, the writing of history, though it could bring rich returns, was expensive to undertake. History, Henry Adams thought, had always been "the most aristocratic of all literary pursuits, because it obliges the historian to be rich as well as educated," and he once told his publisher that he would be sorry to see it pay because it would then "soon become as popular a pursuit as magazine-writing, and the luxury of its social distinction would vanish."[3] There was at first no academic historical profession—Sparks became the first professor of history when he accepted the McLean Professorship of Ancient and Modern History at Harvard in 1839, but another fifty years were to pass before there were more than a dozen such positions—and in any case, the modest salaries of professors bore no proportion to the costs of historical work on a grand scale. George Bancroft estimated in 1872 that he had spent $75,000 of his own money on the research for his series, begun almost forty years before, and he was to invest another $25,000 before he finished. For some years he had two copyists at work for him in London archives. Not only the leisure for extensive labors but the expenses for travel, assistants, copyists, even connections with well-placed and influential persons, were requisites of historical research. History was, then, the prerogative either of leisure-class gentlemen of commanding means or of a few hardy spirits like Sparks and Bancroft, who had the energy for other enterprises as well as history. Bancroft's career in politics and diplomacy delayed his work: his first volume appeared in 1834, his fourth and fifth only in 1852, and it was 1882 when he at last brought out his final two volumes on the making of the Constitution.

Most striking in the historical careers that were started in the decades before the Civil War was the large proportion of historical talents of the first order that went into fields other than American national history. Since the passing of the Founding Fathers and the rise of Jacksonian democracy,

---

3 John Higham, *History* (1965), 70.

the United States had developed in its midst not a ruling
aristocracy but a class of displaced and sometimes frustrated
patricians who found little scope for their energies in political
leadership and felt rather at odds with the main drift of their
society—its increasing materialism and egalitarianism, its
democratic politics and machine government. It was this
class, above all its New England branch, that produced historical writers; and these men, with the notable exception of
Bancroft, were at first attracted not so much to the story of
America, about which they seem to have felt a certain discomfort, but to more dramatic subjects and themes that were
for the most part remote from and in some cases quite
antithetical to the main lines of American development. It is
impressive how far afield the major New England talents
went. Parkman, who stayed closest to native grounds in his
choice of terrain, was nonetheless distant from American
society in his themes: the forest, the Indian character, the
Jesuits, the explorers, the half century of struggle between
the British and French empires for North America. Spain and
Spanish colonization in the New World—subjects that offered
a satisfactory contrast to the United States in the Jackson
era—had a persistent fascination. George Ticknor wrote a
history of Spanish literature. Prescott turned to *Ferdinand
and Isabella,* and went on to *The Conquest of Mexico.* Motley's
interest in the history of Netherlands independence began
with a concern for the history of the Spanish empire. Washington Irving took the history of his native New York only as
the subject for burlesque. When he turned to serious history,
he spent many years on Columbus, *The Conquest of Granada,*
and *The Alhambra* before he wrote on George Washington.
In the post-Civil War period, one of our most eminent historical writers, the Philadelphian, H. C. Lea—another gentleman amateur—carried on with this traditional interest in the
relatively exotic and remote with his great books on the
medieval Church and the Inquisition.

In finding American development a theme sufficiently
grand to sustain the demands of the historian, Bancroft
stood alone among the major writers of his age, as he did in
his Democratic allegiance and his eagerness to play the po-

litical game. But in other respects, as David Levin has shown,[4] he had much in common with Prescott, Parkman, and Motley. All came to historical writing as amateurs, men of letters who had tried their hands at poetry, fiction, or critical essays before they ever wrote history. All came out of the milieu of New England Unitarianism, hoping perhaps to find in the historical process some support for, or alternative to, the pale and fading assertions of their religion. But they also had strong roots in the Puritan past whose traditions gave them a moral impulse toward history—Christianity is distinctly a historical religion, and the Puritans had had a notable passion for history—and also the personal discipline great scholarship required. Avid readers of Scott and Cooper, Wordsworth, Coleridge, and Byron, in some cases of Schiller, Goethe, and Herder as well—but above all, and most attentively of Scott—they were the American counterparts of the romantic historians of Europe. For them the purpose of historical writing was to establish an imaginative relation with the past, not to analyze but to re-create it. What they looked for was experience, not philosophy. Despite the philosophical historians of the Enlightenment, history was still regarded as a literary art whose main aim was to recapture experience. Foremost was the experience of major heroic characters. Character was best portrayed against the background of some sublime natural scene, some militant arena of strife and self-assertion—the forest, the sea, the field of battle— where animal energies and the hardy virtues are at a premium. A social texture was present, but it served mainly as a kind of background or setting for the decisive confrontations, like those of Montcalm and Wolfe, Cortés and Montezuma, Philip II and William of Orange, the climactic scenes arising out of the epics of exploration, colonization, imperial conquest, and revolution. The moral drama of history was told in pictorial terms. The effort at historical discipline—and in their craving for facts, accuracy, and authenticity the romantic historians were strenuous models for their "scientific" successors—rested upon the insatiable quest for the right, the

---

[4] I owe much here to his *History as Romantic Art* (1959).

relevant detail. One looked about for a narrative theme with grand dramatic possibilities, a tale perhaps told before but certainly not well or amply told. One then spared no pains to tell it in more accurate detail, more correctly as well as more vividly, than one's predecessors. The technical or "scientific" side of the work of these men came primarily to this: facts were valued not so much as "evidence," as proofs in some analytic scheme, but as veracious details for the re-creation of some experience.

But the re-creation of experience had a moral context. The romantic writers were trying to establish broad moral lessons. What they found most generally and consistently was progress toward liberty—progress which they interpreted with a distinct Protestant bias, as though all the world had been preparing for nineteenth-century Unitarianism. The medieval inheritance, Latinity, Catholicism, stood as the foe against which the impulse toward progress had to assert itself. Catholicism was frequently characterized as a force of superstition and persecution, its leaders as the colleagues of despots and bigots, men who employed guile and intrigue in the interests of fanaticism. One can hardly help but guess, however, that the romantic historians were fascinated by the pomp and the intricate texture of the Church, which gave them a certain amplitude of range as well as richness in portraiture, and offered the moral complexity, the sinister possibilities, the institutional substance they missed in American history, and that they were grateful for it.

Progress also moved toward modern democracy, even American democracy. Democracy, however, meant the advancing Protestantism of the seventeenth century with its scope for individualism and national independence and its laic control, or the old Whig republicanism of the revolutionary era; it did not mean (except for Bancroft) the new egalitarianism of the 1820's and 1830's. The agents of progress were men who represented in a quintessential way virtues that were also to be found among their people, qualities that could be found in Pitt, William of Orange, Washington. These were simple and natural men, lofty in motive, direct and spontaneous in action, yet full of will, persistent, reliable, endur-

ing, indomitable. As embodiments of virtues that were in some
degree also folk virtues, they were distillations of national
character. The romantic historians believed that national
character had an organic relation to national institutions
and achievements. In particular they thought that the
Teutonic character was in good part responsible for modern
democracy as it evolved in the Netherlands, England, and
America—a theme the scientific historians of a later age
would pick up and adapt to a different set of intellectual
methods. Progressive principles, progressive peoples, natural
impulses, heroic leadership—these were the basic ingredients
of true history.

III

Bancroft, the first great American historian of America,
shared much with the other romantic historians of his age;
but he departed from them in writing a considerably more
philosophical history, shaped by transcendentalism and borne
aloft by the afflatus of German idealism which he brought
back from his student days at Göttingen and Berlin. Above
all, he departed from them by becoming a Democrat in
politics and an egalitarian in philosophy, a supporter of Andrew Jackson and an outspoken foe of the Bank of the United
States—commitments which, though they did not bring the
other Brahmin historians to spurn him, caused some doors
in Boston to be closed to him forever. The basic framework
of Bancroft's ideas—reiterated and reasserted at critical
phases in his story—was quite simple: history taught a lesson, the inevitable movement of human affairs toward the
goal of liberty under providential guidance. In a certain sense,
the challenge he issued to his fellow romantic historians was
a logical one: if it was liberty and democracy that they too
saw in history, why was not the history of the United States,
supposedly the freest and most democratic of all the nations,
the grandest theme of all?

When Bancroft first thought of writing history in 1819,
he remarked significantly that it "has always interested me,
suits well with my theology, and I think I could become useful

by it."[5] When he actually began writing some ten years later, his theology was still not far in the background. As he saw it, the historian was akin to the moral philosopher, and his work should dramatize for the people the significance of their past so that they might better understand their destiny. The unifying principle was progress ordained and planned by God—the advance of liberty, justice, and humanity, all of which were particularly exemplified in American history, where providential guidance had brought together a singularly fit people and fit institutions. The genius of the American people was particularly adapted to liberty, their political order to its advance. American history could be seen as a kind of consummation of all history; Bancroft was supremely confident of the superiority of the United States to other countries, and in particular of the unvarying rightness of the American side in all the issues of the Revolution. The pervasive ideas of his history were made clear in his writings on politics. Intuitively and naturally, he thought, the people express the divine intention. "The popular voice is all powerful with us; this, we acknowledge, is the voice of God." More and more the able young people of the country were learning, he thought, "to reverence the intuitive wisdom of the people." "The universal decision is the nearest criterion of truth. . . . Unmixed error can have no existence in the public mind." It was the merit of such a popular leader as Jackson that he could exercise untutored wisdom, that he knew how to read the popular mind. Lincoln too, Bancroft later saw, was "willing to take instruction" from the people's wisdom.

Though he has been much scoffed at, Bancroft was a formidable historian. The immense and long-sustained popularity of his books testifies too that he was writing the version of their history the American people were looking for, repeating to them, as J. F. Jameson once said, "the things they were saying and thinking concerning themselves." His success not only in giving embodiment to the most general American

---

[5] Levin, *History*, 233; material on and by Bancroft in the following paragraphs, except where otherwise indicated, is from Russell Nye, *George Bancroft: Brahmin Rebel* (1945), especially 87, 92, 127, 139, 167, 188, 304, 306, and from the same writer's valuable brief study of Bancroft's mind, *George Bancroft* (1964), especially 74, 76, 81, 83–84.

idea of American history but also in entering into public life as a party leader, administrator, diplomat, and adviser to Presidents marks him off to a degree uncommon among our historians as a representative American. His history manifests an exceptional ability to marshal a mass of facts and set them into motion, along with a keen understanding—shown, for example, in his glimpses of the importance of the West in American character, and his insight, quite advanced for his time, into the functional character of the party system. Unfortunately it also lends itself to caricature, since his critics are so often tempted to quote the passages that illustrate his intellectual or rhetorical excesses. With its highly formal and self-conscious style and its mindless patriotism, his history frequently reads like an extended historical oration. Telling, for example, of the aftermath of Lexington and Concord, he writes: "With one impulse, the colonies sprang to arms; with one spirit, they pledged themselves to each other 'to be ready for the extreme event.' With one heart, the continent cried: 'Liberty or Death.' "[6] This, as young historians nowadays will surely complain, is consensus history with a vengeance; and one's mind flies with a sense of relief to John Adams's more matter-of-fact estimate that one third of the Americans were against the Revolution.[7]

One's first impulse—though I think it an impulse not quite fair to Bancroft—is to ask whether all that laborious collecting and copying of records and checking of facts came only to *this*. One's second is to wonder whether Bancroft was not, after all, having his little joke, as Henry James would have put it, when he dished up such passages to his readers. Certainly his was not only an intense but also a shrewd and worldly intelligence. Carlyle, after some acquaintance with him, told Emerson that he found him "a tough Yankee man, of many worthy qualities more tough than musical"—which seems a sound appraisal—and then added the more daring suggestion that he had also "a certain small undercurrent of genial humor or as it were *hidden laughter*, not noticed heretofore."

6 *History*, IV, 168; for Jameson, see his *The History of Historical Writing in America* (1891), 104.
7 *Works*, X (1856), 87.

But in the end we return to the likelihood that there is nothing hidden in Bancroft's history, that he was totally sincere in the most rhetorical of his effusions—although in later life he became self-conscious about them and conscientiously pruned them out of his revisions. What seems the soundest interpretation of Bancroft is that his was one of those minds, altogether common and perhaps even representative in America, for which the world of moral philosophy and history, of high ideals and beautiful letters, has only a vague tutelary relationship, though by no means an unimportant one, to reality. In such minds a certain kind of rude and impertinent curiosity is carefully suppressed, and things that are most firmly known as matters of everyday reality are not allowed to intrude themselves upon high thought. Bancroft's remark about the whole continent rising with one spirit reminds us of those for whom the signatures of slaveholders on a most unequivocal declaration of the natural rights of man poses no puzzle. It is a comforting though perhaps not a very animating or militant doctrine that history is under divine superintendence and will in due course deal with the survivals of tyranny and oppression. (Emerson thought that Bancroft and Bryant were "historical democrats, who are interested in dead or organized, but not in organizing, liberty.") It is always consoling to think that evil is temporary. Dissent from the predetermined course of history can be pushed aside: if the entire continent did not cry with one heart, "Liberty or Death," it should have.

About the operation of such preachings in the workaday world Bancroft was not at all deceived, and the whole course of his career shows his ability to keep them in their place. When he returned from Europe at twenty-three, learned and cosmopolitan far beyond his years, he was already considered by Boston and Cambridge Unitarians to have become fancified and overripe. His early experiment in education at the Round Hill School in many ways foretold his later career in its subordination of impulse to practical calculation. He came to Northampton full of Pestalozzian idealism, determined to use new methods to put American secondary education on a footing effective enough to compare, no less, with what the Germans were doing; but when the enterprise was launched, he was soon bored by the day-to-day demands of classroom instruction. Preferring to develop his own scholarship, he sold out his interest in the school at a profit. Later, though he attacked the Bank as a citadel of capitalistic privilege, he was no innocent in the world of enterprise; he managed his own investments and speculations shrewdly enough to build a fortune. He would endorse Jackson and cry out for democracy and egalitarianism, but was quickly disgusted with the coarseness of Jackson's levees where he saw "all the refuse that Washington could turn forth from its workshops and stables." He was quite at home in London among English diplomats and intellectuals, in Berlin among the Junkers, or at his summer house in Newport, where only intellectuals with substantial means could reside. "I like to watch the shouts of the multitude," he wrote at an early age, "but had rather not scream with it." He wrote of American institutions like a visionary, but played the game of the party spoilsmen like a professional. He attacked slavery with eloquence and unquestionable sincerity, but had no difficulty in adjusting himself to the Democratic party of the planters or in supporting the war with Mexico. His biographer, Russell Nye, finds that "beneath his theory lay a substratum of innate conservatism that colored his practice." "The radical who makes war upon everything in which he can discern a fault," Bancroft argued, "becomes destructive, and while he may be of service when it is proper to overthrow, he never knows how to spare or how to rebuild."

When, after more than four decades, Bancroft finished his history, which stopped with the adoption of the Constitution, his once daring espousal of democratic principles had been quite fully domesticated for conservative and nationalist purposes, and his methods of work had been superseded by more critical scholarship; but his books still stand as the greatest monument of the American historical self-consciousness of the nineteenth century. The young rebel of the early 1830's who had shocked the proper Bostonian world had become the literary incarnation of that national genius for indulgent self-acceptance that so often disturbed foreign visitors. For the generation that emerged at the end of the century, his circumspect separation of high ideals from reality became a central object of criticism, and it is not surprising that when Charles A. Beard wrote his iconoclastic book on the Constitution he should still have pointed to Bancroft, then dead almost twenty years, as the archetype of historical mystification.

Francis Bowen, a sturdy exponent of New England conservatism, was among those who found that Bancroft's history showed "a love of country too exalted to be discriminating." It was characteristic that the more orthodox representatives of the New England intellectual class should have responded with less enthusiasm than the reading public at large to the spread-eagle patriotism of Bancroft's volumes. New England Federalism laid down its challenge to Bancroft's vision of American history in the writings of Richard Hildreth —a six-volume enterprise, appearing in two sets of three volumes each in 1849 and 1852, and covering the span of American history down to the Missouri Compromise. A candid rival to Bancroft (who had thus far reached only the middle of the eighteenth century), Hildreth boasted that his was the only work on American history, barring compendiums and abridgments, that covered such a full span of time; and he made it clear, with his jibes at "meretricious rhetoric," the pedantry of German professors, and the "mythic and heroic character" with which the fathers and founders of the republic had been invested, that he was offering an intellectual as well as a commercial alternative to Bancroft. "Of centennial sermons and Fourth-of-July orations, whether professedly such or in the guise of history, there are more than enough," he proclaimed at the beginning of his work. "It is due to our fathers and ourselves, it is due to truth and philosophy, to present for once on the historic stage, the founders of our American nation unbedaubed with patriotic rouge, wrapped up in no fine-spun cloaks of excuses and apology."[8]

In truth Hildreth was one of the most interesting minds to come out of New England, a son of the region who both affirmed and denied his culture. His father, a leading teacher at Phillips Exeter, who had already tried his hand at history,

---

[8] *History*, I, iii; references in the following paragraphs are to Donald E. Emerson, *Richard Hildreth* (1946), 133, 140, 162.

raised his son in the passionate Federalism that informed Richard's work. The son, like so many of his contemporaries, came to history as a kind of literary afterthought. He experimented with law and literature, wrote on philosophical and moral questions, retranslated Bentham's *Introduction to Principles and Morals of Legislation* from the French in which it was originally published, and enjoyed a lively, controversial career for several years as a Whig newspaperman. One of the first of a line of New Englanders—Charles Francis Adams, Jr., and Brooks Adams were in the succession—who rebelled against the New England pieties themselves, he spoke of his own section as a "region of set formality and hereditary grimace," and was capable of wry and subtly humorous thrusts at the clichés of patriotic history. He took a detached view, remarkable in his day, of the struggle between England and the colonies, saw American political controversies rather coolly as a conflict between two sections of the elite classes, and described the adoption of the Constitution in terms that Charles Beard would later find congenial. Though he worked largely from printed documents and did not use the wide range of original sources that Bancroft drew upon, he had a firm regard for accuracy in detail. He had much of the astringent skepticism of Enlightenment historians like Gibbon and Hume, whom he admired, and treated most events with even-handed judgment: the major exception was the struggle between the Jeffersonians and Hamiltonians which he discussed with the ardent partisanship one might have expected of a New Englander born in the year of Jefferson's Embargo. He wrote, however, without Bancroft's flair; his acerbic and matter-of-fact view of things struck a far less resonant note with the public. For all his Federalist loyalties and his Whig journalism, he was not really allied with any major contemporary public force, and his work was not easily usable. He was, a writer in the *Church Review* said in an account of his history, "one of those men ill-adapted to command the special favor of any party, sect, or clique, from a habit he had of probing things to the bottom, stripping off disguises, and stating matters as they seem to him really to have been, careless apparently whom they may tell against, or whose sympathies and antipathies they may conflict with."

Despite their failure with the public, his works long continued to command the respect of historians—among them Henry Adams—but their disappearance from the general public consciousness suggests that they were a good index of what the American reader did not want. Edward Everett, explaining the meager results of his efforts to raise money for Hildreth during the historian's last desperate years, wrote to Charles Sumner: "Personally Mr. Hildreth was but little known here, and his unsympathizing account of the Pilgrim Fathers has prevented his History from being as popular here as otherwise it might have been."

There was indeed a certain perversity about Hildreth. His Federalist materialism, combined as it was with a candid acceptance of class as a historical force, transformed itself rather easily into an almost Marxian conception of historical development. He had never been without social passions: he was an ardent antislavery man and during a sojourn in Florida had written the first antislavery novel, *Archy Moore*, in 1836; he crusaded for temperance and free banking laws, attacked nativism in politics, and wrote a pamphlet against Boston wealth. He had always been candid about his religious skepticism, and stayed aloof from the cozy, mutually congratulatory circles of literary Boston. With time and growing alienation, he became more disposed to challenge the verities of his New England peers as well as those of the American public at large. Disappointed by the reception of his books, and by his rejection on two occasions for the coveted history professorship at Harvard, and distressed by the tightening grip of the slaveholding class on the reins of national power, he produced in 1853 his *Theory of Politics*, which brought out sharply the materialist view of history that had become linked with his utilitarian philosophy and carried his ideas to the brink of a prophetic proletarian radicalism. "The clergy, the nobles, the kings, the burghers have all had their turn," he wrote provocatively. "Is there never to be an *Age of the People*—of the working classes? Is the suggestion too extravagant that . . . the middle of this current century is destined to be that age?" It was a strange question for a Federalist historian to have come to, but the answer that nineteenth-century America was to give was as negative as its response to his books. Hildreth did not live to hear it. Frail in health for many years, he had welcomed the consulship at Trieste to which Lincoln appointed him; he died in Florence at the age of fifty-eight, and was buried there in the Protestant cemetery, not far from Theodore Parker, who had once said of his historical work: "He writes in the interest of mankind. He allows no local attachment, or reverence for men or classes of men, to keep him from telling the truth as he finds it."

IV

"Now," wrote Francis Parkman in 1878, ". . . the village has grown into a populous city, with its factories and workshops, its acres of tenement-houses, and thousands and ten thousands of restless workmen, foreigners for the most part, to whom liberty means license and politics means plunder, to whom the public good is nothing and their own most trivial interests everything, who love the country for what they can get out of it, and whose ears are opened to the promptings of every rascally agitator."[9] He was lamenting "The Failure of Universal Suffrage," and comparing the unhappy situation of modern American democracy with the old-fashioned democracy of the New England village whose government had been safe in the hands of all the adult male inhabitants. Something had been lost, presumably forever, and the loss posed a problem for the exponents of progress: how could one continue to believe in progress if American democracy had passed its apogee some thirty or forty years earlier?

Many historians did, of course, continue to believe in progress; but with something close to unanimity the historical writing of the period from the end of the Civil War to the end of the century shared Parkman's patrician bias and his conservative view of democracy and the lesser breeds. What is striking about the literature of this era, with a terrible Civil War behind it and the hideous problems of industrialism looming larger and larger ahead, is the narrow range of the historians' social sympathies. Parkman himself provides a

---

[9] *North American Review,* 127 (1878), 7.

perfect example of the transition from the romantic historical
writing of the earlier era to the conservative nationalism of
the Gilded Age. More and more, the leading historical talents
of the country were attracted to American national history,
but they acquiesced in it without being comfortable with it.
The nation's recent history had been tainted by failure; its
future seemed uncertain. The historians could, in a way, protest against it without protesting *for* anyone; at least, so it
seems if one thinks of what they usually had to say about
the ordinary farmer or worker, the Negro or the immigrant.
The most radical protest any of them could be found to endorse was Mugwump reform, which led them into a sharp
criticism of the spoilsmen in politics, but that, in turn, only
led to further gloomy reflections about the difficulties or
failures of recent democracy and to righteous condemnation
of demagogues.

The conspicuous and influential historians of the generation that came of age during or just after the Civil War and
dominated the historical writing of the last quarter of the
century were still in the tradition of the wealthy amateurs,
and still largely from the Northeast, though history had
ceased to be a near-monopoly of New Englanders. The lower-
middle-class historian, recruited from the country at large
and bringing, on occasions, more popular sympathies into
historical writing, was only beginning to appear, with the
expansion of the universities. When he read these standard
writers, he found himself still in the atmosphere of New
England Federalism and patrician values. Among leading
writers, the New England tradition was carried on by James
Schouler and John Fiske. Schouler, the Harvard-educated son
of a Scottish immigrant, had been driven to historical work
from his lucrative law practice because of his deafness. John
Fiske, the heir of an old New England Puritan tradition, was
raised by his well-to-do family in Hartford, Connecticut. His
first interest was the new positivist philosophy of Comte and
Spencer, and the task of reconciling evolutionary thought and
religion: while librarian of Harvard he turned to history
because he needed a more profitable outlet for his literary
energies, and he was one of those who made history pay.
Hermann von Holst, the son of a German Lutheran pastor

in the Baltic provinces of Russia, had been educated at Heidelberg and had absorbed a heavy dose of Treitschkean nationalism. As an immigrant to the United States he had for a time been gravely declassed, but had received a professorship at Freiburg and from there was called to teach at Chicago. Germanic intellectual influences were also present in John W. Burgess and his pupil Archibald Dunning. Burgess, who came from a Tennessee Unionist family, was sent away to Amherst for his education and thence to Germany, from which he returned a confirmed Teutonist and an ardent nationalist. His pro-Southern writings on Reconstruction were supplemented by books in which he preached the benefits of imperialism and the exceptional political genius of the Teutonic peoples. Dunning, the brilliant son of a prosperous small-town manufacturer, followed Burgess to Columbia, where he founded a seminar influential in propagating Burgess's anti-Radical views of Reconstruction. James Ford Rhodes, who was raised in the prosperous milieu of the coal-and-iron wealth of Ohio and became a brother-in-law of Mark Hanna, retired from business to write history while still in his thirties. Having made this decision, he moved to Boston— where it must have seemed to him that all proper historians ought to go (one thinks here of the similar removal of William Dean Howells, another Ohioan, many years before). John Bach McMaster, the first historian of the people, was born in Brooklyn and educated in New York, but he came from a family of long Southern residence and rather cosmopolitan interests in banking and trade. He was first an engineer, and taught engineering at Princeton before he settled upon history as his metier, and finally accepted a chair at the University of Pennsylvania.

Little of their concern with contemporary changes made its way overtly and directly into the pages of these writers. Down to the early 1880's the older historians were still engaged mainly with the colonial and Revolutionary periods. In 1882, when Charles Kendall Adams published his *Manual of Historical Literature*, he listed less than a dozen works of much consequence that reached as far as the events of the mid-nineteenth century, and a few years later when Justin Winsor launched his *Narrative and Critical History of Amer-*

ica, a collaborative work that embodied the final synthetic effort of the amateur historians as a group, he assigned only three of its eight bulky volumes to the period after 1789. John Fiske, a popularizer active chiefly in the 1880's and 1890's, took colonial and early American history as his primary theme. The most widely read of his many books—and probably the most influential work on the adoption of the Constitution before Beard's—was *The Critical Period of American History, 1783–1789*, which came out in 1888. But after about 1880 historians tended increasingly to think of the Civil War as the climactic experience of American life and to write histories that not only retold it but looked in retrospect at all national history in terms dictated by Civil War controversies. Among the surviving practitioners of the old tradition of multivolume narrative history, von Holst and McMaster covered the ground from the Revolution to the Civil War, Schouler from the Constitution to Reconstruction; and James Ford Rhodes had gone from the background of the Compromise of 1850 to the age of McKinley and Theodore Roosevelt before he ceased his labors in 1922. Around the turn of the century John W. Burgess and William A. Dunning at Columbia wrote of the middle period (that is, about 1815 to 1860) and of the Civil War and Reconstruction from a point of view that combined nationalism on constitutional questions with pro-Southern views on race and the issues of Reconstruction—views which by now were becoming the national ones.

Most of these writers were affected to some extent by the idea of "scientific" or critical history: there would be no more bowdlerization like that of Sparks, no more historical orations or rearranged quotations as in Bancroft. But they did not relinquish the idea of history as a forum for moral judgments: they were deeply concerned with such questions as Who was right? or Which principles were correct? when they dealt with the background of the Revolution, the adoption of the Constitution, the struggles between Jeffersonians and Hamiltonians, or Jackson and the Whigs. In recounting the background and aftermath of the Civil War, they were concerned with the merits and morality of slavery, the soundness of the idea of a constitutional right of secession, the true nature of the Union, the justice and wisdom of Reconstruction. And here the past was often reshaped by current preoccupations with the problems of industrialism and the city, of agrarian or working-class revolt, of the immense waves of new immigrants that were sweeping into the country. The mobs of the Revolutionary era could be depicted in such a way as to state a general point of view about law and order, Daniel Shays in such a way as to condemn contemporary agrarian radicalism; Jefferson could be used to condemn sentimental democracy and "radical" theorizing, Jackson to discredit spoilsmen, party machines, demagogues, and modern democracy. In short, what the conservative nationalist historians did was to forge a view of the past that needed only to be inverted point by point by the Progressive historians to yield a historical rationale for social reform.

It would be misleading, of course, to suggest that there was a party line among historians whose concerns differed and who on one count or another would have individual and varying views. McMaster, while supporting sound money and Federalist policies, might also celebrate the development of the rights of man, give unusual attention to the history of the common people, and sometimes portray immigrants with sympathy. Schouler might write more warmly about Jefferson than the others. Von Holst, Schouler, and Rhodes might discuss the slavery issue in an abolitionist spirit. But, by and large, this entire generation of writers had much in common; it is possible to draw up a composite view of American history out of their work in which the deviations of individual writers seem of little more than marginal consequence. It was still a history written from a New England or at least a Northeast United States point of view, and influenced directly or indirectly by post-Civil War nationalist conceptions. It embodied the ideas of the possessing classes about industrial and financial issues, manifested the complacency of white Anglo-Saxon Protestants about social and ethnic issues, and, on constitutional issues, underwrote the requirements of property and of national centralization as opposed to states' rights or regional self-assertion.

Critics have noted the stark conservatism of the historiography of this era, and we may well wonder how writers

who were still disturbed by Jefferson could have kept their
poise before Bryan and Altgeld. One thinks of von Holst finding the Declaration of Independence derived from the "crude
theories" of Rousseau; of Fiske, pleading for genealogy and
warning that "by no possible ingenuity of constitution-making
or of legislation can a society made up of ruffians and boors
be raised to the intellectual and moral level of a society made
up of well-bred merchants and yeomen, parsons and lawyers";
of McMaster saying that Jefferson was "saturated with democracy in its rankest form" and remained "to the last day
of his life a servile worshipper of the people"; of Schouler
condemning the activities of "unlettered and boozy foreigners,
the scum of European society"; of Rhodes attributing industrial poverty not to failures in the economy but to "the constantly deteriorating character of the European immigration,"
charging that foreigners had brought the "instinct" of industrial strife to the United States, condemning striking coal
miners as "a mob" whose leisure hours were passed "mainly
in whisky-drinking," and branding T. R. as one who, despite
birth and breeding, appealed to the mob; of Burgess questioning whether the United States could assimilate Slavs, Czechs,
and Hungarians who, being inclined to "anarchy and crime,"
represent "the exact opposite of genuine Americans"; of Dunning bemoaning the "reckless enfranchisement of the freed-
men and their enthronement in power," asserting that "the
negro had no pride of race and no aspirations or ideals save
to be like the whites," and offering this as the sole reason
for his desire for equal treatment. "You may well say," wrote
William E. Dodd even as late as 1919, "why can not historians see things from the people's point of view."[1]

Despite McMaster's pleas for more attention to the common man, the historians of this era gave relatively perfunctory treatment to the farmer, though the country had been
overwhelmingly agricultural up to the time of their own
maturity, and they had a uniformly harsh view of the farmer's discontents, when expressed in inflationary demands.

---

[1] Edward Saveth, *American Historians and European Immigrants,
1875–1925* (1948), 36, 49, 172, 176, 232, 233; Harvey Wish, *The
American Historian* (1960), 141, 216, 221. Dodd quoted in Merle
Curti, "The Democratic Theme in American Historical Literature," *Mississippi Valley Historical Review*, 39 (1952), 9.

As Turner was to show, they consistently underestimated the role of the West. Rhodes, a retired industrialist with the predictable views of his class, had only a slightly more biased view of workers and union activities than was customary among his fellows. Whatever the treatment of the old German and Scandinavian immigration, the Irish and the new immigrants from southern and eastern Europe almost unfailingly fared badly, except for an occasional sympathetic word from McMaster. Issues involving slavery and the Negro received a new formulation after the reconciliationists of the 1880's and 1890's had done their bit to piece the North and South together again. Earlier historians had been abolitionists—slavery was a historically adjudicated issue—but at the same time unmistakably anti-Negro, not only in that they insisted on racial inferiority but strongly espoused the racial case of the Southern whites on every issue except the formality of bondage itself. Historians, responding to the irenical movement of the times, tended to follow what might be called the Rhodes-Burgess compromise, which required the South to concede the immorality and retrograde nature of slavery and the unconstitutionality and unrighteous tendency of secession, while the North was to admit the necessity of white supremacy and white autonomy in the South and grant the wrong-headedness of radical Reconstruction.

Finally, toward the end of the century, with the emergence of the "imperial school" of colonial historians—a gifted group headed by C. M. Andrews, H. L. Osgood, and G. L. Beer—whose teachings coincided with the burgeoning of American imperialism and with a strong new trend toward Anglo-American understanding, even the old partisan version of the Revolution underwent a thorough and circumspect reconsideration in which the policies of George III's ministers were given their first sympathetic review. There were times when it must have seemed that the main enterprise of the standard historians was to repudiate the Revolution and undo the social effects of the Civil War. And the young Progressive historians of the new era might have found an ironic point in their predecessors' disposition to quarrel with so much of the radical and revolutionary American past and their quiet acquiescence in the American present. In 1902, when Charles

Beard arrived as a young doctoral candidate at Columbia, where Burgess, Dunning, and Osgood were flourishing, he found himself plunged straight into this intellectual world; and much of what he wrote from 1904 onward must have been in response to this environment.

V

Among the leading historians at work in the Gilded Age, Henry Adams stands, as he no doubt would have wished to stand, alone—singular not only for the quality of his prose and the sophistication of his mind but also for the unparalleled mixture of his detachment and involvement. His enterprise itself was extraordinary: nine volumes, no less, totaling close to four thousand pages, all devoted, not like the synoptic works of his contemporaries to a half or a whole century or more, but to the administrations of Thomas Jefferson and James Madison, the span of years from 1800 to 1817—a period regarded by the author himself as dreary and unproductive, as an age of slack and derivative culture, of fumbling and small-minded statecraft, terrible parochial wrangling and treasonous schemes, climaxed by a ludicrous and unnecessary war. This was an inexplicable choice of subject for a man whose curiosity and competence ranged so far—inexplicable, at least, if we rely on the guidance Adams himself gives us in his *Education*: "He had even published a dozen volumes of American history for no other purpose than to satisfy himself whether, by the severest process of stating, with the least possible comment, such facts as seemed rigorously consequent, he could fix for a familiar moment a necessary sequence of human movement." One can only wonder if Adams really thought that his choice of the years between the angry departure of John Adams and the arrival of John Quincy Adams—a "familiar moment" indeed to him, and we may ask whether the pun was wholly unconscious—was made for "no other purpose" than to test a certain naïve and ephemeral notion of scientific history; or whether we are not here again dealing with one of the characteristic poses of a mind that was quite as perverse as it was brilliant. It is hard to believe that Adams really thought his only purpose was to test historical science, or even that he designed his history as a kind of reprise of the documents, supplemented "with the least possible comment." What is visible to the reader who knows Adams and the Adamses, is a pilgrimage to the family pieties and a delicate resumption of old family quarrels. The epoch is chosen because John and John Quincy are *not* there—some scruple forbids trying to tackle head-on the history of the Adams presidencies themselves; but they hover in the background, as other men fail to solve the problems they had been denounced or rejected for attempting. They are represented, also, by proxy. "To do justice to Gallatin was a labor of love," wrote this historian who affected to introduce the least possible comment. "After long study of the prominent figures in our history, I am more than ever convinced that for combination of ability, integrity, knowledge, unselfishness, and social fitness Mr. Gallatin has no equal." The moral of Gallatin's life was what interested Adams. As he wrote to Henry Cabot Lodge: "The inevitable isolation and disillusionment of a really strong mind—one that combines force with elevation—is to me the romance and tragedy of statesmanship."[2] The great passion behind Adams's history came from the powerful animating impulse provided by family themes, and by that sense, familiar again and again in the family history and not least in his own generation, of the unenviable fate of really strong minds in America. But the beauty of Adams's history arises in good part because his was no simple or unilateral family vendetta: the presidential Adamses, patriots both for all their angular vanity, had been caught midway between the self-regarding parochialisms of the Virginians and of the High Federalists; and the elegant poise of Adams's detachment derives in part from the even-handed justice that could be dealt out on both sides. Some contemporary reviewers even thought Adams partial to Jefferson, and could find texts to support the interpretation. This was a tribute to subtlety and mixed motives: Jefferson's statecraft ran wholly counter to Adams's values; but Jefferson, for all the estrangement that had taken place,

---

2 William Jordy, *Henry Adams, Scientific Historian* (1952), 47–8.

was an old family friend, and at his worst he must be seen
as a fallen gentleman, while the High Federalists at their
worst were crazed vendettists and reckless conspirators.

In his central concern for nationhood, Adams had something in common with the other amateur writers of his era.
In his feeling for style, he is reminiscent of the literary tradition of Parkman and Bancroft. In his critical methods, his
careful control of emotion, his belief in history as a science
he was more like the school that was now developing in the
academy. But in the singular stamp of his own curiosity, in
a certain delight he took in observing the logic of events, he
stood by himself, and the volumes he produced have been
acclaimed—rightly, I think—as the summit of American
achievement in historical writing. Out of the confusion of the
era he deals with, the dreary debates in Congress, the complex and tedious diplomatic maneuvers, the careers of petty
men who acted according to their characters and great men
who did not, there emerges a narrative full of brilliant passages. One sees the formation of national character, the forging of a country out of the mutual hatreds of clashing
sections, the efforts of a nation of raw farmers to achieve
enough discipline and sophistication and to develop enough
competent leadership to survive and prosper in the savage
world of international politics. There is a strong sense for the
requirements of national power, a consistent and knowing
interest—here Adams was far ahead of his predecessors and
of most of his successors—in what goes on in the heads of
those who wield power, an absorption in the craft of politics,
a frequent note of humor at the sheer absurdity of the American scene.

For Adams, unlike its other advocates, scientific history
was primarily a clue to the human condition. Others might
see scientific history as a surer way of plotting the advance
of mankind toward some freer or better state of things—and
there are in fact a few passages even in Adams that suggest
a momentary concurrence with the idea. But more often than
not, his native mordant alienation asserts itself, and then
one sees his essential view of the matter: scientific history
shows man in the grip of natural impulsions that carry him
to ends determined neither by ideals nor by anyone's well-

formulated purposes but to a destination of nature's own. "History," he wrote in his concluding passage, "has its scientific as well as its human side, and in American history the scientific interest was greater than the human. Elsewhere the student could study under better conditions the evolution of the individual, but nowhere could he study so well the evolution of a race. The interest of such a subject exceeded that of any other branch of science, for it brought mankind within sight of its own end." To a friend he wrote while his enterprise was in progress that he was "at times almost sorry" that he ever undertook to write about Jefferson, Madison, and Monroe, "for they appear like mere grasshoppers kicking and gesticulating on the middle of the Mississippi River. . . . They were carried along on a stream which floated them, after a fashion, without much regard to themselves. . . . My own conclusion is that history is simply social development along the lines of weakest resistance, and that in most cases the line of weakest resistance is found as unconsciously by society as by water."[3]

Adams did not see scientific history as pointing the way to a golden future; neither did he see a happy future for historical writing itself. It was in character for him to be skeptical even about the usability of scientific history, and in 1894, when he was president of the American Historical Association, he sent his colleagues a gloomy presidential message, warning them that the more scientific their history became the less acceptable it would be to the forces of labor and capital, of church and state, and hence the more sure to find itself in crisis, at odds with the world. His own history, echoing as it does with the tired laughter of his remote and sardonic intelligence, was certainly not shaped to be ingratiating, and it lacked the mythic resonances of more complaisant works. For all that, considering its deliberate pace and the austerity of its subject, it did not sell badly—nearly 3,000 sets were sold in the 1890's—but it is questionable how much it was read. Adams may have been indulging in one of his contrarieties when he said "I never met ten men who read my history," but the substantive point was still true:

---

[3] *History*, IX, 224; Harold D. Cater, ed., *Henry Adams and His Friends* (1947), 125.

the work was not notably influential. Basically conservative, it was still not simple enough to be usable by men who could read a dozen other, more accessible conservative historians; basically nationalistic, it was too pessimistic, too preoccupied with failure, too redolent of Adams's blocked and unconsummated patriotism, for the prophets of nationality. And what could either conservative or patriot do with a man who suggested in his *Letter to American Teachers of History* that they might begin by announcing to their class that "their year's work would be devoted to showing in American history 'a universal tendency to the dissipation of energy' and degradation of thought, which would soon end in making America 'improper for the habitation of man as he is now constituted' "?

In his role of historian, as in his other capacities, Adams continued to see himself as a recessive type. "The more I write," he confessed to Parkman in 1884, "the more confident I feel that before long a new school of history will rise which will leave us antiquated. Democracy is the only subject for history"—but again the context showed that he found no hope in this, only the prospect that in another generation the sciences would join "in proving man to have as fixed and necessary a development as that of a tree; and almost as unconscious." When his work was done, he could see little of himself in it. The last volumes had hardly appeared before he was writing to Elizabeth Cameron: "There are not nine pages in the nine volumes that now express anything of my interests or feelings; unless perhaps some of my disillusionment. So you must not blame me if I feel, or seem to feel, morbid on the subject of history. I care more for one chapter, or any dozen pages of *Esther* than for the whole history, including maps and indexes." To J. F. Jameson he wrote: "I would much rather wipe out all I have ever said than go on with more."[4] The whole enterprise, being nothing more than great history, had been a vast disappointment. And was Adams, in confiding this to a leader of the historical profession, indulging in one of his least kindly gestures—a parting word *pour encourager les autres*?

---

[4] Cater, *Adams*, 133–4; Adams, *Letters* (W. C. Ford ed., 1930), I, 468; J. F. Jameson in *American Historical Review*, 26 (1920), 9.

VI

Up to about 1890, when Henry Adams was finishing his history, the major historians of the United States were still working in the tradition of the great amateurs. They were not formally trained to write history, even though some of them, after they had already established themselves as historians, took academic posts and tried to train a few others. But the development of the modern American university, which went on with breathtaking rapidity in the years after 1870, brought into being a whole new class of historians, the academic professionals. In the last two decades of the nineteenth century there took place a sudden transformation of the prevailing model of historical work. A discipline that had once been dominated by well-to-do gentlemen-amateurs inspired by a literary ideal and writing grand narrative history aimed at (if not always successfully reaching) a broad reading public was now rather rapidly taken over by professional scholars, recruited to a striking degree from the middle and lower-middle class, academically trained and academically employed, inspired by the scientific ideal, and writing for the most part highly focused monographic inquiries intended for other professionals. It was not simply that universities and colleges were becoming more numerous: the place they gave to history was growing larger, as they began to cope with the complexity of modern knowledge and as the elective system multiplied the number of courses in college curricula. In the old classical curriculum, history had been taught as something ancillary to the central subjects and had been entrusted to men not primarily concerned with it. Some ancient history, for example, was frequently offered as a background to classical languages. Even as late as 1884, the colleges and universities, then some four hundred in number, still had only about twenty full-time history teachers. Ten years later there were almost a hundred, busily preparing their successors to meet the rapidly growing demand. During the intervening years of growth, the teachers of history, still under the rule of old-fashioned educators who continued to think of history as a marginal subject, were a ludicrously underspecialized

lot who carried on their original work under formidable han-
dicaps. At the very time when Frederick Jackson Turner was
developing the vital ideas in his early essays, he had to offer
courses at Wisconsin in the French Revolution, Primitive
Society, Dynastic and Territorial History of the Middle Ages,
the Constitutional History of the United States, and a seminar
in the History of the Northwest—and it was not every instructor who had Turner's gift for converting such demands
upon himself into an intellectual asset.[5] And yet, at the end
of the century the better universities were beginning to give
the new generation of scholars a professional atmosphere,
and to lay the basis for professional morale. Learned societies
were springing up, scholarly journals and university presses
had been established.

This change coincided with the disappearance of the
older generation of literary historians. Bancroft and Parkman, the last of the great New England romantic historians,
died in 1891 and 1893. To some it must have seemed that a
small number of literary giants had been replaced by a horde
of mediocrities. In 1900 Frederic Bancroft, a historian who
belonged to the fading race of amateurs, reported to Herbert
Baxter Adams that he had lately been reading recent historians and critics and comparing them with those of other
countries and times. "Has it ever occurred to you," he asked
abruptly, "that none of our schools of history has ever produced a historian of special merit as both scholar and
writer?"

Others looked upon this development with resignation.
Writing in 1891 on the course of American historical work,
J. F. Jameson predicted that the coming generation would
produce no classical historian to compare with a genius like
Parkman, but suggested that this should not be regretted.
"If there is not produced among us any work of supereminent
genius, there will surely be a large amount of good second-
class work done; that is, of work of the second-class in respect to purely literary qualities. Now it is the spread of
thoroughly good second-class work—second-class in this

---

[5] Stull Holt, ed., *Historical Scholarship in the United States, 1876–
1901* (1938), 123; cf. 65. On numbers in the profession, see
John Higham, *History* (1965), 4.

sense—that our science most needs at present; for it sorely needs that improvement in technical process, that superior finish of workmanship, which a large number of works of talent can do more to foster than a few works of literary genius. . . . We may even hope that out of improved scholarship may grow in time a superior profundity of thought; for in truth profundity of thought has not been among the merits of our most distinguished historians."[6]

Jameson had summed it up well: "technical process" and finish of workmanship in the interests of a developing science. It was science that, in the post-Darwinian era, had the prestige; and all the social disciplines—anthropology, economics, politics, the new field of sociology, as well as history—were at pains to modernize themselves by bringing their methods into harmony with evolutionary methods, and at the same time to strengthen their status in the academy by affirming whenever possible their scientific character. Now history too, once a branch of literature, must become a science—a science which could aim, in return for whatever qualities might be lost, at greater profundity of thought. But here we must not be deceived: the language of science was ubiquitous, the deference given to it almost universal, but historians did not always mean the same thing when they spoke of it. To some it seemed to mean only zeal in collecting facts and the critical use of sources—though on such counts they were not really far removed from the best of the romantic historians. To others it might mean striving for objectivity, avoiding judgments, staying clear of that open partisanship which was identified with the obsolescent work of George Bancroft. To some it meant concentrating on answering questions about events rather than retelling a narrative, to others simply systematic and quantitative work. In its most demanding form it meant some combination of all of these in order to formulate general laws of historical development.

And yet there were historians who, though they regarded themselves as scientific, objected strenuously to what was implied in this goal. John W. Burgess argued for purely inductive procedures, for the disciplined collecting of facts in

---

6 Holt, *Historical Scholarship*, 281; Jameson, *History of Historical Writing*, 132–3.

their chronological order, on the assumption that their meaning would become clear without the use of hypotheses or
guiding principles. Ephraim Emerton of Harvard, setting
down rules in 1893 for the training of PhD's, reluctantly
allowed for "a brief excursion" into the philosophy of history,
but thought it a "dangerously speculative subject" whose
further pursuit, if there was to be any, could well be put off
to one's mature years. The medievalist George Burton Adams,
protesting against idle speculation in 1909, insisted that
scientific history had one object, and one only: to collect and
classify facts, "to ascertain as nearly as possible and to record
exactly what happened."[7] Anything beyond this was not historical science but merely the philosophy of history. Writers
of this persuasion thought that they understood Ranke, and
they approved of what they thought he stood for: history
wie es eigentlich gewesen. This school, with its firm resistance to all avowed schemes of interpretation, and its disposition to smuggle in its preferences under the pretense of
having no views, constituted a persistent irritant to writers
of Turner's generation, and again of Beard's, who were hot
on the trail of the meaning of history and devoted to explanation and critical analysis. Turner's first speculative paper,
"The Significance of History," brushed this school aside in
his search for explanatory patterns; Beard's famous book on
the Constitution attacked it almost from the start.

The development of another, more theoretically minded
school of scientific history took place at Johns Hopkins in the
1880's, where the influential seminar of Herbert Baxter
Adams introduced some of that dedication and discipline that
he brought back from his studies in Germany. Adams liked
to imagine that his seminar was modeled directly after natural science, and once asserted with ingenuous pride that "the
Baltimore seminaries are laboratories where books are treated
like mineralogical specimens, passed about from hand to
hand, examined, and tested"—an unconscious thrust at his

---

7 On the ideal of scientific history, see John Higham, *History*
92–103; John Herman Randall, Jr., and George Haines IV, "Con-
trolling Assumptions in the Practice of American Historians,"
Theory and Practice in Historical Study, Bulletin 54, Social
Science Research Council (1946), 30–41; A. S. Eisenstadt, *Charles
McLean Andrews* (1956), chapters i, ii.

own vitals that could not have been more deadly if it had been made by some unscrupulous satirist. The Adams school took institutions, especially political institutions, for its subject, and scorning (as it thought) all bias, disdaining the play of feeling in the work of the romantic writers, tried to concentrate on digging out the hard facts of institutional change, and then, through the comparative method, to lay bare the generally applicable principles of evolutionary development. The United States, Adams thought, "will yet be viewed and reviewed as an organism of historic growth, developing from minute germs, from the very protoplasm of state life."[8]

In fact the leading ideas of the Adams school had about the same relation to science that phrenology had to neurology. It refurbished, with biological metaphors and evolutionary language, the old theory, quite familiar to the romantic historians and to others before them, of the Germanic origins of Anglo-American democracy; by disguising Providence in the garb of Evolution, it restored the ancient idea that the events of history go on under providential guidance. But it was a productive school, which had to its credit the rearing of an extraordinary proportion of the next generation's leading historians. Some of its most forceful minds—among them Charles McLean Andrews, Frederick Jackson Turner, and Woodrow Wilson—broke quickly and easily on one count or another with its guiding suppositions, but several remained under lasting debt to its zeal for knowledge and its demand for scholarly patience in unraveling the threads of institutional change.

By the end of the nineteenth century it was evident that the modern university had created a wholly new setting for historical writing, and out of this setting Turner and Beard, the major spokesmen of progressive history, arose. The passion for style prevalent among the narrative writers was now at a discount, in favor of austerity and discipline; but as always there was the need, even in the new modes of work, of readable writers. History was now linked not to romantic fiction or romantic philosophy but to other academic disci-

---

[8] Eisenstadt, *Andrews*, 11. The Johns Hopkins school is discussed at somewhat greater length below, Chapter 2.

plines that were swept along in the Darwinian current—to anthropology, geography, sociology, economics. Historians became more aware of the wide range of subjects that they might attend to—not simply politics but the whole range of human ideas, activities, and institutions. At the same time history was freed of excessive involvement with the religious and sectional debates of the past, and laid upon itself the demand to be objective and critical. More and more the academic writers felt obliged to try to suppress the unsuppressable disposition to judge, and instead to look at historical controversies less to find who was right than to find out how things came about. With the new historians the eternal motive of judgment and vindication did not, of course, by any means disappear; but it became mixed with and overlaid by the motive of analysis and explanation. As the "scientific" monograph replaced the narrative, new imperatives arose. The monograph was the characteristic product of the graduate school, the offshoot of instruction toward the PhD—apprentice work, in a sense. Where the leading historians of the amateur tradition had trained amanuenses and copyists, the leading graduate instructors trained PhD candidates, and the order of service was reversed: the master was now put to the task not of using but of developing the apprentice. The difference was important. The amanuenses had been subordinate to the aims of their employers: they gathered facts, copied documents, but they did not *appear*. Graduate students, on the other hand, were ends in themselves; they wrote their own books which the masters "supervised."

Here is where the leading professionals had their part. In order to run seminars and provide inspiration for the growing number of such students, graduate instructors had to have central, vitalizing ideas, around which a "school" might cohere. And, what is even more to the point, young writers of monographs themselves were hungry for ideas. Their inquiries were often very specialized, very recondite, very limited in scope, sometimes written with an oppressive lack of verve. But we must not imagine that such men were insensate drudges. Precisely because of the narrow confines of their work, they longed to see their monographs take a place as part of some larger, sustained pattern of inquiry. The PhD dissertation had to be justified as a "contribution" to knowl-edge—and the very idea of a contribution suggested a con-summation beyond itself. In the pattern of narrative history, each work, as a work of art, contained its own consumma-tion. In the pattern of monographic history the consumma-tion lay somewhere else, in some grander scheme of ideas, or in the cumulative development of science. And it is here that writers like Turner and Beard performed a function of vital importance. Turner's conception of the frontier process and Beard's of the economic interpretation of politics gave a connected meaning to the multiple events of American history.

Still, the strength of the progressive historians did not depend solely upon the professional appeal of their basic insights; it depended even more upon the mythic appeal of their ideas which reached outside academic walls and touched readers in the general intellectual public. Their work has to be seen as part of a general change in styles of thought that went on inside the academy in the years after 1890 and finally brought the work of academic scholars into a far more active and sympathetic relation to political and social change than it had ever had before. The historical writers of the older generation had commonly looked with incomprehension or stunned resentment at the trends of the times—the devel-opment of industry, the problems of the city, the world of the rebellious farmer, of the worker and the immigrant. Their histories reflect their distaste, their withdrawal, the limits of their social sympathies—in sum, their basic roots in the order of the earlier nineteenth century, when men did not yet believe that the United States would go the way of the other modern nations. Above all, their work reflected the laissez-faire mentality: history was not conceived as a possible in-strument of social change; it had no positive relation to the problems of the present. Turner, Parrington, and Beard be-longed to a generation that was still relatively young during the formative years of the Progressive movement. Turner was in his early thirties, Beard and Parrington in their early twenties, when the great depression of the 1890's—a turning point in the development of the American mind—was at its worst. Wholly post-Civil War and post-industrial, these younger writers were still in an impressionable stage of their intellectual development at the time when the American political system had to make its first major adjustments to the impact of modern industry.

Where the generation before them still thought of our history from a perspective set by the events of the Civil War and Reconstruction and by the moral and constitutional arguments that came with them, the Progressive generation had grown up with American industry, had witnessed the disappearance of the frontier line, the submergence of the farmer, the agrarian revolt, the recruitment of a vast labor force, the great tides of the new immigration, the fierce labor struggles of the 1890's. Their awareness of the whole complex of industrial America was keener, and their sense of the urgency of its problems had been quickened by the depression of the 1890's. They were disposed to think more directly about the economic issues of society, and to look again at the past to see if economic forces had not been somewhat neglected. They were disposed also to think more critically about the ruling forces, about the powerful plutocracy that had been cast up by the national growth of the past thirty years. As academic historians dependent upon their professional income rather than inherited wealth, they were even thrown into uncomfortable juxtaposition with the reigning forces of American society. The raw and arrogant society that had come with the new industry reached down even into the academy and forced them to understand that they lived in no ivory tower, that the professor, at least the professor with new and critical ideas, must in his own way have a reckoning with the world of institutional power. Reared in a society in which angry confrontations between academics and trustees were to become increasingly common, all three of these men —Turner at Wisconsin, Parrington at the University of Oklahoma, and Beard at Columbia—were drawn into and affected by university controversies of varying degrees of acerbity, and each of them left an institution under stress. What these three men did in their writings—again with different strategies and with different intensities of temperament—was to move the thinking of American historians, at first slowly, and then with increasing tempo and commitment, into the controversial political world of the new century and into the intellectual orbit of the Progressive movement. Where the historical writing of the Gilded Age had been marked by its aloofness from if not hostility to popular aspirations, the historical writing of the twentieth century would be, whatever its pretensions to science, critical, democratic, progressive.

PART
II

Frederick Jackson Turner

CHAPTER 2

Turner and the Western Revolt

> *The reign of aristocracy is passing; that of humanity begins. Democracy is waiting for its poet.*
> —Frederick Jackson Turner, 1883 (aet. 21)

> *All the associations called up by the spoken word, the West, were fabulous, mythic, hopeful.*
> —Hamlin Garland

I

WHEN WE THINK of the American West in the 1890's, we think first of its manifest excitements—the revolt of Populism, the climax of the silver issue in the Bryan campaign of 1896. There was also a parallel cultural revolt of similar emotional origins yet gentler, subtler, and considerably more enduring. For a long time the East had condescended to Western culture, and Westerners were tired of being patronized. Mature enough now in their wealth and their cultural powers, they were at last ready to stage a demonstration of their coming of age, to write manifestos proclaiming their cultural independence and promising their future predominance. When Congress authorized a national exposition to celebrate the four hundredth anniversary of Columbus's discovery of America, it was none of the great Eastern cities—not Boston, the passing cultural capital, not New York, the emerging one; not Washington, the political capital, nor Philadelphia, which had appropriately been host to the centennial of the Declaration of Independence in 1876 —but two upstart Western rivals, St. Louis and Chicago, that bid hardest to have the fair, and it was Chicago that won. There the American Historical Association gathered in July, 1893, and there Frederick Jackson Turner, then not quite thirty-two, read a paper on "The Significance of the Frontier in American History" "which was destined," as Charles A.

47

Beard later wrote, "to have a more profound influence on thought about American history than any other essay or volume ever written on the subject."[1]

The political revolt of the West could be heard anywhere in the rhetoric of the nineties. The cultural revolt, carried on for the most part *sotto voce* and scattered in a variety of fugitive sources, is harder to record. But Turner's address was one of two documents symptomatic of the spirit of the new West. While Turner in effect claimed for the West America's historic past, Hamlin Garland's literary manifesto, *Crumbling Idols*, claimed America's cultural future. Garland's little book, published in 1894 by the enterprising new Chicago firm of Stone and Kimball, was almost a counterpart in criticism of Turner's historical essay. Garland, a year older than Turner, was also a native of Wisconsin. Like Turner, he had played the role of the young man from the provinces, although where Turner had gone to the East's most vital academic center at Baltimore, Garland had gone to its old literary center at Boston. With Garland the experience led to a similar reassertion of Western pride, to a rejection of Eastern literary models and standards of judgment. The history of American literature, he argued, is the history "of the slow development of a distinctive utterance." Its greatest impediment was a continuing imitation of English literary models. American literature had been almost wholly provincial down to the Civil War, but at its close, "from the interior of America, men and women rose almost at once to make American literature take on vitality and character." Now the Eastern cities had taken the position once occupied by London, that of an academic center, and the many school-bred Westerners, who were still content to defer to the judgments of the East, wrote imitative works, taking their stand against "the indigenous and the democratic." Against this worship of crumbling idols the Western artist must steel himself. The problem for an American art was not to produce something greater than the past but something different. "Our task is not to imitate but to create."

---

[1] "Turner's 'The Frontier in American History,' " in *Books That Changed Our Minds*, ed. by Malcolm Cowley and Bernard Smith (1938), 61.

In short bold strokes Garland tried to anticipate the new democratic realism (he used the unfortunate term "veritism") that would rise out of the West. The Western writer must learn to see "the wealth of material which lies at his hand in the mixture of races going on with inconceivable celerity everywhere in America, but with especial picturesqueness in the West." For forty years an "infinite drama" had been going on in the wide spaces of the West, as rich a drama as any ever seen on earth. Themes were crying out for their writers —the history, for example, of the lumbering district of the Northern lakes, the subtle changes of thought and life that had come with emergent cities like St. Paul or Minneapolis, the life of the sawmills and shingle mills, the river life of the upper Mississippi, the mixtures of races, the building of the railroads with their trickery and exploitation, the rise of millionaires. "The mighty West, with its swarming millions, remains undelineated in the novel, the drama, and the poem." The coming generation would remedy this: but it must not imitate, it must write of the things it knows, must embrace local color—"Every great moving literature today is full of local color"; look at the Norwegians and the Russians. As Turner argued that local history must be set in the context of universal history, Garland saw that the parochial, once it has been raised to the highest level of expression, has universal merits.

Garland saw the future of American literature coming out of the prairies and forests, from which Turner traced the democracy of the past. "The prairies lead to general conceptions. The winds give strength and penetration and alertness. The mighty stretches of woods lead to breadth and generosity of intellectual conception. The West and South are coming to be something more than big, coming to the expression of a new world, coming to take their places in the world of literature, as in the world of action, and no sneer from gloomy prophets of the dying past can check or chill them." Hence the center of national literary life could no longer be in the East. Literary supremacy would pass from New York to Chicago, as it once had from Boston to New York; and beyond Chicago there lay yet more new centers of literary culture. In the future, American culture would no doubt be more diffuse, but if it would have any center, it would surely not be New York, which, like Boston, "is too near London." "From [the] interior spaces of the South and West the most vivid and fearless and original utterance of the coming American democracy will come. . . . The genuine American literature . . . must come from the soil and the open air, and be likewise freed from tradition."

Turner's single address had more durable fare to offer than the dozen essays that made up Garland's book. Not only did Turner set forth a view of the American character so conceived that the very essence of American nationality was recaptured from the Eastern historians and turned over to the substantial majority of Americans who lived beyond the Appalachians, but he also offered an "explanation," to use his term, of all American history that was distinctly different from previous explanations. His famous paper opens on a strategic note: citing a recent bulletin of the Superintendent of the Census, Turner pointed out that the unsettled area of the United States was now so broken up by the advance of settlers that there was no longer a frontier line. The frontier had disappeared, and this marked "the closing of a great historic movement." Thus far American history had been in large degree the history of the colonization of the West. "The existence of an area of free land, its continuous recession, and the advance of American settlement westward, explain American development."[2]

Turner went on to underscore the central importance of growth and adaptation in American history, with the special feature that the frontier brought a continually renewed reversion to "primitive conditions," which is experienced over and over again. "This perennial rebirth," he asserted, "this fluidity of American life, this expansion westward with its new opportunities, its continuous touch with the simplicity of primitive society, furnish the forces dominating the American character. The true point of view in the history of this nation

---

[2] The address did not appear in book form until the publication of *The Frontier in American History* (1920), 1–38, hereafter cited as *Frontier*. It has been printed in many places, but the most accessible work for readers today, which contains Turner's significant early essays, is Ray Allen Billington, ed., *Frontier and Section* (1961).

is not the Atlantic coast, it is the Great West." Even the
slavery struggle "occupies its important place in American
history because of its relation to westward expansion."

Exclusive attention, Turner complained, had been given
to the germ theory of political institutions—to the study of
European germs maturing in the American environment—
and too little to the demands of the environment itself, for
it was the environment that provided the American elements.
"The frontier is the line of most rapid and effective Americanization." It takes the colonist, a man in European dress
with European habits of thought, strips off the garments of
his civilized past, puts him almost on a par with the Indian,
and disciplines and changes him during his long struggle to
implant society in the wilderness. At first the wilderness masters the colonist; in the end it is mastered by him, as the
apparatus of civilization little by little emerges; but the point
is that the process changes him, and when it is over he is no
longer a European but a new man, an accretion of the new
things he has had to learn and do. "Thus the advance of
the frontier has meant a steady movement away from the
influence of Europe, a steady growth of independence on
American lines. And to study this advance, the men who grew
up under these conditions, and the political, economic, and
social results of it, is to study the really American part of our
history."

Like most of the post-Darwinian thinkers of the nineteenth century, Turner was fascinated by the idea of laying
out the development of civilization in a series of distinct
evolutionary stages; and the beauty of American history,
from this point of view, was the way the stages of social
development appeared and repeated themselves in a clear
pattern. In one of his best images Turner said: "The United
States lies like a huge page in the history of society. Line by
line as we read this continental page from West to East we
find the record of social evolution." The stages are recorded
like the strata in a geological sequence or the order of species
on a phylogenetic scale: first the Indian and the hunter; then
the trader, the pathfinder of civilization; then, successively,
the pastoral stage of ranch life, settled farming communities,
intensive cultivation, and finally the emergence of cities and

manufactures. In a long central passage of the essay Turner spelled out some of the features of these various kinds of frontiers.

In assessing the effect of the frontier on the East and on Europe, Turner argued that the frontier was the primary agency through which the immigrant was Americanized, that it "promoted the formation of a composite nationality for the American people." The important legislation that had developed the powers of the national government was also "conditioned on the frontier." Such matters as the tariff, the disposition of public lands, and internal improvement had traditionally been treated by historians as subsidiary to the slavery question. "But when American history comes to be rightly viewed it will be seen that the slavery question is an incident." (Earlier he had said, with better proportion, "a most important incident.")[3] The demands of the West, the problems arising out of the conquest and settlement of the West, were of such importance that they shaped the slavery struggle itself. The West forged legislation, broke down the sectionalism of the coast, nationalized the federal government. Loose construction of the Constitution gained as the nation marched westward. "It was this nationalizing tendency of the West that transformed the democracy of Jefferson into the nationalizing republicanism of Monroe and the democracy of Andrew Jackson." But the "most important effect of the frontier" was in promoting democracy both in America and Europe. The frontier produced individualism, and "frontier individualism has from the beginning promoted democracy." It was the West that had done most to develop a democratic suffrage.

Above all, the West had promoted mobility and opportunity. "So long as free land exists, the opportunity for a competency exists, and economic power secures political power." Turner saw that "the democracy born of free land" had its limitations too: it went too far in its selfishness and individualism, proved itself intolerant of administrative experience and education, pressed liberty beyond its proper

---

[3] In his "Problems in American History" (1892); *Frontier and Section*, 29.

bounds, showed laxity in regard to governmental affairs, looked indulgently upon speculation and wild-cat banking, and, as the current agitation of the Populists showed, entertained rather primitive notions of finance. In religion and intellectual life the frontier inheritance was also mixed, but invariably powerful. "From the conditions of frontier life came intellectual traits of profound importance," which can be read in the reports of frontier travelers—coarseness and strength, acuteness and inquisitiveness, a practical, inventive turn of mind, quick to find expedients and masterful in its grasp of material things, a "dominant individualism working both for good and evil," an exuberance that comes with freedom, but also a deficiency in artistic sense.

The essay closed with a moving coda, which reverted to the theme of the Columbian Exposition: "Since the days when the fleet of Columbus sailed into the waters of the New World, America has been another name for opportunity, and the people of the United States have taken their tone from the incessant expansion which has not only been open but has even been forced upon them." It would be rash, Turner thought, to say that this expansive quality was at an end: the habit of movement was there, and American energy would continue to demand "a wider field for its exercise." But now it would work without the great gift of free land. "For a moment, at the frontier, the bonds of custom are broken and unrestraint is triumphant. There is not [sic] *tabula rasa*. The stubborn American environment is there with its imperious summons to accept its conditions; the inherited ways of doing things are also there; and yet, in spite of environment, and in spite of custom, each frontier did indeed furnish a new field of opportunity, a gate of escape from the bondage of the past; and freshness, and confidence, and scorn of older society, impatience of its restraints and its ideas, and indifference to its lessons, have accompanied the frontier. What the Mediterranean Sea was to the Greeks, breaking the bond of custom, offering new experiences, calling out new institutions and activities, that, and more, the ever retreating frontier has been to the United States directly, and to the nations of Europe more remotely. And now, four centuries from the discovery of America, at the end of a hundred years of life under the Constitution, the frontier has gone, and with its going has closed the first period of American history."

II

Garland's ingenuous and ill-formed tract, though prophetic on minor points, was soon to be forgotten. As for Turner's address, its immediate reception by the historians at Chicago gave no augury of its future fame, but the tide was running with him: he had struck off a view of American history which appealed both to the particular needs and interests of the rising historical profession and to the American imagination at large. Somehow he had caught in an essay of less than thirty pages what was to become the characteristic American view of the American past. If Turner's paper did not immediately strike his listeners as sensational, it may be because many of them were already sympathetically aware of the Western cultural reaction and because they greeted Turner's assertions as part of the growing concern for the historical study of the West. The idea that the Eastern point of view had failed to account for the development of the continent took on a certain poignancy, to be sure, from sectional resentments. Charles A. Beard later remembered, perhaps with a touch of exaggeration, being "in the bondage of iniquity and the gall of bitterness—at least in the Middle West where I lived at the time Turner read his address," and being convinced that Easterners had been raised on literature assuming "that all of us beyond the Alleghenies, if not the Hudson, were almost, if not quite, uncouth savages."[4]

Westerners were not wrong in thinking that they were often regarded with some disdain by Easterners of the old school. Interregional encounters could be bruising. "I do not like the western type of man," E. L. Godkin had once announced to Charles Eliot Norton, and to another who had written him in praise of California he replied firmly: "No scenery or climate I had to share with western people would charm me." One of Norton's correspondents, the young

---

[4] Beard, "Turner's 'The Frontier in American History,' " 67.

George Edward Woodberry, who had taught for a time early in his career at the University of Nebraska, found that the faculty was sharply split between its Eastern and Western members. His own response suggests why. Nebraska society, he reported to Norton, was "characterized by blank Philistinism intellectually and barren selfishness morally." The undergraduates were "necktieless, often collarless," and sometimes appeared in "shirt fronts of outrageous uncleanness." "This life," he complained in an anxious letter to Norton, "requires a hardihood of the senses and susceptibilities of which you have little conception, I fear. . . . I doubt very much whether the hardihood I gain will not be a deterioration into barbarism, not sinew for civilization."[5]

Such feelings Turner knew, and had opposed with a touch of gentle humor. Years after his famous essay, trying to help a friend phrase a tactful letter that would appease Western sensibilities, Turner unwittingly accounted for much of his own impact. "I have merely tried," he explained, "to put myself in the mental attitude of a sensitive Western man who is apt to be on his guard and looking for trouble when a New England resident explains things to him." Yet, despite the polemical surge behind much of Turner's work, not all Eastern historians were disposed to deny that more attention should be given to the West. At its second meeting in 1885 the American Historical Association called for more suitable measures to preserve materials on Western history. W. F. Poole, an adopted Midwesterner, complained in his presidential address three years later that Easterners had been writing American history without due regard for the importance of the West, and urged them to grow "tall enough to look over the Appalachian range and see what has happened on the other side." At the same meeting Turner's teacher at Wisconsin, William F. Allen, a medievalist who sometimes doubled in American history and whose precepts profoundly influenced the young scholar, thought it important to plead for "The Place of the North-West in General History," and had force-

---

[5] Godkin as quoted by V. L. Parrington, *Main Currents in American Thought* (1930), III, 161; for Woodberry, see Joseph Doyle, "George Edward Woodberry," unpublished dissertation, Columbia University (1952), 157, 168, 215.

fully asserted the central place of the Northwest both in the
imperial struggles of the seventeenth and eighteenth centuries and in the development of American liberty. A young
Eastern historian with Western interests, Theodore Roosevelt,
published in 1889 the first two volumes of *The Winning of the
West,* which Turner praised in the *Dial* as a "vivid portraiture
of the backwoodsman's advance" written "in the light of the
widest significance of the events which he describes."[6]

As is commonly the case with such basic ideas, Turner's
frontier interpretation did not spring into being all at once
out of a single mind. It no more detracts from Turner's originality to point to his predecessors than it does—to risk a comparison with a much grander intellectual construction—to
point out that Marx's system was pieced together out of English political economy, German philosophy, and French utopian speculation. The presence of the unsettled West had
always had a powerful effect upon the minds both of American and foreign observers, and it is no surprise that Turner's
theories were a striking consummation of an old interest rather
than a new departure. Many leading writers, beginning with
Franklin, Jefferson, and Hamilton, had argued that free lands
would act as a kind of relief for unemployed or discontented
labor and as a source of high wages, and this idea became
very widespread in the United States. This, to be sure, was
only a portion of Turner's interpretation; but his central emphasis on westward expansion and open land as forces in
American democracy and the American character had also
been anticipated by others at home and abroad. Hegel, in his
Philosophy of History, had considered that the Mississippi
lands relieved the chief source of discontent in America and
thus guaranteed its existing civil condition.[7] Emerson, in
1844, had observed in his lecture, "The Young American,"
that the Atlantic States had been oriented toward Europe and
commercial culture but that now "the nervous, rocky West is

---

6 Turner to Mrs. Alice Perkins Hooper, February 9, 1916; W. F.
Poole, "The Early Northwest," American Historical Association,
Papers, 3 (1889), 277–300; William F. Allen, *Essays and Monographs* (1890), 92–111; Turner, "The Winning of the West,"
Dial, 10 (1889), 71–3.
7 For references on Turner's precursors in this and the following
paragraphs, see the relevant section in the Bibliographical Essay.

intruding a new and continental element into the national mind, and we shall yet have an American genius." Macaulay in an often quoted letter of 1857 to an early biographer of Jefferson, attributed the stability of American politics to "a boundless extent of fertile and unoccupied land." Yankee prophets of the early nineteenth century like Timothy Dwight and Lyman Beecher had clearly seen the pivotal place of the West in the future culture of America and were intent to claim it for the right brand of Protestantism. Such men did not always think well of the Westerners, but their sense of the process involved was much like Turner's. "In mercy . . . to the sober, industrious, and well-disposed inhabitants," Dwight wrote in 1821, "Providence has opened in the vast Western wilderness a retreat, sufficiently alluring to draw them away from the land of their nativity. We have many troubles even now; but we should have many more, if this body of foresters had remained at home."

A commentator like Tocqueville could hardly fail to see the phenomenon, particularly in its bearing on the American imagination. "The American people," he wrote, "views its own march across these wilds, draining swamps, turning the course of rivers, peopling solitudes, and subduing nature. This magnificent image of themselves does not meet the gaze of the Americans at intervals only; it may be said to haunt every one of them in his least as well as in his most important actions and to be always flitting before his mind." E. L. Godkin had argued in a brilliant essay of 1865 that the phenomena of frontier life were more an effect than a cause of democracy, but that "it has been to their agency more than to aught else, that the democratic tide in America has owed most of its force and violence." To the westward movement Godkin attributed the "prodigious contempt for experience and for theory" that Americans had developed, and he charged it with accentuating their materialism, their anti-intellectual and anticultural feelings and their distrust of history. (Turner was amused when his attention was called to this piece in 1896. "Godkin," he said, "has stolen my thunder.") The ingratiating Southern statesman, Lucius Quintus Cincinnatus Lamar, adumbrated some aspects of the frontier thesis in a memorial speech on Calhoun delivered in 1887. Lord Bryce sounded rather like

Turner two years later when he wrote in his great commentary that "the West is the most American part of America; that is to say, the part where those features which distinguish America from Europe come out in the strongest relief." He also observed that nearly all the best arable land was already occupied, and predicted on this count that the future "will be a time of trial for democratic institutions."

Three years before Turner's address Hubert Howe Bancroft, another historian of the West, had noted that "the tide of intelligence" had always moved from East to West, and had attributed the static character of late medieval Europe to the "lack of free land." He thought that the Anglo-Saxons of America in their westward advance across the continent had "a marked advantage over other nationalities for migration and colonization by virtue of the century-training in backwoods life, and expansion of frontier settlement by constant accessions from the seaboard states. Herein they had developed the practical adaptability and self-reliance inherited from the mother race, so much so as to surpass even that so far pre-eminent colonist element." William Graham Sumner often wrote of American democracy as the product of a particularly favorable "man-land ratio," and forecast that its course would be less smooth as the ratio changed with the exhaustion of the available lands.

Henry George's concern with land use brought him strikingly close to the ideas identified with Turner. In *Progress and Poverty* (1879) he wrote: "This public domain—the vast extent of land yet to be reduced to private possession, the enormous common to which the faces of the energetic were always turned, has been the great fact that, since the days when the first settlements began to fringe the Atlantic Coast, has formed our national character and colored our national thought. . . . The general intelligence, the general comfort, the active invention, the power of adaptation and assimilation, the free, independent spirit, the energy and hopefulness that have marked our people, are not causes, but results— they have sprung from unfenced land. This public domain has been the transmuting force which has turned the thriftless, unambitious European peasant into the self-reliant Western farmer; it has given a consciousness of freedom even to the dweller in crowded cities, and has been a well-spring of hope even to those who have never thought of taking refuge upon it. The child of the people, as he grows to manhood in Europe, finds all the best seats at the banquet of life marked 'taken,' and must struggle with his fellows for the crumbs that fall, without one chance in a thousand of forcing or sneaking his way to a seat. In America, whatever his condition, there has always been the consciousness that the public domain lay behind him; and the knowledge of this fact, acting and reacting, has penetrated our whole national life, giving to it generosity and independence, elasticity and ambition. All that we are proud of in the American character; all that makes our conditions and institutions better than those of older countries, we may trace to the fact that land has been cheap in the United States, because new soil has been open to the emigrant."

At the time of Turner's address America's awareness of its landed heritage stood at a new juncture. Many thoughtful Americans of the 1890's were undergoing a crisis of nerve about the present and future of their country. Even before the beginning of the general depression of 1893, an agrarian depression had set in, followed by the emergence of Populism and the cry for free silver. The possibilities of greater industrial violence too were sounded in the Homestead Strike of 1892 and the Pullman strike of 1894. Renewed agitation over monopoly had stimulated the passage of the Sherman Act in 1890. But the exhaustion of the public lands (then imagined to be much closer than it actually was), the end of the frontier line, seen in conjuncture with the agrarian crisis and labor conflict, posed certain dark questions about the future.[8] What would be the character of American development without the resource of free land, which was believed to have provided a fund of new opportunities and an escape from poverty and unemployment? The eminent American economist, Francis Amasa Walker (who exercised considerable influence on

---

[8] On this crisis in the nineties see my essay, "Cuba, the Philippines, and Manifest Destiny," in *The Paranoid Style in American Politics* (1965), and on the agrarian crisis as a background for Turner's address, Lee Benson, "The Historical Background of Turner's Frontier Essay," in *Turner and Beard* (1960), 41–91; for Walker see 73.

Turner), wrote in 1892 that since public land worth claiming had almost run out, "reluctant as we may be to recognize it, a labor problem is at last upon us. No longer can a continent of free virgin lands avert from us the social struggle which the old world has known so long and so painfully." Leading advocates of immigration restriction, among whom Walker was prominent, were beginning to point to the supposed exhaustion of land as a reason for closing the national gates. Even before the panic of 1893 precipitated the gloom, there was a widespread anxious feeling that the country was nearing a major turning in its history, and that the future might be far more difficult and less endurable than the past—a feeling echoed in Turner's assertion at the end of his address that the first epoch of American history had come to a close. But this anxiety was also a spur to thought, and it prepared the way for new speculation about the meaning of American history.

Turner's friend and contemporary, Woodrow Wilson, was one of those who saw the significance of his ideas. In an essay of 1893, Wilson observed that everything in American development had been modified "when the great westward migration began." A new nation sprang up beyond the mountains, a continental life radically different from that of the first seaboard settlements. "The formative period of American history ... did not end in colonial times or on the Atlantic coast ... nor will it end until we cease to have frontier communities and a young political life just accommodating itself to fixed institutions. That part of our history, therefore, which is most truly national is the history of the West." "The fact that we kept always, for close upon three hundred years ... a frontier people always in our van," Wilson wrote two years later, "is, so far, the central and determining fact of our national history. 'East' and 'West,' an ever-changing line, but an unvarying experience and a constant leaven of change working always within the body of our folk. Our political, our economic, our social life has felt this potent influence from the wild border all our history through. The 'West' is the great word of our history. The 'Westerner' has been the type and master of our American life. Now at length ... we have lost our frontier: our front lies almost unbroken along the great coast line of the western sea. The Westerner, in some day soon to come, will pass out of our life, as he so long ago passed out of the life of the Old World. Then a new epoch will open for us. Perhaps it has opened already. Slowly we shall grow old, compact our people, study the delicate adjustments of an intricate society, and ponder the niceties, as we have hitherto pondered the bulks and structural framework of government."[9]

"Slowly we shall grow old. . . ." The line underscores an important quality of the frontier myth, which, as we shall see, pervades its history: it is adaptable not only to the American's celebration of himself but also, curiously, to his misgivings about America. If the frontier was the making of America, what could ever replace it? The latent pessimism of the frontier view, in sharp contrast to the ebullient optimism attributed to frontier communities, had repercussions in Turner's own intellectual development.

III

Turner's life was like a personal re-enactment of the dialogue that was beginning in his day between the Eastern and Western historians, for he was reared in the frontier country and came eastward for graduate study to one of the primary centers of the historical ideas he eventually overthrew. He was born in 1861 in Portage, Wisconsin, a little town recently planted in the wilderness and not far from the frontier, which still had fewer than 4,500 inhabitants in the early 1880's when Turner left to attend the University of Wisconsin. Of his family background Turner later wrote: "My people on both sides moved at least every generation, and built new

---

9 "Mr. Goldwin Smith's 'Views' on our Political History," *Forum*, 16 (1893), 495–7; "The Proper Perspective of American History," ibid., 19 (1895), 551. Though the first of these articles came hard upon Turner's address, it was, by Wilson's statement, derived from it and not an independent conclusion. "All I ever wrote on the subject came from him," Wilson later declared. "I am glad," Turner wrote to Wilson at the time of the first *Forum* essay, "that you think I have helped you to some of these ideas, for I have many intellectual debts to repay you." See George C. Osborn, "Woodrow Wilson and Frederick Jackson Turner," *Proceedings* of the New Jersey Historical Society, 74 (1956), 218, and Wendell H. Stephenson, "The Influence of Woodrow Wilson on Frederick Jackson Turner," *Agricultural History*, 19 (1945), 250.

communities. . . . My father was named Andrew Jackson
Turner at his birth in 1832 by my Democratic grandfather,
and I still rise and go to bed to the striking of the old clock
that was brought into the house the day he was born, at the
edge of the Adirondack forest. My mother's ancestors were
preachers. Is it strange that I preached on the frontier?"[1]

Andrew Jackson Turner was one of those alert and mobile Americans whose lives figured in his son's essays. Having
come west from the Lake Champlain region of New York in
1855, he started in Wisconsin as a printer, later bought the
newspaper that had employed him, and soon pursued a career
in journalism as well as politics. He became a member of the
state legislature (as a Republican, though he had been raised
as a Democrat), of the state railroad commission, and mayor
of Portage. He also achieved some note as a genealogist and
local historian. In his father's office young Turner learned the
ways of American politics, and in the life around him he
watched the ways of the frontier and developed an appetite
for the outdoors that never left him. In his sixties he recalled:
"I have poled down the Wisconsin [River] in a dugout with
Indian guides . . . through virgin forests of balsam firs, seeing
deer in the river,—antlered beauties who watched us come
down with curious eyes and then broke for the tall timber,
—hearing the squaws in their village on the high bank talk
their low treble to the bass of our Indian polesman,—feeling
that I belonged to it all. I have seen a lynched man hanging
from a tree when I came home from school in Portage, have
played around old Fort Winnebago at its outskirts, have seen
the red shirted Irish raftsmen *take* the town when they tied up
and came ashore, have plodded up the 'pinery' road that ran
past our house to the pine woods of Northern Wisconsin,
have seen Indians come in on their ponies to buy paint and
ornaments and sell their furs; have stumbled on their camp
on the Baraboo, where dried pumpkins were hung up, and
cooking muskrats were in the kettle, and an Indian family
were bathing in the river—the frontier in that sense, you
see, was real to me, and when I studied history I did not keep

1 "Turner's Autobiographic Letter," *Wisconsin Magazine of History*, 19 (1935), 102–3.

my personal experience in a water tight compartment away from my studies."[2]

His memories of the Wisconsin environment, invoked nostalgically in some of his later letters, were strong and formative during his years as a student in Madison. As a junior he wrote his first published work about the vicinity of his birthplace, a "History of the 'Grignon Tract' on the Portage of the Fox and Wisconsin Rivers," and his master's thesis and doctoral dissertation dealt with the early Wisconsin fur trade. "I am placed in a *new* society," he wrote in 1887, "which is just beginning to realize that it has made a place for itself by mastering the wilderness and peopling the prairie, and is now ready to take its great course in universal history. It is something of a compensation to be among the advance guard of new social ideas and among a people whose destiny is all unknown. *The west looks to the future, the east toward the past.*"[3]

The West, the future, and democracy. As the son of middle-class Western culture, and of a politician named after Andrew Jackson, Turner assumed without questioning the ultimate validity and future supremacy of popular democracy. The language of a surviving oration on "The Poet of the Future" Turner delivered as an undergraduate in 1883 sounds to one who is familiar with the idiom of nineteenth-century America as though it might as well have been delivered fifty years before, in the Jacksonian era. "All over the world," young Turner asserted, "we hear mankind proclaiming its existence, demanding its rights. Kings begin to be but names, and the sons of genius, springing from the people, grasp the real sceptres. The reign of aristocracy is passing; that of humanity begins. Democracy is waiting for its poet." Historians, he wrote in his notebook, had traditionally concerned themselves with "noble warriors, & all the pomp and glory of the higher class—But of the other phase, of the common people, the lowly tillers of the soil, the great mass of humanity . . . history has hitherto said but little." Even then Turner thought

---

[2] Ray A. Billington, "Young Fred Turner," *Wisconsin Magazine of History*, 46 (1962), 40.
[3] Ibid., 45; the italicized word is Turner's, the italicized sentence mine.

of what he called "peasant proprietorship"—by which he meant simply the small farmer owning his own land—as the key to the rise of democracy, and hence as the key to America; the nation would have been altogether different had its land fallen into the hands of capitalists, the owners of great estates. "In this simplicity of our land system lies one of the greatest factors in our progress."[4]

At Madison Turner was singularly fortunate in one of his teachers, W. F. Allen, then in his early fifties, who held the professorship of Latin and history. A native of Massachusetts and a graduate of Harvard, Allen had undertaken graduate study in Germany. At Göttingen, he had been influenced by Bancroft's old teacher, A. H. L. Heeren, who was particularly concerned with the history of colonial expansion, the unity of European and American peoples, and a developmental approach to institutions. Allen, who won Turner's enduring affection along with his intellectual interest, taught American as well as ancient and medieval history, and though he was keenly aware of the importance of the West in American development, he taught it against the background of universal history, thus taking it out of the realm of local antiquarianism and putting it into a wide intellectual framework. From the very beginning, then, Turner was directed away from a purely parochial exploitation of his feeling for the West and toward a broad comparative view of history.[5] When he later became Allen's successor in history, his duties required him to duplicate some of his teacher's versatility by offering a wide variety of historical subjects, including the dynastic and territorial history of the Middle Ages. He never ceased to believe that American history had a great deal in common with medieval history; and while this idea in itself may not strike us as a particular telling one, the essential fact remains that Turner

---

4 On the democratic theme in Turner's early years see Fulmer Mood, "The Development of Frederick Jackson Turner as a Historical Thinker," *Publications* of the Colonial Society of Massachusetts, 34 (1939), 290–4, and Smith, *Virgin Land*, 252–3.
5 "My work really grew out of a preliminary training in Mediaeval history, where I learned to recognize the reactions between a people in the gristle, and their environment, and saw the interplay of economic, social and geographic factors in the politics, institutions, ideals and life of a nation and its relations with its neighbors." To Arthur M. Schlesinger, April 18, 1922; cf. Turner to Curti, August 8, 1928.

had the imagination to look at the American frontier and American expansion against the background of other macro-historical changes.

After Turner had taught for a few years at the University of Wisconsin, where he had taken an M.A. and written his thesis on the fur trade, he was prodded into getting a doctorate by its new president, Thomas C. Chamberlin, who hoped to build a more imposing university and wanted more PhDs on his staff. Several Wisconsin students had already gone to Johns Hopkins, then at the peak of its eminence as a center of graduate study, and Turner's decision to follow them in 1888 was fortunate: the new university in Baltimore not only gave him keener intellectual stimulation than he could have had elsewhere in the United States but also gave him the shock of opposition that was needed to precipitate his ideas.

The primary seminar at Johns Hopkins was conducted by Herbert Baxter Adams, German-trained but also a disciple of the English historian E. A. Freeman. Adams adhered to Freeman's notion that history is past politics and to the ideas of the Teutonic school of evolutionary institutional history. But for men like Adams, as for Freeman, "past politics" was generously interpreted: it included heavy doses of legal and constitutional developments, and indeed put a strong emphasis on local institutional history. Influenced by Bluntschli, as well as by such English writers as Freeman, Stubbs, and Maine, Adams shared their concern with establishing a kind of history that would illuminate the problematic nineteenth-century constitutional developments in their own countries. The interest, for example, of a Swiss-German liberal like Bluntschli in the convergence and federation of local political units had obvious points of contact with the problems of American federalism.

The method to be used in such studies was supposed to be rigorously scientific—a comparative method inspired in the first instance by Darwinism and intended to win for history some of the prestige of evolutionary science, but also drawn more immediately from the evolutionary anthropology of Spencer and Tylor and from the techniques of contemporary philology. With the evolutionary anthropologists, the institutional historians believed that human development takes place more or less according to a single, unilinear pattern, and that it is the business of the investigator to trace out the stages in the development of institutions. The Adams school believed firmly in long-range continuities, and in the genetic method. "The science of Biology no longer favors the theory of spontaneous generation," Adams wrote in 1883. "Wherever organic life occurs, there must have been some seed for that life. History should not be content with describing effects when it can explain causes. It is just as improbable that free local institutions should spring up without a germ along American shores as that English wheat should have grown here without planting. Town institutions were propagated in New England by old English and Germanic ideas brought over by Pilgrims and Puritans." If this emphasis on cultural continuity had brought the English historians to see their debt to German institutions, it suggested that Americans should stress their debt to England. "Thus, English historians, Green, Freeman, and Stubbs recognized their fatherland. The origin of the English Constitution, as Montesquieu long ago declared, is found in the forests of Germany."[6]

But the germ theory of democracy, as it has been called, also suggested that democracy had always been present, like the homunculus in the ancient view of human generation, within the political plasm of the Anglo-Saxon peoples, that it would unfold more or less automatically, or organically, wherever the Anglo-Saxon "race" predominated. Actually, the Anglo-Saxon school did not remain formidable for very long. Frederick Seebohm had begun to puncture its notions in the early 1880's, and in 1890 Charles McLean Andrews, one of Adams's own pupils, pointed to the superficiality of the supposed resemblances of the German *tun*, the Anglo-Saxon village, and the New England town. It was not long before the study of early American history would be taken away from the Teutonists by what is known as the "imperial school" of colonial historiography. But what united both was the disposition to look at American history as an extension of English history, a kind of evolutionary conservatism, and an Anglophile bias,

---

6 H. B. Adams, "Germanic Origins of New England Towns," *Johns Hopkins University Studies in Historical and Political Science*, 1 (1883), 8, 10.

none of which was altogether congenial to the spirit of Portage and Madison.

Adams in himself, cordial though he was to Turner, provided a personal summation of the latent differences that were at work in this historical argument. Adams had come out of a solid New England background, and had been sent to Phillips Exeter and Amherst before going to Heidelberg to study under Bluntschli. Just after Turner went back to Wisconsin from Johns Hopkins, Adams too was given an opportunity to move westward, in the form of an invitation to an exceptionally well-paid post at the University of Chicago. Before deciding to stay put, Adams drew a balance sheet of the advantages and disadvantages of moving which sums up the tug of war over social and moral values that was going on between men like him and men like Turner. On Adams's list of the qualities of the two situations there were the following: [7]

BALTIMORE	CHICAGO
Quiet	Rush
Continuity	Broken
Experience	Experiment
Society	New People
Conservatism	Boom
Duty	Advantage
Assured position	All new
Settled	Moving
Identification	Lost

On certain counts Turner could accept the assumptions of the Adams school. Like them he was interested in tracing the development of democracy, and along with most of his contemporaries he shared the general Darwinian cast of mind, the desire to make history more "scientific." In particular, the task of laying out the stages of political and social development seemed of primary importance to him; one of his claims for the particularly revealing quality of American history had its point just here: the constant renewal of social development on the frontier, the constant reversion to primitive conditions brought about by the westward movement, seemed

---

[7] W. Stull Holt, *Historical Scholarship in the United States, 1876–1901* (1938), 157.

to him to make America a singularly good place to study the
basic pattern of social evolution. For a short time after his
arrival at Johns Hopkins he appears to have accepted the
germ theory, writing in 1889 of the "forted village" of the
frontiersmen as a place in which one could still find evidences
of the "old Germanic 'tun,' their popular meetings, 'folkmoots,'
and their representative assemblies, 'witanagemots,' meeting
like the Transylvania legislature." The facts of Western life
"carry the mind back to the warrior-legislatures in the Germanic forests, and forward to those constitutional conventions now at work in our newly made states in the Far West;
and they make us proud of our English heritage." But this
dalliance was not to last long. Even in the same review,
Turner remarked sardonically that "America's historians
have for the most part, like wise men of old, come from the
East, and as a result our history has been written from the
point of view of the Atlantic coast." The younger generation,
he added with confidence, would now step forward to give our
history the proportions required by the movement of the
country's center of gravity into the Mississippi basin. To the
young Westerner, who had seen democratic institutions evolving on the American frontier, the notion that they had come
preformed from the German forest began to seem altogether
factitious. Moreover, Adams's suggestion, as Turner later remembered it, that his seminar on American local institutions
had already "exhausted the opportunities for new contributions in the field of U.S. history and would turn to European
history for its next work" was a direct provocation. With the
West hardly touched, was American history to be thought of
as exhausted? The frontier thesis, Turner explained to Carl
Becker years afterward, "was pretty much a reaction from
that [i.e., the Adams school] due to my indignation." Turner
was far less interested in European germs and the hereditary
side of political evolution than he was in the effects of the
American environment. For a Westerner it was hard to escape
the workings of the massive untenanted continent and the
necessity for men to find ways of coping with it; by comparison the inherited apparatus they brought to it, in ideas, habits,
and institutions, seemed quite frail. ("Into this vast shaggy
continent of ours," he wrote in 1903, "poured the first feeble

tide of European settlement.") The overwhelming American environment must be put back at the center of the story, and the inherited "germs" whether biological-racial or cultural, put in a completely subordinate place.[8]

Turner reacted quite as sharply to the preponderant concern of Eastern historians with the slavery conflict, to the limited forms of constitutional argument it had engendered, and to the sectional myopia of writers on both sides. Too much of American historical imagery had been taken up by the figures of Cavalier and Yankee, and by their selfish sectional quarrels. A new theme was waiting to be exploited, the grand story of Western development. A new figure was waiting impatiently in the wings, the Western pioneer. And the pioneer, though he had faults of his own, would prove to be somewhat more genuinely national in his loyalties and more representatively American. This side of Turner's reaction was registered in a long and shrewd critique, written in the 1890's, of Hermann von Holst's multivolume *Constitutional and Political History of the United States*, a critique which voices Turner's dissatisfaction with the prevailing conservative nationalist history.[9] Pointing out that von Holst, as a German immigrant, had lived his formative years in this country on the Atlantic coast and in New York City, where the specter of Tammany Hall loomed large, Turner concluded that he had missed something essential: "With the healthy democracy of the country and the west he was not familiar." Von Holst had formed his impressions of America during the age of Fiske and Tweed and the Crédit Mobilier scandal. He could see the sectional controversy only from the point of view of the Prussian nationalist, the rise of democracy only from that of the educated Eastern American familiar with its scandals and weary of the spoils system, and the whole work was vitiated by his failure to see the formative effects of the West as "the splendid spectacle of the real growth of national sentiment."

For a man whose usual way it was to deal mildly and

---

[8] Turner, "The Winning of the West," *Dial*, 10 (1889), 71; *Frontier*, 267; on Adams's statement see Wilbur R. Jacobs, ed., *Frederick Jackson Turner's Legacy* (1965), 17.

[9] The essay was not published until the publication in 1965 of *Frederick Jackson Turner's Legacy*, 85–104.

generously with others, Turner's strictures on von Holst were severe, and by comparison his rebellion against Adams's precepts, though firm, was free of acrimony. Indeed, one is impressed most by how much Turner owed to his Johns Hopkins period, even to the provocation he had from Adams, as well as the older man's gentle tutelage. Adams accepted, and perhaps even encouraged, his pupil's Western interests from the beginning. Turner was permitted to expand his master's thesis on the Wisconsin fur trade into a doctoral dissertation, took his degree in 1890, and soon had the pleasure of hearing Adams praise his work before the State Historical Society of Wisconsin.

Other friendships made in Baltimore were of vital importance. Among Turner's teachers was Woodrow Wilson, a visiting lecturer, who as a Southerner shared Turner's feeling that the New England historians had given a false slant to the nation's history and encouraged Turner's emphasis on the West. Wilson also introduced Turner to one of his favorite writers, Walter Bagehot, whose *Physics and Politics* confirmed Turner's interest in the sources of institutional innovation, in the ways in which "the cake of custom" could be broken. Richard T. Ely, who was lecturing on economics, encouraged Turner to think about land economics and directed his attention to the works of Francis A. Walker. Walker had taken much note of the economic and historic effects of "vacant land"; his writing also strengthened Turner's interest in the use of statistics and in devices for more systematic study than historians then customarily engaged in. Albion W. Small, later an eminent sociologist, criticized the neglect of social forces by American historians and impressed upon Turner the importance of working across the constricting boundaries of the social sciences.

During the Hopkins period Turner's reading broadened greatly. It carried him through much of the work of Mommsen, whom he greatly admired, and to J. G. Droysen's *Grundriss der Historik*, a work which owed much to Hegel and from which Turner took some of his conceptions of the social functions of historical writing. By 1892, his interest in land economics had brought him to Achille Loria's *Analisi della Proprietà Capitalista* whose systematic emphasis on expansion, colonization, and free land in relation to capitalism was momentous for the young student. Turner's range, it must be said, was wide. His remarkable essay of 1891, "The Significance of History," was indeed ostentatiously cosmopolitan, being not only full of references to standard English and American historians but studded with citations of German writers like Schelling, Herder, Hegel, Niebuhr, Ranke, Droysen, Roscher, and Knies. The Turner thesis, though based on frontier experience and Western loyalties, had its debt not only to Eastern centers of learning but to ideas imported from England, Germany, and Italy. American democracy may have been born on the frontier, but the Turner thesis was nurtured in Siena and Padua, Göttingen, Berlin, and Jena, Oxford and Cambridge, as well as Portage, Madison, and Baltimore.[1]

IV

The argument, the rhetoric, and the intellectual strategy of Turner's famous frontier essay can best be understood when it is read in context with four other notable essays he wrote between 1891 and 1903.[2] Although his emphatic manner later caused some critics to charge him with an inflexible and dogmatic mind, these five pieces, taken together, are quite impressive for their receptiveness and breadth. In effect, this historian, still in his thirties, charted out a very large part of the course that American historiography was to run for the next generation. Not only did he establish himself as the first writer to break significantly with the H. B. Adams and Burgess schools and the hyper-confident "scientific" history of their era, but he was—even when a certain glibness and imprecision in his own assumptions are duly noted—one of the first in this country to try to make historians more

---

[1] For Turner's Hopkins period, see Fulmer Mood, "Development" and Mood's introduction to *The Early Writings of Frederick Jackson Turner;* see also Jacobs, *Frederick Jackson Turner's Legacy;* and, on Loria's influence, see Lee Benson, *Turner and Beard.*
[2] The others were: "The Significance of History" (1891), "Problems in American History" (1892), "The Problem of the West" (1896) and "Contributions of the West to American Democracy" (1903). All are in Billington's selection, *Frontier and Section,* already cited; quotations in the following paragraphs are from this edition, 12–13, 17, 20, 21, 64, and *Frontier,* 216.

critically aware of their own presuppositions. He anticipated, however briefly and sketchily, the historical relativism that was later to preoccupy Carl Becker and Charles A. Beard. He called, in ringing terms, for a better understanding of the economic aspects of history and of the bearing of economic interests upon politics. In arguing once again that history is not just about politics, diplomacy, constitutions, and battles, not just about the doings of a ruling elite, but must deal with the full range of human activities and with the life of the common man, he anticipated clearly and unpretentiously a central argument later identified with James Harvey Robinson's "New History." Here he repudiated the disposition of the Adams school, following Freeman, to look upon political history as the essence of all history, and spoke boldly for the broadening of the historical enterprise. History was not to be just past politics but also past literature, past religion, and past economics. "History is the biography of society in all its departments." In particular it must embrace, as Thorold Rogers had recently urged in his *Economic Interpretation of History,* the study of economic life, for the meaning of many political events grows out of economic experience. On such counts Turner's preachings, as well as the practice of his historical followers, helped to lay the groundwork for the more aggressive use of the economic interpretation of history that came with Beard's generation.

Turner also made suggestive observations about the American intellectual temper and about the role of immigration. In time he was to be called narrow and parochial, but in the 1890's he was pleading for an understanding of our history in its broader relations that would relieve it of the burden of provincialism. ("How can we understand American history without understanding European history?") He argued that even "local history must be viewed in the light of world history." He took a receptive view of related social disciplines. He had more than a hint of an understanding that history could well become more systematic, more aware of space and quantity, and he was already on the way toward devising the methods that were later to make his seminars so productive. In Germany, where critical speculation about history and its functions had reached a depth far beyond anything in the

United States, Turner's early essays would perhaps have been regarded as intelligent but rather rudimentary, but in the American environment they were impressively original and advanced. Whatever their limitations, his ideas marked a clear step beyond the preconceptions of previous historical writing. In effect what he was doing in these early essays was not just turning attention to the neglected West, but forging a new historical genre, the analytical essay, whose purpose it would be to circumvent the traditional narrative and to try to get at meaning in history. In certain ways, all modern American historical writing follows Turner in his emphasis on posing and defining historical problems, and in his belief that new methods were needed to solve them. Here Turner established himself as the first of the great professionals. Whatever else is to be said about his specific intellectual commitments, it was an achievement for a young historian only a few years past his doctorate to have eschewed both the grand narrative history and the emergent monograph, with its minute investigation of details and its massing of footnotes, to draw up a bold and prophetic new program for American historiography.

In the argument of Turner's early essays it is clear that he shared much of the current enthusiasm for "scientific" history as well as the basic Darwinian assumptions upon which this history was then based. The metaphorical language of the early essays is largely naturalistic, full of references to evolution, development, organs, environment, adaptation, and stages of growth. "Society," Turner proclaims, drawing on Droysen, "is an organism. . . . History is the self-consciousness of this organism." Constitutional forms are "organs," the body politic has its anatomy and physiology, the continent develops "a complex nervous system," the rise of political institutions is a story of the evolution and adaptation of organs, American democracy marks the "origin of a new political species."

Thus far Turner had no quarrel with the evolutionary orientation of the Herbert Baxter Adams school. His break with them grew out of an internal quarrel common to the historical Darwinists. The Teutonic school stressed the unfolding of the "germs" of democratic institutions as a more or less natural process taking place in similar ways in different environments, wherever the Teutonic stock was dominant. Turner broke with the hereditarian, and to a degree with the racist argument underlying this scheme by stressing the fundamental importance of the American environment. Whatever might be said about democracy elsewhere, *American* democracy (and this, though he was sometimes unclear about it, was all he pretended to account for) could not be understood if the native elements peculiar to the American environment were not recognized as central. "This new democracy . . . came from no theorist's dreams of the German forest. It came, stark and strong and full of life, from the American forest."

With this sentence it becomes clear that even though he was throwing overboard its genealogy of democracy, Turner was holding fast to the romantic primitivism of the Teutonic school. Democracy does not yet emerge from society or ideas or from the internal dynamics of human institutions but still comes from a forest—ambling forth, one imagines, like some amiable cinnamon bear. Here, no doubt, much of the appeal of Turner's essays lay in their having aroused once again in a new setting an old and pervasive anti-institutional bias in American thought. Among his other achievements was to put the American historical intelligence into a more direct rapport with a side of the national mind that had fascinated imaginative writers but had received only slight attention from historians. I refer to the enduring American obsession with an escape from society—in the first instance from the society of Europe and then from that society as it was repeated, re-created, and imitated in the American East—into the original innocence and promise of nature, as represented in the vast unspoiled interior of woods and prairies. Americans were the descendants of men who had chosen to make a rupture with the Old World, and had promised themselves to look for the bounty of the New, to make the most of experiencing the start of the world, to make a virtue of having a slender past by becoming the people of the future. With his stress on the "perennial rebirth" of America under primitive frontier conditions, Turner independently arrived at a theme which had been celebrated by many of the major writers—among them Cooper, Thoreau, Melville, Mark Twain—a theme in which the central symbolic figure is a natural and unspoiled man finding his most profound and satisfying relationships with the world of nature and with other natural men—a Natty Bumppo, Huck Finn, or Ishmael. "This," D. H. Lawrence saw in his *Studies in Classic American Literature*, "is the true myth of America. She starts old, old, wrinkled and writhing in an old skin. And there is a gradual sloughing off of the old skin towards a new youth. It is the myth of America." This myth has created, and still creates, its heroes in verse and fiction, but for all the work of Parkman in prenational history, it had as yet in Turner's day found only a slender recognition in national historical writing. The explorer, hunter, trapper, cowboy, yeoman farmer (which of these is emphasized most depends upon the relative strength of the primitive or the pastoral) were still to be given their historical due.

So far as I have been able to learn, Turner was not (with the possible exception of Emerson) directly influenced by any of the imaginative writers—at least none is even casually referred to in his early essays, and there was no point at which he ever wrote of any of them with depth of knowledge or feeling. But his own Western pieties and the political traditions of the country led him in the same direction. Certainly the Edenic myth had its political counterpart in the traditions of American agrarianism. Very few American factions or traditions were altogether free of it, but it had taken its firmest embodiment in the democratic tradition from which Turner himself stemmed. The Jeffersonians had made a great virtue of the old, uncorrupted republican simplicity; the Jacksonians, even as they were tearing up the landscape with the fury of their competitive spirit, hearkened back to it nostalgically; and it had come down in a strong and sometimes militant form in the political agrarianism of the post-Civil War era, culminating in the Populist revolt. Pastoral rather than rawly primitive in its tonalities, the tradition of political agrarianism took for its central figure the worthy yeoman farmer, a symbol perhaps not more than a step removed from that of the hardy pioneer. In Turner's preoccupation with the evolutionary stages by which the frontier of the hunter and trapper were superseded by that of the pioneer settler, and then by the increasingly complex communities of villages and small towns, he was forging a link between the Darwinian mentality of his era and the older mythology of Edenic America—joining hopes and aspirations that were as basic to the American outlook as they were poignantly self-contradictory and self-defeating. But it is this as much as any other quality—and no doubt more than its way of raising so many problems fascinating to the analytical intelligence—that explains our constant readiness to return to the frontier thesis: it touches so directly the American yearning for the simple, natural, unrecoverable past.

V

Turner's view of American history won early acclaim. Raised to prominence by his youthful essays—some of them major substantive contributions to the history of Western state-making in the Revolutionary era and of early national diplomacy—he was soon sought after by other institutions— Princeton, Johns Hopkins, the University of Pennsylvania, Amherst, and the new University of Chicago, then Stanford and the University of California. In 1910, when he was at last lured from Wisconsin to Harvard, Turner also served as president of the American Historical Association at the uncommonly early age of forty-nine. Major publishers wooed him as assiduously as university presidents, and tempted him into signing contracts for several books that he would never be able to write. An impressive roster of young historians made their way to Wisconsin for graduate study under his guidance. The rapid acceptance of his ideas can be laid also to the fact that there was a new public for his writings and for those of his students, a public which was hardly less influential for being small and highly professional. In a very real sense, the Turner thesis and the historical profession grew up together. Although the great day of the wealthy amateurs was coming to a close, the writing of history had only recently become professional, academic, and specialized. The first sound and successful textbook by an American, Alexander Johnston's *History of American Politics,* had been published only in 1879.

As late as 1880 J. F. Jameson could count only eleven professors of history in the country, and the American Historical Association was founded only in 1884. At this stage, it was still possible for one or two exceptionally attractive graduate seminars (or seminaries as they were then called) to have a powerful shaping influence on historical research and thought. Turner's seminar at Wisconsin became for the twenty years after 1890 what Herbert Baxter Adams's had been at Johns Hopkins in the 1880's.

Moreover, American university culture developed with startling rapidity from 1890 to 1910, spreading throughout trans-Appalachian America, drawing strength from the rapid improvement of the state universities, and appealing widely to a new public of potential academics recruited from all parts of the country. The Midwest particularly was now prepared to make a formidable contribution to American culture; in history alone it was producing, in addition to Turner himself, such men as Beard, Becker, Parrington, and James Harvey Robinson. Aspiring academics, coming from the farms and small towns of mid-America, and often from families of modest means, were disposed to respond enthusiastically to Turner's sectional bias and to his mild democratic nationalism, as well as his gift for opening up new areas of historical interest close to their own formative experiences.

Years afterward, in 1926, Turner published one of his most interesting essays on this generation of Middle Western intellectuals, "The Children of the Pioneers." In 1891, Henry Cabot Lodge published in the *Century* an essay that seems to have rankled in Turner's mind over all the intervening years, and Turner's piece was in the nature of a long-delayed answer. Writing on the distribution of ability in the United States, Lodge had made a statistical study of the names listed in Appleton's *Cyclopedia of American Biography* and had come up with the striking conclusion that New England and the Middle Atlantic states had produced together three fourths of the ability of the entire country. Turner pointed out that Lodge had been writing about a generation at whose time of birth much of the Middle West was thinly developed. Examining *Who's Who* for 1923–24, Turner found that he could make formidable claims for the creativity of those born in the North

Central states roughly from 1860 to 1875, whom he called "the pioneer children" of these states. His assumption that the parents of all these children, simply because they were resident in the region, and regardless of their social status or the size and maturity of the community in which they lived, were "pioneers" was simply a part of the mystique of the so-called frontier; and it led to the incongruity of defining such comfortably reared children as, say, Jane Addams, Charles A. Beard, and William Jennings Bryan as "children of the pioneers." Nonetheless, Turner's basic point, as a social historian and an embattled Midwesterner, that his region had produced its full share of leadership in industry, politics, scholarship, science, and the arts, was impressively made by a long roster of distinguished names which evokes much of the intellectual history of the era. Setting forth a strong list of historians alone, Turner remarked on a common quality of their work which he attributed in good part to their regional background: "not only in striking out new lines of investigation, but in interest in the common people; in the emphasis upon economic and social, geographical and psychological interpretation; in the attention to social development rather than to the writing of narrative history of the older type, wherein the heroes were glorified."[3]

Turner was describing here the men of his own generation and that of his earlier students, and perhaps even consciously accounting for some of his own influence. Some evidence suggests that there was among the academic generation Turner trained at Wisconsin a solemn dedication to "democratic" history. That there was a high degree of self-conscious Westernism we can hardly doubt. The quality of this Western sentiment was already registered in the difference between the amateur local historical societies, East and West. The privately financed societies of the East tended to be like social clubs, antiquarian in cast, much concerned with the genealogies and obituaries of their prestigious members, but unconcerned with relations with professional his-

---

3 Turner, *Sections in American History* (New York, 1932), 277–8. His aim in this essay, Turner explained to a friend, was to show "that Eastern fears lest the West should produce only 'barbarian' children [haven't] been fully realized." Turner to Alice Perkins Hooper, March 8, 1926.

torians. The Western societies were dominated by regional rather than family pride, called upon the states for financial support, enlisted the interest of men of affairs with keen promotional spirit, and cooperated with professional historians, particularly those in the state universities. In 1907 the Western professionals were impelled to found their own organization, the Mississippi Valley Historical Association. Turner's own state was an especially strong center of this kind of activity. It had long been the beneficiary of the promotional and collecting genius of Lyman C. Draper, who had begun to put the faltering State Historical Society of Wisconsin on a sound footing as early as the 1850's. With Turner's help, Draper's successor, Reuben Gold Thwaites, made Wisconsin's the best financed of all the state historical societies, and in 1900 Thwaites was at last able to persuade the state to bring the society to the campus of the University of Wisconsin and to put its collections in the same building with the university library. Turner's own work was based in good part upon its splendid materials. More important, his mind refracted the Wisconsin angle of vision. Like many other Western states, Wisconsin had a long history of exploration, Indian trade, involvement in imperial wars, and precarious early settlements. Unlike the Eastern states, it had no claims to individuality and glory based upon contributions to the Revolution or the early Union, but it had a memorable pioneering history. In the West, it has been observed, "local historical and pioneer societies concentrated, almost to the neglect of all else, on the 'golden age' of the pioneer period and territorial days."[4]

When Turner decided, after much painful hesitation, to leave Wisconsin for Harvard in 1910, he was hurt by a few surprisingly tart and unsympathetic letters of reproach from former students for deserting the West. A more genial com-

---

[4] Van Tassel, *Recording America's Past,* 100n; cf. Higham, *History,* 18–19. It is perhaps significant that three of Turner's four major essays of the 1890's appeared first in local periodicals of limited circulation. The famous essay on the frontier appeared first in the *Proceedings* of the State Historical Society of Wisconsin for 1894, though it was reprinted shortly afterward in *The Annual Report* of the American Historical Association. The last of these essays, "The Problem of the West" (1896), came out in the *Atlantic Monthly.*

ment came from Thwaites, who was amused at Turner's account of his early weeks in Cambridge: "To have a man with your Jacksonian ideas established in a mansion on Tory Row comes very near creating heart rupture in this neck of the woods." Heart rupture—the words were not ill chosen; for Turner the experience, which at one point brought him to tears, was rather more like expatriation than professional advancement. "I feel as though I were abandoning a very dear dream," he wrote; and the *Madison Democrat* lamented his departure as "the loss of the acknowledged leader . . . among those who approach American history from the western point of view." Turner found himself well treated at Harvard, after having endured much sniping and denigration from the Board of Regents at Wisconsin. Still, after almost a decade, he wrote: "I am not sure that New England ever accepts anyone, whether 'lion' or not, who doesn't conform and roar in tune with at least some New England key." Although contented, he was never wholly comfortable, and he might easily have understood the point of Herbert Baxter Adams's caution of many years before: "Identification . . . Lost." After an evening spent in the company of Mrs. William James, he reported to his daughter: "I couldn't do more than admire her conversation in brilliant spells of silence." In 1913 he confessed: "I am still a western man in all but my place of residence." But one could always find solace in one's Western identity, and it was confirmed by further observation of life in Cambridge. "There is advantage," he wrote to Becker, "in a region which ferments over one which—doesn't."[5] It was a very American, as well as a Western, judgment.

---

[5] On this move, see Ray Allen Billington, "Frederick Jackson Turner Comes to Harvard," Massachusetts Historical Society *Proceedings*, 74 (1962), 51–2, 75, 81, 82. See also Turner to Alice Perkins Hooper, January 23, 1919. This essay, which sheds much light on conditions at the University of Wisconsin, shows that Turner was moved in part by the hope that his resignation would redound to the ultimate benefit of the university by inflicting a defeat upon the conservative forces in the Board of Regents and the state legislature. To some extent, Turner's departure does appear to have had that effect. I believe also that Turner was afflicted by one of the characteristic fantasies of the nonwriting writer: the idea that moving would help him become productive. He hoped that being at last disengaged from all the familiar affairs of Wisconsin, where he had been chairman of his department for twenty years, and going to an institution in which he did not have a deep personal stake would free him for his own work.

VI

Although his most effective graduate instruction was done in Madison, Turner did not cease to have, even in Cambridge, responsive students. The situation of the graduate seminar and the requirements of the doctoral dissertation gave him perfect ground for his unusual gifts as a teacher. One of the basic needs of professional, specialized history and the supervision of doctoral work was, and is, to work out a historical genre suitable to the talents of large numbers of students who have inquiring minds and sometimes distinguished intellectual abilities but who have at the same time little gift for or interest in narrative history in the grand manner. Turner's interests and perceptions here were as useful as his ideas were congenial. He had the wide knowledge of sources, the patience for factual detail, the new techniques (the use of maps, slides, statistics, soil analysis, the plotting of votes and allegiances), and above all the now established medium of inquiry, the analytical monograph.

Several students have paid tribute to Turner as a teacher. The portrait that emerges is one of a certain openness and generosity of character rather strongly reminiscent of Christopher Newman in Henry James's *The American;* or perhaps of the good American, Cadwallader, in Cooper's *The Travelling Bachelor:* "Truly, there was something so naïf, and yet so instructed—so much that was intellectual, and withal, so simple—a little that was proud, blended with something philosophical, in the temperament and manner of this western voyager. . . ." Students might be struck at the very beginning by Turner's mellow, almost caressing voice, and they would soon respond to the friendly interest behind it— an interest which led in many cases to lifelong attachments— to his non-authoritarian manner, his habit of posing questions rather than offering answers, his unwillingness to tell his students what to think, his lack of pretense and academic snobbery, his way of engaging enthusiastically and immediately with the subject matter without obtruding himself. His lectures, often improvised from whatever sheaf of notes he had at hand or whatever historical problem was uppermost in his mind, might or might not come off; but in the end they had the merit of allowing his students to see his mind spontaneously at work on the subject matter. His seminars, better planned, were well calculated to spur the students to share in his insatiable appetite for facts, his relish for problems.

The whole effect, as Carl Becker reported in a warm tribute, was that of "a lively and supple intelligence restrained and directed by some inexhaustible fund of sincerity, integrity and good will." Presiding over it all was that "intense and sustained interest which an abundance of ideas can alone generate." And this no doubt was the key to Turner's achievement as a teacher, as well as a writer: his sense that American history was still in great part unwritten, his ability to propound large, congenial leading ideas that pointed to whole areas of inquiry, and behind this to marshal a host of specific insights as to how this or that subject might receive a significant treatment. Woodrow Wilson, commenting on a paper of Turner's at the American Historical Association in 1896, hit it off well when he said that Turner was one who gains "the affection of every student of history by being able to do what very few men manage to do, to combine the general plan and conception with the minute examination of particulars; who is not afraid of the horrid industry of his task, and who can yet illuminate that industry by knowing the goal to which it is leading him, and the general plan by which it should be done."[6]

When one looks at the products of Turner's graduate seminars, one is impressed both by the number and professional eminence of his students and by the wide range of subjects they were put to work on. Not only was there Becker himself, but an impressive roster of men and women—almost three dozen of them trained during his years in Madison—who became leading scholars in the history of the West and the territories, the South and slavery, of sectional tendencies in the Eastern states. It is a roster of writers whose names are not, on the whole, recognizable to the general reading public,

---

6 Carl Becker, "Frederick Jackson Turner," in Howard W. Odum, ed., *Pioneers and Masters of Social Science* (1927), 289, 292; Osborn, "Woodrow Wilson and Frederick Jackson Turner," 226.

but whose monographs were, and in some cases still are, the staples of the professional literature and whose cumulative work refashioned American history. The sharp and rather dogmatic form in which the frontier thesis had been set forth in Turner's essays never inhibited significant scholarship dealing with a wide range of problems outside frontier or western history, narrowly construed—problems of foreign policy, political conflict, transportation, immigration, agricultural development, interstate migrations, the disposal of the public lands, constitutional development, even the history of ideas. In effect Turner's own students themselves realized a large part of the program for historical scholarship that he laid down in his ambitious early essays. And, though the training of doctors in American history was sufficiently diffused so that no one historian could lay claim, as Turner's contemporary Franz Boas could for anthropology, to have raised almost singlehanded an entire generation of professionals, Turner was not far wide of the mark. Within fifteen years or less from the presentation of Turner's famous paper at Chicago, his ideas were well on the way to achieving a place in the work of American historians somewhat proportionate to the place the West had long occupied in the American imagination. The historical profession, it was later said, was converted into one large Turner-verein. It is an awkward joke, but it mocks with a certain ironic effect at the passing of the Teutonic school, the abandonment of the German forests in favor of the native woods.

CHAPTER 3

Frontier and Section and the Usable Past

Each age tries to form its own conception of the past. Each age writes the history of the past anew with reference to the conditions uppermost in its own time.
—Frederick Jackson Turner, 1891

. . . *history may hold the lamp for conservative reform.*
—Frederick Jackson Turner, 1911

If the free land did it all, then we are busted when the free land goes.
—Charles A. Beard to Carl Becker, February 4, 193[9?]

I

As one studies the history of the frontier thesis and of Turner's reputation, one conclusion emerges with startling clarity: it is in large part the vagueness, the imprecision, the overstatement in Turner's essays that have given them their plasticity and hence their broad acceptance. Plasticity: it is an intriguing quality of the frontier thesis, and also one of the reasons for using it with care, that it can be invoked to argue for or against almost anything. What it meant at first, emotionally, to Turner we have seen: a way of creating an American self-image in which the frontier and its virtues loomed over everything else, and of making this self-image particularly amenable to the pride and self-assertiveness of the Middle Westerner. Taken this way, it was a doctrine of both national and sectional uses. Its patriotic impulse was susceptible also to being pushed further than Turner himself cared to do by colonizers, imperialists, aggressive promoters of world markets, who could argue, as some did in the 1890's and after, that with continental expansion at an end, the country needed new outlets overseas. (One thinks here of Albert J.

84

Beveridge's reply to those who said that expansion into the islands of the Pacific would be of a different order because these were not contiguous to mainland America. "Not contiguous! Our navy will make them contiguous.") Ever since the days of Cooper the westward movement had been sinking deeper and deeper into the American imagination, and its heroes had become the archetypal American heroes. The slogans of manifest destiny had impressed upon many minds the idea there was something inevitable about it all, something not to be resisted, that Americans were an adventurous outdoor people, for whom some new epic enterprise was practically a biological necessity.[1]

But Turner had not expounded the frontier thesis for imperialist uses, and it was not mainly for such uses that others took it up. He propagated his ideas during the Progressive era, at a time when insurgent democracy and reform cried out for a historical rationale. His immediate predecessors, as we have seen, had been chiefly patrician historians writing in the Federalist-Whig tradition, Mugwump intellectuals who were dismayed at the inefficiency, corruption, and vulgarity of American politics, who scorned demagogues and spoilsmen, and who found in early American democracy, especially in Jacksonian democracy, the prototype of the things they deplored in American life. Turner was one of the first of a new breed of historians who broke with this school, and espoused the democracy created by the common man. It seemed fitting that Turner took a particular interest in the Jackson era, and that he embraced Jacksonian democracy as "strong in the faith of the intrinsic excellence of the common man, in his right to make his own place in the world, and in his capacity to share in government" and as "based on the good fellowship and genuine social feeling of the frontier, in which classes and inequalities of fortune played little part." In Turner, the manliness and hardihood of the Western inheritance seemed to become another sanction for American egalitarianism. "The West believed in the rule of the major-

---

[1] For an illustration, see Walter Hines Page, "The War with Spain and After," *Atlantic Monthly*, 81 (1898), 721–7. On this use of the frontier, see William A. Williams, "The Frontier Thesis and Foreign Policy," *Pacific Historical Review*, 24 (1955), 379–95.

ity. . . ." he wrote. "The East feared an unchecked democracy,
which might overturn minority rights, destroy established institutions, and attack vested interests. . . . The West opened a
refuge from the rule of established classes, from the subordination of youth to age, from the sway of established and
revered institutions."[2] It was, no doubt, a mild and vague
kind of democratic assertiveness, but then the same may in
fact be said about a great deal of the thought of the Progressive era. The change of tone that Turner helped to bring about
can be appreciated only when one has refreshed one's sense
of the way democracy was handled by his more conservative
predecessors. At last the democratic middle-class reformers,
especially those rooted in the agrarian traditions of the Middle
West, were beginning to find a historical basis for their
politics.

But the frontier theme was a double-edged sword: it was
quite as capable of being used by estranged intellectuals to
cut down the myths of American democracy as it was by
patriotic democrats to build them up. Oddly enough, no matter
how it was used, the idea of the formative importance of the
frontier became more and more established, and for a long
time the very men who were digging away at Turner's values
strengthened the impact of his ideas. Whether one praised or
lamented the effects of the frontier, one confirmed the sense of
its fundamental importance. During the years when Turner
was stating and restating the frontier theme, the frontier, as a
figment of American experience, was gradually being drawn
into a battle between American intellectuals and their society.
The modern intellectual class, which in effect came into being
in the United States only around the turn of the century,
lost no time in launching an assault on the national pieties,
an assault which began with the avant-garde reconnoitering
of the "pianissimo revolt" of the nineties, proceeded to the
cannonading of the Little Renaissance of the pre-war era, and
culminated in the unconstrained frontal attack of the 1920's.
On some fronts it was a war of rebels and bohemians, realists
and naturalists, against the conventions and constraints of

---

2 *Frontier*, 302–3; *Sections*, 24–5; for a good estimate of the
change marked by Turner's view of Jacksonian democracy, See
Charles G. Sellers, Jr., "Andrew Jackson versus the Historians,"
Mississippi Valley Historical Review, 44 (1958), 615–34.

Protestant middle-class society and the gentility and timidity of its literature, on others a war of radicals against business society, on still others of metropolitan minds against the village mind, or even, in a few instances, of a self-designated intellectual elite against the mob. But whatever its guises, and whatever was felt to be at stake, the intellectual revolt demanded a re-evaluation of America in which the pioneer heritage was commonly understood to be an issue.

The issue had been posed by the official custodians of Americanism, for whom the frontier virtues were a focal point in America's long-continuing self-celebration. For example, Albert Shaw, the editor of *Review of Reviews,* declared in 1906:[3] "All the conditions of pioneering were such as to create a wonderful spirit of individuality, independence, and self-direction in the average man. Never in the world has there been anything to equal this development of personality, and the capacity for private and individual initiative." This observation led to some predictable advice: the present maturity of the country should not cause the people to abandon their individualist heritage and lose themselves in the search for ways of distributing national wealth.

In mounting their attack on this sort of thing the intellectuals did not find it necessary or strategic to deny the validity of the frontier thesis. They were glad to concede the profound formative influence of the frontier; all they needed to do was to transvalue the values of the Turners and the Shaws. Like Marx with Hegel, Van Wyck Brooks and other critics of the frontier heritage simply inverted Turner's values while using his dialectic. The frontier, they assumed along with him, was a force of the highest importance in the making of America, but those effects that Turner merely acknowledged they chose to stress: the frontier could be invoked to account for our rampant individualism, our crass speculative commercialism, our roughness and coarseness, our vigilantes and our lynch law. Taken in conjunction with Puritanism, it seemed to account for the harshness and stringency of American life, its contempt for the amenities, its anti-intellectualism, for the thwarting, the stunting, the embitterment of its

---

[3] "Our Legacy from a Century of Pioneers," *South Atlantic Quarterly,* 5 (1906), 320.

poets, painters, and thinkers. American development, they agreed, was indeed unique, but it was a unique case of pathology.

Brooks gave classic expression to this view of the matter in his *America's Coming of Age* (1915) and *Letters and Leadership* (1918), and made it central to his stunning study of Mark Twain. He was echoed by many others. Walter Weyl, the *New Republic* editor, considered that the westward movement had given Americans a psychological twist that was harmful to the development of a "socialized democracy"—a conclusion whose substance would probably have won Turner's rueful assent. Zechariah Chafee, the noted authority on civil liberties, writing at the peak of Prohibition lawlessness and Ku Klux Klan intimidation, attributed to frontier influences American hostility to law. Harold Stearns, the spokesman of the expatriate generation, thought the dubious morality of American capitalism derived from the pioneer spirit. John Dewey, discussing Bryan's intervention in the Scopes trial, explained it as the heritage of the frontier's hostility to ideas. Such cultural critics of the twenties as Lewis Mumford, Matthew Josephson, and Waldo Frank blamed the frontier experience for America's inhibitions, her willingness to sacrifice culture to other purposes, her crudeness, her alleged artistic sterility.[4]

A further token of the plasticity of the frontier thesis was its adaptability both to the business mind and the mind of the progressive reformer. To Turner himself, as to most contemporary Progressives, the passing of free land and the industrialization of the country called for new efforts at government regulation of business. Yet to a promoter like E. H. Harriman, as Turner was aware, the captains of industry were the true inheritors of the enthusiasm, hardihood, and imagination of the pioneers; their unconstrained enterprise was the making of America. This contrapuntal play on the frontier theme continued through the 1920's and the New Deal era. Conservatives in business and politics claimed the frontier inheritance. "The frontier still lingers," said Calvin

---

4 On this phase of criticism of the frontier, see Warren I. Susman, "The Useless Past: American Intellectuals and the Frontier Thesis: 1910–1930," *Bucknell Review*, 11 (1963), 1–20.

Coolidge, "the hardy pioneer still defends the outworks of civilization." Herbert Hoover, the prophet of rugged individualism, thought that the greatness of the nation had come from "ceaseless contest with the wilderness in an ever extending frontier."[5] For many critics, this use of the frontier idea still calls up the image of all the businessmen who can be found on the terraces of their country clubs or in the lobbies of the *grand luxe* hotels of Europe lamenting the decline at home of the old pioneer hardihood and bewailing the corruption and decadence of the rest of the world. In this sense, Barry Goldwater looms disquietingly as the last of the frontiersmen.

The New Dealers were disposed to concede, even to insist upon, the importance of the frontier in the past, but reverted to Turner's own proposition that the end of the frontier made new devices necessary. In 1931, the governor of Wisconsin, Philip F. La Follette, invoked Turner by name in attributing the old American freedom and opportunity to free land. "But, in one respect, the frontier was a liability as well as an asset," he pointed out. "For as long as this freedom of movement to new opportunity existed, neither the leaders nor the people were under the pressure of necessity to keep the political, social, and economic processes of American life progressively adapted to changing needs and changing conditions. . . . Today, if we find our freedom restricted and our opportunity denied, we cannot seek a new freedom and a new opportunity by running away from these restrictions and denials into some new territory. We must find our freedom and make our opportunity through wise and courageous readjustments of the political order of State and Nation to the changed needs and changed conditions of our time."[6]

---

[5] For Turner on Harriman, see *Frontier,* 318–19; for Coolidge and Hoover, Susman, "The Useless Past," 10–11.

Turner took comfort in the thought that "even those masters of industry and capital who have risen to power by the conquest of Western resources came from the midst of this society and still profess its principles." He cited, as one example, Andrew Carnegie, who "came as a ten-year-old boy from Scotland to Pittsburgh, then a distinctively Western town." Whatever the tendencies of the steel trust, "there can be little doubt of the democratic ideals of Mr. Carnegie himself." *Frontier,* 264–5.

[6] Quoted in Everett Edwards, *References on the Significance of the Frontier in American History* (1939), 43–4.

The same theme was used (and judging by some verbal similarities borrowed) the following year by Roosevelt's speech writers for his famous Commonwealth Club campaign speech. This statement, drafted by A. A. Berle with the assistance of Rexford Guy Tugwell, was based upon the safety-valve idea, and the disappearance of free land. "Our last frontier has long since been reached, and there is practically no more free land. . . . There is no safety valve in the form of a Western prairie to which those thrown out of work by the Eastern economic machines can go for a new start." Now government intervention becomes the substitute for vacant lands: "Clearly, all this calls for a re-appraisal of values. . . . Our task now is not discovery or exploitation of natural resources, or necessarily producing more goods. It is the soberer, less dramatic business of administering resources and plants already in hand, of seeking to re-establish foreign markets for our surplus production, of meeting the problem of under-consumption, of adjusting production to consumption, of distributing wealth and products more equitably, of adapting existing economic organizations to the service of the people. The day of enlightened adminstration has come."[7]

The pessimism here was not altogether characteristic of F.D.R., who indeed did not see this speech before he delivered it. But the free-land interpretation of American economic history, which did have pessimistic overtones, tended to be linked with stagnationist views of the depression. If the character and vitality of the United States really derived from yeoman farmers and pioneer promoters, how could it be restored, now that free land was gone? Some New Dealers were even taken in by the back-to-the-land movement which was strong in the early 1930's, whose proponents argued that usable land was not in fact gone and that the only way to restore the nation's economic and moral health was to relocate the unemployed on subsistence farms. "Hardly a week goes by," the agricultural writer Russell Lord observed in 1933, "but some new leader

---

[7] Roosevelt, *Public Papers and Addresses* (1938), I, 742–56. In 1935 Roosevelt reiterated his acceptance of the safety-valve idea in a public address. Edwards, ibid., 3. See also Curtis Nettels, "Frederick Jackson Turner and the New Deal," *Wisconsin Magazine of History*, 17 (1934), 257–65.

of public opinion discovers the space between cities as a God-given dump for the unemployed."[8]

As late as 1936, Joseph Schafer, one of Turner's most devoted followers, wrote that "the real American farmer" was "in the truest sense a free man" whose basic character was unchanged by hard times. The small cities, towns, villages, and the countryside, uncorrupted by the big cities, Schafer asserted, "still retain the old primal American virtues. . . . The farmers, from this point of view, are the hope of the nation's future as they have been the chief dynamic force of our country's past."[9] The agrarian myth died hard.

It was only the belated coming-of-age of urban America and the appearance of a new generation of metropolitan historians that finally unseated the Turner thesis in the historical profession. During Turner's lifetime, when his view of America seemed to hold almost undisputed sway among historians, fundamental criticism of his ideas, despite one sharp critique by Beard, was rare. However, during the 1930's and afterward, as though someone had opened the floodgates, a consistent and relentless flow of Turner criticism swept through the historical profession, and it is only in the past ten years or so that there has once again appeared a disposition to revive Turnerism in a chastened form. In a very real sense, despite the preceding decades of experience with industrialism, the urban-industrial mind did not come into its own until after the shock of the Great Depression. Even then it did so rather hesitantly, and it was characteristic than the country waited until the 1960's to accept the fact that modern American problems must be understood as city problems and to begin to disenthrall itself from the dictation of rural and small-town politicians.[1] In the course of the general reconsideration of rural pieties and the agrarian myth made inevitable by the Depression, the Turner thesis also began to be questioned.

---

8 Russell Lord, "Back to the Farm?" *Forum*, 89 (1933), 97–103.
9 *The Social History of American Agriculture* (1936), 271, 293.
1 It is not yet disenthralled. In spite of the Supreme Court's rulings on reapportionment, the small-town mentality still enjoys an overrepresentation that makes it difficult for Congress to take a sympathetic view of the problems of the great metropolitan areas. In 1967, 225 of the 435 members of the House and 56 of the 100 members of the Senate came from towns of 50,000 or less. *Time*, August 11, 1967, 17.

Perhaps the wave of Turner criticism was in some respects no more than a natural response of critical men to a doctrine that seemed all too preponderant and threatened to become ossified. No doubt many of the historians were beginning to respond to the disenchanted view of the frontier expressed by such cultural critics as Brooks and Mumford; but in the surge of optimism and the rediscovery of the folk that came in with the New Deal and the radicalism of the thirties, it had become a moral necessity to look upon the American inheritance with greater affection. Now neither Brooks nor Turner would do. The clash of world ideologies, the battle of Marxism and Fascism, also colored the rising interest in American intellectual history. There was a new emphasis on the role of ideas in history, shaped in part by the effort to mark out what was distinctive in the American mind and what was borrowed; but in any case an emphasis on the history of ideas had to bring some writers into conflict with Turnerian environmentalism. As George W. Pierson asked, in one of the most influential early essays in Turner criticism, "Above all, what happens to intellectual history if the environment be all?"[2] In particular, the development of rather sophisticated techniques of linguistic and philosophic analysis, stemming, on native grounds, largely from the Lovejoy school at Johns Hopkins, struck at the heart of the romantic primitivism latent in Turner's work. If there had been set loose in American philosophy a type of mind capable of distinguishing thirteen varieties of pragmatism, what would it eventually do with the grand, indiscriminate intellectual gestures of Turnerism? It was as though a new Johns Hopkins seminar was to have its revenge at last on the heretic from Portage.

But Turnerism came under fire above all because its premises seemed incongruous with the realities of the Great Depression and the Second World War. Its intellectual isolationism seemed to belong to another age. Turner's celebration of American individualism rang false at a time when too many were suffering from the excesses of the individualists.

---

[2] George W. Pierson, "The Frontier and American Institutions: A Criticism of the Turner Theory," *New England Quarterly*, 15 (1942), 224.

The latent pessimism in the exhaustion-of-free-land theme—an aspect of his ideas that troubled Turner as well as others—was unsuited to the activist mood demanded by any radical attempt to cope with the Depression. The vogue of Marxism among intellectuals turned attention to class conflict and made historians more skeptical of an emphasis on geographic conflict and sectionalism. The idea that the safety valve was gone led some writers to question whether, in the light of the fits of turbulence in our labor history, it had ever been there. Finally, the Depression brought to maturity a new generation of historians from big-city backgrounds and often from ethnic minorities for whom the mystique of rural America was only a phenomenon in the books. Deeply affected, as their teachers could not have been, by the economic collapse and by Marxism, by the global ideological struggle, they moved in an intellectual world in which Turner's Middle Western loyalties began to seem quaint at best, and one can readily imagine them gagging at the sentiment of such essays as "The West and American Ideals" or "Middle Western Pioneer Democracy" and balking at Turner's tribute to "the Boy Scouts who are laying the foundations for a self-disciplined and virile generation worthy to follow the trail of the backwoodsmen."[3] At the time of Turner's death in 1932, Turnerism rested on emotional commitments that were fading.

II

As a writer of substantive histories, Turner's main interest lies in the light his books shed on the implications of his essays. Here the arresting fact is that he wrote no history of the frontier or the West, indeed that he found the writing of history onerous and oppressive and did very little of it at all. For a major historical figure his yield was strikingly lean. Two volumes were published during his lifetime: *Rise of the New West*, which appeared in 1906 as part of the American Nation series, and the essays in *The Significance of the Frontier in American History;* two volumes were published posthumously: the essays brought together in *The Significance*

---

[3] *Frontier*, 358.

of Sections in American History, and a lengthy, unfinished work, *The United States, 1830–1850: The Nation and Its Sections,* brought out in 1935 three years after his death—a total of four books in a working career of almost forty-five years, many of their pages taken up by somewhat repetitive restatements, sometimes even with the same illustrative matter, of a few basic ideas.

If the disparity between his productivity and his reputation and influence troubles us, we may be sure that it troubled Turner even more. The great historians had been in the main figures of steady and lavishly fruitful work. One need not go to such a fountain of energy as Ranke, with his fifty volumes, but need only compare Turner with some of his American contemporaries like McMaster, Rhodes, or Beard to see how humiliatingly small his yield must have seemed to him. In this respect, in having a major reputation and a memorable leading idea but only a minor body of work, he is perhaps most reminiscent of Lord Acton—a man whose high repute, resting on a long and imposing shelf of unwritten books, might well have been considerably diminished if he had ever taken the trouble to do them. Turner enjoyed developing and illustrating his ideas in essays of moderate length, and left some two dozen of them that are rewarding to read. But the writing of full-length works of history, which he felt he ought also to be able to do, bored and oppressed him. His two works of substantive history do however shed much light on his qualities of mind and on the tormenting difficulties of his intellectual development.

When one examines these two books, one is immediately struck by the fact that, for all the charges of overemphasis on the West which have been made against his essays, Turner had much too much common sense to try to write a history of the United States simply in terms of the West, still less of a narrower and more constricting conception like the frontier. The animating idea in these books is not the West, narrowly construed, but sections and sectionalism in American history—an idea which made it possible to give the West the prominent place Turner thought it deserved without putting on it an exclusive or excessive burden. It is indeed this idea, embodied in the title of one of his later essays, "The Significance of the Section in American History," which is the leading idea of Turner's mature working years.

Because of their obvious points of continuity, it is possible to look at the idea of the section as no more than an extension of Turner's original idea about the West and the frontier. The use of the section as a central organizing device still carried on with his commitment to geographical and spatial categories; also the sectional idea was still a good vehicle for pressing his claims for the importance of the West. But in certain respects the section, as a basic theme, represented a partial retreat from the frontier interpretation, since it gave Turner an opportunity to stress the polylateral character of historical development and to dwell on the interplay between sections rather than the single force of the role of the West. One might expect to find a detailed exploration of the suggestions in his essays, but in the index to *Rise of the New West* there is not so much as an entry under "frontier." Nor are we told very much about such leading conceptions of Turner's essays as democracy or individualism. The development of democracy is passed over with a few casual references and in a rather perfunctory two-page sequence on changes in the suffrage; the meaning of American individualism is not explored at all. The history of the common people and their way of life, another demand of the early essays, gets very little attention, while a good deal of space is given to sketches, often nicely drawn, of the leading political heroes—a practice which may have had ample justification, in Turner's scheme, in the truth that they were "democratic" and representative men.

But even here certain vital problems are only touched upon. "We can see the very essence of the west in Henry Clay and Andrew Jackson," writes Turner; but since he is well aware that they were quite unlike each other, we wait with unsatisfied eagerness for the resolution of this commentary on the nature of the West, to be told only that Clay represented the business and propertied interests and Jackson the great masses: "If Henry Clay was one of the favorites of the west, Andrew Jackson was the west itself."[4] There is also relatively

---

[4] *Rise of the New West*, 185, 188.

little feeling for institutions—singularly little for that basic
American institution, the political party, which was undergoing formative changes in the period 1819–29, marked by the
emergence of a new party system. (The chapter labeled
"Party Politics" deals mainly with the personalities and
strategies of four leading figures, John Quincy Adams, Calhoun, Clay, and Jackson.)

Both of Turner's substantive histories are organized in
the same manner: they begin with a series of deft sectional
sketches—New England, the Middle States, the South, the
major segments of the West—and then go on to tell the story
of political events, mainly of legislation in Washington as it
was affected by the demands, the bargains and compromises,
of the several sections, and by the ambitions and strategies of
their outstanding leaders. The merits of the sectional approach
are easy to see here: the country was already big and far from
homogeneous; the sections *were* quite distinct; it is impossible
without becoming tedious to discuss, state by state, the affairs
of twenty-odd states and territories; and even the modern,
relatively homogenized America created by industry and
mass communications still has to be understood in part
through its sectional divisions. The sectional idea does enable
the historian to illustrate different cultural styles. Moreover, much of the politics of the period did take the form of
sectional maneuvering, and the sectional principle helped to
make it intelligible. Other historians, out of sheer necessity,
had resorted to something like the same device. Henry Adams,
for example, a historian perhaps as different from Turner as
one could expect to find, had begun his great history with
regional sketches much in the same fashion—except that
in true New England style he had slighted the West.

But there are also serious limitations to a pronounced
emphasis on sections. An obvious dramatic one, especially important for the narrative historian, lies in the difficulty of
beginning a book with long, relatively static portraits. Turner's
two books are, respectively, one third and more than one half
over before the political action starts. More important from
the standpoint of political history, which was the author's
main concern in these works, sections, for all their significance

in the political bargaining that went on in Congress, are not political centers in their own right—that is, they do not have governors, legislatures, budgets, political foci of their own on their home grounds. States do; and in the attempt to look at the section, the character of American politics at the vital local roots, in the actions of the state legislatures, is likely to be passed over.[5] This is particularly true of the essential efforts of the states in the field of economic development, and of their significant effort to develop a system of mixed enterprise.[6]

The sectional principle of organization, like most such devices, solves certain problems for the historian and makes the solution of others more difficult. Its greatest danger lies in what it may cause him to leave out. It may cause him to play down class or group conflict within the sections. It may cause him to describe people somewhat too much in terms of *where* they were, geographically, not enough in terms of *what* they were, vocationally and socially. It can lead to an underemphasis on those institutions that are characteristic of the whole nation and on which the sections present only variations, or on which the existence of sections sheds only a marginal light—the party system, the legal and constitutional order, the Supreme Court, the pattern of business enterprise, religious organizations and religious style. One is tempted on this count to adopt the rhetoric of the Turnerian exaggerations themselves and to suggest that the true point of view in the history of this nation is not what is merely sectional but what is common to all sections, and that the history of our *national* institutions is the really American part of our history.

---

[5] See Turner, per contra: "Sections are more important than states in shaping the underlying forces in American history." *Sections*, 183.

[6] It would certainly be too much to expect that Turner, whose writing did anticipate so much fruitful work, should have anticipated also the modern emphasis on state enterprise that is associated with such historians as Oscar and Mary Handlin, Louis Hartz, Carter Goodrich, Milton S. Heath, James Neal Primm, and others. But it is true that this whole school had been brilliantly anticipated in 1902 by Guy S. Callender in an article "The Early Transportation and Banking Enterprises of the States in Relation to the Growth of Corporations," *Quarterly Journal of Economics*, 17 (1902), 3–54, of which Turner was aware (*Rise of the New West*, 349).

All in all, *Rise of the New West* is a somewhat disappointing book to have as the only finished work from the hand of a major historian. To say that it was one of the best books in the American Nation series is a comment on the parochial scale of American historical writing and a very limited compliment. The book will hardly bear comparison in its texture—its scope was of course much more limited—with what Henry Adams had done on the chronological period preceding it. Other writings of the same era are more striking for the light they shed on the development of American institutions—one thinks, for example, of Moisei Ostrogorski's *Democracy and the Organization of Political Parties* (1902) or Henry Jones Ford's brilliant and all but forgotten *The Rise and Growth of American Politics* (1898). As a work of prose Turner's has none of the *brio* of George Dangerfield's two volumes written in our own time on roughly the same period. The book was, of course, a commissioned work, representing a type of assignment that proved uncongenial to Turner,[7] a work that had to be forced out of him against all the dictates of his temperament. It has few signs of the argumentative surge and the persuasiveness of his essays, and it shows occasional traces of fatigue. One can only conclude that, faced with the difficult problem of covering a period of rapid and confusing change in a relatively brief work, Turner lost as much as he gained, perhaps more, from his choice of the section as an organizing principle.

As for the second of the two volumes, which must be assessed as a work neither finished nor revised, it was cut out of the same pattern. Unlike the first, it was badly written (some clue to its quality may be found in Turner's effort to dictate it directly out of his voluminous file of notes). But as a work of historical analysis it has a somewhat greater solidity in proportion to its bulk. A brave synthesis of the scholarship of its time, it was impressively well informed, and a professional historian can still find cues in it after thirty years. But the general reader will find it a dead book. Turner believed that history, for all that he tried to do on its "scientific" side,

---

7 For the circumstances under which the book was written, see Ray Allen Billington's Foreword to the Collier Books edition (1962).

is an art; the art of his epoch-making essays was not matched in his histories.

III

His choice of the significance of sections as the leading idea for the second phase of his career may be taken, I think, as a clue to the characteristic problem of Turner's development as a thinker. By about 1910 he had substantially exploited, so far as this could be done through his favored medium of a series of essays, his first insight into the importance of the frontier, and he had already seen the frontier theme win wide historical recognition. For him the theme was now practically exhausted, and he seems to have been casting about for another major line along which he could develop his talents. The disparity between his spendid reputation and his productivity seems to have begun to trouble him, and he apparently hoped for a reprise of his original success with the frontier idea. It is beyond conjecture that his experience in writing *Rise of the New West* had made him acutely aware of the necessity of thinking of American history in sectional terms. In 1907 he read before the American Sociological Society a paper entitled "Is Sectionalism in America Dying Away?" which marked the beginning of a long-term effort to explore the idea of sectionalism—an effort that was climaxed in his lifetime by his essay of 1925 on "The Significance of the Section in American History" and by the detailed exploitation of the theme in his posthumous books.

What the theme of sectionalism meant to Turner is not hard to see. He witnessed with deep and understandable reluctance the easternization of the West, the development of industry, the threat that modern industrialism would homogenize the country, and that the distinctively Western values would disappear. One could see, he wrote in 1908, "that the forces of civilization are working toward uniformity, and that these forces tend strongly to counteract sectionalism in the United States and to promote social unity." But, he went on, sectionalism as well as nationalism was still in evidence, and he added wistfully that it was "too early to predict an Amer-

ican society in which the vast spaces of the United States will
be occupied by a uniform type."[8] It was an important part of
the message of these essays that sectionalism would survive,
would continue to compete with nationalism, and would offer
an alternative to total uniformity.

Again, Turner's answer to the threat of a uniform civilization was couched in geographical rather than sociological
terms: the truly reliable source of pluralism lay not in institutions but in geography. "Geographical conditions," he wrote
in 1908, "and the stocks from which the people sprang are the
most fundamental factors in shaping sectionalism. Of these
the geographic influence is particularly important in forming
a society like that of the United States, for it includes in its
influence those factors of economic interests, as well as environmental conditions, that affect the psychology of a people."[9]

In this respect, in its emphasis on geography, physio-
graphic correlations, and racial "stocks," Turner's mind looks
backward to the post-Darwinian nineteenth-century frame of
mind rather than forward to the modern concern with human
institutions and patterns of thought. He was still mentally
locked into the grand spatial metaphor that had dominated
the first phase of his work. In studying the sectional battles in
Congress during the period 1820–50, he had been concerned
to establish the point that the sectional dialogue did not involve only the North and the South but was also entered into
by the West with a strong and independent voice, that indeed
the Atlantic sections had found it necessary to compete for
Western support. This tripartite bargaining he saw followed
by a more complex bargaining in recent times. One could
indeed find much evidence for this view, and it was certainly
useful to warn that under modern nationalized conditions
historians might fail to see the importance of sectionalism in

---

8 *Frederick Jackson Turner's Legacy*, 184, 186.
9 *Sections*, 288–9. "Most of the political and economic history of
such states as Kentucky, Tennessee, Missouri, Illinois, Indiana,
Alabama and Mississippi can be written in terms of geology."
Legacy, 66. Fortunately no one has tried it. And Turner himself
was ready to concede the inadequacy of such notions. "I think it
clear," he wrote privately in 1926, "that those who believe in
geographic determinism go too far." Billington, *America's Frontier Heritage* (1966), 21.

the past. Unfortunately, however, Turner, unable to resist the temptation to exploit his idea out of all proportion to its consequence, went far beyond this: to him the section was more than a waning but still visible factor in American politics; he insisted that it had survived in full force and even went on to suggest that its importance might be expected to increase. The basically valid idea behind the sectional theme was that the United States is too big to be looked at as a simple nation or even as a federation of states; that it embraces a whole continent of heterogeneous parts, and has become, in effect, a federation of sections. "The significance of the section in American history is that it is the faint image of a European nation and that we need to re-examine our history in the light of this fact. Our politics and our society have been shaped by sectional complexity and interplay not unlike what goes on between European nations."[1] After the First World War, Turner thought that the example of the United States as a federation of sections might be of some use as an example to the world—a League of Sections as a guide to the League of Nations.

But his fundamental and most surprising commitment was to the idea that the country would have a static future in which the role of sections would actually grow larger: "The significant fact is that sectional self-consciousness and sensitiveness is likely to be increased as time goes on and crystallized sections feel the full influence of their geographic peculiarities, their special interests, and their developed ideals, in a closed and static nation."[2]

We may well begin to suspect here that the geography-bound, space-obsessed mind is getting him into trouble. Long before, in 1891, Turner had pointed out that history must adjust to the machine age and cope with economic questions: "The age of machinery, of the factory system, is also the age of socialistic inquiry." But his exaggerated claims for sectionalism show that he had not in fact been able to incorporate into his sense of the recent American past an appreciation of the dynamic quality of industrial life, its voracious appetite

---

[1] *Sections*, 51; cf. 23, 37.
[2] Ibid., 45.

for bureaucratizing and rationalizing (in the Weberian sense) human affairs, its extraordinary ability to break down barriers of space and time. That he should, with his background in the West, have found it distasteful to contemplate an America in which the farming segment of the population would shrink to less than ten percent of the whole, is altogether understandable as a matter of values. But he permitted it to blind him, even in the post-World War years, to the significance of modern industrial mass society. Hence we find him predicting in the early 1920's that the new device, the radio, will of course "diminish localism," but will do nothing to affect sectionalism. We also find him enmeshed in futile Malthusian speculations arising from his fixation on closed space and exhausted land supplies. By the early 1970's, the United States, he thought (he was not alone in holding this idea), would be facing a catastrophe arising from an insufficient food supply, as population pressed upon the now limited amount of land. It would thus be driven to perpetuate its farming regions, and the enforced persistence of agriculture would firmly underpin the survival of sectionalism.[3]

Around 1921, stung by the charge that he had excluded class conflict from his sectional scheme, Turner wrote in an unpublished fragment that sectional contests are quite consistent with class contests and that "to a considerable extent the American class struggle is itself sectional." And then, after a rather confusing passage, Turner asks us to postulate the triumph in the United States of "Bolshevistic labor ideas." "New England," he goes on, "might then divide into Northern and Southern halves according to its economic interests. Assume a combination of Southern New England, the Middle States, and West Virginia, with radical miners of the Mountain States and of the Middle West. Add for full measure a Negro revolution in the South. What would happen? Would not race antagonism afford grounds for sectional divergence between Northeast and South? Would not the Pacific Coast and West North Central States join to resist agricultural ex-

---

[3] *Frontier*, 279, 294, 314; *Sections*, 35; *Legacy*, 84; on the radio, see *Frontier and Section*, 152; *Legacy*, 62. The text of a lecture on sectionalism reprinted here, 52–69, is illuminating. For the appeal of 1891, see *Frontier and Section*, 17.

propriation? Russian experience would seem to say so."[4] At this point the manuscript breaks off, as though Turner was uncomfortably aware that he was descending to nonsense. But one does not learn whether he ever realized that if there were a national triumph of "Bolshevistic labor ideas" and a Negro revolution in the South, no one would in the least care what the internal regional pattern of New England was. What was fundamentally wrong with his insight into sectionalism was not that it lacked validity, but that it lacked the importance with which he so solemnly tried to invest it.

IV

His ruminations on sectionalism convey the detached, unworldly, and unusually gentle quality of Turner's mind, as well as a certain perverse gift he had, when confronted with an uncongenial problem, for irrelevance or disproportion. His was a mind amply endowed with curiosity and perception, and graced by a singular relish for the right detail, the revealing quotation, the fresh and unobserved historical reality. It was, despite its occasional strange excesses, a sensible mind, and it was notably generous, but it was also rather lacking in intellectual passion. Turner's enthusiasm was more like that of a collector of Americana than a critic of the human scene—one thinks of him in his later years, working at the Huntington Library, when he would periodically burst into Max Farrand's office with boyish gusto to report some new discovery that delighted him, much in the spirit of a lepidopterist with a new specimen. Explaining his feeling about history to a Phi Beta Kappa group in 1908, he said: "There is a charm in restoring the past, in compelling the procession of leaders of human thought and action again to traverse the stage of human consciousness, in rescuing from oblivion what is worth the memory of the present day. The events of past years, the institutions that have passed away, the life and manners of societies that are gone, are a precious heritage, not to be wantonly ignored in the heat and bustle of the day. Life becomes a richer thing when it is viewed largely, when it is seen as a

[4] *Legacy*, 78.

continuous movement, reaching back to generations that are gone."[5] One would hardly care to quarrel with what is here, but it is interesting what Turner chose to leave out. "Charm" is not the salient quality that many historians feel in restoring the past. One can only conclude that Turner lacked a strong feeling for the tragedy of history—and also, since very few historians have, it is hardly surprising that he had very little sense for its comedy.

Again, while Turner was moved, and rightly so, by a feeling for the achievement of America, he had little countervailing response to the shame of it—to such aspects of Western development as riotous land speculation, vigilantism, the ruthless despoiling of the continent,[6] the arrogance of American expansionism, the pathetic tale of the Indians, anti-Mexican and anti-Chinese nativism, the crudeness, even the near-savagery, to which men were reduced on some portions of the frontier. He did not fail to acknowledge now and then the existence of such things, but he did neglect to write about them with specificity or emphasis: it was not just that they did not arouse his indignation but that they seem not to have deeply engaged his interest and that he saw no imperative reason why Americans should be encouraged to confront these aspects of their frontier heritage. He saw history partly as science, partly as art, partly as a fountainhead of national and sectional pride, but he used it very sparingly as an instrument of intellectual or social criticism. In 1889, calling for a fuller account of the "progress of civilization across the continent," he said: "Aside from the scientific importance of such a work, it would contribute to awakening a real national self-consciousness and patriotism."[7] Would remorse or self-criticism have any part in this? We are left uncertain. One might perhaps expect a historian who as a young man had poled down the Wisconsin River with Indian guides to have written at least a few poignant lines about the subject of Indian removal in the 900-odd pages of his two books on the middle period. But *Rise of the New West* has a few de-

---

[5] *Legacy*, 169.
[6] "It is a wonderful chapter, this final rush of American energy upon the remaining wilderness." *Frontier*, 312. No doubt, but it was something more than that.
[7] "The Winning of the West," *Dial*, 10 (1889), 73.

tached pages on Georgia's troubled Indian affairs which are retold mainly as an episode in state-federal relations. The Southwestern Indians, Turner blandly tells us, "had developed a very considerable agriculture and a sedentary life. For this reason, however, they were the more obnoxious to the pioneers who pressed upon their territory from all sides; and, as we shall see, strenuous efforts were made to remove them beyond the Mississippi. . . . The secretaries of war . . . made many plans and recommendations for their civilization, improvement, and assimilation. But the advance of the frontier broke down the efforts to preserve and incorporate these primitive people in the dominant American society."

A later passage on Georgia's way of dealing with the Indians closes simply with: "Thus Georgia completed her assertion of sovereignty over her soil both against the United States and the Indians. But this phase of the controversy was not settled during the presidency of [John Quincy] Adams." Indeed it was not, and one looks expectantly to the succeeding volume to see if the excruciating final phases of Indian removal are dealt with, only to find that still less is said: the Indian has almost entirely disappeared as an actor or a victim from American history; the denouement is mentioned in two paragraphs, but again only as an aspect of state-federal relations.[8]

My point, I hope, will not be misunderstood: it is not that the historian is under an obligation to be a muckraker or a moralist, or to venture upon some nagging one-sided quarrel with the behavior of ancestors and predecessors who were morally no frailer than himself. My point is simply that the anguish of history, as well as its romance and charm, is there for the historian who responds to it, and that the response of a historian of the frontier to the Indian problem, as it is sometimes called, is one way of taking his intellectual temperature. It is possible that "the smiling aspects of life," to use Howells's phrase, were those that Turner thought should be featured in historical writing that aimed to awaken "a real national self-consciousness and patriotism"; but it is more likely that his decisions were taken less consciously and deliberately, out of a deep and calm satisfaction with the American past. The

---

[8] *Rise of the New West*, 115, 309–13; *The United States, 1830–1850*, 393–4.

main rebellious note in Turner's work was not a difference with the national history but with the national historians; and even his demand to get the place of the West in American history recognized at last, as against the neglect or indifference or snobbery of the older historians, was, after all, a note of the most genteel insurgency. What is more, his rebellion here was apparently quieted at a relatively early point by its own success. Turner's basic aim, like that of so many historians, was a patriotic one; his main enterprise was a foray in search of the American identity. In a nation where identity had been made uncertain and insecure by social and physical mobility, by immigration and ethnic differences, by sectional clashes, and by the weakness of traditions and of many institutions, Turner was trying to forge a common identity based on the idea of a pioneering spirit and pioneer democracy, and to assimilate it as close to the Western American as the facts of reality would admit. "We need," he said, "a natural history of the American spirit."[9] His was, of course, a gentle and basically humane nationalism, quite adaptable to an international world order, and it would be wrong to picture him as a Treitschke in coonskin. Quite the contrary, it is the blandness of his nationalism that most stands out, as it is the blandness of such social criticism as he attempted, the blandness indeed of his mind as a whole.

Turner's political views were those of a moderate Midwestern progressive, and he succeeded in keeping his detachment even when the winds of controversy were blowing strong. In 1896, as a liberal Democrat, he persuaded himself with some misgivings to vote for Bryan. As for the Populists, though he plainly sympathized with some aspects of their protest, he could never approve of what he considered to be their financial irresponsibility. His coolness in the heat of the battle of 1896 was notable: when he wrote an article on "The Problem of the West" for the *Atlantic Monthly* that year to popularize the frontier thesis, it proved in first draft so remote from the exciting events of the moment that Walter Hines Page had to prevail on him to include more references to the background of the current agrarian uprising. In later days Turner admired T.R. as "the most important single force in the re-

---

[9] *Sections*, 16.

generation of this nation in his day," and a man of "elemental greatness." Woodrow Wilson, who would "also rank with the great ones of this earth," won Turner's approval both for his domestic policies and his war policies; Turner was moved by Wilson's passion for peace and shared the dream embodied in the League of Nations.[1] In his general acceptance of progressive tendencies and progressive leadership, as well as his support for America's role in the war, Turner shared the views of millions of middle-class men and women of good will, and struck a note quite characteristic of the era of T.R. and Wilson.

But all of Turner's later thought was colored by his uneasy resistance to the pessimistic implications of the frontier idea. If, as he had said, American democracy was born of free land and gained new strength every time it touched a new frontier, might it not gradually lose strength after the disappearance of the last frontier, and ultimately die for lack of its distinctive nourishment? He refused to accept this conclusion; yet, having a view of social development founded on spatial expansion rather than the dynamics of institutions, he had difficulty imagining what would keep the American system going; and his positive suggestions, which hung on the persistence of sectionalism and the pioneer spirit, never seemed to bear any proportion to the immense problems he clearly saw ahead. Usually he fell back upon the hope that something would keep the old pioneer spirit alive, that somehow the old ways could be adapted. "This nation was formed under pioneer ideals." "How shall we conserve what was best in pioneer ideals?" Somehow it must be possible to find a way of drawing on these ideals to civilize and reform industrial democracy. "Let us see to it," he urged at the close of an essay written in 1903, "that the ideals of the pioneer in his log cabin shall enlarge into the spiritual life of a democracy where civic power shall dominate and utilize individual achievement for the common good."[2] Almost all experiences were to be tested by the touchstone of the frontier. During the First World War

---

[1] Ibid., 229–32. Turner's view on contemporary politics during his Harvard years were often set down in his correspondence with Alice Perkins Hooper, soon to appear under the editorship of Ray Allen Billington and Walter Muir Whitehill.

[2] *Frontier*, 269, 281, 268.

Turner proclaimed: "It is for historic ideals that we are fighting," and the context made it clear once again that the ideals of the frontier would sustain us in war as they had in peace. The war, Turner thought, made it possible to see more clearly than before the significance of the lives of the pioneers. In a kind of litany at the dedication of a new building of the Minnesota Historical Association in 1918, Turner linked his piety about the pioneers, his feeling about the historian's vocation, and his sense of American nationhood: "As our forefathers, the pioneers, gathered in their neighborhood to raise the log cabin, and sanctified it by the name of home, the dwelling place of pioneer ideals, so we meet to celebrate the raising of this home, this shrine of Minnesota's historical life. It symbolizes the conviction that the past and the future of this people are tied together; that this Historical Society is the keeper of the records of a noteworthy movement in the progress of mankind; that these records are not unmeaning and antiquarian, but even in their details are worthy of preservation for their revelation of the beginnings of society in the midst of a nation caught by the vision of a better future for the world."[3]

Turner did not fail to see that a new America had come into being with the twentieth century: this was indeed one of the implications of the exhaustion of free lands. He devoted much of his presidential address to the American Historical Association in 1910 to underscoring what this meant: the disappearance of the frontier, the massing of capital in large aggregates, the appearance of a large immigrant proletariat, the sharpening of class conflict, the development of world trade and imperialist commitments. Like most Progressives, he was willing to endorse more governmental action to meet these problems: as a safeguard of democracy the now vanished free lands would have to be replaced by a new social resourcefulness. The unrestricted competitive individualism that had been engendered by pioneer conditions was now at odds with democratic ideals and would have to be subordinated to them. He was troubled by the thought that the dangers of social conflict would be greater, not only because the safety valve was closed and "classes are becoming alarm-

<hr>

[3] Ibid., 335, 338–9.

ingly distinct," but also because the prejudices of native-born
employers and the native middle classes against immigrant
workers intensified the struggle. As a boy he had seen the
older immigrants, the Scandinavians, Germans, Irish, English,
and Canadians in the process of Americanization under the
favorable conditions of the frontier. As a young historian he
had witnessed with a certain repugnance and alarm the in-
vasion of the new and less congenial masses of southern and
eastern Europeans, and his comments on the habits and potential influence of the southern Italians, Poles, Russian Jews,
and Slovaks had been sharp and unsympathetic. As he grew
older, his distaste became qualified by compassion. He had
always hoped that a better environment would improve
them. "Even in the dull brains of great masses of these un-
fortunates from southern and eastern Europe," he wrote in
1910, "the idea of America as the land of freedom and of opportunity to rise, the land of pioneer democratic ideals, has
found lodgment, and if it is given time and is not turned into
revolutionary lines it will fructify."[4]

Yet there were moments when it seemed to Turner that
the whole development of the New World, from the freshness of the virgin continent to the assembly lines and blast
furnaces of modern industry marked a gigantic regression—
a regression to a form of society which one might easily wish
to see destroyed. Take Pittsburgh, he once said: there Brad-
dock and his men long ago "were struck by the painted savages in the primeval woods," and now "huge furnaces belch
forth perpetual fires, and Huns and Bulgars, Poles and Si-
cilians struggle for a chance to earn their daily bread, and
live a brutal and degraded life." Reflecting on this contrast
between the woods and the furnaces, he was reminded of
T. H. Huxley, who had found even the best of modern civilization exhibiting no ideal worthy of the name, and was
tempted to think it might be just as well if some "kindly
comet" would sweep the whole thing away. And yet, said
Turner (using—was it for the first time?—the phrase that
John F. Kennedy was to hit upon for the 1960's), if there was

---

[4] *Frontier*, 320–1, 280, 277–8; see Saveth, *American Historians
and European Immigrants*, 122–37, for Turner's views on immigrants.

shock and apprehension in industrial civilization, there was challenge also: "In place of old frontiers of wilderness, there are new frontiers of unwon fields of science, fruitful for the needs of the race; there are frontiers of better social domains yet unexplored."[5]

Turner's sense that the trials of the industrial world might be successfully met was not given substance by any program of his own. He was of course sympathetic to the general direction of the Progressive reforms, and he believed in the advance of government regulation as a necessary condition of reform. But the only particular suggestion he had for the times—aside from his belief that the need for agricultural produce would help to sustain a healthy sectionalism—was breathtaking in its simplicity and its insularity: it was the state university that would keep pioneer ideals alive, translate them into the terms required by industrialism, reaffirm the democratic spirit of the country, keep opportunities open, sustain mobility, provide democratic leadership, and, in the end, "safeguard democracy."[6] The note of naïveté and of Midwestern parochialism in this confidence in the state university is all too plain; yet there is something to be said for it. Turner was among the earliest of modern American scholars to see how important the expert would become in the business of government, and he did realize that modern democracy would require the services of groups of trained experts of the kind he thought the state universities would be particularly well equipped to turn out—lawmakers, administrators, judges, commissioners, and the like—men "who shall disinterestedly and intelligently mediate between contending interests." The University of Wisconsin, as he had had occasion to see, had played just such a role in the reforms of the La Follette era, and had established an intimate and productive relation to the state's political leaders.

In seeking for an intelligent and disinterested class of experts, Turner struck a characteristic Progressive note, somewhat reminiscent of Brandeis's conception that a corps of lawyers with a proper sense of social responsibility would hold "a position of independence between the wealthy and

5 *Frontier,* 299–300.
6 Ibid., 269–89, especially 282–7.

the people, prepared to curb the excesses of either." Turner had also shifted ground: he conceded that the old pioneer prejudice against the expert and the specialist was among the frontier traits that must be abandoned. He thought that if the expert showed enough "creative imagination and personality," he could overcome this residual prejudice and that the new class of experts could best be produced in the state universities because these institutions were the direct inheritors of the democratic spirit. Historians too would have their place among the experts, as shapers of the right kind of social mentality: "A just public opinion and a statesmanlike treatment of present problems demand that they be seen in their historical relations in order that history may hold the lamp for conservative reform."[7]

Of course, Turner expected much more of the state universities than they could give, and they have hardly justified the notion that they would save democracy. There is a certain irony too in the thought that Turner's most memorable manifesto on the state universities as the salvation of democracy was delivered in 1910, the very year when his own discontents with Wisconsin, one of the best of them, drove him to Harvard. It is not hard to be swayed by his belief that modern democracy would need more widespread, and cheaper, public education and that the state universities would contribute both to social mobility and to the sum of social intelligence; but one is struck here, once again, by the imbalance between the major problem he perceived and the minor means he proposed to solve it.

V

Whether there was any relation between the bland and conventional qualities of Turner's mind and his difficulties with his writing and with the development of his talent is a question that must be left to his biographers. There does remain about his career something extraordinary and puzzling: it began with such gusto, such an onrush of inspiration and

---

7 Ibid., 285, 323–4; for Brandeis see his *Business—A Profession* (1927), 337.

major insight, it was encouraged by such prompt recognition, that it is inexplicable to see it foundering before it had even got to mid-passage. Turner's success in conceiving and promoting the frontier theme in the 1890's was never to be followed by any achievement even remotely comparable, and his career becomes an unexpected instance of F. Scott Fitzgerald's sweeping dictum that there are no second acts in American lives. Turner once told his pupil Merle Curti that "a man does not make a fundamental discovery or effect a profound alteration in science after he is thirty."[8] This fixation on youth is extraordinary for a historian: poets and mathematicians are reputed to bloom young, but history is one of those pursuits in which talents usually ripen slowly and in which the highest achievements can be expected in the middle or later years. For Turner, however, the remark has its poignant reality. His basic idea had crystallized when he was about thirty, and during the half-dozen or so years immediately following it had given him the warm, inspired moment that yielded his important early essays. By the time he had reached his early forties, this idea had been exploited about as fully as it could be in illustrative and exhortatory essays, and the further development of Turner's talent now required either that he elaborate it fully in major books of Western history or go on to develop some new central idea. The first Turner could not do; the second he attempted, with results I have already tried to assess, in the notion of sectionalism.

Turner's receptivity, at least, did not wane: he was always prepared to see things he had missed before, or to qualify his formulations. Near the end of his life he told Arthur M. Schlesinger that he thought there was much to be learned from an urban interpretation of American history. But it seems undeniable that Turner's mind, which developed with such rapidity and effect during his thirties developed very little afterward. I trust I have made clear that Turner's early interest in the frontier, though it may have originated in a somewhat parochial concern, was developed with anything but parochial intellectual means. During the 1880's Turner looked eagerly for insight and guidance

---

8 *Early Writings*, 35 n.

from whatever quarter he could find it—not only from books of geography and census reports and observations of native reformers like Henry George, but from English historical writing, German historical thought, and contemporary French scholarship, from statistics, economics, and sociology. He continued, of course, in his later years to call upon historians for this kind of collaboration with other disciplines, but, aside from his efforts to keep up with trends among geographers, he seems to have done rather little of it himself. I find no evidence in his published writings that he followed his early interest in German historical thinkers with any acquaintance with that remarkable efflorescence of sociological work that came in the era of Max Weber. Or, for that matter, that the work of a native social thinker like Veblen, whose experiences and ideas might have been expected to excite his interest, had any effect on him; or that he found anything to learn from other interesting contemporary sociologists like Ward, Ross, or Cooley. Or that he was interested in the emergence of pragmatism, or in the functionalist psychology being developed by John Dewey and related thinkers. Or that he was excited or instructed by native political scientists like Charles E. Merriam, J. Allen Smith, or A. F. Bentley, or, for that matter, Charles A. Beard. Or that the rise of Fabianism in England or of American socialism or later the coming of the Bolshevik Revolution inspired him to any extensive reading in the Marxian tradition. Or that he was at all stirred by the fresh and rebellious American literature of the period between the 1890's and the First World War. Or that he was even intimately concerned with the emergence of the economic interpretation of history, which in this country owed so much to his own earlier suggestions. What he appears to have done, as he dug himself deeper and deeper into the vast materials of Western Americana and kept carefully in touch with the large, proliferating literature of monographic scholarship, was to lose sight of the greater world of ideas that was changing with such rapidity during his middle years. It is tempting to speculate where his mind might have turned if he had taken a cue from any one of a number of major ideas of the era. And though we have no right to try to budget his time, it is tempting too to wonder what might have happened if, in-

stead of writing more essays devoted to showing once again
the importance of the Middle West or the Mississippi Valley,
or to celebrating once again the pioneer ideals, he had written
an essay on, say, the significance of land speculation in American history, or on class stratification on the frontier or (since
he discovered a new interest in the city) on the frontier cities;
or indeed to wonder what his mind might have turned to if he
had been able to forget about geography and physiography, to
abandon his intricate maps, and to read with any of his former
enthusiasm in contemporary sociology and literature, where he
might have found new resources for the distinctive quality
of his insights, which at their best were usually of a sociological character.

What complex of events brought about this arrested development in Turner must remain largely a matter of speculation. Although his productivity even during the 1890's was
not notably high in quantity, it was of such quality as to give
several publishers the impression that in him they might have
found the writer of a whole series of significant works. But
somewhere in his early forties Turner himself must have begun to be aware that something was wrong; certainly he
began to feel with special pain the burden of writing, and he
began to develop so perfectly and completely the syndrome of
the nonwriting writer that the remaining mystery for us must
be not why he did not write the half dozen or so major books
that might have been spun out in pursuit of his insights but
how he managed, as he did, to force out a fairly steady trickle
of short pieces. It is perhaps fairest to think of him not as a
rich productive force full of primal energy who perversely
failed to realize his talents, but rather as a constitutional nonwriter whose work was wrung out of himself at immense
psychic cost.

It is hard to imagine anything that would have made
Turner an easy writer, but domestic tragedy went far to
dampen his spirit. In 1899 the Turners lost two of their three
children, a daughter of five and a son of seven, to childhood
diseases, and in the anguish of this experience, which left
him troubled over the health of his wife, a great deal went
out of him. "I have not done anything, and have not had the
heart for anything," he wrote to Becker at this time. After a

trip to Europe and a hiatus of a few years in his work, the small steady flow of his writing resumed; but a certain resilience was gone, and those who knew him felt that he was never quite the same. If he was not so self-critical as to be unhappy about the somewhat repetitive character of his work, its lack of forward impetus, he was keenly distressed by his inability to get much done, a trait over which the demanding editorship of A. B. Hart might have made him more self-conscious than he had been before. Ray Allen Billington has written a sympathetic and revealing account of Turner's struggles with himself, which mark him with all the stigmata of the prototypical nonwriter. He became haunted by the suspicion, so clear to his biographer, that he was temperamentally "incapable of the sustained effort necessary to complete a major scholarly volume."[9] "I hate to write," he blurted out to a student in later years, "it is almost impossible for me to do so." But it was a self-description arrived at after long and hard experience. In 1901, when he was forty, Turner had signed contracts for nine books, not one of which was ever to be written and only a few of which were even attempted, and his life was punctuated by an endless correspondence with disappointed publishers. For an academic family, the Turners lived expensively and entertained generously, and the income from any of the textbooks he promised to write would have been welcome, but the carrot of income was no more effective than the stick of duty and ambition. Turner's teaching load at Wisconsin was for a time cut down, in the hope that it would clear the way for his productive powers, but what it produced was only a misunderstanding with university trustees. Turner's reluctance to address himself to substantive history was so overwhelming that A. B. Hart, a martinet of an editor who presided with ruthless energy over the authors of the American Nation series, extracted *Rise of the New West* out of him only by dint of an extraordinary series of nagging letters and bullying telegrams. Hart in the end counted this his supreme editorial achievement. "It ought to be carved on my tombstone that I was the only man in the world that

---

[9] Billington's judgment in "Why Some Historians Rarely Write History," *Mississippi Valley Historical Review*, 50 (1963), 15; the facts in the following paragraph are from this account.

secured what might be called an adequate volume from
Turner," he wrote to Max Farrand; and Farrand, one of
Turner's closest friends who watched his agonized efforts to
produce his last unfinished volume in the splendid setting
provided by the Huntington Library, sadly concluded that he
would not have finished it had he lived forever.

Over the years Turner had built up a staggering variety
of psychological and mechanical devices, familiar to all observers of academia, to stand between himself and the finished
task. There was, for example, a kind of perfectionism, which
sent him off looking for one more curious fact or decisive bit
of evidence, and impelled the elaborate rewriting of drafts that
had already been rewritten. There were the hopelessly optimistic plans for what he would do in the next two or twelve
or eighteen months, whose inevitable nonfulfillment brought
new lapses into paralyzing despair. There was an undisciplined
curiosity, an insatiable, restless interest in *everything*, without
a correspondingly lively determination to consummate anything; a flitting from one subject to another, a yielding to the
momentary pleasures of research as a way of getting further
from the discipline of writing. ("I have a lot of fun exploring,
getting lost and getting back, and telling my companions
about it," he said, but "telling" here did not mean writing.)
There was overresearch and overpreparation, with the consequent inability to sort out the important from the trivial—a
small mountain of notes, for example, gathered for a trifling
projected children's book of 25,000 words on George Rogers
Clark. There were, for all the unwritten books, thirty-four
large file drawers bulging with notes on every aspect of American history. There were elaborate maps, drawn to correlate
certain forces at work in American politics. There were scrap-
books, and hours spent filling them. There was summer-session
teaching, often needed to meet family expenses. There were,
as a necessary source of relief, long camping and fishing trips.
(Turner needed the outdoors so much that shortly after his
removal from Madison to Cambridge he set up a tent for a time
on his back porch so that he could sleep out of the house.)
There were the absorbing affairs of the University of Wisconsin
—a duty—and for a long time the burdens of the departmental
chairmanship. There was a crusade against the overemphasis

on college football, a movement to elect a new president. There were the needs and demands of his graduate students, always warmly and generously met ("Turner gives all his time to us, instead of spending it writing books and articles like the others!"), and there was the irresistible lure of over-teaching which caused Turner in 1923–4, his last year at Harvard, to redo the notes for a course which he had given many times and would never give again. There were the professional affairs of the American Historical Association; there were commencement and dedicatory addresses. There were, of course, long letters of explanation to publishers, and other letters setting forth new plans for books. There was indeed an entire set of letters to Henry Holt and Company, examining various possible titles for the last unfinishable volume—letters that the exasperated publishers finally cut off by suggesting that the matter might well wait until the book itself became a reality. Finally, there was, after the possible bounty of his middle age had been lost, a series of wasting and depressing illnesses during his last fifteen years that cut deep into his working time. At the end, Turner was, as always, good-humored and apologetic. There was a last word for Farrand: "Tell Max I am sorry that I haven't finished my book." And one can only hope that he found consolation in the thought that, even without his book, he had redrawn the map of American historiography.

CHAPTER 4

The Frontier as an Explanation

In truth there is no single key to American history.
—Frederick Jackson Turner, 1907

I

I HAVE LEFT to the end Turner's use of the frontier and the many criticisms that have been made of it. A good deal of the confusion that has arisen in the controversy over Turner's ideas can be resolved if one bears in mind the twofold character of his writings. On one side there is what both critics and followers have referred to as his poetic vision. In images of a certain economy and force Turner was giving voice to emotions deeply felt and widely shared—writing, as Henry Nash Smith has said, "with the authority of one who speaks from the distilled experience of his people."[1] Here his achievement must be understood as part of the broader inheritance of romantic nationalism. But this aspect of his work is also linked to the vagueness and imprecision of his formulations, their repetitive, almost incantatory restatement over the years, his tendency to lapse into sentiments of national and regional patriotism. On the other side there are a series of historical and sociological statements about American development which seem to hinge upon fact; in one form or another—whether as he put them or somewhat restated—they do seem to be amenable to the test of evidence, and they have tempted "scientific" historians to exercise their craft upon the Turnerian generalizations in ways that are regarded by those who share the frontier mystique as excessively literal-minded. Hence in this argument there have been mobilized against each other historians of two kinds of intellectual temperament, coinciding with the poet and the positivist that coexisted so uneasily in Turner. And the Turner who deals in fact—or who

[1] *Virgin Land,* 251.

seems to ask us to do so—and the Turner who deals in values are always intertwined in such a way as to make the task of Turner criticism an exercise in nice discrimination.

Historians have debated so long and hard whether the frontier thesis is profoundly valuable or fundamentally misleading that there has been a danger of losing sight of the paradox that it can be both. Here, trying to distill what seems to be of most enduring value in the controversy, I shall work on the assumption that there is indeed something of substantial merit at the core of Turner's views. The most valid procedure with a historical thinker of his kind is not to try to have sport with his marginal failings but to rescue whatever is viable by cutting out what has proved wrong, tempering what is overstated, tightening what is too loosely put, and setting the whole in its proper place among the usable perspectives on our past.

Even Turner's sharpest critics have rarely failed to concede the core of merit to his thesis, and wisely so. For over two hundred and fifty years the American people shaped their lives with the vast empty interior of the continent before them. Their national existence up to Turner's day had been involved with conquering, securing, occupying, and developing their continental empire. It is hard to believe that this process of westward settlement, so demanding, so preoccupying, so appealing to the imagination, so productive of new and rich resources for the economy, could have been carried on for so long without having some considerable effect upon their politics and diplomacy, the pattern of their nationalism, their manners, literature, and their imagination, their habits and institutions. Very little of this has really been in dispute, and if Turner had limited his claims to such terms, had been content to say that the availability of the inland empire and its development must be taken into full account in any well-rounded or complete study of the forces that have shaped the United States, it is doubtful that any reasonable man would have troubled to argue with him.

But it is also doubtful that anyone would have paid any attention. Here I think we can only defer to the soundness of Turner's instincts—as we must in another connection to Beard's—if not to all his reasoning; both men understood that

if a new or heterodox idea is worth anything at all it is worth
a forceful overstatement, and that this is one of the conditions
of its being taken seriously. We have seen that many aspects
of the Turner thesis were stated by other writers before Turner;
but we identify him with this idea not simply because he
stated it more fully but also because he hammered away at it
with a certain obsessive grandeur until everyone had to take
account of it.[2]

What troubled Turner's critics, then, was not the core of
his insight—so useful and appropriate in the setting of American historical writing during the 1890's—but its formulation:
a series of very broad assertions, very vaguely put, seemingly
exclusive of other than frontier and Western forces, and resting heavily upon a Middle Western animus that was irrelevant
to the tasks of historical explanation and impossible for Americans from other regions to share. But before we go on to
consider how much of the Turner thesis may survive the recent
barrage of criticism, it is necessary to return once more to
Turner's mode of statement. Here we must face up to a flat
contradiction: Turner, as a self-conscious theorist of historical causation, was distinctly opposed to one-idea systems. As
a teacher, by the unanimous testimony of his pupils, he was
careful to stress the complexity of history, its multicausal
character, and to avoid dogmatism and oversimplification. In
1907 he said in a lecture: "In truth there is no single key to
American history. In history, as in science, we are learning
that a complex result is the outcome. Simple explanations fail
to meet the case."[3] On other occasions he made similar statements, and I see no reason to doubt that this clear explanation
of his sense of the matter represented his mature judgment.
Yet the whole Turnerian creed is set forth in a series of sharp,
jarring, sweeping assertions that make inordinate demands
upon our belief.

Turner's assertions, it should be said, are not merely those
of a bright young man promoting a new idea, but are repeated

---

[2] "I do not think of myself as primarily either a western historian
or a human geographer. I have stressed those two factors because
it seemed to me that they had been neglected." Turner to Carl
Becker, October 3, 1925.
[3] *Legacy*, 170; this remark was made in a lecture of 1907 published the following year. Cf. *Legacy*, 38–41.

throughout his middle years with little or no modification or explanation:[4]

> This ever retreating frontier of free land is the key to American development.

> The true point of view in the history of this nation is not the Atlantic coast; it is the Mississippi Valley. . . . The real lines of American development, the forces dominating our character, are to be studied in the history of westward expansion.

> The existence of an area of free land, its continuous recession, and the advance of American settlement westward, explain American development.

> The true point of view in the history of this nation is not the Atlantic Coast, it is the Great West.

> And to study this advance, the men who grew up under these conditions, and the political, economic, and social results of it, is to study the really American part of our history.

> The problem of the West is nothing less than the problem of American development.

> The Mississippi Valley has been the especial home of democracy.

> The forest clearings have been the seed plots of American character. . . . This forest philosophy is the philosophy of American democracy.

> This at least is clear: American democracy is fundamentally the outcome of the experiences of the American people in dealing with the West.

> This new democracy that captured the country and destroyed the ideals of statesmanship came from no theorist's dream of the German forest. It came, stark and strong and full of life, from the American forest.

> American democracy was born of no theorist's dream; it was not carried in the *Sarah [Susan] Constant* to Virginia, nor in the *Mayflower* to Plymouth. It came out of the Amer-

---

[4] *Frontier and Section*, 29; *Frontier*, 1, 3, 4, 205, 190, 206–7, 266, 216, 293.

ican forest, and it gained new strength each time it touched a new frontier. Not the constitution, but free land and an abundance of natural resources open to a fit people, made the democratic type of society in America for three centuries while it occupied its empire.

It is these grand verbal gestures that have brought about much of the waste motion in the debate over the frontier. What, for example, are we to make of the statement that free land and the process of Western settlement "explain" American development? An assertion like this is an embarrassing thing to have on one's hands, and it is hardly surprising that when such dicta are referred to, an admirer of Turner will usually intervene, like some alert hostess distraught over a tactless remark, to explain that her guest really did not mean what he said. But what did he mean? We may legitimately indulge Turner, and ourselves, by passing over the complexities that philosophers would surely raise about the meaning of explanation. But still: does Turner's proposition mean that free land and the westward movement are the only major forces in American history that we need to take account of? Or that they are so formidable that they far outweigh all the other forces put together? Or merely that they constitute the largest single force among a variety of forces? And even so, by what calibration do we measure and compare the weight of such grand imponderables as the frontier, as against the nonfeudal inheritance of America, or its Protestant background, or its ethnic mixture? It is probably safest here to fall back on Turner's own remark that there is no single key to American history as evidence that he would in the end have agreed with us that a proposition such as this about the explanation of American history need not be taken seriously as a subject of rational discourse. Its true function was on one side emotional, to protest against the previous neglect of the West, and on the other side promotional, to call attention to the Turnerian propositions.

Again, take Turner's often quoted statement that "the frontier is the line of most rapid and effective Americanization." The context shows what Turner meant: it was at the frontier that European man, rather abstractly conceived, most quickly and surely became the American man—not in itself an implausible suggestion. But if for the moment we turn our attention away from European man to contemplate more concretely the European immigrants who flooded into the United States, the fact will be brought home to us that they had to be Americanized in those portions of America where they happened to settle, and that most of them settled in the cities. (Even as early as 1870 only ten per cent of foreign-born Americans were farmers.) We may leave to students of acculturation the question whether the small minority who went to a frontier were more rapidly and effectively Americanized than those who went to the city—with no more than the suggestion that the matter should not be settled in a circular fashion simply by defining Americanization as that which occurred on the frontier. What is most important is not to let our attention be diverted from the basic facts of urban life by Turner's claims for the superior Americanizing efficacy of the frontier. From the early nineteenth century to the First World War thirty million Europeans were added to the American population. By what process were the ideals of the frontiersmen and the frontier experience transmitted to them and their children? We need not prejudge the question: the frontier had, and has, a profound appeal to the imagination, and something of it may have been conveyed to Italians in Providence and Poles in Hamtramck. Something, but not all, and not in its immediacy; and above all, however it was conveyed, it had to be conveyed through agencies that can be understood only as part of the urban scene. The frontier had a big maw but it cannot be made to ingest everything.

One of the earliest objections to the Turnerian generalizations had to do with the persistent imprecision of their central terms. This was especially, and perhaps most decisively, true of the word "frontier" itself. One may find a certain admirable boldness in Turner's statement on this count: "The term is an elastic one, and for our purposes does not need sharp definition." One may also find merit in it, in the sense that Turner is so often consciously trying to unite and draw together related things rather than to distinguish them: when we are articulate about what we are doing, it is quite as legitimate to combine and relate things as it is to break down and distinguish them. But at length one is impelled to agree with

George W. Pierson's judgment that in a thinker for whom the
"frontier" affords the "explanation" of American history, loose-
ness in using it is a serious problem. Efforts like Pierson's
famous dissections of Turner, which proceed by textual analysis and deal with internal consistency, do not have precisely
the stature of a "refutation" of Turner's views, but they provide a necessary foundation to any attempt to decide how
much use we can make of them. The frontier, to Turner, was
on various occasions the wilderness environment, on others
empty and unsettled land, or the population living in a certain
area, or "the West" generally, or the natural resources found
there, or a social process of settlement and Americanization;
and, in one instance where a stroke of hyper-clarity only underscores the general confusion, Turner repeated the census-
maker's definition as "the margin of that settlement which has
a density of two or more to the square mile."[5]

Criticism based on these vagaries of usage seems to me to
stem from something more than the desire to have a little
semantic fun at Turner's expense. History is neither philosophy nor science, but it is rational discourse that has to proceed in accordance with certain rules, and I am disposed here
to agree with Henry Nash Smith's observation: "Sometimes
. . . Turner's metaphors threaten to become themselves a
means of cognition and to supplant discursive reasoning." To
some readers, for example, it will make a difference whether
Ohio, which can indeed be called a frontier state in 1803, can
still be called a frontier state in 1833—at which point it can
still certainly be called a part of "the West." If the West and
the frontier are loosely identified, then social processes that
were going on in Ohio in the 1830's, and which may be much
the same as the processes general to small-town and rural
America on or off the frontier, all become transmuted into
"frontier" processes. Still worse: if the frontier and the West
mean the same thing, everything that went on west of the Appalachians, and all the natural resources of the West itself
somehow become assimilated to the frontier imagery. Turner

---

[5] See *Frontier*, 3 for Turner on both counts. Two essays by Pierson
are indispensable: "The Frontier and Frontiersmen of Turner's
Essays," *Pennsylvania Magazine of History and Biography*, 64
(1940), 449–78, and "The Frontier and American Institutions,"
New England Quarterly, 15 (1942), 224–55.

himself was troubled by the problem, though he did little to resolve it. Of "the West" he wrote in 1901: "the term has hopelessly lost its definiteness."[6]

The difference here is no mere quibble. The immediate experience of the *frontier,* rather narrowly and literally defined as the meeting place between civilization and the wilderness or as the edge of settlements characterized by a certain low population density, was of necessity the experience only of a very small portion of the whole American population; and as the population of the country became larger through time, it was the experience of an ever shrinking portion. But the experience of growing up in a dynamic and rapidly developing rural environment, common to almost all parts of the country and indeed especially dramatic in the West, was one very widely shared throughout our history. Much of the Turner thesis boils down, in this sense, to the understanding, sound enough, but hardly so distinctive as the frontier rhetoric suggests, that the United States was a rural society before it became an urban one, and that many of its traits were shaped by the requirements of a fast-developing capitalistic agriculture expanding into a rich terrain.

II

The counts on which Turner has been criticized are bewilderingly numerous, though not all are of equal importance. Some of his concerns—like plotting out the "stages of development" through which a frontier area would pass—seem to belong largely to the immediate post-Darwinian intellectual climate in which his ideas were first expressed, and it is not any longer of central interest that his version of a more or less unilinear sequence has been quarreled with by some specialists in frontier history. It will perhaps be more feasible to consider how only a few of his major contentions have fared, and to concentrate on his views concerning the effects of the frontier on democracy and individualism.

Probably the most important is the conception that our democracy is the outcome of the experience of the American

---

[6] *Virgin Land,* 254; *Frontier,* 126.

people in dealing with frontier expansion and the West. In assessing Turner's approach to democracy, certain peculiarities are important to reckon with. The first is a disposition to illustrate but not to define. Perhaps it is easy for a historian to assume that, in writing about democracy for a people who experience and practice it, definition is not necessary. As we shall see, this tendency to circle about the question of democracy without coming to rest on a definition was also one of the problems inherent in Charles Beard's book on the Constitution. A second point is that Turner's real concern was not in fact with democracy as a general phenomenon of political development but only with the distinctive features of American development—a matter to which I shall return. Again, Turner here, as in most situations, has a disposition to synthesize rather than to analyze. He is more interested in combining things that he sees as related than he is in making sharp distinctions between things that can in fact be distinguished. Finally, when he speaks of democracy, he is much more likely to relate it to sentiments and attitudes or to specific historical measures than to the forms of institutions. In particular, he is likely—and this is very American—to identify democracy with egalitarianism. This view of it has obvious limitations: it gives us no way of accounting for societies like England which have a strong deferential social system and a well-developed sense of class but also highly developed democratic institutions. Most of us today are disposed to define democracy as a system of parliamentary government in which there is a universal or nearly universal base of suffrage, in which officeholding is not restricted to a limited class, in which criticism of the policies of the government is tolerated and takes an institutional form in an opposition party or parties, and in which there are adequate formal legal sanctions to protect such criticism. Turner did not show a systematic interest in the development of democracy in this sense, but rather in the history of certain attitudes and issues that reinforced the spirit of egalitarianism.

Turner also finds democracy in American experience intimately associated with "individualism." Insofar as he sees any tension between the two, he sees it only as a product of the modern era, the era after the disappearance of the free lands. "The frontier individualism," he wrote in his famous essay, "has from the beginning promoted democracy." The "democracy born of free land" he sees as being "strong in selfishness and individualism." The old pre-Revolutionary West he calls "a democratic self-sufficing, primitive agricultural society, in which individualism was more pronounced than in the community life of the lowlands." Elsewhere he speaks of "the old democratic admiration for the self-made man, its old deference to the rights of competitive individual development." Democracy was associated with individualism because collective action took place "without the intervention of governmental institutions." Only in the modern post-frontier era, an era Turner speaks of as the era of "organized democracy," do democracy and individualism come into conflict: "Organized democracy after the era of free land has learned that popular government to be successful must not only legitimately be the choice of the whole people" but must also recognize that "specialization of the organs of the government, the choice of the fit and the capable for office, is quite as important as the extension of popular control."[7] When free lands came to an end and the Americans lost their isolation from Europe, they lost their immunity from the costs of mistakes, waste, inefficiency, and inexperience. And with the rise of industrialism they also needed to cope with its ills through social legislation.

More often than not, "democracy" in Turner's writings is an attitude, a spirit, the quality of a certain kind of political or social movement. Jacksonian democracy, for example, was "strong in the faith of the intrinsic excellence of the common man, in his right to make his own place in the world, and in his capacity to share in government." It was the opposite of conservatism: the West brought "a new type of democracy and new popular ideals. The West was not conservative. . . ." It was high-minded: "Western democracy has been from the time of its birth idealistic." It was fraternal: Middle Western democracy involved "a real feeling of social comradeship among its widespread members"; it was "an enlarged neighborhood democracy . . . based upon good fellowship, sympathy

---

[7] *Frontier*, 30, 32, 107, 258, 343, 357, cf. 305–7.

and understanding." It was, of course, anti-aristocratic, since it stood for the predominance of the farmer as against the planter class. Above all it was a quality of the pioneer: "The strength of democratic movements has chiefly lain in the regions of the pioneer." The pioneer was passionately devoted to the ideal of equality, to keeping the road open to opportunity, to circumventing or checking monopoly. He saw no right in the successful to look down on their neighbors, no vested title to superiority.[8]

In other contexts Turner also sees democracy as being an attribute of certain kinds of movements, measures, or institutional forms. "Restless democracy" demanded changes in taxation, in the apportionment of legislative representation between East and West, a broader suffrage. It was also identified with the demand of the frontier for more local self-government. In one passage, which illustrates the breadth of his conception of democracy, Turner linked it with the liberalization of apportionment and the suffrage, with "disregard of vested interests, and insistence on the rights of man," with reform of laws for imprisonment for debt, with "general attacks upon monopoly and privilege," and with Jackson's attacks on aristocracy and "the credit and paper system." Certainly democracy gains impetus in American history as the process of Western settlement grows more and more important. "Already in the first part of the eighteenth century, the frontier population tended to be a rude democracy." Then Jefferson appeared as "the first prophet of American democracy," representing "the Western democracy into which he was born." But it was only with Jacksonianism that frontier democracy finally became the ruling national principle, with Western preponderance under Jackson and William Henry Harrison. It was particularly congenial to the area into which the country moved when it crossed the Appalachians: "The Mississippi Valley has been the especial home of democracy."[9]

Within a certain limited framework, Turner's evocation of the character of American democracy still rings true. The idea that the frontier had much to do with the shaping of

---

[8] Ibid., 302, 210, 261, 345–6, 250–1, 274, 342.
[9] Ibid., 192, 98, 250–1, 31, 190.

American egalitarianism is one of the Turnerian notions that
instantly commends itself to our sense of reality, and indeed
with sufficiently careful qualifications it may outlast the many
criticisms that have been made of it. But its vulnerability is
most acute for students of political development who are interested in the general evolution of modern democracy and for
those who look at the problem of democracy from the standpoint of political theory or constitutional history. Here Turner's
approach does have two grave difficulties, which were pointed
out long ago in notable critiques by Benjamin F. Wright, Jr.,
and which have been expanded by a number of writers since.[1]
The first is that the frontier interpretation isolates the growth
of American democracy from the general development of
democracy in Western civilization, of which it is a part. The
second is that when we try to apply it mechanically as the exclusive, or even the primary, explanation of a variety of problems or phases in the development of American democracy
itself, it yields chiefly a series of stale clichés and misconceptions. One may say that Wright and his successors have been
talking past Turner rather than to him, insofar as they are
concerned with the development of democracy in general,
something Turner never tried to cope with, and not with its
American variations and peculiarities. But Wright's criticisms
serve to remind us that our whole sense of the nature and importance of American variations on democracy can be based
only on a firm sense of its comparative development and upon
an acknowledgment of American borrowings.

"The proper point of departure for the discussion of the
rise of democracy in the United States," Wright argued, "is
not the American West but the European background." American democracy could be understood only as the product of
centuries of development in which the English experience was
an integral part. It was of vital importance that American
civilization had taken its cues from English civilization, and
that in England feudalism had been extinct for many generations before the founding of New England. Again, America's

---

[1] See his "American Democracy and the Frontier," *Yale Review*,
20 (1930), 349–65 and "Political Institutions and the Frontier"
in D. R. Fox, ed., *Sources of Culture in the Middle West* (1934),
15–38.

sources in the Protestant Reformation had shaped its organizational forms on the relatively decentralized and democratic
models that prevailed in the Protestant denominations, and
the American temper had been profoundly affected by attitudes toward power that were bred in the tradition of
dissent. Wright conceded that the frontier probably had a
further democratizing effect, but he pointed out that frontiers do not everywhere produce democratic societies: what
counts more than the frontier environment is the system of
habits and ideas, expectations and institutions, that a people
brings to the frontier. The presence of a frontier did not bring
about in French Canada a political or social system like that
of the United States, nor did it prevent the Dutch from creating a patroon system, or the Spaniards from establishing great
haciendas in Mexico.[2] Even in the United States, slaveholding
planters produced a different society on the southern frontier
from that produced in the Northeast by free labor. One can
best capture the profound consequences of Turner's neglect of
human culture in his stress upon the environment, if one imagines what kind of political society would have been created
on the frontier if it had been settled, say, by Hottentots or
Maori.

Again, while it is probably true that life was frequently
more egalitarian in frontier communities than in settled areas,
the truly significant facts are the brevity of the frontier experience, the relatively small numbers of people who are involved in and directly affected by it, and the readiness with
which, once the primitive stage of settlement is past, the villages and cities only recently removed from their frontier life
reproduce the social stratification, political forms, and patterns

---

[2] In some respects, Turnerians have been able to take comfort in
the findings of comparative frontier studies. A. L. Burt, for example, has argued persuasively that the frontier process had a
considerable democratizing effect on New France, *The Frontier
in Perspective,* ed. by W. D. Wyman and C. B. Kroeber (1957),
59–77, and other frontiers yield similar suggestions. A frontier,
other things being equal, may or may not have some democratizing effect. But none of these findings seem to me to touch the
essential point of Turner's critics. Their point is that the forest
environment does not *create* the essential institutions upon which
democracy rests, and that these institutions are far more effective
than the wilderness or the new lands in establishing the precondi-
tions of democracy.

of leadership and control that exist in similar communities far to the east.

In the forms of government and law, moreover, we do not find, as we might expect, that the West changed Eastern ways, for here the West was imitative rather than innovative. Western settlers were apparently not discontented with the state of constitutional forms in the Eastern regions they had left, for generally they tried to reproduce the types of state and local governments they were familiar with. It is of course true that they reproduced (and in a few cases somewhat strengthened) the democratic aspects of these constitutions—their restraints on the powers of legislators and governors, for example—but they also reproduced their less democratic aspects, including that most fundamental of all checks on popular democracy, judicial review.

Even the effect of the early West on manhood suffrage has been misconstrued. The new states of the trans-Appalachian West did accelerate the broadening of the suffrage, a process already begun in the Revolutionary era before they were settled, but they did not try, and showed no desire, to carry the process beyond the goal previously reached in several of the older states. On one count, Negro suffrage, the new states denied a right that had already been granted by New York and five New England states. It could be conceded that the new states were somewhat advanced in dropping property and religious qualifications for *officeholders,* and in increasing the number of executive and judicial offices elected by popular vote. But in summing up the Western contributions in this area, Wright concluded: "The result of developments in the newer sections seems to have been somewhat to accelerate the rate of growth of the democratic movement, not to change its direction." So far as the right to vote is concerned, Wright's conclusions have been strengthened by later research. Turner had argued in 1903: "It was only as the interior of the country developed that [suffrage] restrictions gradually gave way in the direction of manhood suffrage." Apparently somewhat troubled by the realization that Eastern states were modifying their suffrage requirements at the same time, he found a way of attributing it to Western development: the Western states, he thought, influenced the Eastern ones, partly because the Eastern states feared that unfranchised laborers would move off to areas where they could vote. Chilton Williamson, in his comprehensive history of the suffrage, finds that the facts of suffrage reform in the seaboard states do not fit Turner's argument. The possible drain of population was never a major issue in the discussion of suffrage policies in any Eastern state. What is more important, such states as Vermont, Maryland, and South Carolina had divorced property from suffrage as early as 1812 under circumstances that seemed to owe little to Western influences. Some Western states were not so advanced as legend would have it. Williamson concludes: "In view of the extent to which Western suffrage history was a recapitulation of the suffrage history of the Eastern seaboard, it is difficult to believe that the New West was unique or that it made any new contribution to the growth of suffrage democracy."[3]

Briefly surveying certain focal episodes in American history, Wright pointed out in terms that still seem convincing how unsatisfactory, at point after point, an excessive Western or frontier interpretation of American democracy proves to be. During the century and more before the American Revolution, when the English communities grew in size from straggling settlements to well-populated colonies and pushed the frontier line from the tidewater to the mountains this process did not cause them to make many striking extensions of the democracy they already had; in some respects, especially in the degree of social stratification, egalitarianism actually lost some ground. The first strong new push toward democracy came with the Revolutionary era. In the background of the Revolution, it is true, problems of the West played a part of considerable importance, but in view of the consistent agitational initiatives of Eastern leaders, the predominance of Eastern agitators and propagandists employing ideas not imported from the backwoodsmen but from English Whigs and dissenters and from Continental writers, it would be impossible to assign priority to the West in this movement. The West

---

3 *Frontier*, 250, 30–1; *Rise of the New West*, 175–6; Williamson, *American Suffrage from Property to Democracy* (1960), 208–9, 221–2. For a balanced discussion of the limited contribution of the West to political democracy, see Ray Allen Billington, *America's Frontier Heritage* (1966), chapter vi.

contributed its share to the effort; but in at least two colonies, North Carolina and Georgia, the backwoodsmen were strongly Loyalist. Finally, as Wright remarks, the state constitutions adopted on the seaboard in the revolutionary era "contained nearly all the fundamental principles followed by the state and national governments ever since."

Jeffersonian democracy, again, was more an Eastern than a frontier movement. Turner had written that "Jefferson was the first prophet of American democracy, and when we analyse the essential features of his gospel, it is clear that the Western influence was the dominant element." Jefferson, as Turner had it, was born on the Virginia frontier, and "his father was a pioneer." He was surrounded by democratic pioneer farmers, and became the spokesman of their ideas.[4] During the Revolution his Virginia reforms were intended to throw the political power of the province into the hands of the interior settlers and take it out of the hands of the coastal aristocracy. His presidential regime was an attempt to realize the agrarian ideals of the "Western democracy into which he was born."

Here one may go beyond Wright's criticisms to say that almost everything Turner says about Jefferson, though most of it is still integral in the American gospel, is either badly nuanced, a misleading half truth, or flatly wrong. It is true enough that Jefferson was born on the frontier (where his "pioneer" father, who married into Virginia's upper class was, as Turner knew, the engrosser of a thousand acres, and where he employed a steward and five overseers) and that he spent his first years in a new community. But the rest of his life, including the profoundly formative late adolescent years, was spent in the more sophisticated, thoroughly Anglicized society of Williamsburg, under the social influences of the governing planter class and under the intellectual influences of English Whiggery and the European Enlightenment. His ideas, in this respect, were not markedly different from those of many of his contemporaries in Virginia and in the North, who had always lived on the seaboard. He was a slaveholder, and an integral part of the Virginia planter class, and in slighting the profound moral paradox of the slaveholder's democracy, Turner

---

[4] *Frontier*, 250, 93–4.

falls in line with the tradition, so evasive about slavery and race, of American progressive democratic theory.[5] Jefferson's Virginia reforms, far from laying the ax to the root of Virginia aristocracy, were directed mainly against feudal survivals that had become a distinct nuisance to many planters, and only on one point, religious disestablishment, were they gravely controversial. His brand of democracy, which accepted the conventional notions of balanced government all but universal among the American governing classes, was basically that of a mildly radical English Whig; and the acceptance of an elite leadership, which is evident in his ideas of natural aristocracy and even in his views of the function of education (raking, he said, the true talents out of the "rubbish"), qualified his democratic convictions in a manner not ordinarily associated with militant frontier egalitarians. His presidency embodied agrarian ideals common to great planters and small farmers alike, not to the latter alone, and in relating the history of these ideals, it seems important to say that a coalition of planters and farmers was incapable of applying them successfully in practice or even maintaining them in theory. The changes in Jefferson's views, on this count, are well known. Jefferson himself, like the political movement he created, was complex, fascinating, and paradoxical. The simple rubric of the frontier democrat wipes out all those glorious ambiguities and complexities of his achievement that the serious historian has learned to relish.

The case of Jacksonian democracy was rather different, for Jackson, unlike Jefferson, can indeed be called a Western type, and much of the force as well as the tone of Jacksonian democracy can fairly be attributed to Western influences. But on the whole, Wright forecast later scholarship in emphasizing that Jacksonian democracy was a nationwide movement rather than a sectional one—one need only look at some of Turner's own political maps to see that this was so—and in emphasizing the Eastern provenance of its basic ideas. Wright took an almost malign pleasure in pointing out that Jackson's Tennessee was slow to remove the last of its property qualifica-

---

[5] Staughton Lynd deals rather harshly with Turner and Beard on this count, but I believe his case is basically correct. See his "On Turner, Beard and Slavery," *Journal of Negro History*, 48 (1963), 235–50.

tions for the right to vote, and he might well have enjoyed even more Thomas P. Abernethy's devastating excursions into Jackson and Tennessee democracy, which show how clearly Jackson was aligned against the democratic movement in his own state.[6] Partly because of the obviously national character of Jacksonian democracy, and partly because of its many internal complexities, modern scholarship pays little regard to the notion that it was distinctively a frontier product, and the debate over its meaning has shifted to a concern with the relative importance of its entrepreneurial and labor elements and related questions.[7] Again, the humanitarian reforms that agitated the Jacksonian era, and which very often drew their strength from a very different social constituency from that of the Jacksonians, were parallel to those going on in Europe and strong in the Eastern states. The demand for women's suffrage, pioneered by Frances Wright, a wealthy immigrant Scotswoman, flourished mainly in the East, as did the movements for prison reform, for public schools, for the humane care of the mentally ill; and abolitionism, which had its inception in the East, was not monopolized by either section.

Yet it has been possible to find a way of squaring the facts of American development with Turner's sense—which corresponds with our own—that American democracy owes much to the frontier. *American* democracy: his disciples have been all but unanimous, and I believe wholly right, in pointing out that what Turner was trying to account for was not the evolution of modern democracy in general, but only the distinctive features of its American version.[8] Democratic societies have emerged in so many frontierless countries that it would be bootless to argue that a frontier is essential to democracy as such. In the end it is probably more important to see American democracy as a part of western European democracy than it is to stress its uniqueness—especially to

---

6 See his *From Frontier to Plantation in Tennessee* (1932).
7 On this count, see Sellers, "Andrew Jackson versus the Historians," already cited.
8 "What I was dealing with was in the first place, the *American* character of democracy as compared with that of Europe or of European philosophers." Turner to Frederick Merk, January 9, 1931. The difficulty was that Turner assumed the elements of American uniqueness and did not actually carry out the comparison.

those who are interested in the survival of democracy and who want to understand the most general conditions for its existence. In this sense, the frontier theory will be of little more than marginal concern to the cosmopolitan political theorist who is primarily interested in the institutional foundations of modern democracy. Still, for a student of the American past, the peculiarities of American democracy are as legitimate an object of concern as our manners and morals or the American character or the themes of American literature. If we grant, then, that what is fundamentally at stake in the Turnerian scheme is not the sources of democracy but the element of American uniqueness, we have perhaps arrived at the soundest basis for rehabilitating in some degree the frontier thesis.

Probably the most impressive neo-Turnerian attempt to give a theoretical character to new findings has been that offered by Stanley Elkins and Eric McKitrick.[9] They waste no effort in pretending that the institutions brought to the environment are unimportant—in fact they make such differences an integral part of their theory. Nor do they deny what they call "the absurdities of Turner's logic." But while granting that Turner's insights were "crude in form," they still find in them "in many ways the closest thing we have had to a seminal contribution to the theory of American history." Much of Turnerism they are prepared to give up—but not the central idea that the frontier had a great deal to do with the development of political democracy as a habit and the American as a unique political creature. They start with the proposition that the problem must be approached with a new working—that is, testable—definition of democracy, adapted to the assumption of American uniqueness. What they find is a reality with three main facets: a manipulative attitude toward government shared by large numbers of people; wide participation in public affairs (and by this they do not mean merely voting); and a widespread sense of personal competence to make a difference in the management of affairs. Their primary contribution has been to try to show how these traits develop most quickly during the initial stages of setting

---

[9] "A Meaning for Turner's Frontier," *Political Science Quarterly,* 59 (1954), 325–30, 585–94.

up a new community, a community relatively unencumbered
with the accretions of the past in customs, in clearly assigned
functions, and in the sheer accumulated physical parapher-
nalia of life. Their insight is fortified by an elegantly drawn
analogy with some modern community studies, in which they
are able to compare a housing development which began its
existence well planned and smoothly worked out with one,
more analogous to frontier conditions, where little was adequately prearranged and many serious problems of community life confronted the first settlers. Their findings suggest
that political life can be altered not by the "frontier" in the
narrow and constricted sense of that term, but by the whole
process of moving and resettling, common to America from
the seventeenth century onward, and of forming new communities. The important factors are the new community, the
sudden confrontation of its settlers with a mass of new, unanticipated problems, the presence of a relatively homogeneous population (not necessarily in the ethnic sense, but
in the sense that it is not highly stratified in wealth and
status), and finally the lack of a firmly developed pre-existing
structure of leadership. To imagine the relevant factors at
work, one has to imagine a type of community the authors
believe came into formation over and over again in the Northwest: one which had at first to work and survive, somehow,
without hospitals, churches, schools, and courts, and in which
the functions of the policeman, the judge, the priest, the politician, the teacher had to be improvised and shared, and in
which many citizens were called upon to make new decisions,
assume new functions, and develop the capacity to lead, to
solve problems arising from brigands, Indians, plagues,
locusts, droughts, fires. Then, in a second stage, when a
new kind of leader and a new kind of community morale
has been created, one must follow the same personnel into
the period of developing town life. Now the emergence of
market agriculture, the search for adequate transportation
and credit, the possibilities of land speculation, the avenues
of manipulation, appeasement, and accommodation, the
whole atmosphere of small-town enterprise, give a series of
new opportunities to the alert citizenry that has been called
into being by the processes of first settlement. The authors

suggest that this happened more readily in the Northwest than in the Southwest—here the rigid environmentalism of Turner goes by the board—because planter capitalism in the latter region provided a much firmer and less fluid leadership structure, because the courthouse-clique system of government could more easily be transferred westward from the older South, and because certain regional simplicities and certain features of the plantation economy limit and curtail the second stage of town enterprise. The characteristics of Northwestern development are not here wholly absent, and they manifest themselves in several similarities of political tone; but the substance is different.

Looking, as a kind of postscript, at the frontier of Massachusetts Bay, Elkins and McKitrick find that here, even where a firm leadership structure did exist, it was subjected, whether primarily because of the migratory process itself or because of the frontier or some interaction between the two, to tremendous strains, which resulted in serious modifications, even in the first generation. On the local basis, under the stress of the town's multiple concerns, secular, religious, civil, and military, expanded roles opened for almost everyone. The forms of democracy had indeed been brought in the *Susan Constant* and the *Mayflower*; but since democracy, being more than a matter of forms, is a matter of experience, it is essential to look at the modifications that were made.[1]

1 It is instructive to read Sumner Chilton Powell's remarkable study of an early New England town, with an ear to its echoes of the Elkins-McKitrick categories. "Each town, each leader, was on his own . . . the differences between his own experiences and those of Englishmen who had been living in distinctly different types of English towns . . . special authorizations to meet distinct, often new social problems . . . a community which was active, militant, and demanding on its members . . . many surprises in store for him . . . to be able to blend these contrasting backgrounds into a new whole. . . . Neither his status nor his privileges in his new society remained as clearly defined as it had been in the old borough . . . accomplishing a virtual social revolution in the systems of social and economic status of each community . . . a broad base of responsible citizens . . . an amalgam of English institutional influences, as well as new solutions to new problems. . . . More than 650 orders, 'agreed by the town,' were passed in this period, a staggering number compared with the legislative activities of the Suffolk [England] borough . . . experimenting in government and law, imposing a type of local justice by mutual agreement of all concerned. . . . The townsmen had to change or abandon almost every formal in-

There are, of course, certain limitations on this way of getting at the problem, though they hardly affect the fundamental purpose of the authors, which was to find a way of translating Turner's general assertions about the West and democracy into a set of testable propositions. Like Turner, Elkins and McKitrick do not seek to go outside the self-limiting framework of American uniqueness to answer questions about the character of democracy as such. And even within the American framework, their interest is in *local* democracy. To what extent is the central achievement of the United States—that of uniting what is virtually a continental area under stable representative institutions—accounted for by these forays into local government? Is local democracy the source of democracy in the federal government or vice versa; or are the relations simply reciprocal? Many writers have pointed out that, for all that we may acknowledge about the limitations of democracy, this nation is and has long been more consistently democratic at its center, in its national government, than it is on its varying and heterogenous peripheral elements, its states and localities. This is true partly because the conduct of the national government, under modern conditions, is much more visible and salient for the citizenry than local government; and partly because the two-party system, which does not really exist in many states and localities, does come into play at the national level. Here it may be that the authors have deferred more than one would wish to that piety about local management which is one of the primary features of American agrarianism. Finally, I have some reservations about "participation," beyond voting, as the fundamental test. They can hardly be developed here, but they may be suggested by referring to David Granick's remark concerning participation in Soviet "democracy" that it "consists in participation in everything except basic decision-making."[2] To me it seems that in great modern centralized democracies, direct participation in government (outside of small local matters) be-

---

stitution which they had taken for granted. . . . They made a staggering number of changes . . . they constructed an entirely new type of town." *Puritan Village: The Formation of a New England Town* (1963: Anchor ed., 1965), 3, 4, 13, 18, 20, 26, 73, 107, 112, 118, 119, 143, 179, 181–2.

[2] *The Red Executive* (1960), 196.

comes a hopeless criterion of the efficacy of democratic institutions.

Some confirmation for the Elkins-McKitrick categories at the local level, particularly on the counts of social homogeneity, multiple leadership, and versatility and adaptability of function in the face of new conditions, emerges from the intensive study by Merle Curti and his associates of the life of a Wisconsin frontier county in the period from the 1850's to the 1870's.[3] Setting aside the effort to elaborate Turner's "brilliant and far-ranging but often ambiguous presentations" in favor of a detailed study of frontier life, Curti emerged with a general picture that might have pleased Turner and would probably not have surprised him. It might be disturbing to literal-minded Turnerians that Curti found more democracy in Trempealeau County in the 1870's than in the two previous decades—that is, as it moved away from its pristine frontier condition. It might also be disturbing that the distribution of property in a frontier rural county so closely resembled that of certain nonfrontier rural counties chosen for comparison. But on the whole, in the openness, fluidity, mobility, optimism, and fundamentally democratic ethos that it found, the Trempealeau County study gave some body and substance to the Turnerian picture of the agricultural frontier, not too literally construed.

In sum, we can clarify our search for the validity of Turner's views on the place of the frontier in the making of democracy if we bear in mind that his concern was with the extent to which America is unique or differentiated, and also that he was interested not so much in the basic institutional forms upon which democracy rests as in the formation of the particular activist, egalitarian spirit that seems clearly to have prevailed in the United States. Turner was most vitally interested in, and most sound on, the atmospherics of American democracy. The idea that frontier expectations and problems made a distinctive contribution in this respect still seems valid, so long as it is not permitted, in the interest of our pursuit of uniqueness, to obscure our institutional and intellectual borrowings (of America from England, of the West from the East); or to cause us to neglect, in our concern for

---

[3] *The Making of an American Community* (1959).

popular attitudes, the institutional requirements of democracy, or to overlook the fact that democracy must be a national as well as a local reality. Finally, I believe there is an unfilled gap in the thought of the Turnerians that promises that further inquiry will be rewarding. It is easy to believe them when they tell us that the frontier process greatly spurred democratic feeling and developed, so to speak, the talents of democracy. But Turner failed to solve what may be called the problem of cultural transmission. Most Americans lived where there *had been* a frontier, but only a very small minority actually lived on a frontier or lived through the frontier process themselves. In what ways and to what extent was the experience of the frontier era, and its generation of actual pioneers, transmitted as a live social force to their descendants and successors? How was its characterological residue preserved? In what ways and to what extent were its effects transmitted to the large body of those back east who were remote from the frontier all their lives and who did not even have any family history or legend through which to be exposed to its influence? When such questions have been given more attention, we will no doubt know a great deal more about America; but I suspect that in the attempt to answer them our sense of the impact of the frontier as a democratic force will have been cut down to size.

IV

What of the idea that the frontier promoted individualism? It is doubtful that Turner was as troubled as he could have been by the baffling complexities of this term. There are at least four senses in which it can be used. First, a culture may be called individualistic if it offers favorable conditions for the development of personal assertiveness and ambition, encourages material aspiration, self-confidence, and aggressive morale, offers multiple opportunities for advancement and encourages the will to seize them. Second, it may indicate the absence of mutuality or of common and collective effort, in a society that supposedly functions almost as a conglomerate of individual atoms. Third, it may designate a more or less formal creed in which private action is at a premium and governmental action is condemned—as a synonym, in short, for laissez faire. Finally—and I believe this usage can be quite misleading—it may be used as though it were synonymous with individuality, that is, with a high tolerance for deviance, eccentricity, nonconformity, privacy, and dissent.

Turner certainly used "individualism" in the first three of these four meanings; though I am unsure whether he ever meant to convey also the last of them, it is very likely that this sense of the term was read into him by some of his followers. In the first sense of the term, having to do with morale and creative energy, it seems to me that Turner was entirely right in his claims for the frontier, and that an overwhelming mass of evidence, all of it, to be sure, impressionistic, argues for his case. There is hardly an observer of the United States during the nineteenth century who did not notice the hard, energetic, pushing materialism of the Americans, their ready nose for opportunities, their extraordinary exertions in the pursuit of them; and those who knew the West tended to find these qualities developed there to their highest pitch. The only qualification one might wish to enter here is that the phenomenon, however highly developed on the frontier, was not developed there alone, and that it is likely to be found in any country or region where there is rapid economic development under conditions of freedom. Like democracy, individualism was brought to the frontier.

Moreover, the applicability of the second and third of these senses of the term does not follow automatically from the first. It seems clear that Turner was talking about individualism as a more or less formal creed concerning the proper uses of government when he said that the farmers of the Mississippi Valley began by believing in individualism but, having found their democracy endangered by unrestricted competition, turned away from it to demand regulatory social legislation. Again he describes the pioneer as "impatient of any governmental restriction upon his individual right to deal with the wilderness." More characteristically, and in numerous passages, Turner speaks simply about the enormous assertiveness of Western culture, its resistance to any kind of control. At one point frontier individualism is defined simply as "antipathy to control" and is even characterized as being "antisocial," though on the same page it is credited with having "promoted democracy." Again: "Individualism in America has allowed a laxity in regard to governmental affairs which has rendered possible the spoils system and all the manifest evils that follow from the lack of a highly developed civic spirit."

Finally, in the third sense, society appears almost to lack solidarity, mutuality, or comity: the frontiersman, we are told at one point, knew how to preserve order and was ready to combine *ad hoc*, even illegally, to do it. "But the individual was not ready to submit to complex regulations. . . . *Society became atomic.* . . . The individual was exalted and given free play." In another passage Turner says, defining the "ideal of individualism," that the democratic frontier society was not like a disciplined army where the collective interest destroyed individual will and work. "Rather it was a mobile mass of *freely circulating atoms*, each seeking its own place and finding play for its own powers and for its own original initiative." Elsewhere we are told that this was "not a complex, highly differentiated and organized society. Almost every family was a self-sufficing unit. . . ."[4]

The conception that early Western America was committed to individualism as an economic creed will no longer bear examination. Guy S. Callender, one of Turner's contemporaries, long ago pointed out that "this country was one of the first to exhibit this modern tendency to extend the activity of the State into industry."[5] In fact it was the opening of the West that spurred state promotion of enterprise by creating the need for transportation and other works of internal improvement that the resources of private capital could not manage. Although many Americans had constitutional and political objections to the national government as a promo-

---

[4] *Frontier*, 203, 272, 307, 30, 32, 212, 306, 153; italics are mine.
[5] "The Early Transportation and Banking Enterprises of the States in Relation to the Growth of Corporations," *Quarterly Journal of Economics*, 17 (1902), 111. For a good brief review of some of the findings of modern scholarship on this count, see Robert A. Lively, "The American System," *Business History Review*, 29 (1955), 81–96. See also George R. Taylor, *The Transportation Revolution, 1815–1860* (1951), chapter xvi.

tional agency, very few had similar objections to seeing their state and local governments act in this capacity. They developed an entirely pragmatic approach to governmental as against private promotion which was expressed succinctly by Lincoln: "The legitimate object of Government is to do for a community of people whatever they need to have done but cannot do at all or cannot do so well for themselves in their separate or individual capacities."

It is Turner's account of the "atomic" character of the frontier that has drawn most fire from writers,[6] who have invoked facts of frontier life that Turner knew well but tended to subordinate rather drastically. The frontier experience, with its new problems and its exceptional hardships, was a disciplinary experience, and it inspired a great many collective efforts and fostered habits of mutual aid. The example of the Mormons provides an extreme case of its organizing demands. Turner himself understood that the settlement of the Southwest, in which irrigation was essential, also imposed limits upon individualistic action. But it remains true that the image of the lonely pioneer, or of the isolated yeoman accompanied only by his family, fills too large a part in the Turnerian picture, and subordinates the official, the corporate, and the collective aspects of settlement. The West was in large part explored by men who were acting on commission from one or another arm of government. It was in good part settled under the well-organized supervision of speculators, land companies, and railroads—even Daniel Boone, that archetype of the solitary pioneer, was an agent for a land company. A great deal of westward migration took place in organized groups, moving under a disciplinary code. Planters, for example, moved whole plantation communities *en bloc* into the older Southwest of the cotton boom. On exposed frontiers the necessity for mutual protection against Indians or, on occasion, outlaws, was a powerful force. Cooperative labor was a common feature in log-rollings, house-raisings, and in the cattle roundup. Trials brought solidarity: men joined together to round up the widow's cattle, to plow the ground of a sick neighbor. The

---

6 Notably from Mody C. Boatright, "The Myth of Frontier Individualism," *Southwestern Social Science Quarterly*, 22 (1941), 14–32.

struggle against speculators and railroads and the demands of squatters gave rise to claim associations and land associations, then to movements like the Grangers, the Farmers Alliances, and the Populists.[7] In this sense Turner's belief that when the farmers turned from individualism to the collective demands of Populism they had undergone a change in a hitherto set philosophy is debatable. Private enterprise was always regulated when regulation was felt to be necessary and when the forces of dissatisfaction mustered the necessary political power.

The Western population may have been, in Turner's words, "impatient of restraint" when the restraint, coming from outside their communities and their control, was seen to be inimical to their interests; but they subscribed to no creed that prevented them from using governmental restraint to protect these interests. The frontiersman, in brief, was not ideological about individualism; he left that to his romancers. Nor was his family altogether an atomistic unit. Frontier social organization was a mixture of the familial and the collective, of the private and the governmental, whose devices were arrived at through experience and at the dictates of expediency.

Finally, there is the issue of individuality. It is hard to say whether Turner meant to argue that the frontier was a nursery of individuality as well as individualism, and it is a large question, not to be attempted here, whether individuality flourished in nineteenth-century America. The prevailing view, which stems from Tocqueville, runs to the contrary. Tocqueville was impressed by conformity, enforced by public pressures, as a basic and inescapable American trait. If he was

---

[7] Charles Beard, always a sharp critic of American "individualism," was among those who were skeptical of this side of Turner's work. "I knew in my youth pioneers in Indiana who had gone into the country of my birth when it was a wilderness. My early memories are filled with the stories of log-cabin days—of community helpfulness, of cooperation in building houses and barns, in harvesting crops, in building schools, in constructing roads and bridges, in nursing the sick, in caring for widows, orphans, and the aged. Of individuals I heard much, of individualism little. I doubt whether anywhere in the United States there was more community spirit, more mutual aid in times of need, so little expectation of material reward for services rendered to neighbors." "Turner's 'The Frontier in American History,' " 67–70.

right, and if we are to agree that the basic American traits
were forged on the frontier, we find ourselves in considerable
difficulty, which we can escape only by divorcing the two
terms, individualism and individuality, as fully in our thinking as they are divorced in reality. The metropolis, with its
size, heterogeneity, and anonymity, enjoys a better reputation
for fostering privacy and respecting dissent than the countryside or the small town;[8] though the hard-bitten rural independent is a stereotype not unknown to our literature, and it
may offer a cue to an overlooked side of our life. Individuality
is a precious and fragile thing. Wherever we may conclude
that it was best fostered, it will be useful not to assimilate it
to individualism—for it was individualism that generated the
agencies, and often the animating impulse, that made it possible to submerge the individual.

v

What is said on one side or another about individualism
serves only to remind us how much of the controversy over
Turner is a controversy, only half-articulated and yet very
thinly disguised, over values. On this count, historians are
arguing not just over what it was that went on in history, but
also, and perhaps primarily, how, in the light of what we wish
ourselves to be, we can most usefully think of ourselves as
having been in the past. Turner's views of the American past
are linked on one side to a pastoral agrarian sentimentalism
which, however deeply native, however touching, and indeed
however acceptable on some counts in its emotional commitments, may be very misleading about the facts of settlement,
especially as one approaches the modern era. Again, there has
been a widespread sense that an excessive emphasis on the
frontier encourages American complacency, anti-intellectualism, and anti-Europeanism, and finally that it undercuts the

---

[8] "The pioneer," writes one student of the West, "was most certainly an ill-mannered inquisitor, showing no respect for privacy
as he sought to ease the loneliness of his life and broaden his
cultural horizons with a few tidbits of information." Ray Allen
Billington, *America's Frontier Heritage* (1966), 214.

intellectuals' function of social criticism. Beyond doubt Turner pictured the frontier in bright colors. His disciples are quick to answer that he somewhere mentioned almost every dark aspect of frontier influence that his critics cite—but the point is precisely here: Turner *mentioned* them in passing, and they have the position in his essays only of faint qualifications in a full-throated paean to American virtues. And while he was admitting American cultural shortcomings, he was also at bottom apologizing for them, partly on the old and familiar ground of want of time for cultural achievement, partly on the ground that they were a price well paid for the benefits of the frontier heritage. The whole rationale, as George Pierson has put it, suggested that America and art were perpetually at odds: "If his essays mean what they appear to mean, then the doctrine is that we were most American just when we were least cultivated."

Like most human achievements, American development was a mixed bag of tricks, and any conception that purported to "explain" it might well have undertaken to account for the qualities that Turner's essays slight: the highly commercial character of western settlement, as of American society generally; the speculative spirit of the westward movement, giving adequate attention not merely to the role of the large land speculator but also to the gambling habits of the ordinary farmer; the careless, wasteful, and exploitative methods of American agriculture; the hostility of farmers to "book farming" and scientific improvement; the general waste of resources and the desecration of natural beauty; the failure of the free lands to produce a society free of landless laborers and tenants, its developing class stratification; the rapacity and meanness so often to be found in the petty capitalism of the new towns; the conformist pressures of small-town America, West or East, the assaults on individuality which must be weighed against the individualism of which Turner spoke so highly; the crudeness and disorder, the readiness to commit and willingness to tolerate violence; the frequent ruthlessness of the frontier mind, to which Indians, Spaniards, and Mexicans could testify and which had its repeated reverberations in national policies; the arrogant, flimsy, and self-righteous justifications of Manifest Destiny engendered by American expansionism; the smugness, provincialism, and cant anti-intellectualism common to most of America but especially keen in the West.

Then there was a kind of self-satisfied anti-Europeanism, which Turner himself did not always quite escape. We may find good grounds, of course, for taking some pride in the American achievement of the nineteenth century, and they have hardly diminished in our time, when we compare our political culture to that of Europe from 1918 to 1945. But we must ask whether there cannot be too much of this pride and above all whether it is useful to encourage Americans to play down the deficiencies of their culture or to think of themselves not as a part of Western civilization or of the world community but as a unique and self-contained society perpetually marked off by the frontier tradition from the common fate of modern societies. Here Turner seems to have had no misgivings. It was with evident satisfaction that he wrote of Andrew Jackson: "He had the essential traits of the Kentucky and Tennessee frontier. It was a frontier free from the influence of European ideas and institutions. The men of the 'Western World' turned their backs upon the Atlantic Ocean, and with a grim energy and self-reliance began to build up a society free from the dominance of ancient forms." In his essay of 1910 on "Pioneer Ideals and the State University," Turner found it possible to attribute this type of institution, in which he put such high hopes, entirely to the ideals of pioneer democracy and to avoid all reference to the European ideas and models without which, in fact, it was unthinkable; to avoid also all references to the anti-intellectual pressures under which the middle western state universities so often suffered and of which he was poignantly aware. In the same essay he writes: "It is in the Middle West that society has formed on lines least like those of Europe. It is here, if anywhere, that American democracy will make its stand against the tendency to adjust to a European type." And elsewhere: "By this peaceful process of colonization a whole continent has been filled with free and orderly commonwealths so quietly, so naturally, that we can only appreciate the profound significance of the process by contrasting it with the spread of European nations through conquest and oppression."[9]

It seems important to add that Turner's tendency toward intellectual isolationism was not paralleled in his politics, that in his characteristically open way he embraced Wilsonian internationalism, and that by 1914 he made clear his approval of states like Wisconsin for throwing off the American attitude of "contemptuous indifference" to European social legislation and beginning to study it.[1] But Turner's personal politics, once again, can hardly alter the underlying dynamic of the frontier idea, its drive toward the conviction that America is wholly original, uniquely virtuous, and self-sustaining, its suggestion that America had not just made a contribution to or forged a variation on democracy, but rather had a monopoly of it.

One is driven, in brief, to agree with Pierson's indictment on the relevant counts when he characterizes the frontier thesis as "too optimistic, too romantic, too provincial, and too nationalistic to be reliable in any survey of world history or study in comparative civilization." Other writers might well have added "too conservative"—though this was perhaps part of what Pierson had in mind when he spoke of optimism. Certainly among the considerations that weakened Turnerism in the minds of the post-depression generation was the fear that if they applied the Turnerian insights in substantially the same spirit in which Turner himself applied them, their sense, as historians, of the complexities of American history would be dulled and their capacity as intellectuals to contribute to national self-criticism would be blunted.

Quite inflammatory to many of Turner's critics, I believe, is the way in which the mythology of the frontier is linked to a rugged, masculine, overassertive vision of character which is increasingly seen to be hopeless of emulation under modern conditions and which is felt to impose upon the modern American a character ideal that is both impossibly demanding and

---

[9] *Frontier,* 253, 282, 169–70.
[1] Ibid., 294. On intellectual isolationism see Carlton J. H. Hayes, "The American Frontier—Frontier of What?" *American Historical Review,* 51 (1946), 199–216; and Smith, *Virgin Land,* chapter xxii.

deeply flawed. The mind of the modern American intellectual is nothing if not self-doubting and self-critical, and it is asked by the frontier mythology to live with the humiliating contrast between the imperfect thing it knows it is and the almost superhuman figure of the individualist pioneer. And make no mistake about it: though Turner was a gentle and modest man and his personal politics were pre-eminently Apollonian in tone, humane, and moderately progressive in substance, his version of the frontier cannot easily be dissociated from the heavy, menacing image of rugged individualism and frontier hardihood.

Consider how Turner portrays his pioneer, his frontiersman. Except in matters of art and thought, he is all but omnicompetent, an almost monstrous archetype of aggressive masculinity. He is "independent," he shows all too readily his "love of wilderness freedom," and he is endowed with "stalwart and rugged qualities." He has "coarseness and strength," a "practical, inventive turn of mind," "a masterful grasp of material things," and at the same time "that buoyancy and exuberance which comes with freedom." He has experienced many "hardships and privations" in his life on the frontier, but they have only called out "the militant qualities." He "looks at things independently," with "buoyant self-confidence and self-assertion," addresses himself to life with "energy, incessant activity," he "contends for mastery," "builds empires," leads "a conquest over vast spaces," showing, all the while, "creative vision, restless energy, a quick capacity for judgment and action," which may well have been honed to its keenness of edge by his "fight with nature for the chance to exist." The frontier has given him "a training in aggressive courage, in domination, in directness, in destructiveness," and one need hardly be surprised to find him "masterful and wasteful," a thing of "rude strength and wilful achievement." Yet at the same time this man is an idealist, who "dreams dreams and beholds visions," a force in the "belligerent Western democracy," who has "rebelled against the conventional," who is "conscious of the mobility of his society and glories in it." His is not, then, "the dull contented materialism of an old and fixed society." But his idealism has not the least softened him, since his society is rather like a Darwinian battleground, an arena of rigorous and demanding competition, and he is "the self-made man who, in the midst of opportunity under competitive conditions achieved superiority." "From this society . . . came the triumph of the strongest . . . the prizes were for the keenest and strongest." "He honored the men whose eye was the quickest and whose grasp was the strongest in this contest: it was 'every one for himself.' "[2]

After such fathers, what sons? Indeed, what sons can there be? As if the traits were not demanding enough, Turner's imagery adds to the provocativeness of these frontier demands. The West is portrayed in feminine imagery: she is shaggy and wild, it is true, but also generous, abundant, receptive. When the men of Europe came, she "took them to her bosom," taught them and trained them in her ways, "opened new provinces, and dowered new democracies . . . with her material treasures." She bore great sons: Jefferson, Jackson, and Lincoln. She gave her men wealth and power "vaster than the wealth and power of kings" but at the same time she nourished the "unhappy and oppressed of all lands." "Great and powerful as are the new sons of her loins, the Republic is greater than they." After this it is not surprising to be reminded, concerning the men she reared, that "the rifle and the ax are the symbols of the backwoods pioneer." As the pioneer shoots and hacks his way across the virgin continent, it is natural to expect, too, that the prizes go to "the keenest and the strongest"—that they take "the best bottom lands, the finest timber tracts, the best salt-springs, the richest ore-beds."[3] It is all rather overbearing; and it is again not surprising that the modern intellectual sons of such fathering have been in such haste to rise up and kill the frontier image that they have at times trampled upon what is good and usable in Turnerism.

2 *Frontier*, 15, 18, 22, 30, 37, 65, 70, 78, 153, 154, 209, 210, 211, 214, 249, 256, 263, 269, 270, 271, 355. I have changed a few of Turner's tenses.
3 Ibid., 267, 268, 271.

VI

I have spoken of the important and usable core of truth
in Turner's ideas, but thus far have delineated criticisms with
which in the main I agree. It remains then to say what this
core of truth consists in. It goes well beyond our common
awareness that Turner was the first historian to see clearly
the importance of the West and to insist upon its adequate
recognition, thus breaking in on the fraternal dialogue of the
coastal historians with a fresh voice. Turner's merit hangs in
part upon the fact that he was the first, at least among the influential historians, to understand thoroughly that if the distinctive American pattern and the American character are
worth understanding at all they have to be understood not
alone in the familiar terms of the old narrative history, but in
terms of repetitive sociological processes, and that to understand these processes the historian must lean upon the distinctive types of insight that economists and sociologists bring
to historical development. Turner saw many of the features
of what was *literally* an open society, a society with a growth
before it that was patently irresistible. It rests upon his perception of the intangibles, of the psychological and moral
effects of the West, its role in orienting the American mind
toward space and expansion, giving it a different cast and
direction from the European mind with its deeper roots in
time and its higher fixity; its role in underwriting American
confidence, optimism, and adaptability; the way in which it
peopled the American imagination with a whole gallery of
hero types, and above all of heroes who were not, so to speak,
chivalric or operatic but recruited from the ranks of the common people—the explorer, the prospector, the trapper and the
hunter, the Indian-fighter, the cowboy, the covered-wagon
pioneer, the Western farmer. Turner incorporated into history-
writing an understanding that in the receding and lamented
past the American frontier was different: that in the European complex a frontier was a border, a boundary, a limitation, a place that is costly to defend, and where one might be

called upon to die, whereas in America the frontier was the edge of the new and unused, a source of opportunity, a place where one might earn a reputation or a fortune.

But there is still more than this to be said for him: many of his substantive assertions will have their durability. Here it is important to remember that not all the returns are in, that the work of discovery still goes on; each of the past several decades has been marked by some new turning in the course of historical thought; there is good reason to believe that this process will be continued, that in its course some old ideas will be revived, and some recent ones will prove not very viable after all.

A case in point is the history of the safety-valve thesis, which seems to me to be central for our continued interest in Turnerism. The safety-valve idea, one of the first of the Turnerian notions to inspire detailed new research, prodded an avalanche of criticism from the early 1930's onward, and about ten years ago most historians would have agreed that it was dead or dying. In recent years it has been redefined and I believe quite effectively resuscitated. This may point to a moral, but more than that, it points to a vital process on which the viability of the Turner thesis may in the end depend. There is a certain irony in this: though I believe the idea of a Western safety valve for Eastern discontents was implicit in a great deal of what Turner wrote, there are in his writings only a few relatively brief and casual passages in which he explicitly formulated it, and it has often been thought for this reason to rank among his suggestive throwaways. It is also one of his ideas that is perhaps less distinctively his, insofar as more of the forerunners of Turnerism anticipated the safety-valve idea than any other aspect of his thought. The idea that the frontier was an outlet for the laboring class has been an idea of international consequence, having played an important part in the answer to the haunting question of Werner Sombart, so vital to Marxian theorists, *Warum gibt es in den Vereinigten Staaten 'keinen' Sozialismus?* Turner, in his 1893 essay and elsewhere, seems to have thought of the frontier as a safety valve mainly for the farmer; in 1901 he spoke of "the farther free lands to which the ruined

pioneer could turn." In due course, however, he added the
worker. "Whenever social conditions tended to crystallize in
the East," he wrote, "whenever capital tended to press upon
labor or political restraints to impede the freedom of the mass,
there was this gate of escape to the free conditions of the
frontier. . . . Men would not accept inferior wages and a permanent position of social subordination when this promised
land of freedom and equality was theirs for the taking."[4]

When historians began to criticize the safety-valve idea,
they tended at first to focus their fire upon this notion of a
safety valve for labor discontent. Systematic study of migration produced strikingly little evidence of working-class migration to the West. It was also easy to show that workers
were least able to move during periods of depression and unemployment, or that, quite aside from the lack of farming
skills among most urban workmen, the costs of removal to
the West, the acquisition of land and equipment, were prohibitive. Some writers pointed to explosive episodes in the
history of labor as evidence that the safety valve was not
letting off enough steam. It was also useful for Fred A.
Shannon, in an article confidently titled "A Post-Mortem on
the Labor-Safety-Valve Theory," to point to the characteristic
net migration of the surplus farm population to the cities and
to argue that for the period after 1860 the fast-growing cities
of the United States and the proliferation of industry actually
provided a safety valve for discontent in the *rural* population.
Shannon went so far as to say that the free lands did not even
act as an indirect safety valve by attracting eastern farmers
who might otherwise have gone into the labor force.

The safety-valve idea, however, has benefited in recent
years from the post-war concern with economic growth among
economic historians.[5] The new safety-valve theorists find most
previous formulations and criticisms alike irrelevant. It did
not matter, they say, whether very few Eastern workmen went
west to take up farms, or that the frontier did not prevent
panics, unemployment, farm tenancy, or occasional labor un-
rest. The heart of the problem is elsewhere: did the West have

4 *Frontier*, 21–2, 148, 259; cf. 274–5.
5 For the relevant literature see the section on the safety valve
in the Bibliographical Essay.

an effect on Eastern wage rates, on the level of per capita income, on the development of class consciousness and unionism? Here they arrive at a view of the effects of the free lands rather like Turner's. The role of the West, as they see it, was a many-sided thing, involving not merely new lands for farmers but new resources of every kind—forests, oils, minerals—for exploitation, for investment that created new mines, mills, and factories, new towns and cities. The laboring force for this development had to come from somewhere. So also did the middle classes, the small property owners, professionals, promoters, investors. A new social order was springing up, quite open to talents, and it was the hope and energy and resourcefulness primed by this that made the land so rapidly exploitable and yielded a population of such striking vocational versatility and innovative genius. A tremendous social fluidity of the kind pointed to by Turner was engendered by this process. Cities, fortunes, reputations—not just farms —were built in the West, and if nothing else the West thus served as a great social safety valve for the American middle class, enlarging its opportunities, preventing its proletarianization, sustaining its morale.

Here too a basic anomaly in American economic development has to be considered. The usual situation in countries undergoing industrialization is that a more or less static or perhaps even a declining agricultural sector feeds its surplus laboring population into industry. It is most unusual to find a very rapid industrial expansion going on simultaneously with a considerable growth both in the productive efficiency and the sheer bulk of the agricultural sector of the economy, and yet this is what happened in the United States. (During the great spurt of American industrialization that took place from 1860 to 1900, land in farms more than doubled and the number of those gainfully employed in agriculture increased by almost one half.) Again, where most undeveloped countries are likely to offer an abundance of labor in conjunction with scarce capital and limited resources, the United States had a scarcity both of capital *and* labor but, thanks to its developing inland empire, abundant land and resources. Nineteenth-century Europe, by providing a high level of demand for American staples, sustained prolonged spurts of rapid economic growth, for which Europe was also able to supply capital and immigrant labor. The resources of the American interior were not only lavishly abundant but prime in quality, and were exploited with an intensely progressive technology, with the consequence that the labor applied to them was high in productivity. Constant expansion into new areas, as George G. S. Murphy and Arnold Zellner have put it, kept feeding new "slabs" of rich resources into the more developed sectors of the economy, keeping wage rates high, and sustaining the nineteenth century's highest level of per capita income and highest rate of increase in per capita income. Technological innovation, stimulated by labor scarcity but also by the fluidity of the whole American situation (Stanley Lebergott speaks aptly of "the reckless adaptiveness of the American labor force"), joined with a growing stock of capital and a series of successive rich frontiers to underwrite the high-wage economy. Labor received a higher proportion of the payments to the various factors of production than was common elsewhere, and American real wages were unmatched. While high wages alone do not always suffice to prevent the growth of class-consciousness (as a comparison with Australia, another high-wage economy, will show), they did here create an important material foundation. At the same time the mobility and optimism engendered by American expansion and the opportunities offered by the West probably did their share to deprive the working class of solidarity and even to strip it of many potential leaders. Critics of the safety-valve idea had argued that the West, by helping to draw millions of immigrants to the country, so increased the labor force that by raising supply it undid whatever its expansive processes contributed to raising demand. But it would be an unenviable task to try to prove that the West stimulated as much supply of labor as it did demand for it, and it is undeniable that American real wages always enjoyed a substantial margin over those of the Old World. Moreover, as recent writers point out, a laboring population, supplied by immigrants from low-wage or peasant areas with relatively modest aspirations, came in at the bottom of the social order, taking the poorest jobs and pushing their native predecessors upward in the job hier-

archy and also in the ethnic status hierarchy. Hence the peculiarities of American development, to which the West contributed, created a built-in status elevator, whose effects
can be seen in the ethnic and craft snobberies and the long-
divided organizational pattern of American labor. At the
bottom of the system was an immigrant and unskilled labor
force, poor and exploited, no doubt, but collecting wages that
usually equaled and frequently surpassed their European expectations and experiences. At the top was a skilled native
labor force, privileged with the best jobs, basically middle
class in its psychology and often in its style of living, and
upwardly mobile.

Not only has the safety-valve effect thus been re-argued
but some historians and sociologists, prodded in part by a concern with Turner's categories, have gone on to related insights
which, insofar as they are at odds with Turner's ideas, rather
extend and incorporate than contradict them. This is particularly true of several writers who have concerned themselves
with the general phenomenon of mobility; their work suggests that the frontier process can be considered as a special
instance of the much more general process of constant movement and migration.[6] In the picture these writers draw, the
United States emerges as a vast arena for movement of all
kinds—not just from the East to the frontier but from Europe
to America, from South to North, from farm to farm, from
farm to city, from city to city, from city to suburb, and from
house to house. Turner saw clearly that the frontier was an
important stimulus to all this, and his own writing has in its
way been an equally important stimulus to investigation.
Turner, as Elkins and McKitrick have remarked, "did, after
all, represent the first major effort—after Tocqueville—to deal
with motion as a basic cultural fact in American life."[7] But
what the recent writers have seen is that Turner, by focusing
attention so sharply on the frontier, fell short of exploiting its
more general significance; and they are also more keenly

---

[6] I do not mean to suggest here that Turner's work was the sole
stimulus to an interest in mobility among historians, or even
necessarily the most important one. But among our major historians he was surely the first to have aroused an interest in it.
[7] "Institutions in Motion," *American Quarterly* 12 (1960), 188.

aware that the American habit of movement has continued
in full force even after the disappearance of the frontier.[8] As
recently as 1950 about three quarters of the nation's city
people were living in places where they had not resided in
1940. The movement stirred by the Second World War may
have made this an exceptional decade, but the pattern is only
slightly exaggerated. One is impressed, for example, to learn
that in 1940 the average American farm had been in the same
hands for only twelve years. Or that at age fifty nearly two out
of five native Americans have set up residence outside their
state of birth—a figure which, of course, takes no measure of
the intrastate movement. In recent times the normal pattern
has been for one in five Americans to move from one house to
another *within each year*, and for one in fourteen to migrate
from one county to another. Again, as Elkins and McKitrick
have pointed out, it is not only individuals that have moved
but institutions, and one of the conditions for the survival of
institutions has been their transportability; one of the facts in
their development has been the necessity of changing when
transplanted in order to meet new conditions. The large number of adaptable voluntary organizations illustrates this process—replaceable parts, more or less identical in their mode
of procedure no matter what town they are found in (the
Lions, the Rotary, the Kiwanis); so also do the innumerable
secular functions taken over by the churches. But of course
individuals too are both selected and affected by the migratory
process, in ways that have not yet been fully explored. The
great imaginative book on American movement has not yet
been written. What will it reveal about the effects of movement on the family—on the breakup of extended kinship
groups, the limitation of size in the nuclear family; or about
the pattern of American sociability, or our ways of conformity, our superficial human relationships, our rootlessness, our
carelessness about newly acquired surroundings that Americans can only regard as temporary? What will it tell us about
the pattern of our nationalism, or our status hierarchy?

---

[8] In fact the proportion of native-born Americans living in states
other than that of their birth has actually *risen* in recent decades
over the level at which it was in 1850. Stanley Lebergott, *Manpower in Economic Growth* (1964), 17.

Such considerations not only suggest that much of the Turner thesis can be salvaged but also point to some of the necessary modifications in its form. But let it be clear that in enumerating some of them we are, for the most part, working with familiar elements that can be found in Turner. Turner was not rigorous, but he was circumspect; a Turner disciple is very likely to rise up and argue, with documentation on each count, that the master had anticipated all these points. However, even if we are working entirely with colors that can be found somewhere on Turner's palette, the point is that we are dropping some, toning some down, intensifying and recombining others, so that the resulting picture, for all the similarity of its elements, is quite different from his.

First, I think we must get away from the immediate post-Darwinian frame of mind with its simple categories of man and environment, and consider the whole process of movement in terms of institutions, habits, and ideas. This will help us to accept the fact that democracy and individualism—however we are precisely to define them—had to be brought to the frontier before they could be developed or intensified there. We must abandon the narrow, primitivist conception of the "frontier" as the cutting edge of society where it impinges upon the wilderness—it will be too difficult to balance many social explanations on that fine edge—and think rather of the great West in its relation to American economic development. We must, in short, sacrifice some of the romance of the frontier to our sense of the great American bonanza. We must give up—at least for the moment—the attractive figure of the omnicompetent pioneer with his rifle and his ax as our central actor (we can put him back in later, but he will then fall into his proper marginal place), and accept the fact that the American farmer was a little capitalist, often by necessity a rather speculative one, operating in the new and uncertain Western world along with big capitalists like the land speculator and the railroader. We must not forget or unduly subordinate the role of speculation in Western development. Nor can we think of this development simply as an internal American phenomenon: it must be portrayed in connection with the international market for staples and the international flow of capital and labor. We must give up the excessively agricultural and rural overtones of the thesis as Turner usually stated it,[9] and remember that the rapid emergence of Western towns and cities, with their open, breezy, petty-capitalist atmosphere, were just as much a part of the Western story as agriculture and free land. We must think of the West as a magnificent area for the rapid expansion of middle-class society, and remember that the "pioneer" went westward not to be a self-sufficient yeoman but to find a stronger position in the market, not to live forever in a log cabin or a sod house but to build as soon as possible a substantial frame house, not to enjoy a primitive or wilderness environment but to recreate for himself the American standard of living as he had seen it in the East, and finally, not to forge a utopian egalitarian society but to re-enact the social differences of the older world—with himself now closer to the top. We must do openly what Turner has been criticized for doing implicitly: understand that the West meant not just free land but the whole glorious natural abundance of interior America, its resources of all kinds, including timber, coal, oil, minerals; and that the westward movement involved the conquest of these resources and their incorporation into the machinery of American capitalism. We must get away from the excessive and parochial Midwestern bias and remember that if the frontier process was effective, it ought to have been effective from the days of first colonial settlement, when there was still more frontier and there were fewer people. We must remember that the "Valley of Democracy" had no monopoly on democracy. We must get away from the defeatist overtones of the frontier idea—the notion that democracy and opportunity are so closely linked with the frontier process that the end of free land represents a disastrous major break in history—and contemplate the situation of countries like England whose democracy developed without benefit of an internal frontier. As students of the open society, we must consider what modern sociological inquiry seems to

---

[9] Not always; as urban society formed, Turner once wrote, there were "mill sites, town sites, transportation lines, banking centers, openings in the law, in politics—all the varied chances for advancement afforded in a rapidly developing society where everything was open to him who knew how to seize the opportunity." *Frontier*, 271–2.

find, that the processes of industrial organization yield a rate of social mobility that is no smaller, perhaps notably larger, than that of the old agrarian society. We may do well to drop all rhetorical formulations which suggest that we have found a way either of ruling out alternative explanations or of measuring intangibles against each other—like the statement that the frontier "explains" American development—or the subtle but provocative intellectual demagoguery involved in assertions about "the really American part of our history." Finally, the process of Western development will fall into its proper place if we develop alternative perspectives on American history and simply consider the frontier process in its relation to these other factors, instead of making futile claims for its "importance" as against theirs.

If these other factors are not neglected, the role of the frontier will fall into its proper place. No historian who wants to explain American development or American institutions will want to neglect the fundamentally Protestant character of American society in its formative phases and indeed throughout its history, with all this implies about its dissenting bias, its preference for lay government, its occasional antinomianism, and its penchant for the diffusion of authority outside of a carefully structured hierarchy. Nor will he, without necessarily embracing all of Max Weber's debatable thesis about the Protestant ethic, fail to consider the possible role of the Protestant dynamic and Protestant economic morale—a consideration which may rise in his estimation if he compares the development of the United States with that of Latin America. Neither will he overlook the postfeudal and nonfeudal inheritance of the country, nor forget how much of the heavy weight of feudal apparatus was lost in the Atlantic crossing; nor how little the feudal cast of mind survived among the American upper classes, nor how the corresponding reaction of the middle and lower classes lost in militancy and acerbity. He will, in this respect, think of America as a country that has had patrician leadership but not aristocratic domination. He may wish to consider the effects of selective migration—not merely in the sense that dukes and bishops did not emigrate and that the American population drew mainly upon the

middle and lower orders of Europe, but also in the less demonstrable sense that, since millions more suffered from one form
or another of malaise and oppression than actually removed
themselves, there may have been some selection by psychological as well as social type, with America receiving more than its
share of the exceptionally restless, the exceptionally bold, the
cranky and the intractable. He will not want to stress the forest
environment to the extent of minimizing the English political
heritage or English political thought, nor try to write of the
American mind without reference to Locke and the whole tradition of English Whiggery and English radicalism. The
causes and consequences of the national birth trauma, the
Revolution, will not shrink in his estimation of American
habits, nor will they easily be wrenched out of their Atlantic
context and absorbed into the wilderness. The legalistic, moderate, nonregicidal, and largely nonterroristic character of the
American Revolution will interest him, as well as its impact,
through confiscation and emigration, on the class structure,
and its important quickening of democratic tendencies. He
will concern himself with the origins of the two-party system,
in which Americans pioneered, and the early development of a
pattern of legitimate opposition. He will surely want to take
account of the peculiarities of American federalism, which at
once made it possible to organize a veritable continent under
one political and economic roof and at the same time imposed
certain rigorous limitations upon the political system. When
he deals with American politics and with the development of
this federal system, slavery and race will still loom very large
in his account, and not simply for what they tell about the
foreground of our history—the Old South, the Civil War, Reconstruction, and indeed the racial agitation of recent years—
but also for what they tell us about the dark background and
the deeper recesses of the American conscience. Concentration
on the vastness of the frontier will not cause him to forget
what was once the vastness of the oceans, or that the United
States had not only free land but free security; that isolation
from the European centers of power, compounded by Europe's
own internal divisions and our ability to exploit them, made it
possible to maintain American security and advance American
ends with the expenditure of only a fraction of what the older

nations had to expend and within the framework of a civilian mentality; and that our earlier national objectives were realized at the cost of weak or distracted opposition from Indians, Mexicans, Spaniards, the British only when they were locked in a death-grip with Napoleon, the Central Powers only when war had bled them to exhaustion. When he turns his attention to American economic history, he will have his mind fixed on an area of continental scope with immense spaces to conquer and staggering resources to exploit, organized under a single political system. He will want to remember the highly capitalistic and speculative character that American agriculture assumed, and its long favorable position in a stimulating world market. He will consider the formative effects of material abundance upon a variety of American habits, from child-rearing to military strategy. He will be concerned about the timing and the setting of the nation's entry upon the path of industrialism and the stimuli to economic innovation. He will be interested in the mixed racial and ethnic composition of its labor force, with all that this implies for working-class aspirations, social hierarchies, and political behavior. He will be acutely conscious of a nation constantly mixed and stirred by mobility in all its forms, social and geographic, and with the rootlessness, the restlessness it has implanted within us.

If the simple, primitivist rubric of "the frontier," or even the more open conception of "the West" were allowed to displace all these complex considerations, or cause us to neglect them in our historical thinking, our sense of the American past would be impoverished. But to take account of them does not deprive the frontier process of its place, for it is a part of most of them and interacts with all of them. The great merit of Turnerism, for all its elliptical and exasperating vagueness, was to be open-ended. The frontier idea, though dissected at one point and minimized at another, keeps popping up in new forms, posing new questions to its questioners, always prodding investigation into new areas. Turner once said that his aim had been not to produce disciples but to propagate inquiry. He did both; and the inquiry propagated among critics and friendly revisionists has now reached a volume that overmatches the work of his disciples. This mountain of Turner criticism is his most certain monument. Among all the historians of the United States it was Turner alone of whom we can now say with certainty that he opened a controversy that was large enough to command the attention of his peers for four generations.

PART
III

Charles A. Beard

CHAPTER 5

Beard and the Progressive Mind

> *Wherever we turn in the maze of recent historical investigation, we are confronted by the overwhelming importance attached by the younger and abler scholars to the economic factor in political and social progress.*
> —E. R. A. Seligman, 1902

> *Interpretive schools seem always to originate in social antagonisms.*
> —Charles A. Beard, 1913

I

THE NOTE of vigorous nonconformity rings out sharply among the forebears of Charles A. Beard. His grandfather, Nathan Beard, was read out of a Quaker meeting in North Carolina for marrying a Methodist, and is also remembered to have harbored fugitive slaves there in the underground railroad. Years later he told his grandson: "I ran a one-man church, in which there can be no dissent," and Charles proudly added: "My father continued in that church and I was brought up in it."[1] Nathan's only son, William Henry Harrison Beard, born on a farm in the village of Beardstown in Guilford County, North Carolina, showed his resistance to the mystique of the Confederacy when he fled northward to escape military service in 1861. William Beard made his way to Indiana, where, after working for a time as a carpenter, a clerk, and a schoolteacher, he married and settled on a farm near Knightstown. Quick, versatile, and shrewd, he speculated successfully in real estate, and by 1874, when his son Charles was born, he owned a mill, a bank, and extensive lands, ran a thriving business as a building contractor, and had made a fortune.

Not much more is known about William Beard. Though he had no advanced formal education, he was a voracious

---

[1] Hubert Herring, "Charles A. Beard: Free Lance among the Historians," *Harper's*, 178 (1939), 641.

reader, especially interested in science, an inquisitive and venturesome man who used his leisure to travel and wrote some accounts of his experiences for the press. Among the few works remembered to have been in his large library, perhaps part of Nathan's collection on comparative religion, were Thomas Paine's *Age of Reason* and John W. Draper's *History of the Conflict between Religion and Science*, a popular rationalist classic published in the year of Charles's birth. William Beard was an admirer of Robert Ingersoll, a scoffer at the mistakes of Moses, who prided himself on the role of village skeptic. He was noted also for having made one of his lots available for a camp meeting to local Negroes who had been barred from other sites. A visiting Negro bishop who was turned away from the local hotel was accommodated at the Beard home, in which the moral traditions of Radical Republicanism, elsewhere on the wane, were still taken in earnest.

Like Fredrick Jackson Turner, Charles Beard was brought up in a prosperous Midwestern household where politics and ideas were regularly discussed, but in Beard's background both the feeling of success and proprietorship and the vein of dissent seem to have been stronger. William Beard was a masterful man, full of optimism, who loved to boast about the United States as the land of prosperity and progress. As we follow the course of Charles Beard's life we continue to be aware that his social criticism is that of a man who belongs, both morally and materially, to the possessing classes, to the Beards of Beardstown, of one who, as his friend Hubert Herring put it, "combines the zeal of the crusader with the sound instincts of a good horse-trader." There is about him little of the violent alienation or mordant detachment of such a contemporary as Thorstein Veblen, and one is not surprised to find him making a small-town newspaper pay while still in his adolescence, or in his middle years putting substantial energy into solid textbooks, or, after his abrupt resignation from Columbia, going into the dairy business on two farms in Connecticut. His radicalism, insofar as we can think of him as a radical, was like that of many other writers of the Progressive era, in that it reflected the conscience of the well-to-do as well as the critical spirit of the emerging American intelligentsia. Beard once remarked that the difference between himself and Turner could be summed up in the fact that Turner's father had been named for a Democrat, Andrew Jackson, while his own had been named for the Whig, William Henry Harrison. Beard was raised to assume that respectable Americans would be Republicans. His family's political heritage was close to the intellectual tradition that had come down through the Federalists, Whigs, and Republicans, a tradition which had always embodied a strong vein of economic realism. ("People ask me," Beard once said, "why I emphasize economic questions so much. They should have been present in the family parlor, where my father and his friends gathered to discuss public affairs.")[2] The sense of possession and of firm American identity, so strong among the well-established upper middle class of the Middle West, the note of post-Darwinian rationalism, Radical Republicanism, evangelical conscience, and perhaps even a touch of Quaker dissent—all these mingle strangely and in uncertain proportions in Beard's original intellectual constitution.

In 1884 young Beard was sent to Spiceland Academy, a Quaker school not far from his home. William Beard believed also in training his sons in the management of affairs. In the early 1890's he bought a newspaper, the *Knightstown Banner,* and turned it over to Charles and his older brother Clarence, leaving the boys to write almost all its copy and on occasion to set type as well. From this collaboration Clarence went into the law and Charles, now twenty-one, went off to college at DePauw University. DePauw, then a rather conservative and sectarian Methodist institution, was an improbable place for a good member of the campus Republican club like Charles Beard to get a first acquaintance with a thinker like Karl Marx. But DePauw's professor of political science, the Civil War veteran Colonel James R. Weaver, was one of those original, unorthodox, and uninhibited minds who turn up from time to time in the history of American colleges. He tried to give his students a solid grounding in what would now no doubt be called social science, and, de-

---

[2] Eric F. Goldman, "Charles A. Beard: An Impression," in Howard K. Beale, ed., *Charles A. Beard* (1954), 2, is the source for this remark as well as for the comparison with Turner.

spite his own solid Republicanism, took it upon himself to shake them out of their Hoosier complacencies. He assigned reading in a wide range of political and social thinkers from the Greeks down to Spencer, Bagehot, Buckle, Westermarck, Alfred Marshall, and Marx. In Beard's intellectual life he was a decisive figure; his example probably suggested the possibility of teaching and scholarship as a career. The teacher in turn found the pupil rewarding. "He is full of zeal," he wrote, "fond of investigation, and has a keen insight into truth."

Like so many of the generation that came of age in the 1890's, Beard was deeply affected by the depression that followed the panic of 1893 and by the industrial and political struggles that grew out of it. At the end of his freshman year at DePauw, he visited Chicago—a significant choice for a protected youth of the upper middle class, who might easily have preferred to spend the summer amid the quiet comforts of Knightstown. Chicago, the rawest and the most dynamic city in the United States, was the Midwest's most potent evidence that the Industrial Revolution, with all its terrors, had really descended upon America. Only a few years before, the Columbian Exposition had dramatized the contrast between the city's pretensions, embodied in the artificial White City on the lake, and its realities, stretched out in thousands of squalid and ugly blocks. Chicago was the city of the Haymarket riot and the Pullman strike, of the stockyard horrors that Upton Sinclair would portray in *The Jungle* and the grandiose traction piracy described by Theodore Dreiser in *The Titan*. It was also a scene of protest and critical thought, an arena for men like John P. Altgeld, Clarence Darrow, Eugene Debs, Henry Demarest Lloyd, and a vigorous group of labor-Populists in politics, for a rising school of realists in literature, and for the humanitarian aspirations of philanthropic well-to-do women like Jane Addams. In Chicago young Beard saw working-class miseries that his father's philosophy had never prepared him for and lived for a while near Hull House where rebels and heretics were forever debating the future of the industrial order. He visited the insurgent scholar John R. Commons, listened to speeches by Bryan and Altgeld. Chicago guaranteed that Colonel Weaver's proddings would not be wasted on Beard. When he went back to DePauw he debated on the college team for the right of labor to organize and for a federal income tax.

Upon his graduation in 1898, Beard volunteered for service in the Spanish War, which had just begun. If this seems strangely inconsistent with the hatred of war that colors his later life, or with the criticisms of Western imperialism he would be making only a few years later, it must be remembered that the Spanish War started in a surge of popular idealism over the freedom of Cuba and that at the beginning its imperialist denouement was foreseen by very few. The Wall Street bankers, the big industrialists, the conservative McKinley Republicans were in the main unenthusiastic about this adventure, and found reason to change their minds only near the war's end when some material yield, in the form of new possessions and new trade opportunities, seemed to be forthcoming. Intervention against Spain in Cuba meant taking the side of the underdog; it excited a few potential military adventurers among the young, but it also impelled a man like William Jennings Bryan, for all his moral sentiments and pacifist leanings, to volunteer. The war's main appeal to many Americans lay in the generosity and idealism behind it—so much so that a contemporary like William Allen White later saw in the war enthusiasm the greatest stimulus to the moral awakening of Progressivism. Beard's gesture, then, was only a token of the passion with which he responded to public issues. Fortunately, there was a surplus of volunteers, and his rejection may have spared him embalmed beef as well as the historic irony of serving together with military enthusiasts like T.R. But he was not spared the disillusionment, in his impressionable twenties, of seeing the high moral purpose of 1898 fade into American imperialism in the Philippines.[3]

In 1898 Beard's craving for experience took him to study

---

[3] Beard later took a different view of the matter. Writing of the Spanish-American War in 1914, he said: "Contrary to their assertions on formal occasions, the American people enjoy war beyond measure, if the plain facts of history are allowed to speak." *Contemporary American History, 1877–1913* (1914), 199. The aftermath of the war saw the end of Beard's Republicanism. "I left the G.O.P. on imperialism in 1900 and have found no home anywhere since that year." Beard to Arthur M. Schlesinger, April 7, 1946; Schlesinger memoir, Columbia Oral History Project, 1001.

at Oxford, where he found England in the full tide of change. Keir Hardie was converting the trade unions to the idea of a Labour Party, the Fabians were winning converts, the Webbs had recently published their books on the history of trade unionism and industrial democracy, Charles Booth had just finished his studies of the life and labor of the London poor, Robert Blatchford's *Merrie England,* a popular plea for socialism, was finding hundreds of thousands of readers, and the whole world seemed to be sensitive to social ills and looking for remedies. It was not, however, any of the contemporary books that most impressed Beard, but a work written almost forty years earlier. The book was John Ruskin's *Unto This Last,* a set of four essays which Ruskin himself thought were "the truest, rightest worded and most serviceable things I have ever written." *Unto This Last* actually belonged less intimately to the intellectual spirit of the early 1860's when it was written than it did to the 1890's. When Ruskin's essays first ran in the *Cornhill* magazine, they were partially suppressed because of the unfavorable response, and had to be foreshortened. *Unto This Last* sold less than a thousand copies in the first decade after its publication as a book in 1862, but in the 1890's it began to be read widely and was rapidly approaching its fiftieth thousand at the turn of the century. It was about at this time that Gandhi, who called it "the turning point of my life," first read it; and it was a far more directly influential work among the early leaders of the Labour Party than anything written by Marx.

Ruskin's book was a moral critique of the preconceptions of orthodox economics, a thrust at the philosophy of self-interest which made of man merely "a covetous machine," an attempt to free social thought from the oppressive atmosphere of Malthusianism and Ricardianism, and ultimately to mend the brutalities of English industrialism. Liberated from the dogmatic framework of such classicists as Nassau Senior, who held that it was no business of political economy whether any form of wealth is beneficial to its owner or to society at large, Ruskin spun out in this and other writings a basic social ethic on the strength of which it was possible for him to argue that the state should provide free education for the young, vocational training in government workshops, guaranteed employment, job security, housing and social security for the aged and destitute, minimum wage laws, rent control, income ceilings, and public ownership of transportation. As economic speculation, *Unto This Last* seemed impulsive and naïve, and only the cranky valor of genius could have prompted Ruskin to fling his moral and esthetic preferences into the face of the imposing intellectual edifice of classical economics. But he was trying to restore the conviction that the ultimate test of any economic order is the quality of human life it yields: "THERE IS NO WEALTH BUT LIFE. Life, including all its powers of love, of joy, and of admiration. That country is the richest which nourishes the greatest number of noble and happy human beings; that man is richest who, having perfected the functions of his own life to the utmost, has also the widest helpful influence, both personal and by means of his possessions, over the lives of others." What Ruskin finally achieved, in effect, was to turn the flank of the received economic doctrines not by assaulting their coherence but by destroying their premises, by calling for a more inclusive and humane theory of values, and by insisting on the social relevance of values they had left out of account. In 1860 Ruskin's book was premature—that is to say, prophetic. Forty years later an increasingly forceful demand for social reform gave it a wide audience, and it seems alive and relevant once more today when issues having to do with the quality of life have again taken on a new prominence.

Beard's response to *Unto This Last* may be taken as a clue, I think, not just to the young man, but to the mature scholar. And what is significant in sounding this side of his temper is that Ruskin's was a work much more moral than sociological in its mode of thought, a study in ethical speculation and exhortation that was rather far removed from the economic realism which one associates with the later Beard. Like most interesting and fruitful minds, Beard's was driven by a profound ambiguity, never to be wholly resolved. In his case the ambiguity lay between the moral passions that Ruskin addressed so directly and the desire for detached knowledge and scientific scholarship which Beard voiced on many occasions in his early maturity. At any rate, Ruskin, whom he had first read as an undergraduate, never ceased to move him. More than a third of a century after his English years, when he found the Western world again shaken by a crisis in thought, he harked back to Ruskin as a prophet victorious over the spokesmen of nineteenth-century economics, with its supposedly iron laws. "And who won in the end? John Ruskin or the great and wise of the Victorian age?" Reviled in his own day as a sentimentalist and moralist, Ruskin, Beard thought, had been the true architect of modernity: "The economics taught in the official colleges of Oxford University today is nearer to the economics taught at Ruskin Hall in 1899 than it is to the official economics of that year. . . . Perhaps in the crisis in thought that now besets us it will do some good to take up again 'Unto This Last,' and read it without anger or tears."[4]

The life of politics and social service was at first more alluring to Beard than academic Oxford. He soon fell in with another American five years his senior, Walter Vrooman, whose temperament seems to have appealed to the romantic and the activist in him. Vrooman was a chronic dissenter and agitator, a come-outer who had been on the platform in one place or another since the age of seven when he had toured as "the boy phrenologist." The son of a Kansas judge who had run for office on the Greenback and Prohibition tickets, Vrooman had been reared on grass-roots heresies; he had been a labor agitator in Chicago at the age of sixteen and now might be loosely described as a Christian Socialist. He had drifted from place to place—Pittsburgh, New York, Philadelphia, Baltimore, St. Louis—identifying himself with various kinds of reforms to which he usually contributed more excitement than substance. The collapse of his latest agitations in St. Louis had prompted his wealthy wife to take him to England to regain his health and his nerve, but he was unable even there to stay his hand. At Oxford he and Beard formed the nucleus of a group of reform enthusiasts. Vrooman had thought of setting up in the very shadow of ancient and privileged Oxford a workingman's school which would prepare an elite of working-class leaders to assume the statesmanlike

---

4 "Ruskin and the Babble of Tongues," *New Republic*, 87 (1936), 370–2.

responsibilities required by labor's growing political power. The establishment, which was to be named Ruskin Hall, would be the first of a network of such "colleges" to be opened in large industrial centers. This daring idea, conceived at a time when the free public high school system had not yet been founded in England, was one which Vrooman lacked the tact and the stability to carry through. The task of getting the support of labor leaders, among them Keir Hardie, as well as the endorsement of Oxford dons and Trade Union Councils, fell to Beard. With funds given by Mrs. Vrooman, a large rambling building was leased from Balliol College, and Ruskin Hall opened in 1899. Beard gave the first lecture, taking English constitutional history as his subject.

The following year, Beard returned to the United States, studied for a term under Moses Coit Tyler at Cornell University, and married Mary Ritter, whom he had met at DePauw. But he was soon back in England, working as secretary to Ruskin Hall, a position that enabled him to tour the industrial regions of England and Wales, often speaking as many as five or six times a week, and to spend almost two years in and around Manchester. In 1901, he published his first book, *The Industrial Revolution*, which was intended to introduce working-class readers to the history of nineteenth-century industry, and to the significance and promise of modern technology. A creditable work of condensation and popularization for a young man of twenty-seven, it spoke the mind of an eclectic reformer rather than an agitator or a revolutionary. It is easy for any historian who deals with the Industrial Revolution to treat it merely as a museum of horrors in order to stimulate working-class militancy. Beard, keeping his prophetic intensity under careful restraint, preferred to emphasize the advances in productive potential and the as yet unrealized advantages of industrial modernization. His essential grievance was not against a class, nor even the property system as such, but against the *waste* of energies entailed by modern competitive organization. The book was recognizably Ruskinian in its forthright repudiation of *laissez faire* and its concern for the quality of human life as the test of the economic order. Its practical conclusions were strikingly optimistic. "The charge of inefficiency, weakness, and crudity made against

the present order," Beard wrote, "need not be based upon
sentiment about rich and poor or class jealousy, but upon
mathematical calculations which can be made as soon as
statistical departments turn their attention to the problem.
It is clear to any unprejudiced mind that a reorganization of
industry is both necessary and desirable, not that one class
may benefit at the expense of another, but that the energy and
wealth wasted in an irrational system may be saved to humanity, and that the bare struggle for a living may not occupy
the best hours of the workers' lives."[5]

As a speaker before working-class groups, Beard evidently
saw himself in a different role from that of a writer, even a
writer of a pamphlet on the Industrial Revolution for working-
class audiences. Without the restraints of formal authorship,
he could wax prophetic: he denounced the heartless scholars
who had removed themselves from the plight of the people
for having failed to learn "of God who moves in the hearts of
man, transforming human lives, and lifting men to the sublime heights of self-sacrifice." In the great conquest of the
future, "the triumph over disease, pain, misery, poverty,
wretchedness, and want," the laurels would be won by "the
world's great sages, thinkers, and prophets, yes, even He who
healed wounds and bound up broken hearts in Galilee." His
platform style was militant enough to transport his working-
class listeners. "Aye!" an old man was heard to say after
Beard spoke in the Todmorden Co-operative Hall, "if we'd a
lot o' young fellows like yon'd i' Tormden, we'd turn it upside
down i' a week!"[6]

From 1899 to 1901 Beard turned out a series of articles
for *Young Oxford,* the magazine of the Ruskin Hall enthusiasts, which reveal him almost as much in the role of spiritual
teacher as social agitator. What stands out in these essays,
aside from their high-minded youthful rhetoric, is their humane tone, their lack of rancor or resort to class animus, their
confidence in gradualism and progress. Several of the essays,

---

[5] *The Industrial Revolution* (1901), p. 104. As late as 1930, Beard
wrote: "Science and machinery have made crude class fights
archaic." Bernard C. Borning, *The Political and Social Thought
of Charles A. Beard* (1962), 88.
[6] Harlan B. Phillips, "Charles Beard: The English Lectures, 1899–
1901," *Journal of the History of Ideas,* 14 (1953), 451, 453.

given over to "Men Who Have Helped Us," were short inspirational portraits of Carlyle, Cobbett, Darwin, Mazzini, Morris, and Owen which express an ecumenical admiration for the humane prophets and protestants of the nineteenth century and display no doctrinaire commitments or rigid standards of judgment. (They do, however, show that capacity that Beard would always have in generous measure for a selective use of historical facts in order to put across his message: one would look hard and in vain, for instance, in his treatment of Carlyle, for any sign of the reactionary or the racist; the brutal side of Carlyle is entirely missing.) In these pieces evolution spells progress, science and religion march hand in hand toward fulfillment of "the new morality." Beard drew heavily on those interpreters of evolution like Henry Drummond and Prince Kropotkin who argued the necessity of mutuality and solidarity in the evolutionary process. "The concept of God and the individual," he wrote, "is being supplemented by the more glorious concept of God and the collective life of man." Along with the new, there was a good deal of the old morality: the life, exemplified by his subjects, of firm personal morale, aspiration, and the "splendid discipline of hard work from which parents now-a-days often foolishly wish to free their children." "We all need," Beard wrote, in what may be taken almost as a personal confession, ". . . above all to have continuously before ourselves visions of our own possibilities. . . . We need not only the desire for the valuable, but also the will to be valuable."[7]

At the university Beard studied chiefly with Frederick York Powell, the Regius Professor of Modern History. Although Powell was no democrat ("I hope to God," he once said, "the peoples will never conquer," and he was convinced that the United States would be the scene of the future failure of democracy), he was nevertheless a man of generous social sentiments, compassionate and politically independent despite his Tory sympathies, who encouraged Beard's reform passions, wholly shared his enthusiasm for Ruskin, and gladly lent his aid to Ruskin Hall. Under Powell, Beard began studies in British institutional history, to which he would later

---

7 "William Cobbett, Friend of Man," *Young Oxford*, 2 (1901), 171.

revert for his doctoral thesis. Powell was a man of broad interests—he was responsible for inviting Mallarmé to lecture
at Oxford—but in his historiographical convictions he was a
hard positivist. He saw history not as a branch of literary art
but of science. "The method of history is not different from the
method of physical sciences," he wrote, and he was convinced
that the evolution of political institutions could be explained
with scientific rigor. Historical science demanded that the
historian, whatever his role as a citizen, should be a detached
investigator, seeking the truth for truth's sake. Beard was
rationalist enough to respond to this scientific note in Powell,
and even in his Oxford days we can see in him an uncomfortable duality that was always to haunt him—a duality between the aseptic ideal of scientific inquiry and his social
passions. In his *Young Oxford* essays we find him charmingly
trying to sidestep this problem. Wholly aware of the inspirational and moral character of his biographical portraits from
history, he felt called upon to explain: "In taking up this work
I do not pose as an historian; for it is his duty to leave ethics
alone. . . ."[8] Yet he was too much the social activist to shake
off his feeling that historical knowledge, however "scientifi-
cally" it was gained, ought to serve the common weal by being
made to shed light on the origins and the solution of contemporary problems, and that for this purpose it would have
to be translated into moral terms. For the rest of his life he
would be bedeviled by the opposition between his belief in the
discipline of history as science and his passionate desire to
put it to work as a moral force; and some readers would notice
a strange disharmony between his voluntarism and moralism
and the ironical and mocking determinism of his historical
thought. His difficulty with the place of moral judgments in
history recurs in every phase of his work: it can be seen in
the New History which he promoted at Columbia with James
Harvey Robinson, in the deep, unresolved ambivalence of his
famous book on the Constitution, in his later conversion to historical relativism, and in his polemics on American foreign
policy.

---

[8] Oliver Elton, *Frederick York Powell*, I (1906), 194; *Young Oxford*, 2 (1901), 172.

Beard had sworn in 1900 that he would never stop agi-
tating "till the workers who bear upon their shoulders the
burden of the world should realize the identity of their own
interests and rise to take possession of the means of life."[9]
Briefly he considered remaining in England, where some of
the founders of the new Labour Party had already marked
him as a coming leader; but his decision, made, he later wrote,
"at length and with great reluctance," to return to America in
1902 after three years of English life, and to take up graduate
work in earnest at Columbia University marked not simply a
determination to repatriate himself but also a return to
scholarship from a time of agitation and reform, a lapse from
militancy into detachment. Now, for a brief period, his super-
abundant energies were wholly given over to academic work.
By 1904, his thirtieth year, he had taken his PhD with an
austerely academic thesis on *The Office of Justice of Peace in
England in Its Origin and Development*, and in the autumn of
that year he joined the Columbia department of political
science.

Among Columbia's distinguished roster in law and the
social sciences, Beard was particularly attracted by such men
as James T. Shotwell, James Harvey Robinson, soon to become
the spokesman of the New History, Frank J. Goodnow in
public law, and E. R. A. Seligman in economics. In this urbane
and stimulating environment, he was spurred to put his ideas
about scientific method and the political world into more
systematic form. Meanwhile, he became a celebrated figure
on the campus and flourished as a teacher. "The nicest American I ever knew," Frederick York Powell (who rarely liked
Americans) had said, and the judgment was often echoed at
Columbia. Simple in dress and manner, devoid of pretense and
free of condescension, Beard also had a winning physical
presence; along with striking blue eyes and a benign smile,
which would suddenly illuminate his spare face, he had a
splendidly aquiline nose, which in grave moments could give
him the aspect of a worried eagle. A favorite of many of his
colleagues, he was also perhaps the most popular professor

---

9 Phillips, "Charles Beard," 456.

among the undergraduates, who, in 1909 when Dean J. H. Van Amringe retired, voted in a straw poll for Beard as his successor.

Unlike Turner, Beard did not develop an influential research seminar and hence formed no "school" around himself, but he was at his best in large lecture courses, where students responded to his finished oratorical manner ("an eloquence," Arthur W. Macmahon thought, "that seemed almost imperious") and to his candor on public questions. Irwin Edman remembered Beard in some of his less formal moments, "a lanky figure leaning against the wall, drawling wittily with half-closed eyes," conveying his "passionate concern for an understanding of the realities of government, the economic forces and the interested persons involved in it." "He was clear, he was suggestive, he was witty," Edman added, "but none of these things could quite account for the hold he had on the smug and the rebels alike, on both the pre-lawyers and the pre-poets. I suspect it was a certain combination of poetry, philosophy, and honesty in the man himself, a sense he communicated that politics mattered far beyond the realm commonly called political, and an insight he conveyed into the life that forms of government furthered or betrayed." "There was no one at Columbia in the second decade of the century," John Erskine recalled, "who could rival Beard as an orator. Others excelled him in wit and in the subtleties of civilized conversation, but he had no match in that type of political eloquence which democracy engenders. More than once I heard him address the student body on some question about which I disagreed with him, but while he spoke I could feel persuasion creep over me as it crept over the boys. He had a fine voice, but what carried conviction was his own utter belief, at least for the moment, in what he was saying."[1]

Beard seems to have felt during this period some fear of becoming academic or sterile, or of being absorbed and tamed by institutional life. One day he suddenly turned to Robinson and urged: "Now let's don't get old because when we do we'll be toddling over to that cathedral they're putting over there and spending our last days in the confessional. Let's make

---

[1] Irwin Edman, *Philosopher's Holiday* (1938), 130–1; John Erskine, *My Life as a Teacher* (1948), 93.

sure that we keep young through life." He boasted to Shotwell about his father's role as village atheist in Knightstown, and was apparently impelled to re-enact it at the university.[2] It is significant that more conservative colleagues like Erskine and Shotwell thought of him as "socialistic," an impression he perhaps liked to create, but which is not sustained by his writings.[3] Whatever the meaning of his "socialism," his air of the heretic, the reformer, the radical seems to have helped him to draw an embattled following, which was deeply loyal to him at the critical moment when he resigned in protest and left Morningside Heights.

Though Beard threw himself eagerly into his role at Columbia, and even organized a new undergraduate department of political science, he did not altogether give up his direct interest in public affairs. Progressive reform of a much less heady kind than he had known in England soon began to claim some of his time: he gave long hours as a consultant to the New York Bureau of Municipal Research and took an active part in the National Municipal League. But the outstanding thing about Beard's years at Columbia from 1902 to his resignation in 1917 was his lavish productivity. Aside from very frequent reviews and articles and a half dozen volumes of collected documents and readings, he wrote alone or in collaboration with others no fewer than eleven books. Among these was *An Economic Interpretation of the Constitution of the United States*, which became the most controversial historical work of his generation.

II

Beard's years at Columbia coincided with the Progressive era in national politics. He had come back to a scene of political and social reform that compared in the intensity of its intellectual ferment with the scene he had left in England.

---

[2] Shotwell, Memoir in Oral History Research Project, Columbia University, 62–3.
[3] It is hard to imagine a true socialist, for example, referring to T.R.'s presidential efforts in 1912 as "the candidacy of Mr. Roosevelt on a socialistic platform." *Contemporary American History* (1914), 299.

The first outburst of muckraking came during the years of his doctoral work, and by the time his book on the Constitution appeared, the national mood had grown so suspicious that, as Walter Lippmann put it, the public had a distinct prejudice in favor of those who made the accusations. The political machines and the bosses were under constant fire from political reformers and muckrakers, and all the problems of popular government were being re-examined. Though it had no clear idea what to do about them, the country was in full cry against the great industrialists and the big monopolies. It had become aware too of the pitiful condition of many of the working class—particularly women and children—in the factories, mines, and sweatshops, and was making halting experiments at the legal control of industrial exploitation. Almost every aspect of American life, from sex, religion, and race relations to foreign policy, the regulation of business, and the role of the Courts, was being reconsidered. For eight years Theodore Roosevelt had used the White House as a "bully pulpit" to preach his own version of civic morality and at least to dramatize, if not to exert in any far-reaching way, the powers of the state as opposed to those of capital. The years during which Beard did the immediate research and writing on his famous book coincided with the presidency of William Howard Taft and the exciting insurgency of La Follette and his band in the Senate. These years saw the split among the Republicans, the formation of the Bull Moose party, T.R.'s return to national politics as a presidential contender, the rise of Woodrow Wilson to national prominence, the three-sided election of 1912, and Wilson's election as the first Democratic President since the Civil War who was committed to fundamental reforms.

There was no better moment than the zenith of the Progressive movement for a book dealing with the Constitution as the product of a class conflict, dwelling at great length upon the economic interests and objectives of its framers and advocates, and stressing their opposition to majoritarian democracy. But Beard's book was only one facet of a broad uprising carried on by insurgent scholars since the 1890's against the abstract and conservative style of thought that had prevailed for more than two generations, which Morton White has aptly called the revolt against formalism.[4] Formalist thought, which represented in effect a substantial part of the heritage of the nineteenth century in America, had been long in the making and was well established both inside and outside the academy. Conservative in all its practical implications, it was strong on internal coherence but weak in its descriptive rapport with reality; being fixed and static in its formulation, it was particularly ill equipped to take account of changing reality. It dealt in timeless verities, stated in a very generalized form. In juristic theory, the formalistic mind discussed the political state abstractly, as the product of "the whole people." In legal theory, it took the view that the business of the courts, under a written Constitution, was simply to square legislative acts with the fundamental law, to observe whether or not they fit, and to throw them out if they did not. It left little room for philosophical problems arising from the observable fact that judges did not always see things the same way, and no room at all for the idea that judges, having strong social prejudices, might read these prejudices into the construction of the law. In economic theory, formalism meant classical *laissez faire*, modified perhaps at a few points where modification might work to the interests of industrialists. In the minds of some of its exponents, the lessons of classical economics were reinforced by the lessons of Darwinism: the economy was a natural order whose immanent processes would bring progress if only the struggle for existence and the survival of the fittest were allowed to go on without interference. In philosophy, formalism meant a passive spectatorial approach to knowledge, which accorded well with its equally passive conceptions of social policy. In ethics, for example, one spoke of abstract ethical criteria or of individual moral problems in personal terms, but not about the moral aspects of social systems or the

---

[4] In what follows I have drawn on Morton White's *American Social Thought* (1949) and my essay, "Beard and the Constitution: The History of an Idea," which first appeared in *American Quarterly*, II (1950), 195–213, and is also available in H. K. Beale, ed., *Charles A. Beard*, already cited. In re-creating the intellectual background of Beard's book, I have resorted mainly to works cited in its text or footnotes, which include writings by Pound, Goodnow, Bentley, J. Allen Smith, Seligman, Simons, Myers, Schaper, Ambler, and Libby cited hereafter.

moral ills of industrialism. In history, one wrote about the
heroic, and dealt with systems of ideas as self-contained, but
did not think of political and constitutional history as having
to do with anyone's economic objectives.

Against all this the insurgent scholars had been mounting a strong collective rebellion which can be traced in the
legal realism of Holmes, the economic institutionalism of
Veblen, the instrumentalism of John Dewey, the New History
of James Harvey Robinson, and the revival, by Beard and
others, of the economic interpretation of history. All these
movements, representing attempts to come more closely to
grips with reality, especially with reality in the course of
change, constituted the academic counterparts of muckraking
in journalism and of the literary revolt carried on by the
realist and naturalist writers. The intellectuals of the era were
trying to incorporate in a more general scheme of thought and
in a less polemical context what the muckraking journalists
and the popular novelists were getting at in a more direct
way. And what they were all getting at, if it can be put in a
word, was "reality." Reality was the opposite of everything the
genteel tradition had stood for in literature and the formalistic
thinkers in social philosophy. Reality was the inside story. It
was rough and sordid, hidden and neglected, and being hard
and material and inexorable, was somehow more important
than mere ideas and theories. Reality was the bribe, the
rebate, the bought franchise, the sale of adulterated food, the
desperate pursuit of life in the slums. Reality was what one
did not find in the standard textbooks on constitutional law,
political science, ethics, economics, or history, but could find
in The Jungle, The Octopus, The Titan, Susan Lennox, Wealth
versus Commonwealth, The History of Standard Oil, or The
Shame of the Cities. To portray this hitherto hidden reality
was the aim of every live journalist and novelist; to take account of it in the making of theory was the aim of every
advanced thinker.

What was happening, in effect, was that a modern critical
intelligentsia was emerging in the United States. Modernism,
in thought as in art, was dawning upon the American mind.
Beard's book on the Constitution fittingly appeared in the same
year as the New York Armory show—an event that was far

more shocking to the world of art than Beard's book was to scholars. The new artists, breaking with the placid and derivative craftsmanship that had so long prevailed, were, to be sure, expressionists and individualists where the scholars were inevitably the exponents of a traditional discipline and the prophets of collective action; but what they all had in common was a spirited rebellion against academicism, encrusted conservatism, and gentility, a will to see things afresh and a need for new ideas and new genres.

The rebels against formalism were trying to assert, above everything else, that all things are related, that all things change, and that all things should therefore be explained historically rather than deductively. And for the most part, they were concerned with knowledge as a rationale for social action, not for passivity: they were interested in control. Ideas, the instrumentalists and pragmatists argued, are not mirrors of reality, they are modes of adjustment, plans of action. Philosophy should concern itself with social problems. Economic institutions, the Veblen school held, should be viewed in relation to other aspects of society. Man should be taken not abstractly—as economic man—but concretely, as he actually operates in an institutional setting, particularly in the setting of the price system, absentee ownership, and the large corporation. Judges, said the legal realists, do not merely find law, they make it, and they do so in accordance with their social prejudices and predilections. The development of civilization, asserted a whole battery of historians, including both Turner and Beard, must be charted with a keen eye for the shaping role of economic forces and the incidence of class conflicts. History, the New Historians argued, is not a celebration of past heroes but an instrument for controlling the future.

American political thinkers in the Progressive era were looking for a theory of the state, of the nature of government, that would satisfy the demands of modernist realism and at the same time strengthen the aspirations and strategies of progressivism. The juristic theory of the state, as Beard called it, the notion that the state was made by "the whole people," was at once too conservative to meet the Progressive need for a critical view of government and too abstract to satisfy the Progressive writers' craving for reality, which told them that

the political public is in fact always divided into social interests that quarrel over public issues. On the other side, the
Marxist conception of the state as the instrument of the ruling
class seemed to them, when they thought of it at all, as overgeneralized. They were not socialists; they had no exclusive
sentimental or moral commitment to the proletariat. As reformers, they wanted to believe that they were dealing with a
state system that was accessible to improvement under the existing economic order. As liberals, they would have shrunk
from the conclusion that the existing state should be destroyed
and supplanted by a new one based on a single class. What
they sought was an open and pluralistic theory that would
have the feeling of Marxism for hard realities without its
monolithic implications.

In 1908 there appeared a long, crabbed, difficult, but important book which was to have some influence on Beard and
ultimately a considerable influence on the development of
political science in the United States—A. F. Bentley's *The
Process of Government.* Proceeding from assumptions, closely
related to pragmatism, that anticipated the political and sociological behaviorism of a later day, Bentley had looked for a
realistic and functional method for the understanding of political behavior, and had found it in the group basis of politics.
The common practice of concentrating on the individual in
politics, apart from his group affiliations, Bentley found to be
pointless; similarly pointless were all attempts to deal with
political ideas or emotions apart from their function as expressions of group interests. For Bentley consciousness did not determine group interests, but group interests determined consciousness. "The ideas can be stated in terms of the group;
the groups never in terms of the ideas."[5]

What was true for law was true for the political process.
Law became not the outcome of some disinterested effort to
incarnate abstract principles of justice, but of an effort to

---

[5] *The Process of Government,* (ed. 1935), 206. In a review of
Bentley's book, Beard found its tone excessively polemical, but
praised it for its "attempt to get below formalism," its "very positive feeling for the intimate essence of government," and for
helping "to put politics on a basis of realism where it belongs."
He also thought that Bentley had made "effective use of the idea
of 'group interests,' as distinct from class interests in the Marxian
sense." *Political Science Quarterly,* 23 (1908), 739–41.

systematize and order the relations between interest groups. "Law," Bentley wrote, "is activity, just as government is. It is a group process, just as government is. It is a forming, a systematization, a struggle, an adaptation of group interests, just as government is." Nor did he refrain from applying the same principle to constitutions: everything that could be said of statutory and other forms of law was also true of constitutions, "for constitutions are but a special form of law." In understanding constitutions, the important thing was not to look for abstract repositories of "sovereignty" but for administrative and coercive agencies whose control was fought over by contesting groups. Explain constitutions, Bentley urged, not in the light of the general ideas they are supposed to embody but of the particular groups that forge them. As for the American Constitution, "how can one be satisfied with a theory that comes down hard on the federal Constitution as primarily a great national ideal, in the very face of the struggles and quarrels of the constitutional convention for the maintenance of pressing social interests?"[6]

The phenomena of government, Bentley asserted, are always phenomena of pressure—the push and resistance between groups. And though he did not pretend himself to have "measured" any pressures or counterpressures, he left behind, as his legacy to later political positivists, the promise that political science could indeed hope to measure such forces and thus approximate a scientific understanding of events.

Beard was not much interested in measurement as such, and never cast his lot with the positivist political scientists, but one can see what Bentley's vision of politics meant to him: it combined a realistic conception of interest-group activities with a pluralistic model of power. The state would be in the control of whatever coalition of group interests happened to be strongest at a given moment. And if one were going to try to account for the origins of any particular constitutional system, one would look not in the first instance for the ideas that ani-

---

[6] Ibid., 272, 295, 135. Cf. Beard, *An Economic Interpretation of the Constitution*, 12: ". . . Law is not an abstract thing, a printed page, a volume of statutes, a statement by a judge. . . . A statute . . . separated from the social and economic fabric by which it is, in part, conditioned and which, in turn, it helps to condition, . . . has no reality."

mated it but for the special interests that might expect to gain by it, whose ideas could then be interpreted accordingly. But of the two themes in Bentley's work, it was his realism about politics and law as products of group interests and conflicts that appealed most consistently to Beard. As we shall see, he endorsed Bentley's pluralistic model of power in theory, but in his actual account of the Constitution deviated from it to adopt a dualistic picture of the political struggle which probably owes more to old Populist traditions and to writers like J. Allen Smith. In regarding the struggle over the Constitution as a fight between two broad, more or less homogeneous coalitions rather than an exceedingly complex jumble of special interests, he fell into a trap from which a consistent use either of Bentley or of Madisonian pluralism might have saved him.

Early in 1908 Beard delivered an important formal lecture, one of a series then being being offered by Columbia scholars in various disciplines, which outlines his political thought and shows why he found Bentley congenial. This lecture, published under the title *Politics*, deserves particular attention because it plainly represented a concerted effort on Beard's part to summarize all his views of historical interpretation and political theory in a single persuasive essay, in which both a theory of the state and of the historical process would be knit together. Like the other rebels against formalism, he argued that old modes of explanation were no longer usable: Darwinism had undermined natural rights, for example, as a fixed and an eternal scheme of things, by showing that all things change; science had undercut old-fashioned racial or providential explanations of politics. More and more, men were trying to devise precise notions about causation in politics. Political and legal institutions were beginning to be seen as products of the whole social process, not as consequences of some self-sustained process of abstract reasoning. Political man was no longer divorced from man in his other aspects. "We are coming to realize that a science dealing with man has no special field of data all to itself, but is rather merely a way of looking at the same thing—a view of a certain aspect of human action. The human being is not essentially different when he is depositing his ballot from what he is in the counting house or at the work bench. In place of a 'natural' man, an 'economic' man, a 'religious' man, or a 'political' man, we now observe the whole man participating in the work of government."[7] Political philosophy, far from being the product of pure reason, must be seen as the product of the political system. The state also must be described realistically: "It would seem that the real state is not the juristic state but is that group of persons able to work together effectively for the accomplishment of their joint aims, and overcome all opposition on the particular point at issue at a particular period of time."[8]

Beard's book on the Constitution, published five years later, would consistently take form as an attempt to locate and describe those dynamic groups which were successful in uniting and in overcoming opposition to the making of a new government in 1787–8. In this view the intellectual and traditional foundations of the Constitution would inevitably occupy a less important place in accounting for it than the plans and interests of its most active fabricators. This view of the state was linked in Beard's mind to the possibilities of Progressive reform and to his old complaint against *laissez faire*. The idea that government policies should conform to some kind of "natural" order had been made obsolete by the development of modern business, he argued, and one must take a pragmatic view of what government ought to do: "No student of politics today will attempt to lay down dogmatically what government in all times and places should undertake to do, for he realizes what the government does in practice depends not upon any theory about its proper functions, but upon the will of the group of persons actually in control at any one time or upon the equilibrium that is established through conflicts among groups seeking to control the government."[9] General prescriptions about policy are thrust aside. What is important is: Who has control and what do they want?

---

[7] *Politics* (1908), 6.
[8] Ibid., 20; cf. *An Economic Interpretation of the Constitution,* 10–13.
[9] *Politics,* 26.

III

Although the general drift of legal and political theory pointed toward Beard's book on the Constitution, its premises were not arrived at by any purely logical inference from general propositions. On many counts, the particulars of Beard's argument were anticipated by contemporaries whom in the main he generously acknowledged—so many particulars, in fact, that Beard's work, seen in historical context, seems more like a masterful summation of scattered insights and arguments than an altogether novel work. Beard's more immediate debt to his contemporaries may be set forth under four general headings: the Turner school, the Progressive critics of the Constitution, certain socialist writers, and finally the new school of sociological jurisprudence.

Turner's concern with economic forces and with plotting the geographic lines of political conflict had already led members of his school in the direction in which Beard was moving. Such exponents of regional and sectional analysis as W. A. Schaper and C. H. Ambler had done studies, well known to Beard, of internal sectionalism in South Carolina and Virginia. Beard, though he was never persuaded by Turner's stress on the West or by his praise of individualism, paid deference to Turner's influence by remarking that it had inspired "almost the only work in economic interpretation which has been done in the United States."[1] But the most immediately relevant

---

[1] W. A. Schaper, *Sectionalism and Representation in South Carolina* (1901); C. H. Ambler, *Sectionalism in Virginia from 1776 to 1861;* Beard, *An Economic Interpretation of the Constitution,* 5–6. Schaper, a Westerner, was actually a pupil of the Columbia sociologist Franklin H. Giddings, Ambler of both Turner and U. B. Phillips at Wisconsin.

Some years later, in a review of *The Frontier in American History* (*New Republic,* 25, 1921, 349–50), Beard saluted Turner's "immense and salutary" influence, but criticized his work on several counts: he thought that the emphasis on the West should not be permitted to overshadow "slavocracy, labor, and capitalism"; he doubted that the frontier was the line of the most rapid and effective Americanization, and that the West was as primary as Turner claimed in the development of national legislation or of democratic institutions. He charged Turner, like other "orthodox historians," with having all too little to say about the conflict between the capitalist and organized labor. The Great Depression left him more skeptical than ever about Turner's cordial treatment of frontier individualism, and in 1942 he concluded that in

work of the Turner school was a doctoral dissertation of 1894 out of Turner's Wisconsin seminar by Orin Grant Libby, *The Geographical Distribution of the Vote of the Thirteen States on the Federal Constitution, 1787–8.* Libby's work was plainly affected by current Populist controversy, by similar quarrels between debtors and creditors, and by the currency embroilments that had echoed and re-echoed through American history. Proposing that "a series of studies upon natural economic groupings in American history will be of service to the investigator who desires to understand political history in the light of social and economic forces," Turner commended Libby's work in a preface, in which he also observed that "the present Populistic agitation finds its stronghold in those western and southern regions whose social and economic conditions are in many respects strikingly like those existing in 1787 in the areas that opposed the ratification of the Constitution."

What Libby had done, in a paper which Beard regarded as "the most important single contribution to the interpretation of the movement for the Constitution," was to plot out the geographical distribution of the vote on ratification along lines which marked off an interior resistance movement based on the poor farmer and debtor class as against the pro-Constitution forces of the eastern seaboard. "The state system under the Articles of Confederation," Libby found, "served as a shield for the debtor classes," whereas "the Constitution was carried . . . by the influence of [the] classes along the great highways of commerce, . . . and in proportion as the material interests along these arteries of intercourse were advanced and strengthened, the Constitution was most readily received and most heartily supported." This division, he added, prefigured the later division between the followers of Hamilton and Jefferson.[2]

Among the more radical Progressive writers at least one of Beard's propositions, the antipopular aims of the Consti-

---

this way Turner had "set many historians to thinking that individualism had been the driving force in American civilization," charging that "wittingly or not, he fortified the teachings of Sumner in economics and sociology and of Burgess in political science." *The American Spirit* (1942), 363. See also p. 145 n. above and Beard's essay, "The Myth of Rugged Individualism," *Harper's Magazine,* 164 (1931), 13–22.

[2] Libby, *The Geographical Distribution,* vi–vii, 2, 49.

tution-makers of 1787, had become almost a commonplace. In 1907 J. Allen Smith, a professor of political economy at the University of Washington and a former exponent of radical monetary reforms, published a book, *The Spirit
of American Government,* which discussed at length the
philosophy behind the Constitution. Here Smith set forth the
clearest statement of what might be called the dualistic interpretation of American political thought. To him, American
political history could be described as a long running quarrel
between aristocracy and democracy, with the spirit of democracy embodied in the Declaration of Independence, and
that of aristocracy in the Constitution. His central chapter on
the framing of the Constitution was entitled "The Constitution a Reactionary Document." In it he concluded that the
democratic tendency prevailing at the time of the Revolution
had given way to a period of reaction, during which the Constitution was framed as an embodiment of the reactionary spirit.
The framers of the Constitution were not interested in achieving democracy—government of the people or directly responsible to them; on the contrary this was "the very thing they
wished to avoid." The primary difficulty of current Progressive
politics, Smith saw, was "that we are trying to make an undemocratic Constitution the vehicle of democratic rule."
Although he discussed at length the various devices—the
difficulty of amendment, the complex checks and balances,
and, above all, judicial review—by which the Constitution
was designed to frustrate democracy, Smith did not develop
an economic interpretation of its background. He was content to say that the members of the Federal Convention
"represented . . . the wealthy and conservative classes, and
had for the most part but little sympathy with the popular
theory of government," and to suggest, almost as an afterthought near the end of a long book, that the framers were
"fully alive to the fact that their economic advantages could
be retained only by maintaining their class ascendency in the
government. . . . The Constitution was in form a political
document, but its significance was mainly economic."[3]

---

[3] *The Spirit of American Government* (1907), 28, 29–30, 31, 32,
298–9; I have used the John Harvard Library edition, a photo-
duplicated version with a valuable introduction by Cushing
Strout. Beard's attitude toward Smith's book was curiously aloof,

Within a few years, Smith's book achieved a wide recognition, especially among the followers of Robert M. La Follette, and won a larger readership, as Cushing Strout has remarked, than Herbert Croly's *The Promise of American Life,* which has had much more attention from historians. Many years later, V. L. Parrington concluded that in historical terms, "perhaps the chief contribution of the Progressive movement to American political thought was its discovery of the essentially undemocratic nature of the federal constitution."[4]

Although the "undemocratic" character of the Constitution was a revelation to some Progressive thinkers, they were not in fact making a sharp break with their conservative predecessors. Indeed, the limited regard of the Founding Fathers for popular democracy *in the modern sense,* which is inescapable to anyone who reads any considerable portion of their writings, could hardly be ignored by a scholar. The real issue was what one might choose to make of it. During the long era of predominantly conservative politics from the close of the Civil War to the opening of the Progressive era, the facts of the matter were well known to conservative scholars and publicists. The respectable Mugwump intellectuals, the hard-currency men, the no-nonsense Republicans, the enlightened readers of Godkin's *Nation,* commonly considered that the Founding Fathers had tried to erect barriers against direct popular rule, and they applauded them for it. Smith himself drew heavily on the writings of J. B. McMaster, one of the most conservative of men, and McMaster himself was in a long line of Federalist historians. What the Progressive writers did was to take this staple argument of the conservatives and stand it on its head. Told that contemporary asser-

---

as though he did not want to be identified with Smith's impassioned view of the framers. His preface, which deals most generously with many other precursors, does not discuss Smith's book at all, and there is only one casual citation of Smith (p. 156) in the entire book on the Constitution. Beard had read Smith's book at the time of its publication and wrote a brief review of it, (*Political Science Quarterly,* 23 (1908), 136–7) which is wholly reportorial, containing not a single word of evaluation, agreement, or disagreement. Many years later Beard wrote a letter expressing his admiration for Smith, however. Strout, "Introduction," xlix–lv.

[4] In his Introduction to Smith's posthumously published *Growth and Decadence of Constitutional Government* (1930), xi.

tions of democracy were wrong because they violated the wisdom of the Fathers, the Progressives were now beginning to answer that the Fathers, and with them the Constitution, had been wrong because they tried to stand in the way of the march of democracy. But this argument rested on a distinct agreement as to what the Fathers had been up to. Both sides —with different ends in mind—were prepared to make the American public face up to the contradiction between its reverence for the Constitution and its passion for democracy.

The realism of the conservatives harks back, no doubt, to the hardy realism of the Founding Fathers themselves, and it is echoed at times in the political thought and the historiography of the nineteenth century, especially among writers of the Federalist-Whig-Republican tradition. In the early 1850's Richard Hildreth, writing in this tradition, had anticipated the broad outlines of Beard's argument. Later, a conventional writer like John Fiske did not hesitate to say in his famous book on *The Critical Period of American History* (1888) that "scarcely any" of the framers entertained "what we should now call extreme democratic views," though he was not interested in making a point of it. Woodrow Wilson, in his *Division and Reunion* (1893) put it sharply: "The federal government was not by intention a democratic government. In plan and structure it had been meant to check the sweep and power of popular majorities. . . . The government had, in fact, been originated and organized upon the initiative and primarily in the interest of the mercantile and wealthy classes. . . . It had been urged to adoption by a minority, under the concerted and aggressive leadership of able men representing a ruling class . . . a strong and intelligent class possessed of unity and informed by a conscious solidarity of material interest." William Graham Sumner, an arch-conservative who was never to be outdone in bluff realism, saw the whole course of American history as a conflict between the democratic spirit of the country and its inherited institutions, which were shaped by the legacy of aristocracy and the imperatives of industrialism. "The Constitution-makers," he asserted in an essay written in 1896 or 1897, "were under an especial dread of democracy, which they identified with the anarchism of the period of 1783–1787. They therefore established by the Con-

stitution a set of institutions which are restrictions of democracy." But since the whole genius of the country had been
democratic, "down through our history, ... the democratic
temper of the people has been at war with the Constitutional
institutions." Henry Jones Ford, in his remarkable interpretative work, *The Rise and Growth of American Politics* (1898)
entitled his chapter on the movement for the Constitution.
"The Conservative Reaction," his chapter on its structure "The
Restoration," and his chapter on its philosophy, "Class Rule."
"The constitutional history of the United States," he wrote,
"begins with the establishment of the government of the
masses by the classes."[5]

During the 1890's, as radicals made increasingly pointed
attacks upon the vested interests, this traditionalist conservative answer had been asserted with particular force. In discussing the mentality of the bench and bar in this period,
Arnold Paul has remarked on the tendency "of conservative
spokesmen, in their attempts to hold the line judicially against
majoritarian protest, to insist that the Constitution-makers
themselves were great anti-majoritarians and that to be true
to the Constitution, the judiciary had no alternative but to
apply anti-majoritarian interpretations." This was certainly
true of the single most provocative judicial decision of the
1890's, the case of *Pollock v. Farmers' Loan and Trust Co.*, in
which the Supreme Court invalidated a federal income tax.
Delivering the opinion of the Court, Chief Justice Fuller invoked the spirit of the Founding Fathers as evidence for his
interpretation of a key clause of the Constitution, inferring
that it was "manifestly designed . . . to prevent an attack upon
accumulated property by mere force of numbers." By the turn
of the century this perspective on the Founding Fathers was
hardly an obscure one. In one of the first of the modern textbooks on American political thought, Professor Charles E.
Merriam (himself no conservative), writing in 1903, incorporated it in a very matter-of-fact way. He laid down the
dualistic approach to the thought of the early national period,

---

[5] John Fiske, *The Critical Period* (ed., 1892), 226; Woodrow
Wilson, *Division and Reunion* (1893), 12–13; William Graham
Sumner, *Essays* II, 349–50 and 340–50 *passim;* Henry Jones Ford,
The Rise and Growth of American Politics (1898), 59, 61, 64, 71,
and *passim.*

much as it was to appear in Smith's book, and dealt with the
thought of the Constitution under the caption, "The Reactionary Movement."[6] The view of the ideas of the Fathers expressed by Smith and later to be repeated by Beard was thus
well on its way to becoming a textbook stereotype a full decade
before Beard's book—and was indeed incorporated, as we
shall see, into Beard's own textbook on government published
in 1910. This may help to explain why so few scholars actually
shared the sense of outrage provoked in other quarters by
Beard's argument.

IV

Though some Progressive writers were disposed to deal
with the Constitution as a philosophical dispute over political
theory without close regard to its economic aspects, the same
could not be said of the socialist writers who began to make
a mark on American thought at about the same time. Among
the works by contemporary socialists, Beard cited three that
he thought "deserve study": A. M. Simons's *Social Forces in
American History* (1911) and two books by the muckraker
Gustavus Myers, *History of the Great American Fortunes*
(1909) and *History of the Supreme Court* (1912). Simons, a
former pupil of Turner's who like Beard had taken his cues
from O. G. Libby and who had read J. Allen Smith, set forth
a view of the Constitution that reads like a caricature of
Beard's, couched in the language of vulgar Marxism. Though
Simons was Marxist enough to conclude that the "small ruling
class" that made the Constitution stood for progress because it
brought about a historically necessary unified government, he

---

[6] Arnold Paul, *Conservative Crisis and the Rule of Law: Attitudes
of Bar and Bench, 1887–1895* (1960), 199 n; cf. 28, 80–1, 100–1,
203–4. For Fuller see 157 U.S. 582–3, for Merriam, *American
Political Ideas* (1903), chapter iii.
   Although this view of the matter was becoming a commonplace, I do not mean to say that all Progressives shared it. Herbert
Croly thought the adoption of the Constitution the proudest triumph of American history, even though he was quite prepared to
admit that the Fathers, "in giving some effect to their distrust of
the democratic principle," were guilty of "a grave error," and
bequeathed "a grave misfortune" to the American state. *The
Promise of American Life* (1909), 33; cf. 31–8.

also used the moral accents of the Populists and Progressives: "The organic law of this nation was formulated in secret session by a body called into existence through a conspiratory trick, and was forced upon a disfranchised people by means of a dishonest apportionment in order that the interests of a small body of wealthy rulers might be served." Myers was content to say in his book on great American fortunes only that the Constitution "was so drafted as to take as much direct power from the people as the landed and trading interests dared," but he grew more explicit in the later work. He gave a great deal of attention to the economic interests of some of the Founding Fathers and their associates, made much of the secrecy in which the Constitution was drafted, as well as the superior power of the wealthy and educated classes to persuade. Unlike Beard, he put particular emphasis on great landholders, as opposed to creditors. "The Constitution," he wrote, "was a product of a convention composed mostly of manorial lords or their attorneys and mouthpieces," whose system pointed to a "continuation of the old rule by the great land owners and traders." The Founding Fathers were quite aware of their direct economic interest in the Constitution, and "made no pretense about it in the candor of their private circle. . . . Their acts reveal that the special interests they were furthering were those of a particular class, and that class their own."[7] After this high rhetorical ground had been occupied, Beard's work might well have been looked upon by those who had read Myers as a recession to a more genteel account of the events.

It is ironic that the work of restating and popularizing the economic interpretation of history for Americans and sounding its implications for the Progressive mind was taken up not by any socialist writer, but by Beard's Columbia colleague E. R. A. Seligman. A member of a New York banking family, a distinguished authority on taxation, and past president of the American Economic Association, Seligman was perhaps the ideal man to acquaint American scholars with a doctrine tainted by its association with Marx. In 1901 Selig-

---

[7] Simons, *Social Forces in American History* (1911), 99; Myers, *History of the Great American Fortunes,* 66; cf. 239–40; *History of the Supreme Court* (1912), 133, 92.

man began publishing in the *Political Science Quarterly* a
series of essays which he found to be in such wide demand
that he expanded them into a little book. *The Economic Interpretation of History* (1902) was, in the main, a sympathetic
exposition of this side of Marx's thought, based upon a wide
acquaintance with recent Continental literature on the subject. While emphasizing that Marx was not alone in having
seen the centrality of economic forces in historical development, Seligman not only gave him credit for the most fully
developed statement of the idea but also treated him with a
degree of respect that must have been refreshing to the young
insurgent scholars. "It is safe to say," he asserted, "that no
one can study Marx as he deserves to be studied—and, let us
add, as he has hitherto not been studied in England or in
America—without recognizing the fact that, perhaps with the
exception of Ricardo, there has been no more original, no
more powerful, and no more acute intellect in the entire history of economic science."[8]

The version of the economic interpretation that Seligman
was prepared to defend was the same version, amended and
clarified by Engels not very many years before in letters that
have become classics of the Marxist canon—that is, a version
purged of certain exaggerations and crudities that had sometimes crept into its earlier formulation. Attempting to clarify
his own (and Marx's) understanding of the idea, Engels had
been at pains to state that the economic force was not to be
regarded as the only causal agent in history, but that there
was a reciprocal interaction between political, legal, religious,
philosophical ideas and the economic foundation. In this
two-way process, the efficacy of these ideal forms was not denied, and it was only asserted that in "the last instance" the
decisive factor in history was the economic factor. Seligman's
own formulation of the thesis, cited by Beard and endorsed
with the remark that it "seems as nearly axiomatic as any
proposition in social science can be," is hardly more than a
transcript of Engels: "The existence of man depends upon his
ability to sustain himself; the economic life is therefore the
fundamental condition of all life. Since human life, however,
is the life of man in society, individual existence moves within

---

[8] *The Economic Interpretation of History* (1902), 56.

the framework of the social structure and is modified by it. What the conditions of maintenance are to the individual, the similar relations of production and consumption are to the community. To economic causes, therefore, must be traced in the last instance those transformations in the structure of society which themselves condition the relations of social classes and the various manifestations of social life."[9]

For one whose primary interest is in the development of the Progressive mind, however, a careful reading of Seligman's book will help to make evident the meaning of the economic interpretation of history to many Progressive thinkers: it satisfied at once their craving for "realism" and their desire for a doctrine of progress. What Seligman did in his book was to dissociate the economic interpretation of history from Marx's specific doctrines about the nature and inevitable fate of capitalism and from his single-minded commitment to the proletariat as the carrier of the future. In this way, Seligman was able to detach the economic interpretation from its socialist moorings and make it available to liberal historians for whom it became the counterpart in historical thinking of their pluralistic approach to the state. The connection between the economic interpretation of history and socialism, Seligman argued, was not intrinsic but more or less accidental—resting upon the fact that both had received their aptest formulation by the same man. But it is quite possible, he argued reasonably, to accept the economic interpretation of history, which is descriptive, without arriving at Marx's socialist conclusions, which are teleological and prescriptive. One may even accept the reality of the class struggle without concluding that its end is socialism, as long as one does not accept Marx's economics. In fact, he went on, one may say that a truly sophisticated empirical version of the economic interpretation of history, because it teaches that economic changes transform society by slow and gradual steps, makes the catastrophic and revolutionary aspects—i.e., the socialist aspects —of Marx's theories appear to be exceedingly naïve. The idea

9 Ibid., 64, 142, 3; cf. Beard, *Economic Interpretation*, 15n. Compare Engels's letters to J. Bloch (1890) and H. Starkenburg (1894) in Karl Marx and Friedrich Engels, *Correspondence: 1846–1895* (1935), 473–7, 516–18.

of a sudden revolutionary transition from private property and
private initiative to collective ownership seems then to fly in
the face of the lessons of history.[1]

What was appealing to Seligman—and, we may guess, to
many Progressives—about the economic interpretation of history was that it provided a doctrine of progress. And "progress," indeed, is a word that occurs over and over again in
Seligman's book. The liberal bourgeois version of the economic
interpretation of history seemed to promise that, with the increasing accumulation of capital and the increasing development of a social surplus over the bare needs of the population,
the material foundations would be laid for further social and
moral progress along lines then being advocated by many reformers. This doctrine, Seligman triumphantly asserted, does
not try to rule out the efficacy of moral forces in history but
"endeavors only to show that in the records of the past the
moral uplift of humanity has been closely connected with its
social and economic progress, and that the ethical ideals of
the community, which can alone bring about any lasting advance in civilization, have been erected on, and rendered possible by, the solid foundation of material prosperity."[2] Those
who are familiar with that strain of Progressive thought represented by Simon Patten and Walter Weyl, in which hopes for
the future were founded upon the availability of a social surplus, will readily appreciate the congeniality of this conception of history to the Progressive mind. The main contribution
of socialism to the liberal thought of the Progressive era came
through this urbane but somewhat denatured version of the
economic interpretation of history.

V

A final element that entered into the background of
Beard's book was the development of sociological jurisprudence, which was given particularly sharp relevance by the
current controversy over the role of the courts. Many thoughtful jurists had recently become aware of changes in the social

---

[1] Ibid., 24, 105–10.
[2] Ibid., 133–4.

foundations of law. The beginnings of this awareness in tne United States can probably be traced back as far as 1881 when Oliver Wendell Holmes published his *Common Law*. Holmes had been concerned to establish very clearly the difference, too much slurred over, between one's theories about what the law ought to be and the law as it actually existed. As it was the business of the practicing lawyer to advise his client what to do or not to do without moralizing but by trying to predict what in fact the courts would decide, so it was the business of the legal theorist or historian to concern himself with the actual historical forces that lay behind legal precepts and decisions. As legal thinkers became more and more aware of the changing social context of the law, affected by the problems of industry and urban life, Holmes's view of the matter gained ground. Thoughtful jurists were beginning to interpret the judicial process, and indeed all juristic events, in the light of the underlying social and psychological forces. Judges were no longer seen as sacrosanct figures incorporating the moral sense of the community into law, but rather as former corporation lawyers in black robes—men of flesh and blood making difficult decisions, and often making them against the public interest. "Public thought and feeling have changed," wrote Roscoe Pound in an article which Beard cited as a good sample of the new jurisprudence, "and, whatever the law in the books, the law in action has changed with them." "The history of juristic thought tells us nothing unless we know the social forces that lay behind it."[3]

This realistic, and at times iconoclastic, approach to the law had become linked in the minds of other critics with the demand for reform in the courts themselves, and these critics in turn raised some provocative questions about the Constitution. For a generation the courts had been in the habit of throwing out or crippling important social legislation, often on the grounds of its inconsistency with the Constitution. In the 1890's many people had been outraged when the Supreme Court invalidated a federal income tax law. Then in 1905 in *Lochner v. New York* the Court had struck down New York's ten-hour work law for bakers, and three years later in *Adair*

---

[3] Pound, "Law in Books and Law in Action," *American Law Review*, 44 (1910), 21, 34.

v. United States had done the same to a federal law penalizing employers who required that workers not join unions. At a time when reformers were frequently writing remedial laws into the books only to see them erased by judicial decisions, the intransigence of the state and federal courts took on the same passionately controversial character as it had in the days of the Alien and Sedition Acts or the Dred Scott case, and as it was to do again under the New Deal. Progressives were not usually disposed to think that property rights and social progress were wholly irreconcilable, but the courts were beginning to make them wonder. Inevitably, they began to look more closely into the nature of the judicial process, to conclude that the courts must no longer be regarded as sacrosanct, and to try to find ways of curbing their power. The boldest among them began to argue that constitutions themselves were not sacrosanct, that the making of a constitution was not a sacrament but a political act like other political acts. Since it was the work of thoroughly human men with all the human failings, there was less reason to resist changing it.

Theodore Roosevelt, returning to politics in 1910 with a refurbished radical public image, had demanded the popular recall of state judicial decisions. This proposal, which convinced some of his former friends that he had lost his mind, suggested to horrified conservatives that the wave of Progressive insurgency was now about to break over the last bulwark of property rights, the court system, and brought to a head the argument over judicial power. The air was filled with proposals, of varying degrees of radicalism, for limiting the power of the judiciary and bringing government closer to the popular will. Some writers, like J. Allen Smith, had already been harsh with the practice of judicial review of laws; the years from 1911 to 1914 saw the publication of many more such books—among them F. J. Goodnow's *Social Reform and the Constitution*, W. L. Ransom's *Majority Rule and the Judiciary*, Gustavus Myers's *History of the Supreme Court*, Brooks Adams's *The Theory of Social Revolutions*, and, not least, Beard's *The Supreme Court and the Constitution*.

Among the works by other writers, the one that must command our attention is Goodnow's; the only one that preceded Beard's, it was a study for which he had great regard.

Goodnow, some years Beard's senior on the Columbia faculty, had already made a distinguished reputation as a pioneer in administrative law. Although not a radical by temperament, he was troubled by the thought that twentieth-century United States was governed by eighteenth-century precepts, and hence was caught between a virtually unamendable Constitution and wholly unamenable judges. Thus far the Constitution in its present form had been a substantial bar "to the adoption of the most important social reform measures which have been made parts of the reform program of the most progressive peoples of the present days." He urged that in constitutional law judges should forsake general theories that were applied at all times and under all circumstances in favor of a more opportunistic spirit that gave heed to the pressure of social change. Such an opportunism would be consonant with the lessons that were being taught by the philosophical pragmatists. The impulse behind it had also been strengthened "by the theory of the economic interpretation of history which of recent years has been received with so much favor." Seeing constitutional law entirely subordinated to the demands of defenders of the status quo, and finding the United States almost alone among the modern nations in being denied the possibility of social change because of its judicial institutions, Goodnow was trying to find a way to persuade the courts to take a more liberal view of constitutional interpretation and to adopt a moderate, flexible doctrine of constitutional law that could be reconciled with progress.[4]

One historical issue that was raised very frequently was whether the Supreme Court had been intended by the Founding Fathers to have the power to declare acts of Congress unconstitutional or whether John Marshall had usurped this power when he first asserted it in *Marbury v. Madison*. Beard entered this debate in 1912 with his little book, *The Supreme Court and the Constitution*. What his original expectation was can be disputed. Many years later, when F.D.R.'s proposal for court reform was under debate, Raymond Moley, who had been a student of Beard's in 1915, remembered hearing that Beard had at first hoped to prove that the Court's power of

---

[4] *Social Reform and the Constitution* (1911), v, 3–6, 15–16, 333, 343, and *passim*.

judicial review was *not* planned by the Fathers—a view that
accords with Beard's Progressive sympathies in 1912 and his
admiration for T.R.—but that the historical evidence pushed
Beard to the opposite conclusion. Beard never confirmed
Moley's recollection, and in a brief introduction to the 1938
edition merely recorded his satisfaction that the book had
itself become a historical influence and added rather deceptively that "for practical purposes [it] settled the controversy."
One can only suggest that if Moley was right, and if Beard
had imagined in 1912 that the undemocratic features of judicial review had made the principle unpalatable to the Founding Fathers, he must have forgotten what he had read in J.
Allen Smith or what he himself had written only a few years
before. In the first edition (1910) of his college textbook,
American Government and Politics, Beard had gone on at considerable length about the impatience of the Fathers with unchecked popular rule, and indeed the very same passages now
seemed so appropriate that he used them again without
change in his new work.

At any rate, Beard's findings were clear enough: examining in detail the views of the twenty-five most active and
effective members of the Federal Convention, as well as some
other evidence, he concluded that the Founding Fathers had
indeed meant the Court to have the power to invalidate acts of
Congress. The problem was in fact somewhat more intricate,
the evidence considerably less clear than Beard thought, his
use of his sources more high-handed than he would ever
admit.[5] Even now the evidence does not yield an easy explanation, though the weight of most subsequent scholarship
rests with Beard's conclusions.

The immensely complex issue of judicial review cannot
detain us here. What is most pertinent is the chapter of
Beard's little book entitled "The Spirit of the Constitution,"
because it casts such an unexpected light on the book on the
Constitution which was to appear only a year afterward. In
this chapter Beard, very much in the manner of J. Allen

---

[5] See, for example, Westin's Introduction to the 1962 edition; also
E. S. Corwin's original review, *American Political Science Review,*
7, 329–31 and the same author's book, *Court over Constitution*
(1938), chapter i; also Louis B. Boudin, *Government by Judiciary*
(1932), I, 568–83 and *passim.*

Smith, reviews the fundamentally conservative climate of opinion in which the Constitution was framed. But what arrests our attention, particularly in the light of shrill accusations later levied against Beard—that in 1913 he was merely trying to discredit the Founding Fathers—is the very positive terms in which, in 1912, he portrayed their aims, motives, capacities, and frame of mind. It is true that at one point he declared that the groups behind the Constitution had grown "more and more determined to reconstruct the political system in such a fashion as to make it subserve their permanent interests." But he refrained from suggesting that there was anything reprehensible about this; he even wrote in other passages about this defense of their permanent interests in terms that should have been palatable to his most conservative readers. The Constitution-makers, he said, represented "the solid, conservative, commercial and financial interests of the country," who had been "made desperate by the imbecilities of the Confederation." It was they who stood for "strength and efficiency in government." Their opponents, who stood for its "popular aspects," and who numbered among themselves some radicals who were suspicious of all government, had "pushed to the extreme limits" certain doctrines of individual rights inherited from England. "Anyone who reads the economic history of the time," he asserted with all apparent sympathy, "will see why the solid conservative interests of the country were weary of talk about the 'rights of the people' and bent upon establishing firm guarantees for the rights of property." The members of the federal convention had all had "a practical training in politics." Washington had learned well the lessons of war and mastered difficult problems of administration, the two Morrises had distinguished themselves in grappling with financial problems of unsurpassed difficulty, seven delegates had "gained wisdom" as governors of their native states, and twenty-eight had served in Congress. With their combined training in law, finance, administration, and political philosophy, the Fathers "were equal to the great task of constructing a national system strong enough to defend the country on land and sea, pay every dollar of the lawful debt, and afford sufficient guarantees to the rights of private property." One could hardly surpass this summation: "It is not merely patriotic pride that compels one to assert that never in the history of assemblies has there been a convention of men richer in political experience and in practical knowledge, or endowed with a profounder insight into the springs of human action and the intimate essence of government. It is indeed an astounding fact that at one time so many men skilled in statecraft could be found on the very frontiers of civilization among a population numbering about four million whites. It is no less a cause for admiration that their instrument of government should have survived the trials and crises of a century that saw the wreck of more than a score of paper constitutions."[6]

These words of praise, originally written in 1910 for Beard's textbook in American government, and incorporated without a single word of revision two years later in his book on judicial power, may give pause to those who think that *An Economic Interpretation of the Constitution* was written in the spirit of muckraking, and in that spirit alone. Was it possible that in asserting and then reasserting, for a different and more scholarly audience, these sentiments about the Founding Fathers, Beard was only writing with tongue in cheek? Or must we conclude that there were some decisive ambiguities in the book on the Constitution, arising from a genuine ambivalence in its author, and that it was a somewhat more complex piece of communication than it is usually taken to be?

---

6 *The Supreme Court and the Constitution*, Spectrum Books ed. (1962), 85–92. The greater part of pages 86 to 96 of this work were reprinted, with acknowledgment, from the 1910 edition of *American Government and Politics*, 34–35, 42–49; these passages were retained, unchanged, in the revised edition of this book (1914), which was done after *An Economic Interpretation of the Constitution* was published.

CHAPTER 6

The Constitution as an Economic Document

*In short, it was a war between business
and populism.*
—Charles A. Beard, 1912

*With justification they looked upon the
outcome as the triumph of reason over force
. . . the power of the people to govern themselves on a continental scale by peaceful constitutional processes.*
—Charles A. and Mary R. Beard, 1944

I

An Economic Interpretation of the Constitution begins with
a brief chapter which tells us what the book is against.
It does not question the morals of the Founding Fathers or the
merits of the Constitution as a framework of government;
rather it attacks certain types of historical interpretation.
When one considers this chapter against the intellectual background of the era, it suddenly becomes clear what Beard believed he was doing: he was trying to write a kind of history
that the adult mind could respect. The critical intelligentsia
had arrived on the scene, too secular to take seriously the old
providential explanations of events, too worldly and too free
of chauvinism to believe in past notions about special racial
aptitudes for self-government, too demanding to think that
the claims of science could be met by the "impartial" presentation of naked facts, too realistic to be content with such
abstractions as the juristic theory of the state. The word "abstract" keeps recurring when Beard is telling us what he dislikes; and when he tells what he stands for, we read of
"explanation" and "significance"—two of Turner's favorite
words—but above all of "the critical spirit," "critical interpretation," and "critical analysis." If we are to try to catch in

207

a phrase or two the enduring essence of Beard's contribution
to the study of American history—that which remains when
all the valid criticisms of his work have been taken into account—it is that, along with Turner, he did most to put his
fellow historians not merely to the retelling of stories but to
the study of problems; and that, even more than Turner, he
tried to insure that the problems would be studied in an eminently critical way.

Having stated his rejection of the naïve providential interpretations of a Bancroft, the racism of the Teutonic school,
and the narrow empiricism of the anti-interpretative historians, Beard goes on to acknowledge his affiliations with the
Turner school, especially its receptivity to economic interpretation, and with the intellectual realism of sociological jurisprudence. But above all he reaches back to one of the Founding
Fathers to establish a traditional base for his argument: "The
inquiry which follows," he writes, "is based upon the political
science of James Madison"; and, quoting Madison's formulation of his views in Number 10 of *The Federalist,* he endorses
it as "a masterly statement of the theory of economic determinism in politics." Beard's own version then follows: "Different degrees and kinds of property inevitably exist in modern
society; party doctrines and 'principles' originate in the sentiments and views which the possession of various kinds of
property creates in the minds of the possessors; class and
group divisions based on property lie at the basis of modern
government; and politics and constitutional law are inevitably
a reflex of these contending interests."[1]

With the argument thus posed, Beard surveys economic
and social interests as they stood in 1787, traces the movement for the Constitution to those interests most adversely
affected under the Articles of Confederation, and gives a short
account of limitations on the right to vote. The movement for
the Constitution he attributes to those interests concerned to
see the government control a revenue sufficient to pay the in-

---

[1] *An Economic Interpretation,* 15–16. It was in fact one of the
achievements of Beard's book to discover the importance of *The
Federalist* Number 10, which had hitherto not received much
discussion. See Douglass Adair, "The Tenth Federalist Revisited,"
William and Mary Quarterly, 8 (1951), 48–67.

terest and principal of the public debt, to those seeking commercial regulations advantageous to shippers, manufacturers, and speculators in public lands, and to those seeking to prohibit the state legislatures from resorting to paper money or to acts interfering with the obligations of contracts. Then comes a long chapter, taking up more than a fourth of the whole, tracing the economic interests and holdings of the members of the Federal Convention and giving special attention to their public securities about which Beard had uncovered much new evidence in dusty old Treasury Department records, hitherto unused. We learn that a majority of the framers were lawyers and most came from towns on or near the coast, that not one was drawn from the small farming or mechanic class, and that the overwhelming majority, "at least five-sixths," were directly and personally interested in the outcome of their labors, being economic beneficiaries of the adoption of the Constitution. We learn that forty of the fifty-five who attended had public securities, twenty-four of them in amounts over $5,000, and that fourteen had personalty invested in lands for speculation, twenty-four had money loaned at interest, eleven were investors in mercantile, manufacturing, or shipping businesses, and fifteen were owners of slaves.

After Beard explains the economic implications of the Constitution, he briefly surveys the political doctrines of the framers, stressing their suspicions of majority rule and their "frank recognition of class rights." In the four closing chapters he reviews the fight over ratification in the several states, attempting to establish an economic demarcation between the friends and foes of the Constitution—a "deep-seated conflict" between "a conservative party centered in the towns and resting on financial, mercantile, and personal property interests generally" and "a popular party based on paper money and agrarian interests."[2]

The basic findings of Beard's book, to adapt his own summary of his conclusions, were as follows: the movement for the Constitution was organized by the upper classes whose

---

[2] *An Economic Interpretation*, 292.

investments had been unfavorably affected under the Articles of Confederation—namely, those with money on loan, owners of public securities, and those interested in trade, shipping, or the development of manufactures. Men with a direct personal stake in the outcome of the event initiated the move for a new Constitution, and the members of the Philadelphia Convention that framed it were, with few exceptions, directly and personally interested in economic advantages anticipated from the new system. Similar interests pushed the new Constitution through the state ratifying conventions. The Constitution, as shown both by its provisions and by the explicit statements of its advocates in the Philadelphia Convention in defense of property, "was essentially an economic document based upon the concept that the fundamental private rights of property are anterior to government and morally beyond the reach of popular majorities." Moreover, the process by which the Constitution was adopted was far from democratic: no popular vote was taken on the proposal to hold a Constitutional Convention in 1787; a "large propertyless mass," being altogether unrepresented under prevailing suffrage restrictions, was excluded from a voice in framing the Constitution; and in its ratification by the states about three-fourths of the adult males failed to vote either because of their ignorance or indifference to the issue or their disfranchisement by property qualifications. The Constitution was ratified by a vote of probably not more than one sixth of the adult males, and even then it is doubtful that a majority of the voters who did participate in five of the thirteen states actually approved ratification of the Constitution. The ratification contest aligned on one side substantial personalty interests—i.e., holders of liquid capital— against realty interests, the small farmers and debtors, on the other. The Constitution was thus not created by the "whole people," which was a fiction of the jurists; nor by the states, which was a fiction of Southern nullifiers; but was "the work of a consolidated group whose interests knew no state boundaries and were truly national in their scope."[3]

---

[3] Ibid., 324–5. In counterposing "personalty"—an awkward term —to realty, Beard was adopting old legal language. But by personalty it was clear that he meant liquid capital available for investment.

So much has been said about the substance of the argument in Beard's book that we may be in danger of forgetting that it was an innovation in form, in American experience a new historical genre. It was not a narrative history; the narrative detail was stripped to the bare minimum necessary to remind the reader of the essential facts. It was not tricked out with any of the side effects used by popular historians to provide color or "human interest." It was a scholarly monograph, austere and astringent in form. The monograph, of course, was by now a familiar product of professional scholarship. But Beard's book, probably the first truly exciting monograph in the history of American historiography, achieved its excitement solely through the force and provocation of its argument.

It represented a significant departure too because of its systematic procedure, though here it probably owed much to the efforts of the Turner school to answer general questions by the systematic ordering of historical materials. This side of the book is best illustrated by its long central chapter surveying the holdings and interests of the members of the Philadelphia Convention and thus placing them in the tissue of their economic society. This technique of collective biography —the idea of taking the entire personnel associated with an event or grouped in a parliamentary body at a given moment and of examining their relevant characteristics as a way of shedding light on the social situation they refract—was a method of great potentialities. Even when one admits that Beard's particular execution of it was far from sound, one can see that he anticipated by a full generation both the career-line studies of modern sociologists and the basic idea of "structural history" that has come to be associated with the name of Sir Lewis Namier. This technique is both promising and dangerous: promising because it offers a way of disciplining impressionistic insights by the orderly marshaling of evidence; dangerous because its results, being susceptible to statistical statement, and having a delusive appearance of definiteness and finality, can cause the historian who makes a single important interpretative oversight to build his error firmly into the structure of a whole system of interpretation.

It is also of some consequence here that a kind of anti-intellectualism—a disposition to downgrade or ignore the significance
of ideas—has been charged against both Namier and Beard.

II

Only a few scholars were shocked by Beard's book—after
all, so much of what he had to say had been said before—and
its academic reception was on the whole quite favorable. But
many outside the academy were outraged. A committee of
the New York Bar Association summoned Beard to appear
before it, and took his refusal, he said, as "contempt of court."
Former President William H. Taft denounced the book in
public and suggested to one of his correspondents that Beard
would have been more satisfied by the Constitution if it had
been drafted by "dead beats, out-at-the-elbows demagogues,
and cranks who never had any money." "Filthy lies and rotten
perversions . . . libelous, vicious, and damnable in its influence," was the verdict of Warren G. Harding's paper, the
Marion *Star*, which ran a story on it under the headline:
"SCAVENGERS, HYENA-LIKE, DESECRATE THE GRAVES
OF THE DEAD PATRIOTS WE REVERE." Justice Holmes,
whose famous thrust, "The Fourteenth Amendment does not
enact Mr. Herbert Spencer's *Social Statics*," was cited with
gratitude in Beard's opening chapter, took occasion years
afterward to tell the author that he had not become exercised
about the book "but had supposed that it was intended to
throw light on the nature of the Constitution, and, in his opinion, did so in fact." Holmes's letters, however, suggest that
he thought it threw a deep shadow on the Constitution. In
1916 he had written to Sir Frederick Pollock that one needed
no such evidence as Beard's to believe that the framers "belonged to the well-to-do classes and had the views of their
class. The writer disclaims the imputation of self-seeking
motives yet deems it important to constate all the facts. Except for a covert sneer I can't see anything in it so far." Years
later, after further reflection, he still thought the book a
"rather ignoble though most painstaking investigation of the
investments of the leaders, even if disclaimed. . . . Belittling

arguments always have a force of their own, but you and I believe that high-mindedness is not impossible to man." Holmes also wrote disparagingly of the book in 1916 to Harold Laski, and a dozen years later repeated that it was a "humbug": "I thought Beard's book on that theme a stinker, for all its patient research. For notwithstanding the disavowal of personal innuendo, it encouraged and I suspect was meant to encourage the notion that personal interests on the part of the prominent members of the Convention accounted for the attitude they took." Laski's response to Holmes has its funny side, especially when we recall his essay in the *New Republic*'s symposium of 1938 on *Books That Changed Our Minds*, in which Laski reported that the works of Beard and Parrington had "opened windows for me into the significance of the American tradition as no other books since Tocqueville." In 1916, replying to Holmes's strictures, Laski had written: "I found the book dull, and the considerations a little thin, but I liked his honesty and his serious attention to the documents. And it was a relief to get away from the revelation granted by God to Alexander Hamilton early in 1787."[4]

What shocked or irritated many readers was the most novel of Beard's findings: his emphasis on the holdings of the Founding Fathers in public securities, and the insinuation that their interest in the new frame of government arose in good part out of their expectation that these securities would be worth more under a stronger national system. Was Beard simply trying to say that the Founding Fathers were trying to line their own pockets? Or only that they saw public issues as they did because they had certain kinds of interests? Was he casting a crude muckraker's imputation on their motives,

---

[4] On the reception of the book, see Beard, ibid, viii–ix; Robert E. Brown, *Charles Beard and the Constitution* (1955), 3ff.; Eric Goldman, "The Origins of Beard's *Economic Interpretation of the Constitution*," *Journal of the History of Ideas*, 13 (April, 1952), 244–5. On Holmes and Laski, see *Holmes-Pollock Letters* (1941), I, 237; II, 223 and *Holmes-Laski Letters* (1953), I, 45; II, 1109.
    Beard cherished a certain understandable resentment about the public reception of his book. Writing in 1917 to Arthur M. Schlesinger about the latter's forthcoming dissertation, he warned: "Don't say a word in title or text about economic interpretation or aspects. It's a red rag to the historical bull. It just gives the mob a chance to yell and to peel you. I know from experience. Fools who never read it will damn it." Beard to Schlesinger, May 14, 1917, Schlesinger memoir, Columbia Oral History Project, 294.

or was he trying to offer an economic and sociological account of their ideas?

The book can be read either way, though in the long run it was only the latter interpretation that Beard himself was willing to defend. In the 1935 edition he denied that he had accused the members of the Federal Convention of "working merely for their own pockets." He pointed to a passage in which he said: "The purpose of such an inquiry is not, of course, to show that the Constitution was made for the personal benefit of the members of the Convention. Far from it. . . . The only point considered here is: 'Did they represent distinct groups whose economic interests they understood and felt in concrete, definite form through their own personal experience with identical property rights, or were they working merely under the guidance of abstract principles of political science?' " This is rather cagily put: one might imagine that the alternatives need not be so drastic and that there were additional issues. But it does *seem* to disavow the crudest interpretation of Beard's data. There was another passage of the original text which Beard might also have cited, had he chosen, but which he may have thought embarrassingly equivocal. In closing his long chapter on the economic interests of members of the Convention, he remarks:[5] "It cannot be said, therefore, that the members of the Convention were 'disinterested.' On the contrary, we are forced to accept the profoundly significant conclusion that they knew through their personal experiences in economic affairs the precise results which the new government that they were setting up was designed to attain. As a group of doctrinaires, like the Frankfort assembly of 1848, they would have failed miserably; but as practical men they were able to build the new government upon the only foundations which could be stable: fundamental economic interests." Thus, while the Fathers cannot be praised for their disinterestedness, they can be praised for their practicality, which is seen, unless Beard was writing with tongue in cheek, as being not merely a private but a civic virtue.

No doubt it would be unfair to foist upon Beard a cruder version of his thesis than he was prepared to defend, or to over-

---

5 *An Economic Interpretation*, 73, 151.

look his disavowals and qualifications. But it is still true that
a reader, even a careful reader, might come away with a contrary or at least a mixed impression of what Beard was trying
to say, and it was not altogether arbitrary of Holmes to find
"a covert sneer" in the work. Beard said clearly, at least once,
that he did not see the Fathers as working for their personal
benefit. But it is only a slight promotion of their motives if we
are asked to think of them as working single-mindedly for the
interests of the groups to which they belonged. What conclusion are we to draw when Beard asks us, even in the preface
to the 1935 edition, to turn our attention to the question:
"What interests are behind [theories] and *to whose advantage*
will changes or the maintenance of old forms accrue?"; or
when he suggests in the original text that it is not theories of
justice or the general welfare that are behind changes but
that in certain cases "the direct, impelling motive . . . was the
economic advantages which the beneficiaries expected would
accrue *to themselves first* from their action"; or when he tells
us that he is trying to discover which classes and social groups,
"from the nature of their property, might have expected *to
benefit immediately and definitely* by the overthrow of the old
system and the establishment of the new"; or when he observes that "the amount gained by public security holders
through the adoption of the new system was roughly equivalent to the value of all the lands as listed for taxation in Connecticut"; or when he reminds us that "some of the leading
men outside of the Convention who labored for an overthrow
of the old system were also *directly interested* in the results of
their labors"; or when he summarizes his account of the economic interests of the members of the Federal Convention by
saying that "at least five-sixths" of them "were *immediately,
directly, and personally interested* in the outcome of their
labors at Philadelphia, and were in a greater or lesser extent
economic beneficiaries from the adoption of the Constitution";
or when he concludes that the Constitution "was an economic
document drawn with superb skill by *men whose property interests were immediately at stake*; and as such it appealed *directly and unerringly* to identical interests in the country at
large"; or when, analyzing the vote on the Constitution, he
finds its advocates to be "for the most part, men of the same

practical type [as the members of the Convention] with *actual economic advantages at stake"*; or when he describes the movement for the Constitution as having been launched by "a small and active group of men *immediately interested through their personal possessions* in the outcome of their labors"; or when he once again describes the members of the Convention as "with a few exceptions, *immediately, directly, and personally interested in"* and deriving "economic advantages" from the establishment of the Constitution, and says of the advocates of ratification in the various states that "in large numbers of instances they were also *directly and personally interested* in the outcome of their efforts"?[6]

The book, then, is a document that can be read quite legitimately in two ways: either as an attempt to replace an abstract and rarefied version of the origins of constitutional ideas with an account founded upon economic and sociological realism, or as a crude essay in economic determinism which seeks to reduce statecraft to motives of personal gain (or of class gain so interwoven with personal gain that the distinction loses importance), and in so doing to cast discredit on the Fathers. Are we to accept Beard's one explicit disavowal, or to follow the many contrary passages interspersed through his text? My own conclusion is that we need do neither, but should recognize that the ambiguity in Beard's book was, whatever his conscious strategy, a product of an ambivalence in his mind and temperament. On one side there was Beard the reformer, the moralist, the rebel against authority, the young Beard of Oxford, the Beard who all his days loved the gadfly's role, who was influenced not only by the Progressive hunger for "reality" but also by the iconoclasm, even to a degree the cynicism, of the muckraking milieu, and who in his eagerness to puncture older ways of historical thought could easily stray into a rather crude economic reductionism. On the other side was the Beard of Knightstown, reared in solid Republicanism, himself strongly driven to achievement, a man who admired mastery and control, a scholar disciplined and inhibited by the ideal of scientific history, an American patriot who did indeed revere the practical genius of the Founding

---

6 Ibid., xvii, 17–18, 19, 37, 55, 149, 188, 291, 324–5; all italics are mine.

Fathers and who, in the light of all they accomplished, did not feel that the self-serving side of their work was an unforgivable flaw or that it should be taken to discredit their statecraft.[7]

This ambivalence is in itself not startling, nor was it singular in Beard. Among Beard's contemporaries it can be seen, for example, in the naturalistic writers who condemned the dog-eat-dog morality of the competitive world and yet succumbed to admiration for the mastery of the survivors. One finds it in Jack London's entire career; it colors all of Dreiser's treatment of his tycoon in *The Titan*. At another level it can be seen in the work of a muckraker like Lincoln Steffens, who in his autobiography reported the high regard in which he came to hold the city bosses at the very time he was interviewing them for his muckraking essays on their evil works; and it can be seen in another way in Ida Tarbell, whose devastating book on Standard Oil was followed not long after by works extolling big business leaders. It can be seen, oddly enough, in the Socialist press, whose analyses of capitalism were sandwiched between advertisements for success techniques or for get-rich-quick investments.

Even in his capacity as a reformer, Beard might well have felt the pull of contrary impulses. True, to persuade men to look at the Constitution with less reverence might release social criticism and lower the barriers to reform. Yet many Progressive thinkers (Croly was the best example) were becoming increasingly convinced of the need of a strong, active national state to further their own ends, and accordingly were becoming more critical of the Jeffersonian heritage of weak government and decentralization, more amenable to the Hamiltonian regard for power. One could thus look back on the making of a strong national state, even if somewhat tainted by the immediate personal interests of its founders, as a valuable historical legacy; and in this light the performance of the Fathers was not a thing to be quarreled with. The only thing, in fact, to be quarreled with was just what Beard had at-

---

[7] On the element of the Federalist historian in Charles A. Beard, see Robert E. Thomas, "A Reappraisal of Beard's *An Economic Interpretation of the Constitution of the United States*," *American Historical Review*, 57 (January, 1952), 370–5.

tacked in his opening chapter: historical interpretations too
remote from the real world to take account of the impact of
economic events. What Beard left, then, was a book ambiguous
enough to be read, to his great advantage, in different ways
by different readers. Scholars interested in the problems of historiographical and juridical interpretation could read it one
way, ardent Progressives or Marxists another; and, as Beard
later took a certain ironic relish in pointing out,[8] it could even
be cited, and indeed was, by a conservative judge of the Supreme Court to justify opposition to a new piece of social
legislation. Like many central works of its kind, it was a
plastic object, susceptible to a certain manipulation in the
minds of its audience.

III

The influence of Beard's book seems in retrospect singularly long-lived for a work so controversial and, as it has
proved, so vulnerable. It first took root in the Progressive era
because it was suited to the spirit of protest and the hope for
reform; but it lost none of its appeal to intellectuals and historians in the twenties, an era of pessimism, alienation, and
popular debunking, when it could still be read with complete
sympathy. It is pertinent that Charles Warren's lengthy and
rather awkward book, *The Making of the Constitution*, which
appeared in 1928 and contained the first serious and extended
criticism of some of Beard's ideas, had hardly any impact at
all. Beard's view of the Constitution, at the same time, received
a still wider circulation through the immense popularity of
his and his wife's *The Rise of American Civilization* and
through its use in Parrington's *Main Currents in American
Thought*. The Great Depression and the renewed social struggles of the New Deal era only created a still more receptive
climate of opinion for it. In his Introduction to the 1935 edition, Beard found it necessary to correct himself only on certain points of detail, and looked back on its reception with an

---

8 *An Economic Interpretation*, viii. Beard was probably referring
to Mr. Justice Sutherland's opinion in *Home Building and Loan
Association v. Blaisdell*, 290 U.S. 458–9 (1933).

obvious sense of satisfaction. He insisted that the book had never been intended as a comprehensive history of the making of the Constitution, that its emphasis was clear in advance to its readers, and that he had "simply sought to bring back into the mental picture of the Constitution those realistic features of economic conflict, stress, and strain, which my masters had, for some reason, left out of it or thrust far into the background as incidental rather than fundamental." He insisted too upon the supposed moral neutrality of the book: "No words of condemnation are pronounced upon the men enlisted upon either side of the great controversy. . . . Are the security holders who sought to collect principal and interest through the formation of a stronger government to be treated as guilty of impropriety or praised? That is a question to which the following inquiry is not addressed. An answer to that question belongs to moralists and philosophers, not to students of history as such."

This remark may seem disingenuous: Beard must have known how easy it would be in the political climate of the 1930's for embattled liberals to answer this question; he must have been aware that if you picture a set of men as framing a new government in secret by an illegal process and as reaping personal gains from its acceptance, you do not need to pour on the vinegar of indignant rhetoric to achieve a certain acid flavor. Two years later, when the American Historical Association observed the sesquicentennial anniversary of the Constitution, Beard reiterated his conviction that efforts to deal with the ideas behind the Constitution without reference to the interests involved would be unreal. "I have never said and do not now say that economic considerations determine or explain all history," he asserted, but there are elements of determinism in history, and some of the most important of these are economic forces. In treating such an event as the making of the Constitution by "the persistent association of ideas and interests . . . do we not put men and women on guard against treating their own ideas as having the dogmatic force of divine revelation? Do we not aid mankind in emancipating itself from the idolatry of symbolism that is the essence of government by sheer force?" Beard closed by suggesting that this approach to ideas would "soften the bitterness of conflict and open wide the door for understanding, mediation and adjustment by the use of intelligence."[9]

The notion that Beard's view of the Constitution would somehow be a social emollient might have come as something of a surprise to his auditors; but they could hardly have been surprised by his other reaffirmations. His view of historical interpretation, and of the Constitution in particular, was then at the peak of its influence. A survey of college textbooks in 1936 showed that his thesis, perhaps on occasion slightly modified, had been incorporated by the overwhelming majority of his peers among professional historians, and had become a kind of textbook orthodoxy. In 1938, when a considerable number of intellectuals were queried by the editors of the *New Republic* for its symposium on "Books That Changed Our Minds," Beard's name ranked second only to Veblen's (and ahead of Dewey's and Freud's) among thinkers acknowledged with gratitude, and the two titles most often mentioned by the respondents were *The Theory of the Leisure Class* and *An Economic Interpretation of the Constitution.*

It is a curious fact—one which neither Beard's critics nor his defenders have been eager to acknowledge—that even before the tide finally began to turn against Beard's interpretation, Beard himself had expressed, albeit gently and rather indirectly, some significant misgivings. By the 1940's his opposition to involvement in the Second World War, his increasing awareness of the threat of militarism, his intensified nationalism and growing concern with maintaining the separate integrity of American institutions, seems at last to have refashioned his view of the Constitution itself. Against the background of fascism and the events of the war, America—particularly the older America—looked increasingly attractive. At the same time, the emergence of totalitarianism had made Beard more skeptical of the economic interpretation of history.[1] In 1943, as the war raged, Beard produced a popular

---

9 Ibid., vii–x; Conyers Read, ed., *The Constitution Reconsidered* (1938), 164–6. It is not literally true that the book pronounces no moral judgments. See, for example, the curious innuendo, 227–8; or the verdict that the procedure in Pennsylvania reflected "unseemly haste."

1 See the 1945 edition of his *The Economic Basis of Politics*, chapter v, especially 103–14.

treatise on the American system, *The Republic,* in the form of a series of dramatized "conversations on fundamentals." Now the struggle of interests and classes seemed somewhat less important to Beard than it had in the Progressive era, the necessity of preserving constitutionalism more important. *The Republic* reflected his essential satisfaction with the American form of constitutionalism, which he characterized in appealing terms as "the civilian way of living together in the Republic." The Constitution's effectuality in preventing undue concentration of political power or domination over civilian power by the military now seemed more important to him than it had before, and in his characteristic way he found it possible to read back this assessment of the matter into the days of the Founding Fathers. "Leaders among the framers of the Constitution," he said, "regarded the resort to Constitutional government instead of a military dictatorship as their greatest triumph. In my opinion they were entitled to view their achievement that way." So much evidence had accumulated in his files, he said, of a movement for a military dictatorship during the Confederation period, that he had come to take a "somewhat different view of the Constitution." "One of the interpretations *now generally held,*" he said rather archly, was that the Constitution was "the outcome of a conflict between radical or agrarian forces on the one side and the forces of conservatism or capitalistic reaction on the other." Such a conflict was in fact taking place, but there were three parties, not two, to the struggle—"an influential group on the extreme right of the conservatives" was prepared to resort to the sword and set up a dictatorship, and such an effort, he had no doubt, would have been made had the Constitution failed.[2] For his readers this new view of the matter had the effect of pushing the Founding Fathers from the far right into the center of the political spectrum, and, what is more, of making the adoption of the Constitution much less a victory of capitalism or "personalty" over agrarianism or the debtor classes than a victory of moderate conservative republicanism over military dictator-

---

[2] *The Republic,* 20, 22–6; italics mine. "I sometimes think," Beard wrote in this work (316), "that politics is more of a determining force in history than economics."

ship—an appealing theme in 1943 when a world war was being waged against military dictatorship.

That the evidence of a movement for dictatorship which accumulated in Beard's files does not, in retrospect, seem overwhelmingly impressive, is not of great consequence. What is important is that to some considerable degree he had quietly recanted—and perhaps it is too much to expect a more vigorous and articulate recantation of views that had been inseparable from his reputation for thirty years. In 1944, when Charles and Mary Beard brought out a new popular history, their *Basic History of the United States*, the curious might have taken the measure of Beard's discomfort by comparing the *Basic History* with *The Rise of American Civilization*. In the earlier book the chapter on the Constitution had been entitled "Populism and Reaction"; in the later one it was "Constitutional Government for the United States." In the first, the purpose of the Founding Fathers was "dissolving the energy of the democratic majority"; in the second the system of checks and balances was said to prevent "the accumulation of despotic power in any hands, even in the hands of the people who had the right to vote in elections." The first reproduced Beard's original emphasis on the property holdings of the framers; the second described the men of the Convention simply as a conservative body of merchants, lawyers, and planters, but omitted all reference to public security holdings. Gone from the later work is the account of the economic division over the Constitution; it is replaced only by general labels —"radicals" and "friends of liberty" versus "able defenders." Gone too is the closing exposition of Madison's supposed economic interpretation of politics; it is replaced by the observation that "without drawing the sword in civil war, without shedding a drop of blood, a new plan of government had been proposed, framed, discussed, and adopted."[3] *Je ne suis pas Beardiste!*

In the more conservative postwar intellectual atmosphere

---

[3] I have dealt somewhat more fully with Beard's later retreat from his view of the Constitution in "Beard and the Constitution," already cited, though I neglected there to take note of what I suppose to be his last utterance on the subject, his Introduction to *The Enduring Federalist* (1948); see esp., 28–9. On Beard's changing views see also the essay by Howard K. Beale in *Charles A. Beard*, 115–59.

new critics of Beard's original thesis arose who, not content with his indirect and partial reconsiderations, insisted upon a more direct confrontation with his earlier views, and whose critiques won a much more receptive audience than Charles Warren's neglected work of 1928. Rumblings were evident during the first half-dozen years after the war. Philip Crowl's account of Maryland showed a pattern of behavior on the constitutional issue almost antithetic to Beard's analysis. Similar doubts emerged from William Pool's study of ratification in North Carolina and from Robert Thomas's comparison of the Federalist and Anti-Federalist delegates at the Virginia convention, and Richard McCormick's examination of New Jersey. Beard's version of intellectual history was also reargued. In 1951, Douglass Adair re-examined the political thought of Madison, particularly the Tenth *Federalist* from which Beard had professed to derive the theoretical basis of his work, and emerged with a wholly different view of that document. Four years later, Cecelia Kenyon, in a brilliant study of Anti-Federalist political thought, found the opposition to the Constitution far less geared to democratic premises than one might have expected from Beard's analysis, and struck a sharp blow at that dualistic interpretation of the period upon which Beard's book rested.[4]

But the most telling blows came in 1956 and 1958 in two books given entirely to refuting Beard. The first, Robert E. Brown's *Charles Beard and the Constitution*, is a strange work. Keyed chapter by chapter to the organization of Beard's book, and linked with it step by step in an intimate and lethal *pas de deux*, it argues almost every proposition doggedly and censoriously, for Brown is convinced that Beard tampered with the evidence. One puts it down with the feeling of having lived through an obsessive pursuit, but it is a telling and important book, whose appearance guaranteed that the Beardian view could never again enjoy an unchallenged position. In the second critique, Forrest McDonald's *We the People,* the author went about his work differently: he tried to draw, on the basis of much more detailed researches than Beard's, an alternative portrait of economic interests and their place in the

---

[4] For references to the critical literature on the book see the Bibliographical Essay.

constitutional controversy, a significantly different picture
more closely geared to the workaday world of the 1780's and
to the varied conditions in the states, less fashioned by ideological simplification. In its own way McDonald's is also an
economic interpretation of the Constitution, but his view of
economic realities is at odds with Beard's at point after point.
In the language of the political scientists, McDonald's pluralistic version of the constitutional struggle is Bentleyan (and,
in this sense, Madisonian), where Beard's is in the dualistic
tradition of the Populists, the Progressives, and J. Allen Smith.
Where Beard had presented, at bottom, two opposing coalitions, business and populism, personalty and realty, creditors
and debtors, McDonald emerges with a complex, often overwhelming, variety of political factions and economic groups,
a society cross-hatched with a densely woven tissue of conflicting issues and motives whose residuum is not at all
easy to trace. McDonald finds Beard's picture of the economic
realities of the Confederation period all wrong, and has re-
painted it entirely, using much finer brush strokes and showing a much keener sense for the variety of detail. However,
his palette retains the same somber quality, and he is on one
count closer to Beard than he cares to admit: he apparently
agrees that the making of the Constitution will conform to a
severely economic interpretation, once we have got our economics right. In his most recent book on the period, *E Pluribus
Unum* (1965), he shares with the most animated Progressive
critics of the Constitution the conception that the safest guide
to the Constitutional era is a spirit of smart cynicism, and dis-
tinguishes himself from them only in employing that spirit
not just against the Constitution-makers but against their opponents as well.

IV

The criticisms leveled against Beard's book over the past
two decades are bewildering in their variety, and in their
totality quite formidable. Is there still any point in discussing
his views today, when we know that at the end Beard himself, however quietly and indirectly, abandoned much of his

central thesis, and that even those recent scholars who are
sometimes called neo-Beardians have been careful to put a
certain distance between themselves and Beard?[5] Indeed I
think there is. Beard's own retreat was not wholly articulate.
His interpretations, even some of his data, have been repeatedly argued with, but his critics neglect to account for
the mode of thought that led to them and that made them
plausible for thirty years and more. What is valid and important in the work of his critics has not yet been fully sifted
through, and there are many things that are still to be learned
about the era of the Confederation and Constitution. Moreover, no alternative history of the Constitution has achieved a
comparable intellectual influence. Louis Hartz has suggested
that "Beard somehow stays alive" because, "as in the case of
Marx, you merely demonstrate your subservience to a thinker
when you spend your time trying to disprove him."[6] And this
is Beard's most enduring triumph: he no longer persuades,
but he still sets the terms of the debate, even for those who
are least persuaded.

It has become customary for historians to say simply that
Beard "overstated" or "exaggerated" his case—a formula
which is true enough but which I find unsatisfactory. As
Turner also knew, a certain measure of exaggeration, especially among writers who have a new and heterodox thesis,
is almost a necessity of interpretative historical argumentation,
but I think Beard went far beyond it. The essential question
is whether Beard, by compounding one exaggeration upon another and then presenting the whole result from a skewed
angle of vision, did not leave us with a major distortion, a

---

[5] For example, Jackson T. Main finds a social alignment over the
Constitution that puts him "closer to Beard than to his detractors," but also observes: "Beard can no longer be accepted without serious reservations." *The Anti-Federalists* (1961), 294. E.
James Ferguson, whose learned account of American public
finance from 1776 to 1790 is sometimes called neo-Beardian, gives
but small comfort to Beard's admirers, since he considers the
whole question whether public creditors supported the Constitution a "distortion," even though he finds creditors heavily in its
favor. *The Power of the Purse* (1961), 337–8, 340, 341. "I have
always thought," he writes elsewhere, "that Beard's attempt to
divide the aristocracy at this time according to real and personalty interests was untenable." *William and Mary Quarterly,*
19 (1962), 436; cf. 434.
[6] *The Liberal Tradition in America* (1955), 28.

fundamental misconception of the way in which history
works and power is exercised. Certain positive accomplish-
ments should not be denied. Beard rescued constitutional
scholarship from the atmosphere of mythology and turned it
toward a search, however miscarried in his own case, for the
social and economic sources of the controversy, harking back
in this respect to the Fathers' spirit of cool realism. He bravely
attempted to apply new and more systematic methods to answering the questions he posed. And on two fundamental
counts I believe that he was, for all his difficulty in applying
and controlling his insights, basically right: first, in his sense
that the American society of the 1780's was in fact run by an
elite, or a set of elites, which in a political milieu dominated
by apathy and inertia, took charge of events and framed and
established the Constitution; and second, in his awareness of
the difference between the interests and values of agrarian
society and the cosmopolitan trading classes of the towns, of
the active and dynamic role played by the latter classes in
making the Constitution. His understanding that, as one
moves upward in the scale of wealth and power one finds a
progressively stronger commitment to the Constitution,
though significantly exaggerated, has survived the assaults of
his critics.

And yet—I here introduce and epitomize criticisms that
will occupy us for many pages—there were, aside from a great
many particulars and nuances that altogether are more than
negligible, certain fundamentals upon which Beard went seriously wrong. The first was in giving a central place in his
book and in his whole argument to the holdings of the framers
in public securities. This stratagem—brought about partly by
his sheer delight in having unearthed unused Treasury records but also, I suspect, by a penchant for sly historical muckraking—not only gives these holdings an unduly prominent
place in the story but, more unfortunately, gives the whole
affair an aura of the sinister and the conspiratorial. The
second was in portraying American society as being not
merely divided in its view of the Constitution by wealth and
social position but indeed sharply polarized between, as he
put it, the forces of business and those of populism. Such a
tension did exist in a marked degree in a few of the states

and to some degree in all of them. But to concentrate on it seems to me to divert our attention from what is most significant about the period—and that is its sheer complexity, the variety and specificity of the situations in the separate states, the complex jumble of factions and interests, and above all the presence of a large and heavily populated middle ground occupied neither by rich aristocrats nor poor, debt-ridden, populistic farmers, but by the substantial American middle class, urban and rural. The same is also true of political commitments: Beard's picture of a polarized, wrangling political public leaves out the large numbers of men who were not quite sure what to think of the Constitution, those who changed their minds, those who were not "bitterly" opposed but just moderately skeptical, those who promptly and quietly accepted the outcome; and thus it obscures the gray shadings of the constitutional argument leaving us wholly unprepared for its quick disappearance.

Of more general character are two other difficulties in the work: a lack of clarity about its political theory and its moral stance. Beard's book, after all, is not simply a tight little work of specialized scholarship; it deals with fundamental problems in the evolution of modern democracy. And while it seems to be asserting with considerable vigor a contention about the relationship of the federal Constitution to the democratic forces at work in America in the 1780's, it is inarticulate about the framework of judgment within which this contention is set forth. We are not told what the author means by democracy, either in a twentieth- or eighteenth-century context; nor are we told what we can expect in the way of democratic ideas and procedures at the end of the eighteenth century, or precisely by what standards the theory behind the Constitution or the methods by which it was framed and ratified ought to be judged.[7]

Second, there is a confusion about the role of the historian in his moral capacity, one that troubled Beard throughout his career. I have already suggested that from an early date he had a divided mind about the role of the historian. On one hand, he believed that history ought to be an instrument of social criticism and social progress; on the other, that

---

[7] On these matters see below, Chapter 7.

the historian or political scientist should be governed by the
ideal of scientific detachment and stay clear of moral judgments.[8] Later Beard made some attempt to find a philosophical
position that would resolve this problem, but in 1913 he had
hardly begun to come to terms with it. Here his indecisiveness
about the historian's role was reinforced by his ambivalence
about the Founding Fathers themselves: he was torn between
his unfeigned admiration for their competence, their intellectual realism, their commanding statecraft, and his disposition
to find them high-handed, antipopular, and self-seeking.
Rather than try to resolve this moral ambiguity by putting his
opposed feelings into balance and arriving at some manifest,
tempered standard of moral judgment, Beard was content to
play two roles at once: he could openly praise the Fathers for
their insight and practicality and yet at the same time condemn them, in the main by innuendo, by the "covert sneer"
that Holmes objected to. When Beard said in 1935 that he
had pronounced "no words of condemnation" on the Constitution-makers and that his volume was "strictly speaking, impartial" because it applied "no moralistic epithets to either
party,"[9] he seems to have been wrong in a double sense: this
statement provides a poor description of what he had in fact
done and a questionable conception of what a historian ought
to do. Surely his book communicates a great deal more than
it says. As I have suggested, when one describes men as
thwarting popular majorities while they lined their own
pockets, one does not have to use moralistic epithets to know
that such an account will automatically carry condemnation
in an age of democratic dissent like the Progressive era, or in
any age of aggressive iconoclasm, or social radicalism.

Moreover, Beard did not always keep his guard up. When
he remarked, in discussing Elbridge Gerry's economic interests, that "'barefaced selfishness' was not monopolized by

---

[8] "I wholly agree," Beard had written in 1908, "with my former
teacher and friend, the late Professor Frederick York Powell, 'that
it is not the historian's duty to try to estimate the exact degree
of damnation that should be meted out' . . . I hold that it is not
the function of the student of politics to praise or condemn institutions or theories, but to understand and expound them; and
thus for scientific purposes it is separated from theology, ethics,
and patriotism." *Politics*, 14.
[9] *An Economic Interpretation*, ix–x.

Gerry in the Convention," we get a sudden glimpse of the moral animus that at most points is carefully held in check. But what one should dissent from, I hope it will be clear, is not that the moral animus is there, only that an effort is made to suppress or conceal it. Fundamental questions of constitutional order and stability, of human rights and liberties, of acceptable political procedures, of democratic development, or private gain in places of public service, are questions charged with moral import, and there is no reason why the historian any more than the citizen at large should force himself into a posture of moral neutrality about them. He need not be, indeed ought not to be, merely a dispenser of "moralistic epithets" or a public prosecutor, nor need he necessarily presume to settle the moral questions at issue, but he will do well at least to remember that in his choice and arrangement of facts he is establishing the estimations of reality upon which well-considered moral judgments are based. For example, Beard in an astonishingly casual footnote, states: "The ethics of redeeming the debt at face value is not here considered although the present writer believes that the success of the national government could not have been secured under any other policy than that pursued by Hamilton."[1] Now an interpretative judgment like this is not exactly a moral judgment, but it plainly provides a necessary part of the structural frame within which moral judgments are set. If one makes the premise that, from the standpoint of the common well-being, a firmer national government was necessary and also that Hamilton's way of funding its debt was essential to its success, then one's view of any moral deficiencies that attached to the funding process will be of a wholly different order than if one starts with the opposite premise. Thus, while the historian does not have to set himself up as a moralizer, he is constantly dealing with the substantive setting within which moral judgments are made, constantly trying to provide a sense of the requirements and limitations of social situations, of the effects that actions and decisions have had upon large numbers of people. And while questions about men's intentions and motives have a certain interest in their own right, they are less important

---

[1] On Gerry see ibid., 98 n; on redeeming the debt, 35 n.

than questions about the range of possibilities actually open to historical agents and about the effects of their behavior.

And here Beard's stress on public securities and the motives of the framers was particularly unfortunate. First, in looking at the Constitution against the problems of the Progressive era more than those of the colonial and Revolutionary periods, he rendered himself insensitive to the nuances of language and thought and institutional arrangements by which motives themselves could be correctly seen, and started a long, fruitless, and misleading discussion of the purposes of the Fathers. Still more important, by putting rather too much stress on the question of motives, interesting though it is, he shifted historical attention from what was more vital still: the consequences, intended or otherwise, of what was done. He thus missed the profoundly illuminating historical interplay between what was intended and what was actually achieved.[2]

V

What is valid in Beard's perceptions can be saved if they are put into their proper proportion, and this can best be done by *beginning* with an alternative view of the Constitution and feeding his categories back into the story where they become relevant and only in so far as they seem necessary. Here I

---

[2] There is a splendid passage in one of Engels's clarifications of historical materialism that is appropriate here: "History makes itself in such a way that the final result always arises from conflicts between many individual wills, of which each again has been made what it is by a host of particular conditions of life. Thus there are innumerable intersecting forces, an infinite series of parallelograms of forces which give rise to one resultant—the historical event. This again may itself be viewed as the product of a power which, taken as a whole, works *unconsciously* and without volition. For what each individual wills is obstructed by everyone else, and what emerges is something that no one willed. Thus past history proceeds in the manner of a natural process and is also subject to the same laws of movement. But from the fact that individual wills—of which each desires what he is impelled to by his physical constitution and external, in the last resort economic, circumstances (either his own personal circumstances or those of society in general)—do not attain what they want, but are merged into a collective mean, a common resultant, it must not be concluded that their value = 0. On the contrary, each contributes to the resultant and is to this degree involved in it." Marx and Engels, *Correspondence*, 476–7.

must start from some distressingly old-fashioned premises about the era—premises rather like those Beard himself came to in the end. To me it seems that the central issue of American politics in 1787 was not whether government should protect property—a question over which "radicals" and "conservatives" agreed; nor whether it should advance the interests of personalty as against realty—a question which no historian today takes very seriously; nor how and by whom the public debt should be paid—a question of importance, but not the central one in 1787; nor whether the new government should be more or less democratic than the existing one—a somewhat misleading question into whose reality I will shortly probe. The central issue, around which the others circled like dim and distant satellites, was whether the American union should become a national state. And after the Constitution was framed and ready for discussion, this issue was complicated by a second one: whether the particular national state now proposed would be more likely to destroy or to protect the liberties and the powers of self-government that most Americans thought they had long enjoyed and had just fought a war to keep.

It may be necessary to put ourselves in mind again of the extent to which we can say that the Americans did *not* have a nation under the Articles of Confederation. What they had was what the Articles in fact asserted the Confederation to be: "a firm league of friendship," a loose union, providing mutual citizenship, and giving the central government a bare minimum of the sanctions needed to carry out national functions: the conduct of foreign relations and the power to make treaties or wage war; machinery for settling disputes among the states; the right to regulate the value of coin issued by itself and by the several states; the privilege of asking for money from the states—but not the power to get it; and rather little besides. Since there was no executive power to speak of, there was no center of national leadership. Since there was no power to impose a tariff or regulate commerce, or tax the citizens directly or levy troops, the fiscal and military power of the Confederation and its power to negotiate with other nations were badly crippled. At home its theoretical power to regulate coinage could not resolve a monetary hodge-podge.

To make matters worse—and this point proved in the end to
be quite decisive—constitutional terms requiring the unanimous consent of the states made the Confederation virtually
unamendable, and thus deprived it of an essential mechanism
for self-preservation.

Some of the states were coping quite effectively with their
own affairs. The Confederation did well in moderating disputes between them and even better in laying the foundations
for future Western settlement. But the diplomatic impotence
of the Confederation cast a dark shadow over prospects for
the future, and Americans were not by any means free of
involvement in the European state system. The British still
held seven fortified posts on American soil, embracing every
strategic point on the Great Lakes, from the region of the St.
Lawrence to Lake Michigan, and in this area they were still
effectively and ominously linked with the Indian tribes. In
Vermont they were intriguing with potential American separatists and threatening to bite off a chunk of territory. On the
seas, though they enjoyed access to American markets, they
had shut the Americans out of the rich trade, so vital in the
past, to the West Indies. In the South the Spaniards, also
allied with Indians whom they supplied with arms, held the
mouth of the Mississippi, which they had closed to American
shipping, were busy encouraging Westerners in Kentucky and
Tennessee to quit the Union, and laid claim to a large piece
of American territory in what is now Georgia and Alabama.
They also shut American ships out of the Spanish trade,
which had become important during the Revolutionary War,
and offered to reopen it only on terms which the Americans
in the South and Southwest could not possibly accept—the
continued closure of the Mississippi for twenty-five years or
more.

The American states, after some ups and downs, were
again beginning to enjoy moderate prosperity in the year or
so before the Constitution went into effect, and it is con-
ceivable that they might have gone on for some years more
under the Confederation. But many contemporaries were
afraid that the "imbecilities" of the Confederation, to use
Beard's word, might be fatal to the Union, to order and prosperity, and in the end to liberty. A few were troubled by the

supposed dangers of a monarchical restoration or a military dictatorship, but many seem to have been troubled by the more real danger that the Union would be supplanted by two or three smaller and more tightly organized Confederacies— a prospect that suggested, in modern terms, that the continent would be Balkanized, that its states might enter internecine quarrels, that they might be forced indefinitely to carry on their commerce under extortionate or crippling conditions, and perhaps at last fall victim to reconquest by European powers. The most immediate danger that hung over the Confederation was that of an internal collapse from a sheer failure of morale. Congressmen, disheartened by their continuing ineffectuality, ran up a remarkable record of sporadic attendance, and at last this problem became so acute that for extended periods Congress could not act for lack of a quorum. In January 1786 chairman David Ramsay (who was acting in that capacity because President John Hancock himself had not bothered to show up) sent out a desperate appeal to the state executives in which he said that the delinquency of the states in maintaining representation "naturally tends to annihilate our Confederation. That once dissolved, our States would be of short duration. Anarchy or intestine wars would follow till some future Caesar seized our Liberties, or we would be the sport of European politics, and perhaps parcelled out as appendages to their several Governments."[3]

With this picture in mind, we need not be surprised that many men, even including some who later found grounds to oppose the Constitution, favored a move toward some kind of stronger Union. And if a patriot like Beard, looking back from the relatively detached vantage point of the Progressive era, could still see "imbecilities" in the Confederation (a term also used by Edmund Randolph in the Convention), we need not imagine that a patriot of 1787 had to have a stack of continental securities to come to the same conclusion. Concern about the future of the country was widespread, and it is bootless to try to decide exactly how far it can be called an economic concern, since thoughts of personal gain and loss were mingled with thoughts of the common peace and safety and of the common advantage. But it is also true—and here

---

[3] E. C. Burnett, *The Continental Congress* (1941), 641.

we move into areas where Beard's categories begin to make contact with reality—that the exposure of various segments of the population to these concerns was far from uniform. It should be possible to construct a hypothetical model, taking account of the various forces that impelled men to favor or oppose the Constitution, in which some of Beard's perceptions will have a place, even though not the central place.

The first point to be remembered is that the Americans of 1787 had strong provincial loyalties and thought of themselves as citizens of this or that state as well as having certain occupations and interests. They considered themselves to be members of independent polities, and in these polities most of the forces that normally maintain a political community— including the habit of reckoning common public interests across the barriers of class—were at work. When men thought about civic events, they thought not simply about the state of their own accounts but of the state of New Jersey or Georgia, and often the two were intertwined. Men who lived in such states as Connecticut, Georgia, Delaware, Maryland, and New Jersey did not divide very decisively over the Constitution at all, and within them such differences as we may find between farmers or merchants, debtors or creditors, were not of central consequence. This is not to say that these states had no class divisions or political conflicts, but simply that such conflicts were not deeply or seriously mobilized *by the constitutional issue,* because men on all sides found so much common gain in stronger union. Connecticut and New Jersey, each lacking a suitable port, were at the mercy of the port of New York, and could see large advantages in a strong union that would put the power to regulate commerce in the central government. Delaware, altogether too tiny to go it alone, was similarly dependent upon Maryland and Pennsylvania. The case of Maryland, racked by a political schism in its planter aristocracy, is more complex, and will not yield to quick simplification; but it had only a small if vociferous minority opposed to the Constitution on grounds quite unlike those depicted by Beard. Georgia, as Beard knew, was so haunted by fear of an Indian war that nothing mattered there as against the military advantages of a strong union. In all these states ratification came quickly and easily: it was unanimous in Georgia, New Jersey, and Delaware (despite their over-whelmingly agrarian composition), and went through by mar-gins of three to one in Connecticut and six to one in Maryland.

Setting aside these state-by-state considerations, and try-ing to draw a composite and rather abstract picture of the forces at work for and against the Constitution, we would do well to begin not with the Revolutionary war debt but with the whole Revolutionary experience. An important determining force might be the extent to which men and regions had ex-perienced the Revolution in local terms or in terms of the larger world. Those who had had major political experience in Congress or in foreign capitals and had witnessed the im-potence of Congress during and after the Revolutionary strug-gle, or those who were drawn into political activity for the first time by their sense of the political failure of the Con-federation would be more disposed than firmly rooted local politicians to feel the need of a stronger union. Those whose military experience had been in the Continental line rather than the state militias, and who had marched from state to state and experienced the struggle against British "tyranny" as a continental, common American struggle would be simi-larly disposed. Having come, too, to look with disdain on the state militias as disorderly irregulars and on-and-off patriots, the Continental veterans were sometimes given, in the manner of the recently demobilized, to interpreting civic life in the light of their military experiences. For them, strength and order were at a high premium. Those who lived in areas long occupied or devastated by British forces felt more keenly the necessity of a stronger union; and this, as well as urban and commercial economic interests, may help to explain the higher concentration of Federalists near the seaboard and at certain exposed points of the frontier. Age too is a factor worth ex-ploration. Men who were young enough to have come of age around 1775 when the agitations of a dozen years finally irrupted into open violence found the challenge of organiza-tion and power that came with the Revolutionary War prac-tically coincident with their adult political experience; whereas those who came of age during or before the agitations against British tyranny that quickened after 1763 had had their minds fixed at a formative age more upon the dangers of arbi-

trary governmental power and would be harder to dislodge
from the combative and militant anticentralist republicanism
that the Revolution called into being.

Resistance to the Constitution might well be strongest
among some of the isolates, those remote from military action,
living in relatively self-sufficing agricultural areas but not
endangered by Indians; or among those who had fought only
in the state militias, which sometimes meant sporadic action
to protect local points of vantage. Above all, those who had a
great deal of experience and vested emotional as well as practical interests in state politics and state offices frequently
looked with jealousy upon the creation of a new arena of
federal power, in which they had little interest and no experience, but which threatened to overshadow their local worlds
in prestige and importance and to remove decisions of state
that had long been in their hands. Opponents of the Constitution, in the aggregate, seem to have attracted a higher proportion of those involved only in state politics; advocates of
the Constitution had to draw more heavily in some areas
upon newly concerned amateurs, men from business and the
professions not previously active in politics but now mobilized
by their desire for union. It is also to be remembered that in
some cases the antagonisms of state factions and of leading
personalities, which had their origins in intrastate concerns
quite irrelevant to the merits or defects of the Constitution,
became involved in the argument over its ratification.

But it is at this point that the considerations raised by
Beard must be counted. Beyond doubt the movement for the
Constitution got much of its driving force, perhaps a decisive
measure, from the commercial classes. It was hardly accidental that the first impetus for a stronger central government
came only after Robert Morris, the financier of the Revolution, had repeatedly failed to put the Union on a sound revenue basis. The mercantile class was as close as any to being
unanimous for the Constitution—though we should not fail
to add that it was joined in this (as Beard saw) by its de-
pendents in the towns, the seamen, artisans, mechanics, and
small tradesmen who lived in the orbit of commerce, and (as
Beard did not see) that it was allied to many ordinary farmers
who seem to have recognized that they too had an interest in

trade. When one realizes that in a society in which the Revolutionary debt loomed so large, any merchant of substance and of cosmopolitan interests was likely to hold some public paper, one realizes that support for the Constitution by many public creditors was a function of their mercantile position, not of their concern about their security holdings. If Beard had had detailed information on the commercial experiences and interests of political leaders which was as novel and intriguing, as "hard" and statistically manageable as his evidence from the Treasury records, he might have put much stronger stress on the general interests and experiences of the mercantile classes and less on the public debt. It is often noted that many influential men on the Anti-Federalist side also had large security holdings. However, we need not be surprised that the possession of *large, significant amounts*[4] does have some positive relation to Federalist adherence. E. J. Ferguson considers it "indisputable that as a group the creditors supported the Constitution," and never finds them represented "in a formal statement or petition that did not endorse stronger central government." But he too thinks that to emphasize the question whether creditors on the whole supported the Constitution "constitutes a distortion," and finds the security holders "rather too few in number to serve as the fulcrum upon which to raise a new political structure. To assume that they fathered it, we must suppose them possessed of a degree of power and influence with which they can scarcely be credited. . . . A creditor interest certainly existed—yet it was no more than ancillary to the political development that culminated in the founding of the new government."[5]

---

[4] One of the difficulties in discussing the political role of public creditors is that both Beard and some of his critics count men as security holders without paying attention to the size of holdings in relation to their total business investments, though it is obvious that small holdings would be unlikely to sway political allegiances. See on this count Robert L. Schuyler's "Forrest McDonald's Critique of the Beard Thesis," *Journal of Southern History*, 27 (1961) 73–80, esp. 77–9.

[5] *The Power of the Purse*, 337–8, 340, 285, 341. It is, I believe, debatable whether substantial security-holders were too few in number to be immensely powerful. For example, Ferguson found (278) that in Pennsylvania, where a large portion of the debt was held, there were 434 persons who had more than $1,000 of the public debt. In a small polity, the power of "influentials" in this number could be very great if united. What seems to me more

VI

One of the important misconceptions of Beard's book, derived from the free silver controversies of the 1890's, inherited from the Turnerians, but shared equally by the Progressive and conservative historians of his day, was the notion that the economic situation of the 1780's, insofar as paper money and debts were involved, was quite simply analogous to that of the 1890's. This conception led to the stereotype, embodied in Turner's and Libby's work and taken over by Beard, of the poor debtor-farmers locked in more or less uniform combat from Massachusetts to Georgia in a campaign for cheap money and higher prices against rich merchants, great planters, speculators, and creditors, whose attitudes on such matters were taken to have been rather like those of Wall Street confronted by William Jennings Bryan. Hence, for

decisive is that the security holders were demonstrably *not united* in this capacity. They had many other concerns to take account of; and in states like Pennsylvania, New York, New Jersey, and Maryland, public creditors could not even be sure whether the new government would in fact appreciate their holdings, and therefore had no certain incentive to base their efforts on this issue.

Several writers, beginning with E. S. Corwin in a review of the book published in the *History Teacher's Magazine*, 5 (1914), 65–6, have pointed out that Beard had records of public security holdings only as of 1790. How can we be sure, these critics have asked, that the framers were in any way responding to the possibility of profit from these holdings in 1787, if we do not know that they then had them? Beard himself took note of this problem in a curious footnote (75) in which he remarked that any members of the Philadelphia Convention who bought public paper between the time of the Convention and 1790 would have been speculating, and (a covert sneer here) "it is hardly to be supposed that many of them would sink to the level of mere speculators." Anyway, any of them who actually did so "must have had idle capital seeking investment"! If Beard was only trying to use the public securities of the framers as an index of their general economic position, this latter contention will stand. But if he is trying to tell us that a great majority of them were "immediately, directly, and personally interested in the outcome of their labors at Philadelphia" (149), Corwin's objection raises a real problem for him, which is here only sloughed off with a joke. I am disposed to think with Beard, though for different reasons, that his inability to establish holdings in 1787 as against 1790 is not important. But this footnote reveals once again his failure to think through just what it was that he was trying to conclude from ownership of these securities. On this issue see also *Economic Origins of Jeffersonian Democracy* (1915), 106 n.

Beard, the Constitution, with its prohibitions against money issues by the states and against the impairment of contracts, took on significance primarily as a bulwark against the "populism" of the 1780's. He accordingly pictured a largely unified *national* elite of wealth lined up against the clamorous agrarian masses, the two sides ranged against each other in good part by their opposing interests and convictions about the state of prices and debts, and the putative effects of the Constitution upon them.

More recent writers, among them Richard Lester, E. J. Ferguson, Bray Hammond, and Joseph Dorfman, have done much to correct this view of things. We do not know all we need to know about debts and credits in the late eighteenth century, but certain complications have been at least partially clarified. Despite some unfortunate episodes in the use of paper money, including one in Rhode Island about which historians have written very dramatically, several of the states had had a good deal of success in ameliorating their chronic currency shortages with paper money issues based upon land security. Paper money was indeed controversial, but it was controversial *within* the elites. The leading advocates of paper money in the eighteenth century were not backwoods farmers or doctrinaire demagogues but substantial merchants, leading planters, public officials, and professional men. Debt was characteristically a sign not of poverty but of enterprise, sometimes of daring speculation. There were plenty of rich debtors and solvent farmers.

Ranged against paper money advocates, and intensely prejudiced against what they called "the paper system" in all its forms, were not only some well-to-do merchants and creditors who had suffered from unsuccessful and highly inflationary paper issues but also a great many doctrinaire agrarians like James Madison, Thomas Jefferson, Thomas Paine, and even John Adams. The use of paper money to depreciate debts was widely decried by Anti-Federalist as well as Federalist writers. Anti-Federalist forces were probably too divided in opinion on this issue in most states to take a strong stand on it; and among the many proposed changes in the Constitution, amendments to the paper-money and obligation-of-contracts clauses are conspicuous by their absence. Some

speculators, especially in Maryland and Virginia, had, in effect, financed their speculations by going short, as we would
now say, on public paper, and the prospect of its rapid appreciation in value threatened them with ruin.

Indeed, when one looks at the situation from state to
state, one is impressed by the difficulty of making nationwide
generalizations about the character of economic alignments
as they affected the constitutional issue. The situation in
Massachusetts, in the wake of Shays's rebellion, bears some
resemblance (though not a perfect one) to Beard's picture;
but the situation in Maryland, where the relatively weak resistance was based largely upon a minority of rich planters
who had gone heavily into debt because of speculation, is
quite close to its opposite. On one point we may be reasonably
clear: the Beardian picture of a unified national elite aligned
against a relatively unified, if politically less effective, agrarian debtor mass, simply will not hold in a state-by-state analysis. What we find instead is a series of divided state elites;
and insofar as the attitudes of the agrarian masses can be
rather loosely inferred from the pattern of their representatives' votes,[6] they were divided also.

The situations in the several states are much too complex to lend themselves readily to brief characterization, but
one generalization that will hold better than most is that in
those states where there was a fairly even or at least a sharply
fought division over the Constitution the state elites were
themselves divided. And it will generally be found true that
both elite factions had more than negligible support from the
ranks of the ordinary farmers. Virginia makes an interesting
study. Long ago Robert E. Thomas found, in a study of the personnel of the ratifying convention at Richmond that the
Federalist and Anti-Federalist leaders were members of the
same class, with almost the same average number of slaves
and roughly the same military ranks attained in the Revolution. The slight difference that he found showed the typical
Anti-Federalist to own a larger number of slaves and to repre-

---

[6] We know a great deal about the social and economic position of
the delegates at the ratifying conventions, much less about their
constituencies. Lee Benson has rightly warned against assuming
that public assemblies are simply the electorate in microcosm.
Turner and Beard, 172.

sent counties in which there were more slaves than in those represented by Federalists. With property holdings of all kinds on both sides virtually identical, and with the Virginia elite, for a variety of reasons, split quite evenly, the balance for ratification, as Freeman Hart's work indicates, was swung by representatives of the smaller planters and non-slaveholding farmers from the Shenandoah Valley (14–0 for the Constitution) and the Trans-Allegheny region (13–1). These delegates were sent by a region where debtors (as elsewhere in the state) were common. They wholly violate the pattern of expectation set up by the Turner-Beard categories, and they were acting in accordance with considerations not always taken into account by historians in this tradition. These two western regions of the state were strong in immigrants who did not have the powerful provincial attachments that prevailed among the old planting families. Their representatives were strong in men who had fought in the Continental line. They were eager to see the British get out of the northwestern posts, and would have considered it a good trade to get a national government that could win this end at the cost of getting some of the planters to pay their repudiated debts to British merchants. Their trade routes ran interstate from North to South, and this gave them a strong interest in national power. Having grievances concerning taxation and representation against the state government, many of them considered that the new federal Constitution represented a more equitable departure. Being heavily biased toward the dissenting churches, they were reassured by the promise of religious liberty under the Constitution and did not even seek for additional amendments.[7]

In New York and Pennsylvania the issue of the Constitution became involved with well-developed struggles between leading political factions, struggles which in Pennsylvania were so systematic and continuous as to foreshadow the two-party system. In New York, where majority sentiment against the Constitution seems beyond argument, the opposition was

---

[7] Robert E. Thomas, "The Virginia Convention of 1788," *Journal of Southern History*, 19 (1953), 63–72; Freeman H. Hart, *The Valley of Virginia in the American Revolution, 1763–1789* (1942), chapter x; Forrest McDonald, *We the People*, 255–68.

led by the powerful faction of Governor Clinton. His government had only recently taken advantage of the prosperity of
the state by devising its own funding system in which the
entire state debt was funded and a portion of the continental
debt was assumed and made interchangeable with state securities. The public creditors, of whom there were many in Clinton's camp, thus found their interests tied to the fiscal success
of the state, and New York became one of those states (Pennsylvania was another) in which it was by no means easy for
a public creditor to be sure that the government under the new
Constitution would improve the value of his holdings. In New
York both parties had support from speculators and from
large and small landholders. In New York City, both merchants and the lower classes favored the Constitution; outside
the city, however, sentiment against it was strong; and it was
largely the accumulated weight of ratification by ten other
states, along with whispers that the port of New York might
secede, that persuaded a decisive number of Anti-Federalists
to move over into the camp of the constitutionalists.

In Pennsylvania the opposition to the Constitution was
led by a rich, powerful, and well-knit faction of speculators
and public security owners, headed by Charles Pettit, who
owned over $55,000 in public securities, and Blair Mc-
Lenachan, who owned over $74,000. In Beard's terms the
behavior of these men is incomprehensible, but it was neither
irrational nor devoid of considerations of self-interest. Pennsylvania, prodded by the Pettit faction, had funded both the
state debt and the portion of the national debt owned in the
state on terms favorable to security holders and land speculators, and Pettit's forces were waging a vendetta against
the Bank of North America run by Robert Morris, the leader
of the nationalist faction. It is true that the Pettit group found
strong allies in western Pennsylvania who roughly correspond
to the populist-frontiersman conception of Beard and the
Turnerians (though some of the leaders of this set also were
beneficiaries of speculation). But both sides had a following
among ordinary farmers, and the battle had more to do with
the well-established factionalism of the state than with a
polarized struggle between the rich and the poor.

We may well be persuaded that Beard was right in finding a positive relation between socio-economic position and Federalist convictions. But the limitations of this finding can be seen only when we ask how high a correlation it was. Somewhere along this range a change in quantity may result in a wholly different qualitative picture of the society: it is the difference between a social order that is harmonious and viable and one that is not. If there had been no cleavage within the elite classes over such a fundamental issue, and at the same time no cleavage in the lower, and if the two had been ranged against each other, face to face and class to class, a deep social conflict might have resulted. But where there is a significant cleavage within the elite, and both elite factions draw significant support from the lesser ranks of society, sharp polarization is much less likely to occur, and compromise and accommodation become possible. For the Americans it was a fact of fundamental importance that the Constitution provoked a significant opposition among the wealthy and won a significant support from small farmers, and that these deviants from the Beardian picture were fairly well distributed throughout the country.

VII

Beard's central purpose, by his own account, was to introduce a note of realism into writing about the Constitution; and for his generation, realism meant establishing the point that, even where something so sacred and venerable as the Constitution is concerned, political actions and institutions are not the result of self-contained systems of ideas. There is a dynamic relation between interests and ideas, in which the workings of interests can never be left out of account. As Beard put it in re-evaluating his book in 1937: "In political history, if not in all history, there are no ideas with which interests are not associated and there are no interests utterly devoid of ideas."[8] As early as 1913, he was trying to apply a historical sociology of knowledge, however rudimentary, to the American experience with constitution-

---

[8] "Historiography and the Constitution," in Read, ed., *The Constitution Reconsidered*, 160.

making. It was in keeping with this that in later years he showed such enthusiasm for the work of Karl Mannheim.

It is easy to accept the general proposition that ideas and interests are somehow associated, easy to see that there might still have been some point in asserting it in 1913. But there are some dangers in working with any such formula. The first is that ideas—or all those intangible emotional, moral, and intellectual forces that may roughly be combined under the rubric of ideas—will somehow be dissolved and that we will be left only with interests on our hands. (One cannot quite down the suspicion that Beard and some members of his generation were looking for a way to explain ideas on the assumption that when they were satisfactorily explained they would be properly subordinated.) Then there is the danger that interests will be too narrowly construed: that we will put too much emphasis on the motives and purposes of individuals and groups, not enough on the structural requirements of a social system or on the limitations imposed on men by particular historical situations. There is also the danger of thinking that we know with greater clarity than we do where ideas and interests begin and leave off. The two terms are deceptively simple. Beard seems to have thought of men as simply *perceiving* their interests and then, rather naturally, drifting into the acceptance or the use of ideas that would further them. He does not seem to have recognized, at least not by 1913, that the way in which men perceive and define their interests is in some good part a reflex of the ideas they have inherited and the experiences they have undergone, a blind spot which enabled him to write of the Constitutional era without taking account of the long preceding development of institutional thought in America. Economic interests as such are not always obvious or given; they have to be conceptualized and made the object of calculations or guesses.[9] They have to be weighed against other kinds of interests, sentiments, and aspirations. Ideas themselves constitute interests, in that

---

[9] "Economic man," Marc Bloch observed in *The Historian's Craft*, (1954), 194–5, "was an empty shadow, not only because he was supposedly preoccupied by self-interest; the worst illusion consisted in imagining that he could form so clear an idea of his interests."

they are repositories of past interests and that they present to us claims of their own that have to be satisfied. With ideas, with moral impulses, with cultural forces that could not be closely tied to economic origins, Beard throughout his career was often quite inept. (Note his helplessness, for example, with abolitionism in *The Rise of American Civilization:* there, being too sensible to pretend that it was a direct response to economic interests, he was forced to shrug it off as being really unimportant.)

Finally, the ideas-interests formula led Beard to leave out the whole complex of events that cannot easily be subsumed under one rubric or another, the whole area of *experience* in which ideas and interests are jumbled to a degree that the effort to divorce and counterpose them becomes an artificial imposition upon the realities of history. For the generation of the Founding Fathers, the central, formative, shattering, and then reintegrating experience of civic life was the Revolution, which recast the pattern of their interests and galvanized their inherited store of ideas. And except for Beard's concern with the undeniably important Revolutionary debt, it is the persistent impact of the *Revolutionary experience* that one misses most in his account of the Constitution—and, indeed, the sense of the whole colonial background with its complex institutional development. The bent of his type of interpretation requires that the Constitution be seen as the terminal check or counterpoise to the Revolution and not as its consummation. In his concern with the conflicting material interests left in the wake of the Revolution, he loses touch with the moving force of the Revolutionary commitment. Here, as so often elsewhere, Beard was far less interesting as a historian of ideas, of moral impulses, of literature and culture, than when he wrote about the sweep of economic forces.

CHAPTER 7

The Constitution and Political Thought

> The hope of obtaining, outside of the existing legal framework, the adoption of a revolutionary programme. . . . No special popular elections . . . frank recognition of class rights . . . thorough distrust of democratic institutions . . . no confidence in popular government . . . coup d'état . . . revolutionary plan of procedure . . . precipitous actions . . . unseemly haste . . . not submitted to popular ratification . . . disfranchisement of the masses . . . not created by "the whole people."
> —Charles A. Beard, 1913

> My starting point is "We, the People" . . . [These] are . . . historic words and words of strangely prophetic nature, illustrating the force of ideas in history. In the eighteenth century, they were as revolutionary as any modern phrase which makes timid citizens look under their beds at night. . . . The hard-headed framers of our Constitution . . . spent little time trying to imagine what perfect justice and an ideal society would look like. They refused to try by ideal standards the fruits of necessity and the frailties of human beings. They sought to institute a workable government and a workable society. They put justice into the Preamble of the Constitution; and, if I may make a rash assertion, they made it possible for the American people to have more justice, despite all the black spots on it, than any other people ever enjoyed over such an immense territory for so long a time. . . .
> —Charles A. Beard, 1943

I

IN 1913 Beard found nothing in the ideas of the Founding Fathers that made him feel as close to basic realities as the old Treasury Department records he had enterprisingly turned up. For all the amplitude and moral intensity of po-

246

litical thought in the Revolutionary era, he seems to have believed its residue was not fundamentally important for the Constitution. Whereas his chapter on the economic interests of the members of the Convention runs to almost eighty pages and puts its conclusions in a highly particularized form, his chapter on their "political doctrines" (a revealing choice of terms, since it suggests fixed commitments, academicism, and sterility rather than vital ideas) is a rather perfunctory pastiche of quotations drawn very selectively and sometimes rather out of context from the records of the Convention, and it takes up only one third as much space. Its conclusion, put in a few lines, is simply that despite diversity of opinion on details, *The Federalist* "generalized the political doctrines of the members of the Convention with a high degree of precision." Unfortunately, Beard's own brief discussion of *The Federalist* was not as careful as it was laudatory. In brief, he claimed this treatise as a forerunner of his own: it was, he said, a short but systematic economic interpretation of the Constitution, in fact "the finest study in the economic interpretation of politics which exists in any language." Yet while *The Federalist* was indeed at points touched with a spirit of economic realism, its view of the relation between economic and political realities, as Douglass Adair has since pointed out, gave much more latitude than Beard's to the influence of ideas. In any case, it was not an economic interpretation of politics.[1]

Beard carefully refrained from saying flatly what all his selected data indicated—that the views of the Fathers were "undemocratic." Here his strategic sense was as good as his historical sense was bad: the direct use of this term might have raised troubling questions about anachronism and would certainly have called for an embarrassingly explicit definition. At no point in his book did he explain what one might have expected in the way of democracy in the eighteenth century; nor did he address himself to the difficult task of interpreting the term as it was used by Jefferson's contemporaries. That he did not argues that he thought no

---

[1] *An Economic Interpretation*, 153, 216; see Douglass Adair, "The Tenth Federalist Revisited," *William and Mary Quarterly*, 8 (1951), 48–67.

such interpretation was necessary, because he saw no gap to
be bridged between 1913 and 1787. There is good reason
to conclude that Beard thought of democracy not as a relative matter or as an unfolding historical reality that must
be understood at each point in its temporal context, but as
an eternal absolute. And if it was such an absolute, all
criticisms of or deviations from some abstract and pure
conception of democracy would have substantially the same
stature. It is revealing that in 1929, even after he had had
many additional years for reflection, Beard still held to this
view of the matter. Writing that year about Italian fascist
ideas on democracy, he remarked: "In the condemnation of
democracy there is nothing new, except possibly in the
figures of speech employed. The ancient Greeks said about
all that could be imagined in that line; *the fathers of the
American republic, notably Hamilton, Madison, and John
Adams, were as voluminous and vehement as any Fascist
could desire."*[2] In what Beard suggests, therefore, about the
Founding Fathers on democracy there is always a good deal
more than a hint of this anachronism. The ordinary reader,
approaching the Fathers through his eyes, can easily identify
them with all the other "anti-democrats" he has ever heard
of, and so can drift into thinking of poor old John Adams
as a proto-fascist. Once again, as in J. Allen Smith's *Spirit of
American Government*, we hear John Dickinson praising
limited monarchy, Elbridge Gerry saying "The evils we experience flow from the excess of democracy," Hamilton
saying "The people are turbulent and changing, they seldom
judge or determine right. . . . Nothing but a permanent body

---

[2] "Making the Fascist State," *New Republic*, 57 (1929), 277;
italics added. Beard was somewhat more receptive in 1929 to the
evolutionary possibilities of the corporate state than he had been
in 1913 to the evolutionary possibilities of the American Constitution. "This is far from the frozen dictatorship of Russian Tsar-
dom," he wrote of Mussolini's regime, "It is more like the American check and balance system; and it may work out in a new
democratic direction . . . . Beyond question an amazing experiment is being made here, an experiment in reconciling individualism and socialism, politics and technology." Ibid., 278. Beard,
of course, was not alone among American liberals in giving early
fascism a more indulgent hearing than they would later care to
remember. For the background, see John P. Diggins, "Flirtation
with Fascism: American Pragmatic Liberals and Mussolini's
Italy," *American Historical Review*, 71 (1966), 487–506.

can check the imprudence of democracy," William Livingston saying, "The people have ever been and ever will be unfit to retain the exercise of power in their own hands; they must of necessity delegate it somewhere," Edmund Randolph saying of the difficulties the country faced that "in tracing these evils to their origin every man has found it in the turbulence and follies of democracy," J. F. Mercer objecting to popular election of the lower House on the grounds that "the worst possible choice will be made," and remarks by other delegates in much the same tenor. Beard usually noted, although he did not seem to attach much significance to the fact, that some of those who expressed the sharpest reservations about democracy also had reservations about the new Constitution. Gerry, for instance, refused to sign it and opposed it in Massachusetts; Randolph also withheld his signature, and was converted or seduced to its acceptance in Virginia only at a late hour; and Mercer, another nonsigner, was a forceful Anti-Federalist in Maryland. These unruly realities, along with the support for the Constitution that came from some of the more democratically minded members of the Convention, including Benjamin Franklin and James Wilson, may suggest that, at least within the ruling elite itself on either side, democracy was not precisely the issue.

A good illustration of Beard's procedures was his treatment of the political ideas of Roger Sherman, who had lived in New Milford, Connecticut, where Beard himself spent so much of his life. For Sherman's ideas Beard needed only nine lines. Sherman, Beard reports, believed "in reducing the popular influence in the new government to the minimum," and opposed election of the first branch of the legislature by the people, preferring that this be done by the state legislatures. "The people," he quotes Sherman as saying, "immediately should have as little to do as may be about the government. They want information and are constantly liable to be misled." Here his discussion of Sherman ends. But the Connecticut delegate did have other things to say that might be considered relevant to the spirit and practice of popular government, statements Beard quietly ignores. On the day Sherman issued his seemingly antidemocratic

pronouncement on the role of the people, he also said, concerning elections to the House of Representatives: "If it were
in view to abolish the state governments, the elections ought
to be by the people," adding, however, that if the state governments were to be preserved, the rights of the people
could be secured by their power to elect the state legislatures. On another occasion he spoke out briefly in favor of
the principle of annual elections, which was one of the
leading tenets of contemporary democrats, and further proposed that "the representatives ought to return home and mix
with the people. By remaining at the seat of government,
they would acquire the habits of the place, which might
differ from those of their constituents." On still another he
declared: "Government is instituted for those who live under
it. It ought therefore to be so constituted as not to be dangerous to their liberties. The more permanency it has, the
worse, if it be a bad government. Frequent elections are
necessary to preserve the good behavior of rulers." He went
on to remark that the experience of Connecticut showed that
frequent elections do not undermine stability.[3] The object
of these remarks was to express his opposition to the excessively long terms for senators that were then being discussed, and to say that he would prefer six or four years.

Sherman made other observations and proposals from
which his political views might also be inferred, but these
few citations will serve to illustrate the distance between
Sherman as he actually was and the Sherman so perfunc-
torily put before us in Beard's lines. Beard gives us Sherman
as a crusty antidemocratic ideologue. On the floor of the
Philadelphia Convention, Sherman was a man concerned
with certain complicated problems in the design of government, unsentimental about the infallible wisdom of the
people, but scrupulous in his concern to preserve the processes of popular government as they then existed, a bit

---

[3] Max Farrand, ed., *Records of the Federal Convention* (rev. ed.
1937), I, 48, 133, 362, 365, 423. Sherman, it might be added,
contributed to the greatest single tactical error of the advocates
of the Constitution when he dismissed the proposal for a bill of
rights in the original Constitution on the ground that the powers
of the federal government clearly did not supersede the state
declarations of rights. Ibid, II, 588.

cranky and perhaps at times a bit inconsistent or unwise, but in no way reactionary or sinister.

One more case may do: Beard's treatment of Gouverneur Morris, one of the more outspokenly "aristocratic" delegates. Citing Morris's interest in a freehold property qualification, Beard refers to a passage in which the brilliant and cosmopolitan Pennsylvania delegate urged the need of such a provision to keep the future working class from being mobilized at the ballot. The aristocracy of the future, which Morris feared, would, he predicted, grow out of the House of Representatives. "Give the votes to people who have no property, and they will sell them to the rich who will be able to buy them." Of the existing population, nine tenths were freeholders and would be pleased with the limitation. Beard remarks that Morris "expressed his views freely, always showing his thorough distrust of democratic institutions," cites Theodore Roosevelt's biography for support on Morris's cynicism (Morris, in T. R.'s account, always spoke as though he thought high-mindedness impossible to man), and concludes that what appeared in Morris to be "cynical eccentricity . . . was nothing more than unusual bluntness in setting forth Federalist doctrines."

Morris indeed was very far from being a democrat by any definition; but his very articulateness in the Convention makes it possible to place him more precisely than Beard does. He was notably interested in securing a vigorous executive who would have a close relationship to the people. "Wealth," he said at one point in the debate, "tends to corrupt the mind—to nourish its love of power, and to stimulate it to oppression. History proves this to be the spirit of the opulent." He was worried about the tendency of the Senate, which would be in some respects founded on wealth, to grow too powerful and to overshadow or incorporate the executive. His remedy: "The executive . . . ought to be so constituted as to be the great protector of the mass of the people." The President would have, for example, a large mass of civil appointments to make. "Who will be the best judges whether these appointments be well made? The people at large, who will know, will see, will feel, the effects of them. Again, who can judge so well of the discharge of military duties for the protection and security of the people, as the people themselves, who are to be protected and secured?" It was Morris too who argued: "It is said, the multitude will be uninformed. It is true they would be uninformed of what passed in the legislative conclave if the election [of the President] were to be made there; but they will not be uninformed of those great and illustrious characters which have merited their esteem and confidence." And it was he who said that "the way to keep out monarchical government was to establish such a republican government as would make the people happy and prevent a desire of change."[4] His political utterances in the Convention mark him as one thoroughly convinced of the necessity of balanced government, and hardly less convinced than the other members of the importance of the popular voice in it.

II

A number of perplexities arise when we compare Beard's simple view of the Fathers with the more complex view revealed by closer inspection. Perhaps the best way to break through them is to start, once again, free of his categories. Let us start with the proposition, at first almost too obvious to be interesting, that the main object of the Fathers was to form what they often called a "more energetic" government—that is, a true national state with all the customary powers— without losing the liberties they had. Let us assume, in short, that they were *nationalists* first of all, whose purpose was neither to restrict nor to enlarge democracy. This will help us to remember that what we say about the relation of the Constitution to democracy is likely to elevate the problem of democracy to a position it did not have in the minds either of the Constitution's friends or its opponents. And let us assume further that as nationalists in a country still made up of separate provinces the Fathers found it necessary, like all innovators and reformers, to keep public opinion in mind —and, indeed, references to what would please the people

---

4 Farrand, *Records*, II, 52–3, 31, 35–6.

or what they would approve ripple through the discussions of the Convention. What I would like to suggest is that, contrary to the implications Beard drew from certain scattered texts, the Fathers, though wary of what they thought to be its possible abuses, were not notably dissatisfied with the measure of democracy that already existed in the American states; again, that, under the double necessity of preserving liberty (which they did out of principle) and of pleasing the people (which they did out of a mixture of principle and expediency), they did in fact to some measure, though perhaps in the main inadvertently, advance democratic institutions and practices on a national scale.[5] This requires us to look away for a moment from their intentions and motives to the results, sometimes unanticipated, of their actions. And one of these results was to bring the existing practices of American democratic politics out of the local arenas in which they were operating, and, by creating a national market in political competition, to nationalize and in the end to intensify them. Seen in this light, the Fathers become not the authors of a nationalist Thermidor imposing reaction upon particularist revolutionaries, but rather the architects of a viable national scheme by which the revolutionary impulse toward democracy was taken out of its particularist moorings and made into a continental reality.

If we are to try to characterize the Fathers in the very loose language of political classification, we will find them neither radical democrats (as some Europeans believed) nor ultraconservatives (as many historians in the Populist-Progressive tradition have argued) but moderate Whigs. The central political idea behind the Constitution was a variation of the ancient idea of balanced government. As revolutionaries who felt that they had suffered from tyrannical government, the Fathers were primarily moved by fear of concentrated and arbitrary power. They looked to a skillfully designed balanced government to render impossible the concentra-

---

[5] Cf. the conclusion of J. R. Pole: "Once the Federal government was in operation, its electoral system gave a possibly unintentional but nevertheless an unmistakable impetus to the idea of political democracy." *Political Representation in England and the Origins of the American Republic* (1966), 365, and the discussion, 339–65.

tion of excessive power in any one arm of government or in
any single interest in society. They hoped to achieve such
balance by the separation of powers and by a system of mutual checks—and more sophisticated thinkers among them,
like Madison, considered that this balance in the machinery
of government ought to be paralleled by balance in the
variety of social interests and groups within the society.
The theorists of balanced government believed that a popular
arm, the lower house of the legislature, which would be
based upon a broad suffrage, was indispensable. Counterposed to it, the upper house would be based perhaps upon
a narrower suffrage, and normally upon certain property
qualifications for its members (though this was abandoned
in the federal Constitution where the basic purpose of the
Senate was not to represent property but to represent the
states), which would make it a protective safeguard for
propertied interests and add deliberative "wisdom" to public
counsels. The executive and judiciary would both be independent. Most theorists of balanced government would have
agreed with John Adams that the Executive should not be
embroiled in the factional partisanship of the legislature,
particularly of the upper house, and many of them thought
with Gouverneur Morris that he ought to have a special relationship to, a particular rapport with, the people, which
would add to his strength and to their protection. The independent judiciary, which was to be guaranteed by undisturbed tenure, was thought to have a special relation to the
rule of law—a difficult problem and one which many theorists a hundred years later concluded concealed a trap for
democratic institutions in the form of judicial review. Practically all American Whig theorists agreed on the desirability
of formal guarantees of popular rights.

　　Contemporaneous democrats, on the other hand, sometimes preferred a simple government with a strong unicameral legislature, based on the unrestricted suffrage of free
adult males; they often advocated annual elections as a
means of keeping political leaders close to the popular will.
Pennsylvania's constitution of 1776, with its unicameral
legislature and suffrage limited only to taxpayers (which
meant nearly all adult males), came closest to embodying

PART III: *Charles A. Beard*   255

these principles; and, though it provoked much criticism and was replaced by a bicameral constitution in 1790, it is worth noting that it hardly brought about the destruction of the class system or the subversion of propertied interests. But what is most important is that the difference between a moderate democrat (the word itself was then rarely used to describe one's own political philosophy) and a typical republican in the 1780's was not an inflammatory one.

An understanding of the idea of balanced government helps us to comprehend what such terms as "the people" and "democracy" might mean in the late eighteenth century. No one of any consequence in America doubted that government should be based upon consent, that it should be responsible to the people. By now it was widely accepted that to be politically legitimate a government should be referred to the people for their approval at its beginning. The idea of a convention elected by the people for the sole and specific purpose of ratifying a constitution was a remarkable innovation of their own devising, which was intended to satisfy this scruple about popular consent. "The people," it is true, did not mean all adult males. The Fathers generally accepted the "stake-in-society" conception of suffrage rights—the notion that anyone, to qualify for the right to have a say in the management of the political order, should have some token of permanent attachment to its interest. For all practical purposes, this meant in the American states a freehold or its equivalent; and, of course, in a society in which property was so widely distributed, this disfranchised only a minority of adult whites. Recent research, particularly that of Robert E. Brown, has shown in fact that the easygoing practices of American electoral politics resulted in a very loose enforcement of the qualifications that did exist; that the suffrage was indeed widely available, and was exercised at times to a remarkable degree. In their acquiescent respect for a broad suffrage, the members of the Federal Convention clearly surpassed their predecessors under the supposedly more democratic Articles of Confederation.[6] Nor should we assume

---

[6] In 1784 Jefferson had proposed universal manhood suffrage for the territorial assemblies, but this had been rejected in favor of the then rather stiff requirement of a fifty-acre freehold; this requirement was reaffirmed in the Northwest Ordinance of 1787.

that the desire to keep the freehold requirement had to be inspired by dark reactionary sentiments. To be sure, some of the feeling in favor of property requirements came from fear that mobs might be led to dangerous ends; the mind of the eighteenth-century freeholder had a lively terror of mobs and "demagogues." But a good deal of it came from other, more philosophical premises. Property must be seen from the standpoint of what was being both superseded and built upon in the eighteenth century, and not from the standpoint of the problems facing twentieth-century Progressives in dealing with the large business corporation. In the eighteenth century, political society was conceived as being the voluntary association of those with property. The lack of property was associated with servility, if not with servitude. (Even the radical Levellers of the seventeenth century had not believed in universal manhood suffrage.) To have political competence, it was assumed in Whig theory, a man must stand above being ordered about, or bought or bribed, and this status would be safeguarded by the possession of some property: only in this way would the voter have, it was said (following Montesquieu and Blackstone), "a will of his own."

A still more important point about property and politics must be understood: under the social and political conditions of eighteenth-century America, the appeal to the voice of property was not retrograde in its effects, or even conservative, but tended rather to give a startlingly strong, if unintended, impetus to the development of democracy and political individualism. After all, what the Americans were displacing was not some perfect primitive democracy but rather a set of political institutions brought from England and having a medieval ancestry. Among these was the idea that representation should be given to separate corporate interests, orders, or "estates" in society—hardly the framework for modern democratic organization. What happened during the Revolution, as the Americans drew up new constitutions and in so doing reconsidered their political principles and their techniques of organization, was that they began (especially under the pressure of the large towns, which were on a numerical basis underrepresented) to couple property with numbers, on the ground that numbers (and taxation) formed a rough index of the distribution of property. The townsmen argued that their property was not adequately represented, and proposed to register its weight by the measure of numbers and taxes. Now in a social system in which property was very widely diffused this could, and did, cause the unchallenged authority of property in politics to come to be subtly linked with numbers, and thus to become a channel by which the political weight of numbers was ultimately increased. When, in the development of the states, property became "a sort of substitute for the faded and inadequate idea of the separate 'estate' of an aristocracy with a right to separate representation," the change marked "one of the greatest departures in the origins of modern and democratic government."[7] In the Federal Convention of 1787, though the idea of the explicit representation of property as well as numbers was initially the object of a good deal of concern, it was ultimately abandoned in order to give to the upper house another function: the Senate was instituted not on the principle of the representation of property, but simply to recognize the parity of the several states in one of the two chambers. Property as a qualification for voters found no formal cognizance in the plan for representation, except in so far as the new Constitution paid deference to the requirements already imposed on voters in the constitutions of the states.

In the standard discourse of eighteenth-century politics, "democracy" was not used as it came to be used in the nineteenth.[8] The Fathers spoke rather of "popular government" or "republican government" or "free government." Very few indeed among them were opposed to popular government, and when they criticized democracy, which they classified as

---

7 Pole, *Political Representation*, 170; see this work, *passim*, for a subtle and detailed explication of the changing political role of property.

8 On the meaning of democracy in the Western world, see R. R. Palmer, "Notes on the Use of the Word 'Democracy,' 1789–1799," *Political Science Quarterly*, 68 (1953), 203–6. Also helpful is Robert W. Shoemaker, " 'Democracy' and 'Republic' as Understood in Late Eighteenth-Century America," *American Speech*, 41 (1966), 83–95, though I am unable to follow the author's conclusion that the difference between a democracy and a republic was that between the Articles of Confederation and the Constitution.

one of the varieties of popular government or as one of the elements in mixed government, they almost always had something more limited in mind, because the term democracy was then in a transitional state and was not used consistently. Democracy might mean simply the ancient idea of direct government—the people assembling without the intermediation of representatives to pass on issues of state. Often when men spoke of democracy as unusable or impossible in a large territory, they were speaking in this sense. The idea that democracy was unsuitable to the government of large territories was a fundamental tenet of the age, and one which the Fathers found it essential to controvert. But democracy might also on occasions be used to refer to that part of a mixed government, the "democratical" part, the lower house of the legislature, in which the power of the people was represented. When members of the Convention referred to the troubles of the time as having come from the "excesses" of democracy, they might be referring to mob action (as in the case of Shays's rebellion) or expressing their disapproval of certain types of measures that had received their impetus in the popular assemblies. Edmund Randolph could thus speak of "the democratic licentiousness of the state legislatures."

One must be careful not to assume, then, that invidious references to "democracy" are equivalent to indictments of popular government. It is probably most accurate to say not that the Fathers were antidemocrats but simply that their republicanism had nothing utopian about it. They saw popular government, like other forms, as being attended with certain characteristic failings of its own which they hoped to keep from becoming acute or fatal, and they were trying to devise what Madison called in *The Federalist* Number 10 "a republican remedy for the diseases of republican government."

When the Fathers spoke critically of democracy they were at times implying condemnation of particular policies; they were also, beyond doubt, expressing their reservations about popular wisdom, and they did fear simple majoritarianism as a possible threat to both liberty and property. But they never imagined that the evils of society could be cured by eliminating the popular voice from government. Quite the contrary: all of them—with the possible exception of Hamilton—would have feared the amputation or crippling of the popular house as a threat to a central principle of balanced government and to well-founded popular rights. James Wilson, one of the outstanding juridical thinkers among the Fathers, arguing "strenuously," as Madison's notes record, for the direct election of members of the House of Representatives by the people, declared: "He was for raising the federal pyramid to a considerable altitude, and for that reason wished to give it as broad a basis as possible. No government could long subsist without the confidence of the people." Madison was quick to second him with the remark that he "considered the popular election of one branch of the national legislature as essential to every plan of free government." John Dickinson, undoubtedly one of the most conservative members of the group (Beard mentions him primarily for his belief in limited monarchy and in a freehold suffrage qualification), agreed: it was "essential that one branch of the legislature should be drawn immediately from the people; and expedient that the other should be chosen by the legislatures of the states."[9]

The framers did not, by and large, think that it was by any means impossible to achieve their nationalist goals and construct an "energetic" government within the framework of the popular will, as it then normally found expression; and they were content to plan a government which they thought answered to most popular habits and current practices. The longer they talked about their problems, the more respectful their references to "the people" became. The vain young South Carolina aristocrat, Charles Pinckney (who, Beard tells us, "had no confidence in popular government"

---

[9] Farrand, *Records*, I, 49, 134, 136; see the discussions ibid., I, 48–50, 132–8, 214–15, 358–62; II, 201–5, 215–16. Attempts to impair the normal popular composition of the lower house, or its efficacy, fared badly. Direct election of the members of the House of Representatives was first passed in the Convention by a vote of six to two, with two states divided. Then, after a move to have them chosen by the state legislatures was defeated eight to three, popular election was reaffirmed by a vote of nine to one, with one divided. Annual elections were thought to be impractical, but a motion by Hamilton for three-year intervals went down by seven to three, with one divided. A motion to include a national freehold qualification for electors choosing the lower House was beaten by seven to one, with one divided.

and who indeed did want more checks than some members),
presented an interesting philosophical statement to the Convention during the discussion of the mode of electing senators. Arguing for the choice of senators by the legislatures,
Pinckney observed that the people of the United States were
singular in having "fewer distinctions of fortune, and less of
rank, than among the inhabitants of any other nation . . .
a greater equality than is to be found among the people of
any other country, and an equality which is more likely to
continue." The rest of his discourse made it clear that he was
reconciled to this state of affairs, and proposed to design a
government that accommodated it. "We must, as has been
observed, suit our government to the people it is to direct.
These are, I believe, as active, intelligent and susceptible of
good government as any people in the world."[1] This is not,
as the whole context makes clear, the voice of a sentimental
democrat; but neither is it that of a panicky reactionary.

In short, the Founding Fathers were not democrats in
the sense that many Populists and Progressives were a hundred years afterward: they neither practiced nor professed
the social and philosophical egalitarianism that had become
widespread by Beard's day; and in their own day such views
were still rare among the educated and articulate classes.
Moreover, they did not aspire to bring about the formal
equalization of political power that became an increasingly
powerful motif in American thought a little more than a century afterward and that animated the Progressive demand for
democratization of the Senate, for the initiative, referendum,
and recall, and other political reforms. Such ideals would
have been beyond their ken; and in fact the Supreme Court's
one-man-one-vote decision of 1964 shows how tardy we have
been in trying to implement these demanding ideals, even
in the most rudimentary way. Yet, if we are to avoid being
anachronistic, the deviation of the Fathers from the developing democracy of their own era should not be exaggerated.
The basic achievements in democratic development that had
thus far been brought about they not only accepted but

---

[1] Farrand, *Records*, I, 398, 403–4; cf. *An Economic Interpretation*,
210–11.

cherished: the presence of a parliamentary system with a popular house based upon a broad suffrage; free elections; political and religious rights for minorities. The principal point at which modern democratic thought deviates from them rests on its opposition to the formal qualifications and the multiplicity of checks they wanted to put on majority rule. Most modern democratic thinkers follow them in believing that there ought to be *some* such limits and that the survival of free government in fact depends on them; but whereas most modern democrats are content with the limits involved in securely guaranteed rights of opposition, of dissenters and minorities, the Fathers wanted to go beyond this: practically all of them believed in the existing property qualifications for the suffrage; in addition, they considered that a separate upper house, which would protect substantial property rights and provide a check on a simple legislative majority, was a sound ingredient in a balanced government. If, in the American political spectrum of the 1780's they can with some show of reason be ranked somewhat to the right, it is only because the high aristocrats had been exiled or smashed as a political force during the Revolution, and there was now nothing remaining of far right antirepublican conservatism on an interstate scale. (Hamilton's cool reception in the Convention was a token of this.) In the United States of the 1780's practically the whole political spectrum was taken up by a moderate left and a center.

Moreover, it is important to take note of the fact that the debate over the Constitution, as Cecelia Kenyon has shown, did not take the form of a debate over democracy as such. If we look only for popular rhetoric—for denunciations of aristocrats, special interests, and professional and learned men, and for encomiums on the wisdom and virtue of the common people—I think there is little doubt that we will find much more of it in Anti-Federalist than in Federalist literature. It is also true that, in their whole approach to the problem of representation the Anti-Federalists were raising an important problem of democracy and arguing from what they thought to be the democratic side. But if we are looking for substantive differences in constitutional proposals, we do not, on the whole, find the two sides far apart. Certainly the main argument of the Anti-Federalist leaders was not an argument for simple majoritarianism. They too accepted the idea that majorities can be oppressive. They, as well as the Federalists, believed in a government of checks and balances; in fact some of their leaders insisted vigorously that the Constitution did not contain checks and balances enough. Patrick Henry, supposedly the voice of the people, arguing in Virginia against the Constitution, complained that there was "no check in that government. The President, senators, and representatives, all immediately or mediately, are the choice of the people," and he warned that, in the absence of a hereditary nobility such as Britain had, the government would not incorporate any "real balances and checks . . . only ideal balances."

In proposing alternatives to the Constitution's structure, the Anti-Federalists did not argue for direct popular election of the President or senators or for a unicameral legislature, or attack the possible exercise of judicial review —positions we might expect them to take if they were simply forerunners of modern Progressivism. The attitude of the leading Anti-Federalists toward popular judgment also frequently resembled the attitude attributed by Beard only to the Federalists. "The people," said the leading New York Anti-Federalist, George Clinton, "when wearied with their distresses, will in the moment of frenzy be guilty of the most imprudent and desperate measures," and his colleague, Melancton Smith, thought that "Fickleness and inconstancy . . . were characteristic of a free people." Nor were Anti-Federalist leaders interested in changes that would make possible a government of simple majority controls. As one of their Massachusetts spokesmen put it, they considered that "the sober and industrious part of the community should be defended from the rapacity of the vicious and idle"—a statement that sounds interchangeable with the notions attributed by Beardian scholars to the Federalists. Indeed, one of the purposes of the bill of rights, which the Anti-Federalists so wisely insisted on, was to protect the minority from what the same writer called "the usurpation and tyranny of the majority."[2] At least among the leaders on both sides, then, the argument over the Constitution was an argument between two groups *both* of which were suspicious of simple majority rule.

The Anti-Federalists performed an indispensable function—that of seeing to it that the Constitution received a thorough and demanding scrutiny—and won a major victory on one count, their demand for the inclusion of a bill of rights, on which their arguments seem far more impressive than those of their opponents. But if both sets of leaders were skeptical of popular legislative majorities and in favor of checks and balances, Beard's concentration on the Federalists alone for their views on the subject makes little historical sense.

III

Beard's argument that the procedure by which the Constitution was framed was undemocratic also seems radically out of focus. Like so many of his contentions, it proceeds from several undeniable facts to a misleading conclusion. The leaders of the movement for the Constitution, he argued, being unable to get the Articles of Confederation amended by regular means, set about to have their way by "a circuitous route," the convening of a special Convention ostensibly to revise the Articles (their instructions from the Congress were quite explicit on this count); but actually they hoped to get "outside of the existing legal framework, the adoption of a revolutionary programme." No popular elections, he points out, were held to choose delegates to the Federal Convention—it was easier to persuade the state legislatures to cooperate than it would have been to persuade the people. And of course the delegates were thus chosen by legislative bodies elected under the prevailing limitations on the suffrage and the prevailing property qualifications

---

[2] For the quotations, see Cecelia Kenyon "Men of Little Faith," *William and Mary Quarterly*, 12 (1955), 33–4, 36. The argument is expanded in her invaluable introduction to her anthology, *The Anti-Federalists* (1966).

for legislators. (Beard granted, however, that the wide distribution of real property in the United States created "an extensive electorate" which included "the most dangerous antagonists of personal property.") Once met in conclave, Beard pointed out, the Convention delegates immediately set aside their mandate to revise the Articles of Confederation and, in secret sessions, began to draw up a new instrument of government. The resulting document was sent to Congress, which, without debating or considering it under its own roof, simply referred it to the state legislatures for action. Whereas the Articles of Confederation required that alterations and amendments be framed by the Congress itself and then ratified by every state, the new Constitution was drafted by an alien body acting in excess of its instructions; and the amendment requirements of the Articles were by-passed by the provision in the new Constitution that it could go into effect when ratified by only nine of the states. Quoting John W. Burgess, Beard remarked that the acts of the Founding Fathers, had they been committed by Julius Caesar or Napoleon, "would have been pronounced coups d'état." He quite rightly notes also that Madison, in justification of the procedural short-cuts that had been taken, invoked the right of revolution.[3] But Beard failed to make note of the corollary point that the framers of the Constitution, after all, *were* revolutionaries. After having digested the camel of the Revolution, they could hardly have been expected to gag over the gnat of the unamendability of the Articles of Confederation.

In the states, Beard went on, the Constitution was not submitted to popular referendums but to state conventions assembled for the purpose of ratifying or rejecting it. Since some delegates were uncommitted and uninstructed, it is impossible to know, in many cases, the precise intent behind the people's votes. In the election of delegates—elections in which, by and large, the limitations on suffrage were the same as those governing elections to the lower houses of the legislatures—a large proportion of the adult male population was debarred from participating, though Beard admits that

---

[3] *An Economic Interpretation*, 218, 63; on the relevant matters see chapter viii, *passim*.

more were disfranchised "through apathy and lack of knowledge of the significance of politics" than through lack of property, an important statement to whose implications I will recur. Finally, Beard charges that haste was employed to get the Constitution through in some states (notably Pennsylvania), but at the same time, its fortunes were favored in others, like Maryland and South Carolina, by "deliberations and delays."

The whole story as Beard tells it—tainted by illegality, secrecy, disfranchisement, "unseemly haste," and by the manipulations of a small minority with vested interests at stake—borders on the conspiratorial and the sinister, suggests the unhappiest and most violent hours of some imaginary banana republic. It is topped off by one of Beard's oddest editorial comments: explaining the factors in the success of the Federalists, he remarks that they "had the advantage of appealing to all discontented persons who exist in large numbers in every society and are ever anxious for betterment through some change in political machinery"[4]— which seems to argue that when we finish scourging the Fathers for being conservatives and antidemocrats we should turn around and scourge them for being revolutionaries and demagogues.

Beard's case about the undemocratic way in which the Constitution was made is matched by his account of its undemocratic structural features. Whereas the Founding Fathers saw its checks and balances largely as a means of avoiding an undue concentration of power in *any* hands (including, of course, the power of the popular assemblies) Beard sees it as a means of checking *popular* power alone, and thus transmutes the moderate Whig thinkers of the 1780's into ultraconservatives. All the "undemocratic" features of the instrument thus fall into place for him: the long terms of Senators, the difficulty of amending, the indirect election of the President, the practice of judicial review.

On certain counts Beard was of course right: the Constitution was not intended to create an egalitarian democracy

---

[4] *An Economic Interpretation*, 251.

or to advance simple majoritarianism; it was adopted in a society with limitations on the suffrage, and the procedures by which it was adopted were not, either in formal legal design or in the details of execution, absolutely impeccable. His version of the whole matter here adds strength to the dualistic Populist-Progressive view of the Constitutional era that one finds in J. Allen Smith's work. According to this view, American history is torn by two opposing traditions, the radical one, stemming from the Revolution and expressed in the philosophy of the Declaration of Independence, and the conservative one, stemming from the movement for the Constitution and incarnated in its antimajoritarian features. As the historians of this school would have it, the American Revolution cannot be understood simply as a colonial uprising against British rule, but must be seen too as the outcome of a strong internal class conflict, in which the spirit of democratic protest was unleashed—a struggle, as Carl Becker put it, not only over home rule, but over who should rule at home. The democratic impulse was held to have been articulated by the Declaration of Independence and embodied both in the new Revolutionary constitutions drawn up by the states in 1776 or soon after and in the Articles of Confederation. The spirit of 1787 is thus counterposed to the spirit of 1776, and the Constitution takes its place in the stream of events as the incarnation of the American Thermidor, the repository of reaction.

The idea of a dual tradition has been devastated by recent historical writing—so much so that our major question must be not whether it is correct but by what intellectual legerdemain it came to seem all but axiomatic to a great many scholars of learning and integrity. At the heart of the matter, I think, there lies a latent pattern of insufficiently articulate comparisons. If we are to speak of the Constitution as being undemocratic, a great deal depends upon what actual system of government we are comparing it with, and what span of time we have in mind. In criticizing any political procedure or any actual frame of government with respect to the question, Is it democratic?, it is most important to be clear about the sense in which this question is asked. One may, of course, quite legitimately measure any constitution against an abstract regulative ideal of perfect democracy; but if this is what we are doing, we must—since all actual constitutions fall short of the ideal—be clear about it, and not imply that we are comparing it to other actual constitutions. The Constitution of the United States may be looked at in this abstract way, or it may be compared with other actual constitutions. If we do the latter, which I suppose to be more useful, it is historically most instructive to compare it first with the Articles of Confederation and the state Revolutionary constitutions upon which it built. But here is where historians writing in the dualistic tradition went astray. They began by comparing the supposed philosophy of the Constitution with the supposedly more democratic philosophy of the Declaration of Independence, which was, after all, a high-minded manifesto for a revolution and not a structural plan for a government. Again, in speaking of the Constitution as a recession from democracy, they tend to pass over the limitations of the state constitutions—their religious and property qualifications, for example—and characterize them as "democratic" and "radical" partly because they did make certain reforms embodying the spirit of the Revolution and partly because under some of them certain measures historians regard as "popular" were passed. There has even been a disposition to suggest that under these constitutions power had in fact largely passed into the hands of the ordinary farmers.[5] (There is no doubt that some advocates of the Constitution feared that it would.) However, when the historians turn to the federal Constitution, they tend to

---

[5] If one starts with the image of ultraradical state legislatures, it is then easier to put the alleged ultraconservatism of the Constitution in sharp relief. In 1927 Beard still regarded the state legislatures of the Revolutionary period as dominated by a rather advanced agrarian radicalism. The Revolution, he said, made "the local legislatures, in which farmers had the majorities, supreme over all things." Again he speaks of "the levelling tendencies of local legislatures, generally dominated by farmers," and of the strategy of the constitution-makers to by-pass "the barriers of the populistic state legislatures." *Rise of American Civilization*, (1927), I, 299, 307, 329.

In 1912 Beard had written: "Under the Articles of Confederation populism had a free hand, for majorities in the state legislatures were omnipotent." *The Supreme Court and the Constitution*, 88. This, of course, leaves us with the problem of explaining why these omnipotent populist legislatures so uniformly chose antipopulist delegates to the Convention.

avoid point-by-point comparisons with the state constitutions, or indeed any close comparisons with other actual systems of government either in America or Europe. The Constitution's deficiencies from the standpoint of democratic criteria thus loom larger than life, since its critics had quietly ignored the fact that many of the same deficiencies were present in the "democratic" state constitutions. The "undemocratic" spirit of the federal government can also be established by reference to the disapproval of the democratic state legislatures expressed at times in Convention by the constitution-makers. But this can be done only by ignoring the fact that the constitution-makers, as their appointees, were the creatures of these very legislatures, and presumably had some measure of rapport and political continuity with them.

Of course, all this is quite understandable. The Progressive historians were still suffering, so to speak, from the limitations of the eighteenth-century federal Constitution. Hence it became the archetype for everything that was wrong with American political society, and in discussing its status as of 1787 they dealt with it less in its historical setting than in the setting of the majoritarian philosophy that had emerged among Progressives in American politics during the years after 1890. They became so involved in showing that the Constitution did not measure up to their criteria of democracy that they neglected to ask whether it did not meet most of the criteria that could fairly have been put to it in 1787. In effect, they were passing judgment on it in accordance with universal and utopian rather than historical criteria.

In fact, if the Constitution is measured in contemporaneous rather than anachronistic terms, it fits more comfortably into the Revolutionary tradition. The remarkable thing about the United States in the late 1780's is not the sharp break from a Revolutionary spirit to a constitutional Thermidor but rather the visible continuity both in personnel and philosophy. The Revolution had been brought about with a remarkable economy of violence. The national leaders of 1787-8 were, by and large, men who had been leaders in 1776. Tories had been exiled or silenced, but the children of the

Revolution had not fallen upon or destroyed each other. The sharp break pictured by Progressive historians between the spirit of 1776 and the spirit of 1787 arises from a set of self-deceptive maneuvers. One of these is to exaggerate the radicalism of the Revolution itself and of the Declaration of Independence, which invoked the idea of natural rights not to sustain an advanced notion of general social equality but to assert a more limited proposition: the legal equality of all free men, and hence of Americans with Englishmen. The spirit of the Revolution must be sought for not only in a propaganda manifesto like the Declaration, but in the state constitutions of 1776 and 1777; the latter, being instruments of government, are more properly comparable than the Declaration to the federal Constitution. And here the similarities seem strong. The first state constitutions, with their prevailing bicameral legislatures, their property qualifications (in most states) for voters and for members of the upper houses, and their inequitable legislative apportionments, represented a notable advance toward greater democracy over colonial practices, but they did not embody an advanced democratic radicalism. On the whole, they foreshadow the structure of the federal Constitution more than they contrast with it. The general philosophy of balanced government was accepted by a broad spectrum of leading opinion that embraced such Revolutionary radicals or democrats as James Otis, Samuel Adams, Thomas Jefferson, and Patrick Henry. Nearly everyone of consequence in America shared certain political commitments that would have seemed quite radical anywhere in Europe: a republican system, a written and amendable constitution as the supreme law, guarantees of basic liberties, legal equality, the absence of hereditary privileged orders, representative government, free elections at fixed and frequent intervals. In taking the measure of political differences in this era we cannot allow ourselves to forget that a classic American "conservative" thinker like John Adams was busy defending the "democratic" state constitutions; or that a democrat and libertarian like Thomas Jefferson accepted the Constitution with minor and readily appeasable reservations, and later endorsed the *Federalist* as "the best commentary on the principles of government

ever written."[6] The signers of the Declaration of Independence
did not themselves see the Constitution as representing the
defeat of their views. While it is customary to remark that
only eight signers of the Declaration were at the Federal Convention, it is more important to know that signers of the
Declaration who became Federalists in 1788 outnumbered
those who were Anti-Federalists by six to one. It is another
token of the political continuity of the age that signers of the
Articles of Confederation were in favor of the new Constitution, which supposedly "overthrew" it by a *coup d'état,* by
about four to one, and those customarily described as being in
the "radical" factions during the early Revolutionary era were
also in favor of it, though by a smaller margin.[7] In short, what
the historians in the dualistic tradition asked their readers to
believe is that the breed of men who made the Revolution and
signed or endorsed the Declaration of Independence was defeated and succeeded by men of a quite different breed who
drew up the Constitution and set up the new government. In
fact there is a great deal of evidence to show that both achievements were the works of the same breed of men with the
same basic political philosophy.

IV

Let us now consider what happens to our conception
of the Constitution when we abandon the dualistic tradition of
the Progressive historians and look at it from another point of
view. First, as to procedures: the Constitution was, as Beard
portrayed it, the result of a movement by a strong concerted
minority. But one must ask whether almost all social change,
good or bad, radical or conservative in intent, does not come
about through the activities of just such minorities. John P.
Roche, in describing the Founding Fathers as "a reform
caucus in action" has probably much exaggerated their democratic intent, but I think he is right in suggesting that we will
gain in our understanding of them if we look upon the task

6 *Works* (Ford ed., 1904), V, 434.
7 Jackson T. Main, *The Anti-Federalists,* 259–60.

that faced them as having much in common with the tasks facing innovators and reformers in many other political situations.[8] Their main problems were not ideological but practical. Their main enemy was not populism but inertia. The image of the Fathers as having put over a *coup d'état*, whether propounded by the conservative Burgess or the progressive Beard, is highly misleading, and it is accompanied by an especial inconsistency on the part of anyone who asks us, as Beard does, to look behind legal forms and technicalities to the actual substance of things. The framers, in abandoning their instructions at the outset, and proceeding to draw up a new government instead of making proposals for changing the existing one, were in fact acting illegally, but the taint of illegality is largely purged by other procedural circumstances: the Articles, being in practice unamendable, *had* to be circumvented by a technically illegal act; as a body, the Convention delegates were not self-constituted; they were appointed by the legislatures of the states and recognized by the Congress under the Articles; the procedure by which their proposed new instrument of government was set before the existing Congress, referred by it to the legislatures, and by these to special conventions, popularly elected, hardly conforms to the palace-revolution image evoked by the expression *coup d'état*. The government under the Articles of Confederation was not overthrown but peacefully supplanted; a full cognizance of this fact is essential to any understanding of American political development.

Again, there was, of course, no direct popular referendum on the Constitution. We do not have apodictic certainty as to how the majority of the voters, much less the eligible non-voters, felt about it, though we can hardly forget that the delegates they chose voted in the aggregate about two to one in its favor. Probably many of the voters themselves were unsure—which is one reason why in some cases they were willing to vote for and defer to the final decisions of uncommitted and uninstructed delegates, and why there appears to have been

---

[8] The Revolutionary movement itself was to a striking degree the work of an alert and readily mobilized urban minority.

no outcry against delegates who, in convention, changed their minds. Presumably we would not consider today that the Constitution was less legitimate if we could somehow ascertain that, say, only 45 per cent of the voters actually favored it than if 55 per cent had. What made it legitimate in the minds of contemporaries was not the presence of a putative mathematical majority but the process by which it was referred to the people, the discussion, debate, open criticism, and opposition to which it was subjected, the final compromise on what its opponents considered its major deficiency. It is pointless to be told, as Beard tells us, that there was no popular referendum on the issue unless we are also reminded that none of the other organic national acts of the period—neither the Declaration of Independence nor the Articles—was sanctified by such a referendum, and that the referendum was unheard of anywhere. Neither had the Revolutionary constitutions of 1776 and 1777 been ratified by special conventions elected by the people. This advanced method of seeking for the treasured expression of consent had been first devised by Massachusetts in the making of its constitution of 1780 and followed by New Hampshire in 1784, and in imitating it the Federalists were in line with the most avant-garde thinking on the subject. In putting the Constitution before state conventions chosen solely to ratify or reject it, the Fathers were in fact adopting a procedure that far surpassed previous procedures in its democratic character; and in their concern to establish that the new government would indeed be based upon consent, they brought the process of constitution-making closer to the popular will than in the case of previous instruments of government.

When one looks at the making and ratifying of the Constitution in this light, what seems truly remarkable about it is not its failure (in itself undeniable) to conform to abstractly conceived ideal procedures for the making and adopting of new governments but its long stride forward toward popular legitimation. As R. R. Palmer has remarked, this whole approach to the founding of government was "distinctively American": "European thinkers, in all their discussion of a political or social contract, of government by consent and of sovereignty of the people, had not clearly imagined the people as actually contriving a constitution and creating the organs of government. They lacked the idea of the people as a constituent power."[9]

Not only the procedures but some of the substantive provisions of the Constitution seem different when they are looked at in their proper historical setting. A democratic critic of the American Constitution today will argue that the equal voting power of the states in the Senate, regardless of their populations, and the fact that this provision is unamendable without unanimous consent of the states, ranks high among the features that entitle us to speak of it as being in some respects undemocratic. It is important to remember, however, that the same two features were present in the Articles of Confederation in a still more exaggerated form: for the legislature under the Articles consisted of only *one* house, not a "popular" one, with equal representation of the states; and not only this but all its other provisions were for all practical purposes unamendable. Again, the "undemocratic" Constitution was, in its basic feature of multiple checks and balances, fashioned after the existing "democratic" state governments. Most political leaders, we have seen, accepted such underlying principles, and when the first volume of John Adams's book *Defence of the Constitutions of Government of the United States* arrived at Philadelphia, those members who found time to read it seem to have felt that it represented a fine theoretical statement of what they were trying to do; yet this "conservative" book had been conceived as a defense of the "radical" state constitutions against European criticism. Much has been made of the indirect election of federal officers under the Constitution, and of the way this removed them from the popular will. However, *no* federal officers under the Articles of Confederation were elected by the people—since the members of Congress were appointed by state legislatures and the executive by Congress—and on this count the indirect elections provided by the new Constitution marked a long step closer to the popular will. Only three of the state governors were elected by the people; and since the governors were still feared by early constitution-makers—a residuum of the old battles with the royal governors—their powers were very

---

[9] *The Age of the Democratic Revolution: The Challenge* (1959), 215. See chapter viii, and esp. pages 228–35.

limited. But the stronger nationalists in the Convention—led by Wilson, Gouverneur Morris, and Madison—wanted a strong independent national executive, and thought it would be better assured if it were founded upon a popular vote than if it were derived either from the state legislatures or from the Congress. Their decision on the mode of presidential election did not arise basically from a desire for more or for less democracy but from their passion for national strength: they thought that strong, independent, and capable Presidents would be most likely arrived at through popular election, and after much argument they persuaded the Convention to follow their lead.

In designing a lower house chosen by a broad popular vote, the framers simply imitated the state constitutions. In opening the franchise here to those who in each state were qualified to vote for the members of its own lower house, they accepted the broadest franchise that was practicable. The Senate posed a different problem, since it was not, and was not intended to be, a popular body. Beard's contemporaries had, of course, become acutely aware of the undemocratic character of this body, which had begun to be called a "millionaire's club" in the Gilded Age, and Progressive reformers had mounted a demand for its reform which led to the ratification, in the year Beard's book appeared, of the Seventeenth Amendment providing for the popular election of senators. The very principle of a body constituted not on numbers but on equal representation from each state and thus giving much more weight to a voter from a small state than from a large one, had a profoundly undemocratic potential. But this provision was a response to the sovereignty of the small states and to their fear of being overwhelmed; and, paradoxically, though the actual solution adopted was undemocratic, any other would have been hopelessly unpopular. As to method of choice, the popular election of senators was proposed by James Wilson, but seems to have won little support and was defeated by ten states to one. The framers appear to have considered that an upper house representing propertied and "aristocratic" elements was a wholly appropriate part of mixed and balanced government, and it seemed that senators chosen by legislatures, whose own upper houses already embodied the principle, would reflect it. But it is important to note that the Senate, on this plan, would echo but not intensify the property orientation of the state legislatures. Moreover, the framers moved away from the old idea of formally representing various estates by requiring no property qualifications for Senate membership. The Senate might be thought to represent property, but was not required to *embody* it, and in this respect actually moved a short step away from older and more conservative interpretations of mixed government toward a more open political society.

Indeed on the matter of qualifications for officeholders the new Constitution went well beyond those of the states in specifically barring property or religious requirements. Some of the state requirements for members of the upper house and for governors were substantial. On the count of religious freedom, the Constitution embodied the most advanced thinking of the day; for this it was even criticized by some Anti-Federalists who disliked the tolerant principles it embodied.

The most unsatisfactory feature of the Constitution, the absence of a bill of rights, had also characterized the Articles of Confederation. Here there is no evidence of a design on the part of the framers to recede from liberal principles; but they seem to have thought, quite mistakenly, that the new Constitution would not act with sufficient force upon the individual citizen to make such explicit guarantees necessary, and that, as under the Articles, individuals would be amply protected in the possession of their rights by the bills of rights in state constitutions. This was a costly error; and it was one that opposition compelled them to rectify.

In short, as one reviews the making of the Constitution and its provisions, it seems clear that the framers, determined as they were to get a much stronger national state, knew that it must be referred to the people in order to win strength and legitimacy and that it must continue to have popular support to be workable. Hence, not because they were democrats but because they were nationalists, they brought the central government closer to the people than it or any other had been before, and framed a Constitution ample enough to accommodate further assertions of the democratic spirit.

V

One criticism of Beard's thesis, which is argued by Robert E. Brown but whose important consequences have been on the whole neglected, is that Beard greatly overestimated the intensity of the conflict over the Constitution. At one point Beard characterized the conflict over ratification as "a deep-seated conflict between a popular party based on paper money and agrarian interests, and a conservative party centered in the towns and resting on financial, mercantile, and personal property interests generally,"[1] and so much criticism has addressed itself to the accuracy of this social line-up that relatively little has gone into the question whether the conflict was in fact deep-seated at all. Beard leaves little doubt of his own view: he refers intermittently to a "hot contest," a "battle," a "war," an "antagonism," a "profound division" or a "sharp division," a "clash of interests," and the like. The residual impression is that of a pitched social battle, in which the feelings aroused were in intensity comparable to the importance of the issue at stake.

Of course Beard did not arrive at this view of the matter without evidence: his conclusion about the intensity of the conflict was drawn from two things—the even balance of the two sides in certain states (New York, Virginia, Massachusetts), and the high-pitched rhetoric one finds in the argument, especially among pamphleteers and newspaper writers. But the closeness of the two sides in strength is not to be confused with irreconcilability in the issue over which they fought. And a conscious search for conflict turns our attention largely to those states, vital to success but few in number, in which the issue was close, as against the more numerous states in which opposition to the Constitution was virtually nonexistent. It may also conceal the fact that the movement for the Constitution gained tremendous momentum from very early ratification by several states in which it enjoyed triumphs ranging from two or three to one up to unanimity. In the first

---

[1] *An Economic Interpretation*, 292.

nine states to ratify, after which the Constitution was technically empowered to go into effect, it had been adopted by a
cumulative vote of 725 to 361 delegates. The close and difficult votes that took place in New York and Virginia at the end,
therefore, which guaranteed that it would be actually as well
as legally viable, were conducted under the weight of its preponderant acceptance by the others. That Beard's book fails
to make this clear is attributable to his decision to tell the story
of ratification in geographical order (from North to South)
rather than in chronological order.

A question of more general importance is whether the
rhetoric of the controversy might not be a very poor way to
gauge its intensity. It is right to listen to how men argued over
the Constitution, but would it not be still more enlightening to
observe how they acted? The rhetoric of political controversy is
often very shrill—one might easily conclude, for example,
from a study of the rhetoric of the campaigns of 1896, 1936, or
1964 that the country was divided into two hostile camps
that were about to engage in lethal combat. The eighteenth
century, hardly less than the twentieth, was an age of vigorous
and often exaggerated pamphleteering; and if we are to
penetrate underneath its agitated surface to sound the intensity
of the underyling conflicts, we must find something more than
words alone to use as a measure. And here it seems to me that
the actual picture is almost the opposite of that which Beard
paints for us. The point is not that there was no conflict, for
conflict abounded, but rather that the two sides were reconciled with extraordinary promptitude and ease. Seen from this
perspective, the "hot contests" Beard reports seem remarkable
for their tepidity. Professor Brown may exaggerate when he
suggests that "the Constitution was adopted with a great show
of indifference,"[2] but this bold suggestion seems to me to
bring us closer to the truth.

If we consider that the American people were being asked

---

[2] *Charles Beard and the Constitution*, 170. In retrospect it may
be useful to think of the Constitution as having been framed in
a period of comparative harmony following the common effort
of the Revolution, and, by contrast, of the truly acute crisis of
the early Union as having developed after 1794 and as reaching
a head from 1798 to 1801.

to set forth on the (for them) relatively uncharted sea of national centralization and create a central taxing authority to replace the one they had overthrown, and if we take heed of the experimental character of the whole enterprise, the impressive thing is how lacking in deep-seated acerbity the contest was, how negotiable the issue, how promptly the legitimacy of the new Constitution was accepted by the opposition, once its adoption had been decided.

In understanding the fact that opposition to the new Constitution as such disappeared almost immediately upon its adoption,[3] it is necessary to remember that, for all the malice and suspicion that occasionally flared up, a certain spirit of political comity on basic issues had been achieved among the outstanding leaders on both sides: they were together veterans of the Revolution, and they were accustomed to doing business with each other without resorting to violence and suppression. Symbolic of this comity was the towering figure of Washington, whose presence among the Federalists gave them prestige and offered reassurance to their opponents. Since it was widely assumed that he would stand at the head of the new government, many doubters assumed that it would at least be launched under the best of auspices. Moreover, before the Constitution was drafted, there had grown up a very widespread conviction that a stronger central government was needed, a conviction shared even by many people who were doubtful about the adequacy or safety of this particular plan. In this respect the opposition of many Anti-Federalists was probably more half-hearted than that of their most vociferous leaders. As men who agreed that a general goal was desirable but who had no particular plan of their own, they were in the stance of mere nay-sayers. Their opponents had the initiative, and they were aware of it. Again, the very openness and in most states the amplitude of the debate led to a satisfactory airing of differences and a salutary discharge of doubts and anxi-

---

3 All resistance to it seems to have evaporated in 1789 after the passage of the first ten amendments incorporating basic rights. But it is noteworthy that even before this the voters and legislators seem to have considered that the new Constitution should have a chance to be implemented by its friends. Among the members of the first Congress, representing the eleven states that had ratified, former advocates of the Constitution outnumbered Anti-Federalists by almost three to one.

eties. Anti-Federalists in ratifying conventions sometimes ended by saying that they had been fairly beaten and that they would go home to encourage their constituents to express their loyalty to the new Constitution and their willingness to make it work. The debates in the ratifying conventions were not simply pitched battles between two inflexible parties but sometimes debates and discussions in which persuasion—mediated no doubt by some measure of pure reason but also by the hardboiled politics of bargain and compromise, bribery and flattery—actually brought some men to change their minds. At least sixty delegates who went to the ratifying conventions as Anti-Federalists switched positions, including such outstanding leaders of the opposition as Melancton Smith in New York and Edmund Randolph in Virginia.

Finally, much of the struggle rested upon a misunderstanding, a major failure in strategy and communication, in which the fault clearly lay with the Federalists: the omission of a bill of rights. But here, from the standpoint of their ultimate conciliation, both sides were fortunate in the main issue that divided them, for the issue that meant most to the Anti-Federalists was precisely the one which meant least to the Federalists. It is customary to say that without the promise of amendments to incorporate a bill of rights, the Constitution would not have been accepted. This is easy to believe, but there is a better way of putting it. If a bill of rights had not been left out of the original draft, as one recent student of the era has suggested, "it is probable that the whole anti-federalist movement would from the beginning have been much weaker and would never seriously have threatened the adoption of the Constitution."[4]

Considerable numbers of Americans who were in no wise apathetic about civic issues, were nonetheless unable to take sides sharply over the Constitution, because they could see on one side a need for a stronger central government and could recognize certain unquestionably daring and experimental features. Young John Quincy Adams, then studying law in the office of Theophilus Parsons at Newburyport, wrote in his diary when word arrived that Massachusetts had ratified: "In this

---

[4] Pole, *Political Representation*, 373.

town the satisfaction is almost universal; for my own part, I
have not been pleased with this system, and my acquaintance
have long since branded me with the name of an *antifeder-
alist*. But I am now converted, though not convinced. My feelings upon the occasion have not been passionate nor violent;
and, as upon the decision of this question I find myself on the
weaker side, I think it my duty to submit without murmuring
against what is not to be helped. In our government, opposition to the acts of a majority of the people is rebellion to all
intents and purposes; and I should view a man who would
now endeavour to excite commotions against this plan, as no
better than an insurgent who took arms last winter against the
Courts of Justice."[5] No one has tried to assess their role, but
there were others of similar mind.

V I

It is not quite so difficult to sound the uncertainties of
some men of the articulate governing classes as it is to come
to terms with the apathy of a great many of the people. On
this matter Beard wrote carelessly. After writing of those who
were disfranchised by property qualifications, he conceded:
"Far more were disfranchised through apathy and lack of
understanding of the significance of politics. . . . The disfranchisement of the masses through property qualifications
and ignorance and apathy contributed largely to the facility
with which the personalty-interest representatives carried the
day." He did not come to terms with the possibility that disfranchisement through ignorance or apathy points in precisely
the opposite direction from disfranchisement by formal dis-
qualification. To stress disfranchisement by property qualifications is to hint at an embattled class of underdogs clamoring
for the opportunity to defend their interests by winning a part
in politics. Disfranchisement by apathy (if not by ignorance)
suggests the possibility that great masses of common people
were sufficiently content with the way they were governed
to leave the decision on the Constitution to others. We now
know, thanks to the researches of Robert E. Brown, Richard

---

[5] Brown, *Charles Beard and the Constitution*, 155.

McCormick, J. R. Pole, Chilton Williamson, and others, that access to voting was far more common by the 1780's than was understood in Beard's time. To the degree that this was true, Beard's case on disfranchisement is only diminished in force; but his case on apathy raises a fundamental problem. The more men who were qualified to vote on the Constitution and did not do so, the less possible it is to think of the Constitution as an issue stirring deep-seated social conflicts. And indeed Brown has offered suggestive evidence of quite a different view of the matter: in Philadelphia, where Beard saw "perhaps the hottest contest over the election of delegates that occurred anywhere," the leading candidate got 1,215 votes, and only 1,450 votes were cast out of about 5,000 or 6,000 qualified voters. Twenty-two years earlier, Brown points out, when the population was smaller and the limitations on the suffrage larger, a genuinely hot political contest had drawn out 4,000 votes.[6] Further comparisons of voter turnouts over the Constitution with those in other elections might prove instructive. But it is clear that apathy ranks far ahead of disfranchisement through property qualifications as an explanation of nonvoting. And a widespread failure of the will to vote has serious consequences for Beard's picture of the Constitution as the outcome of a raging social conflict.

The facts about political apathy, however, do not seem to me to fit with the position of those of Beard's critics who argue that we must invert his case and conclude simply that the Constitution was adopted in a thoroughly democratic society. Democracy in any case is relative. But the discovery of a broadly available suffrage does not, in itself, warrant blithe conclusions about the state of democratic development in the

---

6 Beard, *An Economic Interpretation*, 242, 251; Brown, *Charles Beard and the Constitution*, 162.

Beard conceded (242) that nowhere were more than one third of the adult white males disfranchised by property qualifications, and the actual proportion is probably considerably smaller. His estimate that about 160,000 persons took part in the voting has not as yet been much challenged, and it represents about one fourth of the adult white male population. Very likely as much as three fourths of males in this category met the formal qualifications. Voting, of course, was not always convenient or accessible, as it is today, and one cannot fairly infer complete apathy from failure to vote. Probably the fairest way of gauging the heat of the contest over the Constitution would be to tabulate multiple comparisons with other elections.

1780's. Rather than say flatly that the America of the 1780's was a democratic society, I would adopt the characterization adapted by J. R. Pole from Walter Bagehot and describe it as a deferential society: one in which large masses of the people, many of them technically eligible, did not normally and regularly take part in politics, and in which, out of their regard for and acceptance of the role of leading men and leading *families,* drawn from or at least linked to the ruling elite, the common people did not usually clamor for a great deal more participation.[7] Here we come back to one aspect of the period on which Beard's view seems sound, even if drawn out of perspective: the ruling elites, though they always had to come to terms with the broad propertied middle class that voted and acted in politics, still had matters in hand. The Constitution, as a political issue, cut into the ranks of the elites and the public alike; but precisely because it created differences alike within both, instead of aligning them against each other, it resolved itself into a negotiable issue. The difficulty with Beard's view of the matter lay not in his sense of the power of the elites but in his fuzziness about interests and motives and conflicts; and above all in his failure to see that he was arguing, as though it were a specific case against the Constitution alone, a view of things that is true not only here but against all politics, all constitutions, and all societies of any complexity. Democracy in actuality is always very limited as compared with its aspirations and pretensions. The frames of government, the terms of suffrage, all such matters of form, are always operating within social systems, and it is difficult for the level of political democracy to rise above the limitations imposed by economic and social inequality. Differences in wealth and power, in influence and education, that exist in the social system spill over into the political system, and cannot be altogether neutralized by such majoritarian devices as universal suffrage, popular referenda, and the like.

But when we come to this, we come to the realization that the old question whether the Constitution was democratic is a parochial one—parochial both in time and in space. The Progressive reformers of Beard's day, faced with exasperating

---

7 J. R. Pole, "Historians and the Problem of Early American Democracy," *American Historical Review,* 67 (1962), 626–46.

obstacles in the form of legal and constitutional limitations on reforms, retrospectively imposed their problems on those of the Federal era, and in so doing brought a certain new insight into it at the cost of a whole budget of new errors. Their pre-occupations can no longer cause us to fail to see—as Beard himself came to realize—that the Constitution was in fact a phase of American democratic development, a step in the transit of democratic institutions from the local and state level to central government. Nor need it cause us any longer to ignore the avant-garde character of the American political system in the political evolution of the Western world. The truly remarkable thing about the Americans—though we would do well to attribute it more to fortune and necessity than to virtue—was that at a time when the continent of Europe still lay restive under autocracy and when even English democracy was in a rudimentary and emergent stage, they were beginning, in the modern sense of the word, to have politics. That is, they were developing effective pluralities of inter-ests, forums of opinion, a broad popular suffrage, debate and discussion, bargain and compromise. This, with everything it involved for the possible ultimate self-assertion of the com-mon man, was revolutionary, and was rightly so regarded by European contemporaries, who would have been puzzled by the question whether the Constitution was a reactionary doc-ument. Indeed, they would no more have seen that the revo-lutionary impetus of the American experiment had been checked by the Constitution than Western observers in 1921 would have considered that Bolshevism had lost its character or force because of Lenin's New Economic Policy. The United States continued to be regarded as a revolutionary force for more than a generation afterward, even when the Americans might be thought to have been domesticated in the European state system. In 1824 Metternich, who knew what it was to be reactionary, responded to the Monroe Doctrine with a state-ment on what he thought to be the implications of the Ameri-can system: "These United States of America, which we have seen arise and grow, and which during their short youth already meditated projects which they dared not then avow, have suddenly left a sphere too narrow for their ambition, and have astonished Europe by a new act of revolt, more unprovoked, fully as audacious, and no less dangerous than the former. They have distinctly and clearly announced their intention to set not only power against power, but . . . altar against altar. In their indecent declarations they have cast blame and scorn on the institutions of Europe most worthy of respect, on the principles of its greatest sovereigns, on the whole of those measures which a sacred duty no less than an evident necessity has forced our governments to adopt to frustrate plans most criminal. In permitting themselves these unprovoked attacks, in fostering revolutions wherever they show themselves, in regretting those which have failed, in extending a helping hand to those which seem to prosper, they lend new strength to the apostles of sedition, and reanimate the courage of every conspirator. If this flood of evil doctrines and pernicious examples should extend over the whole of America, what would become of our religious and political institutions, of the moral force of our governments, and of that conservative system which has saved Europe from complete dissolution?"[8]

Metternich did not imagine that the United States had undergone any Thermidor with its Constitution of 1787; neither did those radicals, republicans, and constitutionalists who in Europe and Latin America took heart from the American experience. For them the American democracy remained a revolutionary inspiration. More than a century afterward, cramped within the limits of an eighteenth-century constitutional framework, many Progressives, naturally enough, found it impossible any longer to remember or believe in this aspect of the early American republic. For this they can scarcely be condemned out of hand by the present generation. Since the time of the Bolshevik Revolution, it has been hard for most Americans, and especially for those who make our world policies, to recapture the memory of the early United States, Constitution and all, as a revolutionary force.

---

[8] Quoted in Dexter Perkins, *A History of the Monroe Doctrine* (rev. ed., 1955), 56–7.

CHAPTER 8

Reconsiderations

> *Rare indeed is the savant who does not appear to be at war with himself in his own breast.*
>
> —Charles A. Beard, 1934
>
> *Olympian certitude has exploded.*
> —Charles A. Beard, 1940

I

BEARD, a friend wrote, had "a passionate nature that could be swept by great gusts of honest indignation." It was one of these gusts that blew him out of Columbia University in 1917. For several years there had been ill feeling between the Columbia faculty and the board of trustees, which was aggravated by the vain and imperious president, Nicholas Murray Butler. Even before the country was at war, the trustees, yielding to the general spirit of panic, had officiously resolved to investigate the faculty for the taint of disloyalty or subversion. A warmly worded petition from several leading professors failed to deter them, and they were perhaps egged on by Butler's declaration at the 1917 Commencement that, with the nation at war, freedoms of criticism formerly acceptable would now be "intolerable." Beard himself was summoned before a committee of the trustees to satisfy them that he had not, as a sensational newspaper alleged, condoned some inflammatory remarks about the flag made by a visiting speaker. The trustees also charged Beard, as chairman of the department of political science, to warn his colleagues that "teachings likely to inculcate disrespect for American institutions would not be tolerated." "I repeated my order to my colleagues," Beard later reported, "who received it with a shout of derision, one of them asking me whether Tammany Hall and the pork barrel were not American institutions!"

Finally the trustees dismissed the eminent psychologist

J. McKeen Cattell, an inveterate controversialist, and Henry
Wadsworth Longfellow Dana, a professor of comparative
literature, for their opposition to conscription. This act,
coupled as it was with a misleading announcement to the public that the faculty approved the decision, might have been
too much for Beard; but what seems to have made life at the
university finally intolerable for him was Butler's treatment of
Beard's young friend and colleague, Leon Fraser, an instructor
in politics in Columbia College. Taken up by President Butler
and engaged to work for the Association for International
Conciliation, Fraser had been encouraged by the president
himself in his quasi-pacifist views; but when war seemed
imminent, Fraser failed to veer as fast as Butler from visions
of world peace to militant nationalism. He made some critical
remarks about the preparedness camp at Plattsburg, for which
he was brought before the trustees and discharged. Though the
Cattell-Dana case was the ostensible reason for Beard's resignation, his close associates believed that what he saw as
Butler's moral irresponsibility with his own protégé was still
more decisive.[1]

Shortly after Dana and Cattell were sacked, Beard sent
his letter of resignation to Butler. "Having observed closely the
inner life of Columbia for many years," he wrote, "I have been
driven to the conclusion that the University is really under the
control of a small and active group of trustees who have no
standing in the world of education, who are reactionary and
visionless in politics, narrow and medieval in religion." The
status of the professor, Beard protested, had been "made
lower than that of the manual laborer, who, through his union,
has at least some voice in the terms and conditions of his employment." The university was being reduced "below the level

---

[1] The ironies of the Fraser case are too delectable to pass by. Soon
after his discharge for pacifism, he took pleasure in writing on
military stationery to inform the trustees that he had enlisted
in the army. His experiences overseas led to a career in international banking; he became a confidential adviser to Morgan
partners, and in 1936 took a place on the Columbia board of
trustees. There is good evidence that Beard, in this phase of
Fraser's career, came to think of him as a stuffed shirt. On Fraser,
see Matthew Josephson, "The Hat on the Roll-top Desk," *New
Yorker*, 17 (February 14, 1942), 22 ff.; 18 (February 21, 1942),
21 ff.

of a department store." He made it clear that he was himself in favor of entering the war, believing that "a victory for the German Imperial Government would plunge all of us into the black night of military barbarism." But many of his countrymen did not share this view, and their opinions could not be changed "by curses and bludgeons. Arguments addressed to their reason and understanding are our best hope." On the same day, Beard announced his resignation to his large lecture class and told the students that this was his last appearance. They rose and saluted him with volleys of cheers which left Beard silent and overwhelmed, tears streaming down his cheeks.

Though Beard, with his established reputation, was acting from a position of strength, it would be a mistake to underestimate the disinterestedness of his act, as a strong supporter of the war who resigned to defend its opponents, or to minimize his courage in exposing himself to the rapidly mounting malice and hysteria of wartime America, or to forget the contrast between the scrupulous regard he showed for the rights of dissenters and the unabashed and unrestrained enthusiasm with which most of the academic community became nationalistic propagandists. Beard was hardly the first American scholar to resign in solidarity with the victim of an academic-freedom controversy, but he did so at an exceptionally difficult moment; and he was the first to take the offensive and tell the governing board of a major university, in words that all the world could hear, just what he thought of them. It is on such courageous moments of self-assertion that the American tradition of academic freedom has been built.

This was an impassioned act, but also a typically individualistic one. During the year of his resignation, such distinguished contemporaries as John Dewey and Arthur O. Lovejoy were recruiting members to the newly organized American Association of University Professors; but Beard adamantly refused to join—even as he would later refuse, at the peak of his isolationist commitment, to join America First. "I regarded it," he wrote altogether prematurely of the A.A.U.P., "as a futile enterprise when it was begun, and the results have confirmed my suspicions." In Beard's character

there was not only a good deal of the radical but also a touch
of the rebel, with the rebel's impulse toward wholly individual
self-assertion. Though he was by no means withdrawn or
unsocial—a thing his curiosity itself would have prevented—
he frequently preferred to stand alone. He would wear no
man's collar, not even in a fraternal or congenial cause; and
the organized, tame, institutional life of the university scholar
was not for him. A dozen years after his departure from
Columbia he still found the universities wanting: "too much
routine, not enough peace; too much calm, not enough passion; . . . too many theories, not enough theory; too many
books, not enough strife of experience; too many students, not
enough seekers."[2]

Beard's retreat from Columbia to his house in New Milford, Connecticut, did not result in a life of seclusion. He continued for some years to advise the New York Bureau of
Municipal Research. He joined John Dewey, Alvin Johnson,
and James Harvey Robinson in organizing the New School
for Social Research in 1919. A few years later he helped to
establish the Workers Education Bureau of America, whose
purpose was to coordinate the various agencies that had
sprung up in this field in recent decades. In 1921 he took his
family to Europe, and in Paris was at pains to buy several
recent studies of the war guilt question. In 1922 he gave
a series of lectures on this issue at Dartmouth, published
as *Cross Currents in Europe Today*. The same year he
accepted an invitation from Viscount Goto, the Mayor of
Tokyo, to bring his knowledge of municipal administration to

---

2 On Beard's indignation, see Matthew Josephson, "Charles A.
Beard: A Memoir," *Virginia Quarterly Review*, 25 (1949), 586.
For Beard's resignation I have drawn on his own manifesto, "A
Statement," *New Republic*, 13 (1917), 249–50, and the account
by Walter P. Metzger in Hofstadter and Metzger, *The Development
of Academic Freedom in the United States* (1955), 498–502.
For Beard on the universities, see his essay, "Political Science"
in Wilson Gee, ed., *Research in the Social Sciences* (1929),
289–90.

    Beard was at times rather bitter about what he once called
the "temples of respectability," including the American Historical
Association. Denouncing the failure of historians to deal with
capital-labor conflicts, he wrote in 1921 that this "tabu is almost
perfect. The American Historical Association officially is as regular as Louis XIV's court scribes." *New Republic*, 25 (1921), 350.
In fact, his own works were generously received within the profession, and his influence was extraordinary.

bear upon the problems of that city, and a year later he was recalled to advise on the replanning of the city after the great earthquake and fire. His visit to Japan was followed by extended travel in China. In 1927 he accepted an invitation by the American-Yugoslav Society to do a study of the postwar regime in Yugoslavia, and went on to travel in central Europe and the Mediterranean. Of all those American writers who have come to be called isolationists, he was perhaps the least parochial in his awareness of the world.[3]

During the years after his resignation from Columbia Beard fell into a settled way of life at his house and farm. The house, a large, generously designed structure that had once been a boys' boarding school, looked out over the Housatonic River valley from a high hill and accommodated a substantial library. There the Beards' work day, which began soon after dawn, was singularly undisturbed—in the country Beard kept no telephone. In the early 1920's Beard also bought an apartment in New York, which he owned for many years; and there, or in Washington, he spent many winters, though in later years he often went to South Carolina or Arizona. His two small farms brought him some of his deepest satisfactions. Although Beard wrote of agricultural America without sentimentality, there was always in him a bit of the farm boy for whom an investment in the earth had a solidity not matched by paper securities (personalty!) of any kind. By the late 1920's he had accumulated a small fortune, to be only slightly diminished by the Wall Street crash, but it was his farms that he particularly treasured. "With a farm and cows, at least," he once said, "I can go and see to my investments with my own eyes. And if the times get very bad again I can, at least, eat my investments." During the Depression, when the milk producers of Connecticut went on strike, Beard was called upon by Governor Wilbur L. Cross to be chairman of a board appointed to study the milk business and settle the dispute. With that mastery of the practical that he had shown even at Oxford,

---

[3] It is possible, however, that his experience with the minorities problem in Yugoslavia was one of the main sources of Beard's conviction that the age-old problems of Europe are intractable and unamenable to useful intervention. See Mary Beard, *The Making of Charles A. Beard* (1955), 29, and Eric Goldman, *Rendezvous with Destiny* (1952), 282–3.

Beard led in making a settlement, and then in efforts to see that the milk farmers were better schooled in the advancement of their own interests. Again, in 1935, when he still held a few bonds of the Missouri-Pacific Railway, Beard became convinced that the bondholders were being cheated and he organized a bondholders' committee to take on the power of the Van Sweringen railway empire, led his group to the Senate Committee on Interstate Commerce to demand an investigation, and enjoyed the satisfaction of seeing the bankruptcy act modified along the lines he had demanded.

Neither his public interests, his rural existence, nor the ordeal of his growing deafness kept Beard from an active professional life, notable for his kindness to younger scholars. He did not fail to answer scrupulously, with old-fashioned courtesy and often in his own fine hand, a large miscellaneous correspondence, much of it in the form of demands and requests from strangers. He was elected president both of the American Historical Association and the American Political Science Association. To a remarkable degree he enjoyed both the benign stance of the sage and the more heady pleasures of the gadfly. Since his name had become a symbol for academic freedom and bold integrity, he was frequently called upon to lend his name or to draft a manifesto when some question of freedom or conscience was at stake. On occasion, stirred to exercise his commanding eloquence once again, Beard would deliver a sally reminiscent of his speeches to the workers of Todmorden. In 1925, Count Michael Károlyi, the former socialist premier of Hungary, was temporarily admitted to the United States by the State Department only on condition that he not discuss politics. When he was given a dinner by the American Civil Liberties Union in New York City, Beard came to speak. He would not enter upon the merits of any political controversy in Hungary, Beard began, but he would address himself to the state of American rights in the case, and particularly to the decision of the State Department "that we are not morally fit to hear anything that our guest may care to say on any subject. I am here to lift up my voice," Beard went on—and lift it he did, launching into a tirade against the official follies that had become commonplace since the war: "During the past decade officers of the Government of the United States have bullied and beaten citizens and aliens beyond the limits of decency. They have arrested persons without warrant, on gossip and suspicion . . . entered houses and searched premises, inflicted cruel and unusual punishments . . . worthy of Huns and Cossacks. . . . And where have been the pillars of society—the bishops, the clergy, the college presidents, and the self-constituted guardians of American institutions? Where have been the great lawyers—the Erskines of America?—ready to dare the wrath of kings and the stones of mobs, and write immortal pages in the history of Anglo-Saxon jurisprudence? Where have been the judges of the high courts? Echo answers: 'Where.' "[4]

It is an aging generation that can still remember with pleasure opening the morning paper one day in 1935 to read of another of Beard's memorable efforts. The Hearst newspaper chain was in the midst of one of its red-hunting inquisitions directed against schoolteachers in various parts of the country. Learning that Hearst's agents were working to win the endorsement of the National Education Association, some of its leaders invited Beard to address its annual convention at Atlantic City, and Beard, glad to oblige, came up with one of his sterling speeches, a blast that brought the audience to its feet with a tremendous ovation: "In the course of the past fifteen years I have talked with Presidents of the United States, Senators, Justices of the Supreme Court, Members of the House of Representatives, Governors, Mayors, bankers, editors, college presidents (including Charles W. Eliot), leading men of science, Nobel prize winners in science and letters, and I have never found one single person who for talents and character commands the respect of the American people, who has not agreed with me that William Randolph Hearst has pandered to depraved tastes and has been an enemy of everything that is best in the American tradition. . . . There is not a cesspool of vice and crime which Hearst has not raked and exploited for money-making purposes. No person with intellectual honesty or moral integrity will touch him with a ten

---

[4] "Count Károlyi and America," *Nation*, 120 (April 1, 1925) 347.

foot pole for any purpose or to gain any end. . . . Only cowards can be intimidated by Hearst."[5]

The desire for public influence that Beard had shown from his early days was quickened by the Depression. In the 1930's he frequently wintered in Washington, where he met with Senators, Cabinet members, and other government officials, and could sometimes be found offering advice on public issues, occasionally testifying before Congressional committees. Neither his travels of the 1920's nor his public activities of the 1930's, however, interrupted the flow of work from his hilltop—a continuous stream of articles and book reviews, a yield of almost fifty books of history—testimony, in all, to energies of demonic intensity. From the time of his departure from Columbia, his intellectual interests centered on three primary problems: the first, rounding out his economic interpretation of American history, preoccupied him particularly during the 1920's; the second, his growing concern with the problem of historical knowledge, was dominant in the mid-1930's; the last, which gripped him with increasing absorption from the mid-1930's to his death in 1948, was the problem of American foreign policy.

II

In his Columbia days Beard seems to have conceived the grand design of writing a series of monographs offering a complete economic interpretation of American political history on the elaborate scale of his book on the Constitution. Only one more such book was to be written, in fact, but it showed Beard gaining in strength as a historian. *Economic Origins of Jeffersonian Democracy* (1915), a readable, shrewd, often highly illuminating book, was the most solid of his early works. At many points it has been superseded by a proliferating monographic scholarship, but for a long time it was a profound influence on the profession, one of the few works of history that went beyond the immediate events it retold to provoke reflection on the course and meaning of American history as a whole.

---

[5] Quoted by George S. Counts, "Charles Beard, the Public Man," in Beale, ed., *Charles A. Beard*, 245–46.

The keynote of *Economic Origins* can be found in its epigraph, which Beard took from a recent essay by Frederick Jackson Turner: "We may trace the contest between the capitalist and the democratic pioneer from the earliest colonial days."[6] In Beard's book the battle between Jeffersonian Republicanism and Federalism is, *au fond,* simply a battle between capitalism and agriculture, a direct continuation of the struggle over the Constitution. He was at great pains to stress the continuity between the Federalists of 1787–8 and Hamilton's party of the 1790's, between the Anti-Federalists and followers of Jefferson. Hamilton's financial system (and after it, his foreign policies which are its logical corollaries) appears as the consummation of the movement for the Constitution. The members of the Federal Convention of 1787 reappear as friends or members of the Washington administration, whose fiscal policies consolidate the gains of capitalists. The public-security holders reappear as profiteers from Hamilton's fiscal schemes. Stressing these continuities, Beard finds political parties emerging in Congress with rather sharp definition from the very first session when men fell out over Hamilton's plans for funding the national debt and assuming the debts of the states.

At some points we still find Beard pushing his evidence very hard. His proposition about the essential continuity of the personnel of two "parties" seems basically right, though it would be misleading if applied to Virginia, and it should not be taken to suggest that there was direct *structural* continuity between the Anti-Federalists of the constitutional controversy and the Jeffersonian Republican party that emerged in the 1790's.[7] His account of the later political affiliations and

---

[6] In "Social Forces in American History" (1911), reprinted in *Frontier,* 325.

[7] Beard's account in chapter ii of the subsequent party affiliations of the Fathers plays tricks by using two different criteria to classify a man as a Federalist: if he will not qualify for his open partisan loyalties or his position on the main economic issues, he can be made to qualify because he is no democrat, does not "cherish the people." The latter procedure begs an important question: whether the difference between Federalists and Republicans in the 1790's was in fact marked by clear and universal differences in political philosophy. I find particularly suspect his account of such members as Pierce Butler, Elbridge Gerry, Charles Pinckney, Edmund Randolph, John Rutledge, Richard Spaight, Hugh Williamson, and Robert Yates.

views of the members of the Federal Convention, like his
account of their "doctrines" in the preceding book, is an exercise in special pleading. Probably the most vulnerable aspect
of the book is that by concentrating on the most heated spokesmen and ignoring the more placatory or noncommitted, Beard
puts the emergence of clear party patterns of voting much
earlier than many more recent scholars would place them, and
considerably exaggerates the acerbity of the battle over Hamilton's plans for funding and assumption. It is doubtful that
funding was the profoundly divisive issue he made it out to
be; assumption came closer to having this effect, but was less
a question of class conflict, more a question of the adjustment
of conflicting state interests than Beard sees.[8]

   The Economic Origins of Jeffersonian Democracy under-
goes a curious shift in character about halfway through,
marked by an unresolved tension between the way it begins
and the way it ends. The story opens with the battle between
agrarians and capitalists—the same "sharp antagonism
throughout almost the entire country" that had been brought
about by the Constitution—still raging at a fever pitch over
the Hamiltonian system. Since this is described even at the
beginning as "violent," it is hardly surprising that by the
time of the furor over the Jay treaty, opposition has mounted
to "a deep and fervent" dissatisfaction, and that the country is
"sharply divided." The battle lines have not really changed for
Beard: he sees the victory of Adams in the close presidential
election of 1796 as "a victory for the party that had framed

   On some limitations of Beard's argument about the continuity
of the two sides, see Noble Cunningham, Jr., *The Jeffersonian
Republicans: The Formation of Party Organization, 1789–1801*
(1957), 23, and Harry Ammon, "The Formation of the Republican Party in Virginia, 1789–96," *Journal of Southern History*,
19 (1953), 309 ff. However, out of a sample of about 150 leading
persons involved in the battle over the adoption of the Constitution, Jackson T. Main finds support for Beard's general contention: Anti-Federalists became Jeffersonian Republicans in a
ratio of about five to one; Federalists became party Federalists
by about six to one. *The Anti-Federalists*, 260 n.
   The critical remarks on this work by Merrill D. Peterson, *The
Jeffersonian Image in the American Mind* (1960), 314–21, are
penetrating.
[8] On funding and assumption, see Ferguson, *The Power of the
Purse*, 297–305, especially 304–5; 319–25. On the pace of development of party polarization, see Cunningham, *passim*, and
Joseph Charles, *The Origins of the American Party System*
(1956), 91–7.

the Constitution and carried it into effect."[9] But now, just as the acute issues of the Adams administration bring us to a sharp split within the Federalist party (and by Beard's terms in the capitalist elite), and just as the character of the political order is being tested by a really deep political crisis, Beard's whole focus of interest changes. He has begun with the foreground issues of politics: Hamilton's funding, assumption, the national bank, tariffs and taxation, and with the reaction to them of agrarian and capitalist factions. Now, rather suddenly, the leading events and issues of politics slip into the background, and the foreground is occupied by sketches of the political and economic *thought* of John Adams, John Taylor, and Jefferson.

Presumably Beard was only following the drift of his interests rather than some conscious intellectual strategy, but the consequences of this change of focus are important: they cause us to turn away from the grave test of the political order that came with the quasi-war with France, the Alien and Sedition Acts, the split among the Federalists, and the election of Jefferson and to lose the thread of events in the discussion of philosophies—a strange procedure for one who has thus far been urging us to accept an economic interpretation of history. But it is intelligible that Beard has lost his sense of direction if we realize that with the crisis of 1798–1801 we have come to a point in the story at which certain problems have moved into the center of the stage for the account of which Beard's scheme of thought is far from adequate. Then, at the end of the book, when Beard returns to the election of Jefferson, and to an estimation of his policies in relation to the capitalist-agrarian controversy, the work reverts to its original theme. But a sea-change has taken place in the argument. It cannot be said fairly that Beard has contradicted himself, but he has certainly veered off in a new and unexplained direction. It is much as though the historian of class struggles has yielded place to the universal iconoclast, who cannot resist the temptation to take Jefferson down, just as he has done with Jefferson's opponents. (This is one of the qualities which makes Beard's history so much superior to the effusions of wholly partisan historians like Claude Bowers.)

[9] *Economic Origins*, I, 248, 299.

To put it not as Beard did but as a vulgar Marxist might, Beard treats Jefferson as a sell-out. Beard himself carefully avoids such pejorative epithets. He traces the peculiar circumstances of the election of 1800–1 to show that Jefferson, hamstrung by his tie with Burr in the electoral college, needed some Federalist support to become President, and came into office on the strength of a delicate, indirect understanding with certain Federalist leaders. This is seen not as an act of perfidy but as a political calculation based on the necessities of the situation. Jefferson and his advisers, Beard wrote, "decided that the country could not be ruled without the active support, or at least the acquiescence, of the capitalistic interests," and his "practical politics propitiated rather than alienated" these interests. Jefferson "skillfully used and conciliated the very classes that he had denounced."[1] Hence, not only did the Jeffersonians refrain from the quixotry of trying to undo what could not be undone by repudiating or scaling down Hamilton's well-laid schemes for funding and assumption, but they left the Bank of the United States to live out its charter, and they even built up their own faction of bankers. ("I am decidedly in favor," Jefferson wrote, "of making all the banks Republican, by sharing deposits among them in proportion to the dispositions they show.")

Not only the economic issues of the 1790's but the hostile philosophies have thus dissolved. On the subject of majority rule, Beard finds, "it is difficult to see just wherein Jefferson and his party differed from the Federalists."[2] (Here Beard comes to the verge of what would now be called consensus history.) So, while the book starts with capitalists and agrarians almost at each others' throats, it ends on a strangely irenic note: the agrarian leaders have taken over, but they have done very little to change things after all.

At the close of the book, in one of his magisterial summations, Beard concluded: "Jeffersonian democracy did not imply any abandonment of the property, and particularly

---

[1] Ibid., 446, 467.
[2] Ibid., 452. But in chapter ii Beard had worked on a different assumption, since he classified some men politically by their attitudes toward majority rule.

the landed, qualifications on the suffrage or office-holding; it did not involve any fundamental alterations in the national Constitution which the Federalists had designed as a foil to the levelling propensities of the masses; it did not propose any new devices for a more immediate and direct control of the voters over the instrumentalities of government. Jeffersonian Democracy simply meant the possession of the federal government by the agrarian masses led by an aristocracy of slave-owning planters, and the theoretical repudiation of the right to use the Government for the benefit of any capitalistic groups, fiscal, banking, or manufacturing."[3]

The immense distance that has divided the antagonists, the earth-shaking issues over which they have fought, have suddenly and surprisingly shrunk to a marginal difference. This unresolved change of focus underlines the chief weakness of the book: the economic issues of the early 1790's, so important for Beard and invoked as the basic cause of the party cleavage, appear in perspective to have been far milder than those which nearly broke the political system between 1794 and 1801. Political antagonisms became almost unmanageably acute only when complicated by deep emotional issues arising out of foreign policy, the repercussions of the French Revolution, increasing sectional antagonism, and party animosity. Without denying the urgency of the economic differences, it is hard to get away from the independent role played by party organization, by sectional estrangement, even by powerful individual personalities—forces not organic to Beard's system. Here, as in the preceding book, Beard has grasped an important historical force and exploited it with such gusto that other forces of comparable importance have been crowded out of our view. Despite this, he left a work of lasting value.

In a certain sense, Beard's book may be seen as one of the early historical efforts at Progressive self-criticism. This is true not only in that he raised troublesome questions about the adequacy of the Jeffersonian heritage, but that behind his concern about the failure of earlier agrarianism to mount an

3 Ibid., 467.

effective defense of the public interest against the encroach-
ments of capitalism one could also see the signs of his misgivings about twentieth-century Progressivism on the same
grounds, and, in particular, of his persistent skepticism about
Woodrow Wilson's devotion to restoring the old, competitive,
petty-capitalist America. In 1914, while this book was being
written, Beard had published an article on "Jefferson and the
New Freedom" in which this skepticism was made explicit,
and in which he hinted that Wilson's "independent men of
affairs" would be no more successful than Jefferson's farmers
in ruling America.[4] It seems significant that in writing this
book Beard reverted chiefly to works of Federalist historians
and made relatively little use of Jeffersonians. However, by
breaking his story off at 1801, with hardly more than a few
forward-looking remarks on Jeffersonian fiscal policies, Beard
(unlike Henry Adams, who had plotted the ground so brilliantly a quarter of a century earlier, but whom Beard seems
to have used curiously little) did not make the fullest use of
a valid insight: had he gone further and discussed the era
of the Embargo and the War of 1812, he would have been
able to make an even stronger case than he did about the
Jeffersonians' reversal of their original principles, for he would
then have been obliged to discuss how leading Jeffersonians
reversed themselves (by 1806) on the necessity of internal
improvements, how Jefferson violated his own scruples about
centralization and individual liberty in his ruthless enforcement of the embargo, and how Jeffersonian Republican war
policies left the country with a new national bank and a
national debt far greater than the Hamiltonians had ever
contemplated. As a historical ironist, Beard was, though intensely stimulating, still somewhat half-hearted.

Beard never continued with his planned series of monographs in the economic interpretation of American politics,
but he did provide a broad synthesis of American history
conceived in such terms. He reached the peak of his public
influence as a historian with *The Rise of American Civilization*, written with Mary Beard and published in 1927. A two-

---

4 "Jefferson and the New Freedom," *New Republic*, 1 (1914),
18–19. See also Beard's review of Wilson's *The New Freedom*,
Political Science Quarterly, 29 (1914), 506–7.

volume general history which restated the results of much modern scholarship for the common reader, this book was pervaded by a unifying conception rare in such works and was informed by the spirit of contemporary critical thought. Probably the best general history of the United States in comparable dimensions that had thus far been written, *The Rise of American Civilization* was received with all but universal enthusiasm, enjoyed splendid sales, and did more than any other such book of the twentieth century to define American history for the reading public. For a long time, a significant portion of those who took up the professional study of history did so under its influence. Even today, read sympathetically and with care, it yields a fair quota of interesting suggestions and shrewd anticipations of later studies.[5] And yet one returns to it with a distinct sense of disappointment. I found it hard to understand, much less recapture, the sense of excitement I had on reading it for the first time in 1934, when all American history seemed to dance to Beard's tune. The manner is no longer ingratiating, and the matter overpresses the economic interpretation of events to a degree that is fatiguing and no longer enlightening. It is not that the economic interpretation of history has altogether ceased to have its point, but that its impact has been absorbed and it brings no further novelty or illumination to counterbalance the occasional absurdities committed in its name. We are interested in different things now, and the final effect of the book today is much as though a past master at rounders should suddenly appear and thrust himself, self-confidently, into a game of modern baseball.

The style of *The Rise of American Civilization*, and of the succeeding books written in the cycle it began (*America in Midpassage, The American Spirit*), is in marked contrast to Beard's earlier work. In the books on the Constitution and Jeffersonian democracy, presumably for limited professional audiences, Beard had used a severe, almost ascetic medium, well adapted to what he was trying to do, unobtrusive, im-

---

[5] For example: "The American ruling classes, unlike the French bourgeoisie, had already wrested the government from the royal authorities by 1765; their uprising was designed to preserve what they had, rather than to gain something new and untried." *Rise*, I, 187.

mensely competent. Now, reaching for a broader audience and working on a larger canvas, he became expansive, rhetorical, sententious. There was always present in Beard, though carefully suppressed much of the time, a love of the overblown, an affection for rhetoric of a kind that was still heard but beginning to fade in his youth; and along with this penchant for gorgeous prose there came a certain vulnerability to the high-flown, not unmixed with an occasional note of self-dramatization. ("When it is dark enough," he liked to say, "you can see the stars," and on one occasion he announced: "When I come to the end, my mind will still be beating its wings against the bars of thought's prison." He considered, Arthur W. Macmahon recalled, that the greatest lines in English poetry were the closing lines of Shelley's *Prometheus Unbound*.)[6] Now, writing in the grand manner, Beard took on an Olympian tone and devised a medium at once strangely impersonal and yet remarkably wrought-up, a florid popular style, heavy with adjectives, cliché metaphors and stock phrases ("as light as gossamer," "an hour fraught with destiny"), and dotted with occasional archaisms—forsooths, fain woulds, and besoughts—and strokes of ironic condescension. Add to this occasional classical allusions or comparisons —the United States drawn against the background of Greece, Rome, Egypt, the Muslim world, an Ozymandias-aroma of dead empires—and one has a nineteenth-century aura of beautiful letters somewhat incongruous with the sly notes of realism, the occasional modern wise guy's reduction to hard-boiled economic realities that so often mark its insights. It is startling to think that this style was contemporary with *The Sun Also Rises*, and that both books were no doubt enjoyed by many of the same readers. In some aspects of this style one recognizes a persistent American note, which might be called the fallacy of superfluous enumeration: the belief that an intrinsically simple historical proposition acquires depth and force by having the central actors or scenes spelled out at length. Thus when the Beards want to tell us that a certain issue was argued about wherever ideas were discussed, they

---

6 Eric Goldman and Arthur W. Macmahon in *Charles A. Beard*, 7, 221.

write instead: "Each separate battle in the general campaign was carried on by some active group of private citizens driving upon some particular angle, redoubt, turret, or gateway of the mighty structure thrown up by the drift of three hundred years. In a thousand obscure corners, as well as in great open assemblies, the forays and agitations were organized: in city councils, state legislatures, women's clubs, trade unions, grange conferences, reform associations, party caucuses and conventions, the Congress of the United States, the chambers and public rooms of judicial courts, executive mansions, and editorial sanctums."[7]

It is an Olympian Beard who presides over *The Rise of American Civilization,* an observer of the "sweep of economic forces," of the great tides of history that countermand individual wills and mock human hopes and aspirations. The work is filled with a certain wry, sad wisdom, congenial perhaps to the mood of the 1920's, though rather at odds with the dynamic and exhortatory Beard who was to emerge in the 1930's. "All were caught up," he wrote of the political leaders of the Civil War era, "and whirled in a blast too powerful for their wills, too swift for their mental operations." Again: "So dim is the vision of the wisest of statesmen! So far astray do the calculations of the learned and the great lead them!" "Such havoc," he sighs at last, "does fate play with the little schemes of men!"[8]

One quality that made the Beards' book so attractive at first has finally shortened its life: Beard's intellectual daring, his readiness to commit himself on point after point, left him unwilling to rely anywhere on the force of narration alone for his effects; his hunger for understanding, his desire to sound the limits of the economic interpretation, led him to venture an explanation of almost every major phase of American history, leaving his flanks fully exposed to the ravages of later scholarly revisionists. As one advances through American history with the Beards, one witnesses the capture of one "redoubt" after another for the economic interpretation of history. Those familiar with Beard's mind are

---

7 *Rise,* II, 543.
8 *Rise,* I, 596; II, 62, 544.

hardly surprised to find an economic interpretation of Puritanism (the "Protestant revolt against the Catholic system was
strongly economic in character"), but Beard seems to have
had even less patience for certain kinds of ideas than in his
earlier works. He challenged the view that Puritanism was
"essentially religious in character," since he saw its religious
lingo as a mere expedient, "the defense mechanism of men
who were engaged in resisting taxes and other exactions,"
and assured his readers that "the historian need not tarry
long with the logical devices of men in action." Neither the
thought of the seventeenth-century Puritans nor of such a
latter-day figure as Jonathan Edwards seemed to him to require much study. Edwards he treated mainly as a pulpit
spellbinder, his works he regarded as "occult writings."[9] He
went on to portray the American Revolution as an economic
clash between metropolis and colony, marked also by an
internal division among the colonials between conservative
merchants and planters and small farmers and mechanics.
The constitutional controversy was accounted for in terms
substantially similar to Beard's earlier works, the War of 1812
as the outcome (in John Randolph's old words) of "agrarian
cupidity"—the search for "more virgin lands," a better position in the fur trade, and an end to the menace of unfriendly
Indians. Jacksonian democracy was characterized as "a
triumphant farmer-labor party"—a conception in which
Beard had some predecessors and many followers, but one
which has been ravaged by recent research.

What probably left the deepest impress on Beard's
readers was his brilliant interpretation of the Civil War as the
Second American Revolution. He was little interested in
the argument over the morality of slavery, and he dismissed
the agitations of the abolitionists as of small direct consequence because of their lack of appeal to the public.
Neither did legalistic arguments over states' rights and secession detain him, nor the strategems and battles that had
long fascinated military antiquarians. He saw the whole
catastrophe as America's counterpart of the Puritan revolu-

9 *Rise*, I, 28, 31, 148.

tion or the French Revolution—an inevitable battle of rival
social classes ending in a transit of power, a "social cataclysm
in which the capitalists, laborers, and farmers of the North
and West drove from power in the national government the
planting aristocracy of the South." This interpretation was
worked out in substantial detail. The key to the revolution
lay in the battle between capitalists and planters over measures of national policy: tariffs, homesteads, railroad land
grants, banking, and currency. What turned the balance was
that the free farmers, once linked politically with the South,
were lured away and forged into an alliance with the capitalists of the North under the aegis of the Republican party.
With the power of the slaveholders shattered, the Northern
capitalists were able to impose their economic program,
quickly passing a series of measures on tariffs, banking,
homesteads, and immigration that guaranteed the success
of their plans for economic development. Solicitude for the
freedman had little to do with Northern policies. The Fourteenth Amendment, which gave the Negro his citizenship,
Beard found significant primarily as the result of a conspiracy
of a few legislative draftsmen friendly to corporations to
use the supposed elevation of the blacks as a cover for
fundamental law giving strong new protection to business
corporations against regulation by state governments. So
skeptical was Beard about the force of the idealistic and
humane goals of the war, which he saw swallowed up in
the maw of capitalist greed, and so critical was his treatment of the capitalist interests that battened on the war and
on its legislative results, that his interpretation has struck
one student of historiography as unwittingly lending itself
to a pro-Confederate interpretation.[1]

For a generation weary of histories rehearsing the old

---

[1] *Rise*, II, 38–42, 54, 111–14; Thomas J. Pressly, *Americans
Interpret their Civil War* (1954; ed., 1962), 242–3. There is a
large and proliferating literature relevant to Beard's view of the
Fourteenth Amendment. Much of it was touched off by two important articles by Howard J. Graham, "The 'Conspiracy Theory'
of the Fourteenth Amendment," *Yale Law Journal*, 47 (1938),
371–403, and its sequel, ibid, 48 (1938), 171–94. The effect of
Graham's work was, once again, to downgrade the importance
of the search for motives.

constitutional debates about secession or retelling the annals of unremembered battles, this view of the Civil War had the force of revelation. It put American history into the pattern of western European history—we too had our "bourgeois" revolution—and while it offered a new, down-to-earth perspective on the history of American industrialism, it seemed at the same time to explain a great deal of the unfinished business of American society to the critical generations of the 1920's and 1930's. There still seems to be much merit in seeing the Civil War as a social revolution, though the details of Beard's development of the theme have been considerably eroded by later scholarship. Oddly enough, this interpretation finally ceased to appear viable to the Beards themselves. When they wrote their *Basic History* seventeen years later, the Second American Revolution disappeared into the same limbo into which so many other Beardian *aperçus* had gone. Now, though economic issues were not altogether forgotten, the origins of the war were described as an outgrowth of "party strife." The conflict itself was accounted for under the modest and relatively conventional rubric, "National Unity Sealed in an Armed Contest."[2]

III

In the early and middle 1930's Beard underwent an intellectual conversion from a firm adherence to the economic interpretation of history to a form of historical relativism that proved impossible to square with his earlier views. It is hard to say whether this conversion owed anything in the beginning to misgivings about his own work; but it clearly arose in good part out of the disillusionments and fears that came with the 1929 crash and the Great Depression, events which impelled him to reconsider his ideas about the nature of historical writing. He had been raised on the historical thought of the post-Darwinian period when historians were commonly activated by the scientific ideal. The historian, it was then believed, should be, and frequently man-

---

2 *Basic History*, chapters xvi, xvii.

aged to be, objective and detached in relation to his materials. He was thought to have the necessary methods and techniques to put his discipline on a footing comparable to that of the natural sciences. His results, though partial, were felt to have about them the promise of something definitive. History was a meaningful sequence, whose events could be read and interpreted, even put to some positive social purpose. This hope for history was sustained by a social optimism bred by the material progress of Beard's lifetime and by the social reforms of the Progressive era. When a few American historians, led by Beard and Becker, began to mount a campaign for historical relativism, the belief in scientific history had not yet been closely re-examined; and in this respect, as Beard took relish in pointing out, the Americans, mired in their insularity, were all of thirty years behind their co-workers in Europe. Around 1930 Beard became familiar with some of the European writing on the subject, notably with the work of Karl Heussi, Benedetto Croce, and Karl Mannheim, and took on the task of acquainting Americans with this important speculative literature.

Here, though he perhaps thought otherwise, Beard was little more than a gadfly and a popularizer. Most of the philosophers and historians who have written about his work on the problem of historical knowledge have judged it to be not only derivative but fragmentary, obscure, and sometimes contradictory. I find no reason to quarrel with the prevailing judgment; still, it seems to me that the work of both Beard and Becker in this area, by the sheer force of its provocativeness was useful in opening an overdue debate on the nature and terms of historical understanding, a debate which was to unseat the established complacency of the American historical profession about its assumptions. To this debate Beard brought slender philosophical gifts and a sometimes startling disregard for intellectual rigor, but he also brought an earnest, groping, dissatisfied mind, often an enviable degree of intellectual candor. Before concluding that all his efforts were in vain, a student of the subject would do well to reread the famous controversy with Theodore Clarke Smith, in which Beard's openness to heresy and

his humility about what the historian can do contrasts strikingly with Smith's smug dogmatism about the impartiality of
existing historical science.[3]

Beard's first full statement of his position was made in
his presidential address to the American Historical Association in December 1933, in which he called upon the historian to "cast off his servitude to the assumptions of natural
science and return to his own subject matter—to history
as actuality. The hour for this final declaration of independence has arrived. . . ."[4] In urging that history break
with the scientific ideal, Beard did not argue that scientific
method has no place in historical work; he merely expressed
his view of its decisive limitations. He never denied, so far as
I can determine, that historians can make warrantable assertions or establish reliable sequences of fact. On this count he
was careful to distinguish between what he called history
as knowledge and history as thought. "George Washington
crossed the Delaware" is, in his terms, an instance of historical knowledge of a kind that historians can establish in
profusion. Beard readily granted (with consequences for the
rest of his argument that some critics consider fatal) that
"particular phases of history once dark and confused have
been illuminated by research, authentication, scrutiny, and
the ordering of immediate relevancies." "Beyond doubt," he
wrote elsewhere, "scholars of competence can agree on many
particular truths and large bodies of established facts."[5] The
methods that had yielded such results need hardly be abandoned. But: "The historian is bound by his craft to recognize
the nature and limitations of the scientific method and to
dispel the illusion that it can produce a science of history
embracing the fullness of history, or of any large phase, as
past actuality."

It was history as thought—that is, the interpretation and
explanation of large phases of the historical past—which

[3] T. C. Smith, "The Writing of American History in America from
1884 to 1934," *American Historical Review*, 40 (1935), 439–49;
Beard, "That Noble Dream," ibid., 41 (1935), 74–87.
[4] Except where otherwise indicated, quotations in the following
paragraphs are from "Written History as an Act of Faith,"
American Historical Review, 39 (1934), 220–2, 226–8.
[5] "That Noble Dream," 76.

Beard had in mind when he invoked his newly achieved relativist skepticism. What interested him was the conditions of historical understanding concerning major phases of the drama of human existence, interpretations that have a bearing upon basic human loyalties and affect major decisions. And in the effort to achieve such understanding, he argued, no historian can arrive at more than a partial and biased version of the past. Each one is locked into a frame of reference.[6] The truth of a historical work is not timeless or universal but relative to the setting in which it was written; and it can be understood only in that setting.

Beard argued for this conclusion, sometimes rather confusedly, on three different grounds: the historian's need to work with hypotheses and categories, his need to select his facts, and the inevitability of bias. The total bulk of documentation available to the historian, he argued, can only be an incomplete and partial representation of what actually happened. Still, it is unmanageably voluminous. No account, therefore, can simply reproduce the past in miniature. From the vast materials available to him the historian must select. He must arrange what he has selected in some order. And in order to select and arrange, he must work with some preexisting categories of explanation or hypotheses which will tell him what is important. Every act of selection, every choice, is an act of thought, a kind of imposition on the materials. The selection and arrangement of facts "will be controlled by the historian's frame of reference composed of things deemed necessary and things deemed desirable." (Later he added things deemed possible.)[7]

From these methodological and epistemological conclusions Beard moved on rapidly to sociological ones relating to personal and social bias. "Has it not been said for a century or more that each historian who writes history is a

---

[6] This should not be taken to mean that Beard thought that each individual is imprisoned in his own personal and singular frame of reference. He believed that total chaos in historical communication is averted because the number of possible frames of reference is historically and sociologically limited. Beard and Vagts, "Currents of Thought in Historiography," *American Historical Review*, 42 (1937), 480–1.

[7] Beard and Vagts, "Currents of Thought in Historiography," *American Historical Review*, 42 (1937), 480.

product of his age and that his work reflects the spirit of the times, of a nation, race, group, class, or section? . . . Every student of history knows that his colleagues have been influenced in their selection and ordering of materials by their biases, prejudices, beliefs, affections, general upbringing and experience, particularly social and economic; and if he has a sense of propriety, to say nothing of humor, he applies the canon to himself, leaving no exception to the rule. The pallor of waning time, if not of death, rests upon the latest volume of history, fresh from the roaring press."

Somehow the fate of civilization, and the function of historical writing in relation to it, were linked in Beard's mind with the problem of relativism. The unifying and sustaining thread in his conception of history was that it ought to be an agency of social improvement, a guide to civilization. In his earlier phase he had taken comfort in the thought that "scientific" history, with its emphasis (in his own version) on the sweep of economic forces, pointed toward inevitable progress, and yet presumably showed how destiny might be assisted here and there by policy. The idea of progress was confirmed by the history of human advancement, which he saw to be firmly founded on technological gains. Through the ups and downs of history, and in spite of all the setbacks brought about by one or another piece of human folly, Beard had discerned a firm long-range trend toward man's increasing control of his environment, toward a material power that would be more and more put to humane and satisfactory uses. Now, in the wake of the first World War and the Great Depression, when so much of what he believed had been undercut, Beard was much less sure of all this. Thus far it is not hard to follow the course of his thought. But for reasons which he did not make wholly clear, he seems to have thought that historical relativism, chastened and skeptical though it was, offered something more positive than mere skepticism about the finality of historical knowledge. He seems to have believed that it would provide a way of re-establishing, even if in a somewhat less direct way than his diminished optimism, the service of historical writing to human advancement. If this service was to be performed, the historian must be liberated from his fealty to the nineteenth-century scientific ideal.

It is hard to see that he ever made it wholly clear how relativism would serve civilization. Certainly it is possible to argue against him that if historical writing is to be seen as a perpetual series of revisions, each responding to newly emergent frames of reference, its net yield in the way of firm views of the world would be too slight and too evanescent to provide any guides to policy. For whatever reason, Beard apparently dismissed this view of the matter. What is certain is that, in his mind, these speculations about historical knowledge were intimately linked with the future of mankind. He was content to admit, however, as he told his fellow historians, that all their conclusions about meaning and significance in history as a whole rested largely upon acts of faith. In history he saw three basic possibilities: it may be nothing but a chaos, in which case interpretations are impossible; it may move in cycles, as Spengler and others argued; or it may be progressing toward some more ideal order, as imagined by Condorcet, Adam Smith, Marx, Spencer. Since the available evidence is not wholly amenable to any one of these views, the historian "consciously or unconsciously performs an act of faith, as to order and movement, for certainty as to order and movement is denied to him by knowledge of the actuality with which he is concerned." He is not like the scientist, but rather like the statesman dealing with public affairs, in that he must make choices in contingent situations, must act on imperfect knowledge. "His faith is at bottom a conviction that something can be known about the movement of history and his conviction is a subjective decision, not purely objective discovery." Beard's own "guess" as to the movement of history was that it is tending toward "a collectivist democracy" and not a capitalist or proletarian dictatorship—a guess "founded on long trends and on a faith in the indomitable spirit of mankind."

It is not my purpose here to assess the validity of historical relativism, beyond saying that one can find more effectively argued versions than Beard's. In his venture into

philosophy, Beard stumbled over difficulties that are in their
own right quite formidable, and introduced others that were
gratuitous. He seems to have reasoned from the proposition
that the historian cannot know the *whole* past, as it actually
happened, to the conclusion that he cannot make generally
valid assertions about the relations of some of its parts.
At times he seems to have confused hypotheses with value
commitments, the psychological and social origins of a historical interpretation with questions about its intrinsic merits.
He did not define satisfactorily either the nature of the "objective" or "absolute" truth which he said historians could
not achieve or the "relative" truth which he thought could
be established within a particular frame of reference. He
was obscure about the relation between history as knowledge,
whose "scientific" and cumulative character he freely conceded, and history as thought. He often committed himself,
even in developing his relativist argument, to conclusions
("founded on long trends") that seemed by their very nature
to suggest that he had found some objective (nonrelativist)
criteria on which their validity could be established. He
never succeeded in surmounting the basic problem of relativism: that when its own canons of criticism are turned
against it, one opens an endless and dizzying vista of self-
propagating subjectivisms.

It becomes clear, as one reads Beard's speculative writings of the 1930's that his reconsideration of some of his
earlier certainties finally prompted second thoughts about
the economic interpretation of American history with which
he had been preoccupied for about twenty years. His debate
with Theodore Clarke Smith showed that the economic interpretation of history was one of the issues at stake in the
controversy over relativism. Beard's commitment to the economic interpretation of the Constitution gave him a special
spur. His conversion to relativist views seems to have served
more than one function in Beard's development, but among
them, I believe, was that he thought it would enable him
indirectly to acknowledge some of the limitations of his
book on the Constitution—and by implication of all such
special efforts at interpretation—while at the same time
retreating to new and (he might have thought) more tenable

positions in its defense. He had become aware too, if only by seeing what others who did not share his peculiar ambivalence about the Fathers had made out of his interpretation, how frail, imperfect, and double-edged the communication of historical thought can be.

When he made his retrospective defense of *An Economic Interpretation of the Constitution* in the 1935 edition, it was a relativist defense that Beard invoked (and not, I think, a satisfactory one). He pointed to the title itself: he had called his book *an,* not *the,* economic interpretation of the Constitution—which only brings us to wonder whether he thought that several alternative economic interpretations of the Constitution might be equally valid. He also remarked that his readers had been fairly put on guard by the nature of his title as to the special and partial character of the interpretation they were about to be exposed to. There is nothing definitive, he now seemed to be saying, and nothing was ever intended to be, about my view of the Constitution; it is just one of several perspectives from which the Constitution can profitably be seen. "An economic interpretation," he wrote in 1935, "is merely what it professes to be—a version, not the absolute truth, of history."[8]

But Beard's relativism hardly extricated him from the difficulties arising out of previous firm intellectual commitments; indeed, it made new difficulties for him. He had always asserted that he was getting behind appearances to "realities," that he was penetrating high-flown talk, windy abstractions, and insubstantial ideas to get at the "intimate essence" of history. This assumed that there was somewhere a firm point of anchorage from which certain views of history could be assessed as superior to others, that there were some neutral criteria having nothing to do with anyone's value commitments. He now threw this assumption overboard. In his presidential address of 1933 he confidently announced that "the assumption that any historian can be a disembodied spirit as coldly neutral to human affairs as the engineer to an automobile . . . [has] been challenged and rejected." In the past, he insisted, written history that

---

[8] "That Noble Dream," 84.

was "cold, factual, and apparently undisturbed by the passions of the time served best the interests of those who did
not want to be disturbed." But not long afterward, preparing the new edition of *An Economic Interpretation of the
Constitution*, he was back again in the mental framework
of "scientific" history: "Indeed," he there argued, "an economic analysis may be coldly neutral, and in the pages of
this volume no words of condemnation are pronounced upon
the men enlisted upon either side of the great controversy. . . .
This volume is, strictly speaking, impartial. . . . It applies
no moralistic epithets to either party." But his concession
to his own relativism only opened endless prospects of historical subjectivity. His book, he avowed, "does not 'explain'
the Constitution. It does not exclude other explanations
deemed more satisfactory to the explainers."[9] This is an
astounding statement; for the whole bearing of his book
had been to exclude certain other interpretations as superficial and delusive, and his first chapter had been given
over to this contention. It was impossible to maintain that
the book on the Constitution had been in fact written in a
relativist frame of mind. Beard's attempt now to put it in
such a light hinted that he was beginning to have some misgivings, as yet inarticulate, about its adequacy.

Beard also seems to have begun to have his doubts, perhaps inspired by reading Croce, about the idea of causality
in history, upon which the whole conception of an economic
interpretation depended.[1] And though he apparently wavered
over abandoning the whole idea of causality, he was troubled
by the problem of one-way causality in a system of economic interpretation. The economic interpretation of history,
as Beard never ceased to see, has a great deal to recommend
it to the working historian. But it is haunted by a fundamental philosophical difficulty: once the economic interpretation is made sufficiently flexible to survive—that is,
once we admit that all kinds of noneconomic forces have a

---

[9] *An Economic Interpretation*, ix–x, xiii–xiv. Beard's confusion
between being "impartial" as to the merits of historical combatants and "impartial" as to different historical interpretations
is all too characteristic of his approach to such issues.
[1] Some of his difficulties with causation are well illustrated in
The Discussion of Human Affairs (1936).

reciprocal reaction upon the economic base of society—we are confronted with the task of defending the economic interpretation from a kind of eclectic plural system of causation. The Marxists, following Engels, had found an answer by saying simply that "in the last analysis" economic forces are decisive. Again, many a working historian will testify that this corresponds to his instructed sense of the nature of many historical epochs. But if we are looking for a more satisfactory foundation for the priority of the economic, we are still left with a troublesome question: Since all historical causes are presumably also the effects of other events, how do we know when we have arrived at the *last* analysis? It is not easy to find a hitching post in history. Beard had no final answer to this problem. And at one point he seems to have receded quite completely to an idealistic view (in the philosophical sense) of history. In 1932, introducing a new edition of J. B. Bury's *The Idea of Progress*, he began with a flamboyant sentence that in effect repudiated his own intellectual past: "The world is largely ruled by ideas, true and false."[2] The context made it clear that this was no mere impulsive outburst, but a proposition that he was concerned to expound, at least so far as the idea of progress was concerned.

Beard's relativism was in this way connected with a long and leisurely retreat from the economic interpretation of history into historical eclecticism, a retreat that culminated in 1945 in the revised edition of *The Economic Basis of Politics* in which he declared that economic man had now given way to political man, and that under modern conditions economic development might be controlled by political and military leaders. In this later phase of his life, Beard thus wavered about the economic interpretation of history. As a general, systematic proposition, he would no longer undertake to argue for it, and at times he might deviate from its canons in his own interpretations of events. But it would be a mistake to imagine that it had left no traces on him. He never really developed an alternative view of history; on occasions he was quite capable of returning to the

---

[2] J. B. Bury, *The Idea of Progress* (ed. 1932), ix; cf. x–xi, xvii, xix, xxviii.

economic interpretation, and at some points, especially where foreign policies were concerned, he might even revert to a rather crude and vulgarized version.

Both his questioning of the economic interpretation and his new relativist philosophy had something to do with the decline of Beard's optimism. His vision of progress, as we have seen, had always been rooted in his rationalism, his faith in the ultimate sway of material forces. Even in 1901, writing on the Industrial Revolution, he had pinned his hopes on the long-run outcome of increasing material organization and the increasing rationalization of human life. Now, more and more, as the Great Depression and the fear of a new war loomed larger in his thoughts, he relapsed from his role of Olympian observer of an inevitable progress and gave way to the prophet in himself, to his hortatory role, to his interest in the manipulative function of historical ideas. The historian, he seemed to be saying, cannot be content with observing the course of society, he must try to change it. When he began *The Rise of American Civilization* with the words, "The history of civilization, if intelligently conceived, may be an instrument of civilization," he expressed a characteristic ideal that became even stronger with time. But now it became clear to him that historical writing would not perform this function automatically, that it must serve activist criticism and forge a social idealism consonant with the needs of the hour. Historical inevitability, the overruling sway of economic forces, no longer suggested automatic progress but rather the direst of consequences—the certain involvement of the United States in the course of imperialism, and worse still, its certain involvement, through economic ties, with the inevitable wars of Europe. If one wanted to create a collectivist democracy with a system of economic planning designed to minimize or eliminate the danger of entrapment in foreign wars, one had to appeal to the active and shaping role of ideas and ideals. "Slowly it dawns in contemporary consciousness," Beard wrote in 1937, "that historiography so conceived furnishes such guides to grand policy as are vouchsafed to the human mind."[3]

---

[3] Beard and Vagts, "Currents of Thought in Historiography," *American Historical Review*, 42 (1937), 483.

In his middle and later years Beard became increasingly a prophetic voice, come not to tell where history is taking us but to tell us what we must do to take history where we want it.

Despite the ineptitude with which Beard stated his argument for relativism, his writing forced his colleagues to see that systems of historical interpretation can themselves be subjected to historical and sociological analysis, that they must be located not only in place and time but in their social context. It helped to establish the principle that the historian has an obligation to cope with his own bias and clarify his role. No doubt many of the "scientific" historians would have agreed with this proposition, but Beard went beyond it to argue that they would be far more likely to approximate the (to him) unattainable goal of objectivity if they acknowledged and stated their biases openly than if they imagined from the start that their commitment to science somehow made them free of bias. "We do not acquire the colorless neutral mind," he wrote, "by declaring our intention to do so. Rather do we clarify the mind by admitting its cultural interests and patterns—interests and patterns that will control, or intrude upon, the selection and organization of historical materials."[4] Although he had little success in stating an acceptable relativist position, he made a decisive contribution to the dialectic of historical controversy and did much to increase the philosophical self-consciousness of his colleagues. He showed a keener sense than many of his American predecessors and contemporaries of the difficulties of the whole enterprise of historical inquiry. For him relativism was meant to be not a doctrinaire position but a form of

---

[4] "That Noble Dream," 87. "We may say to ourselves and others," Beard privately explained, "that we are not concerned with the good and the beautiful, but in the selective processes of the unconscious we are. I would bring this hidden wish to the surface." To Arthur M. Schlesinger, July 12, 1933, Schlesinger Memoir, Columbia Oral History Collection, 775. Compare, on this count, Beard's attitude with that of one of the distinguished spokesmen of the scientific school, C. M. Andrews. "I have never tried," Andrews wrote in 1943, "to analyze the exact state of my mind and do not care to do so now. . . . I don't know that I have ever before made an effort to find out what kind of mind I had and I am not sure that it is worthwhile doing so now." A. S. Eisenstadt, *Charles McLean Andrews* (1956), 129.

historical skepticism. Some critics have charged him with dogmatism, and it is true that some of his statements on the matter sound oversure, but he was usually oversure in saying only what we cannot be sure about. ("It should be a relief to us," Becker had urged, "to renounce omniscience.") In the end one can hardly help but see in this side of Beard's work, revealing though it was of some of his intellectual limitations, another token of his daring. Here was a man in his middle fifties, standing at the very peak of his reputation as a writer and public figure, who chose, out of a passion for inquiry, to launch upon a fundamental reconsideration of what he and his co-workers were doing—a reconsideration so fundamental that, as he well knew, it might throw into jeopardy some of the suppositions upon which his own achievements rested, and at the same time so unfamiliar that it put him in the unflattering position of the beginner or the amateur. From his forays into the problem of historical knowledge Beard emerges not as a historical philosopher of substance but as an intellectual seeker of admirable persistence and receptivity.

Beard's relativist views suffered, however, not only from their intrinsic defects but from becoming associated with the isolationist writings of his later years. Some critics have even charged that his "frame-of-reference history" was devised *ad hoc* to provide a basis for the abandonment of objectivity that can be seen in his impassioned vendetta against the foreign policies of Franklin D. Roosevelt. That I believe there was some relationship between Beard's hopes for the political role of the historian and his espousal of relativism I trust I have made clear; but the timing of his first interest in relativism suggests that it was impelled more by his reconsideration of past works and events than by a clear anticipation of his future isolationist commitment. Whatever the genetic, psychological relationship between his relativism and his isolationist policies, there is hardly a logical relationship. His critics thought that his relativism, by striking at the sanctions behind "objective" history, had the effect of releasing Beard for full-throated polemics against F.D.R. But historical relativism was psychologically just as consonant with an interventionist as with an isolationist point of view. (Carl Becker's relativism did not keep him from calling for American intervention.) Again,

despite Beard's new-found disposition to shy away from the
idea of historical causation, the whole strategy of his isolationism rested upon the proposition that certain acts of politicians
and bankers conduced or led to ("caused"?) intervention in
foreign wars; and upon the idea that this proposition was not
merely the result of someone's limited angle of vision but was
objectively demonstrable. Moreover, relativism, taken seriously and consistently, calls upon the historian's capacity to
be tentative, upon his humility and his awareness of the location and limitation of his own views; but tentativeness and
humility were qualities notably absent from Beard's last books
about American foreign policy, in which one finds very little of
that "sense of propriety, to say nothing of humor" which Beard
invoked in urging historians to apply relativist canons to their
own work. In this last, tragic, embattled phase of his career,
Beard succeeded mainly in casting a retrospective shadow on
all his previous enterprises by inspiring some historians to
wonder whether the *ex parte* techniques he employed against
Roosevelt had not always been ingredient in his way of writing
history.

CHAPTER 9

The Devil Theory of Franklin D. Roosevelt

More than a hundred years ago, James Madison . . . prophesied that the supreme test of American statesmanship would come about 1930. . . . The test is here now—with no divinity hedging our Republic against Caesar.
—Charles A. Beard, 1948

I

THE LAST, and by far the most intense of Beard's intellectual commitments was to isolationism—or, as he preferred to call it, to American continentalism. His belief that the United States could and should stay clear of the disasters of Europe and Asia eventually drove him back toward an insular American patriotism and impelled him to repudiate much of the radical history of his earlier years. And yet, in his writings on foreign policy, as in his literary vendetta against Franklin D. Roosevelt, Beard displayed much the same style of mind that had characterized his earlier works. In the closing episodes of his career, we still find him given to an excessive preoccupation with the motives and methods of those in power, still disposed to draw a somewhat conspiratorial interpretation of their acts, still trespassing now and then over the border between a sound feeling for economic realism and a crude variety of economic reductionism. As a historian of foreign policy, Beard was an uncertain combination of the disappointed patriot and the village cynic.

War had been a decisive theme in the history of the Beard family. Its comfortable bourgeois position, even the foundations of its Midwestern identity, had originated with his father's act of self-assertion in turning his back on the Confederacy. Certainly this rebellion left no legacy of pacificism: Beard himself at twenty-four followed quite a different path when he tried to volunteer for the war with Spain, and even the experience of seeing the crusade for Cuba *libre* turn into a campaign to subjugate the Filipinos did not quite sour his patriotism. During his years at Columbia, for example, he was by no means a consistent or outspoken critic of imperialism. Again, it has been too little remarked that Beard, like so many others of his generation of academic historians, was quite intensely anti-German. A few experiences on the Continent during his Oxford days had left him with an indelible dislike of "Prussianism" which made it hard for him to be "neutral in thought" in 1914. Like many of his colleagues, he was impatient with Wilson's mild diplomacy, and months before the American declaration of war he believed that "this country should definitely align itself with the Allies and help eliminate Prussianism from the earth." Even when resigning from Columbia in protest against tyrannies brought about by the war fever, he restated his conviction that "a victory for the German Imperial Government would plunge all of us into the black night of military barbarism," and reminded President Butler: "I was among the first to urge a declaration of war by the United States." "I am not and never have been a pacifist," he declared again in 1919. "I never belonged to Mr. Wilson's sweet neutrality band. I did not vote for him in 1916 because I believed his pacifist policies wrong. . . . I was never 'too proud to fight.' "[1]

Although Beard never threw himself into war propaganda with the enthusiasm shown by many of his fellow historians, he made his sentiments clear in a brief appeal for a 1918 Liberty Loan: "America and her allies are now pitted against the most merciless military despotism the world has ever seen. . . . Equipped by forty years' of preparation for armed conquest, fortified by forty years' conspiracy against the democratic nations of the earth, supported by all the engines of destruction that science can devise, the German military machine threatens all mankind. It has made a religion of

---

[1] For Beard's early views on imperialism, see Gerald Stourzh, "Charles A. Beard's Interpretations of American Foreign Policy," *World Affairs Quarterly*, 38 (1957), 112–15; Beard to Butler, October 8, 1917, Minutes of Trustees, Columbia University, vol. 38, 89–90; for the statements of 1917 and 1919 Warren I. Cohen, *The American Revisionists* (1966), 5.

brutality. . . . A German victory means the utter destruction of those ideals of peace and international goodwill which have been America's great reliance, ideals which make life worth living in America or anywhere else."[2] It is tempting to wonder how much different the end of Beard's life would have been if he had taken a similar stand in 1941. But by then he had come to feel that he had been gullible in 1917, and in his fierce determination not to be gulled again he conceived the world of 1939–41 as though it were an exact replay of the earlier war.[3]

During the 1920's historians were preoccupied with the question of war guilt, a matter charged for many of them with special significance because of their own credulous services to wartime propaganda. Revelations of the secret treaties shook their earlier assumptions about the moral issues of the war, and soon Sidney B. Fay, Harry Elmer Barnes, and other revisionist writers were giving the world a version of war guilt in which the self-seeking aims and schemes of the Allies were emphasized and Germany's responsibility much diminished. Beard did not rush to join this movement. In a series of lectures at Dartmouth in 1922, he began to apportion the responsibility between both sides, but he still gave Germany the greater share. By 1925 he had come to assigning Russia and France "a Titan's share" of the war guilt, but was not yet ready to judge American intervention wrong or futile. By now he was disturbed by the guileless ease with which he and his colleagues had taken sides in 1917, and dismayed at the precarious and unsatisfactory character of the peace. He slowly began to withdraw from support for any American involvement in the affairs of Europe—a Continent "encrusted," as he once wrote, in the "blood-rust of fifty centuries"—and to relapse into the old American attitude that Europe is hopelessly corrupt and beyond saving by any efforts. Those who set

---

[2] Cohen, *The American Revisionists*, 17.

[3] This determination not to be fooled twice is a powerful theme in Beard, as in many of the disillusioned enthusiasts of 1917–18. Writing about the war debts in a letter of the late 1920's, he remarked: "I do not think the money will ever be paid back. Probably [the] Morgans will get the American boobs to lend fifty billions more to the European powers and their nationals to loose [sic] in the next war for liberty, democracy, and Christianity. But I am not going to have any more wool pulled over my eyes if I can help it." Beard to Harry Elmer Barnes, June 24, 192[7?].

out to love one country or hate another, he warned in 1922, are "unfit" for correct thinking about international policies. "Moreover, they are usually found shifting their affections with the current of affairs. They are hot lovers one day and hot haters the next, and in deadly peril of becoming a nuisance all the time. It is the man who gets religion the hardest who backslides the hardest." War guilt now seemed less important than the question whether American interventionism had served any good purpose, and he still believed it had because it preserved the European balance of power. It was "decidedly the interest of the United States," he wrote as late as 1926, "to help prevent the rise of any European power to a dominant position." Decisions about foreign policy should be based not upon foreign sympathies but upon a cool calculation of national interest. The country should return to its original disposition to use the European balance of power to national advantage, and should "regard with cold blood all the quarrels of Europe." If the victory of the Entente powers had been desirable, this was not because they were more virtuous than the Central powers but because their victory kept a single power from achieving total domination. At this point Beard was not a spokesman for isolationism; he merely hoped to find discreet and realistic self-regarding criteria for intervention. As late as 1930 he asserted: "The theory that the United States can, in its own interest, refuse to take part in world adjustments becomes more doubtful every day. . . . It can formulate no important policy without affecting the European balance of power."[4]

Such statements, founded on classical conceptions of national interest, were much more realistic than a great deal of contemporaneous writing on the subject. But, as always, there was another side to Beard's mind. At times crass economic interest would re-emerge as the motive power of history. In 1927, Beard opposed foreign investments because they, and not the balance of power, were the source of overseas intervention; he called for heavier income taxes and a program of road, school, and electrical power development that would divert capital from foreign investment to domestic improve-

---

[4] *Nation*, 114 (1922), 289–90; Cohen, *The American Revisionists*, 86–7; Beard, *The American Leviathan* (1930), 733.

ment. Such a program, he concluded in his village-cynic manner, "would reduce our chances of becoming mixed up in the next European adventure in Christian ballistics. If the present rate of foreign investments keep [sic] up, every village skinflint from Maine to California will soon have a hundred-dollar foreign bond paying 8 per cent instead of the 6 per cent local rate, and thus inspired will be [sic] by a holy zeal for righteousness, justice, or whatever the next warlike device may be, which means at bottom a lust to get the money back with interest."[5]

What is discernible in Beard's discussions of foreign policy is a pattern rather similar to that revealed in his treatment of the Founding Fathers. In dealing with the Fathers, he might start, as he did in 1912, with an attempt to give a cool account of the hard problems of their statecraft, and then, as he did in 1913, become all too preoccupied with their motives and their investments in public securities. In discussing foreign policy he would often begin with a sound statement about some of the sobering realities—the limitations of American power, the problems of foreign markets and investments, the dangers of overreaching idealistic aims—and then suddenly emerge with a cranky thrust at the big bankers or their countrywide allies among the village skinflints. To follow Beard through the years is an arresting task: a noble and lofty figure is lecturing us circumspectly on the difficult lessons of history; but every now and then there is a sudden turning, spurred perhaps by a moment of irritation; the mask of detachment drops, and we are abruptly confronted by an angry and suspicious mind. Just as we imagine that we are about to be led down a broad avenue toward some chastening wisdom about the limitations of national power, we are abruptly switched onto some unprofitable byway.

II

The crash and the Great Depression seem to have had a more profound effect on Beard's thinking about foreign policy

---

[5] Cohen, *The American Revisionists*, 99.

than any of the revisionist histories of the 1920's. He had
become convinced that the primary cause of American intervention in 1917 had not been (as some were to conclude) the
sinister machinations of bankers or munition makers but the
more generally shared and more legitimate desire of national
leaders to keep the country from the depression that would
come if it gave up its war trade. But now such a depression
had come anyway. Was it not obviously necessary for the
nation, not only for its domestic well-being but also to avoid renewed engulfment in Europe's wars, to develop an economic
program based upon greater self-sufficiency? Must it not prevent a future President, seeking again to avoid or end a
domestic depression, from plunging the nation into another
war? From 1934 on, almost all Beard's historical writing became programmatic: it was focused upon the paramount goal
of staying out of war, a goal which he pursued with an intensity that dwarfs all the occasional inconsistencies and vac-
illations of his thought.

Beard took pleasure in the early policies of F.D.R., despite
the President's big-navy sympathies, because he saw in them
the promise of a self-sufficing nationalist economic policy, an
eventual collectivist democracy that would be able to stay out
of war by minimizing foreign commitments. He was particularly pleased when Roosevelt scuttled the London Economic
Conference, which confirmed his hope that the New Deal
would seek economic recovery not in foreign trade and investment but in the independent development of its domestic program. But he was always suspicious of Roosevelt, and after
the President's "quarantine" speech of 1937, his hostility
hardened.

In 1934 Beard published two books, the beginning of an
elaborate series of inquiries into foreign policy. The first of
these, *The Idea of National Interest*, an intolerably dull work,
showed some of Beard's characteristic ineptitude with the
history of ideas. He was not attempting here to dishonor or
debunk the idea of national interest, but rather, by giving
examples of its historical uses, to show how it might be made
a firm and durable anchorage for national policy. His aim was
to show that national interest, realistically and broadly defined,

would be a much safer guide to policy than vague notions of
national honor, or demanding and treacherous conceptions of
moral obligations. But to be safe it must be truly national, and
not just geared to the pursuit of private profit for special interests.

Beard tried to make *The Idea of National Interest* an
austerely factual and objective study, reserving to *The Open
Door at Home* the task of presenting his own interpretations
and proposals for a national program. In brief, this program
called for a system of national autarchy calculated to develop
the internal well-being of the country and cut to a minimum
its dependence upon external trade. For its defense, the country should rely upon its geographic isolation and an army
adequate to its defense in the Western Hemisphere. The naval
needs of the country, he believed, would be almost negligible
under a circumspect policy of this kind. The navy he saw
primarily as an instrument of risk-laden exposure to the problems of the outer world. "The one policy that is possible under
a conception which makes the American nation the center of
interest and affection is policy based on security of life for
the American people in their present geographical home."
To surrender our fortunate insular position, he wrote, "for
a mess of pottage in the form of profits on cotton goods, tobacco, petroleum, and automobiles, is to make grand policy
subservient to special interests, betray the security of the
American nation, and prove that we 'deserve to be slaves.' "[6]

Beard's reputation as a student of foreign policy went
into such an eclipse after his attacks on Roosevelt that we
may easily underestimate such a work as *The Open Door at
Home*. Ringing with pertinent warnings against the global
Messianism which has come to be the curse of American foreign policy, the book is by no means either wholly stale or
irrelevant in the 1960's. Beard understood that Americans do
not have the duty, the capacity, or the need to patrol or moral-
ize or democratize the rest of the world, and he was trying
to state the dangers in their overreaching themselves. Whatever his book's weaknesses, it aimed at a respectable object:
to persuade Americans to think of foreign policy not as sub-

---

[6] *The Open Door at Home* (1934), 261, 267; Beard was quoting
John Marshall.

servient to sweeping world-saving ideologies or world-wide
commitments to "democracy" or to peace-keeping efforts beyond the power of their arms and outside the range of their
moral influence, but rather to think first, in the manner of
classical realism, about the requirements of their own security. And security he here defined not as a question of trade
or profit, nor of the defense of formally designed principles of
international law governing neutral rights, but simply as the
long-range pursuit of peace and safety. To achieve these ends,
Beard proposed to reverse the familiar priority between domestic and foreign policies: many times in the past, domestic
discontents had led to war; he now proposed to put the quest
for peace so firmly at the center of American goals as to put
forward as the primary argument for domestic planning that
it would improve our chances of staying out of war.

However, the difficulty in Beard's thought, already evident in *The Open Door at Home*, lay in his findings about the
source of danger to American security. Misled by his current
disposition to overemphasize economic motives and to read
the future in terms of the blasted illusions of 1917, he evaded
the central dilemma of international politics: that the quest
for security involves hazardous competitive confrontations of
power, and is not simply a pursuit of competing interests of
trade and empire.[7] It was this that led him to think that the
primary danger to American peace lay in the sale of cannon
and cotton and the advance of credits to belligerents, and
persuaded him, even in the age of Hitler and Mussolini, that
the possibility of American involvement in war might be
eliminated by abstaining from trade and loans. Despite his

---

[7] Cf. Stourzh, "Charles A. Beard's Interpretations of American
Foreign Policy," esp. 123–32. Beard, Stourzh observes, "remained
under the spell of an economic interpretation in spite of his
formal repudiation of economic determinism and his acceptance
of a voluntaristic set of ideas. . . . The outstanding feature of
Beard's brand of economic interpretation of politics, whether in
1913 or in 1934, was its un-Marxian stress, implicit or explicit,
on the economic *motives* of individuals or groups. This insinuation of the acquisitive instinct as the most crucial attribute of
human nature lies at the very bottom of Beard's incapacity to
take into account the genuinely political aspects of foreign policy.
It was one of the reasons which led him to see in American
foreign policy little else but the continuation beyond the water's
edge of the economic quests of individuals and groups making up
American society."

new-found skepticism about historical generalization, he ventured a "tentative law" governing such matters: "The degree of probability that the United States will become involved in any war arising anywhere in Europe or Asia bears a direct relation to the extent of the economic interests possessed by American nationals in the affected area, and in the fortunes of the respective belligerents."[8] One need think only of the Second World War, or the wars in Korea or Vietnam, not to speak of American experience in 1812 and 1898, to see the limitations of this "law"—a law drawn (and many would say even here incorrectly) from the single experience of 1917.

In February 1935, Beard expressed his recurrent pessimism and his irrepressible suspicions of F.D.R. in a remarkable article on "National Politics and War" which illustrates his disposition to see the threat of war as arising solely from internal, domestic causes. At the outset he addressed himself to the significance of the "Roosevelt upheaval" in American life and the future of the now prostrate Republican party as a viable opposition. Looking to past experience, he found that twice before in American history the "party of wealth and talents" had been overwhelmed at the polls—under Jefferson in 1800 and under Jackson in 1828. (He would not count Wilson's victory in 1912, since it was a minority victory, a political fluke.) On both occasions the victory of the popular party had finally been reversed by two forces: war, and "the inexorable movement of American business enterprise." The war of 1812 had in effect liquidated Jeffersonian democracy, undercut its principles, and re-established Federalist policies. Jacksonian democracy too, in the long run, developed a faction which would rather risk civil war than make concessions to the growth of business enterprise. It fell into the hands of

---

8 *The Open Door at Home*, 269. In 1935, urging a policy that would develop a more secure economy at home, Beard wrote: "Surely such a policy is as defensible . . . as, let us say, one that leads to the killing of American boys in a struggle over the bean crop in Manchuria." Manfred Jonas, *Isolationism in America, 1935–1941* (1966), 72. It is sometimes hard to tell whether such passages represent Beard's idea of the essential problems of foreign policy or whether they are meant only to serve as rhetorical gestures; or indeed whether in his case this distinction can always be made.

the planters, who in the end preferred to take their section out of the Union rather than bow to the demands of business interests. The Civil War, which nearly shattered the Democratic party, returned the country to that whole complex of policies—of banks and tariffs and bonded indebtedness—that the original Jacksonians had opposed. Again when the Democrats, thanks to a Republican split, slipped into power under Wilson and launched upon another episode in reform, they were checkmated by the war of 1917; and once more, as a consequence of the war, "the party of business enterprise emerged more triumphant than ever."

Now the country was living once again under a third Democratic upheaval. Would this be, at last, the "permanent revolution"? With a bow to the admitted uncertainty of things, Beard hazarded that it would not: none of the basic institutions of capitalism had been unseated, and at the end of the present Depression, "if it ever ends, the concentration of wealth in the United States will doubtless mark a new high point in the evolution of the American economy." Likewise the Republican party would survive. True, should the Democrats achieve recovery, the Republicans would face a very bleak short-run future. But Beard was plainly more persuaded that the Depression would continue, or even grow worse, and that the Democrats would probably not advance to further radical measures, such as the nationalization of the banks. Instead, tradition and experience suggested that "a wider spread of economic calamity will culminate in a foreign war, rather than in a drastic reorganization of domestic economy." Roosevelt's actions, particularly his navy program, confirmed this prospect. "Judging by the past and by his actions, war will be his choice—and it will be a 'war for Christianity against Paganism' this time." It might be objected, Beard said, that nations do not deliberately make war; but what is to the point is that statesmen, who make the effective decisions, do decide for policies that lead to war and often resort to strong foreign policies in preference to strong domestic policies—witness the way the Cleveland and McKinley administrations had used, respectively, the Venezuela crisis and the Spanish war. "This is not saying," Beard concluded in a memorable passage, "that

President Roosevelt will deliberately plunge the country into a Pacific war in his efforts to escape the economic crisis. There will be an 'incident,' a 'provocation.' Incidents and provocations are of almost daily occurrence. Any government can quickly magnify one of them into a 'just cause for war.' Confronted by the difficulties of a deepening domestic crisis and by the comparative ease of a foreign war, what will President Roosevelt do? Judging by the past history of American politicians, he will choose the latter, or, perhaps it would be more accurate to say, amid powerful conflicting emotions he will 'stumble into' the latter. The Jeffersonian party gave the nation the War of 1812, the Mexican War, and its participation in the World War. The Pacific war awaits."[9]

It is a chilling note of prophecy that Beard strikes here, and it is prophetic not only for the world but for himself: in this article he wrote the scenario for the rest of his career, for the unrelenting battle he was to wage against an event which he had forecast as all but inevitable. He had also set down the basic historical assumption upon which his critiques of American foreign policy were to proceed: the United States goes to war not in response, whether right or wrong, to anything other nations do; it goes to war as a part of its own cycle of domestic politics, because statesmen who prefer strong foreign policy to strong domestic policy seek war, or at least seek the conditions under which they can stumble into war. For the dialectic between nation and nation he had substituted a dialectic between internal and external policies.

In assessing Beard's isolationist views of the mid-1930's, one must remember that he by no means stood alone; he was in the main stream of liberal and radical opinion at least until the outbreak of war in 1939, and probably right up to the fall of France in 1940. By the mid-1930's almost all American liberals were convinced that no important principle or value had been served by the military intervention of the United States in 1917, and that private interests, notably bankers with a large stake in Allied loans, were primarily responsible for it. A large body of revisionist historical literature was

9 "National Politics and War," *Scribner's Magazine*, 97 (1935), 65–70. Cf. *The Idea of National Interest* (1934; ed. 1966), 433–4.

capped in 1935 by the investigations of the Nye Committee, which again laid the impulse toward American intervention at the door of international bankers and munitions makers, the "merchants of death." When Mussolini invaded Ethiopia in the same year, Congress hastily passed the 1935 Neutrality Act, which authorized the President, where he found that a war existed, to ban the sale or transportation of munitions to any belligerent and to warn American citizens (the *Lusitania* still haunted the legislators) that they traveled on belligerent ships at their own risk. The Neutrality Act of 1936 also forbade loans to belligerents.

As fascism swept over Spain and Ethiopia, and as the savagery of the Nazis toward the Jews gave stronger intimations of the ultimate horror that lay in wait, some antiwar liberals became troubled about the adequacy of the neutrality laws and were impelled to think about the need for collective action against aggression. But proposals for collective security to halt fascism were dimmed by Anglo-French "neutrality" policies in the Spanish Civil War and then by Munich. It was hard to argue for American initiative when those even more immediately endangered by aggression were not providing it. Above all, most American liberals were convinced by the experiences of the First World War and by the subsequent political conflict of the 1930's that American democracy could not survive another such effort. The idea that democracy would collapse under the stress of a major war was one of the most pervasive clichés of the 1930's; it was held by men along a wide spectrum of political opinion from Norman Thomas to such conservative isolationists as Robert A. Taft. Skeptics saw no point in a war to stop fascism abroad if it was all but certain to bring fascism or military dictatorship at home. "Nothing is more likely," wrote the editors of the *New Republic* in the fall of 1937, "than that the United States would go fascist through the very process of organizing to defeat the fascist nations." Beard, writing in the same journal a few months later, voiced his "firm conviction" that the United States could not prevent war in Europe, and that if it took part in another general European war, "no matter what the alleged pretexts or the alignment of powers may be, that participation will mark the end of democratic institutions in the United States. Some forms may survive, as of the Roman Republic, but the spirit and substance will be destroyed."[1]

The dilemma facing American liberals on the eve of the war was indeed a difficult and a cruel one. On one side was their fear of another war, with all its horrors, and of the prospect that it would put an end to democracy in America as well as elsewhere; and their now deeply ingrained desire not to lend themselves to a repetition of the follies of 1917–18. On the other was their increasingly acute fear of the triumph of fascism in all Europe, with its own threat to American survival, and their disposition, newly heard but growing stronger, to ask whether, in order to help turn back the threat of fascism, the United States ought not, while it still had potential allies, take the risks connected with a policy of collective security.

What marked Beard off from many of his contemporaries was that he saw no dilemma at all. He took higher ground than most of his fellow liberals: he could see nothing at stake for American security in the impending conflict; and such moral difference as he could find between the contending powers was not big enough to warrant American partisanship. He could see only a battle between the ruthless old imperialisms of Britain and France and the ugly new aggression of the fascist powers. "My trouble," he wrote in March 1936, "lies in the fact that greed, lust and ambition in Europe and Asia do not seem to be confined to Italy, Germany and Japan; nor does good seem to be monopolized by Great Britain, France and Russia." He was sure, he wrote the following month, that one could expect Hitler to make "a sudden and devastating attack, East or West," but he did not see why this should be regarded by Americans as any part of their business. Wisdom dictated a policy of strict neutrality. The neutrality laws were based on

---

1 For the *New Republic*, see Jonas, *Isolationism*, 81; Jonas has many illustrations of the belief that American democracy would end with the next war. For Beard, see his essay "Collective Security," *New Republic*, 93 (February 2, 1938), 358. In 1939 he wrote that it was "as certain as death and taxes that civil liberty would perish in the United States as soon as war is declared." "We're Blundering Into War," *American Mercury*, 46 (1939), 398. But by 1943 Beard had come to the conclusion that the war would not destroy American democracy. *The Republic*, 253.

a good principle and should be made mandatory; he hoped they would not only bar the sale of munitions and credits to belligerents but would also be extended to impose a restriction on sales to neutrals engaged in reselling to belligerents.[2] When war came the country ought to retire to the storm cellars.

The Nye Committee's revelations and the debate over neutrality legislation touched upon Beard's sensitivities both as a historian and as an isolationist, and in 1936 wrung from him a strange, tortured little book, *The Devil Theory of War*. Plainly the Committee's findings reawakened his penchant for the somewhat conspiratorial view of events that colors his book on the Constitution, his fascination with motives, his passion for the inside story, the "intimate essence" of history. He considered the Nye report in some ways even more revealing than the opening of the European archives in 1917 and after, and in one of his broad sardonic strokes he suggested that in forty or fifty years "even Respectable Citizens" might absorb some of its lessons. With a cautious bow to his own relativist pronouncements, he warned that the Nye revelations did not in any final sense tell what "caused" American intervention in 1917—a matter the human mind could not entirely comprehend. (Beard was clearly troubled by the difficulty of dismissing the idea of cause in history and then, in effect, asserting that the country had gone to war because bankers and politicians took it there.) He warned too—like a man fighting the strongest tendencies of his own mind—against the popular notion that wicked men make war. (He was to say just the opposite about F.D.R. ten years later.) Politicians and bankers, he argued, do not operate in a vacuum: it is the whole society that seeks buyers, jobs, and profits. War comes out of the pursuits of peace. "War is not the work of a demon. It is our own work, for which we prepare, wittingly or not, in the ways of peace. But most of us sit blindfold at the preparation."[3]

---

[2] Jonas, *Isolationism*, 105–6; Bernard Borning, *The Political and Social Thought of Charles A. Beard* (1962), 237; on the neutrality laws see Beard, *The Devil Theory of War* (1936), 122.
[3] *The Devil Theory of War*, 11–13, 29. Although he said that wicked men do not make war, Beard wrote in 1937 that since the American people had not been prepared in 1914 for foreign intervention, "it took time for Woodrow Wilson to manoeuvre the nation into war." Borning, *Political and Social Thought*, 233.

Beard then launched into a rehearsal of the Nye Committee's evidence on the importance of the war loans to the Allies, and their central place in America's wartime prosperity. "The country," he concluded concerning 1914–17, "faced an economic smash at home or intervention"; but did this decision really "pay" the nation—the nation as a whole, as distinguished from "profit-seeking bankers"? Now again the country was in the midst of still another economic crisis much graver than that of 1914, faced with the prospect of another world war, and with the temptation of more war "prosperity." Would Americans now prefer to stay out, or to gamble again on wartime profits that would be followed by another, still bigger crash? Rejecting both the militant defense of neutral rights that had failed in 1917 and the collective pursuit of peace conducted arm in arm with corrupt imperialist powers, he urged: "I think we should concentrate our attention on tilling our own garden." And this was why he favored the most sweeping mandatory neutrality laws. They would be difficult to enforce, he admitted. "But enough of them can be so enforced as to prevent the bankers and politicians from guiding the nation into calamity as in 1914–17." But here—as indeed in his stress upon war loans, to the exclusion of every other consideration leading America to war—Beard was back with the devil theory of war that he had started out to decry, back indeed with that notion of an arcane and sinister "reality" behind events, in which he had believed in 1913. Manfred Jonas concludes—rightly, I believe—that in this respect Beard's book "contributed greatly to fixing the onus of guilt on the already suspected parties. It thus had the effect of advertising, rather than refuting, the devil theory."[4]

In his peroration to *The Devil Theory of War*, Beard posed the issue that would occupy Americans for the next five years. If the United States was to go to war, he pleaded, let it not be because of "backstairs dealing and manipulating," but for some open public object, openly agreed upon. "If we go to war, let us go to war for some grand national and human advantage openly discussed and deliberately arrived at, and not to

---

[4] Ibid., 93, 123; Jonas, *Isolationism*, 153; cf. Borning, *Political and Social Thought*, 220.

bail out farmers, bankers and capitalists or to save politicians from the pain of dealing with a domestic crisis."[5] It was what lay behind these words that more and more separated Beard from his generation of liberals in the years to follow. Not only could he see no "grand national and human advantage" in a war against the Axis, but he found it impossible to see how any American of good will and intelligence could on this count disagree with him. In 1939 Beard attributed much of the pressure for collective security to "resident foreigners" who were treating the United States as a boardinghouse, the foreign-born and their offspring. He minimized the danger of German and Italian domination of the Atlantic, asserted that the European powers could themselves easily stop Germany and Italy "within forty-eight hours" if they were truly interested in doing so, and argued: "For the government of the United States to operate on the ostensible fiction that a mere test of despotism and democracy is at hand would be nothing short of childish." "To entangle ourselves," he concluded, "in the mazes and passions of European conflicts and tie our hands to British and French manipulators on the remote contingency of a German and Italian domination in the Atlantic seems to me to embrace immediate calamities when the possibility of security and peace in this hemisphere is clearly open to us. If this be immorality, the foreigners now boarding here and the home-grown missionaries can make the most of it."[6]

The clearer the lineaments of the Nazi state became, the less Beard seemed to be concerned with what was happening outside the United States. In 1940 he published a brief historical apologia for his proposed policy of "American Continentalism," under the title *A Foreign Policy for America*. It was his misfortune that this work, completed by April, was published almost simultaneously with the fall of France. At the very moment when every American was being forced to confront the implications of a possible Nazi victory for the future of his country and the world, Beard, who had always wanted so much to make history relevant to the present, had given his

---

[5] *The Devil Theory of War*, 123, 124.
[6] "We're Blundering Into War," 392, 299, and *passim*.

readers a manifesto on foreign policy in which Hitler was
barely mentioned,[7] in which the problems that would come
with an Axis victory were given no consideration at all, and
in which the real contemporary villains were American "in-
ternationalists" and "imperialists." Beard had always been
convinced, as he now put it, that "foreign policy is a phase of
domestic policy, an inseparable phase." This is an important
insight, but if it is exploited to the exclusion of the even more
basic truth that foreign policy is also a response to the actions
of other states, it can become an instrument of distortion.
Most of Beard's later writings on foreign policy come back
repeatedly to a single theme: the United States never goes to
war because of anything that is happening outside its borders,
but because politicians want to evade a domestic crisis or
bankers and munitions makers want outlets for their capital
and products. Although in his earlier days he had argued that
the quest for national security is in good part a response to
happenings in the outer world, he withdrew from this insight
from the mid-1930's onward. During the very years when the
future Axis powers were ravaging Ethiopia, Spain, and China,
and when Hitler was preparing the ground for his horrendous
gamble, Beard became increasingly preoccupied with the
search for domestic villainy. In the end his sights were trained,
as they had to be, upon F.D.R.

III

Beard's last two books, *American Foreign Policy in the
Making, 1932–1940* (1946) and *President Roosevelt and the
Coming of the War, 1941* (1948) devoted over nine hundred
pages to a detailed historical polemic intended to prove that,
from an early date, F.D.R. practiced deceit on the American

---

7 Beard makes one passing reference (p. 9) to Sumner Welles's
recent visit to "the Italian and German dictators," but they do
not otherwise appear. During 1938 and 1939 Beard had consistently minimized the possible threat of the Axis powers to the
United States, and dismissed talk about possible fascist penetration of the Western Hemisphere as "the new racket created to
herd the American people into President Roosevelt's quarantine
camp." Borning, *Political and Social Thought*, 241 and chapter
xiv, *passim*.

people, promising them peace while leading them gratuitously into war, and that finally, having failed in his other moves toward war, he provoked the Japanese into the attack on Pearl Harbor. Roosevelt's motives—to save Britain at whatever cost to the American people and to their constitutional forms, and in so doing to aggrandize his own power—had been abominable; his methods had been deceitful; the results of his policies had been disastrous.

George Leighton, in a sympathetic account of Beard's writings on foreign policy, refers to Beard as "an attorney with a brief and with his country as his client."[8] To assume that this brief was in fact of service to the country would beg the question, but the phrase is otherwise apt: these last two books were indeed a legal brief, a statement of the case for the prosecution, cast in a mold more suitable to an adversary proceeding than to a historical inquiry. As Beard told this story of duplicity in pursuit of Caesarism, the influence of bankers and munitions makers' loans vanished, and now at last the explanatory pattern based upon the events of 1917 was laid aside.[9] Instead of the mischief-makers turned up by the Nye Committee, Beard had discovered a more visible and, in some quarters, a more acceptable villain in the person of Franklin D. Roosevelt.

Much has been written about Beard's use of omission, distortion, and innuendo in these books:[1] but absorption in such details may cause us to lose sight of his grand strategy. By concentrating attention largely upon the plans and devices of the President, Beard turned away from the world events to which Roosevelt was responding, from the genuinely trying dilemmas of foreign policy that he had to solve, and from the

---

[8] Leighton, "Beard and Foreign Policy," in Beale, ed., *Charles A. Beard*, 161.

[9] "I was right," Beard wrote to Oswald Garrison Villard during the closing year of the war, "in saying that the war was on the way, but I was foolish in laying such emphasis on economic aspects of the business. Man hasn't sense enough to pursue economic interests consistently." In fact, he added, the war proved mainly that "man seems bound to have a berserk rage every so often—a senseless berserk rage, and I regard it as a mistake to gloss that fact over. Look at Hitler." Beard to Villard, July 18, 194[5].

[1] Notably by Basil Rauch in *Roosevelt: From Munich to Pearl Harbor* (1950); see also Herbert Feis, *The Road to Pearl Harbor* (1950), and Samuel Eliot Morison, *By Land and by Sea* (1953), 337–45.

basic question of how the national interest should have been defended. By writing voluminously about intentions, criticisms, suspicions, stratagems, evasions—in brief, about the clouded moral atmosphere in which power functions—he succeeded in giving the whole story the aspect simply of a study in the immorality of Roosevelt's statecraft. We are back again, once more, as we were with the Founding Fathers, caught up in an excessive preoccupation with motives. Even in the wake of Hitler, Beard was reverting to the muckraker's approach to foreign policy, probing once again for the sordid "reality" that must always lie beneath the surface. (Indeed his last book, subtitled "A Study in Appearances and Realities," was entirely organized around this dualistic conception.) By not setting out the alternatives Roosevelt faced, each with its own costs and dangers, Beard weighted the scales against him in a way that would be fatal to the reputation of almost any political leader faced with a comparable decision. His relatively sketchy treatment of what was going on in Europe and Asia left Roosevelt's objectionable decisions in high relief, as though they had been made in a vacuum. By posing certain questions and avoiding others of equal and greater importance, he diverted attention from the problem whether American national interests or the interests of mankind were in fact at stake, a stratagem that from the start reduced Roosevelt to the level of a mere meddler in the affairs of an intractable world.

Hardly any of Roosevelt's advocates have denied that Beard and his other detractors were right in making their grave charges about the uncandid character of his leadership. Roosevelt did not tell the public the truth about what he expected, what he planned, what he was doing. After the fall of France, he surely knew that his repeated promises to avoid war might prove impossible to keep. And though he never took any step in the Atlantic that was far out of line with the current state of public opinion,[2] it seems clear too that he was

---

[2] Roosevelt was a maker of public opinion, but he was not disposed to defy it, and his actions in this respect were keyed to national sentiment. In March 1941, 70 per cent of the public thought it more important to help England than to keep out of the war; in November 1941, more than 70 per cent were willing to risk war with Japan rather than let her continue her aggressions.

content to work with, and upon, the ambivalence of the American public mind—which was intensely eager for British survival and German defeat but almost as eager to stay out of the war—rather than to put the whole case, as he saw it, frankly before the public. Sometime before the summer of 1941 he plainly decided that the United States must sooner or later—preferably sooner—enter the war, and his whole course of action in the Atlantic, as he moved steadily from neutrality to nonbelligerency to quasi-belligerency to undeclared war, suggests that he was trying, not only to aid Britain, but also to create the circumstances and incidents that would overcome public opposition to the final step. The aggressive character of his policies—the use of American convoys and the beginnings of naval hostilities with Nazi submarines—might have been expected to force a declaration of war by Hitler; but the Fuehrer, mindful of 1917, refused to oblige, and at the time of Pearl Harbor American progress toward full-scale belligerency was still halting and uncertain. In this sense— but I believe in this sense alone—Pearl Harbor came as an end to troublesome uncertainties.

The general course and purport of Roosevelt's policies in the Atlantic theater were obvious enough, and it can hardly be denied that they had, step by step, the overwhelming endorsement of the public and of national leaders. The pivot of Beard's book, therefore, was the Pacific theater, where war finally came. There the preliminaries were not followed with the same close general attention as the events in the Atlantic, and there the charge of surreptitious dealings and disastrous failure could be pushed to best advantage. The actual outbreak of the war poses a complex issue for historians, for the policies and performance of the Roosevelt administration are acutely vulnerable. In the then existing state of American military intelligence the disaster at Pearl Harbor should have been avoidable. It is possible to argue also that American diplomacy vis-à-vis Japan was impatient and inept, and that a further postponement of the showdown, which was in fact Roosevelt's objective, might have been attainable. It is more difficult to argue, as Beard did, that granting the expansionist aims of Japan, the war could have been entirely avoided without jeopardy to long-range American security, and extremely difficult to argue that the situation was a case of flagrant unilateral provocation by the United States.[3]

What one misses in Beard's account is a systematic statement of the alternatives facing Roosevelt. The danger on one side was that if Germany and Japan should win, the United States would stand alone, facing two immense and aggressive military empires in the Atlantic and the Pacific. The danger on the other was that to try to stop one or both would mean almost certain ultimate involvement in the war. And the point at which military-strategic realities required that Roosevelt should act, *if* this eventuality were unavoidable, was not likely to be the point at which congressional leaders or the American public would accept the necessity of war. (It does not seem to have occurred to Beard that F.D.R.'s undeniably devious leadership at certain moments reflected not his Caesaristic aspirations but the difficulties of a democratic politician confronting the force and unhampered initiative of Caesaristic powers.) One would never learn by reading Beard alone that the Japanese had arrived at a determination to gain American acquiescence in their plans or to precipitate war; one might never see that Roosevelt was given the alternative either of becoming, by providing materials, a partner in Japan's plans for imperial expansion in China and Southeast Asia, or of putting economic pressure upon her to desist, at the almost certain risk of driving her to widen the war. Had Roosevelt, by continuing trade, abetted the gradual conquest by Japan of Dutch, French, and British centers of power in the Southwest Pacific, he would have sapped the Allied cause everywhere, and would have laid himself open to domestic critics for having been a feeble custodian of American security. Had he intervened, however, against Japanese conquests of territories *not* belonging to the United States, he would have had to enter the war on grounds that many Americans could not

---

[3] Beard did not endorse, though he also did not reject, the view that F.D.R. deliberately exposed the fleet at Pearl Harbor in order to invite a Japanese attack. He said only that while Roosevelt argued that acts of war had been committed against the United States, "in reality the said acts were secretly invited and even initiated by the armed forces of the United States under his secret direction." *President Roosevelt and the Coming of the War*, 583.

accept as legitimate and would have waged war with a divided country behind him. From this dilemma the Japanese, unwisely as events showed, rescued him by striking at Pearl Harbor and the Philippines.

While the war was being waged, Beard, like other isolationists, gave it his support, but when it was over he promptly returned to his original view that it had been futile and unnecessary. And on this view hangs the final meaning and consequence of his books on foreign policy. If we can see a valuable result or historical necessity in America's participation in the war, Beard's questions, absolutely central for him, about the motives and details of F.D.R.'s leadership become less vital for us. For his part, Beard was prepared to follow to the end the implications of his argument. "Out of the war," he wrote in 1948, "came the triumph of another totalitarian regime no less despotic and ruthless than Hitler's system, namely, Russia, possessing more than twice the population of prewar Germany, endowed with immense natural resources, astride Europe and Asia, employing bands of Quislings as terroristic in methods as any Hitler ever assembled, and insistently effectuating a political and economic ideology equally inimical to the democracy, liberties, and institutions of the United States. . . . Since, as a consequence of the war called 'necessary' to overthrow Hitler's despotism, another despotism was raised to a higher pitch of power, how can it be argued conclusively with reference to inescapable facts that the 'end' justified the means employed to involve the United States in that war?"[4]

In this passage Beard, as he points up the direction of his own thought, throws down the gauntlet to Roosevelt's defenders. He asks them to put aside the interests of the rest of humanity, which he believed the United States simply lacked the power to advance or sustain and from which he believed its fate really could be separated, and to address themselves solely to American national interests. And then he poses the ultimate question. After all, *if* the Russian system and the Nazi system were on an absolute moral par, *if* the Soviets

---

4 *President Roosevelt and the Coming of the War* (1948), 577.

did in fact represent an even more formidable threat to America than Hitler, *if* their system had no greater latitude for internal liberalization and democratization than the Nazi system, and *if* life in the world with them promised no significantly greater chance of peaceful coexistence—then the notion that something had been gained for America from the war was a delusion and the whole Rooseveltian adventure was proved to be the fraud that Beard had anticipated over a decade before when he wrote: "The Pacific war awaits." The basic political tendency underlying this conclusion was precisely that which had in the intervening years driven a wedge between Beard and his liberal friends. His profound animating hatred of F.D.R., his conspiratorial view of historical events, his idea that this whole episode in human history should be looked at strictly from an American nationalist point of view, and the conviction that the war had accomplished nothing at all, were to become the staple assumptions of the far right wing. These preconceptions had brought Beard to the verge of allegiances that he must himself have thought strange: he would find himself taking pleasure at Chicago *Tribune* editorials, praising Herbert Hoover, conferring with Henry Luce, supplying memoranda to Republican congressmen.

Though I believe the force and persistence of his early "socialism" has sometimes been exaggerated, Beard had surely always occupied a place on the political spectrum considerably to the left of center. No doubt he would have described himself as a liberal (in the modern American rather than the classic sense of the word), and on occasions he had spoken of his belief in "collectivist" democracy. Now his responses to the war were pulling him steadily toward the right, cutting him loose from his moorings in traditional American liberalism, and setting him adrift on political tides that might have carried him, had he lived beyond 1948, into unfamiliar and uncomfortable waters. Beard was deeply troubled, as many responsible minds have been, by the possible effects of the President's war-making power on the fate of American constitutionalism. His heightened nationalism and his newly awakened impulse to defend American constitutionalism against the menacing inheritance of Rooseveltian Caesarism, helped to push him toward the mild, acquiescent conservative views of such later works as *The Republic, The Enduring Federalist* and the Beards' *Basic History of the United States,* in which he seemed to be retreating with a certain muffled embarrassment from his earlier writings. But the suspicious and somewhat conspiratorial approach to history that at times had shown itself in his work had now come full circle: a style of thought which gave heart to Progressivism when he was exposing the machinations of the Founding Fathers had become congenial to postwar ultraconservatives and Roosevelt-haters, now that he was exposing the machinations of F.D.R. His penchant for finding the rotten core in the fruits of history finally brought him to turn upon his earlier works, and his intense lifelong devotion to pursuit of the "reality" that underlay appearances at last consumed itself.[5]

During his fight against Roosevelt's policies Beard had begun to drift into a new political orbit. Although he had endorsed the isolationist organization, America First, he refused to join it, and he became uncomfortably aware that it was acting as a magnet for "native fascists," a breed he never ceased to detest. He was spared the painful embarrassment of appearing on the platform with some leaders of the German-American Bund only when friends persuaded him at the last minute to cancel a speech he had engaged to give at an America First meeting in Hartford. His increasing alienation from the main stream of liberal sentiment and from old friends troubled him deeply. "All the people I have always liked," he once regretfully said, "seem to be on the other side," but he would not let this dim his independence or his self-confidence. As differences deepened, he found himself spurned or denounced by cherished associates of the past. In 1944 Lewis Mumford, whom he had once helped, wrote a dreadful, wounding attack on him in a letter to *The Saturday Review*, in which Beard was described as having become "a passive—no, active —abetter of tyranny, sadism, and human defilement," guilty of a self-betrayal and corruption "comparable to that which

---

[5] At least one commentator, George Leighton, has remarked that Beard's last book had "much of the quality of the book on the Constitution. The two were alike in their method, their attack on the conventional view," as well as in their indication of the need for further research and their power to evoke wrath. "Beard and Foreign Policy," 184.

placed a novelist of Knut Hamsun's dimensions on the side of the Nazis."[6] Beard was also deeply hurt to be treated discourteously by a few historians when he appeared at a wartime meeting of the American Historical Association, though the political scientists gave him a cordial reception.[7] A sense of persecution finally gripped him, and the closing years of his life found him more than ever in an embattled state of mind. It is a crusty and suspicious note that runs through Beard's surviving correspondence of the war and postwar years, the note of a man who feels himself surrounded by venality, treachery, timidity, and incompetence, but who in the face of it all maintains his own courage and assurance. Perhaps the worst part of it for him was not the feeling, now quite familiar, of opposing a sinister and scheming officialdom, but the sense of being surrounded by the literary lackeys of power. The country needed, he thought in 1943, "an exposé of the Wilson-F.D. mythology, but most of the people who deal with foreign affairs are subsidized by the Carnegie peace–slush fund and live by keeping up the mythology." Carnegie's "peace money," he said, had done "incalculable damage to minds and morals." He was convinced that he and other critics of the Pearl Harbor disaster and wartime diplomacy were being shut off from important documentary information that was available to the "official" historians—"the vestal virgins" he called them, "who guard the sacred tradition." He was so convinced that "no big N.Y. publisher will touch anything that does not laud the Saint" that he denied them the chance to turn him down by taking his books on Roosevelt's foreign policy directly to the Yale University Press.[8]

As all other issues shrank in significance when compared with the necessity of telling the public the truth about Pearl

---

[6] Leighton, "Beard and Foreign Policy," 183, on Beard and the minority report; Josephson, "Charles A. Beard: A Memoir," 591, 602, and the same writer's *Infidel in the Temple* (1967), 413–14; *Saturday Review*, 27 (December 2, 1944), 27; see also November 11, p. 12, 13, and December 16, p. 15. "The Sat. Lit Rev. performances are shocking," Beard wrote calmly to Oswald Garrison Villard, January 31, 1945, "but I am used to it now."
[7] Alfred A. Knopf Memoir, Oral History Collection, 147–8.
[8] On Carnegie money, Beard to O. G. Villard, November 25, 1943, September 8, 1945; on publishers and vestal virgins, Beard to H. E. Barnes, May 23, 1947, January 14, 1948.

Harbor, Beard found himself in a totally alien political environment. He thought Herbert Hoover "courageous" for speaking out on the manner in which the country got into the Pacific war, and in 1944 had two long talks with Henry Luce, preparatory to writing a sharp article on Pearl Harbor for *Life*, which, to his disappointment, Luce decided not to use. In the election of 1944 he saw himself as forced to choose between "the Peanut of Pawling" and "the Madhatter of Washington," and felt uncertain, he wrote Oswald Garrison Villard, as to whether he could vote for Norman Thomas, for "he too is a world-saver." He expected little from Congress on Pearl Harbor: "I hope that Congress demands the truth, but does Congress want the truth?" The State Department, he said in the autumn of 1947, is "now our prize madhouse." The Truman administration pleased him no more than its predecessor. In early 1947 he thought that he discerned in the Truman policies "a project to invade Russia by way of Turkey, now that the opportunity to fight Russia in China has exploded," and he saw nothing constructive even in the Marshall Plan. "The Democrats," he concluded as 1948 began, "are playing the old game of crisis and trying to wring one more victory out of the bloody shirt! Having brought the country to the verge of disaster, they want to complete the job." Truman, he believed, was looking for another "Pearl Harbor in the Mediterranean or Palestine."[9]

What sustained Beard in these years was his arduous labors on his Roosevelt books, and the signs he sometimes saw that Roosevelt's reputation might yet be destroyed. The rumbles over George Morgenstern's exposé, *Pearl Harbor: The Story of the Secret War* (1947), gave him hope: "The pseudo-intellectuals who have been trying to terrorize everybody who questions the official myths are now getting frantic," he wrote, "and well they may be, for the whole structure is crumbling and the high-brows are tearing one another's hair out." "The myth of the Savior is fading," he joyfully wrote Harry Elmer Barnes in early 1948, and with his own last book well launched, he had a final moment of keen expectation: "The

---

[9] Beard to Villard, October 20, 1944; March 9, April 15, September 8, 1947, January 17, 1948; Beard to Barnes, January 6, 1948.

country seems to be in a mood to consider the question of how we were secretly governed by our great *Fuehrer!*"[1] When he died in the summer of that year it was with the sense of repose that comes to a man who has done his duty under the greatest of difficulties.

IV

Today Beard's reputation stands like an imposing ruin in the landscape of American historiography. What was once the grandest house in the province is now a ravaged survival, afflicted, in Beard's own words, by "the pallor of waning time." As an admirer of Charles A. Beard approaches the house that Beard built—a pile of formidable proportions and a testament to the vaulting ambitions of its architect—he can hardly fail to feel a twinge of melancholy. True, its lofty central portion, constructed in the days when the economic interpretation of history was flourishing, remains in a state of partial repair, and one suspects that several of the rooms, with a little ingenious improvisation, might still be habitable; but it has become shabby and suggests none of its former solidity and elegance. The east wing, inspired by historical relativism and showing a little sadly the traces of a wholly derivative design, is entirely neglected. The west wing, dedicated to continental isolationism, looks like a late and relatively hasty addition; a jerry-built affair, now a tattered shambles, it is nonetheless occupied from time to time by transient and raucous tenants, of whom, one is sure, the original owner would have disapproved.

As one looks back upon it, Beard's professional life takes on more and more the aspect of a daring gamble—though, as a critic of speculative enterprise, he might have laughed at such a notion. But Beard did take moral and intellectual risks: he had never been content with the role of the historian or the academic alone; he had always hoped to be politically relevant, had always aspired to become a public force, and even more than the part of the sage he relished the part of

---

1 Beard to Villard, February 9, 1947; to Barnes, January 6, 1948; to Villard, April 13, 1948.

the public moralist, the gadfly, the pamphleteer. With his ready pen and wide knowledge, his strong intellectual self-confidence and his tireless energy, he had made himself foremost among the American historians of his or any other generation in the search for a usable past. And yet any man who makes written commitments year after year on difficult public questions will live to find some of his views evanescent and embarrassing and to see his own words quoted with telling effect against himself. Beyond this, the inevitable risk of the publicist, Beard took a further and more gratuitous risk: he finally geared his reputation as a historian so closely to his political interests and passions that the two were bound to share the same fate. This foe of the speculators put everything he had on the line, and though he had a long run at the tables, in the end he lost. As he once wrote about Henry Adams, "He wanted to achieve great things and was oppressed by his own and the general ignorance. What was the poor devil to do in the circumstances?"[2]

For those of us who came of age in the 1920's or 1930's, and for whom *An Economic Interpretation of the Constitution* and *The Rise of American Civilization* were books of profound and decisive importance, the decline of Beard's reputation has not been a thing to be witnessed with pleasure, nor indeed can it be by any other historian who has ever shared Beard's hope that somehow the past might be mobilized to strengthen or enlighten his passion for the public interest. One longs to restore the earlier Beard, who is still remembered as a man of extraordinary kindliness, courage, and honor. And somehow, quite aside from the fate of his works, he does remain appealing—a man so clearly bred out of the native grain, and yet once so cosmopolitan in his interests and experiences; a bearer of something like folk wisdom, and yet a scholar of broad learning; a radical who was also a patriot in the classical and untarnished sense of the word. One prefers to think of him in this way—as a productive scholar who was also an intrepid public spirit, as the patron and guide of younger colleagues, the distinguished and embattled defender of civil and academic liberties, the scourger of Hearst, the

---

[2] Beard to Carl Becker, May 14, 193[2?].

spokesman of the native decencies—and one remembers that the life of a man does not end as a series of propositions that can simply be assessed and found true or false, but as a set of lingering resonances that for our own sake we must be attuned to hear. Some scholars choose to live their lives, usefully enough, amid the clutter of professional detail. Beard aimed to achieve a wisdom commensurate with his passion, and to put them both in the public service. No doubt he would rather have failed in this than succeeded in anything less.

PART
IV

V. L. Parrington

CHAPTER 10

Economics and Criticism

> *Officially I am a teacher of English litera-*
> *ture, but in reality my business in life is to*
> *wage war on the crude and selfish materialism*
> *that is biting so deeply into our national life*
> *and character. . . .*
> —V. L. Parrington to the Rev. L. N.
> Linebaugh, June 16, 1908

> *He was concerned only with* nuances.
> —V. L. Parrington on Henry James

I

THE MOST striking thing about the reputation of V. L. Parrington, as we think of it today, is its abrupt decline. On
the appearance in 1927 of the first two of its three volumes,
his *Main Currents in American Thought* won a more prompt
and enthusiastic acceptance than the first important works
of Turner and Beard. Liberal critics hailed it as a major work,
and even the old-fashioned academic guardians of American literature were cordial. In the 1930's, the book had an
influence that matched Turner's essays on the frontier and
Beard's study of the Constitution; but where the controversies
over Turner and Beard enlisted ardent combatants and in
time provoked a large and fruitful literature, Parrington,
after a few salient essays, was little scrutinized, and now tends
to be overlooked. It is hard to re-create the excitement generated by *Main Currents* in the years between 1927 and the
mid-1940's. In a famous essay, "Reality in America," written
in 1940, Lionel Trilling attributed to Parrington "an influence
on our conception of American culture which is not equaled
by that of any other writer of the last two decades." Parrington's ideas, Trilling remarked, "are now the accepted ones
wherever the college course in American literature is given
by a teacher who conceives himself to be opposed to the genteel and the academic and in alliance with the vigorous and
the actual. And whenever the liberal historian of America

349

finds occasion to take account of the national literature, . . .
it is Parrington who is his standard and guide. . . . Parrington
formulated in a classic way the suppositions about our culture
which are held by the American middle class so far as that
class is at all liberal in its social thought and so far as it
begins to understand that literature has anything to do with
society."[1]

Even as late as 1950, when Parrington's reputation had
gone far on its course of decline (hastened by Trilling's wither-
ing verdict that his mind was "rather too predictable to be
consistently interesting"), Henry Steele Commager in his
The American Mind professed that his deepest intellectual
debt was to Parrington "whose great study of American
thought has long been my inspiration and whose disciple I
gladly acknowledge myself." Commager's judgment that
Main Currents was "a magnificent tract calling upon Americans to be true to their past and worthy of their destiny" was
widely shared among his colleagues in the historical profession. At about the same time a poll of American historians
showed that among all books in their field published between
1920 and 1950 Parrington's was the most highly esteemed,
enjoying a narrow margin over Turner's frontier essays and
a substantial one over the Beards' *Rise of American Civilization*.[2]

For those of us who were young in the 1930's and who
responded to the democratic idealism of the Progressive tradition, this enthusiasm is easy to recall. Historians were just
beginning to show a renewed interest in the history of ideas
in America, and Parrington became available on the eve of
a strong resurgence of concern with the subject, which was
in turn stimulated by his own work. Reading him for the first
time in 1938, I found his volumes immensely rewarding. What
other historian had written about American letters with such
a wealth of democratic enthusiasm? What other writer had
covered the whole span of American letters from 1620 to the
end of the nineteenth century in a work which had so much

---

[1] Trilling, "Reality in America," first published in *Partisan Review*, 1940, reprinted in *The Liberal Imagination* (1950), 3.
[2] Commager, *The American Mind* (1950), ix, 303; John W.
Caughey, "Historians' Choice," *Mississippi Valley Historical Review*, 39 (1952), 289–302.

of a personal stamp on it, and yet with so consistent an effort to put American writing into its social setting? As Howard Mumford Jones remembered it, Parrington "seemed for a time almost to obliterate literary histories": "Who can forget the tingling sense of discovery with which we first read these lucid pages, followed his confident marshalling of masses of stubborn material into position, until book, chapter, and section became as orderly as a regiment on parade! Readers in 1927 felt the same quality of excitement, I imagine, as Jeffrey experienced when in 1825 young Macaulay sent his dazzling essay on Milton to the *Edinburgh Review*. All other histories of literature were compelled to pale their intellectual fires. . . . Here was a usable past, adult, reasonable, coherent."[3]

Parrington indeed seemed at first wholly admirable, at least until one engaged oneself in the study of one of his idiosyncratic interpretations. Much that we learned from Parrington in the years after 1927 could perhaps have been learned in less partisan form from other writers. But we knew of few other writers of literary history who we thought could do much for us. Moses Coit Tyler's four volumes (1878, 1897), which in any case only reached 1783 and thus left out nine tenths of what we knew as American literature, were relatively inaccessible and had fallen into undeserved neglect. A book like Barrett Wendell's *A Literary History of America* (1900) we had been taught to laugh at by various critics of the genteel tradition, and without troubling to read it we concluded that we had nothing to learn from it. There were other surveys, most of them old-fashioned, academic, rather thin. Few people, I suppose, actually read the *Cambridge History of American Literature* (1917). Parrington, on the other hand, was salient and accessible, and had a live idea. He seemed much the most interesting, as well as inspiring, among the comprehensive writers on American literature— the one with whom a historian, a political scientist could find rapport. And many of us did at first learn a good deal from him—perhaps much that still lingers in the intellectual heritage of the prewar generations, unacknowledged not (one hopes) out of lack of gratitude but because this debt has

---

3 *The Theory of American Literature* (1948), 140, 141-2.

been so overlaid by other influences and so attenuated by the passing of time that it can no longer be distinguished and given voice.

During the 1940's Parrington rather quickly ceased to have a compelling interest for students of American literature, and in time historians too began to desert him. He is still widely read, of course, in fact more widely read in the paperback era than he was at the peak of his influence; but I suspect that he is read primarily as an object rather than a subject— that is, his work is one of those monuments by which one can take one's bearings as one finds one's way across the historic terrain of American thought, and it no longer has the force of authority or inspiration. Recently, in teaching a graduate seminar on American historiography, I discovered that students quickly became engaged once again in the complex debates over Beard on the Constitution and Turner on the frontier, but I could find no way to interest them in Parrington. A generation that has been reading Jean Genet, Henry Miller, and William Burroughs sees Parrington (along with so many others) as an incomprehensible square.

Yet, if we want to understand the presuppositions of the American Progressive mind and trace what has happened to it, we must again interest ourselves in a book which, as Alfred Kazin has put it, "represents the most ambitious single effort of the Progressive mind to understand itself." In fact, I found on rereading *Main Currents* little of the disappointment or boredom that afflicted me with the Beards' *Rise of American Civilization*, though I must confess that what now gave the work its interest for me was not so much in what I found there as in the intellectual games Parrington set in motion, the mild pleasure I found myself taking in the study of the architectonics of his book and its determined intellectual strategy. I could see once again some of the qualities that had made the book attractive. Parrington's was that rare thing among works of scholarship—a deeply felt book, full of vitality and passionate concern. He was, too—though I think my own generation did not at first quite see the full significance of this—a gifted melodramatist, and most of us at one time or another crave a bit of intellectual melodrama, well done and closely cued to our prejudices of the moment. Parrington also had a distinctive style; and for anyone who has to read widely among historical monographs and surveys and in the literature of "social science," the presence of any personal note, of any style, even if it is a comic oddity like Veblen's or somewhat mannered and oratorical like Parrington's, is a welcome thing. Parrington's writing was courtly, self-conscious, a little over-formal, at times repetitive almost to the verge of echolalia, and at a few points his metaphors come along so fast that they seem to trip over each other, but it was still much better writing than one characteristically found in academic historians. It had an insistent, persuasive rhythm, and a certain masculine energy that was well suited both to his tendentious judgments and to the affectionate evocation of his heroes. Although he was not a writer of great biographical precision—his heroes tend to melt into each other and his villains do the same—some of his sketches, like his fierce account of Cotton Mather, were quite memorable even if not quite just. He could hit off rather well from time to time some aspect of a familiar figure—as when he spoke of Emerson's "superlative mastery of the sententious sentence" or of Whitman's "somewhat truculent pose of democratic undress" or when he called John Adams a "political counterpart of Dr. Johnson" or John Randolph "an arch individualist in opinions as other Americans were in acquisitiveness." He was one of the first literary historians to see the importance of the dawning Melville revival, and the first to see the significance of Brooks Adams. He had a good eye for the focal quotations in his subjects, and he seemed to know so much about so many writers one had never heard of, like Nathaniel Ward, John Pendleton Kennedy, and Nathaniel Beverley Tucker. At times his down-to-earth iconoclasm hit the mark cleanly, as in his treatment of the Davy Crockett legend. Now and then his perceptions seemed keener than those of other Progressive historians—he was one of the first, for example, to have a glimpse of the importance of the entrepreneurial and acquisitive side of Jacksonian democracy, and was perhaps the first to show interest in recovering the qualities of the antebellum Southern mind. Finally there were a few sharp evocative sequences that economically summoned up a whole era, such as his account of the Great Barbecue of the Gilded Age, in which he re-created the ugliness and rapacity of the times through physical portraits of its leading figures. Whatever was wrong elsewhere, there was an imaginative quality in such passages that one hardly found in the work, say, even of so sound and learned a historian of American writing as Moses Coit Tyler.

Still, the decline in Parrington's reputation is as easy to account for as its eminence. Quite aside from the limitations of the Progressive imagination and from certain vulnerable idiosyncrasies in his interpretations, his book was designed neither as a history of political thought nor as a viable history of literature. Nor was it conceived as a many-sided history of the main currents in American thought: it was no part of Parrington's purpose, for example, to account for philosophic, scientific, or legal thought. Even with theology he had lost patience, despite his long sequence on the Puritans and his early desire to become a Presbyterian minister, and it commanded his interest only in a fitful and superficial way. Oddly enough, despite the importance of historical writing in American literature and its relevance to the democratic theme, he did not try to deal seriously or at length with the major historians. Only at a few points, and again superficially, was he concerned with esthetic thought, and when he came to Poe, perhaps the first American to develop a distinctive and considered esthetic, and certainly the first to develop one of consequence for the literature of the Western world, his response was to throw up his hands.

Essentially, Parrington's three volumes are a history of the literary aspect of American politics and of the most overtly political aspects of American letters. "I have undertaken," he explained, "to give some account of the development in American letters of certain germinal ideas that came to be reckoned traditionally American. . . . I have chosen to follow the broad path of our political, economic, and social development, rather than the narrower belletristic; and the main divisions of the study have been fixed by forces that are anterior to literary schools and movements, creating the body

of ideas from which literary culture eventually springs."[4]
Parrington's assumption that the experience recorded in *belles
lettres* is more restricted in range—"narrower"—than experience in the political realm, and that literary ideas are in some
way subordinate or posterior to political ideas led him to a
rather stark politicization of literature. This conception, congenial to many minds nurtured in the Populist-Progressive
tradition, became congenial again in the 1930's when the
prospects of a proletarian literature were being widely and
solemnly discussed and when Marxist critics like Granville
Hicks, V. F. Calverton, and Bernard Smith seemed at times to
be echoing Parrington's methods and some of his judgments;
but it proved to be one of the less durable ideas in the history of criticism. Parrington's most eager reception was probably always among left or liberal intellectuals whose primary
passion was not for literature.

In this sense Parrington's was a one-dimensional book,
yet it was not this so much that made him *passé*—Americans
are used to one-dimensional books on their literature, and
some of the best have been of this order—but rather that the
dimension he settled upon was fatal to his survival. For all
his honest efforts to serve that which was up-to-date and
modern, and to give aid and comfort to the avant-garde of
his early maturity, which was represented by the struggle
of realist and naturalist writers for acceptance, his seems
now to have been a strikingly premodernist sensibility. The
type of criticism and literary history he represented had
always been under fire, and with the increasing academic
influence of the New Criticism in the late 1930's and early
1940's, literary interest turned sharply away from the
biographical, historical, sociological, and moral aspects of
literature and toward just those aspects that Parrington was
least concerned with: toward a close and exclusively interior
analysis of texts, toward a preoccupation with language and
with the mythological and symbolic aspects of writing, toward
the literary manifestations of the unconscious and the irrational. By the early 1940's a complete critical jargon had

[4] I, iii.

come into being which sounded as though it had been con-
trived in a world wholly alien to that of Parrington and his
generation; and by then the very idea of *any* kind of literary
history, as opposed to criticism, was decidedly on the defensive.

Moreover, aside from the effects of the New Criticism,
readers were becoming interested in a kind of writing that
made the pale modernism of Parrington's era seem to belong
to the nineteenth century. The new postwar modernism, with
its sensationalism, its love of extremes and violence, its affection for the picaresque and the anti-hero, its interest in mad-
ness as a clue to the human, its candor about sexuality and its
belief that the modes of sexuality embody or conceal symbols
that are universally applicable and revealing, its sense of outrage, its distrust of institutions, its profound destructive intention, its persistent and almost hypnotic fascination with
the deepest abysses of the human personality, seemed in many
ways to be a transvaluation of everything Parrington cared
about, and it thrust writers of Parrington's type so sharply
backward into the past that he now seemed (and with a certain truth) to have merged into the genteel tradition, to have
become an old-fashioned moralist. Even the radical tendency
of the new modernism had next to nothing in common with
the radicalism of Parrington's time. Where a Parringtonian
looked askance upon established institutions as the possible
agencies of human exploitation, judged issues from the standpoint of a certain sentimentality about the people, and questioned the inherited idea of progress only with sad regret,
the radicalism of the new writing moved increasingly toward
a ruthless individualism or a thoroughgoing anarchism, a
complete indifference or hostility to the principles by which
institutions are constituted, a mordant skepticism about progress, and a disposition to see the mass of men with more
revulsion than pity. The mind of a man like Parrington was
suspended, in honest doubt and hesitation, between the world
of the progressive agrarian or bourgeois and the world of the
supposedly ascendant proletariat. The mind of literary modernism is convinced beyond doubt or hesitation of the utter
speciousness of bourgeois values, and it is altogether without
hope, usually without interest, in the proletariat.

To those who were raised on the New Criticism, with its great show of analytical precision and its frequent academic fussiness, or to those who were wholly responsive to the latest phase of modernist writing, it seemed unlikely that a historian or biographer working with Parrington's preconceptions could tell them anything *they* wanted to know about Whitman, Emerson, or Thoreau; a world of sensibility, responsive to such writers as Eliot, Pound, Joyce, and Lawrence, had come into being in which his critical canons seemed quite irrelevant. Perhaps the last moment at which Parrington's kind of concern for the moral and social function of literature was likely to strike some positive response would have been during the first few years after the outbreak of World War II, when critics like Archibald McLeish in *The Irresponsibles* (1940), Van Wyck Brooks in *Opinions of Oliver Allston* (1941), and Bernard De Voto in *The Literary Fallacy* (1944) attacked certain modern writers, among them Eliot, Pound, Hemingway, and Faulkner, for having failed to affirm the values of Western democratic culture. (It was in this period that Brooks likened Joyce to "the ash of a burnt-out cigar.") But this was only a passing mood. The war, the bomb, the death camps wrote finis to an era in human sensibility, and many writers of the recent past were immolated in the ashes, caught like the people of Pompeii in the midst of life, some of them in curious postures of unconsummated rebellion.

II

Troubled though it was, the world in which Parrington lived now seems one of comparative innocence and certainty. He was born in 1871 in Aurora, Illinois, where his father, a lawyer, was county clerk. The family was of English descent, Parrington's grandfather, John, having emigrated from Yorkshire in the late 1820's, and it had kept alive a tradition of English working-class radicalism. John Parrington had left England during a time of economic and social upheaval, when memories of Peterloo were still strong and rancorous. The introduction of new machinery had caused particularly acute distress among the hand-loom weavers of the industrial North, an unusually literate and militant segment of the working class, and the Parrington family came from the industrial town of Barnsley, about twenty miles north of Sheffield, a center of radicalism where the workers had rioted just about at the time of the Parringtons' departure. Apparently an individual rebel as well as a political radical, John Parrington was an admirer of Tom Paine. He left his family a legacy of hatred for conservative England that can still be felt in his grandson's work. "It was an England," Parrington believed, "fit only to leave—for the economic underling at least; and once my grandfather reached America hatred for the old home seems to have crept into his heart. My father shared this feeling and to the end of his life thought ill of England; and I think rightly, for that old tory England richly deserved the hate of free souls." Immigrants to America, Parrington wrote in *Main Currents*, "very likely transmitted to their children a bitter hostility to the ways of an aristocratic society, the residuum of old grievances," and however conjectural this was for other immigrant families, it was certainly true for his own.[5]

Parrington's father, John William, was born in the village of Gorham Corners, Maine, a dozen miles from Portland, where John Parrington had set up a small carpet-weaving mill. Although the family was impoverished not long afterward by John's death, the little community rallied around the widow and her four children in a warm-hearted fashion, and Parrington was raised to remember gratefully "the essential humanity that underlay the hard and niggardly life of that older New England."[6] With the help of neighbors it was even possible to send John William to a local academy and to Waterville College (now Colby) from which he graduated in 1855. He then emigrated to Illinois, where he found a

---

[5] I, 136. On working-class conditions, with particular glimpses of Barnsley, see E. P. Thompson, *The Making of the English Working Class* (1964), *passim*. For a touching illustration of some of the hazards of engaging in social protest in England at this time, see the letters between the Rev. Humphrey Price and Jeremy Bentham; Bentham, *Works* (ed. John Bowring, 1848), VI, 43–8.
[6] On the family legacy, see Parrington's untitled biographical memoir, written for his children, dated February 1918. All reminiscent and self-characterizing statements from Parrington in the following pages, unless otherwise documented, are from this memoir, in the possession of Vernon Parrington, Jr.

place as principal of the high school in the town of Aurora. There he married Elizabeth McClellan, the daughter of a Scotch-Irishman of abolitionist views who had left the Baptist ministry to take up without much success a variety of trades. Parrington served as captain in the Union Army from 1863 to 1866, was wounded in the second attack on Petersburg, and was brevetted out at the rank of lieutenant colonel. He returned to begin the practice of law and to enter politics as a Republican. For a while, after he became clerk of the court of Kane County, Parrington moved to Geneva, Illinois, but he believed that his health required an outdoor occupation, and in 1877, when Vernon, his second son, was six, he took his family to eastern Kansas, and there on a farm in the little village of Americus not far from Emporia, the young Parrington had the earliest social experiences he could remember.

Americus, which Parrington recalled as a "crude and ugly" town, was in a corn-growing area of the prairies, flat, hot in summer, icy in winter, alternating between dust and muck in the dry and wet seasons. There, between the farm chores and the rural schoolhouse, Parrington got his first sense of the world; and if he later responded to Hamlin Garland's evocation of farm life—Garland, he wrote, "was no frontier romantic but a sober historian"—it was because Garland's *Son of the Middle Border* re-created to such a striking degree the circumstances of Parrington's early boyhood experience: the small, ugly farmhouses, the hazards of the cold and drought, and also the intermittent moments of warmth and liveliness, the pleasures of hunting, the promise of growing crops, and the spring flowers.

Although he could feel a good deal of nostalgia about his own boyhood, in which a warm family life always sustained him, the drabness and hardship of farm life were also unforgettable, and when Parrington begins to account for the impact of the frontier on literature he refers straight off to its spirit of "bitterness," and some form of the word bitter occurs no less than seven times in two pages. "It was no holiday job," he wrote, "to subdue an untamed land and wrest abundance and comfort from a virgin soil. Only for the young who can project their hopes into the future is it endurable; for the middle-aged and old it is a heart-breaking task. The history of the western frontier is a long, drab story of hardship and privation and thwarted hopes, of men and women broken by endless toil, the windows of their dreams shuttered by poverty, and the doors to an abundant life closed and barred by narrow opportunity. It is true that the prairies took no such toll as the forests had taken; the mean and squalid poverty through which Lincoln passed was not so common along the Middle Border as it had been along the frontier. Nevertheless a fierce climate and a depressing isolation added their discomforts to a bleak existence. The winds were restless on the flat plains, and the flimsy wooden houses, stark and mean, unprotected by trees and unrelieved by shrubbery, were an ill defense against their prying fingers. In winter the blizzards swept out of the North to overmaster the land, and in summer the hot winds came up from the Southwest to sear the countrysides that were rustling with great fields of corn. Other enemies appeared, as it were, out of a void. Endless flights of grasshoppers descended . . . and when they passed the earth was bare and brown where the young wheat had stood. Armies of chinch-bugs came from nobody knew where, and swarming up the tender cornstalks left them sucked dry and yellow. It is nature's way to destroy with one hand what it creates with the other; and for years the western farmers were fighting plagues that had possessed the prairies before the settlers came."[7]

Americus had been settled in the 1850's during the great pre-Civil War struggle over the soul of Kansas, and the frontier, taken literally as the cutting edge of settlements, had moved far to the West when the Parringtons reached town, but they might have been justified in thinking of themselves as frontiersmen. Around them there were still large patches of untilled vacant land. If Parrington's

---

7 III, 260; on bitterness, 288–9. In his *Son of the Middle Border*, Garland, Parrington said, "has captured . . . truly the life that I knew and lived; every detail of discomfort and ugliness and rebellion which he sets down vividly I can match from my own experiences."

acknowledgment of intellectual kinship or indebtedness
to Turner was made only casually,[8] it was perhaps because
the Turnerian sense of the reality and importance of the
frontier and its relation to democracy was a part of his
experience long years before Turner's first essay was written, and what the historian had to say did not have, for
him, any of the force of revelation. In the 1880's Americus
was still quite primitive, still raw physically and socially,
and any glimpse of beauty or cultivation that anyone
might find there—any touch of what Parrington would
come to call romance—had to be found through some
weighty effort of the imagination or put there through
some assertion of will. The new house the family had
built in 1879—"a house that even the softening touch of
years could not beautify or render other than bleak and
inhospitable"—stamped itself on Parrington's memory as
a thing that "in its naked ugliness . . . seems to me to
symbolize those years of farm life, which in spite of the
romance which youth discovers in the crudest reality,

---

[8] It was only when "Professor Turner drew attention to the creative influence of the frontier on American life that the historians
were provided with a suggestive working hypothesis" to explain
American democracy, Parrington believed. III, 404; cf. III, 159,
287. "I have a high regard for Professor Turner," he wrote in
1924, "although I fear his work has long since been done. Perhaps you can tell me why the last ten years of his life have been
so barren. It was away back about 1894 that he announced his
doctrine of the influence of the frontier, and he has done little
since." To T. S. Laush, November 19, 1924. Of course no historian of ideas who put as much stress on imported intellectual
systems could be regarded as a Turnerian, and Parrington did
not make very much of the frontier impact on American letters.
"I gave, in reality, serious consideration to the whole question of
frontier influences," he explained to one correspondent, "but I
could not forget that ostensibly I was writing a history of ideas
as expressed in literature, and so when I had followed the development of such things as frontier humor in David Crockett, I
convinced myself that I had pushed my field to the limit." To a
confidential source, March 7, 1928. As a former teacher, Parrington probably had something to do with the interests that led
Lucy Lockwood Hazard to write *The Frontier in American Literature* (1927), one of the first studies of its kind. Parrington
hailed her book for doing so much to uproot "the lingering prejudice in favor of the pernicious genteel tradition which has
come down as a heritage from New England Victorianism" and
commended her for her tart critique of Emerson. To Lucy Lockwood Hazard, February 10, 1927; cf. *The Frontier in American
Literature*, viii, 149–53.

I was never so romantic as to believe were years of pleasant or desirable existence." If, in the Parringtonian esthetic, beauty sometimes seems to be a thing rather outside of and counterposed to "reality," it may be because beauty was something rarely to be found on the prairies, not a natural and organic effect of the surroundings, but a thing attained by effortful self-cultivation. That Parrington consciously schooled himself to surmount the dry ugliness of Americus we can hardly doubt. The prairie came alive with flowers in the spring, and he developed a love for them and a passion for gardening. Except for music, there was hardly an art or craft that did not fascinate him. At an early age he learned to paint, and he never lost interest in art. For a long time he wrote poetry, and for several years it was his major creative interest. In time he took such keen pleasure in architecture that he pursued the study of it for years, and formed his book almost compulsively on architectonic principles. He developed an interest in craftsmanship and carpentry that seems appropriate to an admirer of William Morris, and designed and helped to construct two of the houses in which he lived. Even in dress he was, as his father had been, meticulous during his early and middle years, and, for a Western farm boy, faintly dandyish; and to those who met him, for all his generous and democratic manners, he presented the aspect of an old-fashioned gentleman with aristocratic tastes and a fondness for elegance. A good deal of the somewhat awkward but tender concern about the place in life of esthetic values that can be found in his work may have grown from his sense of the *separateness* of art from the social and physical world, of the immense effort required to achieve some beauty, and perhaps from a lingering uncertainty about the legitimacy of such effort in the face of the world's visible injustices and unmet needs.

In 1884 Parrington's father, who had been an active member of the local Republican machine, was elected to a judgeship in the probate court, and the family moved to Emporia. Parrington and his brother John were sent to the College of Emporia—first to its preparatory department and then to the collegiate division. A tiny church "college" sponsored by the Presbyterians, Emporia offered the familiar classical curriculum—heavy doses of Greek, Latin, and mathematics, drearily taught, along with careful schooling in the Bible and "Christian Evidences." Committed to old-fashioned pedagogy and religious fundamentalism, the college, though Parrington was grateful for it and even quite happy under its regime, gave next to nothing in the way of intellectual stimulation. It was, he recalled, "a sterile world," closed to ideas, in which the teachers were "zealous to keep us from all new and unorthodox views." His real education in these years seems to have been largely self-conducted. A voracious reader, he found himself at last in the presence of a city library with resources commensurate with his appetite, and he plunged vigorously into a course of self-directed reading in which the Victorian novel loomed large. His intellectual promise seems to have impressed his parents, for after three years of Emporia College they strained their resources to send him to Harvard, where he spent two more years and graduated, along with Oswald Garrison Villard and William Vaughn Moody, in the class of 1893.

At best Parrington's Harvard experience can be characterized only as a provocative disaster. In the 1890's Harvard was still an educational outpost of proper Boston, and although it did have a certain receptivity to bright young men from outside its sphere, it expected them to knock at its doors and wait. Some did; Bernard Berenson, less than ten years out of the Polish Pale, had made his way in, and so had others. But some combination of pride and vulnerability seems to have made it impossible for Parrington to make the necessary overtures, and he never recovered from his feeling of being an outsider. "An inferiority complex," he later wrote—of Howells, whose problem in this respect was much less acute than his own— "is a common mark of the frontier mind that finds itself diffident in the presence of the old and established."[9] He had encountered, he thought, a degree of snobbery totally unfamiliar in Americus or Emporia, and he linked this snobbery

---

[9] Howells himself offers some insight into the situation of the "jay," the unclubable outsider at Harvard, in his novel, *The Landlord at Lion's Head* (1897).

to the wealth of State Street that lay behind the university. "I could have made friends had I tried," he later observed, "but I didn't try, being as proud and independent as I was poor." Although he studied with a few adequate instructors —among them Barrett Wendell (whose literary history would so often be contrasted with his) and George Herbert Palmer whose instruction in philosophy he thought first-rate—he seems to have received little more from the classroom than he did from the social or intellectual life of the undergraduates, and once again, as in Emporia, his education became in large part a matter of lonely reading, now in the Harvard library. A barely controlled resentment of Harvard and of the Brahmin culture it served lingered in his mind and occasionally broke through the surface of his history. On the occasion of the twenty-fifth anniversary of his class in 1918, Parrington wrote to the class secretary for the benefit of his classmates: "The past five years I have spent in study and writing, up to my ears in the economic interpretation of American history and literature, getting the last lingering Harvard prejudices out of my system," a remark which seems to stray into the disingenuous in order to arrive at the provocative, since it is hard to see how Parrington could ever have acquired any Harvard prejudices. "I become more radical with each year," Parrington continued, "and more impatient with the smug Tory culture which we were fed on as undergraduates. I haven't been in Cambridge since July, 1893. Harvard is only a dim memory to me. Very likely I am wrong in my judgment, yet from what little information comes through to me I have set the school down as a liability rather than an asset to the cause of democracy. It seems to me the apologist and advocate of capitalistic exploitation—as witness the sweet-smelling list of nominees set out yearly for the Board of Overseers."[1]

---

[1] *Secretary's Sixth Report, Harvard College Class of 1893* (1918), 220–1. In his letter for the report of 1923, Parrington relented a little, since he appears to have recognized that in this age of conformity Harvard was sending out more than its share of critical young intellectuals. Of his own vintage, he singled out Oswald Garrison Villard: "He is the only member of our class whom I really envy. What a gorgeous time he must have, laying on at every smug and shoddy respectability that crosses his path!"

The mark of Parrington's Harvard experience is evident in his treatment of Puritan and Brahmin culture. Two generations of Harvard scholarship, he remarked in the course of some biting observations on Kenneth Murdock's study of Increase Mather, had covered the traces of the Mathers with apologetics because "a consciousness of dealing with Harvard worthies would seem to have laid the writers under certain inhibitions." He blamed Harvard for what he considered the moral downfall of Lowell: Parrington speaks of "the dun professorial period of his life, when Harvard laid hands on him and came near to reducing him to its own ways," and conjectures that Lowell's dislike of Thoreau might have been "prodded by the consciousness that Thoreau had refused to make terms with Harvard culture as he had done." In writing of the Gilded Age, Parrington protested against New England's "cultural dictatorship over American letters," charged that "New England parochialism had become a nation-wide nuisance," and felicitated Hamlin Garland for having had the good fortune to enroll at the Boston Public Library instead of Harvard. "Only a New England historian," he thought, could write as naïvely as John Fiske on the town meeting as the source of American democracy, and he took an unmistakable pleasure in contemplating the abolitionist Wendell Phillips's last memorable encounter with Harvard when Phillips tactlessly read out a list of the movements of humanitarian reform to which Harvard had contributed nothing. Harvard was but one, in some ways the most objectionable, of a bad breed. Parrington had good reason not to be enamored of the academy in America, and believed, as he remarked in another connection, that "provocative thinking and the American university seem never to have got on well together."[2] It is tempting to speculate how much better served he might have been at one of the good state universities—to imagine, for example, that he might have gone, like Carl

---

In an undated letter plainly of his later years Parrington admitted to mixed feelings. "I suppose I love Harvard too, and as we are usually the nastiest to those we love best, I prove my affection by speaking somewhat despitefully of Harvard's ways." But his operative injunction about Harvard was firm: his son was *not* to go there.

[2] I, 98; 460, 465–6; III, 52–3, 124, 146, 211, 292.

Becker, another Kansan, to study at Wisconsin, and might have come, as Becker did, under the influence of Frederick Jackson Turner. But for Kansans out of New England, Harvard seemed the obvious place to send a son.

Parrington's isolation at Harvard underlines a significant quality in his education. It might be taken as pejorative and would be literally inaccurate, after his five years of instruction at the collegiate level and his Harvard B.A., to say that Parrington was an autodidact. But he was left closer to the autodidact's condition and feeling about learning than one might infer from his Harvard degree. The College of Emporia had offered him the bare drill-master's fare of the old-time church-dominated small-town college, and what stimulation Harvard had to offer, in the era of James and Royce, he had largely missed. What he got from Harvard, in the main, was a feeling for pedagogy. Harvard had led the way in developing the elective system and in surmounting the curse of the old-fashioned classroom recitation, and Parrington picked up certain cues there—particularly, he acknowledged, from Barrett Wendell and Lewis Gates in English —which helped make him an outstandingly successful university teacher. Still, it does seem true that he never developed a close relationship with any leading teacher who could take an interest in the development of his mind or help him break down his native shyness. Parrington was self-educated to a degree beyond the conventional sense in which this must be said of every educated man. What he knew he learned mainly from his enthusiastic and self-directed reading, first in the library at Emporia and then at Harvard, and this set a pattern he was to follow the rest of his life. When one compares Parrington's experience in this respect with that of Beard, who went from the heady classes of Colonel Weaver at DePauw to Frederick York Powell at Oxford and then back to study with the urbane and distinguished graduate faculty at Columbia, or with that of Turner, who was so fortunate as to find W. F. Allen at Wisconsin and then to go on to Johns Hopkins at the moment when it had the most effective graduate school in the country, Parrington can be seen

as one of the most underprivileged of our famous academic
men, a veritable waif of scholarship; and one gets a keen
sense of the lonely courage and the dogged will that sustained him during his long years in the Siberian outposts of
academic life before he finally arrived at the University
of Washington. But if he appears also as an original, a kind
of direct, native, self-made writer, one begins to understand certain of his qualities: his resentment of heartless
establishments and the intellectuals who flourish in them,
his love of the grand and difficult terms of criticism, his
aspiration to cover in almost encyclopedic fashion such
a great range of American literature, his formal and self-
conscious style.

Intellectually, perhaps the most important consequence of his Harvard years was the secularization of
Parrington's mind. At the College of Emporia, where evolution was still taboo, he had not rebelled against the prevailing doctrines. (His first recorded essay was an entry
in an oratorical competition entitled "God in History.")[3]
But during his long hours of independent reading in the
Harvard library, he began to feel the fascination of contemporary writers on evolution. Henry Drummond, the
author of *The Ascent of Man* and a famous popular recon-
ciler of evolution and religion, became his "chief guide,"
and he was soon led on to Herbert Spencer, particularly
to his *Data of Ethics*, "the first book of Victorian speculation to make a deep impression on me." Under these influences the orthodoxy inculcated at Emporia began to
crumble, and when Parrington returned to join the faculty
of his college it was as a dissenter (presumably a secret dissenter with such secret discomforts as we can only guess at)
from its most cherished assumptions.

At twenty-two Parrington was engaged by Emporia College, at a salary of $500, to teach English and French—a posi-
tion he readily accepted because it was the only one available
and he wanted to be near home. As yet he had no vocation for
teaching. His father had wanted him to enter teaching and,

---

[3] *College Life*, the weekly college newspaper, gives the text of
this oration, February 21, 1891.

as he said, he "drifted into it"; but it soon appears to have commanded his earnest interest, since we find him promptly, but tactfully, pressing for more English courses in the curricula of American colleges.[4] He was probably fortunate to have a job, for the stark depression of 1893 was about to begin. Since his father's term as a probate judge had now expired, the Parringtons shared in the general insecurity, and the family was dependent upon his pension and the income from the farm. Things had not been good for the farmers for several years past, but now, as the price of corn fell to little more than twenty cents a bushel, the condition of many of them became desperate. Long afterward, recalling the stress of these years, Parrington remembered warming himself "by the kitchen stove in which great ears were burning briskly, popping and crackling in the jolliest fashion. And if while we sat around such a fire watching the year's crop go up the chimney, the talk sometimes became bitter about railroads and middlemen, who will wonder? We were in a fitting mood to respond to Mary Ellen Lease and her doctrine of raising less corn and more hell."

The Populist movement began to gain ground, and in Parrington's mind the significance of the Western scene that he had known since boyhood became clear. The Republican party, so long the enthusiasm of his father, he now began to see as an organization of grafters, men who had waved the bloody shirt and talked patriotism "while the . . . politicians were making off with the spoils." A new feeling about his family's experience on the farm began to awaken in him and, as he later wrote, he saw his family's role as essentially that of frontiersmen, with whom he was proud to identify himself. "In the most receptive years of my life I came under the influence of what, we are coming to see, proved to be the master force in creating the ideals which are most deeply and natively American—the influence of the frontier with its democratic sympathies and democratic economics. From that influence I have never been able to escape, nor have I wished to escape. To it and to the spirit of agrarian revolt that grew out of it, I owe much of my understanding of American history and

---

[4] *College Life*, October 30, 1893.

much of my political philosophy." The times reawakened Parrington's lively sense of injustice. Any resident of a Western town like Emporia might number among his friends several old farmers who, at the end of a virtuous life of hard work and trial, had nothing to show for it, and at the same time might know one or two mean and grasping local bankers or tradesmen whose unrelinquished power and comfortable situation in the midst of the general distress seemed enviable and hateful. Such a man was Major Calvin Hood of the Emporia National Bank, who was vividly described by William Allen White, a domineering figure with his "hard, cruel mouth, rapacious and hungry," his seemingly endless resources, and his tight web of influence controlling from one center the spheres of politics, business, the church, and, of course, the local college, where a radical young instructor might quickly come to his attention. Generous to his friends, ruthless to his enemies, Hood, as White put it, was, in little, the perfect surrogate and symbol of the world of concentrated power that lay outside the sphere of Emporia and Americus; he was Jim Hill, Jay Gould, Andrew Carnegie, John D. Rockefeller—and, for the radicals swinging into the orbit of the Populist movement, his presence put the reality of flesh and bile into abstract resentments.[5] In his own mind Parrington could draw the contrast between his family's friend, Old Pa Cook, an honest farmer who worked sixteen hours a day and died at seventy, a failure, and Major Hood, "a mean, small, grasping soul, who never missed a Sunday morning sermon or failed to skin a neighbor on Monday. . . . As a boy I hated Major Hood unreasoningly; as a young man I hated him because he tried to put pressure on me when I turned Populist." And so, under the stress of the nineties, Parrington forsook the political orthodoxy of Republicanism as he had forsaken the doctrinal orthodoxies of Emporia College.

Parrington did not turn Populist overnight, and he did not, as has commonly been said, run for a minor office on the Populist ticket,[6] but his latent rebelliousness was brought to

---

[5] White, *Autobiography* (1946), 263, 266–8, 353, 441.
[6] Parrington did run in the spring of 1897 for a school board position on the Citizen's ticket, and was not surprised or disappointed by his defeat. I do not know to what extent the Citizen's ticket was a Populist creation.

life. His first impulse, he recalled, "was to dismiss the [Populist] leaders as a lot of farmer cranks." But in the depths of his mind were "old grievances that still rankled" and the new agrarian radicalism began to make sense to him. "I gave increased attention to the agrarian proposals, gaining thereby my first real insight into economics and political science. I was convinced then—and I have never seen any cause to doubt my conclusions—that the Populists were fighting the battle of democracy against an insolent plutocracy, defending the traditional American principles against a feudal industrialism." He began now to "hate the Republican party with its sordid and corrupt Mark Hannas, because it had sold itself to big business; and I came to hate big business because of its brutal hoggishness." In 1896 Parrington voted for Bryan. William Allen White, who had known Parrington and his brother John at the College of Emporia, later recalled arguing with the young instructor over the merits of the Bryan campaign. Unpersuaded, White went on to write his famous sally against agrarian radicalism, "What's the Matter with Kansas?" but years afterward concluded that Parrington had been right: "He knew the eternal justice of it. He was right and I was wrong. He just had a better brain than I, that was all."[7] By 1897 Parrington, previously aloof about politics, attended a Kansas Populist convention as chairman of Emporia's First Ward delegation. He was also writing cautious but politically engaged essays for the college paper, appealing for the interest of educated men in affairs of state, attacking government by businessmen, invoking the social criticism of Ruskin and Morris.[8]

---

7 Walter Johnson, *William Allen White's America* (1947), 91. Parrington's recollections were similarly cordial. Despite White's famous editorial, he wrote in 1928: "An Emporia editor would have been in hot water if he had turned Populist. . . . During that campaign I was inclined to Populism—as I still am—and I felt that Will had also in him the makings of a Populist." To Paul W. Partridge, October 6, 1928.

8 "Some Political Sketches," *College Life*, April 17, 24, May 1, 25, 1897. Parrington's "sketches," which were written under the eye of the senior members of the college faculty, and also, perhaps, under the eye of Major Hood, hardly preached straight Populist gospel, though there may have been an element of aesopian communication in them. Parrington began by complaining that educated men take too little interest in affairs of state and by suggesting that this might be an increasingly serious

After four years of teaching at Emporia, Parrington, discouraged by his wretched pay (now $700 a year) and poor prospects, moved on to a position as instructor in English and Modern Languages at the University of Oklahoma in Norman. The depressing terrain in the vicinity of Norman was so utterly without attractive physical features that in retrospect the Kansas prairies took on a certain charm. Parrington arrived in a great dust cloud, walked through "a stretch of burnt-up slovenly village," and proceeded on a long and unshaded plank sidewalk, whose nails had been partially drawn out by the extreme heat, to the patch of brown prairie where the single red brick structure of the university had been built. "How crude and bare and vulgar the place was, one who has never seen the southwest could not imagine."

In this unpromising milieu Parrington was to toil for eleven years. It was not in his resilient nature to wilt or grow sullen, and the picture one gets of him in this period is one of health, toughness, adaptability, and astonishing buoyancy. Always a good athlete—he had played baseball briefly as a semiprofessional and during his faculty days at Emporia College had occasionally played, under the loose or nonexistent athletic rules of the period, on its football team—he now took over for a few hard-driven years the unsalaried position of coach of the Oklahoma football team, a job which required

---

matter in an age when grave new problems—among them the question "how far shall men born naked into the world be saddled by the product of past toil stored up in the form of capital?"—must be met. The ideal lawmaker for the republic was not the businessman. The strong have always taken good care of themselves, and wealth is arrogant; the impulses that make the good businessman are not good for the affairs of state. Unfortunately, however, men of culture, trained in the universities, did not provide an ideal alternative; they had not been in the habit of taking a leading part in public affairs, and had not shown themselves to be practical, although they had a valuable knowledge of history and political economy. Parrington vested his hopes in a third type of man—in which it is not hard to see a prototype of those "idealists" who win his approval in *Main Currents*: public leaders who have "sympathy for men," and who place human rights above the rights of property. But such leaders would need broad ideas about public policy, which, he suggested, they would be able to get from the university. In these essays one can see the Mugwump ideal of disinterested civic dedication, modified by a touch of Populist social idealism and a dawning respect for expertise—in short, a moderate and fairly representative statement of the themes which were to become dominant in the thought of the Progressive era.

that he also act as athletic director, manager, trainer, referee, and publicity writer. "Everything Parrington touched he seemed to vitalize," wrote a later annalist of Oklahoma football. Introducing the powerful cross-blocking he had seen at Harvard, Parrington developed a strong winning team; but after three years of exhausting success he asked to be relieved of his coaching duties. In the meantime he had been responsible for the organization of the tiny English Department. The catalogue of 1906 shows that it still had only three members, and that Parrington not only joined the other two in teaching English composition and had sole responsibility for advanced composition but that in various years he offered as well: English literature from Spenser to Pope, English literature from Johnson to William Morris, two courses in Shakespeare, a course on Tennyson and Browning, one on Ruskin and Morris, others on the novel in the eighteenth century, the novel in the nineteenth century, and the French Revolution in English poetry.

In the evenings, often at first after long afternoons on the gridiron, he wrote verse, some of which he published in the newspapers. In 1901 he married Julia Williams, a young woman of cultivated New York background who had come to Norman with her family from Kansas City, Missouri; and for fourteen months in 1903–4, while his patient bride waited at home because they were too poor for both of them to go, he made a grand tour of England and France, marked by prolonged reading spells in the British Museum and the Bibliothèque Nationale, and by careful and elaborate studies of English gardens. (A few years afterward, in a disastrous campus fire, all his notes from this venture were destroyed, along with the manuscript of a novel he had begun.) He appears to have won the regard of the university's president, who commissioned him in 1907 to prepare a report, in aid of their building program, on styles in contemporary college architecture in the United States. Parrington surveyed various existing plans and submitted a neatly designed version of a new campus. "Personally," he observed in a characteristic note, "I feel that we talk too much about a big university and too little about a beautiful university. To prefer the utilitarian and to assume that the utilitarian must necessarily be ugly, and conversely that the beautiful is useless and therefore effeminate, is one of our national heresies."

At the end of his long spell of generous service, Parrington lost his job in what must surely be one of the most scandalous episodes in American academic history—and one which may help us to comprehend his impatient view of America's Puritan heritage. Oklahoma, which had been in the most rudimentary stage of its territorial development when Parrington went there, became a state in 1907, with serious consequences for the state university. The new governor, a Bryan Democrat, was catering to the Methodist Episcopal Church, South, some of whose leaders were engaged in a cabal against a large part of the faculty. Their purpose was clearly to get rid of its Yankee members educated at Eastern universities and to replace them with a more congenial faculty, including a healthy portion of coreligionists. After a brief but strident crusade against professors who smoked, danced, or played cards, the Christian reformers had their way, and the president and fourteen members of the faculty, including Parrington, were summarily fired. (Among them was the head of the department of philosophy, who was replaced by an eighth-grade teacher from the Tulsa school system.) Parrington's personal ways were what might have been called wholesome, even by Southern Methodist standards: he did not drink or play cards, and he cared little for dancing, though he might have been one of the "cigarette fiends" who aroused the indignation of one of the insurgent pastors. He fought hard for his job, and collected letters of testimony to his character and his usefulness that were both touching and impressive, but his assiduous efforts were futile. Only a few months after moving into a new house designed by himself (after the Elizabethan cottage), and partly built by his own labors, he was jobless and without resources. Even a portion of the salary owed to him was never collected. For a moment he thought of returning to Harvard—Harvard again, after all—to work for a one-year doctorate. He wrote a long, careful letter to the secretary of the graduate school, appealing for aid and explaining his desire to study the influence of the

Renaissance on English prose, to compare changes in prose with the development of English architecture, and also to compare what he called "English-colonial literature"—that is, American, Canadian, and Australian writing—with English writing. But Harvard, which had done little enough for him earlier, when it was feasible, must have looked askance at such an imaginative but impracticable suggestion from a man of thirty-seven who had already been teaching for fifteen years, and, understandably, he was rejected once again. Fortunately, Parrington found a job at once at the University of Washington at a salary of $1,500, slightly lower than at Oklahoma. The change proved much to his advantage; both the physical and the social climate at Seattle were congenial, and there Parrington found warm colleagues in political science and history, like J. Allen Smith, and Joseph B. Harrison, and later younger men in his own field, among them E. H. Eby, who was to write the introduction to his posthumous third volume. Above all he found himself at last living in an environment of great natural beauty.

In this heartening new life the political man in Parrington began to take on more coherent intellectual form. All that had shaped his radical sentiments—the radical legacy of his English grandfather, the social resentments of his Harvard period, the protest spirit of the Populist 1890's, the long years of academic service under the surveillance of fundamentalists and tenth-rate politicians—began to come into focus in a more systematic, rather militant view of literature and politics. When he left Norman, as he remembered, "the economic interpretation of history had not yet risen for me, but it lay just below the horizon and was soon to become the chief luminary in my intellectual sky. My new interest in American literature opened a fresh field for me and in that field I applied the economic interpretation more and more rigidly."

In the encouraging companionship of academics of some distinction, Parrington began to gain confidence in himself and to develop new interests. He had never taught American literature, but now it began to absorb him, and he plunged into it with the fresh energy of a novice. Around 1910, he began to think of a big book on American letters, and in 1913

PART IV: V. L. Parrington

he started work on it in earnest. Until the eve of publication, when his publishers suggested a change, he intended to call it *The Democratic Spirit in American Literature: 1620–1870*— a title that proclaimed his selective and limited intentions and might perhaps have helped, if he had kept it, to soften some of the criticism he was to receive. As an epigraph for the work, he once planned to use a few words of Carl Becker's he had copied from *The Dial*: "The business of history is to arouse an intelligent discontent, to foster a fruitful radicalism."[9] The Progressive era was in full swing. Everyone was talking, during the formative years of this book, of the new democracy and the new freedom. And indeed in this country, with its long history of democratic aspiration, why should there not be a grand history of thought and letters celebrating the democratic theme? Why should not someone, at last, use the history of letters to illuminate national life and thought, and discuss literature, in the tradition of Sainte-Beuve and Taine, as an index of a civilization? Like his predecessors, Parrington planned to view literature through biographical-critical sketches, but now the biographies would serve as the connectives between the themes of literature and the motives of society.

Neither the entire boldness of Parrington's undertaking, nor its importance as a stimulus, nor the enthusiasm with which it was greeted, nor its final eclipse, can be understood unless we recall the state of scholarship in American literary history and the history of ideas, as well as the state of criticism, at the time he did his work. In the years from 1913 to 1927 a few American scholars, including some of the Europeanists and the philosopher A. O. Lovejoy, were writing sophisticated and distinguished studies in the general history of ideas; but among those who worked in American history, this field had excited scant interest. Parrington had only two predecessors of note, both able, self-taught amateurs of scholarship, Edward Eggleston and Moses Coit Tyler, a novelist and a Congregational pastor. Neither had won adequate recognition, nor had they succeeded in founding a scholarly tradi-

---

[9] The line occurs in Becker's review of James Harvey Robinson's *The New History*, *The Dial*, 53 (1912), 21.

tion of work in the history of ideas, though both Beard and Becker had taken some steps in this direction. There was in fact so little regard for this kind of history, *as history,* that *Main Currents,* even though it received the Pulitzer Prize in the field, was not at first taken by most historians to be a historical work, and (except for an obscure magazine in Parrington's own state) was not reviewed by the professional historical quarterlies.

A whole shelfful of comprehensive histories of American literature had accumulated by 1927, most of them stereotyped, uncritical, textbookish, and, in one way or another, parochial. In a noted essay of 1924, "A Call for a Literary Historian," Professor Fred Lewis Pattee complained that these works were so uniform that he could dictate one to a stenographer in three days.[1] College teachers of American literature were still fighting for the legitimacy of their subject, which was looked upon with disdain by most departments of English. American literature was not usually an important part of the undergraduate curriculum, and in many colleges it was not taught at all. Even graduate work in the subject was extremely limited. Harvard, Parrington's unloved alma mater, one of the largest and best graduate schools in the country, located at the geographical heart of American literary culture, had sponsored only negligible research in the field: of all the PhD theses presented to the English Department down to 1926, only four dealt with North America, and one of these was on Canadian literature. Until 1929 there was no learned periodical given entirely to studies in American literature. Specialized studies were still rare, and sound modern biographies of many of the figures Parrington wrote about (including the central figure of Jefferson himself) were not to be had. He knew very well that he was venturing again and again upon untrod ground. "The inadequacies of the present study," he wrote modestly, "I am painfully conscious of: its omissions, its doubtful interpretations, its hasty generalizations, its downright guesses; but in the present lack of exact knowledge of the history of American letters, I do not see how such in-

---

[1] In Norman Foerster, ed., *The Reinterpretation of American Literature* (1928), 3; the essay first appeared in the *American Mercury,* June 1924.

adequacies can be avoided."[2] It was, in fact, a primary function of his book, a function even of its abundant errors, to stimulate a new intensity of interest in American intellectual history.

In criticism too, some of Parrington's most startling judgments become more understandable if we remember the state of American writing at the time his work was being done. Among accessible critics, the reigning figures during these years were Van Wyck Brooks and H. L. Mencken, both of whom Parrington read. It is hard to say how much influence they may have had upon him—he must have been proof against Mencken's jocose and irresponsible conservatism—but insofar as they affected him they might well have helped to lead him astray. Their common disposition to hold the Puritan heritage at fault for some of the most decisive failings of American culture played to one of his weaknesses; and for all that can be said for them, they may have encouraged a disposition to carp at certain writers and to launch all too easily upon wholesale deprecation.[3] On the other side of the critical fence were Irving Babbitt and Paul Elmer More, who, with their reactionary political ideas, must have been quite inaccessible to Parrington, if he read them at all; and such writers of influence as Joel Spingarn and Stuart Sherman seem not to have much interested him. The critical mentality which we would recognize as contemporary was just coming into being in the United States. A whole battery of writers born within a half dozen years on either side of 1900—among them Edmund Wilson, Kenneth Burke, Allen Tate, Newton Arvin, Yvor Winters, F. O. Matthiessen, R. P. Blackmur, Lionel Trill-

---

[2] II, x. Parrington was intensely conscious of the rudimentary state of American literary study. "Pretty much everything is yet to be done in the field of [the] History of American Literature," he wrote in 1924, though five years later he remarked with satisfaction that "the study of American Literature is becoming respectable." To Elias T. Arnesen, November 17, 1924; to George E. Hastings, March 1, 1929.

[3] On this tendency in Parrington, see Chapter 11, 408 *ff.* One may wonder, for example, if Parrington's treatment of James (see below, 394) might not have been given some encouragement from the following by Brooks (*The Pilgrimage of Henry James*): "Magnificent pretensions, petty performances!—the fruits of an irresponsible imagination, of a deranged sense of values, of a mind working in a void, uncorrected by any clear consciousness of human cause and effect."

ing, Cleanth Brooks—men without whose collective achievement our present sense of literature and the function of
criticism would be impoverished and unrecognizable, had not
yet begun to publish criticism. In most cases, their earliest
important critical writings came roughly in the years 1930-40,
during which the premises of literary evaluation, as well as
the national feeling about literature, were undergoing rapid
change. At the very time when readers were becoming acquainted with Parrington's volumes, therefore, a new set of
receptivities, a new sensibility belonging to another moment
than his own, were in the process of formation. His volumes,
published only at the end of his life, had been conceived in
a quite different literary world from that into which they were
launched, and the ground under his feet shifted almost immediately. It is a comment on the function of *Main Currents*
that, appearing as it did at such a focal moment in the development of American letters, of criticism and literary knowledge, and belonging as it did so much more to the past than
to the future, it was still able for a time to strike so congenial
a note with many intelligent readers, and that by the force of
its provocation it could exercise quite so much effect.

Here too one must be impressed by the solitary courage,
the discipline, the sustained determination of this professor
of English as he carried on in obscurity, and despite the handi-
cap of an underequipped and inadequate library, with this
improbable enterprise, the likes of which no one had ever undertaken for American literature—a comprehensive history of
national letters from the Puritans to the most recent past,
which, even in the unfinished form in which he left it after
labors of sixteen years, and ten years of discouraging rebuffs
from publishers, came to three volumes and more than 1,300
pages. At the time Parrington began it, he was almost totally
unknown, and had published little besides a few verses in the
daily press, and at the time he finished it he had added to
these only about a dozen book reviews and a few articles. Seen
against this background, Parrington, with his singular vision
of his task, his undismayed persistence, and his isolated and
unpracticed energy, appears to be less a typical product of the
academy than a phenomenon of natural talent, another of

those lonely American originals who are made to seem somewhat overstrained and bizarre by their excessively firm grip on
some too limited segment of the truth, and who finally succeed
not in giving us the grand revelation they have hoped to find,
but at least in telling something about themselves, and hence
something native and vital about America after all.

III

The sources of Parrington's ideas are not entirely clear,
but we can see how the sense of literature expressed in *Main
Currents* has its cognates in the views of art and reality that
run through some other writers of the Populist-Progressive
era. Here it is important not to be oversystematic. Parrington
was no esthetician. He was only slightly more interested in
formal philosophy than he was in theology or science, and it
would be as wrong to attribute to him a finished or consistent
esthetic doctrine as it would be to expect one from him. But
if we are willing to deal with a tendency of mind, a general
drift of sensibility, rather than to hope to find identities of
taste or judgment, it becomes possible to find his place in the
stream of literary thought and to mark out his affinities with
certain other writers, no two of whom were entirely alike in
their approach to art and no one of whom he approved un-
reservedly.

Parrington proclaimed his indebtedness to Hippolyte
Taine, whose four-volume *History of English Literature*
(1864) had appeared in translation in England in 1874 and
was reissued in the United States in 1886. For a time Taine
enjoyed a certain regard among many critics in the United
States, including some of the most genteel and conservative,
but his mind belonged rather more to the post-Darwinian positivistic climate than to the era in which Parrington began to
write. For Taine literary history was not self-sufficient but had
somehow to be made amenable to the methods of science.
This was his chief link to Americans like Parrington, but perhaps also a reason for the ephemeral character of his influence. His approach to literary history might well have been
expected to excite a generation that found intellectual enlight-

enment and liberation in Herbert Spencer—precisely the experience of Parrington and Hamlin Garland.[4] His leading idea —that all forces behind literary movements can be reduced to the interplay of race, milieu, and moment—would not be taken very seriously for very long; but Taine did set a kind of precedent for later writers who were concerned to establish the idea that literature is largely a product of society, that a work of literature is a social document amenable to the methods of the social historian. I suspect that Parrington's obligation to Taine did not go much beyond this, though it is quite possible that it was in Taine that he first happened to encounter a model for a biographical approach to literature— a grand, comprehensive literary history, organized in a series of compressed discussions of leading writers and their works. When he actually discusses English writers, Taine does not seem the *terrible simplificateur* that a bare statement of his "theory" may suggest. His mind was, though more positivistic, less sociological than Parrington's, his concern with intrinsic literary values greater, his range of interests wider, his attention more closely directed to the work of art itself. He was much more interested than Parrington in literature as an aid to national characterization—"race"—much less in the phenomena of politics and class. Taine himself, in fact, was almost antipolitical, but the kind of literary history he encouraged tended to substitute biography for criticism, the man for the work. Flaubert had complained of Taine and Sainte-Beuve that they did not pay enough attention to the work of art in itself, to "composition, style, briefly what makes for Beauty." Turning away from the literary text itself, and from the task of criticism, the literary history written in this tradition was disposed to *use* the literary work to elucidate the man,

---

[4] Garland tells of his first encounter with Taine one summer in a cabin in the Dakotas: "Day after day I bent to this task, pondering all the great Frenchman had to say of *race, environment,* and *momentum* [sic] and on the walls of the cabin I mapped out in chalk the various periods of English society as he had indicated them. These charts were the wonder and astonishment of my neighbors whenever they chanced to enter the living room, and they appeared especially interested in the names written on the ceiling over my bed. I had put my favorites there so that when I opened my eyes of a morning, I could not help absorbing a knowledge of their dates and works." *A Son of the Middle Border,* 307.

which was its primary object. And in Parrington's own variation, the elucidation of the man became first and foremost the elucidation of his civic role and his political ideas.

Considerably more important for Parrington than Taine was the Victorian tradition of moral-esthetic criticism represented by Carlyle, Ruskin, and Morris; among these it was Morris who was most significant. In Morris, Parrington found a socialist who had a coherent theory of art, and who shared Parrington's wariness of the threat of concentrated state power. Here was a writer of authority who recognized fully the interplay between art and social forces, but whose esthetic passion put him above the charge of subordinating art to propagandistic intent, a writer who could explain how commercial society was damaging and destructive to art, who developed a democratic esthetic of uncompromising egalitarianism in which the true roots of art are seen to be in the joyous labor of the ordinary man. At the moment, Parrington recalled in his memoir, when the rising flame of radicalism in him needed only a little fuel, "William Morris came bringing that fuel. In lovely prose with its suggestion of mediaeval beauty, he laid bare the evils of industrialism: how it was destroying art and bringing upon society the blight of universal ugliness; how it reduced the free artist workman to a machine slave; how it took away the chance of happiness in one's work and therefore in one's life; and how before art should be born again men must be free to do their work in their own way." The one vital principle that Parrington could not in the end bring himself to accept, however it might accord with his agrarian prejudices and his dislike of political centralization, was the anti-industrial side of Morris's thought. Although in writing of Bellamy he noted that Morris had spoken of *Looking Backward* as "a horrible cockney dream," he concluded that "Bellamy was far more modern and realistic in his understanding of the part the machine will play in the society of the future."[5]

By the time he began his book, Parrington's ideas were largely formed. In reading he had paid close attention to the struggles of certain of his contemporaries who were involved

[5] III, 237, 311–12.

in the development of realism and naturalism and the novel of social criticism. Among these were William Dean Howells, whom he treated more sympathetically than did most of the writers of the 1920's; Hamlin Garland, whose personal and intellectual experience bears a closer resemblance to Parrington's than that of any other imaginative writer; and Frank Norris, whose *Responsibilities of the Novelist* Parrington found "boldly, magnificently" stated, even if colored by the writer's "immense faith in the finality of his own conclusions." These were, again, writers who shared certain very broad tendencies, without having precisely the same sensibilities or theories of literature. But what Parrington found sympathetic in them—the point at which they confirmed the drift of his own mind—seems reasonably clear. They quickened his belief, a belief for which he had already found Taine congenial, that art is a product of its social milieu, and that literature can therefore become a means of studying society, as well as the conviction he had found in the Victorian cultural critics that art and life should serve each other, that art has moral responsibilities which in the final analysis are social responsibilities. They confirmed in him a disposition to believe in the central importance of what he would have called "reality"—in the feeling that that which is observed has some kind of superiority to that which is "merely" imagined. Further, they suggested at times that form and style can to a significant degree be dissociated from the matter or substance of art, and that matter is more important—by the same token that an excessive preoccupation with style or nuances or with distinctively individual concerns is superficial, effete, unworldly, "romantic," as compared with a robust engagement with the real, the material, the sociological.

Howells, Parrington suggested in a revealing sentence, "came late to an interest in sociology, held back by the strong literary and aesthetic cast of his mind." The assumption here of a powerful opposition between the social and the esthetic sense is characteristic. Here one finds, and not surprisingly, a parallel between Parrington's approach to literature and Beard's to politics—above all in their common conviction that there is some hard core to history, some basic substance, and that ideas and literature, all phases of culture, are somehow secondary to it or derivative from it. Finally, and of particular importance, early realist writers seem to share the uncomfortable feeling that there is probably some kind of tension or opposition between truth and beauty that must, as far as is possible, be overcome or reconciled by strenuous devices; but that if there is at the end any irreducible conflict between them, it is truth that is the ultimate end of art. The opposition between truth and beauty was their way of expressing that dichotomy between content and form which their esthetic was incapable of surmounting. Truth, at any rate, was the key word for them, and they kept calling for truth in art as if they really expected some compatriot to step forward and take a firm stand for falsehood.

Howells tried to persuade them that when the matter was rightly understood, this opposition between truth and beauty did not exist. "What is unpretentious and what is true is always beautiful and good, and nothing else is so." "Realism is nothing more and nothing less than the truthful treatment of material." "We must ask ourselves before we ask anything else, Is it true?—true to the motives, the impulses, the principles, that shape the life of actual men and women?" But some of the difficulties of all this began to appear when he also wrote: "There is no greatness, no beauty, which does not come from *truth to your own knowledge of things*"—a passage which only hints at the problems that arise from the fact that the artist perceives truth at a variety of levels and proceeds in a variety of ways to express it.[6]

---

[6] Howells, *Criticism and Fiction and Other Essays*, ed. by Clara M. and Rudolf Kirk (1959), 10, 38, 49, 69; italics added.

Early American realistic and naturalistic writers were so embattled in behalf of verisimilitude that most of what was implied in this involuntary concession by Howells seems to have escaped them. Truth to a writer's "own knowledge of things" covers a great many ways of fiction. No doubt, for example, the stylized novels of Ivy Compton-Burnett try to state "truths" about English society, but these are surely of a different order and differently conveyed than the truths stated by Arnold Bennett. In America, again, the truth about the small town (to choose two authors Parrington appreciated) in Sherwood Anderson is another thing from the truth as seen by Sinclair Lewis. Even in social science this principle sometimes applies: the American scene as understood by Thorstein Veblen has more in common with the human scene as understood by Jonathan Swift than it does with the American scene portrayed in Robert H. and Helen M. Lynd's

It was the responsibility of the novelist, Frank Norris urged, to give people the truth: "The people have a right to the Truth as they have a right to life, liberty, and the pursuit of happiness. It is *not* right that they be deceived with false views of life. . . ." And in a passage quoted with some reservation by Parrington, Garland recalled the resolution of his own sense of the proper view of literature: "Obscurely forming in my mind were two great literary concepts—that truth was a higher quality than beauty, and that to spread the reign of justice should everywhere be the design and intent of the artist. The merely beautiful in art seemed petty, and success at the cost of the happiness of others a monstrous egotism."[7] Parrington might well have been disturbed by the implications of this—as he put it in a puzzling remark, Garland's "will to remain objective weakened"—but Garland had posed in a rough way the problem of the Populist-Progressive sense of literature, bringing to the surface the note of stern social moralism that accompanied its humane purposes.

A realistic, robust, masculine literature, it was thought, pointed away from estheticism and aristocratic prejudice, and laid the mental and moral basis for democracy and social reform without involving the writer in the trap of mere tractarianism. By 1893 Howells had come to believe that "any conscientious and enlightened fiction" would somehow show the need for and the way to socialism. Any art, Howells had written in *Criticism and Fiction*, which "disdains the office of teacher is one of last refuges of the aristocratic spirit which is disappearing from politics and society and is now seeking to shelter itself in aesthetics. The pride of caste is becoming the pride of taste; but as before it is averse to the masses of men. . . . It seeks to withdraw itself, to stand aloof; to be distinguished, and not to be identified. Democracy in literature is the reverse of all this. It wishes to know and to tell the truth, confident that consolation and delight are there. . . .

---

books on Middletown. A work like C. Wright Mills's *White Collar*, though it purports to be in the tradition of empirical sociology, is in fact an expressionistic work voicing the author's horror at what goes on in large offices and at what he sees as the particular spiritual impoverishment of the salaried middle class.
[7] Norris, *The Responsibilities of the Novelist* (originally published 1903) in *Complete Works* (1929), VII, 8–9; Garland, *A Son of the Middle Border*, 374.

Neither arts, nor letters, nor sciences, except as they somehow, clearly or obscurely, tend to make the race better and
kinder, are to be regarded as serious interests. . . ." The real
American muse, Norris had insisted, is a Child of the People;
she will lead you, he had promised the novelists of the future,
"far from the studios and the aesthetes, the velvet jackets and
the uncut hair, far from sexless creatures who cultivate their
little art of writing as the fancier cultivates his orchid. Tramp-
ing along, then, with a stride that will tax your best paces,
she will lead you . . . straight into a world of Working Men,
crude of speech, swift of action, strong of passion, straight
to the heart of a new life, on the borders of a new time. . . ."
"The realist or veritist," said Hamlin Garland in *Crumbling
Idols*, "is really an optimist, a dreamer. He sees life in terms
of what it might be, as well as in terms of what it is; but he
writes of what is, and, at his best, suggests what is to be, by
contrast. . . . He sighs for a lovelier life. . . . With his hate
in his heart and his ideal in his brain the modern man writes
his stories of life. They are not always pleasant, but they are
generally true, and always they provoke thought." The fiction
of the future, he thought, "will grow more democratic in outlook and more individualistic in method."[8] Realism, truth,
democracy, a new time, a lovelier life—these were key terms
of art.

IV

One can readily trace similar concerns in Parrington's
work. At some time during the years when the rising generation of realist and naturalist writers were having their first
important successes, his hard-won, self-conscious, and rather
brittle youthful estheticism appears to have snapped and to
have given way to something that was very close to its opposite. I do not mean to suggest that he now became in-
different to the values of art, but that he became increasingly
fearful that they were capable of standing in the way of

---

[8] Cf. Howells on enlightened fiction in Everett Carter, *Howells
and the Age of Realism* (1954); Howells, *Criticism and Fiction*,
87; Norris, *Responsibilities*, 159–60; Garland, *Crumbling Idols*,
143–4, 42.

something more important: the values of social morality.
It is true that he expressed quite clearly his doubt about the
proposition that art must serve social morality, or, as he
rather loosely put it, that "it must teach rather than amuse,"
and it is easy to see why he took comfort in Morris not for
preaching that art must serve social reform but rather for
promising that social reform would engender a finer art.
He was capable of reproaching several writers, including
some he admired, for putting propaganda above art—of dismissing such books as Garland's *A Spoil of Office* as being
"a social tract rather than a work of art"—and he had a
certain saving skepticism about young writers "enthusiastic
for revolt as a profession."[9] Now and then, as in his estimation of Cabell, he appears even to have returned to the impulse evident in his youthful estheticism, and he was never
at any time willing to defend the bald proposition that the
values of art ought to be regarded as inferior to any social
concern. Nonetheless, he was capable of treating particular
works, or even the entire *oeuvre* of a particular writer, as
though this proposition was his basic canon of criticism. He
seemed to rule out whole areas of human experience, including some of the most tenderly personal and some of the
most significantly universal, as being beneath the dignity
of serious art and unworthy of the attention of serious writers.
In this way, while he dismissed some books for having been
propaganda rather than art, he also dismissed others, including those of Hawthorne and James, for not having the
proper social concerns.

Parrington's basic aim was to define a writer's milieu,
his style of life, his class affiliations, and finally his political
ideas, especially insofar as these ideas had a bearing on the
development of American democracy. Ultimately, Parrington's judgments are moral, but his test of a writer's morality
is not the integrity of his mind in relation to his art but the
breadth and warmth of his social sympathies and the ap-
propriateness of his subject matter as defined by the canons
of critical realism. Of some interest here is his view of
Howells, a writer whom he treated more generously on the

---

[9] III, 249, 385–6.

whole than most of the critics of the 1920's and whose conversion to "socialism" he admired. Despite his regard for Howells's human warmth, Parrington still thought, as many other critics have, that Howells's concern for the commonplace weakened his work and rendered it trivial, that "it does not probe the depths of emotional experience." But one begins to be shaken, on reading further, to find that he regards Howells as having been "a specialist in women's nerves, an analyst of the tenuous New England conscience, a master of Boston small-talk," and one is rather taken aback when he remarks concerning one of Howells's better books, *The Rise of Silas Lapham,* that it fails "when endless pages are devoted to the ethical subtleties of a woman's accepting the hand of a man who the family had believed was in love with her sister," thus concentrating his disdain on one of the most successful moments in Howells's writing. What business does a writer have, Parrington seems to ask, to occupy himself with such trifles? But perhaps nothing illustrates better for most critics the limitations of his view of literature than his two-page dismissal of Poe as a writer "quite outside the main current of American thought" and his leaving him, as he put it, "with the psychologist and the belletrist." Again, when he condemns Hawthorne for lacking the imagination of a healthy romantic because he did not rise to the romance of Salem's trade, for neglecting "to lift his eyes to the horizon beyond which the hurrying ships were seeking strange markets," and for turning them in "upon a shadowy world of half unreal character," for overlooking "the motley picturesque in the foreground of the actual, in order to brood over an old adultery and twist it into theological sin," we are prompted to wonder why he wrote at all about a figure like Hawthorne, whose literary pre-eminence may be arguable, but surely not on such grounds as this.

A certain rigidity was undoubtedly introduced into Parrington's approach to literature at the very time that his political views were taking form. Here perhaps his intellectual association with J. Allen Smith was of some importance. Smith, eleven years Parrington's senior, had been born in Missouri of Virginia emigrants, had studied law and had then turned to economics. Always a radical, he had published a heretical doctoral thesis on monetary reform, *The Multiple Money Standard,* during the Bryan campaign, and had lost his job at Marietta College because of his political views. In 1897 he moved to the University of Washington, where before long he became active as a reformer in local politics and in 1912 declined an offer to run for governor on the Progressive ticket. It was in 1907 that he published his *The Spirit of American Government* about the undemocratic character of the Constitution and the undemocratic intentions of its framers—the book which, along with Beard's, Parrington saw as constituting the primary contribution of Progressivism to political thought. A single-minded political reformer, Smith was not a friend likely to encourage Parrington's regard for the autonomy of art. He was, as Cushing Strout describes him, "a man of limited cultivation" who "owned a library exclusively composed of works in the subjects he taught," and who "had no taste for serious literature or music."[1] He was the true founder of that Progressive dualism I have already discussed in Chapter 5 in connection with the work of Beard, but he had none of Beard's covert or suppressed Federalism, and shared none of Beard's ambivalence about the Founding Fathers, of whose work he took a more unequivocally conspiratorial view. It was of course the similarity between the findings of the two men that struck Parrington; Beard's book on the Constitution, appearing just at the time when he was settling down to concerted work on *Main Currents,* came as a complete confirmation and enlargement of what he had learned from Smith, and strengthened his ingrained suspicion of establishments and their spokesmen and manipulators.

During these years at Seattle it seemed very clear who were one's friends and one's enemies, and the discussion of literature became part of a social struggle, in which the theory and uses of literature were understood to be a weapon. Within the halls of the university itself Smith, with Parrington's sympathy, was embattled, and Parrington himself experienced some tension with his own department. In 1917 Smith fell afoul of the university's president, who was more

---

[1] Introduction to *The Spirit of American Government,* xxii.

interested in developing a business school than in the study of pure economics and who drastically cut back Smith's department, arbitrarily isolating and humiliating one of the most distinguished members of the faculty.[2] At the same moment Parrington was incensed against his colleagues in the English department, who, in the time-honored manner of English faculties, took a dim view of American literature, its place in the curriculum, and even its demands on library funds. It was in the course of this controversy that Parrington prepared an essay, "Economics and Criticism" (1917), for a proposed volume of English department studies, which shows how far he had gone toward a rather stark economic interpretation of literature.[3]

Assailing "the conservatism of scholarship," Parrington took up the case for "the economist" in literature—the "upstart" inspired by rude materialism who digs into the dirt under the flower garden. "The economic interpretation of things is in the air," he proclaimed. ". . . It is fast becoming for us both the law and the prophet." The time has come when we are pulling the clothes off things and stripping them to "the naked reality." "Literature is the fair flower of culture, but underneath culture are the deeper strata of philosophy, theology, law, statecraft—of ideology and institutionalism—resting finally upon the subsoil of economics. We may begin as critics but we end up as historians." He was quite out of patience, he confessed, with the old-fashioned scholars, the classicists and philologists. Aristotle's *Poetics* no longer had much help to give toward understanding the world, and there ought to be something more important to students of English literature than the Teutonic origins of the language. The humanists in literature were more attractive, but there was something vital missing in them. "Do they understand the origin and significance of those very ideas which they study so lovingly? Ideas are not godlings that spring perfect-

---

[2] "I deeply resented the shabby treatment he received from the late administration. . . . He was too little appreciated by the ruling group at the university . . . the small men who had too few brains to estimate his worth." Parrington to Elfreda Smith, his colleague's daughter, May 16, 1927; J. Allen Smith papers, University of Washington.

[3] "Economics and Criticism," ed. by Vernon Parrington, Jr., *Pacific Northwest Quarterly*, 44 (1953), 91–105.

winged from the head of love; they are not flowers that bloom in a walled garden; they are weapons hammered out on the anvil of human needs." It is the economist—by which term it is clear that Parrington here means not the professional economist but the critic who applies economic insights to letters—who understands this best. The economist is "a humanist who has gone further and seen deeper." Although he cannot explain everything, he at least understands the "subtle compulsions" under which the artist works, and when we come to study the habitat of literature, the system of ideas and institutions in which the artist moves, the economist is truly master. "He has only to apply the familiar principles of the economic interpretation of history to his literary documents in order to measure in which degree they reflect the current ideology. He cuts under the feet of the humanist to the property basis of ideas and institutions. In every society, he discovers, property is sovereign." He penetrates through the veil of taste and convention. He may of course underestimate at times the force of ideas and ideals, but "that the mainspring of the struggle is the economic is plain as the way to parish church." In a passage reminiscent of Howells on "the pride of caste" converting itself into "the pride of taste," Parrington continued: "Polite culture is a translation of economics into caste terms. Good taste is no other than a by-product of property. Standards and canons of excellence, types and forms and conventions of art, are no more than the sublimation and embodiment of current aristocratic practice. How could it be otherwise?"

Having laid down these principles, Parrington went on at length to show how they might apply to English and American literature. Here it may be enough to repeat what he had to say about Shakespeare. Shakespeare (who is contrasted unfavorably with the hardy radical, Milton) turns out to be, on these canons, the product of a courtier society, a creature of the "insolent toryism, masterful and arrogant," that "stalked across the Elizabethan stage." "Shakespeare was the cleverest of climbers and necessarily he stood cap in hand in the presence of gentlemen. The dramatist of universal human nature, the poet of all time, was eager to assert his servility by befouling all underling human nature. His

draft on posterity he readily sold for present favour. The
Warwickshire peasant caught the insolent class consciousness of his patron. . . . Where in the ample pages of Shakespeare do we find the London of reality that was gathering
its strength to pull down both court and courtier? . . . He was
more concerned to become the first citizen of Stratford than
to hold the broadest realms of poesy in fee."

Have we ever heard anything like this before? In fact
we have: it is very reminiscent of Mark Twain's reaction
in *Innocents Abroad* to the "cringing spirit" of the great
artists of the past when he first saw them in the museums of
Europe: "Their nauseous adulation of princely patrons was
more prominent to me and chained my attention more surely
than the charms of color and expression which are claimed
to be in the pictures."[4] But for Parrington to have struck the
same note seems all too much like self-caricature, and it
may indeed be true that he began to have some misgivings
about the way his case was put, since he did not attempt
to publish this essay elsewhere when the planned collection
of English department essays was abandoned.[5] His essay

---

[4] Cf. also the later Tolstoy on Shakespeare: "The content of
Shakespeare's plays . . . is the lowest, most vulgar view of life,
which regards the external elevation of the great ones of the
earth as a genuine superiority; despises the crowd, that is to say,
the working classes; and repudiates not only religious, but even
any humanitarian efforts directed toward the alteration of the
existing order of society." *Tolstoy on Art*, ed. by Aylmer Maude
(1924), 446.

[5] His son, in publishing the essay after more than thirty-five
years, remarked that it was uncharacteristically belligerent and
doubted that Parrington thought it was a satisfactory statement
of his "materialism." "Economics and Criticism," 97. In the
preface to his third volume, Parrington remarked: "I hold no
brief for a rigid scheme of economic determinism. I recognize
the rich culture potentialities that inhere in individual variation
from type, and I realize that the arts are likely to receive their
noblest gifts from men who should be classed biologically as
cultural sports or variations from the cultural type." But in
looking for the typical, these variations, he went on, were not
significant for their own sake, and he saw nothing to regret in
his treatment of Poe. III, xx–xxi.

Parrington was not the only American of his period to stumble
over an economic approach to literature. In 1910, inspired by
E. R. A. Seligman's *The Economic Interpretation of History*,
Brander Matthews took as the subject of his Presidential Address
to the Modern Language Association, "The Economic Interpretation of Literary History." The result was not distinguished. See
Matthews, *Gateways to Literature, and Other Essays* (1912),
35–56.

marks out, nonetheless, the hard core of feeling upon which
the "economic interpretation of literature" rested, and rather
rudely foreshadows the aggressive but inarticulate esthetic,
the reductionist animus, that was to be the hallmark of the
liberal historians.

Surely this quality was not Parrington's alone, but one
widely shared in the tradition of Progressive history. Here
Parrington and Beard, for example, seem to be kindred
spirits. One of Parrington's happiest moments came from a
review by Beard, in which the democratic realism of Parrington's first two volumes was greeted with cries of enthusiasm. Although Beard had some reservations about the
book, chiefly for its neglect of natural science, he thought
that Parrington had "revealed the substance from which
literary culture springs" and had sent "exhilarating gusts
through the deadly miasma of academic criticism." Parrington, he suggested, "is about to start an upheaval in American
literary criticism. He has yanked Miss Beautiful Letters out
of the sphere of the higher verbal hokum and fairly set her
in the way that leads to contact with pulsating reality—that
source and inspiration of all magnificent literature. No
doubt, the magpies, busy with the accidence of Horace, the
classical allusions of Thoreau, and the use of the adverb by
Emerson, will make a big outcry, but plain citizens who believe that the American eagle could soar with unblinking
eyes against the full-orbed noonday sun if he had half a
chance will clap their hands with joy and make the hills
ring with gladness."[6]

Perhaps one should close this disturbing chapter in the
history of taste while the hills are still ringing, but it remains

---

6 Beard, "Fresh Air in American Letters," *Nation*, 124 (1927),
560, 562; oddly enough, Beard's review of Parrington appeared
back to back with a review of the Beards' *Rise of American Civilization*, in which Carl Becker showed the same hearty enthusiasm
and took a similar tone of jazz-age robustness. "It is often difficult," he said, "to recognize the ancient lady Clio, famous for
her spotless flowing robes. She is off stage so much of the time!
Her hair is bobbed, and you can see her bare knees if you care
to look, for she rolls 'em too, and will in any company as like
as not be seen tapping a cigarette or fumbling for a lip-stick. It's
all right with me. What the lady loses in dignity she gains in
appeal—sex maybe." Ibid., 560.

to suggest that these two writers were linked not simply in mutual approval, but upon a view of literature that could result at times in strikingly similar verdicts. One illustration may do. More or less at the same time, and of course writing in complete independence, Parrington and Beard were coming to terms with Henry James, the latter giving him a brusque paragraph in *The Rise of American Civilization*, the former a few pages in *Main Currents*.[7] Both historians condemn James for what they regard as preciosity and aristocratic yearnings, and both are animated by the same democratic nationalism and outraged Americanism, the same hearty masculine impatience with refinement and esthetic truck. Beard had this to say:

"For the poignant middle class of seasoned families, equally distressed by the doings of the plutocrats and the vulgarisms of democracy, spoke Henry James. The grandson of a millionaire, a whole generation removed from the odors of the shop, and granted by good fortune a luxurious leisure, James steered his way into a more rarefied atmosphere, normally as the sparks fly heavenward. In a loftier altitude he found many superior people 'cultivated' in taste, languid in habits, and desirous of elegant manners if they had not fallen heir to them in a natural way. Of such upper class persons and for them, James wrote most of his novels, using the crude, rising bourgeoisie of America to emphasize the prettiness of the English landed aristocracy which had subdued even its latest cotton-spinning recruits to some accord with manorial taste. Possessing an assured income from fixed investments, he took time in his writing to evolve a meticulous and fine-spun style, one so vague and so intricate that it moved even his brother, William, the pragmatic philosopher, to explode in a letter to the novelist: 'Say it out, for God's sake.' Accustomed by his position to the society of people not wholly engrossed in business, James found a home in England, where at last, during the World War, he renounced his American citizenship and became a subject of King George."

---

[7] *Main Currents*, III, 239–41; *Rise*, II, 441.

In Parrington's pages James turns up only a little less briefly and even more ignominiously. A man for whom "life was largely a matter of nerves," James "fled from reality" and became "a pilgrim to shrines other than those of his native land," a fatal mistake for his work, since it is unhealthy for the artist "to turn cosmopolitan." The key to James was that he was never a realist but rather "a self-deceived romantic, the last subtle expression of the genteel," oppressed by an "unconscious inferiority complex" before the long-established social order of Europe, a writer whose romanticization of European culture "worked to his undoing." "From the external world of action he withdrew to the inner world of questioning and probing; yet even in his subtle psychological inquiries he remained shut up within his own skull-pan. His characters are only projections of his brooding fancy, externalizations of hypothetical subtleties. He was concerned only with *nuances*. He lived in a world of fine gradations and imperceptible shades. It is this absorption in the stream of psychical experience that justifies one in calling Henry James a forerunner of modern expressionism. Yet how unlike he is to Sherwood Anderson, an authentic product of the American consciousness!"

These passages, which expose the vulnerable underside of the environmental approach to literature, reveal both men at their worst, writing about a major writer in whom their interest was relatively casual, and about whom they could not command enough detachment even to see the necessity of being fair. But they also raise a question that has from time to time haunted radical criticism, especially in America: how does one preserve that tincture of rage, that energetic indignation which makes social protest possible, without at the same time succumbing to a certain puritanism about beauty and pleasure, or to a raw political sociologism that resists everything rare and individual? Parrington thought it among the primary limitations of the genteel tradition that its literary historians had "an exaggerated regard for esthetic values," that they did not "enter sympathetically into the world of masculine intellectual and material struggles," and that they "sought daintier fare than polemics"— thus reiterating that characteristic American male reproach of absorption in the effeminate and the unreal that had so long been made against men of complex and delicate sensibility. In his defense it must be said that he did not pretend to shed light upon the creative act itself or to be a critic. "With aesthetic judgments I have not been greatly concerned," he wrote—which could surely not have been an attempt to deny that his book contained such judgments, but only an invitation not to regard them as essential or take them altogether seriously. Presumably he meant only to remedy the failures of literary gentility by looking steadily at the "masculine" and material values in literature, and to do this by writing a history of our political expression as though it were a history of literature. He was concerned, he hoped to make clear, "with the total pattern of American thought—the broad drift of major ideas."[8] But just as he failed to see that a history of literature must not (and in his case did not) avoid esthetic judgments, he failed to see that the history of political ideas too, even when we look for its total pattern, is composed of particularities; that to discern its drift, no matter how broad, is a task which requires, as good criticism does, a certain delicacy of touch.

---

[8] I, vi; II, i; III, xx.

CHAPTER 11

Criticism and Political Thought

> To enter once more into the spirit of those
> fine old idealisms, and to learn that the prom-
> ise of the future has lain always in the keeping
> of liberal minds that were never discouraged
> from their dreams, is scarcely a profitless
> undertaking. . . .
> —V. L. Parrington

> To love ideas is excellent, but to under-
> stand how ideas themselves are conditioned
> by social forces is better still.
> —V. L. Parrington, 1917

I

THE METHOD and design of Parrington's *Main Currents*
discloses a marked disproportion between his object and
the means to reach it. He insisted that he was not making
esthetic judgments or writing a conventional history of
literature, but he included so many writers whose political
ideas were inconsequential that their presence could be
justified only by their stature as imaginative writers; and it
is hardly necessary to say that he did in fact, as one must,
make some judgments about their worth as writers. On the
other hand, he chose to leave out or subordinate a few writers
who had political ideas of decisive importance, a procedure
which impaired his scheme as a plan for a history of political thought. The work is thus haunted throughout by an
unresolved ambiguity, a suspension between political thought
and literature. That the undefined area where literature
and politics intersect is a legitimate subject need not be disputed. But to write well about our political-literary culture
requires a fine feeling for the nuances of ideas which was
hardly the strongest quality of the Progressive mind. Much
too often we are left with the sense that Parrington has not
succeeded in finding the relation between politics and litera-

ture, but only in putting them into awkward juxtaposition. His method, moreover, was biographical, and biography requires a certain patience with the individuality of the materials as well as a feeling for the nature of each subject's development, which was hardly feasible within the framework of his plan. These difficulties are related to the other basic defects of *Main Currents:* its lack of penetration in depth, of historical specificity, and—as a corollary of this last—of a feeling for the actual historical *movement* of ideas.

Consider first the plan of Parrington's book. It is a series of biographical-intellectual portraits linked together by several explanatory connective sequences. The portraits number almost a hundred, and if the author had lived to complete the scheme sketched out in the table of contents of his third volume, he would probably have needed still a fourth volume, and would have added some forty more. Here the very nobility of his conception became an obstacle: his plan required him to read so extensively that penetrating inquiry was possible only at a few points, and to write with such rigid compression that not a single writer could get extended discussion. Where his model, Taine, had felt free to take seventy pages or more for an author, Parrington allowed himself in the longest of his sketches to take no more than fourteen or fifteen. In order to include scores of minor literary figures of hardly more than incidental and symptomatic significance for the development of American thought, he had to neglect the dynamics of the basic ideas, and to cut his portraits of central political writers to a pattern so cramped that he could not seriously deal with them: it is all but impossible, for instance, to cope in fifteen pages with the complexities, nuances, and changes in John Adams's thought, or with the subtle problems of interpretation posed by Jefferson. And for James Madison, a thinker of absolutely central importance, Parrington found no place at all, aside from a few pages in an account, itself far too perfunctory, of *The Federalist.*

The ambiguity of Parrington's intent and the multiplicity of his sketches go far to explain his difficulty in getting below the surface. His tendentious purpose and the simple dualism of his scheme help to explain the abstractness, the static quality in his conception of intellectual development. At the beginning of his admiring sketch of Roger Williams, Parrington makes a significant suggestion that sums up a major premise of his work. Williams, he concludes, though in manner and speech a Puritan controversialist, was really "contemporary with successive generations of prophets from his own day to ours"—a forerunner, in fact, of Locke and the natural-rights school, of Paine and the French romantics, of Channing and the Unitarians, of Emerson and the transcendentalists. *Main Currents*, indeed, has a very full quota of forerunners and precursors, and as one reads with an eye for its sense of intellectual filiations and continuities, the significance of the metaphor in Parrington's title emerges: we are in the presence of two great historical currents that course through our history, the currents, roughly speaking, of democratic and antidemocratic thought. Through changing intellectual assumptions and through various phases of manner and speech, we deal in substance, always and recurrently, with the same age-old controversy. The major thinkers of the past are summoned up, in effect, as contemporaries of each other and ourselves. The colonial Americans, for example, were "old-fashioned only in manner and dress," and the subjects they dealt with were at heart "much the same themes with which we are engaged and with which our children will be engaged after us." Whitman, enlisted for democracy, was "fighting the battle of 1790 over again." The great debate of the Progressive era "was the struggle of 1789 over again."[1] Even the Puritans must be understood in this way as thoroughly preformed moderns, for if we discard their strange manner and dress to interest ourselves solely in the matter of their arguments, "and if we will resolutely translate the old phrases into modern equivalents, if we will put aside the theology and fasten attention on the politics and economics of the struggle, we shall have less difficulty in discovering that the new

---

[1] III, xxv, 83.

principle for which those old Puritans were groping was the
later familiar doctrine of natural rights. . . ."[2]

The suggestion that the theological forms of Puritan
thought are like transient fashions in dress, and that we will
understand the true content of Puritan thought better if we
brush aside Puritan theology, is the counterpart, in intellectual history, of Parrington's canon in literary theory that
esthetic judgments are of incidental concern and belong to
the "narrower belletristic." There is, as he sees it, a hidden
core, a basic substance, to history; and once we have found
this, the essential thing, we have reached reality and have
come to the point at which the actual contemporaneity of
history can be clearly perceived. The true significance of our
ancestors lies just here: in their contemporaneity.

There is, of course, a sense in which Parrington's disposition to abstract from the specificity of historical events
can be defended. Later struggles for democracy have something in common with earlier struggles for democracy—*if*
indeed we can be sure that that is what they actually were—
and it would be impossible to generalize at all if it were
impermissible to look for such resemblances. In Parrington's
history, however, the conviction of the similarity seems to
have *preceded* an examination of the particularities of events,
and at times to have taken the place of such an examination.
His method, then, is governed not simply by the defensible
assumption that our ancestors had something in common
with us but by the far less defensible one that the respects
in which they will be found to differ from us are of little
consequence. The result is that in his search for the hard core
of "reality" Parrington's view of things becomes, paradoxically, increasingly abstract, and we get carried further and
further away from what was really on the minds of Roger
Williams, John Cotton, and their successors. For example,
in his long sequence on Puritan thought Parrington found
occasion only for fleeting mention of the Half-Way Covenant
and the troublesome problems of church polity it was meant

---

[2] I, i, 6. One is reminded here of Beard's belief that Puritan religious thought was "the defense mechanism of men who were
engaged in resisting taxes and other exactions" and his confidence that "the historian need not tarry long with the logical
devices of men in action." *Rise*, I, 31.

to solve. These problems may have been frippery to the Progressive mind, but they were meat and drink to the Puritans; indeed the Puritans' ideas of church polity provided the conceptual model for their understanding of civil polity, and without them their political theory cannot be understood. We may profitably turn our attention, as Parrington suggests, to "the politics and economics of the struggle" but to "put aside the theology," as he also enjoins us, will only guarantee that we will never comprehend them at all. It is this lack of concern with the immediate terms on which intellectual problems present themselves to the makers of history that accounts for our failure to get from Parrington a feeling for the movement of ideas, their change in function in different situations. One looks to him in vain for an account or explanation of just how Puritanism gave way to latitudinarianism and to the skeptical thought of the Enlightenment, how transcendentalism emerged in the Unitarian environment, or how the laissez-faire ideas that seemed so radical in some of the left-wing Jacksonians turned up in such an ultraconservative guise forty years later when people were reading Herbert Spencer. In *Main Currents* ideas do not develop, they only recur.

Some of the static quality in the work comes from Parrington's very passion for form and proportion. As E. H. Eby reports, his love of architecture carried over into his book and determined the structure he would give it. One need only look at the Table of Contents of his first volume to see how this urge toward design affects its organization. It is full of counterpoise—the stewards of theocracy versus the independents, the Mather dynasty versus the liberals, Edwards as against Franklin, the mind of the Whig against the mind of the Tory, and, among the later political thinkers, "The English Group" against "The French Group," the Constitution against the Declaration of Independence. Each sketch is touched off by some key designation upon which everything depends. As Professor Eby writes, Parrington began with a thesis, fixed in a phrase, a sentence, or a revealing figure, and he was so habituated to follow the dictates of this formula that "his ability to write would be blocked until he had in

mind a perfectly crystallized concept expressible at the maxi-
mum in one sentence." For a long time he was suspended
over the Gilded Age, but could not get on with his writing
until the indispensable title occurred to him. Finally, after
some weeks, he showed relief. "I have found the phrase," he
said: "I will call it the Great Barbecue"—and so the work
went on.[3] The advantages of this mode of presentation are
clear enough: one always knows where one is in Parrington's
volumes, and the atmosphere of each scene, the role of each
actor, is firmly fixed at the beginning. Its disadvantage hangs
on the fact that history itself does not take place architectoni-
cally, but with a fluid dialectic of its own. It is capricious,
asymmetrical, organic, rather than geometrical; and if it is
to be likened to architecture it is more like a church by
Gaudi than one by Wren. Ideas appear, make their mark in
one context, begin to change form, and then sometimes,
rather suddenly, change function also. The architectonic
conception, then, for all the obvious merits it had in organizing an accessible popular work, accounts in some part for the
static feeling one gets, the sense that in his love of counterposing sets of ideas Parrington has all too often neglected to
get them into motion.

II

The sheer size of his cast of characters required Parrington to paint a large number of portraits, but the limited and
predetermined nature of his interest in his writers, his belief
that many of the specifics of their intellectual lives were not
of enduring importance, left him with only limited means by
which to render their features. He painted with a palette
confined, by his own decision, to a few stark primary colors
and permitted himself only the broadest and boldest strokes
of the brush. It became necessary for him to classify almost
every writer in relation to certain very broad categories
drawn from the spheres of political, literary, and intellectual
history. Such terms as realism and romanticism, conserva-

[3] III, vi.

tism, liberalism, and individualism thus took on a saliency
in his writing that is unfortunately not matched by their
clarity or sharpness of definition. He knew that these terms
are difficult and imprecise, and he tried to take honest cognizance of the fact by putting them in the plural—which
was a way of acknowledging their multiple meanings but not
of coming to grips with them. This device accounts for a
noticeable awkwardness in his abstractions, his references
to the "liberalisms implicit in the Puritan Revolution," or
the "liberalisms implicit in Plymouth Congregationalism,"
"the inchoate idealisms of English Puritanism," the "diverse
liberalisms" that were being stifled by the Massachusetts
Bay oligarchy, "the liberalisms involved in Luther's premises,"
"the nineteenth century with its cargo of romanticisms," and
indeed of the whole complex of "ebullient romanticisms"
with which his second volume was concerned. He found it important to place the individual writer in relation to these
large tendencies in thought, which were sometimes almost
personified, as when he said of Godkin: "His realism was a
profound discouragement to his idealism."[4] Now and then
these abstractions rattle against each other: "Overseas liberalisms had flourished in the soil that proved inhospitable to
overseas conservatisms, and it was these European liberalisms that provided the mold into which ran the fluid experience of America to assume substantial form." It is almost as
though Parrington at a late point in his work had read Arthur
O. Lovejoy's famous paper of 1924, "On the Discrimination
of Romanticisms," and had taken its lesson, if not exactly
to heart, at least into his rhetoric, and had gone through his
text and changed many of his key terms from the singular
to the plural.[5]

    Parrington also worked with a set of fundamental count-

---

[4] III, 160; cf. I, 11, 13, 26, 72, 397; II, 473.
[5] It is possible that Parrington (though he disliked the Modern
Language Association and did not take its periodicals) might
have read Lovejoy's essay. It appeared in *PMLA*, which is often
seen, if not always read, by university teachers of English. In
this essay Lovejoy asked what could be done to diminish a confusion of terminology "which has for a century been the scandal of literary history and criticism," and suggested, among other
devices, that "we should learn to use the word 'Romanticism' in
the plural." *PMLA*, 39 (1924), 229–53. See Lovejoy's *Essays in
the History of Ideas* (1948), 234–5.

ers, or basic elements of characterization, which he tended to combine and recombine as he thought the merits and defects of his subjects warranted. It is the frequent recurrence of these counters that in the end gives the impression of similarity in his portraits of so many of his heroes and villains. Perhaps the most important of them was that treasured personal quality designated as idealism, which he found prominent in almost all the heroes of his book. "The idealist," as he put it, "has always seen deeper into the spirit of America than the realist."[6] An all but indispensable attribute of true greatness, idealism was fortunately not in short supply, and Parrington found writers aplenty upon whom he could lavish his affection.

Both Thomas Hooker and Roger Williams were men of "fine idealism,"[7] Williams indeed because he anticipated so many "idealisms of the future," among them those of Emerson, Channing, and Paine. Paine too, though a realist in his handling of facts, was "a thoroughgoing idealist in aim." Jefferson, "far more completely than any other American of his generation . . . embodied the idealisms of the great revolution." It was fortunate that he was an idealist, since his idealism was badly needed to leaven the strong materialism of his times. His ally, the journalist Freneau, was "an idealist who cared only for the *res publica*." Cooper too was "at heart an idealist" and in fact paid "a great price for his idealism." Greeley was "an incorrigible idealist," and so was Edward Bellamy, and oddly enough, Sinclair Lewis. John Brown was "a primitive idealist of rugged mold," Theodore Parker a man of "frank idealism," Margaret Fuller a woman of "romantic idealism." Charles A. Dana, another Brook-Farmer, was a spoiled idealist: "disappointed with idealism, he turned materialist," and therein lay his downfall. E. L. Godkin was "at once an idealist and a realist" and his intellectual history is largely comprehended in his change from one to the other. Hamlin Garland, more consistent, was "an idealist of the old Jeffersonian breed." Such characters were

---

[6] I, 368.
[7] I, 53. Because Parrington's characterizations of individual writers are easy to find in the relevant chapters, I have here documented only those quotations which, having no obvious place, would be hard to find.

a necessary counterpoise to numerous men of quite another
breed. Thomas Hutchinson had not "the faintest spark of
idealism," John Trumbull "was not a political idealist," and
Hamilton (it seems hardly necessary to say) "was without a
shred of idealism, unless a certain grandiose quality in his
conceptions be accounted idealism." Federalists in general do
badly here: "One might as well look for the sap of idealism
in a last year's stump as in John Marshall," and Fisher Ames
"naturally . . . regarded every idealist, the Rousseaus and
Paines and Jeffersons, as 'democratick babblers'" and the
enemies of law and order.

Some of Parrington's other counters were deployed in
his assessments of motives. His are moral as well as intellectual portraits, perhaps moral portraits primarily. We
should not cavil at the presence of such evaluations. It is
only that Parrington's attributions of motive are so one-
sided and so predictable. Orthodox Puritans, Tories, Federalists generally fail to win his admiration for one or more
of three failings: profit, power, and pride. Even Samuel
Sewall, kindly and neighborly though he was, probably stood
unintelligently against all popular movements because of his
"subconscious concern for his material interests." In Cotton
Mather nothing "can obscure the motive of personal ambition," and vanity provides "the sufficient explanation" of his
various political activities; he came by it legitimately because his father, Increase, had been "ambitious and self-
seeking," "wanting in self-denying love." The Tories were
moved by vanity and arrogance: "Their most cherished
dream was the institution of an American nobility, with the
seal of royal favor set upon their social pretensions."[8]
Thomas Hutchinson was "avaricious of power, even more
than of money," and his entire philosophy, a compression
of Toryism, represented simply "the will-to-power of the
wealthy." The conservative John Dickinson, "as a large
property owner, . . . hastened to the defense of the principle of self-taxation"—which leads one to wonder if this
was not a view also sympathetic to small property owners

[8] I, 194.

in America. A strong conservative like Francis Hopkinson, who joined the Revolution but later became a stout Federalist, is easily accounted for: "His Whiggery was probably commercial in origin, a reflection of the economic interests of the merchant class with which he mingled." The "mendacious" Anglican clergyman, Samuel Peters, a strong advocate of episcopacy whose "better qualities were corroded by overwhelming conceit," was a man with "all the arrogance of a lord." John Marshall was easy to understand: "His financial interests overran state boundaries and his political principles followed easily in their train, washing away all local and sectional loyalties." Webster, for all his rich native endowment, was, after all, "the greatest corporation lawyer of the day, certain to be found defending vested interests, never on the side of the leaner purse." The one great disinterested act of Webster's life, the Seventh of March speech, in which he sacrificed his provincial reputation and exposed himself to the fury of New England reformers in his eagerness to preserve the Union, Parrington, in common with many other writers, saw as merely another token of his hopeless materialism.

To find a certain unchristian pride in some Puritan leaders or a concern for money among rich merchants and their legal spokesmen or a note of class arrogance in the Tory rich puts no strain on our credulity, and independent study might bring us to similar judgments. But the same kind of moral realism does not infuse Parrington's judgments of his idealists and humanitarians, who are not only free, as we might well suppose, of the desire for gain, but of vanity and ambition as well. Thomas Hooker, seen as a man of democratic sympathies, was "a simple man in worldly ambitions as well as in origin, not given to climbing or feathering his own nest." John Wise, the village democrat, was "uninfected by the itch of publicity that attacked so many of his fellow ministers." Crèvecoeur, though he yielded in the end to his Loyalist sympathies, was at heart a frontier democrat, "devoid of petty ambition and local prejudice," and, strangely enough, "an embodiment of the generous spirit of French revolutionary thought." Samuel Adams preferred politics to profits: "He was no self-seeking politician, but a man of vision," and "all cynical and sordid interpretations of his strange career" are beside the point. Freneau was "wholly free from lust of economic aggression, either for himself or for his class. . . . There was no envy in the soul of Freneau, and no self-seeking." As for Joel Barlow, another sound republican, "politics for profit was a sorry spectacle to him," even though he was an agent for a speculative land company. One of the few non-idealists to join this company—Parrington had a disposition to be a little tender to Southern spokesmen—was Alexander Stephens, who was "never selfishly ambitious."

If idealists were sometimes a bit sharp, they had the best of excuses. If they failed to be lovable, they had provocation. Freneau, for example, was often ruthless, and his writings reveal him as "a good hater"; but after all, "it was an age of partisan ruthlessness, and if Freneau was a fierce partisan it was because the new hope then whispering to liberals was in danger of being stifled by selfish men who feared it. . . . If like Sam Adams he was given to robbing men of their characters, it was due to no personal or selfish motives; those great ones whom he lampooned so fiercely, he believed were enemies of the new order." And so with Sam Adams: "To stimulate what we call today class consciousness was a necessary preliminary to a democratic psychology. . . . The ways of the iconoclast are rarely lovely, and the breaking of idols is certain to wound sensitive souls." If Adams also robbed men of their characters, as Hutchinson charged, it was because the respect that attached to men like Hutchinson was a part of their authority. "For the good of America their power must be destroyed. Doubtless Adams was ungenerous in attack; certainly he was vindictive in his hates; but the cold record as we read it today justifies one in the belief that the men whom he attacked were tools of the ministry and must be struck down if the rights of Massachusetts were to be preserved." It is only where William Lloyd Garrison was concerned that Parrington paused to give thought to the problems of ruthless radical prophecy. Single-minded men like Garrison and John Brown, he remarked, "sometimes do succeed in moving mountains; but unfortunately they leave a great scar, and the débris litters the whole countryside." And even after the waste of the level-ing, other mountains may arise, for out of Emancipation came the Fourteenth Amendment, due process of law, and the whole apparatus of capitalist exploitation. Here, for a moment, we get a glimpse of the difficulty of things: "The devil under-stands the ways of the world too well to become discouraged at a temporary set-back, for if righteousness succeed in break-ing the bonds that bind a generation, he knows that the market place carries an ample stock of new cords to replace those that are broken."

In characterizing his idealists and reformers, Parrington broke with the environmental determinism as well as with the search for motives that colors his accounts of his villains. Power, pride, and profit move the conservatives and possessors and they can always be understood, sometimes with and some-times without sympathy or a note of admiration, by reference to their location in society. For idealists it is necessary to derive their motive power from some more mysterious and inaccessible inner resources, since society, as Parrington con-ceives it, does not seem in itself to generate the reform impulse in the way that it generates self-seeking. Roger Williams simply "lived in the realm of ideas," and "his actions were creatively determined by principles"; Franklin transcended his environment and in a rare way "freed [himself] from the prejudice of custom . . . a free man who went his own way with imperturbable good will and unbiased intelligence"; Wil-liam Cullen Bryant's nature was "self-pollenizing." Wendell Phillips came out of morally backward Back Bay, but did not accept its prejudices because "something deep within him, a loyalty to other and higher ideas, held him back. . . . An in-stinctive love of justice held him back."[9]

One of the most persistent themes in Parrington has to do with the unintellectual character, the ignorance, the limited interests of the writers he dislikes and of many others as well.

---

[9] If I give little stress to this gap in Parrington's "environmental" view of ideas, it is because it has been more than once com-mented upon, and is well documented by Robert A. Skotheim and Kermit Vanderbilt, "Vernon Louis Parrington: The Mind and Art of a Historian of Ideas," *Pacific Northwest Quarterly*, 53 (1962), 102–4.

The charge often made against critics who work exclusively in American studies that they overestimate American writing is one that can never be responsibly pressed against Parrington. He looked at the faults as well as the virtues of American writers—and what an imperfect lot they are, especially if they stand in the traditions of Puritanism, Federalism, Brahminism, or modern conservatism. No anti-American from another literary culture would be likely to draw up a more consistent list of limited men. It begins with the substantial Puritan diarist, Judge Samuel Sewall, whose "intellectual interests were few," who "cared nothing for pure literature, and was unacquainted with the English classics," whose mind ran to things "either occult or inconsequential," and who was "quite without imagination"—and it goes steadily on from there. That pillar of the Puritan order, Increase Mather, "was quite unread in the political philosophers and wholly ignorant of major principles," having read none of the major writers from Locke on. "Ideas in the abstract held no interest for him." As he had a conventional mind, he was "incurious intellectually." His son Cotton Mather "knew no other political philosophy than that of the obsolete theocracy in which he had grown up," and his work was "barren of ideas." Even the undeniably learned Jonathan Edwards suffered stultification because he remained "isolated in Massachusetts" and was denied the opportunity of mingling with "the leaders of thought in London." The royal governor, Thomas Hutchinson, though a historian of parts, had not even read Locke, was "little given to intellectual interests," and "his knowledge of political classics was of the slightest." He was "only an unintelligent politician who served the hand that fed him." John Dickinson shared the regrettable quality of many men versed in the law, of knowing little else. "He rarely refers to political authorities." Unlike Hutchinson, he *had* read Locke, but he ignored him. In the end, though a cultivated lawyer, Dickinson emerges as "in no sense a serious political thinker." His "Fabius" letters in defense of the Constitution contain "not a single illuminating comment." The Tory satirist Jonathan Odell fares still worse: "Of any valid or reasoned philosophy, social or political, he was as wanting as a child." He was a man of "vast ignorance." Alexander Hamilton, though perspicacious and admittedly a "great master of modern finance," was otherwise lacking: he was "not a political philosopher in the large meaning of the term," comparing badly with John Adams in his knowledge of history and with Jefferson in his studies of politics. (He compares badly also with Thomas Paine, who was likewise not to be compared with Adams as a student, but who somehow "absorbed ideas like a sponge.") The mind of Timothy Dwight, president of Yale and pillar of Connecticut Federalism, "was closed as tight as his study windows in January." It is true that he read widely in rationalist writings, "but he read only to refute." The Connecticut Wits, to whom Parrington had given some special attention, "were not devoid of cleverness, but they were wanting in ideas. They were partisans rather than intellectuals." Perhaps in emulation of Dwight,[1] "they sealed the windows of their minds against the disturbing winds of doctrine that were blowing briskly," and rather gratuitously "chose to remain too ignorant to be interesting." National independence, with its new problems, did little to quicken the minds of men who stood in this tradition. The easygoing Justice John Marshall, we are hardly surprised to learn, "was wholly wanting in intellectual interests. Strangely ill-read in the law, he was even more ignorant of history and economics and political theory. . . . There is no indication that he had ever heard of the Physiocratic school of economics, or had looked into the writings of Rousseau or Godwin or Paine. The blind sides of his mind were many," though what he did see and understand he at least grasped firmly. The Virginia lawyer and biographer William Wirt was "curiously ignorant of the economic and political philosophy of agrarianism," though it flourished around him, and he "was little given to abstract speculation on the rights of man." Jefferson Davis had "little intellectual curiosity." Even the learned immigrant scholar Francis Lieber was a victim of legalism and of "his failure to investigate the economics of politics." The Charleston intellectual, Hugh Legaré, was a similar case: he had "read too many law books" and speculated too little on politics. "Immersed in his codes, he had forgotten to inquire into the hidden springs of sovereignty," and "in his contempt for practi-

---

[1] Or even of Increase Mather, who also "closed the windows of his mind against the winds of new doctrine."

cal politics he had neglected to study even the primer of economic determinism"—a strong reproach to a man who died
five years before the *Communist Manifesto* was written.
Legaré accepted the economics of Adam Smith, but was seriously handicapped by "his ignorance of the economics of John
Taylor." Henry Clay, as we might by now expect, was "unread
in history and political theory," and if this is true one need
hardly be surprised to find Andrew Jackson, for all that can be
said for him on other counts, "almost wholly lacking in political and social philosophy." Augustus Longstreet, the Georgia
writer, "had no intellectual curiosity and was incapable of
rigorous intellectual processes." Washington Irving, for all
his gaiety and humor, "was lacking in a brooding intellectual-
ity." Justice Story was another of those lawyers who troubled
Parrington for being too immersed in their law books:
"Against such a mind, deeply read in the law and with scanty
knowledge of economics and political theory, the waves of
liberal and romantic thought broke impotently." Whittier,
though approved on other counts, "felt rather than thought,"
being a man of "conscience rather than intellect," who never
thought about economics and appears not to have read even
such supposedly congenial writers as Rousseau, Paine, and
Jefferson. We need not look for anything better from Longfellow: "There was little intellect in Longfellow, little creative
originality. . . . The winds of doctrine and policy might rage
through the land, but they did not rattle the windows of his
study to disturb his quiet poring over Dante." Hawthorne's
notebooks provide "the occasional record of one who lived an
unintellectual life. . . . Few books are referred to; systems of
thought lie beyond his ken. Compared with the thinkers and
scholars of his time he is only an idler lying in wait for such
casual suggestions as he may turn into stories." Lowell, again,
had "no interest in ideas, only a pottering concern for the
text. . . . Scarcely an important movement of contemporary
thought awakened his interest. . . . He never took the trouble to
ground himself in the elements of politics," and "of American
constitutional history he was as ignorant as a politician."
Thomas Bailey Aldrich, an embodiment of "intellectual sterility," was worse: "Of many things that concern men greatly

he was very, very ignorant. Of the American people beyond the Hudson River, he knew nothing. Of social economics he knew nothing." Sarah Orne Jewett, for all her strivings for realism, "was as ignorant as her Maine fisherfolk of the social forces that were blotting out the world of her fathers," and Mary Wilkins Freeman's thinking "on social questions was still in its teens." She had a warm heart, "but her inadequate knowledge of economics served her ill." The fact that Theodore Dwight Woolsey's speculations on the state were thought to be significant is only "added confirmation of the shallowness of the Gilded Age." Indeed most of the critics of the Gilded Age, including some very well-meaning ones, were "ill equipped . . . intellectually lean and impoverished" as the result of too much constitutional debate, "uninstructed idealists with no understanding of *Realpolitik*." The entire self-constituted educated leadership of the Gilded Age consisted of "second-rate men—mediocre minds cramped by a selfish environment, imbued with no more than a property-consciousness."[2] John Hay was a perfect example of this, the product of an education that "seems to have been faulty." George William Curtis, one of its finer and saner spirits and a most useful man, was still "not a great scholar and not an acute critic," and "never a serious student of politics in the broader sense . . . an inadequate political philosopher . . . as helpless in diagnosing the evil as Lowell or Norton." Even the distinguished Godkin, a man of such wide range and once so well in touch with things, turned out to be in the end "a very ignorant or shallow critic, blinded by his prejudices . . . he seems [by the 1890's] to have done no serious reading in economic theory for half a century." John Fiske, though once intellectually curious and a brilliant popularizer of science, was a poor interpreter of the American past, having "an inadequate knowledge and an inadequate philosophy. . . . The economics of historical change he seems never to have considered, and his analyses of social forces are never acute or penetrating."

Ignorant as they were, the members of the Puritan-

---

[2] III, 137–8, 178–9.

Brahmin-Tory-Federalist tradition produced a heavy portion of anachronisms. John Winthrop was "unable to adapt old prejudices to new conditions," Samuel Sewall "refused to go forward with the changing times," Increase Mather came to be mocked at in Boston because "he had outlived his age," and his son Cotton was "an anachronism in his own day"; Jonathan Edwards, "the greatest mind of New England, had become an anachronism in a world that bred Benjamin Franklin." Thomas Hutchinson "never understood the assertive capitalism that was rising about him." The Tory Jonathan Boucher spoke with "the voice of seventeenth-century Cavalier England." John Dickinson was "incapable of understanding current economic forces either in England or in America," and belonged "in that older world in which he was bred." John Trumbull remained "an echo . . . throughout his life." The mind of the Old South, though Parrington found some sympathy for its resistance to centralized power, was still found to be "so archaic . . . as to appear singular." One of its keenest critics, Whittier, so much esteemed for his honest conscience, was still "fast becoming an anachronism in industrial New England." Hawthorne "lived in the shadow of a Puritan past," and seemed wholly anachronistic. By the time of the 1870's and 1880's "the incurious Boston mentality missed pretty much everything vital and significant in American life." Thomas Bailey Aldrich "traveled back a hundred years." Godkin, with his archaic program of reading, certainly "did not go forward to meet new times." Henry Adams even "seemed to himself a somewhat pathetic anachronism."

It is not that Parrington was singularly ungenerous. Quite the contrary: he usually welcomed the chance to make even his less favored subjects sympathetic or understandable. Moreover, the art of deprecation, as applied to standard American writers, was well developed among the critics of his time—Brooks and Mencken stand out here, but there were others—and Parrington was writing in a common idiom. Nor was he so wrong in his estimates: he was neither the first nor the last writer to find a certain flabbiness of thought and thinness of sensibility in some of the men he dealt with, and his acid judgments frequently seem not wide of the mark. What does trouble me in these estimates is their essential sameness, the predictable uniformity of his reproaches, the forceful, if rather indirect suggestion that most of these writers suffered from the same combination of vanity and selfishness, the same lack of robustness and realism, and that they would all have been cured in roughly equal measure if they had infused themselves with large doses of "idealism" and then read liberally in the Physiocrats, Rousseau, Jefferson, and John Taylor of Caroline County.

I am tempted also to offer the unprovable guess that Parrington was extraordinarily preoccupied with the idea of men ill prepared for their tasks, insufficiently educated, and unreceptive to ideas coming from outside their own tradition. The modest tone in which he spoke of his own omissions, doubtful interpretations, and hasty generalizations seems to me to be truer to the man than the hauteur with which he appeared to dispose of one uncongenial writer after another. But his role was, by his canons, a difficult one. He had committed himself to a kind of economic realism which, by his own reckoning, appeared to require a firm foundation in economic "reality"—a thing he constantly sought in those he read. Yet his own notions of economics were not well grounded. When he refers to a parochial windbag like John Taylor as the source of some arcane or indispensable wisdom on economic matters, or classifies Bastiat with Louis Blanc and Proudhon as a "left-wing" economist, or when he tells us that part of the trouble with Hawthorne was that he "never grappled with economics *as Thoreau did*," or again when he imagines that Hamilton, as an avid reader of Adam Smith, stood in the tradition of English liberalism instead of seeing him as a bridge between the older mercantilism and the new economic nationalism of Friedrich List, I begin to wonder if he must not have been half-aware of the contrast between the state of his own preparation in economics and the stringent demands he made upon other American writers.[3] In this sense, Parrington had cast himself in a role he particularly disliked—that of the "narrow belletrist" writing upon matters concerning which the wisdom of "the economist" seems more important. He preached with the desperation of a minister who doubts his own salvation.

---

[3] II, x, 449; I, 296; the italics are added.

III

It remains only to look at the main currents of American thought as Parrington saw them. His characteristic procedure was to describe certain major ideas or tendencies that came from Europe—English Independency and Whiggery, French romantic theory, the laissez-faire ideas that rose with modern industry and commerce, nineteenth-century science as it affected social and literary thought, the various strains of Continental utopianism or collectivism—and to examine their course in the American environment. Usually he saw two sets of ideas as being brought into direct and blunt confrontation. He was fascinated, as many writers had been before him, with the battle waged in Puritan New England between dissent and a rigid system of doctrine, and then between what he took to be the correlated principles of aristocracy and democracy. "Unfortunately," he wrote, "the liberal doctrine of natural rights was entangled in New England with an absolutist theology that conceived of human nature as inherently evil, that postulated a divine sovereignty absolute and arbitrary, and projected caste divisions into eternity—a body of dogmas that it needed two hundred years' experience in America to disintegrate."[4] The first part of his work was concerned with the long continuing clash between liberal political philosophy and "reactionary theology" culminating in a rather rapid deterioration of the Puritan system at the close of the seventeenth and the early decades of the eighteenth century.

Outside New England a similar process of liberation took place, but against less resistance. There, various European immigrants reacted more directly to the stimulus of the new environment and a great population of yeomen developed the philosophy that was to be characteristic of America for a hundred years or more. "It was to these scattered and undistinguished colonials that French romantic theory was brought by a group of intellectuals in the latter years of the [eight-

---

[4] This section draws in some part on Parrington's own summaries. See I, iii–vii, 5–15, 51–3, 179–90, 267–91, 397–8; II, xix–xx, xxiii–xxix, 3–5; and for particular quotations, I, iv, 180, 185, 284, 288, 289; II, 28; III, xxiii, 3.

eenth] century, a philosophy so congenial to decentralized society that it seemed to provide an authoritative sanction for the clarifying ideals of a republican order, based on the principle of home rule, toward which colonial experience was striving." Now this French romantic theory, which was "spreading widely through the backwoods of America," provided a view of human nature antagonistic to the Puritan view, a new view of man as potentially excellent, capable of indefinite development. It argued for a government circumscribed in its powers and for a social policy that deferred to the great and virtuous mass of yeomen farmers. At the same time, English liberalism was fortifying itself in the commercial towns, promulgating a philosophy based on the values of the market place, stressing competition, seeing human nature as being above all acquisitive, ministering to the needs of those who profited from commercial expansion.

Parrington traces these currents of thought through two sharply counterposed sets of thinkers, matched in pairs at almost every point along the way. On one side are the stewards of the theocratic order, such men as John Winthrop, John Cotton, and the Mathers, followed in a later age by Jonathan Edwards, who tried to infuse new life into a dying Calvinist orthodoxy. In later political debates these men were followed by the more conservative Whigs like John Dickinson, by outright Tories like Thomas Hutchinson, and by the architects of the new coercive state, the exponents of commercialism and minority control symbolized and led by Alexander Hamilton. Against them is the camp of the idealists—the independents, dissenters, liberals, democrats, humanitarians—represented at their best by Roger Williams, Thomas Hooker, and John Wise as opponents of the theocracy; by Franklin, Jefferson, and Paine as spokesmen of the more secular, enlightened, democratic, and humane movements of the eighteenth century.

In dealing with the political thought of the Revolution, Parrington was modest and candid. He realized how puzzling the event was for historians (it remains so even now), but in his own stab at accounting for its thought he followed the traditions of Progressive historiography, emphasizing the role of "liberal impulses in the background of the American mind" which had been precipitated into militancy by the crisis in the British Empire after the Seven Years War. An ungainly coalition of aggressive, profit-minded town merchants, aristocratic planters in debt to English merchants, and frontier liberals who stood for republican principles had brought about the Revolution. It was the last faction, he concluded, that provided the revolutionary dynamic. "In every colony the party of incipient populism had been checked and thwarted by royal officials; and it was this mass of populist discontent, seeing itself in danger of being totally crushed, and its interests ignored, that provided the rank and file of armed opposition to the King."

The period of state-making and internal debate that followed the Revolution, Parrington accounted for on lines substantially like those drawn by Beard and J. Allen Smith. What was unique in his own account was chiefly his sense of the derivation of the ideas in the debate. For him the opposition to the new Constitution was founded not in old ideas of English republicanism qualified by American experience but rather in "the humanitarian theory of the French thinkers." He saw the opponents of the Constitution as being handicapped in the great debate because the principles of French romanticism and Physiocratic agrarianism were not yet sufficiently known and accepted on American soil, and because the principles of democracy had not yet been clarified by Jacobinism. The leading English authorities like Locke, at best aristocratic republicans, were of no use to emergent democracy. Lacking discipline and cohesion as well as a developed political theory, the populists lost to "the money group," which was able to "overwhelm the silent majority with clamorous argument" and to establish "the coercive state." Still, on the merits of the matter, and even without quite enough French theory to draw on, Parrington thought the Anti-Federalists had much the better of the case. As political thinking, he saw very little in *The Federalist,* which is "of interest only to students of constitutional law and practice," and must be seen as a "frankly partisan" attempt to stave off popular rule and underwrite government by the minority. In striking contrast, Richard Henry Lee's Anti-Federalist pamphlet, *Letters from the Federal Farmer,* is so outstanding for its "calmness and fair-mindedness" that it "ill deserves the name partisan."

Jefferson's victory in 1800 at last put liberalism in the saddle, and greatly extended the influence of French humanitarian thought. However, it left the eighteenth-century aristocratic class still in possession of the vantage points of polite culture. Eventually the new romanticism of the middle class shouldered aside the aspirations of both gentlemen and farmers. The flourishing romanticism of the years from the War of 1812 to the Civil War is the theme of Parrington's second volume. Romanticism in different guises prevailed in the South, in New England, and on the Western frontier; but its real strength Parrington somehow found to rest in the middle class. Colonial America had been static, rationalistic, inclined to pessimism; the nineteenth century was ebulliently optimistic, and though it usually saw human nature as acquisitive rather than good or evil, it was content to find it so. Southern romanticism, stemming from Scott, deserted Jefferson for Calhoun, developed the slaveholders' ideal of a Greek democracy—"the most romantic ideal brought forth by our golden age of romance." The idea of Greek democracy was an ingenious one, but it fatally left out of account the middle class that finally destroyed it. The middle states, eclectic in culture, were fundamentally an expression of the mind of Philadelphia and New York. For a long time, under the leadership of Boston Federalism, New England rejected French ideas, and hence lost itself in a morass of reaction; but finally, in the age of Channing, it caught up first with Rousseau and other French thinkers to produce the Unitarians, and then with German idealism to produce the transcendentalists. On the frontier, a coonskin democracy came forth, at once intensely acquisitive and intensely egalitarian. Jacksonian democracy too, Parrington believed, owed a great deal to French thought, but at this point in history he apparently felt it had begun to lose its pertinence to economic society, for Jacksonianism, though "it imposed upon America the ideal of democracy to which all must hereafter do lip service,... lost its realistic basis in a Physiocratic economics and wandered in a fog of political equalitarianism."

The Civil War broke the last obstacle to a consolidated

capitalism. After Appomattox, "a slave economy could never again thwart the ambitions of the capitalistic economy." Particularism was dead; the future belonged to the machine, to the centralized state, to those who knew how to seize, possess, and enjoy. Americans fell upon the riches of the continent like a gang of frontiersmen invited to a grand barbecue. More sensitive souls might gag at the sight, but few of them had any animating philosophy that would inspire them to resist the depredations of the gluttonous individualists. After the long spell of optimism that had come with the romantic era, the combination of industrial capitalism and modern science once again undermined the foundations of hope. A new pessimism, founded not like colonial pessimism on Calvinist theology but on modern mechanistic philosophy, swept over the American mind. Parrington's third volume was concerned both with the implications of this pessimism and with the countervailing promise of critical realism, of the signs of revolt among intellectuals and artists.

IV

His point of view, Parrington explained in a disarmingly candid introduction, was "liberal rather than conservative, Jeffersonian rather than Federalistic, and very likely on my search I have found what I went forth to find, as others have discovered what they were seeking." This avowed partisan dualism accounts in some part for the signal importance that matters of intellectual genealogy had for him. If he considered an intellectual tradition like Calvinism to be bad, he was also rather likely to find that it had a fixed and monolithic character, and little or no capacity for development. Since it could not be expected to evolve, it would have to be overthrown or rejected, and this destructive task would have to be carried out by men stemming from an altogether different tradition. Opposing ideas demand opposing ancestries. Calvinism he thus saw not as having grown gentler and more receptive to modification under the stress of late seventeenth- and eighteenth-century changes, but as having been "grotesque and illiberal to the last," and as having been "finally rejected" by natural rights thinkers and democrats.[5] Although he did have some insight into the positive historical relation between Puritan thought and the natural rights philosophy, Parrington put his primary emphasis upon the opposition between them. His tendency to see two sets of completely opposed ideas in conflict made it impossible for him to see the shared Calvinism of Roger Williams and John Cotton, the basic similarity of the ideas of Thomas Hooker and the Massachusetts theocrats, or the common Whiggery behind the friends and opponents of the Constitution. It also led him to some bizarre notions of intellectual genealogy, of which the most important are the idea that early American dissent had its intellectual foundations in Lutheranism and the idea that the American democratic tradition had its primary animating sources in "French romanticism."

While the settlers of Massachusetts Bay were strong Calvinists, resting their theocracy on firm Calvinist foundations, Parrington imagined that the Pilgrims at Plymouth were far more democratic Separatists drawing their inspiration from Luther. "The teachings of Luther," he wrote, "erected on the major principle of justification by faith, conduced straight to political liberty. . . ." These teachings embodied "the spirit of uncompromising individualism that would eventually espouse the principle of democracy in church and state." Hence Radical Separatists turned naturally to Luther rather than Calvin. Roger Williams could be understood both as "a follower of Luther and a forerunner of French romantic thinkers." Parrington seems to have consulted too exclusively some of Luther's early utterances on "the liberty of the Christian man" and to have ignored entirely the later phases of his political development. The Luther who said: "I would rather suffer a prince doing wrong than a people doing right" makes no appearance in his calculations. In comparing the political impact of Lutheran and Calvinist thought he was almost pathetically unsure. He overemphasized the clarity and constancy of the political theories of both men, as well as overstating their differences from each other as political thinkers.

---

[5] I, i, 13, 15.

But above all, he put the case the wrong way round. There
had been more margin in Calvin than in Luther for a theory
of popular resistance to absolute authority; and in Holland,
France, Scotland, England, and finally America, it was Calvinist thinkers who had actually made progress toward finding
a theological foundation for popular rights. Perhaps more important for the historian of ideas, by ascribing the source of
democratic tendencies to Lutheranism, Parrington had turned
away from one of the most interesting tendencies in late sev-
enteenth- and eighteenth-century thought—the emergence of
a strong doctrine of natural rights within the Puritan tradition itself.[6]

Parrington belonged to a generation that found it especially hard to look at the Calvinists in detached historical terms.
He had experienced too keenly the ugly little tyrannies of rigid
religion at Emporia and again at Oklahoma. Along with so
many others of his time, he had emancipated himself from
religion with the aid of Darwin and Spencer; and while it is
by no means impossible for a predominantly secular mind to
enter imaginatively into the Puritan experience (one need
think only of the wholly secular Perry Miller in this respect),
there were very few among the liberal minds of Parrington's
generation who could have looked upon such an effort of
imagination as anything other than an abject return to the
intellectual manacles they had just broken. In the wake of
their emancipation, Puritanism meant little more than harsh
theology, aristocratic or theocratic politics, the stultification
of natural human impulses, prudery and intolerance, superstition, and burnings for witchcraft. In criticism, at the same
time, Mencken and others were lashing away at the funda-
mentalist assumptions of large segments of American culture,
and were stigmatizing Puritanism, along with frontier influences, for having warped and desiccated American literary
culture. The modern rediscovery of the American Puritans,

---

[6] I, i, 11–12, 70. In his approach to Luther, Parrington seems to
have passed by the standard authorities and turned to an un-
reliable study by Luther H. Waring, *The Political Theories of
Martin Luther* (1910), and to have ignored the course of Luther's
thought after 1525. See Esther E. Burch, "The Sources of New
England Democracy," *American Literature*, I (1929), 115–30.

which owes so much to the work of scholars like Samuel Eliot Morison, Kenneth Murdock, Clifford K. Shipton, and Perry Miller had barely begun when Parrington was at work. Here, then, Parrington was only shaping his own variation of the view of Puritanism commonly shared by emancipated American intellectuals during the years when his volumes were being written.

Today historians of Puritanism can see many aspects of Puritan society that were not of interest to Parrington's generation, and find themselves fascinated by complex changes in the texture of a dedicated and disciplined community that took place under the stress of time and circumstances. Here, almost as in some kind of laboratory experiment, a sect can be seen evolving into a church, and one can observe the tension between utopian piety and the imperatives of organization, between the claims of the deterministic doctrine of election and the hortatory and evangelical side of religion, between the desire to create a church of true saints and the pressures, pleasures, and profits of the world. One can see how the Puritan community—pressed first by the dissenting sectaries and then by the awakeners in its own midst, shaken by profound internal problems of church polity, moved by the religious and political struggle with English authority, menaced by latitudinarian and Arminian thinkers, challenged at last by science and the rise of secularism—changed character within a few generations, and how the ministerial class struggled to cope with these changes and yet in some ways cooperated in bringing them about. To those who bear in mind the pristine aims of the first Puritan emigrants, what is impressive is the gradual yielding of the old order. Even by the time the Half-Way Covenant was adopted in the 1660's the Puritan community was no longer the same, and the succeeding decades were so filled with change that the Mathers themselves could not avoid being swept along with the tides.

For writers of Parrington's generation and of his stamp of mind, little of this had reality or significance; and they tried to find what sympathy they could for a few Puritan rebels on the ground that they prefigured modern democracy. Hence to

Parrington the God-intoxicated Roger Williams was "more concerned with social commonwealths than with theological dogmas," a man whose religion "issued in political theory rather than in theological dogma," who was "primarily a political philosopher rather than a theologian," and who indeed anticipated the principles of "local home rule, the initiative and the referendum, and the recall." Again, Thomas Hooker's basic intellectual similarity to the other stewards of the Puritan theocracy disappears in Parrington's treatment, and Hooker too emerges if not as a secular mind at least as a radically democratic thinker.[7]

Distracted by this single-minded concern for democracy and dissent, Parrington failed to see much significance in the fascinating change that swept over the Puritan community. He paid no attention when even the Mathers went with the tide, espousing toleration and refusing to defend the old ways of their tribe. Instead, like so many other writers, he used the Mathers only as "anachronisms" who personified the old order. In seeking for the causes that overthrew Puritanism from without, Parrington and many of his contemporaries passed up the profound changes that were taking place within. And something in his populistic bias made it impossible for him to see what the process of change was like. For example, writing of the early eighteenth century, Parrington suggested to his readers that although rationalism "might be excluded from the minister's study, it spread its subtle infection through the mass of the people," though what actually happened was closer to the reverse. Here again it is the common people that become the vehicles of virtue, just as in the Revolution it is invariably the popular party that provides strength and as later it is in the "backwoods" of America that Physiocratic social idealism spreads. Calvinism is undermined not by the increasing cosmopolitanism of the towns, by science or latitudinarian speculation, but first by the native kindliness of

---

7 On Williams, see Alan Simpson, "How Democratic Was Roger Williams?" *William and Mary Quarterly*, 13 (1956), 53–67; on Williams's supposed secularism, see Mauro Calamandrei, "Neglected Aspects of Roger Williams' Thought," *Church History*, 21 (1952), 239–56. For Hooker, Perry Miller, "Thomas Hooker and the Democracy of Early Connecticut," *New England Quarterly*, 4 (1931), 663–712.

the New England village and then by the philosophic assaults of Rousseau.[8]

Rousseau: perhaps the most persistent and, for him, fundamental of Parrington's ideas was that American democratic thought was basically French in origin. Throughout his first two volumes impulses derived from what are loosely called "French romanticism" and "French humanitarianism" are invoked to account for the democratic proclivities of one writer after another. Even the dissatisfaction with Calvinism that could be seen in the eighteenth century is traced not to the English Arminians and latitudinarians but to a "fresh impetus from the new social philosophy of France." But if we look for the particular French writers upon whom all this influence depends, the only names we find mentioned are Rousseau, the Physiocrats, and, collectively, "the Jacobins." Parrington passes over a vast tradition of English latitudinarian and rationalist thought to make of Rousseau the fundamental secularizing influence. What undermined Calvinism, he thought, was the teaching of Rousseau that men are naturally good and that evils come from society, an idea that quickened the revolt against "every form of arbitrary authority," theological and political. Even a colonial who had no direct contact with such speculative thought could hardly escape being affected by it. Again, in the nineteenth century, "French liberalism" is given the central role in the formation of New England Unitarian culture; in a somewhat disguised garb, "the gospel of Jean Jacques presently walked the streets of Boston and spoke from its most respectable pulpits under the guise of Unitarianism." In fact Unitarianism discreetly "accomplished for New England what Jeffersonianism had accomplished for the South and West—the wide dissemination of eighteenth century French liberalism." As to politics, Parrington, being unable to find much power in the English backgrounds of American democratic thought, had to ascribe democracy in the Federalist era to the Jacobins, who he thought were necessary to "clarify" its principles for Amer-

---

8 I, 148–51, 185. For an early attempt to clarify the decline of old-fashioned clerical influence from about 1680 to 1740, see Clifford K. Shipton, "The New England Clergy of the 'Glacial Age,'" *Publications* of the Colonial Society of Massachusetts, 32 (1937), 24–54; this essay was originally written in 1933.

icans. He concluded that if only the American debate over the Constitution had taken place five years later than it did, "after the French Revolution had provided new democratic theory, the disparity of intellectual equipment [that is, between Federalists and Anti-Federalists] would have been far less marked." Indeed, he regarded the enthusiasm for the French Revolution as "the first great popularization of democratic ideals in America."[9]

The notion that Rousseau was a major source of the ideas of the Declaration of Independence and of democratic thought in the Jeffersonian era was, again, no peculiarity of Parrington's. Many historians and men of letters writing in the Federalist tradition—most of them shockingly ignorant of Jefferson—had taken up this idea as one of a number of ways (so they thought) of discrediting the Virginian as a wild theorist of the French type, and by the sheer force of repetition it gained ground. John Morley, for example, had been persuaded by such writers that the ideas and phrases of the Declaration of Independence came from Rousseau's writing, and many American writers would have followed Lowell in referring to Rousseau as "the father . . . in politics of Jefferson and Thomas Paine."[1] No doubt this notion of a Rousseauian influence got much of its impetus from the memory of the enthusiasm shown among many Jeffersonian Republicans for the French Revolution, though it was a mistake to identify this enthusiasm for the *event* with an immediate conversion to its ideology or to forget how short-lived the enthusiasm was. But above all, the defenders of Jefferson made a mistake in inverting this Federalist version of intellectual history by simply accepting the idea of the Rousseauian Jefferson and holding that the impact of Rousseau was, after all, an excellent thing.

[9] I, 151, 279, 281, 324; II, 322.
[1] On the Rousseauist image of Jefferson, see Merrill D. Peterson, *The Jefferson Image in the American Mind* (1960), 44, 117, 133, 214, 269; for Morley and Lowell see Lewis Rosenthal, "Rousseau in Philadelphia," *Magazine of American History*, 12 (1884), 46.

Parrington saw Rousseau as having cut an extraordinarily wide swath in the American mind. Thoreau, for example, was "a child of Jean Jacques," Melville "a spiritual child of Jean Jacques," and even Sinclair Lewis was "an echo of Jean Jacques and the golden hopes of the Enlightenment—thin and far off, no doubt, but still an authentic echo."

No serious student of early American thought has in fact been able to find that Rousseau had any considerable influence here, and it is doubtful that there was a single American thinker of any consequence who professed to owe him anything of importance.[2] The Anglo-American tradition of republicanism had taken on a firm character before Rousseau began to write (the *Social Contract* appeared in 1762) and long before his works were known here. He was occasionally read by Americans, but rather infrequently cited, and then often as the object of disdain, or even, especially after about 1800, of revulsion. His abstract approach to the majority will was quite uncongenial to the particular problems of representation that were of utmost concern in America, and it would have been a rare American democrat who could have seen in him much more than a spirited but vague confirmation of sentiments they found expressed more clearly and usably in Anglo-American writing. The major American writer who seems to have known him best was John Adams, and Adams detested him. Jefferson took little or no interest in him, and even Paine, who is supposed to have followed him, found him seriously wanting in guiding principles. It is doubtful that any American democrat who read Rousseau did not imagine that he could get a better intellectual foundation for his political aspirations from more congenial and accessible English sources. The really interesting question is not whether Rousseau had much influence in America but why he struck so few resonances in the American mind.

---

2 One had only to seek carefully for the influence of Rousseau in American political thought in order to be able not to find it. Howard Mumford Jones, whose exhaustive study, *America and French Culture, 1750–1848*, appeared the same year as Parrington's first two volumes, concluded that, as to political theory, "the influence of Rousseau was negligible." P. 369 n; cf. 572. Carl Becker, in his *Declaration of Independence* (1922), which, unlike Jones's book, was available to Parrington but which was not cited in his bibliography, remarked: "It does not appear that Jefferson, or any American, read many French books. So far as the 'Fathers' were, before 1776, directly influenced by particular writers, the writers were English, and notably Locke." Ed. 1942, 27. See also the finding of Lewis Rosenthal, "Rousseau in Philadelphia," 46–55. Paine is sometimes cited as owing much to Rousseau. He did think that Rousseau's works were full of an elevating spirit of liberty, but he also found that they "leave the mind in love with an object [liberty], without describing the means of possessing it." *Rights of Man* in *Complete Works* (ed. 1954), II, 75.

Finally, the notion, so central for Parrington, that American democratic thought owed its economic rationale to the
influence of the Physiocrats can be regarded only as a gratuitous intrusion on the facts. Parrington considered the thought
of a striking number of his heroes to have been shaped by the
economic ideas of the Physiocrats, beginning with the seminal
trio of Franklin, Paine, and Jefferson, and going on to Barlow,
Crèvecoeur, John Taylor, and Cooper. The Southern mind as a
whole also had "a frank bias towards . . . Physiocratic agrarianism." Various Americans who were not to be classed as
openly Physiocratic had "a pronounced bias" toward Physiocratic views of society (Emerson), or were, however informal
in their thinking, still Physiocrats by derivation (Jackson,
since Jacksonianism was merely "John Taylor's economics
written into the law of the land"), or were instinctive "step-
sons" of the Physiocrats without reading them (Greeley), or
had at least "a Physiocratic dislike of middlemen" (H. C.
Carey), or arrived along an independent path at identical
conclusions (Henry George). When the Physiocrats cannot
be found, Parrington misses them. Whitman, whom he admired, was, he thought, a superb latter-day representative of
Enlightenment thought, but "there was wanting only a physiocratic economics to make it perfect"; and a whole host of
writers whom he did not admire were reproached for ignoring
or never having gone to school to the Physiocrats.

Had Parrington spoken of physiocracy simply to refer to
a generally agrarian cast of thought, there would be little to
differ with, for the agrarian bias of so much of the American
mind is undeniable; but there are several passages which
make it clear that he meant that specific doctrines of Physiocratic economics, including the *produit net*, the principle of
laissez faire, and the proposal of the *impôt unique*, were
literally taken over by American followers. To Jefferson, he
asserted, "the appeal of the Physiocratic theory of social
economics [was] irresistible," and the "strongest creative influence on the mature Jefferson" came from Quesnay and
Du Pont de Nemours, along with a few other French writers.
The struggle between Jeffersonian and Hamiltonian economics was an American version of "a conflict between the

rival principles of Quesnay and Adam Smith, between an agrarian and a capitalistic economy." It was "the Physiocratic conception that explains [Jefferson's] bitter hostility to protective tariffs, national banks, funding manipulations, the maturity of credit, and all the agencies which Hamilton was skillfully erecting in America." Accordingly, "Jeffersonian democracy as it spread through Virginia and west along the frontier assumed a pronounced Physiocratic bias."[3]

In fact Parrington understood the Physiocrats no better than he understood Luther, and was no more successful in finding American followers for them than he was for Rousseau. The Physiocrats were not fundamentally interested in expressing a sentimental agrarianism or in laying the basis for a humanitarian social economics. They were trying to rescue the *ancien régime* from its fiscal difficulties by devising an economic theory which would justify it in taking adequate tax revenues from landed proprietors. Neither their absolutist political principles nor their ideas about the virtues of a single tax upon the revenue of the land—perish the thought!—were congenial to the American agrarian mind. The warm regard for agricultural life which Parrington attributed almost wholly to them could have been drawn from any of a score of writers in the ancient tradition of pastoral poetry.[4]

Taken superficially, Parrington's version of intellectual history seems to have been inspired by a kind of Anglophobia that disposed him to accept readily enough the English ancestry of ideas he disliked but caused him to minimize or even deny the English ancestry of ideas he approved. This feeling is charmingly laid bare near the end of his third volume where, discussing the importance of the Progressive attack on the Constitution, he remarks that the myths that had gathered about it were dispelled by the work of J. Allen Smith and Beard, and that "the document was revealed as English

---

[3] I, 346; II, 10.
[4] The supposed influence of the Physiocrats is the subject of my essay, "Parrington and the Jeffersonian Tradition," *Journal of the History of Ideas*, 2 (1941), 391–400; see also the Introduction by Gilbert Chinard to *The Correspondence of Jefferson and Du Pont de Nemours* (1931).

rather than French"—as though this were indeed a revelation, and also the last word in condemnation.[5] A hatred of
Tory England was, of course, a vital part of his family inheritance, and it may have been confirmed by the anti-English
feeling that was commonplace in the Populist movement. Yet
it could be argued that Parrington was at the worst deeply
ambivalent about England and English culture, since his own
debt to the Victorian moralists was considerable and his
response to the country, when he was at last able to visit it,
was one of instant affection. More important than his anti-
English feeling, I suppose, was his partisan dualism, his un-
controllable passion for schematization, and his flimsy
knowledge of the very "sources"—Luther, Rousseau, the Physiocrats—he liked to invoke. But the consequence is unmistakable: a whole series of misleading suggestions in which the
traditions he most wanted to celebrate—the traditions of
early dissent, of Jeffersonian and Jacksonian democracy, and
of secular enlightenment—are desiccated and shorn of even
so much of their true history as might have been recoverable
in the light of the scholarship of Parrington's day. To make
way for Luther, Quesnay, Du Pont, and Rousseau it was
necessary to minimize or ignore America's inheritance from
Coke, Milton, Locke, and Sidney, not to speak of a throng of
lesser writers, now interesting perhaps mainly to specialists
in the history of thought but once of central importance to
American rationalists, revolutionaries, and democrats: those
English Arminians, latitudinarians, Whigs, and radicals who
were the true precursors and shapers of the American mind.

V

In his first two volumes, Parrington's work seems a strong
and clear illustration of the Whig interpretation of history: it
is avowedly partisan, it takes the side of dissenters and protestants against establishments, of democrats against aristocrats, of revolutionaries against old regimes; it seems to be
telling a story of steady progress, pointing toward a certain
satisfaction with the enlightened ideas of the present. But

[5] III, 409.

then, as it reaches and passes the Civil War, its mood changes. The third volume, which one reviewer labeled a study in disillusionment, is afflicted by that awareness of defeat that so often beclouds the agrarian mind. It becomes tainted with a certain wistfulness or melancholy, and yields now and then to a note of pessimism. Here we find Parrington arriving at a common ground with Turner. Both men had the same misgivings, arising from the decline of agrarian America, the disappearance of the frontier and free land, the same fear that American democracy, once separated from its agrarian and particularist base, might be doomed to go down before the machine and the city. On this count a common strain of poignant nostalgia underlies their thought: while they might be able to see the inevitability of industrial culture and the modern state, neither could find it in himself, as Beard could in the 1930's, to embrace modernity in the hope that it would lead to a democratic collectivism; and of course neither lived to the era of the New Deal, which constituted a kind of test case for the agrarian liberal mind.

Parrington shrewdly understood that the liberalism of the Progressive era to which he belonged was "the spontaneous reaction of an America still only half urbanized," and "an attempt to secure through the political state the freedoms that before had come from unpreempted opportunity" on the frontier. He thought about the possibility that his social ideals could be achieved only under socialism, and though I believe that he remained much more the Jeffersonian liberal than the Marxist, he seems to have arrived at a generous, undoctrinaire, ecumenical radicalism which, seeing no enemies on the left, reached out to embrace many varieties of protest that were hospitable in spirit even if not quite congenial in doctrine. There is no doubt that his private sentiments were more radical than his book, and he might have enjoyed the brief burst of radical literary criticism that came after his death. He had a high regard "for critics of the left wing," he wrote in 1928 to a radical critic, "for long ago I learned that they were far more likely than conventional critics to have some insight into *Realpolitik*, and to be able to judge men and programs in the light of underlying principles." To the same correspondent, who had referred to him as "a diluted Marxian," he replied that the remark was "pretty near the truth—at least I was a good deal of a Marxian and perhaps still am, although a growing sense of the complexity of social forces makes me somewhat distrustful of the sufficiency of Marxian formulae." His use of the term liberal in *Main Currents*, he also explained, was a considered one: "I could see no harm and some good in using the term, and warping it pretty well to the left. As a matter of fact, in my first draft I used the word radical throughout, and only on revising did I substitute the other."[6] But his idea of Marxian intellectual filiations was an extremely loose one if one may judge by his belief that the thought of the later Wendell Phillips exemplified "pretty much all of Marxism" and that William Dean Howells was "the first distinguished American man of letters to espouse Marxian socialism."[7]

If Parrington's agrarianism was overlaid with some sympathy for proletarian socialism, it was more surely and profoundly affected by a quite contradictory perennial anti-institutional strain in American thought which verges toward anarchism. In him the old American fear of centralized power, echoed repeatedly in his references to "the coercive state," was very much alive. Characteristic here was his response to Herbert Spencer, whom he had first read in the early 1890's. Seeing in Spencer an intellectual liberator for his secularism and his anticlericalism, Parrington was also attracted, as no Marxist could be, by Spencer's view of state power. In his enthusiasm for the note of anarchism that he found there, a total dislike of governmental authority that accorded with his own feeling about "the coercive state," he found it easy to overlook the less congenial side of Spencer's mind, its laissez-faire complacency and social Darwinism. Always a little indulgent to those conservatives whose views were founded in opposition to state authority, he welcomed the anarchist and nonconformist elements in Spencer, his passion for individual liberty and his faith in progress, and overlooked his hostility to all plans for human welfare. Spencer, he thought, had achieved

---

6 Letter to a confidential source, February 24, 1928; on "half-urbanized" liberalism, III, 404.
7 Parrington seems not to have owned any work of Marx, though he had a full set of the works of William Morris.

"a fresh justification, based on the findings of Victorian science, of the master principles of eighteenth-century speculation; its individualism, its liberalism, its passion for justice, its love of liberty and distrust of every form of coercion," and concluded that Spencer's final deductions were such "as to warrant a disciple of Jefferson in becoming a disciple of Spencer."[8]

His regard for localism and for all who resisted the centralized state accounted in good part for the tenderness with which Parrington, despite his antipathy to slavery, racism, and caste exclusion, treated certain spokesmen of the South. "I was at particular pains," he explained, "to present the doctrine of States' Rights sympathetically, partly because it has had too little recognition and partly because the States' Rights men were the best liberals of the time."[9] Calhoun—whom he struck off splendidly as "a potential intellectual whose mind was unfertilized by contact with a generous social culture"— was too harsh a spirit to win his approval. But he did see much to admire in Calhoun's elaboration of the states-rights doctrine, and found his great mistake to lie in linking its fate to the doomed institution of slavery and so mobilizing against it American idealism and liberalism. "What Calhoun so greatly feared has since come about," he wrote. "He erected a last barrier against the progress of middle-class ideals—consolidation in politics and standardization in society; against a universal cash-register evaluation of life: and the barrier was blown to bits by the guns of the Civil War." For Parrington the truly admirable Southern spokesman was Alexander H. Stephens, a figure many other historians nave found attractive. A gentle, selfless patriot, whose career exemplified "the passionate love of freedom," Stephens was so highly principled, as Parrington read his mind, that he refused to

---

[8] III, 197–201; Arthur A. Ekirch, Jr., sees clearly this side of Parrington in "Parrington and the Decline of American Liberalism," *American Quarterly*, 3 (1951), 295–308.

[9] Eric F. Goldman, "J. Allen Smith," *Pacific Northwest Quarterly*, 35 (1944), 209, quoting a letter to Ross L. Finney, January 23, 1929.

Parrington was also doubtful whether the Constitution could survive the changes that the near future would bring. "My own view is that it will not, and that when the masters of society think the time has come to throw it on the scrap heap they will do it." To Howard Lee McBain, December 18, 1928.

sanction the use of extraconstitutional powers even in the urgent crisis of war. "He was of an earlier generation, instinctively hostile to all consolidation," and even though he failed to understand the economic basis of politics, he was worthy of a characterization which, coming from Parrington, was almost the ultimate accolade: the doctrine upon which his *Constitutional View of the Late War between the States* was based was "the doctrine which Paine and Jefferson derived from the French school, namely, that a constitutional compact is terminable."

Parrington's feeling about the power of government was founded, it must be said, on a lifetime of hard experience during which he had rarely, if ever, seen authority acting in an enlightened, flexible, and humane way. He had moved from his Republican family into the tight little environment of Emporia College, whose windows (as he might have said) were certainly closed against the winds of doctrine, and where everything went on under the encompassing eyes of the Presbyterian Church and Major Hood; from there he had gone first to Harvard, which he found impenetrable, and then to Oklahoma, where he endured the ruthless cabal of the Methodists and political hacks, and finally to Washington, where he saw J. Allen Smith so shabbily treated. Arriving at maturity as a young agrarian in the era of Harrison and Cleveland, and finishing his book in the age of Harding and Coolidge, when the hopes of Progressivism seemed to have been blasted, he had seen little to suggest that somewhere a reliable center of power existed where the needs of the common man were a matter of vital concern. What experience taught him, and what the Jeffersonian tradition instilled, may have been confirmed in more self-conscious philosophical terms by J. Allen Smith, whose distrust of centralized government had led him to conclude by 1923 that "the only way to secure any real democracy in this country is to check the growth of federal power" and that democracy "is possible only where there is the largest practicable measure of local self-government." (On these grounds Smith refused to support a federal child-labor amendment.)[1]

---

[1] Goldman, "J. Allen Smith," 210, 212.

Parrington, E. H. Eby concluded, "feared above all . . . the cancer of power. 'Man,' he used to say, 'has never proved himself worthy of an unrestrained control of his fellows, nor has any special group of men ever been dominant without injustice to others.'" This distrust of state power, which I believe would have made Parrington ultimately resistant to Marxism, made him somewhat skeptical even of the possibilities of Progressivism. He understood that, to achieve their ends, the Progressives needed the power of the state, and also that the cry of states' rights was being used by businessmen to protect themselves against reforms; but he was afraid that the state apparatus was always more likely to be captured by the vested interests than by the people. The centralized state, he wrote to a fellow reformer in the year of his death, was certainly coming, but he was troubled about it: "Wherever power is lodged a great struggle for control and use of that power follows. When one controls the political state, whatever one wants can be done under cover of the law and with the sanction of the courts. Have you been able to convince yourself that the corporate wealth of America will permit the centralized political state to pass out of its control and become an agent to regulate or thwart its principles? The entire history of federalism shows clearly that the business interests of the day desired first, to create a strong state; second, to control that state; and third, to transform it into an agent of a class. . . . You see the dilemma in which I find myself. We must have a political state powerful enough to deal with corporate wealth, but how are we going to keep that state with its augmenting power from being captured by the forces we want it to control? I agree . . . that taxation is a vital problem, but how are we going to tax our masters?"[2]

To such questions Parrington offered no easy optimistic answers. His own economic realism seemed to point to the defeat of his social aspirations. The philosophy of Jefferson and John Taylor, he sadly remarked in his last volume, had

---

[2] Goldman, "J. Allen Smith," 209. Cf. Woodrow Wilson in 1912: "If monopoly persists, monopoly will always sit at the helm of government. I do not expect to see monopoly restrain itself. If there are men in this country big enough to own the government of the United States, they are going to own it." *The New Freedom* (1913), 286.

been "buried in the potter's field," and he was not confident
or dogmatic enough to predict a better turning, though he had
not given up every hope in the liberals and radicals of his
own time. With his love of balance and proportion, his taste
for elegance, his awakened secularism, and his affection for
the ideals of humanitarianism and progress, Parrington belonged intellectually, as he fully realized, to the eighteenth
century. For him the American Enlightenment remained the
high point in national thought, and it was a warm compliment
on his part, if wistfully conceived, to speak of Walt Whitman
as "the afterglow of the Enlightenment"—as though Whitman
represented not a beginning in poetry but a lovely echo in
philosophy. Though he preferred the ebullience of the early
optimistic reformers, he showed a certain gentle sympathy for
the pessimism of men like Melville and Henry and Brooks
Adams, men who, like himself, were caught on some receding
wave of history: courageous, honest, sometimes rebellious
minds who faced with poise the fatality of extinction. Whether
later turnings of American history would have given him any
comfort we cannot know, for he died suddenly during a trip to
England in the summer of 1929. It seems a pity that he should
have been denied some years more to finish his work and enjoy
the fame that had come to him, and it would have been instructive to see him balance his humane ideals against his
distrust of the consolidated state in the era of centralizing
reform that was about to dawn.

PART
V

The Aftermath

CHAPTER 12

Conflict and Consensus in American History

> *Every other enlightened nation of the earth is at this moment divided between great opposing principles; whereas here, if we except the trifling collisions of pecuniary interests, everybody is of the same mind except as to the ordinary immaterial question of a choice between men.*
> —James Fenimore Cooper, 1828

> *There was strife—bitter, persistent strife—almost everywhere. . . . What was the cause of the malaise? Why was the surface of public life so brittle?*
> —Bernard Bailyn on "The Origin of American Politics," 1967

I

THE PIVOTAL idea of the Progressive historians was economic and political conflict. Since conflict is a universal presence in history, they were hardly the first to discover it. But Turner began, in a somewhat ambiguous form, to give an unaccustomed emphasis to conflict and to put it to new kinds of uses; what he began was carried out more wholeheartedly by Beard and Parrington, and was taken up between 1910 and 1950 by a generation of historians who applied it to every area of American history. "We may trace the contest between the capitalist and the democratic pioneer from the earliest colonial days," Turner asserted in his presidential address to the American Historical Association, and Beard seized upon this statement as the epigraph for his *Economic Origins of Jeffersonian Democracy* and expounded its implications in *The Rise of American Civilization*. The cast of characters might vary slightly, the image or the definition of the capitalist and the democratic pioneer might shift somewhat from one historical age to another, but in essentials the plot

437

remained the same. Parrington summed it up in a passage written for but never used in his *Main Currents*: "From the first we have been divided into two main parties. Names and battle cries and strategies have often changed repeatedly, but the broad party division has remained. On one side has been the party of the current aristocracy—of church, of gentry, of merchant, of slave holder, or manufacturer—and on the other the party of the commonalty—of farmer, villager, small tradesman, mechanic, proletariat. The one has persistently sought to check and limit the popular power, to keep the control of the government in the hands of the few in order to serve special interests, whereas the other has sought to augment the popular power, to make government more responsive to the will of the majority, to further the democratic rather than the republican ideal—let one discover this and new light is shed on our cultural tendencies." One thinks here too of the most succinct and famous expression of this theme in our modern literature—John Dos Passos's "All right we are two nations."

Somewhere around 1950 the tide began to run out for this view of our history, and conflict as a vitalizing idea began to be contested by the notion of a pervasive American consensus. Probably the last distinguished historical studies to be written squarely in the Progressive tradition were Arthur Schlesinger, Jr.'s, *The Age of Jackson* (1945), which portrayed the main issues of the Jackson period as the result of conflict between the business community and the rest of the community, and Merrill Jensen's inquiry into the Confederation period, *The New Nation* (1950), which restated the view, familiar to readers of Beard and Becker, that this era should be seen as a contest between two persistent political forces that could be labeled radical and conservative.

In part the swing away from conflict history was a response to a new political environment, and a new intellectual mood. The collapse of Europe, the horrors of the war and the death camps, brought about a revulsion from European society and politics, a disposition to look once again for the promise of the future on native grounds, a revival of the old feeling that the United States is better and different. But even Europe, as the war began to recede into memory, looked different, less subject to ideological polarization than it had been in the prewar period. The cold war brought a certain closing of the ranks, a disposition to stress common objectives, a revulsion from Marxism and its tendency to think of social conflict as carried *à outrance*. The apocalyptic end of capitalism so widely expected during the 1930's had not been brought by the war—nor had the precipitate end of American democracy the isolationists had so confidently predicted. Instead of the expected catastrophic depression, an unprecedented economic boom followed the war, and the star of Keynes rose as that of Marx waned. Even the bomb, the most disquieting reality of the era, set in motion a current of conservatism, insofar as it made men think of political change with a new wariness and cling to what they had. The outburst of McCarthyism, instead of provoking a radical response, aroused in some intellectuals more distaste than they had ever thought they would feel for popular passions and anti-establishment demagogy. The populism of the right inspired a new skepticism about the older populism of the left. While Daniel Bell was writing about the end of ideology in the West, historians were returning to the idea that in the United States it had hardly ever begun.[1]

But the change in the historical mood was not simply a response to the new political environment. Ideas have an inner dialectic of their own. The Progressive historians and the generation of historical specialists that worked under their inspiration had pushed polarized conflict as a principle of historical interpretation so far that one could go no further in that direction without risking self-caricature. The pendulum had to swing in the opposite direction: if we were to have any new insight into American history, it began to appear that we had to circumvent the emphasis on conflict and look at the American past from another angle.

---

[1] On the postwar international political situation, see Raymond Aron, "Nations and Ideologies," *Encounter*, 4 (1955), 24–33; Daniel Bell, "The End of Ideology in the West," in *The End of Ideology: On The Exhaustion of Political Ideas in the Fifties* (1960), 369–75; for the disposition of literary intellectuals at the same time to reconsider their most extreme moods of alienation, see the *Partisan Review*'s symposium, "Our Country and Our Culture," separately published as *America and the Intellectuals* (1953).

Once the swing away from Progressive historical thought had begun, it went on with startling rapidity. As early as 1959, John Higham complained of a "cult" of consensus whose devotees were homogenizing American history. Consensus history, as Higham saw, marked a return to the insights of Tocqueville, a reversion to his interest in American uniqueness, to a concern with the absence of polarized class conflict and of correspondingly deep ideological differences. Tocqueville had seen the distinctiveness of the American character and social system as stemming from the absence of a feudal heritage. As he saw it, the recruitment of the population from dissenters and radicals and other circumstances of national development had assured a democratic condition from the beginning: hence there was no need in America for a democratic revolution, with the lasting hostilities or the grand ideological systems that such a revolution sets in motion. There was only a gradual (and, Tocqueville thought, Providential) unfolding of the pristine democratic condition. Equality of condition among Americans became increasingly prevalent in a distinctively democratic society, stamped with an undeniable mediocrity of culture, but also with widespread affluence and orderly ways.

The uneasy concern Higham expressed with the prevalence of consensus history was a reaction to efforts, particularly by Louis Hartz and Daniel Boorstin, to generalize the consensus idea, to give it the positive status of a theory of American history. But the main strength of the idea, considered as a reaction to the legacy of the Progressive historians, came not so much from their works as from a whole series of concurrent special studies that broke sharply with the Progressives' patterns of interpretation.[2] These studies, I believe, may be regarded as a related and convergent but quite independent development. Their authors chipped away at various parts of Progressive history, while writers like Hartz and Boorstin were simultaneously trying to write more general works that would suggest how a new version of our history might look.

---

[2] For the leading works see the Bibliographical Essay.

The decade and a half that followed 1950 was extraordinarily rich in revisionist historical writing. Historians roamed up and down the whole range of American history, and made one lightning foray after another upon preserves that had been assumed to be quite firmly staked out for the older views. I have already discussed the assaults on Beard's view of the Constitution. A simultaneous and almost equally effective campaign was staged against related views of the Revolution that had been developed by Progressive historians. The idea that an internal class conflict was a central force in the Revolution was now seriously questioned; the prevalence of a widely available suffrage was conclusively demonstrated and the demand for "democracy" on the part of the underprivileged minimized; the existence of a profound and consistent division between "radicals" and "conservatives" throughout the period was riddled with criticism. Finally, one of the basic tenets of Progressive writers, the notion that political and constitutional ideas were merely opportunistic improvisations masking fundamental economic interests, was shown to be a rather superficial and almost philistine version of the actual subtle relation among ideas, interests, and attitudes.

At the same time new writers on Jacksonian democracy found many flaws in the views that had held sway for a generation. The Progressive notion of Jacksonian democracy as a national democratic uprising was coolly shattered by voting studies, and the idea of Jacksonian democracy as a farmer-labor coalition became less and less plausible, as the entrepreneurial backgrounds and ideas of some of the "labor" spokesmen and the behavior of the labor constituency were examined. A better understanding of the fresh entrepreneurial forces behind Jacksonian "radicalism" required a new view, and a more critical one, of the Jacksonian assault on central banking. Serious studies of Jacksonian rhetoric and symbolism opened up new ways of understanding the inner tensions between the old republicanism of early America and the entrepreneurial passions of this age of economic growth and speculative investment. Quantitative studies pointed to the importance of religious, ethnic and cultural factors, as well as social class, in the party alignments. The Progressive tendency to think of a homogeneous capitalist class or "business community" also came under fire when the view of Reconstruction that had been formulated by Charles A. Beard and Howard K. Beale was re-examined. The Progressive historians had thought of Radical Reconstruction as the result of efforts by a more or less homogeneous capitalist class, a kind of power elite, to use the Radical Republicans to enact a business program and to forsake the social idealism of the earlier Republican movement. Several new studies found a far from homogeneous capitalist class pursuing divergent policies and divided over support of the Radicals. And as the unity and power of the leading capitalists was somewhat minimized, other factors in the situation—the importance of party goals and imperatives, the persistence of abolitionist idealism, the survival of wartime passions, the role of inherited ideas and sentiments—became once again an important part of the story. Again, as one moved on closer to the present, Populism and Progressivism too began to seem more complex than they had to the older generation of historians. Once more, American radicalism seemed to have a pronounced entrepreneurial base; social struggles were marked by broad coalitions of shifting interests rather than by the persistence of a simple polarized division; and sociological, ethnic, and cultural forces were recognized as indispensable to a full understanding of events.

If there is a single way of characterizing what has happened in our historical writing since the 1950's, it must be, I believe, the rediscovery of complexity in American history: an engaging and moving simplicity, accessible to the casual reader of history, has given way to a new awareness of the multiplicity of forces. To those who find things most interesting when they are simple, American history must have come to seem less interesting in our time; but to those who relish complexity, it has taken on a new fascination. When we look at the diffuseness of what has taken their place, we may appreciate once again the allure of the Progressive schematizations, but we can hardly continue to believe in them. The Progressive scheme of polarized conflict has been replaced by a pluralistic vision in which more factors are seriously taken into account. To a degree, the direct impact of economic forces has in some cases been downgraded; but I do not think that the force of the new historical writing lies primarily here. Indeed, had the Progressive historians been saying nothing more than that economic forces were somewhat underestimated, they could be said to have won the day, for few historians now are likely to repeat that neglect of material factors that sometimes characterized their predecessors. What is distinctively new is that ideas and attitudes as forces in history have returned and are now being explored as explanatory categories in a novel way. The old Progressive antinomy between ideas and interests, between appearances and reality, has been dissolved; and what has begun to appear in its place is an ability to recapture the meaning of ideas in history by seeing how they function in their pragmatic institutional settings and by following their course of development in periods of social change. An excellent illustration of this is in the recent work of Bernard Bailyn in plotting out the way in which ideas and attitudes must be taken into consideration if we are to hope to understand the background and the effects of the American Revolution.

What recent historical writers have done is to find the significance of new subjects—new not in the sense that no one had ever touched upon them before, but that they had had either to be excluded or made merely incidental in the histories both of the Progressive historians and their predecessors because these subjects did not fit their conceptual schemes, or because the methods required to write about them significantly had not yet been devised. The whole religious, ethnic, and racial complex of American life has been re-examined—not in isolation, but as an integral part of political life. Immigration, acculturation, nativism, race, slavery, mobility, status tensions—in short, the entire sociological penumbra of political life—has become an organic part of historical thinking. Much of this is the result of ideas and methods that have come from outside the historical discipline proper. Both Freudianism and the sociology of knowledge have made historians more aware of the emotional and symbolic aspects of behavior. Functional analysis in sociology, especially as made accessible in the work of

Robert K. Merton, has had a marked impact on the minds of many of the younger historians. Even so specialized a development as the public-opinion poll has caused some historians to reconsider much of what they have said about mass political behavior in the past. The incursion of quantitative methods, though still low in yield of new interpretations as compared with the energy and resources that have been put into it, at least provides more severe ways of testing old generalizations, and has resulted in turning attention to fresh problems. Very little of this work has been made accessible to the general intellectual reading public, partly because the new history has not produced a central symbolic idea comparable to Turner's on the frontier or a readable synthesis comparable to *The Rise of American Civilization* or *Main Currents in American Thought.* But it has unmistakably toppled the classic works of the Progressive tradition and has released both the speculative capacity and the research energies of a generation of first-rate professionals.

II

The remarkable monographic uprising of the 1950's had hardly started before a few prescient writers began to try to provide a generalized theoretical framework for what they sensed would be a new episode in historical awareness. The work of the two leading consensus theorists, Louis Hartz and Daniel Boorstin, though not presumably a source of the specialized studies I have mentioned, represented a parallel development, a transitional effort to find a new comprehensive meaning in American history.[3] New, and in a sense

---

[3] I must warn unsuspecting readers that in discussing the so-called consensus school I am discussing a tendency with which my own work has often been associated. I suppose the first statement, however brief and inarticulate, of the consensus idea in this period was in the Introduction to my book *The American Political Tradition* (1948), and it is developed fragmentarily in other writings, not least in some of my comments on Beard above in chapters 6 and 7. However, I have resolved not to discuss my own work in these pages; and I hope my present attitude toward consensus history is clarified here, so far as an essentially ambivalent attitude can be said to be clarified. I trust it will be clear that while I still find use for insights derived from consensus history, it no longer seems as satisfactory to me as it did ten or twenty years ago.

old: both writers consciously reverted to Tocqueville's sense of the ineluctable singularity of American development, his stress on the preformed character of our democratic institutions, the importance of the democratic revolution that never had to happen. In both, the old question, Why is there no socialism in America?, is translated into an even more inclusive question: Why is there no political theory in America? Their works are distinctively books of the postwar era, works which could not have been written in the 1930's when Americans were still absorbed in their domestic conflicts and when the preconceptions of Progressive historical writing were still persuasive. The efforts of Hartz in *The Liberal Tradition in America* (1955) and Boorstin in *The Genius of American Politics* (1953) come from the search for a usable past consistent with the sense of the world brought by the war, and responsive to the problems of foreign policy in the early phases of the cold war. Boorstin is primarily concerned to affirm the unexportability of American ways. Since America has no political theory, he argues, no philosophy of democracy, she has none to purvey to the world. Her very uniqueness makes it folly to imagine that she can expect others to adopt her practices. Hence there is a grave danger in trying to impose them on the world or to compete with the Russians in the realm of ideology. We must find a way of "defending our institutions without insisting on propagating them. . . . We must refuse to become crusaders for conservatism in order to conserve the institutions which have made America great." Hartz, perceiving also that Americans must not define world issues in terms of their own special experience, puts the question differently, but gives the same answer: whether or not America has anything to "export," he argues, it is certainly not the right thing. With Boorstin he goes back to an old idea about America's mission: it is her part to influence the world, if she can, not by proselytizing, nor by arms or money, but by the force of example. As the quintessentially liberal nation, the United States, if it learns to understand itself and others adequately, can act only as the world's liberal model: "Russian development," Hartz writes, "has turned its back on the Western concept of personality while American development, even in its provincialism, rests still on that concept. . . . The hope for a free world surely lies in the power for transcending itself inherent in American liberalism."[4]

Hartz's *The Liberal Tradition in America* (1955) is perhaps the most important attempt to generalize the implications of the idea of an American consensus. America, he finds, was always a liberal community; it never had to fight the historic opponents of liberalism. Tocqueville was right: lacking a feudal past, America was "born free," and needed no democratic revolution to become democratic. The American Revolution itself was a colonial revolution only, marked by an astonishing traditionalism and legalism in its leading ideas. The basically liberal-bourgeois ideas of Europe had been transported to America and here were given (on this count Turner too was right) an exceptionally open environment in which to develop virtually unopposed. In the absence of feudal reactionary traditions and feudal patterns of dominance and submission, the principles of bourgeois liberalism, as embodied in the intellectual heritage of Locke, enjoyed here an almost exclusive control of the spectrum of political belief. Absorbed in constitutionalism, America developed, in place of a class of political thinkers, a class of argumentative lawyers. Lacking the opposition of feudal classes, American bourgeois thought never had to develop a keen militant spirit to match its self-confident rhetoric; hence, in contrast to the European bourgeoisie, it had no corresponding militancy to communicate to the working class. The working class, so little affected by the dreams of socialism, became preoccupied with individualistic opportunity and advancement, not with class solidarity and class struggle. In the nation's formative years, virtually everyone, even the nascent industrial proletarian, had "the mentality of an independent entrepreneur."[5] Politics too was different for American work-

---

4 Boorstin, *The Genius of American Politics* (1953), 189; cf. 4, 184–7. Hartz, *The Liberal Tradition in America* (1955), 305, 309. "It is the battle against the Communist revolution in its current phase which has brought to the fore the peculiar orientations of a nation 'born free.'" Ibid., 304–5.
5 *The Liberal Tradition in America*, 89; quotations in the following paragraphs are from pages 78, 91, 101, 250.
Hartz's emphasis on freedom as a theme in Tocqueville is some-

ers. In England and on the Continent the working class had to fight its way into the political community; here universal manhood suffrage was achieved *before* there was a significantly numerous proletariat.

Without an important socialist tradition, the main American critique of capitalism was shaped by the agrarian tradition, as articulated first by Jefferson and John Taylor; but this was only the complaint of profit-making agriculture against opposing interests, a defense of the capitalist farmer against other capitalists. Despite interesting deviants like George Fitzhugh, strong aristocratic opposition to the bourgeoisie and true programmatic or intellectual alternatives were also absent, for there was no class of ruling grandees with a history of privilege before the law, no military or clerical allies of the aristocracy, no magnificent patrons of high culture and systematic thought. In American history we find only a class of frustrated aristocrats, exercising little influence and no independent power.

With so many elements of the European struggle missing, Americans delude themselves when they try to underline the acerbity of their class conflicts. Americans in the Whig tradition might imagine themselves to be classic conservatives, just as Americans in the agrarian tradition might fancy themselves to be radical critics of capitalist ways. But when the political spectrum is laid out against the spectra of European countries, it can be seen in its naked brevity, its simplicity, its lack of range. All American thinking, except for a brief, luminous, creative, but basically deluded reactionary episode arising out of the proslavery argument, is huddled around the Lockean center. The liberal community develops practically nothing but liberal thought; its differences, intellectually speaking, are largely fabrications. The Progressive historians have been comically credulous in taking them so seriously: "The Progressive historians, working with the concept of social revolt, fortified with a mass of erudition all the misunderstandings the average American in the midst

what different from Tocqueville's own. Tocqueville was impressed by equality rather than freedom as an American attribute. See, for example, *Democracy in America*, Part II, Book II, chapter i, and *passim*.

of 'Americanism' had about himself. They discovered a genuine American 'revolution,' they unearthed a 'class conflict' between 'agrarian and capitalist,' they forgot the Southern reaction, and made the rise of American democracy practically impossible to understand." "Our progressive historians," Hartz adds in one of his striking sentences, ". . . have not produced a study of American thought: they have produced a replica of it."

The influence of Hartz's book reflects the importance, indeed the classic centrality, of his ideas. His development of his theme is witty and often aphoristic, yet heavily allusive, repetitive, and somewhat overargued. Since he reminds us that we can hardly know the uniqueness of anything without the relevant comparisons, his book is in fact an elaborate and closely textured contrast between American and European political thought. His method keeps us constantly in mind of possible American cognates of European thinkers whose significance lies in the fact that we cannot find them. "Jackson," he tells us in a characteristic sentence, "was not another edition of Flocon, Jefferson another version of Ledru-Rollin." In discussing the limits of the Shays rebellion, he writes: "Indeed what American liberalism offers Shays is a fixed acceptance of Locke deeply antagonistic to anything like the vision of Babeuf and Maréchal." When we read a sentence like this we know at once that we are not being asked to consider what Shays was actually thinking about, but that we are reading a kind of historical shorthand, in which the possibilities and nonpossibilities of the American political order are being demarcated by reference to the *missing* schemes of thought. It is a highly rationalist and intellectual approach to the ways of a nonintellectual people.

If Hartz, loosely speaking, represents the intellectual wing of consensus history, Daniel Boorstin, in *The Genius of American Politics* and later works, represents its anti-intellectualist wing, and in this respect is perhaps more characteristically American. Whereas Hartz, with his easy and knowing allusions to European political thinkers of the second and third rank whom most of us have never read and have not, in some cases, even heard of, seems like some splendid exotic bird, cruelly forced to live on the coarse and indigestible flora of America, Boorstin is the American eagle himself, flourishing in his proper habitat. In Hartz one often detects a note of exasperation with the false consciousness of American thinkers, with their failure to recognize their common Lockean bonds, above all with the sparse intellectual diet they provide. Where he asks us to understand, as a condition of knowing America, the limitations of American political thought, Boorstin asks us not only to understand but to celebrate them.

Boorstin's work is reminiscent of Turner's—not, of course, of Turner's struggle between frontiersmen and capitalists, but of his quest for the fountainhead of American uniqueness. In Boorstin the frontier becomes a source not of agrarian conflict but of American conservatism. Since he never assigns so exclusive a significance to the frontier, he does not share Turner's worries about the drying up of the distinctive resources of the American system. American values, as he reads them, are too deeply rooted: they *precede* the frontier process, and hence are not altogether dependent upon it. Boorstin scrupulously observes that the distinctive genius of American democracy "comes not from any special virtue of the American people but from the unprecedented opportunities of this continent and from a peculiar and unrepeatable combination of circumstances." It is these circumstances that have given an indelible stamp to American institutions, for whose wisdom, in true Burkean spirit, Boorstin advises Americans to have a proper regard. This wisdom teaches that values emerge out of experience, not out of philosophy: "We do not need American philosophers because we already have an American philosophy, implicit in the American Way of Life." A deep current of feeling runs through American life which protects Americans from the excessive and dangerous demands of individual genius and heady ideas; it is seen in "the difference between Washington and Napoleon; between Roosevelt, Truman, and Eisenhower on the one hand and garret-spawned illuminati like Lenin, Mussolini, and Hitler." Americans are right in not being willing to pay the price demanded by high cultural achievement: "The European concept of culture is basically aristocratic. . . . European culture, most of it at least, is the heritage of a pre-liberal past. For all their magnificence, the monuments of that past are products of a culture with which we, fortunately, are in no position to compete. It is surely no accident that we have accomplished relatively little in the arts of painting, sculpture, palace and church architecture, chamber music, and chamber poetry. It is equally no accident that we have contributed so little in political philosophy."[6]

III

"It may seem strange," a foreign observer has suggested, "that American historians should be moved to take sides over the very question of whether there are any sides to take."[7] Even after fifteen years the controversial hyperbole that so often comes with a new idea has not entirely disappeared. A few of the embattled younger historians still seem to imagine that they are being asked to see the American past as stripped of all significant conflict and to accept a historical rationale for political tameness or passivity by denying the reality of past and present issues.[8]

It is indeed true that consensus history arose at a moment of conservative retrospect in our national history, and that such a moment was more conducive than periods

---

6 *The Genius of American Politics*, 162, 163–65, 184; *The Americans: The Colonial Experience* (1958), 154.

It is always a delicate question how much emphasis to put on American uniqueness. "The colonies," Boorstin writes, "were a disproving ground for utopias." (*Ibid.*, 1) This seems to me incontestable, but I would have thought the same could be said about most of human history.

7 J. R. Pole, "The American Past, Is It Still Usable?" *Journal of American Studies*, 1 (1967), 77.

8 I should perhaps point out that historians were debating consensus history some years before Lyndon B. Johnson's methods began to be referred to as consensus politics, and almost all historians have avoided confusing the historical issue with the question of Johnson's politics. It would indeed have been fatal if this matter had had to bear the burden of Johnson's reputation among the intellectuals. The extent to which Johnson's approach to consensus departs from the American pattern is illuminatingly discussed by David S. Broder, "Consensus Politics: End of an Experiment," *Atlantic*, 218 (1966), 60–5; see also the critique by Hans J. Morgenthau, "Where Consensus Breaks Down," *New Republic*, 154 (January 22, 1966), 16–18.

of political radicalism to a reconsideration of Progressive
history. It is also true that there are moments in consensus
writing that seem to warrant the suspicions of radical
historians. For example, when Daniel Boorstin asks us to
regard with what seems to many of us an excessive satisfaction, the pragmatic mindlessness that he finds characteristic of American society, or when he asks us all too
baldly to celebrate "the marvelous success and vitality of
our institutions," we begin to feel a twinge of that irritation with the consensus idea that John Higham gave vent
to some years ago. But if the essentially political revulsion
from consensus history has some warrant, it is still no
more than a marginal consideration. In any case, it rests
upon certain intellectual confusions. It is always possible,
but not, I think, desirable, to find too simple an identification between past and present problems—a conclusion to
which Charles Beard's book on the Constitution stands as
permanent testimony. To take a strong stand for Negro
rights today, for example, it is not necessary to find a long
history of effective slave rebellions; to be deeply concerned
over the problem of poverty, it is not necessary to show either
that we have degenerated from an idyllic past or, for that
matter, that poverty in the past was much worse than we
ever imagined it. Again, it is a mistake to assume that the
consensus idea is intrinsically a *prescriptive* one which com-
mits us to this or that particular arrangement. It is a part
of the *descriptive* task of the historian or political scientist
to find and account for the elements of consensus in any
situation, but he is not required to endorse what he
finds. He may analyze society in functional terms, but this
does not require him to assume that no arrangements are
dysfunctional. If the matter is seen this way, I believe it
will be understood that the idea of consensus is not intrinsically linked to ideological conservatism. In its origins I
believe it owed almost as much to Marx as to Tocqueville,
and I find it hard to believe that any realistic Marxist historian could fail to be struck at many points by the
pervasively liberal-bourgeois character of American society
in the past. Many aspects of our history, indeed, seem to
yield to a "left" consensus interpretation, and some radical

historians have in fact begun to see it that way. Presumably, insofar as the idea of consensus has permanent validity, it will be detachable from any particular political tendency and will prove to be usable from more than one point of view.[9]

Finally, I see little point in denying that, for all its limitations, consensus as a general view of American history had certain distinct, if transitional merits. Coming when it did, it was an indispensable corrective force as well as an insight of much positive value. To the degree that the consensus school returned to the Turnerian theme of American uniqueness, it began to confront the problem Turner glimpsed but did not really try to cope with, the task of getting this theme into its necessary comparative frame. Above all, the consensus historians rediscovered the differentness of our history, reasserted a regard for its niceties after it had undergone too many simplifications, saw its continuities after its discontinuities had been grossly exaggerated, returned to an understanding of its pragmatic and pluralistic character, and forced us to think about the importance of those things Americans did not have to argue about.

Once all this has been granted, I think the important ground on which consensus as a general theory of American history should be quarreled with is not its supposed political implications but its intrinsic limitations *as history*. Having come into being as a corrective, the idea of consensus as an interpretative principle has the status of an essentially negative proposition. It demarcates some of the limits of conflict in American history, and underlines some other difficulties in the historical legacy of the Progressives, but as a positive principle it does not go very far. As J. R. Pole

---

[9] Irwin Unger has pointed out that some of the New Left historians have made use of the notion. "The 'New Left' and American History," *American Historical Review*, 72 (1967), 1251–3. My own assertion of consensus history in 1948 had its sources in the Marxism of the 1930's. Political struggles, as manifested in the major parties, I argued, had "always been bounded by the horizons of property and enterprise. . . . American traditions . . . show a strong bias in favor of equalitarian democracy, but it has been a democracy in cupidity rather than a democracy of fraternity." *The American Political Tradition*, viii.

has put it, "The idea of consensus was useful as a direction-finder. It is not an explanation."[1] It has somewhat the same relation to historical writing as an appropriate frame has to a painting: it sets the boundaries of the scene and enables us to see where the picture breaks off and the alien environment begins; but it does not provide the foreground or the action, the interest or the pleasure, the consummation itself, whether analytical or esthetic. It has been developed as a counter-assertion more than as an empirical tool. Sociologists and political scientists have also been interested in the phenomenon of consensus, and it is instructive to see how they approach it.[2] They have asked such down-to-earth questions as: How much agreement is required for an effective consensus? Whose participation in a consensus really counts? Who is excluded from the consensus? Who refuses to enter it? To what extent are the alleged consensual ideas of the American system—its preconceptions, for instance, about basic political rights—actually shared by the mass public? (So far as the masses are concerned, what we call consensus is often little more than apathy.) Their questions and their answers are, of course, mainly contemporary, and they have the advantage of opinion poll data as well as the usual descriptive apparatus of the historian. But they raise some interesting questions about the past: they are acutely aware of the complex texture of apathy and irrationality that holds a political society together, and they help us to realize how incidental for many purposes are explicitly formulated theoretical commitments.

Consensus is certainly an idea of some uses, but it will

---

[1] Pole, "The American Past," 75.

[2] See, for example, V. O. Key, *Public Opinion and American Democracy* (1961), Part I, and Herbert McCloskey, "Consensus and Ideology in American Politics," *American Political Science Review*, 58 (1964), 361–82. Among sociologists a difference over conflict and consensus also became a major problem of the 1950's. Much of the sociological work of the postwar years was dominated by the functionalism of Talcott Parsons and Robert K. Merton, which was disposed to stress the role of values in integrating society and to use consensus as an explanatory principle. This was questioned by Lewis Coser, who emphasized the functional character of conflict in social change and later by Ralf Dahrendorf. For relevant items see the Bibliographical Essay.

be more fruitful when it is taken not as a satisfactory general theory or as an answer but as a whole set of new questions about the extent to which agreement prevails in a society, who in fact takes part in it, and how it is arrived at. We can distinguish, for example, the constitutional consensus which exists when an effectively overwhelming majority of the politically active public accepts the legitimacy of the legal-constitutional order in which it finds itself. One can also speak of a policy consensus, which exists when an issue moves, at least for a time and perhaps permanently, out of the area of significant controversy. Americans now of middle age can remember how social security passed in no more than twenty years from the status of an almost visionary social reform to a controversial issue, and then to an established consensual position.

Finally, there is a subtler, more intangible, but vital kind of moral consensus that I would call comity. Comity exists in a society to the degree that those enlisted in its contending interests have a basic minimal regard for each other: one party or interest seeks the defeat of an opposing interest on matters of policy, but at the same time seeks to avoid crushing the opposition, denying the legitimacy of its existence or its values, or inflicting upon it extreme and gratuitous humiliations beyond the substance of the gains that are being sought. The basic humanity of the opposition is not forgotten; civility is not abandoned; the sense that a community life must be carried on after the acerbic issues of the moment have been fought over and won is seldom very far out of mind; an awareness that the opposition will some day be the government is always present. The reality and the value of comity can best be appreciated when we contemplate a society in which it is almost completely lacking—for example Spanish political culture on the eve of the civil war of the 1930's as we find it portrayed in the opening chapters of Hugh Thomas's brilliant history, *The Spanish Civil War*. In Spain the center dwindled and fell apart, and the extremes were occupied by reactionaries, lay and clerical, and radicals or nihilists with burning anti-clerical passions; neither side had more than the faintest residual sense of the humanity of the other. Where Spain might be taken as the example of a society that failed to de-velope comity, the Weimar Republic is a case history of its gradual, but accelerating, breakdown.

The waxing and waning phases of comity shed consider-able light on American history. The period of the Revolution, which drove out or silenced Americans of Loyalist persuasion and united most politically active Americans in a common cause, brought about a high measure of comity that was of great value in helping them surmount the difficult prob-lems of political organization and real antagonisms of in-terest. Even the debates over the Constitution, sharp though they were, did not destroy it. But during the 1790's the political leaders, prodded by their particularist passions, groping uncertainly and not always successfully toward the still ill-formulated principle of legitimate opposition, and embroiled to a remarkable degree in the material and ideological issues arising out of the French Revolution and the ensuing war, entered upon a brief period of violent political emotion in which comity dwindled and a disruption of the Union seemed possible. Having once survived it, they made their way slowly out of this situation, and the period during which the second American party system grew and flourished was one of predominant comity, in which the gift for conciliation became highly developed. The story of the 1850's, however, is one of the steady dissipation of comity, climaxed by the coming of the Civil War. Not all groups were equally or fully included in the system. Catholics felt themselves to be outsiders, and won acceptance only very slowly and by degrees. The so-called new immigrants during the period of post-Civil War industrialization were in the same position, and finally found their incorporation in the system of comity only in the twentieth century. Negroes have never been given a real part in the covenant of comity. A great deal of the severity of our present crisis arises from the fact that they have not been able to fight or bargain their way in, and they have learned to find their exclusion intolerable.

IV

The efforts of Professors Hartz and Boorstin to generalize the consensus principle and raise it to the level of a theory may give us some cues as to where to depart from it. Hartz's book suffers from reducing its account of American development largely to questions of political thought, at the very time that he proclaims that political thought in this country has never amounted to much. Though he is right again and again in his learned comparative observations about the elements that are missing from the American scene, he cannot, with this device, get around to telling us quite enough about what is there. Again, despite all his sound warnings not to take American thinkers too seriously, and certainly not at their face value, he seems disposed at points, just because the categories of political theory are so central for him, to take their thought a bit too seriously himself; he defines sets of ideas which might best be understood when keyed closely to specific American controversies, and to the party structures and *their* institutional imperatives, as though these ideas were sustained and animated intellectual entities in their own right. Hence his reification, for example, of Whiggery and of Lockeanism.[3] One misses, again, in a book that deals with what is uniquely American, two of our vital unique characteristics: our peculiar variant of federalism and our two-party system. Without a focus on federalism, we are tempted to downgrade unduly the fierceness of the parochial and particularist feelings that went into many of our political conflicts. Without the parties, we not only downgrade the inventiveness of the American political system—for we were the pioneers in the development of the modern popular party and of the system of two-party opposition—but we miss the chance to see how conflict was both channeled and blunted in American history. Finally, while Hartz has been careful to remind us that the liberal community did not eliminate conflict, we may still ask whether, using his canons, we can explain or

---

[3] See on this account the comments of Eric L. McKitrick, "Is There an American Political Philosophy?" *New Republic*, 132 (April 11, 1955), 22–5.

give an adequate account of those conflicts that did take place. Certainly the gravity of political conflicts cannot be measured by the extent to which they do or do not give rise to systematic political theory. Consensus, to be effective, must be a matter of behavior as well as thought, of institutions as well as theories.

While Boorstin's work, insofar as its argument resembles Hartz's, is afflicted with the same difficulties, it is to him that we owe such an extended use of consensus as an overarching explanatory principle that we can say that its limits have already been quite substantially explored. Where he is most successful in the two volumes of *The Americans* which we thus far have, it is chiefly as a social historian writing about selected aspects of our social life in which conflict is not uppermost. He has an exceptional gift for discerning in the variegated aspects of life a distinctive American style, for explicating the significance of American pluralism and the American pragmatic cast of mind. Where he most typically fails is in dealing with the fundamental problems of American political culture with which he began. He is highly suggestive, for example, on American military technique in the Revolutionary era, but leaves much to be desired in dealing with the origins and character of the American Revolution. He is so intensely set on minimizing the effects of ideas in history (Beard, in contrast, seems an almost pure idealist) that he becomes decisively misleading when he deals with classes of men among whom ideas were passionately held, like the Puritans, or among whom they were also most seriously and effectively consulted and used, like the Founding Fathers. As his work has progressed, he has turned his back on the basic problems of political conflict in our history, and often of social conflict as well. *The Americans: The National Experience,* for example, does not even mention the war over the Bank of the United States,[4] or many other controversial episodes and movements, though it continues to be entertaining and illuminating on such subjects as Frederic Tudor, the "Ice King," who discovered the usability and marketability of ice, or on

---

[4] Andrew Jackson appears in this book chiefly as a notorious duelist and as a symbol of American boosterism; Nicholas Biddle appears briefly as a promoter of hotels.

granite quarrying, or the balloon frame house, or the organization of the early factory, or what he prefers to call "the Know-how Revolution." However, in following such concerns Boorstin has not resolved the problem of conflict, he has simply abandoned it.

One of the greatest difficulties that confront the interpretative historian is that he must not just steer clear of ideas that seem false but must refrain from overextending those that are true. There is nothing in the idea of consensus, to be sure, which requires that we deny the reality of conflict, and Hartz himself has been careful to say that "the argument over whether we should 'stress' solidarity or conflict misleads us by advancing a false set of alternatives."[5] Yet I think it is a valid comment on the limits of consensus history to insist that in one form or another conflict finally does remain, and ought to remain, somewhere near the center of our focus of attention. Our attention to conflict is not just a requirement of the drama of all truly interesting history—that is to say, a requirement of historical esthetics—but also a necessity of historical knowledge. History deals with change, and in change conflict is a necessary, and indeed a functional, ingredient. It is one thing to say that a school of historians has overstressed a certain type of conflict or has misconceived social alignments, but another to write conflictless history. Americans, it is true, have not had to debate in any very serious way the merits of popular government or private property, or the grand systems of European political theorists. But they have had a steady diet of major political controversy, and we do not have to look very hard to find conflict in our history. The American nation was born in an age of almost constant stress and crisis that lasted from 1763 to 1788, during which its people experienced a dozen years of agitation over imperial policies, several more years of warfare and harassment, and during this time were stirred by intense debates over new state constitutions and two new federal constitutions. Afterward, about once in each generation they endured a crisis of real and troubling severity. The

---

Union was in some danger of division during 1798–1801; it was in serious trouble during the years 1807–14 and again in 1832. It was racked by such grave differences in the 1850's that it finally broke in two. It went through a touchy crisis again in Reconstruction, climaxed by the events of 1876–7. It was deeply disturbed in the 1890's and again in the 1930's. And now, in the 1960's, it is in the midst of a dangerous major crisis the outcome of which I hesitate to try to predict. Surely these episodes evoke a record of significant conflict to which we cannot expect to do justice if we write our history in terms of the question whether or not Americans were disagreeing with John Locke.

There are three major areas in which a history of the United States organized around the guiding idea of consensus breaks down: first, I believe it cannot do justice to the genuinely revolutionary aspects of the American Revolution; second, it is quite helpless and irrelevant on the Civil War and the issues related to it; and finally, it disposes us to turn away from one of the most significant facts of American social life—the racial, ethnic, and religious conflict with which our history is saturated.

I would not propose to lose what is valid in the insight into America's happy circumstance of having been "born free," of not having to throw off the incubus of a feudal tradition and feudal establishments; nor would I quarrel with the perception that on some counts American thought in the Revolutionary era had a remarkably legalist and traditionalist —that is to say, conservative—cast. Certainly the pattern of the American Revolution was different from that of the Puritan, French, and Russian revolutions. But will it do to conclude that since Americans were in this sense born free, they had no revolution at all? Oddly enough, I believe our answer to this question will be clearer and more exact if it is properly equivocal. If we conclude that the American Revolution lacked a true revolutionary character because of the traditionalism of its *ideas*, we may miss a vital point. This Revolution represented the inheritance of the most radical ideas in Western civilization: the Protestant Reformation, the Puritan Revolution, the Glorious Revolution, the whole

tradition of English dissent and radical criticism. Taken out
of its parochial setting, it was the agency of some explosively
radical ideas; not only because of its threat to the principle
of legitimacy and to colonialism but also because it took the
demand for popular government out of the realm of slogans
and rallying cries and showed that it was actually susceptible
to being translated into living institutions and being made
to work. If our test for a revolution is the formation of a
radically new ideological system, or regicide, or a widespread
lethal terror, the American Revolution will not qualify. But
if our criterion is the accelerated redistribution of power
among social classes or among various social types, a pragmatic disrespect for vested interests, the rapid introduction
of profoundly important constitutional changes, we must
reconsider it. The Tories may have been almost as devoted
to Locke as the revolutionaries, but perhaps as many as
60,000 of them found what the revolutionaries stood for to
be so intolerable that they left the American states never to
return, and thousands of others risked their reputations, fortunes, and lives to fight against it. It does seem to have made
an effective difference; and Washington's generation, looking
back over the years of battle, sacrifice, and turmoil from 1763
to 1801, would surely have been puzzled at efforts to portray
their age as one of bland unity. People who are "born free"
may have to make remarkable exertions to stay that way.

Yet many Americans were born in slavery. And the
phenomena of slavery and race—everything associated with
the Civil War and its aftermath—have had to be incorporated
sideways and almost by stealth into the consensus view of
our history. Even more than the Revolution, the Civil War
has been a stumbling block for the consensus theorists, as
it was for their Progressive predecessors. The Progressives,
with their disposition to set "democratic" agrarian against
capitalist and to play down the issues of slavery and race
that cut across this alignment, usually failed to confront the
importance of slaveholding leadership in American democracy;
and their tendency to see the issues of the Civil War and Reconstruction as a struggle between agrarianism and capitalism
led them to some stark oversimplifications and to underplaying
the moral and intellectual side of the struggle. The consensus

theorists falter in a different way over this massive, inconven-
ient reality of the nineteenth century. It is an understatement,
though a candid one, when Professor Boorstin concedes:
"For us who boast that our political system is based on compromise, on the ability to organize varied regions and diverse
institutions under a single federal union, it [the Civil War]
offers considerable embarrassment." Here he is surely even
more right than he realizes: we can hardly fail to see the
irony when Americans, after having experienced the most
costly and deadly internal failure among the great states of
the nineteenth century, begin to wring their hands over the
inability of the European peoples to control their class conflicts. Yet Boorstin's most urgent interest in the Civil War,
as expressed in *The Genius of American Politics*, is not
so much in learning how it came about or what it cost as
in learning why it never became a "free-for-all for political
theorists"—an interesting concern, but to most of us a highly
specialized one. (Hartz too considers as "the remarkable
thing" about the Southern reaction the smallness of its impact
on American political thought.) In their fascination with the
failure of even so terrible a war, founded in such irreconcilable social antagonisms, to stimulate fundamental efforts in
political theory, both authors tend to lose sight of the basic
challenge it puts to the consensus idea. Consensus, after all,
is supposed to be a matter of the workings of institutions,
not just of harmony in thought; and the Civil War, taken as
a test of institutions, is a major instance of tragic collapse.
One may differ as to whether to call the impassioned arguments of the North and South "ideological" differences—but
if this was not an ideological conflict (and I think it was),
we can only conclude that Americans do not *need* ideological
conflict to shed blood on a large scale. In the face of this
political collapse, what does it matter if Professor Hartz re-
assures us that, because the Southern states were simply ad-
hering to their own view of the Constitution which they
incorporated into the Confederate constitution, the Civil War
does not represent a real failure of the American consensus?
What does it matter if we say, as Henry V. Jaffa has suggested, that both sides read the same Bible, prayed to the
same God, and considered themselves to be fighting for the

same cause for which George Washington fought?[6] I can best put my own dissent by suggesting a cartoon: a Reb and a Yank meet in 1865 to survey the physical and moral devastation of the war. "Well," says one to the other consolingly, "at least we escaped the ultimate folly of producing political theorists."

I am struck too by the importance of those kinds of conflict which the Progressive historians lost sight of in their emphasis upon the polarized opposition of classes, and which the consensus theorists also neglect in their concern to deny the Progressives: the ethnic, racial, religious, moral conflict with which American life is permeated. Certainly American history, even without feudalism and socialism, has been far from bland. In fact, a magnificent book could be written on violence in American life—the story of our early mobs and rebellions; the long, ruthless struggle with the Indian; our filibustering expeditions; our slave insurrections; our burned convents and mobbed abolitionists and lynched Wobblies; our sporadic, furiously militant Homesteads, Pullmans, and Patersons; our race lynchings, race riots, and ghetto riots; our organized gangsterism; our needless wars. What can, of course, raise such a book above the level of a mere description of certain sensational aspects of our history is the need to explain why the extraordinary American penchant for violence has been so sporadic, channeled, and controlled that it has usually bled itself out in the isolated, the local, and the partial, instead of coalescing into major social movements. How do we explain why, long before this country had a large, militant organized labor force, it had some of the bitterest and most violent strikes in the history of international labor movements? Why, without organized militarism or an established and influential military caste, have we so loved generals in politics? Why have we entered with such casual impulsiveness into wars with England, Mexico, Spain, and North Vietnam?

6 Boorstin, *The Genius of American Politics*, 99–100; on Hartz, see *The Liberal Tradition in America*, 148; cf. 18–19, 172, and Pole's comments, "The American Past," 75; for Jaffa, "Conflicts within the Idea of the Liberal Tradition," *Comparative Studies in Society and History*, 5 (1963), 276. Jaffa, it should be made clear, was in fact asserting, not denying, fundamental conflicts in our history.

With the instructive effects of the debate over consensus history behind us, we can return to the assessment of conflict in American life and thought without going straight back to the arms of the Progressives. We can avoid what made them most vulnerable: their sometimes too exclusive reliance on geographical or economic forces, their disposition to polarize, to simplify, to see history as the work of abstract universals, to see past conflicts as direct analogues of present conflicts, their reductionist stress on motives, their tendency toward Manichaeanism, their occasional drift toward conspiratorial interpretations of events. We can do more justice to the role of parties and other institutions; we are in a position to write more sophisticated accounts of types of conflict they ignored; we will almost certainly be able to do better with the complex issues of slavery and race. We can achieve a better and fuller understanding of the importance of ideas than Beard and Turner did, and in dealing with ideas we can achieve a much clearer sense of their historical and institutional settings and their actual functions than was possible for Parrington's generation.

V

As more and more historians become aware that conflict and consensus require each other and are bound up in a kind of dialectic of their own, the question whether we should stress one or the other may recede to a marginal place, and give way to other issues that are at stake: the dualism of the Progressives as against the tendency of their successors to see so many forces at work that historical explanation seems to dissolve; the renewed interest in the argument over the effectiveness of ideas and states of mind, the tendency to take more account of the symbolic aspects of politics,[7] the search for new methods. But as one looks at the productive historiographical arguments of the past two decades, one cannot fail to see that historians are responding in their own way to the sense of crisis that is so pervasive in our time. Here the issue

---

[7] On this count see my *The Paranoid Style in American Politics* (1965), viii–ix, 86–92, and *passim*.

is an old one: they are troubled about their own role and function, caught between their desire to count in the world and their desire to understand it. On one side their passion for understanding points back to the old interest in detachment, in neutrality, in critical history and the scientific ideal. But the terrible urgency of our political problems points in another direction, plays upon their pragmatic impulse, their desire to get out of history some lessons that will be of use to the world. And at this point we seem closer than we might have imagined to Bancroft, and to his contemporaries among the romantic historians who believed that they were finding instructive moral lessons in history. Beard himself appears not quite so far from Bancroft as he would have thought, at least at the beginning of his career; but he went a significant step further, and in proposing not just to draw general moral lessons about the direction and meaning of history but to forge specific recommendations for policy upon which he believed the life and death of American democracy depended, he became our supreme tragic example of the activist mind in history.

It will always be possible to argue over these two views of the historian's role—and in the end most historians will be persuaded less by the arguments than by the dictates of their temperaments. In the American temperament there is a powerful bias toward accepting the pragmatic demand upon history: it is hard for us to believe that there is such a thing as a truth that cannot be made useful. The urgency of our national problems seems to demand, more than ever, that the historian have something to say that will help us, and the publisher's puff on the jacket of almost every historical work of any consequence tries to suggest its relevance to the present. Against this, the professional case for detachment seems at first overwhelmingly strong. Most of us think we have other and better criteria of a historical work than its usefulness as a source of battle cries or slogans, even in the best of causes. Unlike economics and sociology, history is not, in the jargon of our time, a policy science, and rather than deploring this as a limitation, we may seize upon it as a luxury. Again, it is easy to point to the dangers of committed history, of which Beard provides so poignant an example. The activist historian who thinks he is deriving his policy from his history may in fact be deriving his history from his policy, and may be driven to commit the cardinal sin of the historical writer: he may lose his respect for the integrity, the independence, the pastness, of the past.

Such are the risks; and yet let us not deceive ourselves: the case for the historian *engagé*—and I mean here the case for him *as a historian,* not as a public force—also has its strength. It is not just that great histories have been written —witness Churchill and Trotsky in our age—by embattled participants. We must go beyond this to admit that, while there are few instances of historical insight in the direct and immediate service of public policy, there are innumerable instances of a vital connection between strong public concerns and distinguished historical work. The marvelous vitality that French historiography has derived from the controversial heritage of the French Revolution is a case in point. But the leading interpreters of America have also been, in this extended sense of the word, *engagé*—they have been committed to the historical realization of certain civic values, even in some cases to specific ends. At their worst they may stray into a culpable present-mindedness, like Beard striking at the stale constitutionalism of 1913 through the Constitution of 1787, or Parrington assimilating Roger Williams and Thomas Hooker to the democratic insurgency of the Progressive era. But this present-mindedness, though it has been responsible for major errors, has often brought with it a major access of new insight—bearing error and distortion not in arbitrary solitude but in a kind of fertile if illicit union with intellectual discovery. At their best, the interpretative historians have gone to the past with some passionate concern for the future; and somehow—the examples of Tocqueville and Henry Adams may encourage us—they have produced from the inner tensions of their minds an equipoise that enables them to superimpose upon their commitment a measure of detachment about the past, even to reconcile themselves to having knowledge without power.

The great fear that animates the most feverishly committed historians is that our continual rediscovery of the complexity of social interests, the variety of roles and motives of political leaders, the unintended consequences of political actions, the valid interests that have so often been sacrificed in the pursuit of other equally valid interests, may give us not only a keener sense of the structural complexity of our society in the past, but also a sense of the moral complexity of social action that will lead us toward political immobility. Since a keen sense of history begets a feeling of social responsibility and a need to act, this is not necessarily the case; but history does seem inconsistent with the coarser rallying cries of politics. Hence I suppose we may expect that the very idea of complexity will itself come under fire once again, and that it will become important for a whole generation to argue that most things in life and in history are not complex but really quite simple. This demand I do not think the study of history can gratify. As practiced by mature minds, history forces us to be aware not only of complexity but of defeat and failure: it tends to deny that high sense of expectation, that hope of ultimate and glorious triumph, that sustains good combatants. There may be comfort in it still. In an age when so much of our literature is infused with nihilism, and other social disciplines are driven toward narrow positivistic inquiry, history may remain the most humanizing among the arts.

Bibliographical Essay

THIS ESSAY is not intended as a comprehensive guide to the relevant literature, nor is it a complete list of the sources to which I have referred. It is chiefly meant to expand the documentation in my footnotes and to indicate sources that have been most important for me. However, some items of less importance are included, primarily for the convenience of other writers, because they have been hitherto unknown or too little known. For example, while I have tried to be brief in my account of materials on Turner and Beard, both of whom have been well bibliographed, I have stretched my sequence on Parrington to include his book reviews, of which up to now there has been no identification. Periodicals cited repeatedly have been abbreviated as follows:

AH, Agricultural History; AHR, American Historical Review; APSR, American Political Science Review; AQ, American Quarterly; JEH, Journal of Economic History; JHI, Journal of the History of Ideas; JPE, Journal of Political Economy; JSH, Journal of Southern History; MVHR, Mississippi Valley Historical Review; N, Nation; NEQ, New England Quarterly; NR, New Republic; PHR, Pacific Historical Review; PMHB, Pennsylvania Magazine of History and Biography; PNQ, Pacific Northwest Quarterly; PSQ, Political Science Quarterly; SAQ, South Atlantic Quarterly; VQR, Virginia Quarterly Review; WMH, Wisconsin Magazine of History; WMQ, William and Mary Quarterly; YR, Yale Review.

HISTORICAL WRITING BEFORE TURNER

I CANNOT PRETEND that in preparing for my impressionistic survey of the background in American history I have read my way all through the voluminous works of our major historians. I did, however, go back, and in each case with pleasure, to four

great writers: Bancroft, Parkman, Hildreth, and Henry Adams.
In addition to my reading in them, I found a few books outstandingly useful. On Bancroft I consulted Russell Nye's *George Bancroft: Brahmin Rebel* (1955); Nye's briefer study of Bancroft's
thought in the American Thinkers Series, also somewhat con-
fusingly entitled *George Bancroft* (1964), is a very good discussion of Bancroft's mind. On Parkman I was enlightened by
Mason Wade, *Francis Parkman, Heroic Historian* (1942), and
Otis Pease, *Parkman's History: The Historian as Literary Artist*
(1953). Howard Doughty, *Francis Parkman* (1962) is a superb
study. See also Wilbur Jacobs, ed., *The Letters of Francis Parkman*, two volumes (1960). On Hildreth, see Donald E. Emerson,
Richard Hildreth (1946). On Henry Adams there is a long shelfful
of books. I mention only his *Education* (1918), the volumes of
Ernest Samuels's biography (1948, 1958, 1964), and pre-eminently
William H. Jordy, *Henry Adams: Scientific Historian* (1952), which
is much better than its title promises.

General guides

The scholarship of the present generation has at last made it
possible to write in an informed way about the development of
American historical writing. John Higham, et al., *History* (1965)
is a good guide to the period since history-writing became professional. More comprehensive are Michael Kraus, *The Writing of
American History* (1953), a revision of an earlier history (1937),
Harvey Wish, *The American Historian* (1960) and H. Hale Bellot's
manual, *American History and Historians* (1952). Herman Ausu-
bel traces historical speculation as seen in the presidential
addresses to the American Historical Association in *Historians and
their Craft* (1950). The interpretative essays in W. T. Hutchinson,
ed., *The Marcus W. Jernegan Essays in American Historiography*
(1937) are still good; those in Donald Sheehan and Harold C.
Syrett, *Essays in American Historiography in Honor of Allan
Nevins* (1960) are uneven. J. Franklin Jameson, *The History of
Historical Writing in America* (1891) is a series of four interpretative essays representing the historical thought of the early
days of the profession. Carl Becker's essays in *Everyman His Own
Historian* (1935) are eminently readable; he is good on Henry
Adams, unfair to Bancroft. The essays by various hands in John
Higham, ed., *The Reconstruction of American History* (1962) are
helpful. David W. Noble, *Historians against History* (1965) is a
provocative critical work tracing certain themes from Bancroft
to the recent past.

Special Studies

Peter Gay, *A Loss of Mastery* (1966) is penetrating on the
Puritan historians. David D. Van Tassel, *Recording America's*

Past (1960) is a mine of information on the development of historical studies from 1607 to 1884, the pre-professional period. John Spencer Bassett, *The Middle Group of American Historians* (1917) deals with the era of Sparks and Bancroft. David Levin, *History as Romantic Art* (1959) is excellent on Bancroft, Prescott, Motley, and Parkman. W. Stull Holt is good on the emergence of the profession in *Historical Scholarship in America 1876–1901* (1938), an edition of the letters of Herbert Baxter Adams, and in his essay, "The Idea of Scientific History in America," *JHI*, 1 (1940), 352–62. Edward Saveth, *American Historians and European Immigrants 1875–1925* (1948) is definitive on its subject. A. S. Eisenstadt, *Charles McLean Andrews* (1956) is an illuminating study of the outstanding product of the scientific school at Johns Hopkins. Burleigh Taylor Wilkins, *Carl Becker* (1961) is a distinguished study, as is Cushing Strout's critical account of relativism in Becker and Beard, *The Pragmatic Revolt in American History* (1958). On some aspects of style in recent historical writing see David Levin, *In Defense of Historical Literature* (1967). Robert H. Skotheim, *American Intellectual Histories and Historians* (1966) is a survey dealing mainly with writing in this field since the time of Tyler and Eggleston. Among essays that have helped me are C. Vann Woodward, "American Attitudes toward History," an inaugural lecture delivered at Oxford in 1955; Oscar Handlin, "The Central Themes of American History," in *Relazioni del X Congresso Internazionale di Scienze Storiche* (1955), 143–66; Merle Curti, "The Democratic Theme in American Historical Literature," *MVHR*, 39 (1952), 3–28; and Charles Crowe, "The Emergence of Progressive History," *JHI*, 27 (1966), 109–24.

The Social Science Research Council has sponsored a series of inquiries into the state of our historical writing. Particularly good, in Bulletin 54, *Theory and Practice in Historical Study* (1946), is the masterly essay by John Herman Randall and George Haines IV on "Controlling Assumptions in the Practice of American Historians," which deals with basic trends in thought since the 1870's. See also Bulletin 64, *The Social Sciences in Historical Study* (1954), which is described as "a product of group thinking," and the stimulating essays in *Generalization in the Writing of History* (1963).

I have benefited from reading some American contemporaries, notably H. Stuart Hughes, *History as Art and as Science* (1964) and Morton White, *Social Thought in America* and *Foundations of Historical Knowledge* (1964). There is a splendid collection of essays on the views of historians on their craft in Fritz Stern, ed., *The Varieties of History* (1956), and another on views of basic issues in historical philosophy in Hans Meyerhoff, ed., *The Philosophy of History in Our Time* (1959). It would be tedious to cite specifically and at length, but ungracious to omit all reference to what I have learned from reading among the speculative and critical books of R. G. Collingwood, E. H. Carr, Herbert Butterfield, Marc Bloch, Peter Geyl, and J. G. Renier, on the problems of history and the ways of historians in dealing with them.

TURNER

Turner's writings

Turner's four books, *Rise of the New West* (1906), *The Frontier in American History* (1920), *Sections in American History* (1932), and *The United States, 1830–1850* (1935) are discussed in the text. Fulmer Mood has edited *The Early Writings of Frederick Jackson Turner* (1938), which includes the doctoral dissertation on the Indian trade. The most accessible edition of Turner's important early essays, and indeed of his major essays generally, is now Ray Allen Billington's, *Frontier and Section* (1961). Out of the many hundreds of fragments left by Turner among his papers, Wilbur R. Jacobs has printed and annotated in *Frederick Jackson Turner's Legacy* (1965) a good selection of the most significant, including the important early critique of von Holst and some extremely illuminating bits on sectionalism. His introduction also supplies some biographical information.

I spent too brief a period with Turner's voluminous manuscripts at the Henry E. Huntington Library. The most revealing of his letters, as they bear upon his work, have already been fairly well exploited in previous studies, and others are soon to be published in a collection of his correspondence with Alice Perkins Hooper, edited by Ray Allen Billington and Walter Muir Whitehill. In interpreting Turner's intentions, at least as he elucidated them in retrospect, I have tried to make good use in particular of the following illuminating letters: to William E. Dodd, October 7, 1919; to Arthur M. Schlesinger, April 18, 1922; to Carl Becker, December 16, 1925, and February 13, 1926, May 14, 1927; to Merle E. Curti, August 8, 15, and 27, 1928. The few Turner papers at the Harvard College Library are mainly letters to Turner, among which the most interesting are those from Walter Hines Page, Theodore Roosevelt, and Woodrow Wilson.

Bibliographical

In addition to the Turner bibliography by Edwards, already cited, there are good introductions to the whole frontier controversy. The best of these is Billington's *The American Frontier*, second ed., (1965), a pamphlet available from the American Historical Association, which provides a running commentary on the literature from a standpoint sympathetic to Turnerism but not uncritical. See also the excellent bibliographical notes to Billington's *America's*

Frontier Heritage (1966). Also useful are: Gene M. Gressley, "The Turner Thesis—a Problem in Historiography," *AH*, 32 (1958), 227–49, and Walter Rundell, Jr., "Concepts of the 'Frontier' and the 'West,'" *Arizona and the West*, I (1959), 13–41. Still of value is E. E. Edwards's *References on the Significance of the Frontier in American History* (1939), a mimeographed publication of the United States Department of Agriculture Library. Fulmer Mood is helpful on the history of the word frontier and on the concept of the frontier in two articles in *AH*, 19 (1945), 24–30 and 22 (1948), 73–83, but John T. Juricek has made an exhaustive investigation, "American Usage of the Word 'Frontier' from Colonial Times to Frederick Jackson Turner," in *Proceedings* of the American Philosophical Society, 110 (1966), 10–34; Juricek concludes, among other things: "Before Turner 'frontier' had meanings that were concrete, if often difficult to apply. With his work the word became abstract, and his early followers made it even more so."

Biographical, Personal, and Intellectual

The main course of Turner's career has already been much clarified by three articles by Ray A. Billington, whose full-scale biography is forthcoming: "Young Fred Turner," *WMH*, 46 (1962), 38–48; "Frederick Jackson Turner Comes to Harvard," Massachusetts Historical Society *Proceedings*, 74 (1962), 51–83, which goes beyond the scope of its title; and "Why Some Historians Rarely Write History," cited in the text. For his later years see Max Farrand, "Frederick Jackson Turner at the Huntington Library," *Huntington Library Bulletin*, 3 (1933), 157–64. Extremely valuable is Fulmer Mood, "The Development of Frederick Jackson Turner as a Historical Thinker," *Publications* of the Colonial Society of Massachusetts, 34 (1939), 283–352. See also Constance L. Skinner, ed., "Turner's Autobiographic Letter," *WMH*, 19 (1935), 91–103. The two essays by Lee Benson in his *Turner and Beard* (1960) are valuable in locating Turner's views against the economic speculation of the 1890's and in establishing his debt to Loria. On Turner's place in post-Darwinian sociology and historiography, see Rudolf Freund, "Turner's Theory of Social Evolution,'" *AH*, 19 (1945), 78–87, and Gilman M. Ostrander, "Turner and the Germ Theory," *AH*, 32 (1958), 258–61. Alan C. Beckman, "Hidden Themes in the Frontier Thesis," *Contemporary Studies in Society and History*, 8 (1966), 361–82, supplies a venturesome psychoanalytic interpretation, based, I believe, on insufficient evidence, of Turner's difficulty in writing; he also illustrates the use of the oedipal romance in Turner's rhetoric, and here I believe he is on more secure ground. On Turner as a post-Darwinian thinker and on the importance of biological metaphors in his thought, see the excellent article by William Coleman, "Science and Symbol in the Turner Frontier Hypothesis," *AHR*, 72 (1966), 22–49.

The biographical introductions by Jacobs, *Frederick Jackson Turner's Legacy*, and Mood, *Early Writings*, have important material. On Turner as a teacher and friend, Carl Becker's sketch in H. W. Odum, ed., *American Masters of Social Science* (1927), is unsurpassed. For other statements that offer both personal and intellectual estimates, see Merle Curti, "The Section and Frontier in American History" in S. A. Rice, ed., *Methods in Social Science* (1931) and the same author's "Frederick Jackson Turner" in the series *Historiadores de América* published by the Instituto Panamericano de Geografía e Historia (1949). Also significant are Robert E. Riegel, "American Frontier Theory," *Cahiers d'Histoire Mondiale*, 3 (1956), 356–80; Avery Craven's essay in *The Marcus W. Jernegan Essays in American Historiography* (1937); and U. B. Phillips, "The Traits and Contributions of Frederick Jackson Turner," *AH*, 19 (1945), 21–3. On Turner's influence through his teaching, see W. R. Jacobs, "Frederick Jackson Turner—Master Teacher," *Pacific Historical Review*, 23 (1954), 49–58. The uses and rejection of Turner by intellectuals are discussed by Warren I. Susman in the essay cited in the text, while the state of opinion about Turnerism in the historical profession is systematically surveyed by George W. Pierson, "American Historians and the Frontier Hypothesis in 1941," *WMH*, 26 (1942), 36–60, 170–85.

Turner's forerunners

Herman C. Nixon deals with a few but by no means all of Turner's forerunners in "The Precursors of Turner in the Interpretation of the American Frontier," *SAQ*, 38 (1929), 83–9. The long background of the safety-valve idea is discussed by Carter Goodrich and Sol Davison, "The Wage Earner in the Westward Movement," Part I, *PSQ*, 50 (1935), 161–85, and Henry Nash Smith, *Virgin Land* (1950), chapter XX. See also Rush Welter, "The Frontier West as Image of American Society: Conservative Attitudes before the Civil War," *MVHR*, 46 (1960), 593–614. For Hegel, see W. Stull Holt, "Hegel, the Turner Hypothesis, and the Safety-Valve Theory," *AH*, 22 (1948), 175–6. For Lamar, Wirt Armistead Cate, "Lamar and the Frontier Hypothesis," *JSH*, 1 (1935), 497–501. For H. H. Bancroft, *Essays and Miscellany* (1890), 43, 185–6. For Sumner, Edith H. Parker, "William Graham Sumner and the Frontier," *Southwest Review*, 41 (1956), 357–65. The passage from Henry George is from *Progress and Poverty* (New York ed., 1920), 387–8. Turner was familiar with this book as early as 1887, but the importance of this passage seems first to have been brought to his attention by Achille Loria's work; see Jacobs, *Frederick Jackson Turner's Legacy*, 15–16. See also William M. Tuttle, Jr., "Forerunners of Frederick Jackson Turner: Nineteenth Century British Conservatives and the Frontier Thesis," *AH*, 41 (1967), 219–28.

Turner's critics

Turner's logic and his use of terms are subject to close analysis by George W. Pierson in two classic articles of first importance: "The Frontier and Frontiersmen of Turner's Essays," *PMHB*, 54 (1940), 449–78, and "The Frontier and American Institutions," *NEQ*, 15 (1942), 224–55. Of comparable importance as a critique of Turner's views on the frontier and democracy are two articles by Benjamin F. Wright, Jr., "American Democracy and the Frontier," *YR*, 20 (1930), 349–65, and "Political Institutions and the Frontier, in D. R. Fox, ed., *Sources of Culture in the Middle West* (1934), 15–38. The sharpest challenge to Turner's version of frontier individualism is that of Mody C. Boatright, "The Myth of Frontier Individualism," *Southwestern Social Science Quarterly*, 22 (1941), 14–32. Boatright brings together various kinds of evidence for the sense of collectivity and mutuality on the frontier—material of a kind, it should be said, that Turner was quite well aware of but which he tended to minimize. The romantic and primitivist elements in Turner are emphasized by Henry Nash Smith, *Virgin Land* (1950) and in his article, "The West as an Image of the American Past," *University of Kansas City Review*, 18 (1951), 29–39. Turner's inheritance from the agrarian myth is made clear in my book, *The Age of Reform* (1955), which also tries to show the limitations of the frontier thesis in the interpretation of the Populist movement. Some light on frontier anti-intellectualism may be found in my *Anti-intellectualism in American Life* (1963), and Arthur K. Moore, *The Frontier Mind: A Cultural Analysis of the Kentucky Frontiersman* (1957). For a nice demonstration of the way in which cultural heritage influences behavior on the frontier, see Richard H. Shryock, "British versus German Traditions in Colonial Agriculture," *MVHR*, 26 (1939), 39–54.

Turner's partisans

Turner's ideas have been expounded and defended in various writings by Ray Allen Billington, who combines a sympathetic view of the master with readiness to modify his views on significant counts. See his essay, "The Frontier in American Thought and Character," in A. R. Lewis and T. F. McGann, *The New World Looks at its History* (1963) and *The American Frontier*, already cited. Also illuminating on Turner's methods and ideas is Wilbur R. Jacobs's essay in W. R. Jacobs, J. W. Caughey, and Joe B. Frantz, *Turner, Bolton, and Webb* (1965). Essays already cited by Curti, Craven, Becker, and Phillips are sympathetic. Of central importance in the attempt to adapt Turnerism is the two-part essay, discussed in the text, by Stanley Elkins and Eric McKitrick, "A Meaning for Turner's Frontier," *PSQ*, 59 (1954), 321–53,

565–602. Merle Curti's study of Trempealeau County, Wisconsin, *The Making of An American Community* (1959), finds some support for the Turnerian view of the frontier and democracy, but the author scrupulously points out that the site was chosen not for its representativeness but for its convenience and that the findings are in some respects qualified. John D. Barnhart, *Valley of Democracy* (1953), a historical study of the Ohio Valley, 1775–1818, is a valuable frontier history, but I fail to see that it was in fact designed to test the Turner categories. The author believes that the history of democracy in the early Ohio Valley "gives us an historical basis for the hope that we as a people may continue to have a history of our own, a history that is unique." A vigorous brief defense of the Turner thesis is presented by H. C. Allen, "F. J. Turner and the Frontier in American History," in H. C. Allen and C. P. Hill, eds., *British Essays in American History* (1957).

Comparative Frontiers

The frontier concern has been immensely fruitful in stimulating comparative study, though at present its implications for the Turner thesis on the American frontier remain somewhat equivocal. There are good essays on other frontiers, some of which give support to the idea that the frontier process is intrinsically democratizing, in Walker D. Wyman and Clifton B. Kroeber, eds., *The Frontier in Perspective* (1957), along with some important critical essays on the American frontier; those by Thomas Perkins Abernethy and Paul W. Gates raise important questions about the Turner thesis. Two good assessments of the growing literature in this field are Marvin Mikesell, "Comparative Studies in Frontier History," *Annals of the Association of American Geographers*, 50 (1960), 62–74 and Dietrich Gerhard, "The Frontier in Comparative View," *Comparative Studies in Society and History*, 1 (1959), 205–29. See also Herbert Heaton, "Other Wests than Ours," *JEH*, 6, Supplement (1946), 50–62, and Paul F. Sharp, "Three Frontiers: Some Comparative Studies of Canadian, American, and Australian Settlement," *PHR*, 24 (1955), 369–77. Relevant on this theme is the comparison of the United States and Australia by Carter Goodrich, cited below under safety-valve essays.

The Safety-Valve Controversy

Carter Goodrich and Sol Davison opened the assault on the labor-safety-valve idea with two articles, "The Wage Earner in the Westward Movement," *PSQ*, 50 (1935), 161–85 and 51 (1936), 61–116, showing both the long history of the doctrine and the difficulty of finding direct evidence in selected instances of successful westward migration by workingmen. See also Murray Kane, "Some Considerations on the Safety Valve Doctrine, *MVHR*,

23 (1936), 169–88. Clarence H. Danhof, "Farm-Making Costs and
the 'Safety Valve': 1850-1860," *JPE*, 49 (1941), 317–59, and
"Economic Validity of the Safety-Valve Doctrine," *JEH* Supplement (1941), 96–106, has emphasized the prohibitive costs to
working men of moving and establishing a farm. Fred A. Shannon,
"A Post-Mortem on the Labor-Safety-Valve Theory," *AH*, 19 (1955),
31–37 argues that the real safety valve lay in the opportunities
opened up by the growing cities for surplus farm labor.

These articles, along with some of the rejoinders they brought
from Turner's followers, are bibliographed and sharply com-
mented on by Ellen von Nardroff, "The American Frontier as a
Safety Valve—The Life, Death, Reincarnation, and Justification
of a Theory," *AH*, 36 (1962), 123–42, who argues that the rate of
economic growth, the high wages and low class-consciousness in
the United States are indeed related to the frontier process. Von
Nardroff draws in part upon Norman J. Simler, "The Safety-Valve
Doctrine Re-Evaluated," *AH*, 32 (1958), 250–7, who has corrected
some of Shannon's calculations and has argued that the westward
movement raised eastern wages and also provided a "social safety
valve" for the middle classes, and in part upon George G. S. Murphy
and Arnold Zellner, "Sequential Growth, the Labor-Safety-Valve
Doctrine and the Development of American Unionism, "*JEH*, 19
(1959), 402–21, who emphasize the role of successive "slabs" of
rich Western resources in increasing the number of jobs and
raising per capita income in the United States. On this count I
find Douglass C. North, "International Capital Flows and the
Development of the American West," *JEH*, 16 (1956), 493–505,
very helpful. See also Donald L. Kemmerer, "The Changing Pattern of American Economic Development," *JEH*, 16 (1956), 575–
89. Carter Goodrich, "The Australian and American Labour Movements, *Economic Record*, 4 (1928), 193–208, suggests that the
level of wages alone may not suffice to explain differing labor
mentalities in two frontier countries, and points to other historical
forces. On wages, mobility, and the mentality of American labor,
I am much indebted to Stanley Lebergott's learned and spirited
volume, *Manpower in Economic Growth* (1964). H. J. Habakkuk's
elegantly argued study, *American and British Technology in the
Nineteenth Century* (1962), is indispensable on innovation and
labor scarcity and is instructive for students of the safety-valve
problem. Brinley Thomas, *Migration and Economic Growth*
(1954), is also helpful in setting the problem of labor migration
in its international economic setting; on the social escalator effect
of immigration, see pp. 118–19.

Mobility

The importance of the phenomenon of movement in America
has been studied in a series of essays by one of Turner's major

critics, George W. Pierson: "The Moving American," YR, 44 (1954), 99–112; "The M-Factor in American History," AQ, 14 (1962), 275–89; "Under a Wandering Star," VQR, 39 (1963), 621–38; "A Restless Temper . . . ," AHR, 59 (1964), 969–89. Everett S. Lee has looked at the phenomenon from a sociologist's standpoint, "The Turner Thesis Re-examined," AQ, 13 (1961), 77–87. The same theme is dealt with by Allan Bogue, "Social Theory and the Pioneer," AH, 34 (1960), 21–45. Eric McKitrick and Stanley Elkins have dealt suggestively with the effect of mobility on institutions in "Institutions in Motion," AQ, 12 (1960), 188–97.

Earl Pomeroy, "Toward a Reorientation of Western History: Continuity and Environment," MVHR, 41 (1955), 579–600, argues forcefully that Turner overemphasized environment at the expense of cultural continuity. For a similar view, see Louis B. Wright, Culture on the Moving Frontier (1955), and the works of Pierson and Wright, already cited. Carlton J. H. Hayes, "The American Frontier—Frontier of What?" AHR, 51 (1946), 199–216, stresses the intellectual isolationism of an overemphasis on America's frontier development as against its Atlantic inheritance. A number of historians have quarreled with Turner's version of the frontier process itself. Among these I have found the works of Thomas Perkins Abernethy especially illuminating. See his Three Virginia Frontiers (1940); "Democracy and the Southern Frontier," JSH, 4 (1938), 3–13; and Frontier to Plantation (1932). Robert F. Berkhofer, Jr., "Space, Time, Culture and the New Frontier," AH, 38 (1964), 21–30 emphasizes strongly the overpowering weight of Eastern cultural institutions and aspirations, including commercial aspiration, on the frontier. The role of speculation has been developed by many writers, among whom I have found the works of Paul W. Gates especially rewarding. See, for example, his "Role of the Land Speculator in Western Development," PMHB, 60 (1942), 314–33, and "Frontier Estate Builders and Farm Laborers" in The Frontier in Perspective, already cited. Francis S. Philbrick is sharply polemical against Turner in his The Rise of the West, 1754–1830 (1965), 336–74, 379–87.

The most ambitious attempt to extend the frontier idea is represented in the writing of Walter Prescott Webb, especially in The Great Frontier (1952), a work which, by the author's testimony, was conceived quite independently of Turnerism. This book, which attempts to interpret modern world history in terms of the exhaustion of frontiers, has had relatively little influence. Webb's The Great Plains (1931) is also among the most interesting of the frontier books.

The frontier is an imense presence in American literature, and not merely in those writers who, like Cooper and Mark Twain, wrote directly about the frontier experience. For secondary studies, see Ralph L. Rusk, The Literature of the Middle Western Frontier, two volumes (1925); Dorothy A. Dondore, *The Prairies and the Making of Middle America* (1926); and Lucy Lockwood Hazard, *The Frontier in American Literature* (1927).

BEARD

Bibliographical

There are two excellent bibliographies of Beard's writings, though unfortunately neither is arranged chronologically: one by Jack Frooman and Edmund David Cronon in Howard K. Beale, ed., *Charles A. Beard* (1954), another by Bernard C. Borning in *The Political and Social Thought of Charles A. Beard* (1962). Beale's essay on "Beard's Historical Writings," in the first of these volumes, gives valuable information about their sales and distribution. It is instructive to learn that over 5,500,000 copies of his textbooks were sold, and an estimated grand total of all books of over 11,000,000, but that *An Economic Interpretation of the Constitution* had sold at that point (1954) somewhat less than 8,000. Among works other than textbooks, by far the most widely circulated were *The Republic* (over 4,200,000) and the Beards' *Basic History of the United States* (over 640,000)—so that the later, and somewhat repentant, Beard reached a larger and perhaps different public than the earlier rebel and iconoclast. The list of articles and books about Beard bibliographed both in the Borning and Beale volumes is usefully supplemented by John C. Rule and Ralph D. Handen, "Bibliography of Works on Carl Lotus Becker and Charles Austin Beard, 1945–63," *History and Theory*, V (1966), 302–13. Some measure of Beard's impact on the historical profession is provided by Maurice Blinkoff, *The Influence of Charles A. Beard upon American Historiography* (1936).

Biographical

Beard did not want to have a biography written. He felt that he had expressed himself voluminously in published writings and did not want his works interpreted in the light of personal information—an approach to his own life which seems at odds with the canons of his relativism. Some time around 1939 he systematically destroyed his personal papers. He also destroyed the manuscripts of books written in collaboration with his wife, so that the exact circumstances of their very congenial co-authorship cannot be established. In the absence of a large body of personal materials, a full-scale, intimate biography cannot be written. There are, however, bits of Beard's correspondence in the memoir of Arthur M. Schlesinger in the Oral History Collection at Columbia University. There are also a few letters in the papers of Carl

Becker, Cornell University Library, and some interchanges, quite illuminating for Beard's views on foreign policy in the 1940's, in the papers of Oswald Garrison Villard, Houghton Library, Harvard University. However, the most extensive body of letters I have seen is the letters of Charles and Mary Beard to Harry Elmer Barnes in the library of the University of Wyoming. The letters of Mary Beard, written after Beard's death, are of some biographical value. There are interesting glimpses of Beard in some of the memoirs in the Columbia Oral History Collections by Alfred A. Knopf, Guy Stanton Ford, Herbert Claiborne Pell, William Harvey Allen, and James T. Shotwell. Some family materials are available on microfilm at the library of Beard's alma mater, DePauw University. They contain few letters, but they have documentary information and clippings on Beard's family background and his early life, his experiences as a teacher, Ruskin Hall and his English lectures; his relations with Columbia University, the New School for Social Research, the American Political Science Association, and the American Historical Association; his speeches and public services; the reception of his books; and his foreign travels. There are also family photographs.

Among published works, Mary Beard provides some family background and information and documents on Beard's early travels in Japan and Yugoslavia in *The Making of Charles A. Beard* (1955), which seems to be a fragment of an unfinished biography, abandoned when hardly begun. See also the introduction by his son, William Beard, to a selection from Beard's writings, *The Economic Basis of Politics and Related Writings* (1957), for further biographical data. Bernard Borning's study of Beard's thought, already cited, is a sound scholarly work which amounts almost to an intellectual biography. I am much indebted to it. There are important personal reports and recollections by various persons who knew Beard in Beale, ed., *Charles A. Beard*, including a moving account of Beard as a teacher, by Arthur W. Macmahon. Cushing Strout has biographical material as well as critical observations in *The Pragmatic Revolt in American History* (1958). See also two personal sketches: Matthew Josephson, "Charles A. Beard: A Memoir," *VQR*, 25 (1949), 585–901; and Hubert Herring, "Charles A. Beard: Free Lance among the Historians," *Harper's Magazine*, 178 (1939), 641–51; as well as Josephson's recollections in *Infidel in the Temple* (1967). Some points in Josephson's article, especially having to do with Beard's background and his death, are challenged in letters from Mary Beard to Harry Elmer Barnes, October 12, 1949, and January 24, 1951. On Beard's undergraduate education, the best source is Merle Curti's sketch of Colonel James R. Weaver, "A Great Teacher's Teacher," *Social Education*, 13 (1949), 263–7. It is also in his *Probing Our Past* (1955). Among the more interesting comments, though not reportorial, is that of Perry Miller,

"Charles A. Beard," *N*, 167 (1948), 344–6. Beard's place in the history of American liberalism in the subject of intermittent attention in Eric F. Goldman, *Rendezvous with Destiny* (1952). A valuable sidelight on Beard may be found in his appearances before Congressional Committees. These are best bibliographed by Borning (p. 278), who, however, missed an interesting apperance on March 20, 1935, *Hearings before the Senate Committee on Interstate Commerce*, 74th Congress, 1st sess., on S. R. 71 (1939), 2–36, an obscurely placed item which the diligent researches of Edwin G. Burrows turned up for me. It provides an interesting view of Beard under pressure.

The Oxford Period

There is a file of *Young Oxford* in the Yale University Library. Beard's book on *The Industrial Revolution* (1901) is more generally available. Harlan Phillips, *Walter Vrooman: Restless Child of Progress*, unpublished Ph.D. dissertation, Teachers College, Columbia University (1954), is good on Vrooman and Ruskin College. See also Phillips's articles, "Charles Beard, Walter Vrooman, and the Founding of Ruskin Hall," *SAQ*, 50 (1951), 186–91, and Burleigh Taylor Wilkins's account (with texts) of Beard's reminiscent letters, "Charles A. Beard on the Founding of Ruskin Hall," *Indiana Magazine of History*, 52 (1956), 277–88. See also Wilkins's "Frederick York Powell and Charles A. Beard," *AQ*, 11 (1959), 21–39. Oliver Elton is illuminating on Beard's mentor at Oxford in *Frederick York Powell*, 2 vols. (1906).

The Columbia Period, 1902–17

The astonishing thing about Beard's work in this period is its volume, which testifies not only to extraordinary energy, facility, and discipline but to breathless speed. His M.A. essay, *The Present Status of Civil Service Reform in the United States* (1903), is available in the Columbia University Library. His doctoral dissertation, *The Office of Justice of the Peace in England* (1904), must of necessity have been hurriedly done; it was reviewed rather severely by the distinguished medievalist Charles Gross in *AHR*, X (1904–5), 440–1. In 1906 Beard edited a book of sources *An Introduction to the English Historians;* in 1907–8 he published, with James Harvey Robinson, a textbook in two volumes, *The Development of Modern Europe;* and during 1908–9 the two published their two-volume book of *Readings in Modern European History*. Beard's thoughtful lecture, *Politics*, important for the student of his intellectual development, was published in 1908. In 1909 Beard also edited his own *Readings in American Government and Politics*, and in 1910 published his excellent textbook, *American Government and Politics*, which stated some of his ideas on the Founding Fathers. In 1912 he published his *American City Government*, as well as *The Supreme Court and the Constitution*, which is discussed in the text; I have used the Spectrum edition (1962) of this book with an Introduction by Alan Westin. In the same year he edited (with Birl E. Shultz) *Documents on the State-wide Initiative, Referendum and Recall*. Hard upon all this came his memorable book *An Economic Interpretation of the Constitution* (1913), which was followed the next year by *Contemporary American History* and (with Mary Beard) *American Citizenship*. In 1915 came *Economic Origins of Jeffersonian Democracy*. During this period Beard published ten articles in the *Political Science Quarterly* alone, and, by my rough count, sixty-five book reviews of works on history and politics.

The Columbia Controversy

There is a good brief account of Beard's resignation in its general setting by Walter P. Metzger in Richard Hofstadter and Walter P. Metzger, *The Development of Academic Freedom in the United States* (1955). See also the unpublished Columbia University doctoral dissertation by Carol Gruber on the academic man in wartime, *Mars and Minerva* (1968), for the fullest account of the Beard controversy. Important documents are Beard's account, "A Statement," *NR*, 13 (1917), 249–50, and his letter of resignation in *School and Society*, 6 (1917), 446–7. Earlier charges against Beard in the flag dispute were denied by fifty-three of his students in a signed letter, "What Professor Beard Said" *NR*, 7 (1917), 18, testifying to "the high order of his scholarship, his genuine devotion to the best of American ideals, and above all to his unfailing habit of sane and measured utterance. . . ."

The Controversy over An Economic Interpretation of the Constitution

This book should be read in the 1935 edition, with Beard's explanatory introduction. The various works drawn upon by Beard in arriving at this work are discussed in the text. Among important books written in the Beardian tradition on the constitutional era see Merrill Jensen, *The New Nation* (1950) and *The Articles of Confederation* (1940). Jackson T. Main is still sympathetic in his important study, *The Antifederalists* (1960), and E. James Ferguson partly so in *The Power of the Purse*. On Ferguson see the review by Stuart Bruchey, *WMQ*, 19 (1962), 429–34, and the author's answer, ibid., 434–8. The major critiques of Beard have been those of Robert E. Brown, *Beard and the Constitution* (1956), and Forrest McDonald, *We the People* (1958). The latter work was the subject of extended controversy between McDonald and Main in *WMQ*, 17 (1960), 86–110, and of pertinent comment by Robert L. Schuyler in *JSH*, 27

(1961), 73–80. See also, for an alternative economic interpretation, McDonald's *E Pluribus Unum* (1965). Lee Benson reviews Beard and his critics in *Turner and Beard* (1960) and makes some important methodological suggestions.

The path by which Beard arrived at the ideas in this book is traced by Eric Goldman, "The Origins of Beard's *Economic Interpretation of the Constitution, JHI*, 13 (1952), 234–49, and by my own essay, "Beard and the Constitution," *AQ*, 2 (1950), 195–213, upon which part of chapter V is based. Beard's role in bringing attention to the tenth *Federalist* is emphasized, and his interpretation of it is disputed in Douglass Adair, "The Tenth *Federalist* Revisited," *WMQ*, 8 (1951), 48–67. Robert E. Thomas rightly perceives the element of the Federalist historian in Beard, but I believe greatly overestimates its importance in "A Reappraisal of Charles Beard's *An Economic Interpretation of the Constitution*," *AHR*, 57 (1952), 370–5. There have been several sharp criticisms of Beard's conception of the intellectual and constitutional history of the 1780's. One of the earliest and most important of these was Cecelia Kenyon's "Men of Little Faith: the Anti-Federalists on the Nature of Representative Government," *WMQ*, 12 (1955), 3–43; it should now be supplemented by the more extended discussion of Anti-Federalist thought in the Introduction to her anthology, *The Antifederalists* (1967). See also her essay on radicalism and democracy in the Revolutionary era, "Republicanism and Radicalism in the American Revolution: an Old-Fashioned Interpretation," *WMQ*, 19 (1962), 153–82. Benjamin F. Wright, Jr., has emphasized the continuity between the Constitution and previous fundamental law and has vigorously attacked the conceptions of Progressive dualism in *Consensus and Continuity, 1776–1787* (1958). I am much indebted to this little book, as I am to Richard B. Morris's article criticizing the Beard-Jensen tradition, "The Confederation Period and the Historian," *WMQ*, 13 (1956), 139–56, and to the same author's analysis of the Populist-Progressive school, "Class Struggle and the American Revolution," *WMQ*, 19 (1962), 3–29. Stanley Elkins and Eric McKitrick in "The Founding Fathers: Young Men of the Revolution," *PSQ*, 76 (1961), 181–216, emphasize the Constitution as a consummation rather than a negation of the Revolution. Viewing the whole period in a comparative perspective, Robert R. Palmer sees it substantially the same way in *The Age of the Democratic Revolution*, I, *The Challenge* (1959), chapters VII–IX, esp. 214–17, 228–35. Another writer who perceives the continuity of Revolution and Constitution is Hannah Arendt, *On Revolution* (1963), especially chapter IV. The efforts of historians to understand early American democracy are shrewdly discussed by J. R. Pole in "Historians and the Problem of Early American Democracy," *AHR*, 67 (1962), 624–46. The same author's more recent book, *Political Representation in Eng-*

land and the Origins of the American Republic (1967), is a work
of fundamental importance in tracing the evolution of majority
rule in America. Bernard Bailyn takes issue with the intellectual
tradition of the Progressive historians in "Political Experience
and Enlightenment Ideas in Eighteenth Century America," *AHR*,
67 (1962), 339–51. See also Martin Diamond, "Democracy and
The Federalist: a Reconsideration of the Framers' Intent," *APSR*,
53 (1959), 52–68; John P. Roche, "The Founding Fathers: A
Reform Caucus in Action," *APSR*, 55 (1961), 799–816; Forrest
McDonald, "The Anti-Federalists, 1781–1789," *WMQ*, 46 (1963),
206–14; and Cecelia Kenyon, " 'An Economic Interpretation of the
Constitution' after Fifty Years," *Centennial Review*, 7 (1963),
327–52.

State studies

I have not attempted, in reconsidering Beard's book, to read
systematically in the internal history of the states, but a few
items stand out that are either focused directly on his thesis or
otherwise shed light upon it. One of the earliest was Philip Crowl,
Maryland During and After the Revolution (1943), in which
Beard's own assistance is acknowledged, but which discerns a
pattern of division markedly different from Beard's. Another was
Robert E. Thomas's "The Virginia Convention of 1788," *JSH*,
19 (1953), which systematically demonstrates the economic and
sociological homogeneity of the leadership of the two sides, as
manifest in the members of the ratifying convention. Richard
McCormick's study of New Jersey, *Experiment in Independence*
(1950), is illuminating on a state in which no serious controversy
took place. William C. Pool, "An Economic Interpretation of the
Ratification of the Federal Constitution in North Carolina,"
North Carolina Historical Review, 27 (1950), 119–41, 289–313,
and 437–61, collects systematic information on the delegates in
the manner of Thomas; and though Pool does not seem to me to
generalize with high precision from his data, he leaves little
doubt that Beard's version of the controversy is not fully borne
out in this state. Forrest McDonald's *E Pluribus Unum*, already
cited, is challenging on the situation in Pennsylvania. Linda
Grant De Pauw, *The Eleventh Pillar* (1967), a study of New York,
proceeds as though Beard's socio-economic categories are practically irrelevant; and though I am not persuaded by all her
generalizations (she certainly goes too far in finding some kind
of triumph for the Anti-Federalists in ratification), she is successful in cutting the issue between the two factions down to size.
A valuable supplement and corrective is the unpublished Columbia
University MA thesis (1966) by Edwin G. Burrows, *The Meaning
of Federalism and Anti-Federalism: New York and the Constitu-*

tion, which also sheds a good deal of light on the validity, at least in one state, of the analytical categories suggested by Elkins and McKitrick in "The Founding Fathers," already cited. A new study is needed for Massachusetts, though I have been much enlightened by Oscar and Mary Handlin, "Radicals and Conservatives in Massachusetts after Independence," *NEQ*, 17 (1944), 345–55, and by Robert East "The Massachusetts Conservatives in the Critical Period," in R. B. Morris, ed., *The Era of the American Revolution* (1939), 349–91, as well as Robert E. Brown's researches on earlier developments as reported in *Middle Class Democracy and the Revolution in Massachusetts, 1691–1780* (1955).

Writings of the 1920's and 1930's

Besides *The Rise of American Civilization* (1927) which is discussed at some length in the text, Beard amplified his ideas in *The Economic Basis of Politics* (1922). A curious feature of this book, which was based on lectures given at Amherst in 1916, is its omission of Karl Marx from the names of those who developed an economic interpretation of history and politics; Beard discusses Aristotle, Machiavelli, Locke, Madison, Daniel Webster, and Calhoun as proponents of this idea, but not Marx or Engels. In 1945, this book was reissued with a long chapter on "Economics and Politics in our Revolutionary Age," which records Beard's responses to bolshevism and fascism as they bear upon the economic interpretation of politics and marks a notable retreat from his earlier views. The text of this work is reprinted, along with other portions of Beard's work bearing on the same theme in William Beard's edition, *The Economic Basis of Politics and Related Writings* (1957). Beard's general survey of modern American government (with William Beard), *The American Leviathan* (1930), is one of his better books. Always a sharp critic of "American individualism," Beard wrote a scathing brief dissection of *The Myth of Rugged Individualism* (1932), a sort of answer to Herbert Hoover. His resistance to individualism is also manifest in his treatment of Turner in *Books That Changed Our Minds* (1938), ed. by Malcolm Cowley and Bernard Smith. His sympathy for the idea of planning is evident in a series of books he wrote on the New Deal with George H. E. Smith, among them *The Future Comes* (1933), *The Recovery Program* (1934), and *The Old Deal and the New* (1940); but his most considered account, as a historian, of the 1930's is his *America in Midpassage*, two vols. (1939), written with Mary Beard as a part of the series started with *The Rise of American Civilization;* it is illuminating on many of his views on both domestic and foreign policy. Beard's resistance to the old idea of trustbusting and his sense

that the New Deal was floundering in its return to this exploded
idea is clear in a memorable article, "The Anti-Trust Racket,"
NR, 96 (1938), 182–4. Beard's receptiveness to planning and
to the enlarged role of government in modern life is discussed
by Borning, especially chapter V.

Beard and Historical Relativism

The essential documents here are Beard's Presidential Address to the American Historical Association, "Written History
as an Act of Faith," *AHR*, 39 (1934), 219–27; "That Noble
Dream," *AHR*, 41 (1935), 74–87; "Currents of Thought in Historiography," written with Alfred Vagts, *AHR*, 42 (1937), 460–
483; and his book, *The Discussion of Human Affairs* (1936).
Beard's influence was also strong and his written contribution
of much importance in the Report of the Committee on Historiography set up by the Social Science Research Council in
1946; see Merle E. Curti, ed., *Theory and Practice in Historical
Study*, SSRC Bulletin No. 54 (1946). Some of Beard's problems
with relativism are aired in *The Open Door at Home* (1934) and
in the opening sequences of *The Devil Theory of War* (1936),
discussed below. His break from historical scientism and his
espousal of a sweeping idealism is interestingly manifest in his
Introduction to the 1932 edition of J. B. Bury's *The Idea of Progress*. Elias Berg, *The Historical Thinking of Charles A. Beard*
(1957), published in Stockholm, is incredibly scholastic in its
procedures, but it is useful nonetheless. For critiques of Beard,
see Maurice Mandelbaum, *The Problem of Historical Knowledge*
(1938), Morton White, *Social Thought in America* (1949),
especially chapter XIV, and Cushing Strout, *The Pragmatic
Revolt in American History*. See also Whitaker T. Deininger,
"The Skepticism and Historical Faith of Charles A. Beard," *JHI*,
15 (1954), 573–88; Harry J. Marks, "Ground Under Our Feet:
Beard's Relativism," *JHI*, 14 (1953), 628–33; and Lloyd R. Soren-
son, "Charles A. Beard and German Historiographical Thought,"
MVHR, 42 (1955), 274–87. Theodore Clarke Smith's essay, "The
Writing of American History in America, from 1884 to 1934,"
AHR, 40 (1935), 439–49, attacked Beard and prompted his
piece, "That Noble Dream." Among historians who find an
intimate relation between Beard's relativism and his political
views are Samuel Eliot Morison, "Did Roosevelt Start the War?
History Through a Beard," *Atlantic Monthly*, 182 (1948), 91–7,
which appears in a different version in *By Land and by Sea*
(1953), and Chester M. Destler, "Some Observations on Contemporary Historical Theory," *AHR*, 55 (1950), 503–29. Some
of Beard's intellectual indebtednesses are discussed by Gerald D.
Nash in "Self-Education in Historiography," *PNQ*, 52 (1961),
108–15.

Beard and Foreign Policy

Beard's periodical writings in this area, as in several others, are voluminous, and I have not tried to go much beyond his primary books. Here the basic works are *The Idea of National Interest* (1934); *The Open Door at Home* (1934); *The Devil Theory of War* (1936); *Giddy Minds and Foreign Quarrels* (1939), which is in fact a short pamphlet based upon an article for *Harper's*; *A Foreign Policy for America* (1940); and the two books on Roosevelt: *American Foreign Policy in the Making, 1932–40* (1941), and *President Roosevelt and the Coming of the War, 1941* (1948). Relevant here also is Beard's testimony before Congress on a couple of occasions; see Borning, *Political and Social Thought*, 278, for references. See also his articles, "National Politics and War," *Scribner's Magazine*, 97 (1935), 65–70, which is discussed in the text, and "We're Blundering Into War," *American Mercury*, 46 (1939), 388–99. The setting is made clear in two books, Warren I. Cohen's excellent *The American Revisionists* (1966) and Manfred Jonas, *Isolationism in America, 1935–1941* (1966). Also helpful were Wayne Cole, *The America First Committee* (1953); Walter Johnson, *The Battle Against Isolation* (1944); and Selig Adler, *The Isolationist Impulse* (1957). See also Adler's "The War Guilt Question and American Disillusionment, 1918–1928," *Journal of Modern History*, 23 (1951), 1–28; and Wayne S. Cole, "American Entry into World War II: A Historiographical Appraisal," *MVHR*, 43 (1957), 595–617. A penetrating critique is that of Gerald Stourzh, "Charles A. Beard's Interpretations of Foreign Policy," *World Affairs Quarterly*, 28 (1957), 111–48. Among the many historians of the pre-Pearl Harbor period who are directly or inferentially critical, Basil Rauch is most explicit in *Roosevelt: From Munich to Pearl Harbor* (1950). See also Samuel Eliot Morison's "Did Roosevelt Start the War?" already cited. I have profited from reading Roberta Wohlstetter, *Pearl Harbor: Warning and Decision* (1962). Beard's views on navalism and on the effects of internal politics on foreign policy were very much influenced in 1931 and afterward by the work of a young radical German historian, Eckart Kehr, whose book, *Schlachtflottenbau und Parteipolitik* (1930), was called to his attention by his son-in-law, Alfred Vagts. See the Introduction by Hans-Ulrich Wehler to Kehr's posthumous volume of essays, *Der Primat der Innenpolitik* (1965), especially 8–9, and Beard's "Making a Bigger and Better Navy," *NR*, 68 (1931), 223–6, reprinted in his *The Navy: Defense or Portent?* (1932), and in *The Economic Basis of Politics*, already cited, 121–8.

Thomas C. Kennedy, "Charles A. Beard and the 'Court Historians,'" *Historian*, 25 (1963), 439–50, takes issue with Beard's allegation that important documents were being withheld from

critical historians like himself and made available only to more
or less "official" spokesmen. Peter A. Soderberg, "Charles A.
Beard and the Radical Right," *Teachers College Record*, 68 (1967),
631–9, makes it clear that Beard's anti-Roosevelt writings have
never succeeded in endearing him to the far right, for which he
is a figure of all but diabolic dimensions.

Beard's later writings, other than foreign policy

The American Spirit (with Mary R. Beard) (1942), the last
of the cycle begun with *The Rise of American Civilization*, is a
dreary book on the intellectual history of the United States in
terms of the idea of civilization, which besides displaying that
ineptitude with the history of culture which so often characterized Beard, shows a new note of complacent nationalism. *The
Republic* (1943), subtitled *Conversations on Fundamentals*, cast
in the form of a dialogue, was one of Beard's most readable books.
In various passages it incarnates that retreat from his earlier
iconoclasm which is often in evidence in this period of his life.
Aside from splendid sales in its regular edition, this book was
taken up by *Life* magazine and distributed in an edition of over
4,000,000. *The Beards' Basic History of the United States* (1944),
which also represents Beard's retreat toward what John K. Gal-
braith has called the conventional wisdom, contrasts interestingly
in its interpretations with *The Rise of American Civilization*, whose
sales were considerably smaller, but whose intellectual influence was much greater. *The Enduring Federalist* (1948) is a
selection, acompanied by an affectionate introduction. Of the three
authors of this treatise Beard wrote understandingly (p. 34):
"This is not to say that they were never disingenuous, that they
never 'shaded' their facts, or that they never revealed any prejudices. Such perfection is beyond mortal power. But even their
stoutest foes had to admit that they kept the great argument on a
high level of basic assumptions, frankness and practical reasoning." Was this also a comment on his own aims and limitations?

PARRINGTON

Parrington's writings

Unpublished papers are mentioned below among biographical
materials. The three volumes of *Main Currents in American
Thought* comprise: I, *The Colonial Mind, 1620–1800* (1927); II,
The Romantic Revolution in America, 1800–1860 (1927); III,
The Beginnings of Critical Realism in America, 1860–1920
(1930). Parrington sought a publisher for *Main Currents* from
1917 onward, and was several times rebuffed. In 1924 it was accepted by a university press, which, however, asked for a $500

subsidy toward publication. It was then accepted by B. W. Huebsch, but because the publisher was having financial diffi- culties, he was unable to keep his commitment. Van Wyck Brooks, who had read it for Huebsch, recommended it to Harcourt, Brace, where it finally found lodgment in 1925. The essays on Cabell and Sinclair Lewis reprinted in vol. III had appeared independently in 1921 and 1927. Parrington's account of "The Puritan Divines," chapter III of *The Cambridge History of American Literature*, Vol. I (1917), is abbreviated from portions of *Main Currents*, and passages from the major work are also incorporated into his In- troduction to *The Connecticut Wits* (1926), an anthology.

Parrington's essay, "Economics and Criticism," written in 1917, remained unpublished until edited by Vernon Parrington, Jr., in *PNQ*, 44 (1953), 91–105. An essay, "The Development of Realism," appeared in *The Reinterpretation of American Literature* (1928), edited by Norman Foerster. Although Parrington seems to have published a number of poems, of which I have read sev- eral in manuscript, I have seen only one in print; it appears in *College Life*, the College of Emporia weekly, January 13, 1896. Some of his poems were published in Kansas newspapers, some in the old *Life*. See also his undergraduate oration "God in His- tory," *College Life*, February 21, 1891, interesting for its con- ventionality. Other essays of the Emporia years are "The Position of English in College Curricula," ibid., October 30, 1893; "On Novel-Reading," November 18, 1895; "Plain English vs. Pedantry," January 13, 1896; and the series, "Some Political Sketches," April 17, 24, May 1, 15, 25, 1897. In addition to these, see Parrington's Introduction to J. Allen Smith's, posthumous *The Growth and Decadence of Constitutional Government* (1930). To the 14th edition of the *Encyclopaedia Britannica* (1929) he contributed articles on "Nathaniel Hawthorne" and "American Literature to the End of the Nineteenth Century," and to the *Encyclopaedia of the Social Sciences* (1930) an article on "Brook Farm." He also wrote an introduction to the 1929 edition of Ole Rölvaag's *Giants in the Earth*. Among other minor writings are an article, "On the Lack of Privacy in American Village Homes," *House Beautiful*, 13 (1903), 109–12, and a twelve-page report, published as a pamphlet, "On Recent Developments in American College Archi- tecture" (1908).

There are brief *unsigned* reviews by Parrington, identified from his own list, in *N*, of the following: Santayana's *Philosophi- cal Opinion in America*, vol. 109 (1918), 614; Stephen Leacock's *The Unsolved Riddle of Social Justice*, 110 (1920), 772; Boris Brasol, *Socialism vs. Civilization*, 110 (1920), 860a; C. H. Douglas, *Economic Democracy*, 111 (1920), 19; Stella S. Centre, *The Worker and his Work*, 111 (1920), 59–51; O. F. Boucke, *The Limits of Socialism*, 111 (1920), 304; Richard Roberts, *The Un- finished Programme of Democracy*, 111 (1920), 330; J. M. Meck-

lin, *An Introduction to Social Ethics*, 111 (1920), 381; Edgar
Dawson, *Organized Self-Government*, 112 (1921), 796.

There are the following *signed* reviews, all in ibid.; C. E.
Merriam, *American Political Ideas, 1865–1917*, 112 (1921) 342–3;
Irwin Edman, *Human Traits and their Social Significance*, 112
(1921), 558–9; Kenneth B. Murdock, *Increase Mather*, 122
(1926), 453–4; Herbert Gorman, *Hawthorne: A Study in Solitude*,
125 (1927), 482–3; Mark Van Doren, ed., *Samuel Sewall's Diary*,
126 (1928), 22; Howard Mumford Jones, *America and French
Culture, 1750–1848*, 126 (1928), 454, 456; Charles A. Beard, ed.,
Whither Mankind, 127 (1928), 621–2; Ralph and Louise Boas,
Cotton Mather, 128 (1929), 137–8.

Parrington also reviewed the following: "Some Farmer-Labor
Books" (a miscellany), *Pacific Review*, 1 (1920), 434–7; Edith
Wharton, *The Age of Innocence*, ibid., 2 (1921), 157–60; Sinclair
Lewis, *Main Street*, ibid., 1 (1921), 607–10; Carl Van Doren, *The
American Novel*, ibid., 2 (1921), 516–18; Waldo Frank, *The Re-
Discovery of America*, in *Bookman*, 59 (1929), 441–2.

Among the above reviews those which seem to me to reveal
most about the development of Parrington's mind and taste are
those of books by Van Doren, Murdock, Douglas, Roberts, Beard,
and Wharton. His reviews of 1920 and 1921 reveal a somewhat
more radical spirit, though undoctrinaire and receptive, than *Main
Currents* itself. I do not know whether his radicalism, undoubtedly
raised to a new pitch by the war period and its aftermath, actually
waned somewhat by the time *Main Currents* was published. What
does seem true is that in the process of revision he tended to tone
it down.

Parrington not only reviewed for the *Nation* on occasion but
read it regularly; his other most favored periodical was the
Freeman.

Biographical

There is no adequate biographical account of Parrington, and
the best is his own, a revealing unpublished fifty-page memoir
dated 1918, which takes the story of his life to 1908. This memoir,
and Parrington's letters, in the possession of his son, Vernon Parrington, Jr., are my main biographical sources; they are not yet
available for general consultation. There are also a number of
passages with autobiographical resonances in *Main Currents*, of
which the most important is a sequence in vol. III, 401–13. E. H.
Eby's introduction to vol. III, v–xvii, has valuable comments and
the same author's sketch in the *Encyclopaedia of the Social Sciences* is helpful. There is not much additional information in the
appreciations by Joseph B. Harrison, a pamphlet, *Vernon Louis
Parrington: American Scholar* (1929), or in Russel Blankenship,
"Vernon L. Parrington," *N*, 129 (1929), 141–2, and William T.
Utter, "Vernon Louis Parrington," in W. T. Hutchinson, ed., *The*

Marcus W. Jernegan Essays in American Historiography (1937). Stephen Colwell, "The Populist Image of Vernon Louis Parrington," *MVHR*, 49 (1962), 52–66, corrects certain notions about Parrington's Populist activities in the 1890's, but only at the cost of minimizing the impact of Populism on his thinking; it is contradicted here by Parrington's account of himself. There are biographical gleanings in Parrington's writings for *College Life*, cited above, and in the *Reports* of the Secretary, Harvard College Class of 1893, for 1899, 1910, 1918, 1923. On the years in Norman there is very little, but see Roy Gittinger, *The University of Oklahoma, 1892–1942*, and Jimmie L. Franklin, "That Noble Experiment: A Note on Prohibition in Oklahoma," *Chronicles of Oklahoma*, 33 (1965), 19–34. The inquisitorial spirit that precipitated Parrington's departure from Norman is illuminated by four articles on the situation at the university in the *Outlook* for April 11, September 5, October 3, 17, 1908. On Parrington and Oklahoma football, Harold Keith, *Oklahoma Kickoff* (1948), is ample, if perhaps a little legendary at points. There is no account of Parrington at the University of Washington; but on J. Allen Smith see Thomas G. McClintock, "J. Allen Smith: A Pacific Northwest Progressive," *PNQ*, 53 (1962), 49–59, Eric F. Goldman, "J. Allen Smith: the Reformer and His Dilemma," *PNQ*, 35 (1944), 195–212, and Cushing Strout's excellent introduction to the John Harvard Library edition of *The Spirit of American Government* (1965). I have not seen McClintock's unpublished doctoral dissertation, *J. Allen Smith and the Progressive Movement: A Study in Intellectual History*, University of Washington, 1960.

Information about intellectual influences on Parrington is fragmentary, and the cues in the extensive bibliographies of *Main Currents*, will not take us far. Taine's importance, it seems to me, could easily be overemphasized, and he is not mentioned as a major force in Parrington's Memoir. But Parrington did owe something to Taine, and I found it helpful to browse in Taine's *History of English Literature* and to read René Wellek, *A History of Modern Criticism: 1750–1950*, vol. IV, *The Later Nineteenth Century* (1965) chapter 2, as well as Sholom J. Kahn, *Science and Aesthetic Judgment: A Study in Taine's Critical Method* (1953), Edmund Wilson, *To the Finland Station* (1940), chapter VII, and especially Harry Levin, *The Gates of Horn* (1963), chapter I. Parrington mentions his debt to Spencer and to Henry Drummond in his manuscript memoir, and his interest in Carlyle and Ruskin is clear (he had read *Unto this Last* by 1897), but his primary intellectual mentor was, he reported, William Morris; one may guess that it was *Hopes and Fears for Art* that affected him most, though he no doubt read *News from Nowhere* and many other writings.

Parrington's main intellectual obligation in interpreting American development was of course to J. Allen Smith, to whom

Main Curents is dedicated, especially to *The Spirit of American Government* (1907), and then to Beard's *An Economic Interpretation of the Constitution*. This influence is discussed particularly in I, 279–91, and III, 408–12, but also in his posthumous Introduction to Smith's *The Growth and Decadence of Constitutional Government* (1930). His treatment of the political history of Puritanism is similar to that in James Truslow Adams's anti-Puritan *The Founding of New England* (1921), and it is instructive to compare his view of the struggles of the Federalist era with that of Claude Bowers, *Jefferson and Hamilton* (1925), a fellow Jeffersonian partisan whom he had read. It is possible that Parrington was indebted to Georg Brandes's six-volume *Main Currents in Nineteenth Century Literature* (1872–90; available in English, 1901–05) for suggesting his title, but probably for little else; the final title was arrived at after correspondence with Harcourt, Brace editors, and it is not clear to me whether it was actually suggested first by Parrington. Parrington cites (III, 52–3) Santayana's "The Genteel Tradition in American Philosophy," which was first published in the *University of California Chronicle*, 13 (1911), and it was evident that it had an important effect on his conceptions of New England culture, as it did upon that of many other writers. He adopted two of Santayana's phrases, "genteel tradition" itself, and "winds of doctrine." It is also likely that Santayana's rather disdainful version of this aspect of American culture was reinforced by Van Wyck Brooks (who drew upon him too); Parrington had read Brooks's *The Ordeal of Mark Twain* (1920) and *The Pilgrimage of Henry James* (1925). Parrington's immediate indebtedness to Moses Coit Tyler's four volumes is clear; though he took a very different view of the Puritans from Tyler, he deeply appreciated Tyler's work, which he once described as "urbane, witty, catholic in knowledge and sympathy," *Pacific Review*, 2 (1921), 516–17. It would be rewarding to undertake a detailed comparison of Parrington's and Tyler's treatment of individual writers. Parrington also greatly admired Carl Van Doren's *The American Novel* (1921); cf. *ibid.*, 2 (1921), 516–18.

Reception of Main Currents

Bernard Smith's essay in *Books that Changed Our Minds* (1938), ed. by Malcolm Cowley and Bernard Smith, quite rightly dwells on the extraordinary applause with which *Main Currents* was greeted by reviewers of varying points of view, including many ordinarily identified as conservative. In frequency of mention, among authors nominating books for the essays in *Books that Changed Our Minds*, Parrington was roughly on a par with such seminal authors as Spengler and Whitehead, and with Lenin and I. A. Richards.

The near-unanimous enthusiasm of reviews is well illustrated by Parrington's scrapbook. Aside from the praise by Beard, quoted in the text, *Main Currents* was found to be as "accurate as sound scholarship should be" by Henry Seidel Canby, *Saturday Review*, 3 (1927), 925–6, who had some reservations only about its lack of esthetic judgment; was praised as a great book, with some cautious reservations by Percy H. Boynton, *NR*, 51 (1927), 181–2; was coupled by T. V. Smith with the Beards' *Rise of American Civilization* as "two great studies of American culture," *International Journal of Ethics*, 38 (1927), 112–15; and was conceded even by Kenneth Murdock, whom Parrington had treated rather sharply, as "having real merits" within its limits, *YR*, 17 (1928), 382–4. Henry Steele Commager found it "the finest piece of creative criticism in our literature," *The Symposium*, 2 (1931), 122–8. In retrospect, the most impressive of the reviews was that of Morris R. Cohen, *NR*, 65 (1931), 303–4, on the publication of volume III. Though generous in his estimate—he found the whole work to be done one of "rich and illuminating insight" and worthy to be put beside Tocqueville—he made a large number of pertinent general criticisms which I believe to be, almost point by point, correct.

The sales of *Main Currents* offer a challenge to those who would measure the "influence" of a work by the market place, and also an illuminating comparison of book-buying habits before and after the paperback revolution. In their first two years, volumes I and II sold somewhat less than 3,500 sets, and the typical annual sale of these volumes during the 1930's, when one supposes that Parrington was at the peak of his influence, was around 600 sets. Volume III usually sold a bit less than the two finished volumes. In 1939 Harcourt, Brace brought out a less expensive edition in which the three volumes were bound together. In its first year the one-volume edition sold 4,800; it reached a peak of 7,000 in 1946; and had sold, as of mid-1967, 83,000 altogether. In 1955, on the rising wave of paperback publication, the publishers brought out paperback editions of volumes I and II, which sold almost 10,000 copies each their first year and have since then usually sold 5–7,000 yearly. Volume III, which was not republished in this form until 1963, has had fewer readers. To mid-1967 their overall paperback sales were: I, 96,000; II, 87,000; III, 10,000. All in all, from the beginning 304,000 volumes have been sold in various editions. In 1962, the thirty-fifth anniversary of publication, *Main Currents* was bought by almost as many readers as during its entire first decade, 1927–36.

The intellectual milieu

Alfred Kazin offers a shrewd appraisal of Parrington and puts him in his literary and intellectual setting in *On Native Grounds* (1942). Henry Steele Commager's view in *The American Mind* (1950) is appreciative. On the state of criticism and the

history of ideas in America at the time Parrington was at work,
William Van O'Connor, *An Age of Criticism, 1900–1950* (1952),
is helpful, and Richard Ruland, *The Rediscovery of American
Literature* (1967), is excellent. For a broader context still, see
William K. Wimsatt, Jr., and Cleanth Brooks *Literary Criticism:
A Short History* (1957), chapters XXI, XXIV. Much is told about
the state of scholarship in American studies and certain special
problems in the relevant period in Howard Mumford Jones, *The
Theory of American Literature* (rev. ed., 1965), and in his *Ideas
in America* (1944), especially the essay "The Drift to Liberalism
in the American Eighteenth Century." Parrington is not discussed,
but the literary background of his working years is illuminated by
Henry May, *The End of American Innocence* (1959), which deals
with the years 1912–17. Bernard Smith's *Forces in American
Criticism* (1939) is an informal history written from a Marxist
point of view and one basically sympathetic to Parrington's intention. The literary atmosphere in which Parrington reached the
peak of his acceptance is surveyed at length in Daniel Aaron,
Writers on the Left (1961), and somewhat comparable, though
Marxist rather than Jeffersonian, tendencies in criticism are illustrated by Granville Hicks, *The Great Tradition* (rev. ed., 1935),
and V. F. Calverton, *The Liberation of American Literature* (1932).
A rough counterpart of these books in the Progressive era was
John Macy's *The Spirit of American Literature* (1913); I have
no idea whether Parrington was acquainted with this socialist
critic, though he owned a copy of the Modern Library edition
(1913). Parrington is set in the context of other writers on the
history of ideas in the United States by Robert A. Skotheim, *American Intellectual Histories and Historians* (1966). See also John
Higham, "The Rise of American Intellectual History," *AHR*, 56
(1951), 463–71, and "American Intellectual History: A Critical
Appraisal," *AQ*, 13 (1961), 219–33, as well as the same writer's
passages on Parrington in Higham, et al., *History* (1965).

Parrington criticism and commentary

In point of its timing and influence, no Parrington criticism
was more important than Lionel Trilling's essay, "Reality in America," in *The Liberal Imagination* (1950); however, readers particularly interested in Parrington would do well to read the longer
essay from which the remarks on Parrington were adapted for
this book; it appeared as "Parrington, Mr. Smith and Reality," in
Partisan Review, 8 (1940), 24–40. Granville Hicks, "The Critical
Principles of V. L. Parrington," *Science and Society*, 3 (1939),
443–60, is a perceptive account of certain limitations in Parrington's Jeffersonianism, though it loses its persuasiveness when it
begins to argue that a more inclusive and assertive Marxian determinism would have cleared up Parrington's problems. The essay

by Alfred Kazin, cited above, is amply critical, and it sets forth the reasons for the further waning of Parrington's reputation which it confidently forecast in 1942. A characteristically forthright assault on Parrington by the late Yvor Winters ("brutally crude thinking . . . vulgar floridity . . . obsolete before it was written") appeared in his *The Anatomy of Nonsense* (1943) and may be most conveniently found now in the Winters omnibus, *In Defense of Reason* (1947), 556–64. David W. Noble emphasizes the regressive aspect of Parrington's Jeffersonianism in *Historians against History* (1965). Arthur A. Ekirch, Jr., sees clearly and sympathizes with the anti-statist elements in Parrington's philosophy in "Parrington and the Decline of American Liberalism," *AQ*, 3 (1951), 295–308. The close analysis of Parrington's rhetorical technique in Robert A. Skotheim and Kermit Vanderbilt, "Vernon Louis Parrington: the Mind and Art of a Historian of Ideas," *PNQ*, 53 (1962), 100–13, is valuable; this is an indispensable study. For a tempered defense of Parrington's liberalism, see Merrill D. Peterson, "Parrington and American Liberalism," *VQR*, 30 (1954), 35–49. I am not much persuaded by the comparison set forth by Louis Filler, "Parrington and Carlyle," *Antioch Review*, 12 (1952), 203–16.

Probably the first of a number of efforts to test Parrington on various particulars was Esther E. Burch's article, "The Sources of New England Democracy," *American Literature*, 1 (1929), 115–30, which is directed entirely at Parrington's belief that Lutheranism was the source of the democratic tendency in New England dissent; though it does not deal at much length with the substance of Luther's thought, it suggests how much at variance Parrington was with the best Luther authorities of his own period. The literature in which the limitations of Parrington's view of the Puritans are indirectly and inferentially shown has now become enormous, and it would be pointless to try to list very much of it. His views are made the object of some direct discussion in most of those that follow. For his notion of the secular and democratic elements in Roger Williams, see Alan Simpson, "How Democratic was Roger Williams?" *WMQ*, 13 (1956), 53–67; Mauro Calamandrei, "Neglected Aspects of Roger Williams' Thought," *Church History*, 21 (1952), 239–58; and Perry Miller's introduction to his documentary selection, *Roger Williams* (1953). Thomas Hooker's forward strides toward democracy and the extent of his philosophical differences with the rulers of Massachusetts are minimized by Perry Miller in "Thomas Hooker and the Democracy of Early Connecticut," *NEQ*, 4 (1931), 663–712, which is most conveniently accessible in his *Errand into the Wilderness* (1956). Parrington's version of the Mathers, and incidentally of John Wise, is most effectively contested by Clifford K. Shipton, "The New England Clergy of the 'Glacial Age,'" *Publications* of the Colonial Society of Massachusetts, 32 (1937), 24–55, an important paper; and less

elaborately in "A Plea for the Puritans," *AHR*, 40 (1935), 460–7.
Parrington's dualism, as manifested in his treatment of the Declaration of Independence and the Constitution, is sharply challenged by Douglass Adair, "The Tenth *Federalist* Revisited," *WMQ*,
8 (1951), 48–67. Parrington's conception of a major Physiocratic
influence in American thought is the primary concern of my
own essay, "Parrington and the Jeffersonian Tradition," *JHI*, 2
(1941), 391–400. Robert A. Skotheim in two articles, "Environmental Interpretations of Ideas by Beard, Parrington and Curti,"
PHR, 33 (1964), 35–44, and "The Writing of American Histories
of Ideas: Two Traditions in the XXth Century," *JHI*, 25 (1964),
257–78, is concerned with the disposition of historians of ideas in
the Progressive tradition, among them Parrington and Beard, to
attribute passivity (i.e., a response to "interests") to ideas they
dislike and an active power to ideas they like.

The preponderantly English (as opposed to French) backgrounds of American radical and dissenting thought have been
assessed in innumerable works, and it may suffice to cite only a
few of the most important recent books: for latitudinarian thought,
Conrad Wright, *The Beginnings of Unitarianism in America*
(1955), and the works of Perry Miller generally, and especially
his remarks in *Jonathan Edwards* (1949), 108 ff.; for historical
thought, Trevor Colbourn, *The Lamp of Experience* (1965); for
political thought, Bernard Bailyn's *Ideological Origins of the
American Revolution* (1967); for humanitarian reform, Frank
Thistlethwaite, *The Anglo-American Connection in the Early Nineteenth Century* (1958).

CONFLICT AND CONSENSUS

Revisionist Literature of the 1950's: The Revolution

It is impossible to cite more than a small portion of the most
significant works of this period. Many of them are dealt with
above in connection with the critiques of Beard on the Constitution. There is a very extensive literature on revisionism in the era
of the American Revolution. An excellent account of it is given
by Jack P. Greene, "The Flight from Determinism: A Review of
Recent Literature on the Coming of the American Revolution,"
SAQ, 51 (1962), 235–59. See also Edmund S. Morgan, "The
American Revolution: Revisions in Need of Revising," *WMQ*, 14
(1957), 3–15, and Peter Marshall, "Radicals, Conservatives, and
the American Revolution," *Past and Present*, 23 (1962), 44–56.
Clinton Rossiter writes in a consensus vein in his *Seedtime of the
Republic* (1953). The revolutionary impact of the American Revo-
lution is stoutly argued by Robert R. Palmer, *The Age of the*

Democratic Revolution, Vol. I: *The Challenge* (1960), and in his essay, "The Revolution," in C. Vann Woodward, ed., *The Comparative Approach to American History* (1968). The whole question is viewed circumspectly by Richard B. Morris in *The American Revolution Reconsidered* (1967). This book may be profitably contrasted with J. F. Jameson, *The American Revolution Considered as a Social Movement* (1926). For an interesting effort to rehabilitate some aspects of the Progressive historians' view of the Revolution, see Gordon S. Wood, "Rhetoric and Reality in the American Revolution," *WMQ*, 23 (1966), 3–32. Of decisive importance on revolutionary thought is Cecelia Kenyon, "Republicanism and Radicalism in the American Revolution," ibid., 19 (1962), 153–82. Two works of basic importance, not only for the light they shed on the Revolution itself but for the suggestiveness of their approach to the place of ideas in historical analysis are Bernard Bailyn, *The Ideological Origins of the American Revolution* (1967) and *The Origins of American Politics* (1968).

Jacksonian Democracy

A brilliant and distinctive embodiment of the Progressive views is Arthur Schlesinger, Jr.'s, *The Age of Jackson* (1945). A similar point of view can be found both in the Beards' *The Rise of American Civilization* and in the elder Schlesinger's essay on Jacksonian democracy in *New Viewpoints in American History* (1922). One of the major monographic incarnations of this view, still valuable, is Dixon Ryan Fox, *The Decline of Aristocracy in the Politics of New York* (1919). As of 1958, the criticisms of this view were well bibliographed by Charles G. Sellers, Jr., "Andrew Jackson Versus the Historians," *MVHR*, 34 (1958), 615–38, and there is a good recent essay on the subject by John William Ward in John Higham, ed., *The Reconstruction of American History* (1962). Aspects of the entrepreneurial view of Jacksonian democracy are developed in my essay, "William Leggett, Spokesman of Jacksonian Democracy," *PSQ*, 48 (1943), 581–94, and more clearly in the chapter on Jackson in *The American Political Tradition*. For a more extended statement of this view see Bray Hammond's major work, *Banks and Politics in America* (1957), and his essay, "Jackson, Biddle, and the Bank of the United States, *JEH*, 7 (1947), 1–23; also the treatment of economic writers of the period in Joseph Dorfman, *The Economic Mind in American Civilization*, II (1946), *passim*. On the importance of wage-earners, see Dorfman's "The Jackson Wage-Earner Thesis," *AHR*, 54 (1949), 296–306, and Schlesinger's reply, ibid., 54 (1949), 185–6. On Jackson's role see Richard B. Morris, "Andrew Jackson, Strike-Breaker," *AHR*, 55 (1949), 54–68. The most satisfactory study of workingmen's movements in this respect is Walter Hugins, *Jacksonian Democracy and the Working Class* (1960), and its

bibliography accounts for the most important items in the literature.

On the politics of Jacksonianism, see Richard P. McCormick's
important articles, "Suffrage Classes and Party Alignments: A
Study in Voter Behavior," *MVHR*, 46 (1959), 397–410, which
minimizes the effects of the suffrage extension and again questions the role of sections and classes in the pattern of voting, and
"New Perspectives on Jacksonian Politics," *AHR*, 65 (1960), 288–
301, which questions the notion of a democratic "uprising" at the
polls in the Jackson era. See also his *The Second American Party
System* (1966). A further challenge to Progressive historiography
in this area may be found in Lee Benson's *The Concept of Jacksonian Democracy* (1961); more recently, three articles by F. O.
Getell shed new light on this controversy and give some comfort
to historians in the Progressive tradition: "Money and Party in
Jacksonian America," *PSQ*, 82 (1967), 235–52; "Sober Second
Thoughts on Van Buren, the Albany Regency, and the Wall Street
Conspiracy," *JAH*, 53 (1966), 19–40; "Spoils of the Bank War,"
AHR, 70 (1964), 35–58.

Reconstruction

The older view is expressed in the relevant chapters of Charles
and Mary Beard's *The Rise of American Civilization* (1927) and
in Howard K. Beale's *The Critical Year* (1930; rev. ed., 1958). The
attack on the Beardian notion of a unified capitalist class can be
found in Stanley Coben, "Northeastern Business and Radical Reconstruction," *MVHR*, 44 (1959), 67–90, Robert P. Sharkey,
Money, Class and Party (1959), and Irwin Unger, *The Greenback
Era* (1964). Andrew Johnson's tactics and his relation to capitalist support are treated with a newly critical perspective by Eric
McKitrick, *Andrew Johnson and Reconstruction* (1960), and W. R.
Brock, *An American Crisis: Congress and Reconstruction, 1865–67*
(1963). The importance of partisan political, as against purely
economic factors in Reconstruction is suggested by David Donald's
quest for the centers of support for the Radicals in *The Politics of
Reconstruction, 1863–67* (1965). New points of view have been
incorporated critically in a masterful brief statement, *The Era
of Reconstruction, 1865–1877* (1965), by Kenneth M. Stampp,
who also bibliographs more of the relevant literature than I can
account for here. On the literature, see also Bernard Weisberger,
"The Dark and Bloody Ground of Reconstruction Historiography,"
JSH, 25 (1959), 427–47.

Consensus Theorists

The most important attempts to state the general implications
of the idea of consensus are those of Louis Hartz and Daniel J.
Boorstin. The ideas set forth in Hartz's *The Liberal Tradition in*

America (1955) had been developed by the author in a series of articles that appeared in 1952 in the *APSR* and the *Western Political Quarterly*. A portion of Boorstin's *The Genius of American Politics* (1953) also appeared in *WMQ* in 1950. Further development of Boorstin's ideas may be found in *The Americans: The Colonial Experience* (1958) and *The Americans: The National Experience* (1965); the second of these works marks an almost complete turn from political to social history. On the first of these volumes see "History and the Distrust of Knowledge" by Bernard Bailyn, *NR*, 139 (1958), 17–18, and the review by Cecelia Kenyon, *WMQ*, 16 (1959), 585–9. Boorstin expresses a more critical view of many aspects of contemporary American life in *The Image* (1961). Hartz's ideas are discussed by himself, and by Marvin Meyers, Leonard Krieger, and Henry V. Jaffa in *Comparative Studies in Society and History*, 5 (1963), 261–84, and by Hartz again in "American Historiography and Comparative Analysis: Further Reflections," ibid., 5 (1963), 365–78. For an excellent brief statement of Hartz's views, see his essay, "The Rise of the Democratic Idea," in *Paths of American Thought* (1963), ed. by Arthur Schlesinger, Jr., and Morton White. There is an astute review of his book by Eric McKitrick, "Is there an American Political Philosophy?" *NR*, 132 (1955), 22–5. John Higham accounts for the decline of Progressive history and the rise of consensus in *History* (1965), chapters V and VI. Among other statements of the role of consensus, see the Introduction to my *The American Political Tradition* (1948) and its chapters on Jefferson, Jackson, and Lincoln. See also W. B. Hesseltine, "Four American Traditions," *JSH*, 27 (1961), 3–32.

The most notable critique of consensus history is that of John Higham in "The Cult of the 'American Consensus,' " *Commentary*, 27 (1959), 93–100, and "Beyond Consensus: The Historian as Moral Critic," *AHR*, 67 (1962), 609–25. J. R. Pole, "The American Past: Is It Still Usable?" *Journal of American Studies*, 1 (1967), 63–78, is a witty essay on contemporary American historical thought. In "The North and South of It," *American Scholar*, 35 (1960), 647–58, C. Vann Woodward, writing largely about race, argues that America has made up in the "indigenous tensions of her peculiar heritage" what she lacked in class conflict. There is also a large relevant literature, pro and con, of which I am familiar with the following: J. Rogers Hollingsworth, "Consensus and Continuity in Recent American Historical Writing," *SAQ*, 61 (1962), 40–50; Burl Noggle, "Variety and Ambiguity: The Recent Approach to Southern History," *Mississippi Quarterly*, 17 (1963–4), 21–35; Samuel P. Hays, "The Social Analysis of American Political History, 1880–1920," *PSQ*, 80 (1965), 373–94; Dwight W. Hoover, "Some Comments on Recent United States Historiography," *AQ*, 17 (1965), 299–318; Harvey Wish, "The American Historian and the New Conservatism," *SAQ*, 65 (1966),

178–91; A. S. Eisenstadt, "The Perennial Myth—Writing American History Today," *Massachusetts Review*, 7 (1966), 757–99; Kenneth McNaught, "American Progressives and the Great Society," *JAH*, 53 (1966), 504–20; W. R. Brock, "Race and the American Past: A Revolution in Historiography," *History*, 52 (1967), 49–59. Gene Wise, "Political 'Reality' in Recent American Scholarship: Progressives versus Symbolists," *AQ*, 19 (1967), 303–28, discusses the new disposition of historians to see the symbolic aspects of political life, a theme that runs through several of the essays of my own *The Paranoid Style in American Politics* (1965). The mixed reception of consensus history by left historians is accounted for by Irwin Unger in "The 'New Left' and American History," *AHR*, 72 (1967), 1237–63; some of the anguish, in my opinion gratuitous and self-imposed, through which a few left historians have put themselves over consensus history, is illustrated by Norman Pollack, "Hofstadter on Populism: A Critique of *The Age of Reform*," *JSH*, 26 (1960), 478–500.

One of the failures, thus far, of most historians who have written on the conflict-consensus controversy, has been to take sufficient notice of a convergent interest among political scientists and political sociologists, who have looked at this argument in terms of the prevalence of certain democratic norms among the electorate, the extent to which the supposed basic principles of the American consensus are in fact adhered to by the electorate, the relative weight of elite and mass in a consensus, and other questions of trans-national significance. A good beginning here is Herbert McCloskey, "Consensus and Ideology in American Politics," *APSR*, 58 (1964), 361–82, and McCloskey, Hoffmann, and O'Hara, "Issue Conflict and Consensus Among Party Leaders and Followers," ibid., 44 (1960), 406–27. V. O. Key deals with important related issues in his *Public Opinion and American Democracy* (1961), especially Part I. Seymour M. Lipset has relevant observations on the economic and social prerequisites of democratic development in *Political Man* (1960); see also the discussion by Ernest S. Griffith, John Plamenatz, and J. Roland Pennock "Cultural Prerequisites to a Successfully Functioning Democracy," *APSR*, 50 (1956), 101–37. The functional character of conflict is emphasized by Lewis Coser in *The Functions of Social Conflict* (1956), and by Georg Simmel in his classical essay, *Der Streit* (1908), reprinted in *Conflict and the Web of Group Affiliations* (1964), and the issue of class conflict is discussed in Ralf Dahrendorf, *Class and Conflict in Industrial Society* (1959). Several of the essays by Daniel Bell in *The End of Ideology* (1960) are relevant. See also the essay by Robert A. Dahl in *Political Oppositions in Western Democracies* (1966) and J. W. Prothro and C. W. Grigg, "Fundamental Principles of Democracy: Bases of Agreement and Disagreement, *Journal of Politics*, 22 (1960), 276–94.

Index

Abernethy, Thomas P., 135
abolitionism, 22
Acton, Lord, 44
Adair, Douglass, 223, 247
Adair v. United States, 201–2
Adams, Brooks, 21, 353; *The Theory of Social Revolutions*, 202
Adams, Charles Francis, Jr., 21
Adams, Charles K.: *Manual of Historical Literature*, 25
Adams, George Burton, 35
Adams, Henry, 22, 31–3, 35, 96, 412; *Education*, 30; *Letter to American Teachers . . .* , 34
Adams, Herbert Baxter, 36, 38–9, 65–8, 77, 80
Adams, John, 4, 17, 30–1, 239, 248, 254, 295, 353, 409, 425
Adams, John Quincy, 30–1, 279
Adams, Samuel, 269, 406
Adams school, 38–9, 66–9, 72
Addams, Jane, 170
agrarian-capitalist conflict, 293–8, 447, 460
agrarian crisis of 1890's, 59–66, 75
agrarianism: *see* farmer; Physiocratic agrarianism; Populism
Aldrich, Thomas B., 410–11, 412
Alien and Sedition Acts, 202, 295
Allen, William F., 55, 64
Altgeld, John P., 28, 170
Ambler, C. H., 190

America First, 287, 341
American Civil Liberties Union, 290
American Historical Association, 33, 47, 55, 76, 77, 117, 219, 288 *n.*, 290, 306
American Revolution, 7–10, 17, 29, 162, 235–6, 256, 264, 266, 268–9, 302, 415–16, 418–23, 441, 443, 446, 455, 459–60
Americus, Kansas, 359–61
Ames, Fisher, 404
Andrews, C. M., 29, 39, 66
Anglo-Saxon, 66; *see also* Teutonism
Anti-Federalists, 223, 233, 236–9, 249, 260–3, 276–82, 293
antimajoritarianism, 85–6, 182, 195, 257–63
Articles of Confederation, 208, 210, 266, 271; state system under, 191, 231; socio-political complexities of, 232–7, 263–4, 273

Bagehot, Walter, 282; *Physics and Politics*, 70
Bailyn, Bernard, 443
Baltimore, 67
Bancroft, George, 11–13, 15–20, 36, 37, 207, 464
Bancroft, Hubert Howe, 58

i

Bank of the United States, 15, 296

banking laws, 22

Barlow, Joel, 406

Barnes, Harry E., 320, 343–4

Beale, Howard K., 442

Beard, Charles A., xi–xvii, 21, 29–30, 41, 72, 77, 94, 126, 437, 441, 451; *An Economic Interpretation of the Constitution . . .* , xi, 181, 183 n., 187 n., 188, 189, 207 ff., 311–12; *The Rise of American Civilization*, xi, 218, 222, 298–304, 314; on frontier thesis, 48, 54, 190 and n.; on American individualism, 145 n.; family background of, 167–9; social criticism of, 168; nonacademic enterprises of, 168–9, 288–92; political background of, 168; Quaker schooling of, 169; at De Pauw, 168–170; and Spanish-American War, 171 and n., 318–19; on American imperialism, 171 n., 319; Oxford years of, 172–9; influence of Ruskin on, 172–4; moralist-scientist ambivalence of, 173, 177, 178, 214–18, 227–230, 322, 335–6; at Cornell, 175; *Industrial Revolution*, 175–176; at Ruskin Hall, 175–7; *Young Oxford*, essays of, 176–177, 178; selective use of historical fact by, 177, 231–43, 249–52, 263; evolutionism of, 177, 304–17; *The Office of Justice of the Peace in England*, 177, 179; Columbia period, 179–181; controversy, 285–8; personability of, 179–80; "socialism" of, 181 and n., 196, 205–6 n., 340; productivity of, 181; and revolt against formalism, 183–4; influence of political realist school on, 186–8; on law, 187 n; dualism in political theory of, 188, 226–7, 265–70, 304–17; *The Economic Basis of Politics*, 188, 313; on political philosophy, 188; on function of government, 189;

influence of Turner school on, 190–1, 208; on Libby paper, 191; influence of Progressive constitutional critics, 191–6; influence of socialist scholarship on, 196–200; influence of sociological jurisprudence on, 200–206, 208; *The Supreme Court and the Constitution*, 202–6; on thought of Madison, 208, 247; on property as basis of government, 208; historiographical innovations of, 211; critical reception of *Economic Interpretation*, 212–13 and n., 214–216; influence of thought of, 219–20; partial recant of thesis by, 220–2, 225; *The Republic*, 221, 341; *Basic History of the U.S.*, 222, 304, 341; critical works in reaction to, 233–6; summary criticisms of *Economic Interpretation*, 226–30; ideas-interest formula of, 243–245, 247; conception of democracy, 247–52; on Mussolini regime, 248 and n.; on political views of the Founding Fathers, 248–52; on procedures for framing Constitution, 263–5, 270–3; on structure of Constitution, 265–6, 266–70; and ratification conflict, 276–82; on Columbia University trustees, 286; individualism of, 287, 288 and n.; New Milford years of, 288–292; Dartmouth lectures of, 288, 320; *Cross Currents in Europe Today*, 288–9; travels in Europe, Asia, 288–9; on 1920's Hungarian controversy, 290–1; on Hearst 1930's Red hunts, 291–2; 1920's economic interpretation of, 292, 298–9, 301–2, 310; *Economic Origins of Jeffersonian Democracy*, 292–8; on agrarian-capitalist conflict, 296–7; stylistic contrasts in work of, 299–301; *America in Midpassage*, 299; *The American Spirit*, 299; on Puritanism, 302; interpretation of Civil War

Beard, Charles, A. (*continued*)
of, 302–4; 1930's relativism of,
304–17; isolationism of, 316–
328, 330–4, 339–44; anti-Prus-
sianism of, 319–20; and foreign
policy, 322–44; hostility to
F.D.R., 323–8, 334–40; *The Idea
of National Interest*, 323–4;
The Open Door at Home, 324–
326; and American messianism,
324–5; on economic motives for
war, 325–6, 332–4; "National
Politics and War," 326–8; on
demise of democratic institutions, 329–30; *The Devil Theory
of War*, 331–3; *A Foreign Policy
for America*, 333–4; *American
Foreign Policy in the Making*,
334; *President Roosevelt and
the Coming of the War*, 334;
modification of war thesis by,
335 and *n.*; on outcome of
W.W. II, 339; *The Enduring
Federalist*, 341; decline of rep-
utation of, 341–6; death, 344;
on Parrington's *Main Currents*,
392 and *n.*; on Henry James,
393
Beard, Clarence, 169
Beard, Mary, xi, 175, 222, 298
Beard, Nathan, 167
Beard, W. H. H., 167–8
Becker, Carl, xi–xii, 72, 77, 80, 82,
266, 305, 316, 365–6, 375
Beecher, Lyman, 57
Beer, G. L., 29
Belknap, Jeremy: *History of New
Hampshire*, 9
Bell, Daniel, 439
Bellamy, Edward, 403
Bentham, Jeremy, *Introduction to
Principles and Morals of Legis-
lation*, 21
Bentley, A. F.: *The Process of
Government*, 186–8
Berenson, Bernard, 363
Berle, A. A., 90
Beveridge, Albert, 84–5
Bluntschli, Johann, 65
Boone, Daniel, 7, 144
Boorstin, Daniel, 440, 444, 451,
461; *The Genius of American
Politics*, 445, 448–50; *The
Americans*, 457
Botta, Carlo, 10
Boucher, Jonathan, 412
Bowen, Francis, 20
Bowers, Claude, 295
Brooks, Van Wyck, 87–8, 377,
412; *America's Coming of
Age*, 88; *Letters and Leadership*,
88; *Opinions of Oliver Allston*,
357
Brown, John, 403, 406–7
Brown, Robert E., 255, 276, 280;
*Charles Beard and the Constitu-
tion*, 223, 277 and *n.*
Bryan, William Jennings, 28, 47,
88, 170, 171, 370
Bryce, Lord, 57–8
Burgess, John W., 25, 26, 28, 30,
37, 264
Burke, Edmund, 9
Burr, Aaron, 296
Butler, Nicholas M., 285–6
Butterfield, Herbert, 7

Calhoun, John C., 57
Callender, Guy S. 143
Calverton, V. F., 355
*Cambridge History of American
Literature*, 351
Cameron, Elizabeth, 34
capitalism, 88–9 and *n.*, 159–60,
293–8, 447, 460
Carlyle, Thomas, 17, 177, 381
Carnegie, Andrew, 89 *n.*, 342
Cattell, J. McKeen, 286
Chafee, Zechariah, 88
Chamberlin, Thomas C., 65
Chicago, 47, 48, 70, 170
Chicago, University of, 67
China, 338
Civil War, 7–8, 24, 26–7, 42, 302–
304, 326–7, 417, 429, 431, 455,
460–2
Clark, George Rogers, 116
Clay, Henry, 95, 410
Clinton, George, 242, 262
Coleridge, Samuel Taylor, 13
Columbia University, 30, 42, 285–
288

Columbian Exposition of 1893, 47–8, 53, 170

Comity, American, 278, 454–5

Commager, Henry Steele: *The American Mind*, 350

Commons, John R., 170

Compromise of 1850, 26

Comte, Auguste, 24

Confederation: *see* Articles of Confederation

Connecticut, 25, 234

consensus history, 17, 296, 438 ff.; intellectual wing of, 445, 446–448, 456–7; anti-intellectual wing of, 445, 448–50, 457; limitations of, 452–4, 459; and idea of comity, 454–5

conservatism, 23–5, 27–8, 194–5

Constitution: as product of class conflict, 21, 182, 187, 188, 189, 190–206, 266, 447; influence of West on construction of, 52; ratification struggle for, 191, 209, 240–3, 276–82, 416; radical Progressive thought on, 191–6, 266; socialist thought on, 196–200; and sociological jurisprudence, 200–6; socio-political background of, 208–9; 231–7; economic interest of framers of, 209, 226–7, 236–43; political doctrines of framers of, 209, 248–55, 257–61, 264, 269; related to nationalism, 231, 234, 252; and paper money issue, 238–40; and idea of balanced government, 253–5, 267; and property-suffrage relationship, 255–6, 276, 280–2; and property-representation relationship, 256–7, 275; bill of rights of, 262–3, 275, 279; procedure for framing of, 263–5, 270–3; structural features of, 265–6, 273–6; dualistic view of era of, 266–70; as expression of eighteenth-century political avant garde, 282–4

Coolidge, Calvin, 88–9

Cornell University, 175

Cotton, John, 6

Crédit Mobilier scandal, 69

Crèvecoeur, Michel de, 405

Croce, Benedetto, 305, 312

Croly, Herbert: *The Promise of American Life*, 193

Cross, Wilbur L., 289

Crowl, Philip, 223

Cuba, 171

culture, American, 449–50

Curti, Merle, 112, 140

Curtis, George William, 411

Dana, Charles A., 403

Dana, Henry W. L., 286

Dangerfield, George, 98

Darrow, Clarence, 170

Dartmouth College, 288, 320

Darwinism: *see* historical evolutionism

Davis, Jefferson, 409

Debs, Eugene V., 170

Declaration of Independence, 10, 28, 47, 192, 266–7, 270, 424

Delaware, 234

democracy, American, 14, 23, 28, 159; influence of frontier on, 52, 57, 63–4, 121–2, 125–41; neo-Turnerian theories of, 136–140; and the intent of Constitution, 192, 282–3; contextual meanings of, 248–52, 283; and eighteenth-century political discourse, 257–61

Democratic Party, 326–8, 343

De Pauw University, 169

depression: of 1890's, 41, 59, 170, 368; Great, 92, 208, 304, 322–323, 327

De Voto, Bernard: *The Literary Fallacy*, 357

Dewey, John, 88, 184, 220, 287, 288

Dickinson, John, 248, 259, 404, 408, 412

Dodd, William, 28

Dorfman, Jay, 239

Dos Passos, John, 438

Draper, John W., 168

Draper, Lyman C., 79

Dred Scott case, 202

Dreiser, Theodore, 170, 217

Droysen, J. G., 70
Drummond, Henry, 177, 367
dualistic interpretation, 192–3, 266–70
Dunning, W. A., 25, 26, 28, 30
Dwight, Timothy, 57, 409

East: European orientation of, 47–8, 54, 56–7; cultural contribution of, 77–8; antimajoritarianism of, 85–6; voting rights in, 131–2
Eby, E. H., 374, 400
economic institutionalism, 184
economic interpretation, 72, 190–200, 244–5; *see also under* Beard, Charles; Constitution; Parrington, Vernon
Edwards, Jonathan, 4, 302, 408, 412
egalitarianism, 126, 128–9, 132, 260
Eggleston, Edward, 375
Elkins, Stanley, 136–40, 157–8
Elliot, Jonathan, 10
Ely, Richard T., 70
Emerson, Ralph Waldo, 17, 18, 56, 75, 353, 357, 426
Emerton, Ephraim, 38
Emporia College, 362–3
Engels, Friedrich, 198–9, 313
England, 66, 126, 129, 172–5, 256–7, 357–8, 425
Enlightenment, 13, 21
Erdman, Irwin, 180
Ethiopia, 329
Everett, Edward, 22
evolutionism: *see* historical evolutionism

farmer, 28, 41, 63–4, 75, 91, 153–154, 267 and *n.*
Farrand, Max, 103, 116, 117
fascism, 220–2, 248 and *n.*, 329–330, 333–4
Fay, Sidney B., 320
Federalist, The, 208, 223, 247

Federalists, 31–2, 85, 223, 226–7, 236–43, 248–61, 263, 270, 276–282, 293
Ferguson, James, 225 *n.*, 237
Fiske, John, 24, 28, 69, 365, 411; *The Critical Period of American History, 1739–89*, 26, 194
Flaubert, Gustave, 380
Force, Peter: *American Archives*, 10
Ford, Henry Jones: *The Rise and Growth of American Politics*, 98, 195
foreign policy, American, 171 and *n.*, 318–44
formalism, 183–8
Founding Fathers, 190–206; economic interests of, 209, 215, 226–7, 236–43; political aims of, 248–55; party affiliations of, 293 and *n.*
Fourteenth Amendment, 212, 303 and *n.*, 407
France, 295, 320, 330, 333, 336, 423-5
Frank, Waldo, 88
Franklin, Benjamin, 249, 407, 412
Fraser, Leon, 286 and *n.*
Freeman, E. A., 65
frontier: process in history, 41, 50–4; economic impact of, 56, 153–61, 163; political impact of, 52, 57–8, 136–40, 161–3 449; closing of, 57–61, 90, 93; negative influence of, 52–3, 86–90, 147–8; myth, 61, 149–51, elasticity of definition of, 123–5; effect of, on democracy, 125–141; effect in Europe, 130 *n.*; individualism and, 141–6; impact of, on literature, 359–60 and *n.*, 361 and *n.*
Freeman, Mary Wilkins, 411
Freneau, Philip M., 403, 406
Fuller, Margaret, 403
Fuller, Melville W., 195

Gallatin, Albert, 31
Gandhi, Mohandas, 172

Garland, Hamlin, 47, 49, 50, 365, 380, and *n.*, 382, 384, 403; *Crumbling Idols*, 48; *Son of the Middle Border*, 359; *A Spoil of Office*, 386
Garrison, William L., 406–7
Gates, Lewis, 366
George, Henry, 59, 113; *Progress and Poverty*, 58
Georgia, 105, 133
germ theory of political institutions, 38–9, 51, 66, 68–9, 73–4
German-American Bund, 341
Germany, 15, 25, 38, 64, 66, 68–69, 319–20, 329, 330, 337, 338–340
Gerry, Elbridge, 228–9, 248, 249
Gibbon, Edward, 21
Gilded Age, 30, 43, 365, 411
Godkin, E. L., 54, 55, 57, 402, 403, 411, 412
Goldwater, Barry, 89
Goodnow, Frank J., 179; *Social Reforms and the Constitution*, 202–3
Goto, Viscount, 288
Granick, David, 139
Great Britain, 330, 335, 337
group basis of law, 186–7
guaranteed employment, 172–3

\amilton, Alexander, 213, 248, 293–5, 408–9, 413
\amiltonians, 21, 191, 293
Hammond, Bray, 239
Hamsun, Knut, 342
Hancock, John, 233
Hanna, Mark, 25
Hardie, Keir, 172, 175
Harding, Warren G., 212
Harriman, E. H., 88
Harrison, Joseph B., 374
Harrison, William H., 128
Hart, A. B., 115–16
Hart, Freeman, 241
Hartz, Louis, 225, 440, 444; *The Liberal Tradition in America*, 445, 446–8, 456–7
Harvard University, 10, 11, 22,

64, 79–81, 117, 363–7, 373–4, 376
Hawthorne, Nathaniel, 386, 387, 410, 412, 413
Hay, John, 411
Hearst, William Randolph, 291
Heeren, A. H. L., 64
Hegel, G. W. F.: *Philosophy of History*, 56, 70, 87, 230 *n.*
Henry, Patrick, 10, 262
Herring, Hubert, 168
Heussi, Karl, 305
Hicks, Granville, 355
Higham, John, 440, 451
Hildreth, Richard, 20–3, 193; *Theory of Politics*, 22
historical evolutionism, 4, 26, 30–33, 37–42, 65–6, 177–8, 183, 188, 304–17
historical relativism, 304–17
historiography, American: Progressive, xii–xvii, 6–7, 14–15, 41–2, 191–200, 437–44, 447–8; amateur, 11–12, 24; professional, 11, 35–42; romantic, 15, 18–20, 36, 464; scientific, 26, 30–3, 37–42, 178; interpretive, 37–8, 211, 224; dualistic tradition of, 191–200, 463; idea of conflict in, 437–8, 458–9, 462; idea of consensus in, 438, 442, 443, 444 *n.*, 445 ff.; revisionist, of 1950's, 441–4
Hitler, Adolf, 330, 334, 337, 339–340
Holmes, Abiel, 9–10
Holmes, Oliver W., 9, 184, 212–13, 215; *Common Law*, 201
Holst, Hermann von, 24–5, 27–8, 70; *Constitutional . . . History of the U.S.*, 69–70
Hood, Major Calvin, 369
Hooker, Thomas, 403, 405
Hoover, Herbert, 89, 340–1
Hopkinson, Francis, 405
Howells, William Dean, 25, 363, 383–3; *Criticism and Fiction*, 384; *The Rise of Silas Lapham*, 387
Hull House, 170
Hume, David, 21
Hungary, 290–1

Huntington Library, 103, 116
Hutchinson, Thomas, 403, 404, 406, 408, 412
Huxley, T. H., 109

immigrant, 27–8, 41, 52, 60, 108–109, 122–3, 156–7, 358
imperial school, 29, 66
imperialism, 25, 171, 334
Indian, American, 12, 104–5
individualism, 52–3, 141–6, 159, 419
individuality, 142, 145–6
Industrial Revolution, 170, 175
industrialism, 41, 42, 88–9 and n., 154–7, 170, 304
Ingersoll, Robert, 168
instrumentalism, 184, 185
Irving, Washington, 12, 410
isolationism, 328–44
Italy, 248 and n., 330

Jackson, Andrew, 15, 19, 27, 52, 95–6, 134–5, 148, 410, 438, 448
Jacksonian democracy, 85, 128, 133–4, 239, 269, 292, 326–7, 353, 441
Jaffa, Henry V., 461
James, Henry, 4, 81, 393–4
James, William, 366
James, Mrs. William, 80
Jameson, J. F., 16, 34, 36–7, 77
Japan, 335, 337–9
Jefferson, Thomas, 27, 28, 30–2, 52, 133–4, 239, 269, 292, 296–298, 403, 404, 409, 447–8
Jeffersonian democracy, 128, 133–134, 292–8, 326–7
Jeffersonians, 21, 191, 293
Jensen, Merrill: *The New Nation*, 438
Jewett, Sarah O., 411
Johns Hopkins University, 38, 65, 68, 70
Johnson, Alvin, 288
Johnson, Lyndon B., 450 n.
Johnston, Alexander: *History of American Politics*, 76
Jonas, Manfred, 332

Jones, Howard M., 351
Josephson, Matthew, 88
judicial review, 131, 202, 203–4, 262
judiciary, 195, 200–6, 260

Kansas, 174, 359–61
Károlyi, Count Michael, 290
Kazin, Alfred, 352
Kennedy, John F., 109
Kennedy, John P., 353
Kenyon, Cecelia, 223, 261
Keynes, John Maynard, 439
Kropotkin, Prince, 177
Ku Klux Klan, 88

labor, 101–3, 153–8
La Follette, Phillip, 89, 182
laissez faire, 21, 175, 183, 189
Lamar, L. Q. C., 57
Laski, Harold, 213
Lawrence, D. H., 75, 357
Lea, H. C., 12
League of Nations, 101
Lease, Mary Ellen, 368
Lebergott, Stanley, 156
legal realism, 184–8
Legaré, Hugh, 409–10
Leighton, George, 335
Lester, Richard, 239
Levin, David, 13, 16 n.
Lewis, Sinclair, 403
Libby, Orin G.: *The Geographical Distribution of the Vote . . . on the Constitution*, 191
Lieber, Francis, 409
Lippmann, Walter, 182
List, Friedrich, 413
literary criticism, 377–8, 381, 394–5
literary history, 351, 355–6, 375–376
literature, American: history as, 4, 13–14, 375–6; New England influence on, 12–13, 20–3, 365, 418–23; birth of, 48; universal *v.* parochial in, 49, 365; frontier influence on, 49–50, 359–60,

literature (*continued*)
361 *n*.; 363; tardy academic
recognition of, 376; and moral-
aesthetic criticism, 381; realistic,
naturalistic, 381–5; economic in-
terpretation of, 389–92, 426–7;
democratic and antidemocratic
currents in, 398, 418–27
Livingston, William, 249
Lloyd, Henry Demarest, 170
Lochner v. New York, 201
Locke, John, 162, 408, 447, 448,
449, 460
Lodge, Henry Cabot, 31, 77
London Economic Conference,
323
Longstreet, Augustus, 410
Lord, Russell, 90–1
Loria, Achille: *Analisi della Prop-
rietà Capitalista*, 70–1
Lovejoy, Arthur O., 287, 375, 402
Lowell, James Russell, 365, 410
Luce, Henry, 340, 341
Luther, Martin, 402, 419–20

Macaulay, Thomas, 57
MacLeish, Archibald, 357
Macmahon, Arthur W., 180, 300
Madison, James, 4, 30, 188, 208,
223, 239, 397
Main, Jackson T., 225 *n.*
Mannheim, Karl, 244, 305
Marbury v. Madison, 203
Marshall, John, 9, 203, 404, 405,
409
Marshall Plan, 343
Marx, Karl, 56, 87, 109, 172, 197–
200, 451
Marxism, 22, 92, 93, 186, 197–
200, 313, 429–30
Maryland, 223, 234, 235, 240
Massachusetts, 47, 240, 276
Mather, Cotton, 3, 5, 353, 404,
408, 421–2
Mather, Increase, 365, 408, 412,
421–2
McCormick, Richard, 223, 281
McDonald, Forrest: *We the Peo-
ple*, 223; *E Pluribus Unum*, 224

McKinley, William, 26
McKitrick, Eric, 136–40, 157–8
McLenachan, Blair, 242
McMaster, John B., 25, 27, 28, 94,
193
Melville, Herman, 353
Mencken, H. L., 377, 412
mentality, American, 5–8, 50–4,
57, 74–5, 86–90, 141–6, 152,
157, 449, 464
Mercer, J. F., 249
Merriam, Charles E., 195
Merton, Robert K., 444
messianism, American, 324–5
Metternich, Prince, 283–4
Mexico, 19, 130
Midwest, 77–8, 168–70
Minneapolis, 49
Mississippi Valley Historical As-
sociation, 79
Missouri-Pacific Railway, 290
mobility, 52, 53, 157 and *n.*, 158
modern realism, 184–8
modernism, postwar, 356–7
Moley, Raymond, 203–4
Mommsen, Theodor, 70
monograph, 40–1, 211
Monroe Doctrine, 283
Monroe, James, 52
Moody, William Vaughn, 363
Morgenstern, George: *Pearl Har-
bor . . .*, 343
Morris, Gouverneur, 251–2, 254
Morris, Robert, 236, 242
Morris, William, 362, 370, 381
Motley, J. L., 12
Mugwump reform, 24, 85, 193
Mumford, Lewis, 88, 341
Murdock, Kenneth, 365
Murphy, George G., 156
Mussolini, Benito, 248 and *n.*,
329
Myers, Gustavus: *History of the
Great American Fortunes*, 196,
197; *History of the Supreme
Court*, 196, 202

Namier, Sir Lewis, 211
National Municipal League, 181

nationalism, 24–5, 27–8, 99, 231, 234, 252
nationalization of government, 52
nativism, 22
Nebraska, University of, 35
Negro, 28, 29, 131, 168, 302–3, 451, 455
Neutrality Act, 324
New Deal era, 88–91, 218, 323
New Criticism, 355–6, 357
New England, 12–13, 20–4, 27, 67, 80, 129, 131, 138 *n.*
New Hampshire, 9
New History, 72, 180, 184, 185
New Jersey, 223, 234, 235
New Milford, 288
New Republic, 220, 329
New School for Social Research, 288
New York, 12, 201, 234, 241–2, 276, 277
New York Armory Show, 184–5
New York Bar Association, 212
New York Bureau of Municipal Research, 181, 288
New York City, 47, 69, 242
Niles, Hezekiah: *Principals . . . of the Revolution . . .*, 10
Norris, Frank: *Responsibilities of the Novelist*, 382–5
North Carolina, 133, 168, 223
Norton, Charles Eliot, 54
Nye, Russell, 19
Nye Committee, 329, 331–2, 335

Odell, Jonathan, 408
Ohio, 25
Oklahoma, University of, 42, 371–373
Osgood, H. L., 29, 30
Ostrogorski, Moisei: *Democracy and the Organization of Political Parties*, 98
Otis, James, 269
Oxford University, 172–5

Paine, Thomas, 239, 403, 404; *Age of Reason*, 168
Palmer, George Herbert, 364
Palmer, R. R., 272

"paper money" issue, 238–40
Parker, Theodore, 23
Parkman, Francis, 12, 23, 36
Parrington, Elizabeth, 359
Parrington, John, 357–8
Parrington, John William, 358–9, 362, 368
Parrington, Julia, 372
Parrington, Vernon L., xi–xvii, 41, 77, 437; *Main Currents of American Thought*, xi, 218, 349–57; 374 ff.; on Progressive movement, 193; critical, popular acclaim of, 349–52; decline of, 352, 354; merits of, 353–4; failings of, 354; on intention of *Main Currents*, 354–5; politicization of literature by, 355, 396, 398–400; and the New Criticism, 355–7; and postwar modernism, 356–7; family background of, 357–9; Anglophobia of, 358, 427–8; Kansas boyhood of, 359–62; and impact of frontier, 359–60 and *n.*, 361 and *n.*, 363, 368; esthetic of, 362, 380, 382, 389–95; interests, tastes of, 362; as Emporia College student, 362–3, 366–7; Harvard experience of, 363–7, 373–4; "self-education" of, 366–7; as Emporia College teacher, 367–8, 371; and Populist politics, 368–370; "Some Political Sketches," 370 *n.*, 371 *n.*; at University of Oklahoma, 371–3; European travels of, 372; at University of Washington, 374–5; literary history at time of work of, 375–377; on inadequacies of *Main Currents*, 376–7; literary criticism at time of work of, 377–8; influence of Taine on, 380–2; influence of moral-aesthetic criticism on, 381; realist-naturalist contemporaries of, 381–5; on Morris, 381; on Howells, 382, 386–7; economic interpretation of, 385–6, 389–91, 426–432; basic aim of, 386; on Poe, Hawthorne, 387; "Economics and Criticism," 389–91 and *n.*;

Parrington, Vernon L. (*continued*)
on Shakespeare, 390–1; Beard's
review of work of, 392 and *n.*;
on Henry James, 394; biographical method of, 397–8, 403–13;
architectonic organization of,
401; use of rhetorical abstrac-
tion by, 402; categories of characterization of, 403–13; counterposing of ideas by, 414–15,
418–23; treatment of Revolutionary period by, 415–16, 418–
423; treatment of Civil War period by, 417, 426–9; treatment
of post-Civil War period by,
418, 429–32; political dualism
of, 418–19, 429–33; on Puritanism, 418–23; and Rousseauian
romanticism, 423–5; and Physiocratic agrarianism, 426–7; fear
of centralized power of, 430–3
Parsons, Theophilus, 279
Pattee, Fred L.: "A Call for a Literary Historian," 376
Patten, Simon, 200
Paul, Arnold, 195
Pearl Harbor, 335, 337, 338, 342–
343
"peasant proprietorship," 64
Pennsylvania, 241–2
Pennsylvania, University of, 25
Peters, Samuel, 405
Pettit, Charles, 242
Philippines, 171
Phillips, Wendell, 365, 407
Physiocratic agrarianism, 416,
426–7
Pierson, George W., 92, 147
Pilgrims, 5
Pinckney, Charles, 259–60
pluralistic interpretation, 188; *see
also* consensus historiography
Poe, Edgar Allan, 354, 387
Pole, J. R., 281, 282, 452–3
political parties, 96, 98, 293, 326–
328, 455, 456
political realism, 186–9
political theory, 445
*Pollock v. Farmers' Loan and
Trust Co.*, 195
Pollock, Sir Frederick, 212
Pool, William, 223

Poole, W. F., 55
Populism, 47, 53, 59, 75, 106, 145,
170, 188, 368–9
positivism, 24, 178, 187
Pound, Roscoe, 201
poverty, American, 451
Powell, Frederick Y., 177–9
pragmatism, 185, 186
Prescott, W. H., 12
progress, 200; and pastoral ideal,
7; and nineteenth-century
American history, 7–8, 14–15
Progressive era: socio-political
background of, 180–2; revolt
against formalism, 183–5; political scholarship of, 185–206,
282–3
Progressive historiography: *see
under* historiography, American
Prohibition, 88
property: related to suffrage, 132,
255–6, 263–4; and social progress, 202, 205; as basis of government, 208; related to representation, 256–7, 275–6
Protestantism, 14, 130, 161–2
Pullman strike of 1894, 59, 170
Puritanism, 5, 9, 13, 302, 354,
398–400, 402, 404, 418–23

racism, 29; *see also* Teutonism
Ramsay, David: *History of the
Revolution of South Carolina*,
9, 233
Randolph, Edmund, 233, 249, 258,
279
Randolph, John, 302, 353
Ranke, Leopold von, 38, 94
Ransom, W. L.: *Majority Rule
and the Judiciary*, 202
Realpolitik, 411
Reconstruction, 12, 24–5, 26–7,
28, 42, 442, 460
Republican Party, 326–8
Rhodes, James Ford, 25, 27, 28,
29, 94
Ricardo, David, 198
Robinson, James H., 72, 77, 178,
179, 184, 288
Roche, John P., 270

Rogers, Thorold: *Economic Interpretation of History*, 72
romanticism, 13–20, 28, 416, 417, 423–5, 464
Roosevelt, Franklin D., 90 and *n.*, 203, 316, 318, 323, 324, 326–8, 331
Roosevelt, Theodore, 26, 171, 182, 202, 204; *The Winning of the West*, 56
Rousseau, Jean-Jacques, 28, 404, 417, 423–5
Royce, Josiah, 366
Ruskin, John, *Unto This Last*, 172–4, 370, 381
Ruskin Hall, 174, 175, 176–7
Russia, 25, 320, 330, 339–40

safety-valve theory, 57–61, 90, 93, 108–9, 153–8
Sainte-Beuve, Charles, 380
St. Louis, 47
Sanderson, John: *Biography of the Signers of the Declaration of Independence*, 10
Schafer, Joseph, 91
Shaper, W. A., 190
Schlesinger, Arthur M., Jr.: *The Age of Jackson*, 438
Schouler, James, 24, 27, 28
scientific history, 4, 26, 30–3, 37–42, 178; *see also* historical evolutionism
sectionalism, 52, 69, 94–7, 99–103, 190
Seebohm, Frederick, 66
Seligman, E. R. A.: *The Economic Interpretation of History*, 197–200
Senior, Nassau William, 172
Seventeenth Amendment, 274
Sewall, Samuel, 404, 408, 412
Shakespeare, William, 390–1
Shannon, Fred A.: "A Post-Mortem on the Labor-Safety-Valve Theory," 154
Shaw, Albert, 87
Shays, Daniel, 27, 240, 448
Sherman Act, 59
Sherman, Roger, 249–50

Shotwell, James T., 179
Simon, A. M.: *Social Forces in American History*, 196–7
Sinclair, Upton, 170
slavery, 19, 22, 29, 51, 52, 69, 240–241, 302–3, 460
Small, Albion, 70
Smith, Adam, 410, 413
Smith, Bernard, 355
Smith, J. Allen, 188, 202, 204, 266, 374, 389; *The Spirit of American Government*, 192–3, 248, 388; *The Multiple Money Standard*, 387–8
Smith, Melancton, 262, 279
Smith, Theodore Clark, 305
socialism, 181 and *n.*, 196–200
sociological jurisprudence, 200–6
Sombart, Werner, 153
South, 29, 49, 302–4
South Carolina, 8–9, 190
Southern mentality, 353, 412, 417
space, as basic to American imagination, 5–7
Spain, 12, 329
Spanish-American War, 171
Sparks, Jared, 9, 11; *Diplomatic Correspondence of the . . . Revolution*, 10; *The Writings of George Washington*, 10
Spencer, Herbert, 24, 212, 380; *Data of Ethics*, 367
Stearns, Harold, 88
Steffens, Lincoln, 217
Stephens, Alexander, 406
Strout, Cushing, xii, 193
structural history, 211
suffrage, 131–2, 135, 255–6, 263–264
Sumner, Charles, 22
Sumner, William G., 58, 194–5
Supreme Court, 195, 200–6, 260

Taft, Robert A., 329
Taft, William H., 182, 212
Taine, Hippolyte: *History of English Literature*, 380–2, 397
Tammany Hall, 69
Tarbell, Ida, 217
tariff, 52

Taylor, John, 295, 410, 413, 447
Tennessee, 25
Teutonism, 25, 66, 73–4, 83, 208
Thomas, Norman, 329
Thomas, Robert, 223, 240
Thoreau, Henry D., 357, 365
Thwaites, Reuben Gold, 79, 80
Ticknor, George, 12
Tocqueville, Alexis de, 9, 57, 145, 157, 440, 445, 446
transcendentalism, 15
Trilling, Lionel, 377; "Reality in America," 349–50
Truman, Harry S., 343
Trumbull, Benjamin, 10
Tucker, Nathaniel B., 353
Tugwell, Rexford G., 90
Turner, Andrew Jackson, 62
Turner, Frederick Jackson, xi–xvii, 29, 36, 38, 39, 41, 437; *The Significance of the Frontier in American History*, xi, 47–8, 50 and *n.*, 55 *ff.*; awareness of space in thought of, 6, 72, 100–2; "The Significance of History," 38, 71; historical perspective of, 41–2, 59–60; 1893 address of, 47–8, 50–4; on free land and American development, 50–3, 121, 153–4; frontier thesis of, 50–4, 74–5, 84 *ff.*; evolutionism of, 51, 65, 67, 73, 75–6, 120; on the Westerner, 55, 148; intellectual precursors of, 56 and *n.*, 57–61, 85; birth, background of, 61–3; "The History of the Grignon Tract . . ." and "The Poet of the Future," 63; schooling of, 63–4 and *n.*, 65; at Wisconsin, 64–5, 77, 79, 80 *n.*; Johns Hopkins period of, 65, 68, 70–1 and *n.*; and Adams school, 66–9, 70; doctoral thesis of, 70; seminal essays of, 71–4, 76, 79 *n.*; on provincialism, 72; and origins of democracy, 74, 85–6, 95, 121–2, 127, 128, 135 *n.*, 148; early acclaim of, 76–7; at Harvard, 76, 79–81; 80 *n.*; "The Children of the Pioneers," 77; defense of the Midwest, 77–78 and *n.*; on the pioneer, 78,

107, 108, 128, 142, 148, 150–1; on New England, 80; characterized, 81–3, 103, 116; on history, 84, 104; criticisms of premises, formulations of, 84–93, 103, 118–25, 146–51; on Jacksonian democracy, 85, 128, 148; on the Western inheritance, 85–6, 95, 121; diminution of influence of, 91–3; on Boy Scouts, 93; "The West and American Ideals," 93; "Middle Western Pioneer Democracy," 93; *Rise of the New West*, 93, 95, 98, 99, 104–5, 115; small output of, 93–4, 99; *The Significance of Sections in American History*, 93–4, 97, 100–6; *United States, 1830–1850 . . .*, 94; and American individualism, 95–7, 125–7, 141–6; underemphasis of national institutions by, 96–7; quality of work of, 98–9; "Is Sectionalism in America Dying Away?," 99, 100; on importance of geography, racial stock, 100, 121; on industrialism and urban growth, 101–3, 108–11, 160 *n.*; on class struggle, 102–3, 108–9; lack of social criticism in work of, 103–6, 146–7; on Indian removal, 105; "The Problem of the West," 106; on T. R., 106–107; political views of, 106–7, 149; pioneer bias of, 107–11, 149–51; on immigrants, 109; on specialization, 110–11; champion of state univeristy, 110–111; arrested development of, 111–14; creative impedimenta of, 114–17; on term "frontier," 123; on individualism, 127, 142–3; on suffrage, 131; on Jefferson, 133; on Jackson, 148; "Pioneer Ideals and the State University," 148; intellectualism of, 148–9; salvageable portion of thesis of, 152–3, 159–64; on safety-valve theory, 153–8; on Libby paper, 191; on pioneer-capitalist contest, 293
Turner school, 170–1, 208, 211

Twain, Mark, 391
Tweed, William M., 69
Tyler, Moses Coit, 175, 351, 354, 375

Unitarianism, 14, 18, 423
urbanization, 91, 159–60
Utilitarianism, 20

Van Armitage, J. H., 180
Van Sweringen railway empire, 290
Veblen, Thorstein, 113, 184; *Theory of the Leisure Class*, 220
Villard, O. G., 343, 363
violence, in America, 171 *n.*, 324–330, 462
Virginia, 133–4, 190, 223, 240–1, 276, 277
Vrooman, Walter, 174–5

Walker, Francis A., 59–60, 70
War of 1812, 298, 302, 326
war guilt, 320–1
Ward, Nathaniel, 353
Warren, Charles: *The Making of the Constitution*, 218, 223
Washington, George, 10, 12, 205
Washington, University of, 374–5
Washington, D.C., 47
Weaver, Colonel James R., 169–70
Weber, Max, 113, 161
Webster, Daniel, 405
Weems, Parson, 10
Welles, Sumner, 334 *n.*
Wendell, Barrett: *A Literary History of America*, 351, 364, 366
West, 29, 47–9, 51–4, 86–90
Westerners, 54–5, 60–1
Weyl, Walter, 88, 200

White, Morton, 182, 183 and *n.*
Whitman, Walt, 353, 357, 398
White, William Allen, 171, 369; "What's the Matter with Kansas?," 370
Williams, Roger, 5, 6, 398, 403, 407, 419, 422
Williamson, Chilton, 132, 281
Wilson, James, 249, 259
Wilson, Woodrow, 39, 60–1 and *n.*, 70, 82, 182, 298, 319, 326; *Division and Reunion*, 194
Winsor, Justin: *Narrative and Critical History of America*, 25–26
Winthrop, John, 412
Wirt, William, 409; *Patrick Henry*, 10
Wisconsin, 48, 79
Wisconsin State Historical Society, 79
Wisconsin, University of, 42, 61, 64–5, 76, 79, 80 *n.*, 116–17
Wise, John, 405
Woodberry, George E., 55
Woolsey, Theodore D., 411
Workers Education Bureau of America, 288
World War I, 107–8, 285–7, 329
World War II, 220–1, 322–44, 438–9
Wright, Benjamin F., Jr., 129–31
Wright, Frances, 135

Young Oxford (magazine), 176, 178
Yugoslavia, 289 and *n.*

Zellner, Arnold, 156
Zenger, John Peter, 5

About the Author

Richard Hofstadter, DeWitt Clinton Professor of American History at Columbia University, was born in Buffalo, New York, in 1916. He received his B.A. from the University of Buffalo, and his M.A. and Ph.D. from Columbia University, where he was awarded a William Bayard Cutting Travelling Fellowship for 1941-2. He taught at the University of Maryland from 1942 until 1946, when he joined the History Department of Columbia. He has lectured widely at colleges and universities in the United States and Britain, and in 1958-9 served as Pitt Professor of American History and Institutions at Cambridge University. The first of his books on American History was *Social Darwinism in American Thought,* published in 1944. His most recent book is *The Idea of a Party System.*

Titles by Richard Hofstadter available in Vintage Books are *The American Political Tradition, The Age of Reform* (won the Pulitzer Prize in history), *Anti-intellectualism in American Life* (received the Pulitzer Prize in general non-fiction, the Emerson Award of Phi Beta Kappa, and the Sidney Hillman Prize Award), *The Paranoid Style in American Politics.* He is the editor of the three-volume *Great Issues in American History: From Settlement to Revolution 1584-1776* (with Clarence L. Ver Steeg), *From the Revolution to the Civil War 1765-1865, From Reconstruction to the Present Day 1864-1969.*

VINTAGE POLITICAL SCIENCE
AND SOCIAL CRITICISM

V-428   ABDEL-MALEK, ANOUAR   *Egypt: Military Society*
V-625   ACKLAND, LEN AND SAM BROWN   *Why Are We Still in Vietnam?*
V-340   ADAMS, RUTH (ed.)   *Contemporary China*
V-196   ADAMS, RICHARD N.   *Social Change in Latin America Today*
V-568   ALINSKY, SAUL D.   *Reveille for Radicals*
V-365   ALPEROVITZ, GAR   *Atomic Diplomacy*
V-503   ALTHUSSER, LOUIS   *For Marx*
V-286   ARIES, PHILIPPE   *Centuries of Childhood*
V-511   BAILEY, STEPHEN K.   *Congress Makes a Law*
V-604   BAILYN, BERNARD   *Origins of American Politics*
V-334   BALTZELL, E. DIGBY   *The Protestant Establishment*
V-335   BANFIELD, E. G. AND J. Q. WILSON   *City Politics*
V-674   BARBIANA, SCHOOL OF   *Letter to a Teacher*
V-198   BARDOLPH, RICHARD   *The Negro Vanguard*
V-185   BARNETT, A. DOAK   *Communist China and Asia*
V-270   BAZELON, DAVID   *The Paper Economy*
V-60   BECKER, CARL L.   *The Declaration of Independence*
V-563   BEER, SAMUEL H.   *British Politics in the Collectivist Age*
V-199   BERMAN, H. J. (ed.)   *Talks on American Law*
V-211   BINKLEY, WILFRED E.   *President and Congress*
V-81   BLAUSTEIN, ARTHUR I. AND ROGER R. WOOCK (eds.)   *Man Against Poverty*
V-508   BODE, BOYD H.   *Modern Educational Theories*
V-513   BOORSTIN, DANIEL J.   *The Americans: The Colonial Experience*
V-358   BOORSTIN, DANIEL J.   *The Americans: The National Experience*
V-621   BOORSTIN, DANIEL J.   *The Decline of Radicalism: Reflections on America Today*
V414   BOTTOMORE, T. B.   *Classes in Modern Society*
V-44   BRINTON, CRANE   *The Anatomy of Revolution*
V-625   BROWN, SAM AND LEN ACKLAND   *Why Are We Still in Vietnam*
V-234   BRUNER, JEROME   *The Process of Education*
V-590   BULLETIN OF ATOMIC SCIENTISTS   *China after the Cultural Revolution*
V-578   BUNZEL, JOHN H.   *Anti-Politics in America*
V-549   BURNIER, MICHEL-ANTOINE   *Choice of Action*
V-684   CALVERT, GREG AND CAROL   *The New Left and the New Capitalism*
V-30   CAMUS, ALBERT   *The Rebel*
V-33   CARMICHAEL, STOKELY AND CHARLES HAMILTON   *Black Power*
V-664   CARMICHAEL, STOKELY   *Stokely Speaks*
V-98   CASH, W. J.   *The Mind of the South*
V-556   CASTRO, JOSUE DE   *Death in the Northeast*
V-272   CATER, DOUGLASS   *The Fourth Branch of Government*
V-290   CATER, DOUGLASS   *Power in Washington*
V-551   CHEVIGNY, PAUL   *Police Power*
V-555   CHOMSKY, NOAM   *American Power and the New Mandarins*
V-640   CHOMSKY, NOAM   *At War With Asia*
V-554   CONNERY, ROBERT H. (ed.)   *Urban Riots: Violence and Social Change*

V-420	CORNUELLE, RICHARD C. *Reclaiming the American Dream*
V-538	COX COMMISSION *Crisis at Columbia*
V-311	CREMIN, LAWRENCE A. *The Genius of American Education*
V-519	CREMIN, LAWRENCE A. *The Transformation of the School*
V-734	DANIELS, R. V. *A Documentary History of Communism*
V-237	DANIELS, R. V. *The Nature of Communism*
V-638	DENNISON, GEORGE *The Lives of Children*
V-746	DEUTSCHER, ISAAC *The Prophet Armed*
V-747	DEUTSCHER, ISAAC *The Prophet Unarmed*
V-748	DEUTSCHER, ISAAC *The Prophet Outcast*
V-617	DEVLIN, BERNADETTE *The Price of My Soul*
V-671	DOMHOFF, G. WILLIAM *The Higher Circles*
V-603	DOUGLAS, WILLIAM O. *Points of Rebellion*
V-645	DOUGLAS, WILLIAM O. *International Dissent*
V-585	EAKINS, DAVID AND JAMES WEINSTEIN (eds.) *For a New America*
V-390	ELLUL, JACQUES *The Technological Society*
V-379	EMERSON, T. I. *Toward a General Theory of the First Amendment*
V-47	EPSTEIN, B. R. AND A. FORSTER *The Radical Right: Report on the John Birch Society and Its Allies*
V-692	EPSTEIN, JASON *The Great Conspiracy Trial*
V-661	FALK, RICHARD A., GABRIEL KOLKO, AND ROBERT JAY LIFTON *Crimes of War: After Songmy*
V-442	FALL, BERNARD B. *Hell in a Very Small Place: The Siege of Dien Bien Phu*
V-423	FINN, JAMES *Protest: Pacifism and Politics*
V-667	FINN, JAMES *Conscience and Command*
V-225	FISCHER, LOUIS (ed.) *The Essential Gandhi*
V-424	FOREIGN POLICY ASSOCIATION, EDITORS OF *A Cartoon History of United States Foreign Policy Since World War I*
V-413	FRANK, JEROME D. *Sanity and Survival*
V-382	FRANKLIN, JOHN HOPE AND ISIDORE STARR (eds.) *The Negro in 20th Century America*
V-224	FREYRE, GILBERTO *New World in the Tropics*
V-368	FRIEDENBERG, EDGAR Z. *Coming of Age in America*
V-662	FREIDMAN, EDWARD AND MARK SELDEN (eds.) *America's Asia: Dissenting Essays in Asian Studies*
V-378	FULBRIGHT, J. WILLIAM *The Arrogance of Power*
V-264	FULBRIGHT, J. WILLIAM *Old Myths and New Realties and other Commentaries*
V-354	FULBRIGHT, J. WILLIAM (intro.) *The Vietnam Hearings*
V-688	FULBRIGHT, J. WILLIAM *The Pentagon Propaganda Machine*
V-461	GARAUDY, ROGER *From Anathema to Dialogue*
V-561	GALIN, SAUL AND PETER SPIELBERG (eds.) *Reference Books: How to Select and Use Them*
V-475	GAY, PETER *The Enlightenment:The Rise of Modern Paganism*
V-277	GAY, PETER *Voltaire's Politics*
V-668	GERASSI, JOHN *Revolutionary Priest: The Complete Writings and Messages of Camillo Torres*
V-657	GETTLEMAN, MARVIN E. AND DAVID MERMELSTEIN (eds.) *The Failure of American Liberalism*
V-451	GETTLEMAN, MARVIN E. AND SUSAN, AND LAWRENCE AND CAROL KAPLAN *Conflict in Indochina: A Reader on the Widening War in Laos and Cambodia*
V-174	GOODMAN, PAUL AND PERCIVAL *Communitas*

V-325   GOODMAN, PAUL   *Compulsory Mis-education and The Community of Scholars*

V-32   GOODMAN, PAUL   *Growing Up Absurd*

V-417   GOODMAN, PAUL   *People or Personnel* and *Like a Conquered Province*

V-247   GOODMAN, PAUL   *Utopian Essays and Practical Proposals*

V-606   GORO, HERB   *The Block*

V-633   GREEN, PHILIP AND SANFORD LEVINSON (eds.)   *Power and Community: Dissenting Essays in Political Science*

V-457   GREENE, FELIX   *The Enemy: Some Notes on the Nature of Contemporary Imperialism*

V-618   GREENSTONE, J. DAVID   *Labor in American Politics*

V-430   GUEVERA, CHE   *Guerrilla Warfare*

V-685   HAMSIK, DUSAN   *Writers Against Rulers*

V-605   HARRIS, CHARLES F. AND JOHN A. WILLIAMS (eds.)   *Amistad 1*

V-660   HARRIS, CHARLES F. AND JOHN A. WILLIAMS (eds.)   *Amistad 2*

V-427   HAYDEN, TOM   *Rebellion in Newark*

V-453   HEALTH PAC   *The American Health Empire*

V-635   HEILBRONER, ROBERT L.   *Between Capitalism and Socialism*

V-404   HELLER, WALTER (ed.)   *Perspectives on Economic Growth*

V-450   HERSH, SEYMOUR M.   *My Lai 4*

V-283   HENRY, JULES   *Culture Against Man*

V-644   HESS, KARL AND THOMAS REEVES   *The End of the Draft*

V-465   HINTON, WILLIAM   *Fanshen: A Documentary of Revolution in a Chinese Village*

V-576   HOFFMAN, ABBIE   *Woodstock Nation*

V-95   HOFSTADTER, RICHARD   *The Age of Reform: From Bryan to F.D.R.*

V-9   HOFSTADTER, RICHARD   *The American Political Tradition*

V-317   HOFSTADTER, RICHARD   *Anti-Intellectualism in American Life*

V-385   HOFSTADTER, RICHARD   *Paranoid Style in American Politics and other Essays*

V-686   HOFSTADTER, RICHARD AND MICHAEL WALLACE (eds.)   *American Violence, A Documentary History*

V-429   HOROWITZ, DE CASTRO, AND GERASSI (eds.)   *Latin American Radicalism*

V-666   HOWE, LOUISE KAPP (ed.)   *The White Majority: Between Poverty and Affluence*

V-630   HOROWITZ, DAVID   *Empire and Revolution*

V-201   HUGHES, H. STUART   *Consciousness and Society*

V-514   HUNTINGTON, SAMUEL F.   *The Soldier and the State*

V-241   JACOBS, JANE   *Death & Life of Great American Cities*

V-584   JACOBS, JANE   *The Economy of Cities*

V-433   JACOBS, PAUL   *Prelude to Riot*

V-332   JACOBS, PAUL AND SAUL LANDAU (eds.)   *The New Radicals*

V-459   JACOBS, PAUL AND SAUL LANDAU, WITH EVE PELL   *To Serve the Devil: Natives and Slaves*, Vol. I

V-460   JACOBS, PAUL AND SAUL LANDAU, WITH EVE PELL   *To Serve the Devil: Colonials & Sojourners*, Vol. II

V-456   JONES, ITA   *The Grubbag*

V-451   KAPLAN, LAWRENCE AND CAROL, MARVIN E. AND SUSAN GETTLEMAN   *Conflict in Indochina: A Reader on the Widening War in Laos and Cambodia*

V-369   KAUFMANN, WALTER (trans.)   *The Birth of Tragedy* and *The Case of Wagner*

V-401   KAUFMANN, WALTER (trans.)   *On the Genealogy of Morals* and *Ecce Homo*
V-337   KAUFMANN, WALTER (trans.)   *Beyond Good and Evil*
V-482   KELSO, LOUIS O. AND PATRICIA HETTER   *Two-Factor Theory: The Economics of Reality*
V-470   KEY, V. O. JR.   *The Responsible Electorate*
V-510   KEY, V. O.   *Southern Politics*
V-341   KIMBALL & MCCLELLAN   *Education and the New America*
V-582   KIRSHBAUM, LAURENCE AND ROGER RAPOPORT   *Is the Library Burning?*
V-631   KOLKO, GABRIEL   *Politics of War*
V-661   KOLKO, GABRIEL, RICHARD A. FALK AND ROBERT JAY LIFTON (eds.) *Crimes of War: After Songmy*
V-361   KOMAROVSKY, MIRRA   *Blue-Collar Marriage*
V-675   KOVEL, JOVEL   *White Racism*
V-215   LACOUTURE, JEAN   *Ho Chi Minh*
V-459   LANDAU, SAUL, PAUL JACOBS, WITH EVE PELL   *To Serve the Devil: Natives and Slaves*, Vol. I
V-460   LANDAU, SAUL, PAUL JACOBS, WITH EVE PELL   *To Serve the Devil: Colonials & Sojourners*, Vol. II
V-367   LASCH, CHRISTOPHER   *The New Radicalism in America*
V-560   LASCH, CHRISTOPHER   *The Agony of the American Left*
V-399   LASKI, HAROLD J. (ed.)   *Harold J. Laski on the Communist Manifesto*
V-426   LEKACHMAN, ROBERT   *The Age of Keynes*
V-638   LEVINSON, SANFORD AND PHILIP GREEN (eds.)   *Power and Community: Dissenting Essays in Political Science*
V-280   LEWIS, OSCAR   *The Children of Sánchez*
V-421   LEWIS, OSCAR   *La Vida*
V-370   LEWIS, OSCAR   *Pedro Martínez*
V-284   LEWIS, OSCAR   *Village Life in Northern India*
V-634   LEWIS, OSCAR   *A Death in the Sánchez Family*
V-637   LIBARLE, MARC AND TOM SELIGSON (eds.)   *The High School Revolutionaries*
V-392   LICHTHEIM, GEORGE   *The Concept of Ideology and Other Essays*
V-474   LIFTON, ROBERT JAY   *Revolutionary Immortality*
V-661   LIFTON, ROBERT JAY, RICHARD A. FALK AND GABRIEL KOLKO (eds.) *Crimes of War: After Songmy*
V-690   LIFTON, ROBERT JAY   *History and Human Survival*
V-384   LINDESMITH, ALFRED   *The Addict and The Law*
V-533   LOCKWOOD, LEE   *Castro's Cuba, Cuba's Fidel*
V-469   LOWE, JEANNE R.   *Cities in a Race with Time*
V-659   LURIE, ELLEN   *How to Change the Schools*
V-193   MALRAUX, ANDRE   *Temptation of the West*
V-480   MARCUSE, HERBERT   *Soviet Marxism*
V-502   MATTHEWS, DONALD R.   *U. S. Senators and Their World*
V-552   MAYER, ARNO J.   *Politics and Diplomacy of Peacemaking*
V-577   MAYER, ARNO J.   *Political Origins of the New Diplomacy, 1917-1918*
V-575   MCCARTHY, RICHARD D.   *The Ultimate Folly*
V-619   MCCONNELL, GRANT   *Private Power and American Democracy*
V-386   MCPHERSON, JAMES   *The Negro's Civil War*
V-657   MERMELSTEIN, DAVID AND MARVIN E. GETTLEMAN (eds.) *The Failure of American Liberalism*
V-273   MICHAEL, DONALD N.   *The Next Generation*

V-19   MILOSZ, CZESLAW   *The Captive Mind*
V-669   MINTZ, ALAN L. AND JAMES A. SLEEPER   *The New Jews*
V-615   MITFORD, JESSICA   *The Trial of Dr. Spock*
V-316   MOORE, WILBERT E.   *The Conduct of the Corporation*
V-539   MORGAN, ROBIN (ed.)   *Sisterhood is Powerful*
V-251   MORGENTHAU, HANS J.   *The Purpose of American Politics*
V-57   MURCHLAND, BERNARD (ed.)   *The Meaning of the Death of God*
V-274   MYRDAL, GUNNAR   *Challenge to Affluence*
V-573   MYRDAL, GUNNAR   *An Approach to the Asian Drama*
V-687   NEVILLE, RICHARD   *Play Power*
V-377   NIETZSCHE, FRIEDRICH   *Beyond Good and Evil*
V-369   NIETZSCHE, FRIEDRICH   *The Birth of Tragedy* and *The Case of Wagner*
V-401   NIETZSCHE, FRIEDRICH   *On the Genealogy of Morals* and *Ecce Homo*
V-689   OBSERVER, AN   *Message from Moscow*
V-642   O'GORMAN, NED   *Prophetic Voices*
V-583   ORTIZ, FERNANDO   *Cuban Counterpoint: Tobacco and Sugar*
V-285   PARKES, HENRY B.   *Gods and Men*
V-624   PARKINSON, G. H. R.   *Georg Lukacs: The Man, His Work, and His Ideas*
V-128   PLATO   *The Republic*
V-648   RADOSH, RONALD   *American Labor and U. S. Foreign Policy*
V-582   RAPOPORT, ROGER AND LAURENCE KIRSHBAUM   *Is the Library Burning?*
V-309   RASKIN, MARCUS and BERNARD FALL (eds.)   *The Viet-Nam Reader*
V-719   REED, JOHN   *Ten Days That Shook the World*
V-644   REEVES, THOMAS and KARL HESS   *The End of the Draft*
V-192   REISCHAUER, EDWIN O.   *Beyond Vietnam: The United States and Asia*
V-548   RESTON, JAMES   *Sketches in the Sand*
V-622   ROAZEN, PAUL   *Freud: Political and Social Thought*
V-534   ROGERS, DAVID   *110 Livingston Street*
V-559   ROSE, TOM (ed.)   *Violence in America*
V-212   ROSSITER, CLINTON   *Conservatism in America*
V-472   ROSZAK, THEODORE (ed.)   *The Dissenting Academy*
V-288   RUDOLPH, FREDERICK   *The American College and University*
V-408   SAMPSON, RONALD V.   *The Psychology of Power*
V-431   SCHELL, JONATHAN   *The Village of Ben Suc*
V-403   SCHRIEBER, DANIEL (ed.)   *Profile of the School Dropout*
V-375   SCHURMANN, F. and O. SCHELL (eds)   *The China Reader: Imperial China, I*
V-376   SCHURMANN, F. and O. SCHELL (eds.)   *The China Reader: Republican China, II*
V-377   SCHURMANN, F. and O. SCHELL (eds.)   *The China Reader: Communist China, III*
V-394   SEABURY, PAUL   *Power, Freedom and Diplomacy*
V-649   SEALE, BOBBY   *Seize the Time*
V-662   SELDEN, MARK AND EDWARD FRIEDMAN (eds.)   *America's Asia: Dissenting Essays in Asian Studies*
V-637   SELIGSON, TOM AND MARC LIBARLE (eds.)   *The High School Revolutionaries*
V-279   SILBERMAN, CHARLES E.   *Crisis in Black and White*
V-681   SNOW, EDGAR   *Red China Today*

V-365   ALPEROVITZ, GAR   *Atomic Diplomacy*

V-604   BAILYN, BERNARD   *The Origins of American Politics*

V-334   BALTZELL, E. DIGBY   *The Protestant Establishment*

V-198   BARDOLPH, RICHARD   *The Negro Vanguard*

V-60   BECKER, CARL L.   *The Declaration of Independence*

V-494   BERNSTEIN, BARTON J. (ed.)   *Towards a New Past: Dissenting Essays in American History*

V-199   BERMAN, HAROLD J. (ed.)   *Talks on American Law*

V-211   BINKLEY, WILFRED E.   *President and Congress*

V-512   BLOCH, MARC   *The Historian's Craft*

V-513   BOORSTIN, DANIEL J.   *The Americans: The Colonial Experience*

V-358   BOORSTIN, DANIEL J.   *The Americans: The National Experience*

V-621   BOORSTIN, DANIEL J.   *The Decline Of Radicalism: Reflections on America Today*

V-44   BRINTON, CRANE   *The Anatomy of Revolution*

V-98   CASH, W. J.   *The Mind of the South*

V-311   CREMIN, LAWRENCE A.   *The Genius of American Education*

V-190   DONALD, DAVID   *Lincoln Reconsidered*

V-379   EMERSON, THOMAS I.   *Toward a General Theory of the First Amendment*

V-424   FOREIGN POLICY ASSOCIATION, EDITORS OF   *A Cartoon History of United States Foreign Policy Since World War I*

V-498   FRANKLIN, JOHN HOPE   *From Slavery to Freedom: History of Negro Americans*

V-368   FRIEDENBERG, EDGAR Z.   *Coming of Age in America*

V-264   FULBRIGHT, J. WILLIAM   *Old Myths and New Realities*

V-463   GAY, PETER   *A Loss of Mastery: Puritan Historians in Colonial America*

V-400   GENOVESE, EUGENE D.   *The Political Economy of Slavery*

V-676   GENOVESE, EUGENE D.   *The World the Slaveholders Made*

V-31   GOLDMAN, ERIC F.   *Rendezvous with Destiny*

V-183   GOLDMAN, ERIC F.   *The Crucial Decade—and After: America, 1945-1960*

V-95   HOFSTADTER, RICHARD   *The Age of Reform: From Bryan to F.D.R.*

V-9   HOFSTADTER, RICHARD   *The American Political Tradition*

V-317   HOFSTADTER, RICHARD   *Anti-Intellectualism in American Life*

V-385   HOFSTADTER, RICHARD   *The Paranoid Style in American Politics and Other Essays*

V-540   HOFSTADTER, RICHARD and CLARENCE L. VER STEEG (eds.) *Great Issues in American History, From Settlement to Revolution, 1584-1776*

V-541   HOFSTADTER, RICHARD (ed.)   *Great Issues in American History, From the Revolution to the Civil War, 1765-1865*

V-542   HOFSTADTER, RICHARD (ed.)   *Great Issues in American History, From Reconstruction to the Present Day, 1864-1969*

V-591   HOFSTADTER, RICHARD   *Progressive Historians*

V-630   HOROWITZ, DAVID   *Empire and Revolution: A Radical Interpretation of Contemporary History*

V-514   HUNTINGTON, SAMUEL P.   *The Soldier and the State*

V-242   JAMES, C. L. R.   *The Black Jacobins*

V-527   JENSEN, MERRILL   *The New Nation*

V-623   KRADITOR, AILEEN S.   *Means and Ends in American Abolitionism*

V-367   LASCH, CHRISTOPHER   *The New Radicalism in America*

V-560   LASCH, CHRISTOPHER   *The Agony of the American Left*

V-488   LYND, STAUGHTON   *Intellectual Origins of American Radicalism*

V-502   MATTHEWS, DONALD R.   *U. S. Senators and Their World*

V-552   MAYER, ARNO J.   *Politics and Diplomacy of Peacemaking*

V-386   McPHERSON, JAMES   *The Negro's Civil War*

V-318   MERK, FREDERICK   *Manifest Destiny and Mission in American History*

V-84   PARKES, HENRY B.   *The American Experience*

V-371   ROSE, WILLIE LEE   *Rehearsal for Reconstruction*

V-212   ROSSITER, CLINTON   *Conservatism in America*

V-285   RUDOLPH, FREDERICK   *The American College and University: A History*

V-394   SEABURY, PAUL   *Power, Freedom and Diplomacy*

V-279   SILBERMAN, CHARLES E.   *Crisis in Black and White*

V-52   SMITH, HENRY NASH   *Virgin Land*

V-345   SMITH, PAGE   *The Historian and History*

V-432   SPARROW, JOHN   *After the Assassination: A Positive Appraisal of the Warren Report*

V-388   STAMPP, KENNETH M.   *The Era of Reconstruction 1865-1877*

V-253   STAMPP, KENNETH M.   *The Peculiar Institution*

V-110   TOCQUEVILLE, ALEXIS DE   *Democracy in America*, Vol. I

V-111   TOCQUEVILLE, ALEXIS DE   *Democracy in America*, Vol. II

V-103   TROLLOPE, MRS. FRANCES   *Domestic Manners of the Americans*

V-516   ULAM, ADAM B.   *The Unfinished Revolution*

V-540   VER STEEG, CLARENCE L. and RICHARD HOFSTADTER (eds.) *Great Issues in American History, 1584-1776*

V-265   WARREN, ROBERT PENN   *The Legacy of the Civil War*

V-605   WILLIAMS, JOHN A. and CHARLES F. HARRIS (eds.)   *Amistad 1*

V-660   WILLIAMS, JOHN A. and CHARLES F. HARRIS (eds.)   *Amistad 2*

V-362   WILLIAMS, T. HARRY   *Lincoln and His Generals*

V-208   WOODWARD, C. VANN   *Burden of Southern History*

V-340 ADAMS, RUTH (ed.) *Contemporary China*
V-286 ARIES, PHILIPPE *Centuries of Childhood*
V-185 BARNETT, A. DOAK *Communist China and Asia*
V-620 BILLINGTON, JAMES H. *Icon and Axe: An Interpretive History of Russian Culture*
V-44   BRINTON, CRANE *The Anatomy of Revolution*
V-250 BURCKHARDT, C. J. *Richelieu: His Rise to Power*
V-391 CARR, E. H. *What Is History?*
V-628 CARTEY, WILFRED and MARTIN KILSON (eds.) *Africa Reader: Colonial Africa*, Vol. I
V-629 CARTEY, WILFRED and MARTIN KILSON (eds.) *Africa Reader: Independent Africa*, Vol. II
V-556 CASTRO, JOSUE de *Death in the Northeast: Poverty and Revolution in the Northeast of Brazil*
V-518 CHILDE, V. GORDON *The Dawn of European Civilization*
V-526 DEHIO, LUDWIG *The Precarious Balance*
V-746 DEUTSCHER, ISAAC *The Prophet Armed*
V-747 DEUTSCHER, ISAAC *The Prophet Unarmed*
V-748 DEUTSCHER, ISAAC *The Prophet Outcast*
V-471 DUVEAU, GEORGES *1848: The Making of A Revolution*
V-611 FONTAINE, ANDRE *History of the Cold War*, Vol. I
V-612 FONTAINE, ANDRE *History of the Cold War*, Vol. II
V-475 GAY, PETER *The Enlightenment: The Rise of Modern Paganism*
V-277 GAY, PETER *Voltaire's Politics*
V-685 HAMSIK, DUSAN *Writers Against Rulers*
V-114 HAUSER, ARNOLD *The Social History of Art* through V-117 (four volumes)
V-630 HOROWITZ, DAVID *Empire and Revolution*
V-201 HUGHES, H. STUART *Consciousness and Society*
V-514 HUNTINGTON, SAMUEL P. *The Soldier and the State*
V-550 JENKINS, ROMILLY *Byzantium: The Imperial Centuries A.D. 610-1071*
V-50   KELLY, AMY *Eleanor of Aquitaine and the Four Kings*
V-628 KILSON, MARTIN and WILFRED CARTEY (eds.). *Africa Reader: Colonial Africa*, Vol. I
V-629 KILSON, MARTIN and WILFRED CARTEY (eds.). *Africa Reader: Independent Africa*, Vol. II
V-728 KLYUCHEVSKY, V. *Peter the Great*
V-246 KNOWLES, DAVID *Evolution of Medieval Thought*
V-83   KRONENBERGER, LOUIS *Kings and Desperate Men*
V-215 LACOUTURE, JEAN *Ho Chi Minh*
V-522 LANGER, WILLIAM L. *European Alliances and Alignments*
V-364 LEFEBVRE, GEORGES *The Directory*
V-343 LEFEBVRE, GEORGES *The Thermidorians*
V-587 LEWIN, MOSHE *Lenin's Last Struggle*
V-474 LIFTON, ROBERT JAY *Revolutionary Immortality: Mao Tse-Tung and the Chinese Cultural Revolution*
V-487 LIFTON, ROBERT JAY *Death in Life: Survivors of Hiroshima*
V-533 LOCKWOOD, LEE *Castro's Cuba, Cuba's Fidel*
V-92   MATTINGLY, GARRETT *Catherine of Aragon*
V-689 OBSERVER, AN *Message from Moscow*
V-733 PARES, SIR BERNARD *The Fall of the Russian Monarchy*
V-525 PARES, SIR BERNARD *A History of Russia*

V-285   PARKES, HENRY B.   *Gods and Men*

V-719   REED, JOHN   *Ten Days That Shook the World*

V-176   SCHAPIRO, LEONARD   *The Government and Politics of the Soviet Union* (Revised Edition)

V-745   SCHAPIRO, LEONARD   *The Communist Party of the Soviet Union*

V-375   SCHURMANN, F. and O. SCHELL (eds.)   *The China Reader: Imperial China,* I

V-376   SCHURMANN, F. and O. SCHELL (eds.)   *The China Reader: Republican China,* II

V-377   SCHURMANN, F. and O. SCHELL (eds.)   *The China Reader: Communist China,* III

V-681   SNOW, EDGAR   *Red China Today*

V-312   TANNENBAUM, FRANK   *Ten Keys to Latin America*

V-322   THOMPSON, E. P.   *The Making of the English Working Class*

V-724   WALLACE, SIR DONALD MACKENZIE   *Russia: On the Eve of War and Revolution*

V-206   WALLERSTEIN, IMMANUEL   *Africa: The Politics of Independence*

V-298   WATTS, ALAN   *The Way of Zen*

V-557   WEINSTEIN, JAMES   *The Decline of Socialism in America 1912-1925*

V-106   WINSTON, RICHARD   *Charlemagne: From the Hammer to the Cross*

V-627   WOMACK, JOHN JR.   *Zapata and the Mexican Revolution*

V-81   WOOCK, ROGER R. and ARTHUR I. BLAUSTEIN (eds.)   *Man against Poverty: World War III*

V-486   WOOLF, S. J. (ed.)   *European Fascism*

V-545   WOOLF, S. J. (ed.)   *The Nature of Fascism*

V-495   YGLESIAS, JOSE   *In the Fist of Revolution: Life in a Cuban Country Town*

VINTAGE BIOGRAPHY AND AUTOBIOGRAPHY

V-658   ALINSKY, SAUL D.   *John L. Lewis: An Unauthorized Biography*

V-250   BURCKHARDT, C. J.   *Richelieu: His Rise to Power*

V-725   CARR, E. H.   *Michael Bakunin*

V-746   DEUTSCHER, ISAAC   *The Prophet Armed*

V-747   DEUTSCHER, ISAAC   *The Prophet Unarmed*

V-748   DEUTSCHER, ISAAC   *The Prophet Outcast*

V-617   DEVLIN, BERNADETTE   *The Price of My Soul*

V-225   FISCHER, LOUIS (ed.)   *The Essential Gandhi*

V-132   FREUD, SIGMUND   *Leonardo Da Vinci*

V-147   GIDE, ANDRE   *If It Die*

V-499   GOODMAN, PAUL   *Five Years*

V-449   GRAY, FRANCINE DU PLESSIX   *Divine Disobedience*

V-268   JUNG, C. G.   *Memories, Dreams, Reflections*

V-50   KELLY, AMY   *Eleanor of Aquitaine and the Four Kings*

V-728   KLYUCHEVSKY, V.   *Peter the Great*

V-581   KRAMER, JANE   *Allen Ginsberg in America*

V-215   LACOUTURE, JEAN   *Ho Chi Minh*

V-677   LESTER, JULIUS   *The Seventh Son*, Volume I

V-678   LESTER, JULIUS   *The Seventh Son*, Volume II

V-280   LEWIS, OSCAR   *Children of Sánchez*

V-634   LEWIS, OSCAR   *A Death in the Sánchez Family*

V-92   MATTINGLY, GARRETT   *Catherine of Aragon*

V-490   MYRDAL, JAN   *Confessions of a Disloyal European*

V-624   PARKINSON, G. H. R.   *Georg Lukacs: The Man, His Work, and His Ideas*

V-373   PAUSTOVSKY, KONSTANTIN   *The Story of a Life*

V-133   STEIN, GERTRUDE   *The Autobiography of Alice B. Toklas*

V-100   SULLIVAN, J. W. N.   *Beethoven: His Spiritual Development*

V-287   TAYLOR, A. J. P.   *Bismarck: The Man and the Statesman*

V-256   WILDE, OSCAR   *De Profundis*

V-106   WINSTON, RICHARD   *Charlemagne: From the Hammer to the Cross*